A DICTIONARY OF

ENVIRONMENTAL

Quotations

A DICTIONARY OF
ENVIRONMENTAL
Quotations

Compiled by
BARBARA K. RODES
and
RICE ODELL

SIMON & SCHUSTER
A Paramount Communications Company

New York London Toronto Sydney Tokyo Singapore

Academic Reference Division
Simon and Schuster
15 Columbus Circle
New York, New York 10023

Printed in the United States of America

printing number
1 2 3 4 5 6 7 8 9 10

ISBN 0-13-210576-4

Library of Congress Cataloging-in-Publication Data

A Dictionary of environmental quotations / compiled by Barbara K.
Rodes and Rice Odell.
   p.   cm.
   Includes index.
   ISBN 0-13-210576-4
   1. Nature—Quotations, maxims, etc.—Dictionaries. 2. Ecology—
Quotations, maxims, etc.—Dictionaries. I. Rodes, Barbara K.
II. Odell, Rice.
PN6084.N2D53   1992
333.7—dc20
                                       92-3055
                                        CIP

CONTENTS

CONTENTS

PREFACE

This *Dictionary of Environmental Quotations* collects quotations about the interactions of human beings and the natural environment and presents them in an easy-to-use reference format. Throughout history, people have commented—rhapsodically, humorously, glibly, wisely, acidly, worshipfully, provocatively—on the earth and all it contains. We hope that this book delights, provokes, and informs a diverse audience of researchers, scholars, speech writers, and devotees of quotations.

The word *environmental* in the title refers to the whole complex of factors that act upon an organism or community to determine its form and survival. It embraces human responses to natural systems, pollution, land use, and wildlife. As William V. Shannon put it in *The New York Times* many years ago: "The environment is not just one more factor to be considered along with dozens of others in making social and economic decisions. The environment is not a crisis or a problem at all. Rather, it is a context in which all crises and problems have to be analyzed."

Concern for the environment greatly increased in the 1960s, as the selection of quotations here shows. But respect for nature and ideas about the special relationship between humankind and nature—two central components of environmentalism—have appealed to people in many cultures throughout the ages.

The approximately 3,700 quotations in this book, drawn from proverbs and poems, speeches and scientific papers, philosophical works and bumper stickers, reflect that vast range of human interest in the environment. The quotations are organized in 143 categories arranged alphabetically from Acid Rain to Zoos.

Within each category, we put the quotations in chronological order, as best we could determine. If we were uncertain about the date, we attempted to place the quotation approximately, sometimes by educated guess. Entries from books precede entries from periodicals and broadcasts.

But this is more than just a compendium of quotations. Because the entries within each category are arranged chronologically, the book serves as a chronicle of environmental thought across the centuries. Especially in quotations drawn from recent decades, it provides verbal snapshots of the evolution of a powerful, controversial movement that has sparked a long, slow transformation in social values. Our intention, then, is as much to define the environment and issues related to it as to offer an assortment of quotations.

In developing this collection, we have drawn on our combined experience of fifty years working in environmental groups and for environmental causes. Some of our choices are unapologetically idiosyncratic, and we regret the need to leave out many illuminating quotations. We invite readers to submit favorite selections that we might have overlooked (send them to our publisher at the address listed on the copyright page) for future editions of the dictionary.

Although we encourage the reader to browse, the indexes will make it possible to find quotations on subjects of particular interest and to track the views of particular politicians, philosophers, poets, and ordinary citizens. Most of all, we invite the reader to savor, to learn, to be challenged by the vast range of environmental concern and human response.

ACKNOWLEDGMENTS

Among the many people who have helped us form this collection, we would like especially to thank Carla Langeveld and Fannie Mae Keller. Thanks are also due to Charles E. Smith, Paul Bernabeo, and Stephen Wagley at the Academic Reference Division of Simon and Schuster.

Barbara K. Rodes
Rice Odell

Washington, D.C.
January 1992

A DICTIONARY OF

ENVIRONMENTAL

Quotations

1 ACID RAIN

1 Acid Rain Is a Bad Trip
   BUMPER STICKER

2 Once the "cumulative loading" of acids deposited in these areas through the years has exhausted the environment's limited neutralizing capacity, severe effects follow very quickly with the addition of small, previously inconsequential quantities of acid.
   GREGORY WETSTONE, *Environmental Law Reporter* 10, 1982

3 The fact that the amount of acid rain we are adding every year hasn't necessarily changed dramatically doesn't mean you won't reach a dramatic endpoint.
   ROY R. GOULD, testimony, U.S. Senate Committee on Environment and Public Works, 25 May 1982

4 Let us dismiss out of hand that we can lime the northeast quadrant of a continent. . . . If you take an acid lake and lime it, you do not now have a normal lake; you now have a limed, formerly very acid lake, with a very peculiar water chemistry and a very peculiar biota as a result.
   HAROLD HARVEY, on the use of lime to counteract the effects of acid rain, *Adirondack Life*, September–October 1982

5 I would suggest it is a good way to manage a fish hatchery but a lousy way to manage an environment.
   HANS MARTIN, director, Air Resources Branch, Environment Canada, on the use of lime in lakes to counteract acid rain, speech, Soil Conservation Society of America conference, Burlington, Vt., 25 October 1982

6 Saying sulfates do not cause acid rain is the same as saying that smoking does not cause lung cancer.
   DREW LEWIS, U.S. presidential adviser, quoted in *New York Times*, 14 September 1985

7 The [U.S.] Administration has itself been of not two but several minds on this issue. It is divided between those who want to see action, those who are skeptical that the science justifies the expense, and those who oppose environmental regulation as an act of faith. It is further divided between those who accept that the U.S.A. has a legal obligation to Canada to act, and those who see the whole issue as a Canadian conspiracy to increase electrical exports. This mildly schizophrenic frame of mind has made our work with the Administration a pathway fraught with pitfalls and digressions.
   ALLAN E. GOTLIEB, Canadian ambassador to the United States, on the problem of acid rain originating in the United States and falling in Canada, speech, University of Southern California, 1988

8 Acid rain spares nothing. What has taken humankind decades to build and nature millennia to evolve is being impoverished and destroyed in a matter of a few years—a mere blink in geologic time.
   DON HINRICHSEN, *Earth Report*, 1988

9 As your neighbor, you're [the U.S.] my friend. I give you the benefit of the doubt. The test of our friendship is that I don't have the right to pollute your front lawn or dump garbage in your back yard. I told [the U.S.] Congress, "We're your best friend. Why are you doing this [sending acid rain] to us?"
   BRIAN MULRONEY, Prime Minister of Canada, quoted in *USA Today*, 26 August 1988

1

10 We can't keep studying this thing to death: we're got to do something about it.
DREW LEWIS, U.S. presidential adviser, quoted in "Acid Rain," World Wildlife Fund special report, 1990

2 AESTHETICS

1 See one promontory (said Socrates of old), one mountain, one sea, one river, and see all.
ROBERT BURTON (1577–1640), *The Anatomy of Melancholy*, part 1

2 Her mighty lakes, like oceans of liquid silver; her mountains, with their bright aerial tints; her valleys, teeming with wild fertility; her tremendous cataracts, thundering in their solitudes; her boundless plains, waving with spontaneous verdure; her broad deep rivers, rolling in solemn silence to the ocean; her trackless forests, where vegetation puts forth all its magnificence; her skies, kindling with the magic of summer clouds and glorious sunshine;—no, never need an American look beyond his own country for the sublime and beautiful of natural scenery.
WASHINGTON IRVING (1783–1859), on America, quoted in Norman Foerster, *Nature in American Literature*, 1923

3 The landscapes were like a violin bow that played upon my soul.
STENDHAL, (Henri Beyle, 1783–1842), on his travels, *Vie de Henri Brulard*, 1890

4 To the attentive eye, each moment of the year has its own beauty, and in the same field, it beholds, every hour, a picture which was never seen before, and which shall never be seen again.
RALPH WALDO EMERSON (1803– 1882), *Nature*, 1836

5 Miller owns this field, Locke that, and Manning the woodland beyond. But none of them owns the landscape. There is a property in the horizon which no man has but he whose eye can integrate all the parts, that is, the poet. This is the best part of these men's farms, yet to this their warranty-deeds give no title.
RALPH WALDO EMERSON (1803–1882), *Nature*, 1836

6 The enjoyment of the choicest natural scenes in the country and the means of recreation connected with them is a monopoly . . . of a very few rich people. . . . For the same reason that the water of rivers should be guarded against private appropriation and the use of it for the purpose of navigation and otherwise protected against obstruction, portions of the natural scenery may therefore properly be guarded and cared for by government. . . . The establishment by government of great public grounds is thus justified and enforced as a public duty.
FREDERICK LAW OLMSTED (1822–1903), "The Yosemite Valley and the Mariposa Big Trees: A Preliminary Report," 1865

7 If a certain assemblage of trees, of mountains, of waters, and of houses that we call a landscape is beautiful, it is not because of itself, but through me, through my own indulgence, through the thought or the sentiment that I attach to it.
CHARLES BAUDELAIRE (1821–1867), *Curiosités esthétiques*, 1868

8 No synonym for God is so perfect as Beauty. Whether as seen carving the lines of the mountains with glaciers, or gathering matter into stars, or planning the movements of water, or gardening—still all is Beauty!
JOHN MUIR (1838–1914), quoted in Edwin Way Teale, *The Wilderness World of John Muir*, 1954

9 The hours when the mind is absorbed by beauty are the only hours when we truly live.
RICHARD JEFFERIES (1848–1887), *The Life of the Fields*, 1884

10 To know one's landscape, to feel in sympathy with it, is often to be at peace with life. When all the world seems wrong and the burdens overwhelming he can look out on the familiar fields and hills or get among them and give way to their beauties of form and color as a resource within himself that will be an ever-present power of recuperation.
RICHARD E. DODGE, *Journal of Geography* 13, 1915

11 It is the love of country that has lighted and that keeps glowing the holy fire of patriotism.

And this love is excited, primarily, by the beauty of the country.
J. HORACE MCFARLAND, 1908, quoted in Garrett De Bell, ed., *The Environmental Handbook*, 1970

12 Not one cent for scenery.
JOSEPH G. CANNON (1836–1926), speaker of the U.S. House of Representatives, squelching a request for funds for a federal conservation effort, quoted in Blair Bolles, *Tyrant from Illinois*, 1951

13 Ordinarily the demands of utility are imperative and scenic beauty where it stands in the way must yield.
HIRAM CHITTENDEN, *Pacific Monthly*, January 1910

14 [The essence of what] we call America lies not so much in political institutions as in its rocks and skies and seas.
PAUL STRAND (1890–1976), 1920, quoted in the Paul Strand Exhibition, National Gallery of Art, Washington, D.C., 1990–1991

15 Indifference to the aesthetic will in the long run lessen the economic product . . . attention to the aesthetic will increase economic welfare.
JOSIAH STAMP (1880–1941), *Some Economic Factors in Modern Life*, 1929

16 I think that I shall never see
A billboard lovely as a tree.
Indeed, unless the billboards fall
I'll never see a tree at all.
OGDEN NASH (1902–1971), *Song of the Open Road*, 1933

17 The greatest beauty is organic wholeness, the wholeness of life and things, the divine beauty of the universe. Love that, not man apart from that.
ROBINSON JEFFERS (1887–1962), "The Answer," 1938

18 Our ability to perceive quality in nature begins, as in art, with the pretty. It expands through successive stages of the beautiful to values as yet uncaptured by language. The quality of cranes lies, I think, in this higher gamut, as yet beyond the reach of words.
ALDO LEOPOLD (1886–1948), *A Sand County Almanac*, 1949

19 The concept of public welfare is broad and inclusive. . . . The values it represents are spiritual as well as physical, aesthetic as well as monetary. It is within the power of the legislature to determine that the community should be beautiful as well as healthy, spacious as well as clean.
WILLIAM O. DOUGLAS (1898–1980), U.S. Supreme Court justice, *Berman* v. *Parker*, 1954

20 Less is more.
LUDWIG MIES VAN DER ROHE (1886–1969), on modern architecture, in *New York Herald Tribune*, 28 June 1959

21 Many people live in ugly wastelands but in the absence of imaginative standards most of them do not even know it.
C. WRIGHT MILLS, *Power, Politics, and People*, 1963

22 I look forward to an America which will not be afraid of grace and beauty, which will protect the beauty of our natural environment, which will preserve the great old American houses and squares and parks of our national past and which will build handsome and balanced cities for our future.
JOHN F. KENNEDY (1917–1963), speech, Amherst College, 26 October 1963

23 The machine turned Nature into an art form. For the first time men began to regard Nature as a source of aesthetic and spiritual values.
MARSHALL MCLUHAN, *Understanding Media*, 1964

24 Billboards are the art gallery of the public.
BURR L. ROBBINS, quoted in Peter Blake, *God's Own Junkyard*, 1964

25 We must not only protect the countryside and save it from destruction, we must restore what has been destroyed and salvage the beauty and charm of our cities. . . . Once our natural splendour is destroyed, it can never be recaptured. And once man can no longer walk with beauty or wonder at nature, his spirit will wither and his sustenance be wasted.
LYNDON B. JOHNSON (1908–1973), special message to Congress on conservation and restoration of natural beauty, 8 February 1965

26 To the extent that we create or maintain beauty through an ordered diversity, we will

also enhance the stability, health, and productivity of America.
RAYMOND F. DASMANN, speech, Columbus, Ohio,1966

27 Sporadic White House interest in "natural beauty" is so superficial as to be dangerous. The public is gulled into thinking problems are being met. Natural beauty is cosmetics conservation. Instead of applying pancake makeup to the landscape, we should be stopping cancer.
SPORTS ILLUSTRATED, 6 December 1967

28 Making a town more beautiful and more human can lessen tensions and friction. Any city *can* do it; any city *would do well* to do it.
LADY BIRD JOHNSON, *Reader's Digest*, September 1968

29 Beauty created by Nature is equal in value to, and to be accorded reverence equal to that of the beauty of music, art or poetry of man, and experts are available to testify as to degrees of natural beauty just as they are able to testify to the quality of mortals' art.
DAVID SIVE, conference on law and the environment, Warrenton, Va., September 1969

30 One cannot assess in terms of cash or exports and imports an imponderable thing like the turn of a lane or an inn or a church tower or a familiar skyline.
JOHN BETJEMAN (1906–1984), quoted in *The Observer*, 20 July 1969

31 Fight blight, burn a billboard tonight.
DAVID R. BROWER, quoted in John McPhee, *Encounters with the Archdruid*, 1971

32 There can be no greater moral obligation in the environmental field than to ease out the living space and replace dereliction by beauty.
FRANK FRASER DARLING, *Wilderness and Plenty*, 1971

33 What is curious about this singular acknowledgment of landscape for other than economic values is that its political justification is not primarily a matter of "taste" or aesthetics, but rather of egalitarian public service, having to do with recreational opportunity and, to a lesser extent, ecological "balance" as a subsidiary rationale.
CHARLES E. LITTLE, in James N. Smith, *Environmental Quality and Social Justice in Urban America*, 1974

34 Out of our human needs, perhaps, will come the strongest argument for preventing the blind destruction of the plant world and its natural habitats. This will not simply be for utilitarian reasons but increasingly because of the demand for that natural solace which the green world and unspoiled scenery provide.
ANTHONY HUXLEY, *Plant and Planet*, 1975

35 We believe that ugliness begets ugliness and that nature's beauty, once destroyed, may never be restored by the artifice of man.
CARL CARMER, quoted in *Harper's*, December 1977

36 The good news is that Americans will, in increasing numbers, begin to value and protect the vast American landscape. The bad news is that they may love it to death.
CHARLES E. LITTLE, in *The American Land*, 1979

37 The first act of awe when man was struck with the beauty or wonder of nature was the first spiritual experience.
HENRYK SKOLIMOWSKI, *Eco-Philosophy*, 1981

38 Of all values . . . landscape most forcefully reinforces the traditional love of agriculture and distrust of artifice.
JOHN R. STILGOE, *Common Landscape of America, 1580 to 1845*, 1982

39 It seems to me that aesthetics is an area of immense ethical failure. We have a thousand times more ecological consciousness than aesthetic consciousness and we have a hundred times more consciousness of the issues of social equity in the ownership and use of land. Yet, aesthetics has no parity with equity and with ecology, even though aesthetics, more than any aspect of the land ethic, feeds the spirit in direct ways.
CHARLES E. LITTLE, *American Land Forum*, Summer 1986

40 We recognize defeated landscapes by the absence of pleasure from them.
WENDELL BERRY, *What Are People For?: Essays*, 1990

41 People need a model. If they can see a place become beautiful, they're inspired to act.
MARION STODDART, *Countryside*, Winter 1990

42 The beauty of nature affected me almost as profoundly as a religious "born again" experience. The whole of nature unfolded in

front of my eyes. I am not a religious person but you could describe me as an ecopantheist.
PERTTI SALOLAINEN, Finnish foreign trade minister, describing childhood visits to his family cottage on the Finnish coast, *Sierra*, May–June 1991

3 AFFLUENCE
See also   20 CONSUMERISM, 79 LIFESTYLE, 110 POVERTY

1 He who knows what sweets and virtues are in the ground, the waters, the plants, the heavens, and how to come at these enchantments, is the rich and royal man.
RALPH WALDO EMERSON (1803–1882), *Essays, Second Series,* 1844

2 But we need to remind ourselves, in our quest for immediate subsistence and wealth, that while a bird in the hand is worth two in the bush, birds breed in pairs and nest in bushes.
PAUL SEARS, *Deserts on the March,* 1947

3 An indefinitely rising material standard of living has nearly the same effect on the biosphere as an indefinitely rising population. . . . A basic change in values in which increase in material wealth is not so highly rated must accompany any solution to the problem of economic growth.
MAN'S IMPACT ON THE GLOBAL ENVIRONMENT, report of the Study of Critical Environmental Problems, 1970

4 It's the rich who wreck the environment . . . occupy much more space, consume more of each natural resource, disturb ecology more, litter the landscape . . . and create more pollution.
JEAN MAYER and T. G. HARRIS, *Psychology Today,* January 1970

5 Nothing would be more dangerous today to the human future than if the American standard were to be achieved in country after country.
NORMAN COUSINS, *Saturday Review,* 20 June 1970

6 Environmental degradation is not, of course, *inherent* in rising affluence. Only the particular forms and methods of production and consumption to which our society has become accustomed degrade it. Rising affluence can and should be a source of environmental enhancement.
NEIL H. JACOBY, in Clifton Fadiman and Jean White, eds., *Ecocide,* 1971

7 One way to be rich is not to want anything.
KENNETH E. BOULDING, in Anne Chisholm, *Philosophers of the Earth,* 1972

8 A society that is declining materially may be ascending spiritually. . . . The loss of our affluence will be extremely uncomfortable and it will certainly be difficult to manage. But in some respects, it may be a blessing in disguise, if we can rise to this grave occasion.
ARNOLD TOYNBEE (1889–1975), *London Observer,* 14 April 1974

9 "Wealth" and "poverty" are but names we give to two extreme kinds of ecological niche.
PAUL COLINVAUX, *The Fates of Nations,* 1980

10 None of us can evade the responsibility that comes with our high standard of living; we all take advantage of the amenities of civilized life in pursuing our individual values and interests. Since it is modern commerce, industry, and technology that make these amenities possible, each of us is a consumer and user of what the natural world can yield for us. Our well-being is constantly being furthered at the expense of the the good of Earth's nonhuman inhabitants.
PAUL W. TAYLOR, *Respect for Nature,* 1986

11 The logic of our present thinking—that we should increase in numbers and, especially, in material wealth and ease—leads inexorably in the direction of the managed world. It is, as a few rebels have maintained, a rut, a system of beliefs in which we are trapped. When Thoreau declared that the mass of men lead lives of quiet desperation, it was to this rut that he referred. He went to live at Walden Pond to prove how little man needed to survive—$61.99¾ for eight months, including the cost of his house.
BILL MCKIBBEN, *The End of Nature,* 1989

12 We, all of us in the First World, have participated in something of a binge, a half century of unbelievable prosperity and ease. We may have had some intuition that it *was* a binge and the earth couldn't support it, but aside from the easy things (biodegradable detergent, slightly smaller cars) we didn't do much. We didn't turn our lives around to prevent it. Our sadness is almost an aesthetic response—appropriate because we have marred a great, mad, profligate work of art, taken a hammer to the most perfectly proportioned of sculptures.

BILL MCKIBBEN, *The End of Nature*, 1989

13 An Innu hunter's prestige comes not from the wealth he accumulates but from what he gives away. When a hunter kills caribou or other game he shares with everyone else in the camp.

DANIEL ASHINI, Innu spokesman, in Julian Burger, *The Gaia Atlas of First Peoples*, 1990

14 Assuming conservatively that four calories of animal feed are needed to produce one calorie of animal product, the developed world—with only 25 percent of the world's population—in effect consumes at least 40 percent of the total world "primary" food supply in caloric terms.

ROBERT S. CHEN, *Environmental Impact Assessment Review* 10, no. 4, 1990

15 Ethiopia reminds us that there are still people for whom food is primarily a means to biological survival. Here . . . food has come to mean much more: status, authority, entertainment, style, possibly religion.

BARBARA EHRENREICH, *The Worst Years of Our Lives*, 1990

---

4 AGRICULTURE

See also   58 GREEN REVOLUTION,
77 LAND USE, 99 PESTICIDES,
120 RURAL AREAS, 122 SOIL

---

1 That land pays avarice and doth what is askt of it, even
That which hath unto the heats twice lain and twice to the hoar-frosts:
Thence are immense harvests and granges fill'd to the bursting.

VIRGIL (70–19 B.C.), *Georgics*, Book 1

2 Whoever could make two ears of corn, or two blades of grass, to grow upon a spot of ground where only one grew before, would deserve better of mankind, and do more essential service to his country, than the whole race of politicians put together.

JONATHAN SWIFT (1667–1745), *Gulliver's Travels*, 1726

3 Ill fares the land, to hastening ills a prey,
Where wealth accumulates, and men decay.

OLIVER GOLDSMITH (1730–1774), *The Deserted Village*, 1770

4 Give a man the secure possession of bleak rock, and he will turn it into a garden; give him a nine years lease of a garden, and he will convert it to a desert.

ARTHUR YOUNG (1741–1820), *Travels*, 1787

5 An extensive speculation, a spirit of gambling, or the introduction of any thing which will divert our attention from Agriculture, must be extremely prejudicial, if not ruinous to us.

GEORGE WASHINGTON (1732–1799), letter to Thomas Jefferson, 1 January 1788

6 I hope, some day or another, we shall become a storehouse and granary for the world.

GEORGE WASHINGTON (1732–1799), letter to Marquis de Lafayette, 19 June 1788

7 To own a bit of ground, to scratch it with a hoe, to plant seeds, and watch the renewal of life—this is the commonest delight of the race, the most satisfactory thing a man can do.

CHARLES DUDLEY WARNER (1820–1900), *My Summer in a Garden*, 1870

8 There are two spiritual dangers in not owning a farm. One is the danger of supposing that breakfast comes from the grocery, and the other that heat comes from the furnace.

ALDO LEOPOLD (1886–1948), *A Sand County Almanac*, 1949

9 What remains of our native fauna and flora remains only because agriculture has not got around to destroying it.

ALDO LEOPOLD (1886–1948), *Round River*, 1953

10 Any land, even a mountaintop, can be brought into cultivation if enough money and labor are put into it.
   WILLIAM PADDOCK and PAUL PADDOCK, *Famine 1975!*, 1967

11 In the days of the scratch-plow, fields were distributed generally in units capable of supporting a single family. . . . [T]o use the new and more efficient plow, peasants pooled their oxen to form large plow-teams. . . . Thus, distribution of land was based no longer on the needs of a family but, rather, on the capacity of a power machine to till the earth. Man's relation to the soil was profoundly changed. Formerly man had been part of nature; now he was the exploiter of nature.
   LYNN I. WHITE, JR., *Science*, 10 March 1967

12 The battle to feed all of humanity is over. In the 1970s the world will undergo famines—hundreds of millions of people are going to starve to death.
   PAUL EHRLICH, *The Population Bomb*, 1968

13 Given the present capacity of the earth for food production, and the potential for additional food production if modern technology were more fully employed, the human race clearly has within its grasp the capacity to chase hunger from the earth—within a matter of a decade or two.
   DONALD J. BOGUE, *Principles of Demography*, 1969

14 It is hard to see how there can be any meaningful modernization of food production in Latin America and Africa south of the Sahara unless land is registered, deeded, and distributed more equitably.
   LESTER R. BROWN, *Seeds of Change*, 1970

15 My reply to the prophets of agricultural utopia is: When you can adequately feed the 3.6 billion people we have now . . . come back and tell us how you'll feed the 7 billion we'll have by the year 2000. Until you can do that, why don't you just shut up and get back to work?
   PAUL H. EHRLICH, speech, Second World Food Congress, The Hague, June 1970

16 A developed Agriculture is a fabulous polluter;

As development gets faster, then the problem gets acuter.
We are loading up the planet with a lot of nitric trash,
And if nitrogen falls off its cycle—wow! is that a crash.
   KENNETH E. BOULDING, "The Ballad of Ecological Awareness," in M. Taghi Farvar and John P. Milton, eds., *The Careless Technology*, 1972

17 In simplest terms, agriculture is an effort by man to move beyond the limits set by nature.
   LESTER R. BROWN and GAIL W. FINSTERBUSCH, *Man and His Environment: Food*, 1972

18 The signs of the "agridollar," big-business fantasy of the [Nixon administration Secretary of Agriculture Earl] Butz mentality are all present: the absenteeism, the temporary and shallow interest of the landrenter, the row-cropping of slopes, the lack of rotation, the plowed-out waterways, the rows running up and down the hills. Looked at from the field's edge, this is ruin, criminal folly, moral idiocy. Looked at from Washington, D.C., from inside the "economy," it is called "free enterprise" and "full production."
   WENDELL BERRY, *The Unsettling of America*, 1977

19 There are biological limits imposed by available energy, soil fertility, soil moisture and, above all, the genetic capacity of the plants to transform raw materials into products desired by man. We must conclude that there is a biological limit to the amount of yield a plant may produce which in the future will constitute a severe barrier to further increasing crop yields per acre. Then, yield increases must come by increasing the level of protection afforded against plant pests.
   PERRY ADKISSON, February 1977

20 Low risk—*not* high yield—is the name of the game in subsistence agriculture. Low inputs, diverse crops, multiple plots, dooryard gardens, nearly self-sustaining poultry and livestock, and low but certain-to-get-something yields: these are all reflections of the harsh fact that the subsistence farmer cannot absorb a single failure.
   JACK EWEL, report for Agency for International Development, 1 April 1977

21 In addition to the obvious physical limitations of land and water, the economic, political, and social barriers to ideal productivity and distribution are profound. The inadequacy of market structures: the difficulty of transferring technology; the massive quantities of capital, energy, and water needed to bring uncultivated land into production; the threat of ecological damage; the inertia of tradition and custom; and the uneven distribution of usable land in relation to the distribution of the world's population—all these factors seriously limit the availability of food for those in need.

U.S. HOUSE OF REPRESENTATIVES SELECT COMMITTEE ON POPULATION, "World Population: Myths and Realities," report, October 1978

22 Ten years from now, Americans could be as concerned over the loss of the nation's prime and important farm lands as they are today over shortages of oil and gasoline.

SHIRLEY FOSTER FIELDS, "Where Have All the Farm Lands Gone?," 1979

23 It is not difficult to imagine a time when technology will no longer be able to offset the decreasing land under cultivation.

THOMAS A. SLOAN, in David W. Orr and Marvin S. Soroos, eds., *The Global Predicament*, 1979

24 Growing crops is easier than building castles, yet there are many castles in our world and not enough crops.

PETAK SAEOUNG, World Environment Day/ International Year of the Child Poster Contest, Environment Liaison Centre, Nairobi, Kenya, 23 January 1979

25 Those interested in the long-term health of the land need only stand on the edge of a stream after a rain and watch a plasma boil and turn in the powerful current below and then realize that the vigorous production of our fields is, unfortunately, temporary. Since we initiated the split with nature some 10,000 years ago by embracing enterprise in food production, we have yet to develop an agriculture as sustainable as the nature we destroy.

WES JACKSON, *New Roots for Agriculture*, 1980

26 A society stressed by warfare, hunger, internal turmoil, and corruption, or obsessed with modernization to the point that it ignores the fate of its agricultural lands, will be fortunate if the productivity of its land does not diminish significantly in the decades ahead.

COUNCIL ON ENVIRONMENTAL QUALITY and U.S. DEPARTMENT OF STATE, *The Global 2000 Report to the President*, July 1980

27 We are mining the soil of its fertility, and are draining oil and gas fields of their wealth to get the energy to do that. . . . We can't afford to let our food system just "run out" some day.

ROBERT RODALE, *Organic Gardening*, September 1980

28 Visualize a strip of land half a mile wide stretching from New York to California. That is one million acres—the amount of important farmland converted to other uses and irreversibly lost to agriculture every year in the United States.

COUNCIL ON ENVIRONMENTAL QUALITY and U.S. DEPARTMENT OF AGRICULTURE, *National Agricultural Land Study*, 1981

29 To understand the source of one's next meal is to understand one's own political vulnerability.

MICHAEL KRAMER, *Three Farms*, 1981

30 The abundance of food in America in 1981 is being achieved at a very high cost—not so much in dollars, but in soil, in irreplaceable underground water, in squandered oil, wasted gas and environmental degradation that nature will be able to repair only many decades after the current American food machine grinds to a halt.

ROBERT RODALE and THOMAS DYBDAHL, *Cry California*, Summer 1981

31 The starving and undernourished can only be fed by intensifying present agricultural production, and science will play a key role in achieving this goal.

FRANK PRESS, *Washington Post*, 30 December 1981

32 I have now come to the point where if I see a totally black field I get sick. I feel good now

only when I see a real messy field that's *just covered* with crop residue.

MILO HANSON, in Joe Paddock, Nancy Paddock, and Carol Bly, *Soil and Survival*, 1986

33 Unless national governments are prepared to wage the war against hunger on a far broader front, it may not be possible to arrest the decline in per capita food production that is undermining the future of so many poor countries.

LESTER BROWN, *The Changing World Food Prospect*, Worldwatch Paper 85, 1988

34 Agriculture is native not merely when native peoples are the farmers. It is fully native when a diversity of locally adapted organisms function within its fields, lending them yield stability and ecological resilience.

GARY PAUL NABHAN, *Enduring Seeds*, 1989

35 The agriculturist seeks to homogenize the environment. *Homo* is a good name for us—homogenizer of landscapes. When you plow, you homogenize, because you've destroyed the plant-soil interactions, plant-water interactions. And when you move to a chemical approach to agriculture, that's further homogenization, because you have the herbicides that knock out all the weeds.

WES JACKSON, quoted in *Atlantic Monthly*, November 1989

36 Fessing up to addictions and seeking treatment has become a fact of contemporary life, and farmers are not about to be left out. Maybe we'll end up naming the nineties the Detox Decade.

RICHARD NILSEN, on organic farming, *Whole Earth Review*, 1990

37 [Some agriculturalists] are working to create systems that display all four of the things we want to learn from nature: energy efficiency, cyclicality, diversity, and self-regulation.

EVAN EISENBERG, *New Republic*, 30 April 1990

38 A principal problem facing agriculture during the next 40 years is that current techniques cannot provide the food output and diet improvement that the world will need. Unless we choose to plow up the entire planet and to urge more people into labor-intensive primary agriculture, we must squeeze greater

yields from existing acres in ways that will remain environmentally friendly indefinitely.

HOWARD A.SCHNEIDER and WILL D. CARPENTER, *Environmental Science and Technology*, April 1990

39 The major alteration of the Earth's surface is through agriculture. But only recently have people begun to ask questions about the resulting impact on biological diversity.

STEPHEN GLIESSMAN, *Business Week*, 18 June 1990

40 This concentration on a few species at the expense of crop diversity makes us extremely vulnerable to catastrophic interruptions in the food supply, through natural or engineered disaster.

JEAN MAYER, *Business Week*, 18 June 1990

41 You can still make a small fortune in agriculture. Problem is, you got to start with a large one.

JIM HIGHTOWER, former Texas agriculture commissioner, *Buzzworm*, September–October 1990

42 The only difference between a pigeon and the American farmer today is that a pigeon can still make a deposit on a John Deere.

JIM HIGHTOWER, former Texas agriculture commissioner, *Buzzworm*, September–October 1990

43 It took a couple of million years for this land to evolve to the state it is in today, and it took 48 hours to destroy it. One of the things that bothers me the most is that we get up in arms over destruction of the rain forest, when the natural habitats in North America have been all but eliminated. We don't seem to be upset about destroying the things in our own backyard.

BUZZ HOAGLAND, on a farmer plowing up the largest remaining stretch of virgin prairie in northeast Kansas, *New York Times*, 23 November 1990

5 AIR
See also   6 AIR POLLUTION

1 Fresh air keeps the doctor poor.
DANISH PROVERB

2 The first Care in building of Cities, is to make them airy and well perflated; infectious Distempers must necessarily be propagated amongst Mankind living close together.
JOHN ARBUTHNOT (1667–1735), *An Essay Concerning the Effects of Air on Human Bodies,* 1733

3 This blue wilderness of interminable air.
GEORGE GORDON, LORD BYRON (1788–1824), *Cain,* 1821

4 Three months of camp life on Lake Tahoe would restore an Egyptian mummy to his pristine vigor, and give him an appetite like an alligator. I do not mean the oldest and driest mummies, of course, but the fresher ones. The air up there in the clouds is very pure and fine, bracing and delicious. And why shouldn't it be?—it is the same the angels breathe.
MARK TWAIN (Samuel Langhorne Clemens, 1835–1910), *Roughing It,* 1872

5 World-mothering air, air wild,
Wound with thee, in thee isled,
Fold home, fast fold thy child.
GERARD MANLEY HOPKINS (1844–1889), "The Blessed Virgin Compared to the Air We Breathe"

6 Those who desire air and quick recovery should go to the hills, where the wind has the scent of sunbeams.
RICHARD JEFFERIES (1848–1887), *The Life of the Fields,* 1884

7 Let the clean wind blow the cobwebs from your body. Air is medicine.
LILLIAN RUSSELL (1861–1922), quoted in *Reader's Digest,* March 1922

8 Every American in every city in America will breathe clean air [by early in the next century]. Ours is a rare opportunity to reverse the errors of this generation in the service of the next. It's time to clear the air. . . . The wounded winds of north, south, east and west can be purified and cleansed, and the integrity of nature can be made whole again.
GEORGE BUSH, on his clean-air plan, quoted in *Washington Post,* 13 June 1989

9 For the first time in my life, I saw the horizon as a curved line. It was accentuated by a thin seam of dark blue light—our atmosphere.

Obviously, this was not the "ocean" of air I had been told it was so many times in my life. I was terrified by its fragile appearance.
ULF MERBOLD, West German space shuttle astronaut, quoted in Francesca Lyman, *The Greenhouse Trap,* 1990

10 The air is the ultimate global commons—mixed and moved around the globe by the winds; shared by all living things; used and reused for many different purposes. It not only sustains life but, in the ozone layer, shelters it from the harsh ultraviolet rays of the sun and buffers the Earth from extremes of hot and cold. The air must increasingly be seen as a common resource, not a common sewer.
BUSINESS WEEK, 18 June 1990

11 One can exist for days without food or water or companionship or sex or mental stimulation, but life without air is measured in seconds. In *seconds.*
CASKIE STINNET, *Countryside,* Winter 1990

---

6 AIR POLLUTION
See also 1 ACID RAIN, 5 AIR,
71 INDOOR ENVIRONMENT, 97 OZONE LAYER, 104 POLLUTION,
105 POLLUTION CONTROL,
106 POLLUTION PREVENTION

---

1 Irritations of the eyes, which are caused by smoke, over-heating, dust, or similar injury, are easy to heal; the patient being advised first of all to avoid the irritating causes. . . . For the disease ceases without the use of any kind of medicine, if only a proper way of living be adopted.
AETIOS (c. 535), *Tetrabiblon,* Sermo 2

2 Ill air slays sooner than the sword.
RATIS RAVING, c. 1450

3 [London was cloaked in] such a cloud of sea-coal, as if there be a resemblance of hell upon earth, it is in this vulcano in a foggy day: this pestilent smoak, which corrodes the very yron, and spoils all the moveables, leaving a soot on all things that it lights.
JOHN EVELYN (1620–1706), *A Character of England,* 1659

4 That Hellish and dismall Cloud of SEA-
COAL . . . so universally mixed with the otherwise wholsome and excellent Aer, that her
Inhabitants breathe nothing but an impure
and thick Mist accompanied with a fuliginous
and filthy vapour, which renders them ob-
noxious to a thousand inconveniences, cor-
rupting the Lungs, and disordring the entire
habits of their Bodies; so that Catharre
. . . Coughs and Consumptions rage more in
this one City than in the whole Earth besides.
JOHN EVELYN (1620–1706), on London, *Fumi-
fugium*, 1661

5 Fly the rank city, shun its turbid air:
Breathe not the chaos of eternal smoke
And volatile corruption.
. . . and tho' the lungs abhor
To drink the dun fuliginous abyss
Did not the acid vigor of the mine,
Roll'd from so many thundring chimneys,
tame
The putrid salts that overswarm the sky;
This caustic venom would perhaps corrode
Those tender cells that draw the vital air. . . .
While yet you breathe, away! the rural wilds
Invite.
JOHN ARMSTRONG (1709–1779), *The Art of Pre-
serving Health*, 1744

6 Hell is a city much like London—
A populous and smoky city.
PERCY BYSSHE SHELLEY (1792–1822), *Peter Bell
the Third*, 1819

7 The idiosyncrasy of this town is smoke. It rolls
solemnly in slow folds from the great chimneys
of the iron-foundries, and settles down in
black, slimy pools on the muddy streets.
Smoke on the wharves, smoke on the dingy
boats, on the yellow river—clinging in a coat-
ing of greasy soot to the house-front, the two
faded poplars, the faces of the passers-by.
REBECCA HARDING DAVIS (1831–1910), *Atlantic
Monthly*, April 1861

8 The centralisation of population in great cities exercises of itself an unfavourable influence; the atmosphere of London can never be
so pure, so rich in oxygen, as the air of the
country; two and a half million pairs of lungs,
two hundred and fifty thousand fires,
crowded upon an area three to four miles
square, consume an enormous amount of oxygen, which is replaced with difficulty.
KARL MARX (1818–1883), *Das Kapital*, 1867

9 Experimental evidence is strongly in favor of
my argument that the chemical purity of the
air is of no importance.
L. ERSKINE HILL, quoted in *New York Times*,
22 September 1912

10 There is a midland city in the heart of fair,
open country, a dirty and wonderful city nes-
tling dingily in the fog of its own smoke. The
stranger must feel the dirt before he feels the
wonder, for the dirt will be upon him in-
stantly. It will be upon him and within him,
since he must breathe it, and he may care for
no further proof that wealth is here better
loved than cleanliness.
BOOTH TARKINGTON (1869–1946), *Growth*,
1915

11 I had rather raise up one man to front the
world than half a hundred dependents that
dare not breathe the outside air.
LOUIS J. HALLE, JR., *Spring in Washington*,
1947

12 Our Georgian forerunners [in England] . . .
ignored the natural smells of sweat and dung
and dirt as we ignore the artificial smells of
petrol fumes and industrial effluents.
JOHN GLOAG, *Georgian Grace*, 1956

13 The Ford engineering staff, although mindful
that automobile engines produce exhaust
gases, feels these waste vapors are dissipated
in the atmosphere quickly and do not present
an air pollution problem.
DAN J. CHABEK, Ford engineering spokesman, March 1953, quoted in Ralph Nader,
Unsafe at Any Speed, 1965

14 I would like to begin this morning by reading
you a little weather report: ". . . dirty water
and black snow pour from the dismal air
to . . . the putrid slush that waits for them below." No, that is not a description of Boston,
Chicago, New York, or even Washington,
D.C. It is fromDante's *Inferno*, a 600-year-old
vision of damnation. But doesn't it sound familiar? Isn't it a forecast that fits almost any
large American city today? . . . Don't we really risk our own damnation every day by destroying the air that gives us life? I think
we do.
LYNDON B. JOHNSON (1908–1973), signing the
Air Quality Act of 1967

6 AIR POLLUTION

15 Something is wrong with what we are doing and not doing if you can fly over any city or town in this vast nation, with the possible single exception of Los Angeles, and be greeted by plumes looping in the wind when there is a wind, or streaming out slowly on calm days, looking like so many tattered and tired gray, black or red banners—proclaiming the dogged durability of obsolescence and decay. And you can.

> JOHN T. MIDDLETON, director, National Center for Air Pollution Control, speech, Air Pollution Control Association convention, 12 June 1967

16 One of the first laws against air pollution came in 1300 when King Edward I decreed the death penalty for burning of coal. At least one execution for that offense is recorded. But economics triumphed over health considerations, and air pollution became an appalling problem in England.

> GLENN T. SEABORG, Atomic Energy Commission chairman, speech, Argonne National Laboratory, 1969

17 It is important to remember that our respiratory system was developed, in the course of evolution, in an environment which was precisely fitted to support this system. In nature, the air is free of toxic substances that might, in contact with the rich blood supply in the lungs, readily penetrate into the body or damage the self-protective processes in the lungs. Having evolved in such an environment, the human body is not well equipped to tolerate the presence of any other airborne substances that affect bodily functions.

> BARRY COMMONER, testimony, U.S. Senate Public Works subcommittee, 27 October 1969

18 The sulfur oxides, hydrocarbons, carbon monoxide, oxides of nitrogen, particulates, and many more contaminants amounts to compulsory consumption of violence by most Americans.

> RALPH NADER, in John C. Esposito, *Vanishing Air*, 1970

19 The pervasive environmental violence of air pollution has imperiled health, safety, and property throughout the nation for many decades.

> RALPH NADER, in John C. Esposito, *Vanishing Air*, 1970

20 Air pollution (and its fallout on soil and water) is a form of domestic chemical and biological warfare.

> RALPH NADER, in John C. Esposito, *Vanishing Air*, 1970

21 They said there was no such thing as an air pollution problem and, if there were, it wasn't the automobile that caused it, and if it were the automobile that caused it, they could easily cure it.

> WALLACE L. MINTO, on a visit to one of the big automobile manufacturers, testimony, U.S. Senate Public Works subcommittee, 1972

22 Not a single representative [of the auto industry] came forward with the idea that any of the power systems were viable and a good alternative to the combustion engine. . . . The point I am making, you have made your bed, and now you have to sleep in it.

> HOWARD BAKER, U.S. Senator, on auto industry prototype-car demonstrations on Capitol Hill, hearings of Senate Public Works subcommittee, February–March 1972

23 The automobile companies are spending too much money on goodwill and too little on trying to see if there is an alternative to the internal combustion engine.

> WILLIAM P. LEAR, testimony, Senate Public Works Committee subcommittee, February–March 1972

24 It happens that those who are most susceptible [to air pollution] are the very young and the very old—not, as some would suggest, peculiarly squeamish groups whose interests the society can afford to compromise if it begins to look like it might be expensive to protect them.

> LOIS JEFFREY, speech, University of North Carolina, 1 November 1973

25 It is clear that the enforcement of clean air standards is wasted on smokers; however, it also appears impossible to maintain clean air standards in the presence of smokers. If we are really serious about clean air, the use of tobacco must be controlled as well as pollution from automotive and industrial sources.

> ROBERT J. NAUMANN, letter to *Science*, 26 October 1973

26 We still have too much air and water pollution and we still need to work to reduce it.

But we also need to put the problem of pollution into a historical as well as scientific perspective. It's not as frightening to hear some overzealous environmentalists say that air pollution is rapidly destroying civilization when we realize that people have lived in much dirtier air throughout history. We know that the ancient Greeks, who were considered highly civilized, either cooked with a fire in the middle of a stone floor or under a ceiling. They lived in fumes that must have been a thousand times worse than our worst air pollution.

RONALD REAGAN, quoted in Charles D. Hobbs, *Ronald Reagan's Call to Action*, 1976

27 As a holding action, you could say [the Clean Air Act] has been successful. There are more cars and more industry, but the problem is not appreciably worse.

DAVID HAWKINS, *Washington Post*, 31 December 1979

28 We all live downwind.

BUMPER STICKER, 1980s

29 Approximately 80% of our air pollution stems from hydrocarbons released by vegetation. So let's not go overboard in setting and enforcing tough emissions standards for man-made sources.

RONALD REAGAN, quoted in *Sierra*, 10 September 1980

30 Mt. St. Helens has contributed more sulfur dioxide than has been released in the last ten years of automobile driving.

RONALD REAGAN, quoted in *Science*, 28 November 1980

31 You cannot affirm the power plant and condemn the smokestack, or affirm the smoke and condemn the cough.

WENDELL BERRY, *The Gift of Good Land*, 1981

32 Who believes the world is about to come to an end because of smokestack and automobile emissions? How many people think they are going to die from dirty air? The real popular concern is for environmental aesthetics, not with health risks.

WALL STREET JOURNAL, editorial, 25 August 1981

33 The air [in Manchester, England] is so polluted that you wake up in the morning listening to the birds cough.

ANONYMOUS, quoted in letter to *Le Monde*, 6 August 1982

34 If we don't take in air every few minutes, we die, but the air we are taking in is killing us.

JANE WAGNER, *The Search for Signs of Intelligent Life in the Universe*, 1987

35 For instance, the average American car driven the average American distance—ten thousand miles—in an average American year releases its own weight in carbon into the atmosphere. Imagine each car on a busy freeway pumping a ton of carbon into the atmosphere, and the sky seems less infinitely blue.

BILL McKIBBEN, *The End of Nature*, 1989

36 The President I don't think cares whether people burn ethanol or methanol, compressed natural gas or Chanel No. 5, so long as we get these pollution reductions.

WILLIAM K. REILLY, on President Bush's call for a move toward more clean-burning fuels for automobiles, "This Week with David Brinkley," ABC-TV, 18 June 1989

37 Now's the time for someone in the [Bush] administration to start telling the public that driving in America is about a lot more than just carbon dioxide.

WALL STREET JOURNAL, editorial on a proposed air pollution control law, 15 January 1990

38 In a country where the vast majority of air pollution comes from energy use, much of that from transportation, we are trying to achieve clean air through a law that has little say over how much energy we use or how we get around.

JESSICA MATTHEWS, on the Clean Air Act, *Washington Post*, 17 October 1990

39 A fuming smokestack is the perfect symbol of our national dilemma. On one hand, it means the jobs and products we need. On the other, it means pollution.

AMERICAN GAS ASSOCIATION, advertisement, *Sierra*, January–February 1991

40 The Grand Canyon is to the United States what Notre Dame is to France. Its a worldwide symbol of our country's spirit and beauty.

WILLIAM K. REILLY, invoking the Clean Air Act to protect visibility in the parks, *Washington Post*, 1 February 1991

7 ANIMAL RIGHTS
See also 69 HUNTING

1 To relieve an animal of pain or danger is a biblical law.

TALMUD, Sabbath,128b

2 We can judge the heart of a man by his treatment of animals.

IMMANUEL KANT (1724–1804), *Lectures on Ethics*

3 Have the wild things no moral or legal rights? What right has man to inflict such long and fearful agony on a fellow-creature, simply because that creature does not speak his language?

ERNEST THOMPSON SETON (1860–1946), *Wild Animals I Have Known*, 1895

4 Higher animals and to some extent plants that have complex behaviors and life cycles, all with vast power requirements, were not developed for man's enjoyment, by accident, or even through some quirk of evolutionary procedure.

HOWARD T. ODUM, on legal rights for natural objects, *Environment, Power and Society*, 1971

5 It is not inevitable, nor is it wise, that natural objects should have no rights to seek redress in their own behalf. It is no answer to say that streams and forests cannot have standing because streams and forests cannot speak. Corporations cannot speak either; nor can states, estates, infants, incompetents, muncipalities or universities. Lawyers speak for them, as they customarily do for the ordinary citizen with legal problems.

CHRISTOPHER D. STONE, *Southern California Law Review* 45, Spring 1972

6 I am quite seriously proposing that we give legal rights to forests, oceans, rivers and other co-called "natural objects" in the environment—indeed, to the natural environment as a whole.

CHRISTOPHER D. STONE, *Southern California Law Review* 45, Spring 1972

7 The voice of the inanimate object . . . should not be stilled. . . . [B]efore these priceless bits of Americana (such as a valley, an alpine meadow, a river, or a lake) are forever lost or are so transformed as to be reduced to the eventual rubble of our urban environment, the voice of the existing beneficiaries of these environmental wonders should be heard.

WILLIAM O. DOUGLAS (1898–1980), U.S. Supreme Court justice, *Sierra Club* v. *Morton*, 19 April 1972

8 The critical question of "standing" would be simplified . . . if we fashioned a federal rule that allowed environmental issues to be litigated . . . in the name of the inanimate object about to be dispoiled, defaced, or invaded by roads and bulldozers and where injury is the subject of public outrage. Contemporary public concern for protecting nature's ecological equilibrium should lead to the conferral of standing upon environmental objects to sue for their own preservation.

WILLIAM O.DOUGLAS (1898–1980), U.S. Supreme Court justice, *Sierra Club* v. *Morton*, 19 April 1972

9 Power to all the people. What we must . . . do . . . is incorporate the other people . . . the creeping people, and the standing people, and the flying people and the swimming people . . . into the councils of government.

GARY SNYDER, on extending rights to animals, *Turtle Island*, 1974

10 Their [animals'] interests are allowed to count only when they do not clash with human interests.

PETER SINGER, *Animal Liberation*, 1975

11 It can no longer be maintained by anyone but a religious fanatic that man is the special darling of the whole universe, or that other animals were created to provide us with food, or

that we have divine authority over them, and divine permission to kill them.
PETER SINGER, *Animal Liberation*, 1975

12 We must give [dolphins] rights as individuals under our laws [with] complete freedom of the waters of the earth.
JOHN C. LILLY, *Oceans*, March 1976

13 We should go beyond proving the rights of animals to live in utilitarian terms. Why don't we just admit we like having them around? Isn't that answer enough?
OLAUS MURIE, quoted in Donald Worster, *Nature's Economy*, 1977

14 So we're dealing with a broadening, really, of our framework of moral reference.
MICHAEL FOX, on endowing animals with rights as an extension of the process of liberation for blacks and women, quoted in *Washington Star*, 28 April 1978

15 It bothers me that society has no ethic for dealing with animals. We have a few rules. Kill them humanely. Don't torture them. About two years ago, I thought we were really moving to an ethic by which people could have a respectful relationship with the other species on earth. But now I'm really not sure. It doesn't seem to be happening.
JOHN R. CLARK, quoted in *Conservation Foundation Letter*, May 1978

16 The basis of all animal rights should be the Golden Rule: we should treat *them* as we would wish them to treat *us*, were any other species in our dominant position.
CHRISTINE STEVENS, quoted in Michael Fox, *Returning to Eden*, 1980

17 Just as we have progressed beyond the blatantly racist ethic of the era of slavery and colonialism, so we must now progress beyond the speciesist ethic of the era of factory farming, of the use of animals as mere research tools, of whaling, seal hunting, kangaroo slaughter and the destruction of wilderness.
PETER SINGER, Prologue, *In Defense of Animals*, 1985

18 There is no ethical basis for elevating membership of one particular species into a morally crucial characteristic. From an ethical point of view, we all stand on an equal footing—whether we stand on two feet, or four, or none at all.
PETER SINGER, Prologue, *In Defense of Animals*, 1985

19 The whole creation groans under the weight of the evil we humans visit upon these mute, powerless creatures. It *is* our hearts, not just our heads, that call for an end to it all, that demand of us that we overcome, for them, the habits and forces behind their systematic oppression.
TOM REGAN, in Peter Singer, ed., *In Defense of Animals*, 1985

20 The most cruel environmental threat comes from the environmental movement itself as we see the animal rights laws systematically destroy our way of life and violate our right as aboriginal peoples to our traditions and values.
RHODA INUKSU, Inuk spokeswoman, testimony, World Commission on Environment and Development, Ottawa, Canada, 26–27 May 1986

21 Without animal research, medical science would come to a total standstill.
LEWIS THOMAS, *Reader's Digest*, June 1990

22 Get a feel for fur: Slam your fingers in a car door.
ANONYMOUS, on the use of steel traps to capture fur-bearing animals, cited in *Audubon*, November 1990

---

8 AUTOMOBILES
See also   62 HIGHWAYS

1 [A car is] a rampacious grizzly bear on the average highway, snorting and stinking.
J. HORACE MCFARLAND, letter to E. Mills, 20 April 1912

2 In American towns, it was thought more important to have a car which is a public asset than a bathroom which is private.
D. W. BROGAN, *The American Character*, 1944

3 Everything in life is somewhere else, and you get there in a car.
E. B. WHITE, *One Man's Meat*, 1944

4 No other man-made device since the shields and lances of the knights quite fulfills a man's ego like an automobile.
WILLIAM ROOTES, quoted on "Who Said That?," BBC TV, 14 January 1958

5 The automobile has not merely taken over the street, it has dissolved the living tissue of the city. Its appetite for space is absolutely insatiable; moving and parked, it devours urban land, leaving the buildings as mere islands of habitable space in a sea of dangerous and ugly traffic.
JAMES MARSTON FITCH, New York Times, 1 May 1960

6 In short, the American has sacrificed his life as a whole to the motorcar, like someone who, demented with passion, wrecks his home in order to lavish his income on a capricious mistress who promises delights he can only occasionally enjoy.
LEWIS MUMFORD, The Highway and the City, 1963

7 The current American way of life is founded not just on motor transportation but on the religion of the motorcar, and the sacrifices that people are prepared to make for this religion stand outside the realm of rational criticism.
LEWIS MUMFORD, The Highway and the City, 1963

8 Except the American woman, nothing interests the eye of American man more than the automobile, or seems so important to him as an object of esthetic appreciation.
A. H. BARR, JR., on displaying "pop art" that incorporated pieces of old automobiles, 1963

9 The car has become a secular sanctuary for the individual, his shrine to the self, his mobile Walden Pond.
EDWARD McDONAGH, quoted in Time, 10 May 1963

10 Climbing into a hot car is like buckling on a pistol. It is the great equalizer.
HENRY GREGOR FELSEN, To My Son—The Teen-Age Driver, 1964

11 The car has become an article of dress without which we feel uncertain, unclad, and incomplete.
MARSHALL McLUHAN, Understanding Media, 1964

12 The first thing an American does when he gets a little ahead is to buy an auto, and the second thing he does is to drive it over the horizon.
WALT A. ROSTOW, to Soviet general at the Johnson-Kosygin conference, Glassboro, N.J., 23 June 1967

13 François Nourissier in his recent book, The French, decries what he calls "the absurd tyranny of the automobile." But as we approach the problems associated with the automobile we must certainly keep in mind that the tyranny we associated with it has, in fact, been brought on by a love affair with the automobile and the mobility which it produces. It is only in the stage of disenchantment with the love affair that we begin to identify the relationship as one of tyranny.
M. CECIL MACKEY, 25 October 1968

14 In all this automania, there lurks the danger of a slowly diminishing quality of existence, of a fading appreciation of the experiences cars have usurped from the bodies and senses of men.
EDWARD AYRES, What's Good for GM, 1970

15 The automobile and the American public are locked in a life and death struggle. The car is robbing the American people of their land, air, minds and their very lives.
KENNETH P. CANTOR, in Garrett De Bell, ed., The Environmental Handbook, 1970

16 I think it is absolutely ridiculous for 100,000 Americans living in the same urban center to try to go to the same place for the same purpose at the same time, as each drives a ton and a half of metal with him. I just think that is utterly stupid from an economic point of view and from a human point of view.
WALTER REUTHER, quoted in Conservation Foundation Letter, June 1970

17 The automobile is the woman in technological man's life; his mistress, wife and mother.
KAISER NEWS, no. 5, 1971

18 An automobile is a suit of armour with two hundred horses inside; anyone who has one is a Knight: anyone who doesn't is a peasant.
  KENNETH E. BOULDING, in Anne Chisholm, ed., *Philosophers of the Earth: Conversations with Ecologists*, 1972

19 The bicycle is a vehicle for revolution. It can destroy the tyranny of the automobile as effectively as the printing press brought down despots of flesh and blood. The revolution will be spontaneous, the sum total of individual revolts like my own. It may have already begun.
  DANIEL BEHRMAN, *The Man Who Loved Bicycles*, 1973

20 [The freeway driving experience is] chillingly impersonal, suicidally frenetic, and so vacuous as to make [Los Angeles] inhabitants appear as the robots of a city that has become a puppet of technology.
  NEIL MORGAN, quoted in *New York Times Magazine*, 15 April 1973

21 Cars are here to stay. The idea that cars are a sex symbol or a status symbol foisted on the public by the magic of advertising is a myth. It would be hard to find much sex or status in the Model T—the car that started it all.
  HENRY FORD 2D, *New York Times*, 28 November 1973

22 The model American male spends more than 1,500 hours per year on his car; driving or sitting in it, parking or searching for it; earning enough to pay for the vehicle, the tolls, the tyres, the insurance or the highway taxes.
  IVAN ILLICH, *The Ecologist*, February 1974

23 We can't afford to rely on selling 9 to 11 million cars a year. It has some of the overtones of a one-crop economy in South America.
  RALPH NADER, testimony, Senate Commerce Committee, 12 March 1975

24 Mass transportation is doomed to failure in North America because a person's car is the only place where he can be alone and think.
  MARSHALL MCLUHAN, quoted in *Newsweek*, 22 September 1975

25 Trains are not any more energy efficient than the average automobile, with both getting about 48 passenger miles to the gallon.
  RONALD REAGAN, quoted in *Chicago Tribune*, 10 May 1980

26 The development of the automobile, for instance, had large effects on road-building industries, on the geographical structure of cities and retail trade, on the hotel and motel industry, on the oil industry, on international trade, and even on sexual patterns, fertility, and family life. All these effects may have mixtures of "goods" and "bads," so that the ultimate assessment is extraordinarily difficult.
  KENNETH E. BOULDING, speech, American Association for the Advancement of Science, Washington, D.C., 3 January 1982

27 I have an "Ecology Now" sticker on a car that drips oil everywhere it's parked.
  MARK SAGOFF, *Earth Ethics*, Summer 1990

28 Thanks to the automobile, cities no longer have to dispose of tons of horse manure every day.
  VIRGINIA I. POSTREL, *Reason* magazine editor, speech, City Club of Cleveland, Ohio, 19 June 1990

29 The distinction between the "natural," that is, nonhuman, and the "artificial" is not really very important. An automobile, I have often said, is a species just like a horse. It just has a more complicated sex life and it has detachable brains which guide it. The genes of a horse are contained in the stallion and the mare; the genes of the automobiles are in human minds, plans, perhaps computers, and so on, that organize the process of production in the womb or the factory.
  KENNETH E.BOULDING, in Norman Myers, *Gaia Atlas of Future Worlds*, 1990

---

9 BIODIVERSITY
See also   38 ENDANGERED SPECIES

---

1 All nature is so full that that district produces the greatest variety which is the most examined.
  GILBERT WHITE, *The Natural History of Selborne*, 1789

2 Diversity, be it ever so little, has value in relieving stress.
  FRANK FRASER DARLING, *Daedalus*, Fall 1967

3 We need to appreciate that a species, of whatever form, is life, is a unique manifestation of life, the final product of some evolutionary development.

IRSTON R. BARNES, quoted in *Conservation Foundation Letter*, 24 January 1968

4 The environmental source of uncertainty lies almost entirely in the organic world outside mankind, almost entirely indeed in the world of microbes. We cannot foretell the whole future of infectious disease. We can however make an important prediction about its effects on man. It is that man's future prospects are proportionate to the amount of genetic diversity he maintains among the interfertile members of his own species. In this respect, more than in any other, the loss of any primitive and apparently unsuccessful tribe affects the future of mankind as a whole. In this respect mankind is one.

C. D. DARLINGTON, *The Evolution of Man and Society*, 1969

5 We must shun uniformity of surroundings as much as absolute conformity of behavior, and make instead a deliberate effort to create as many diversified environments as possible.

RENE DUBOS, *The Ecologist*, October 1970

6 It is often said that variety is the spice of life. No intelligent investor confines his money to one or two shares. No one can sit stably and comfortably on a chair with two legs. No one remains fully healthy on a restricted diet. These facts are obvious, but the larger analogy that a varied base is vital for human existence fails to achieve recognition.

PRINCE BERNHARD OF THE NETHERLANDS, Founder President of World Wildlife Fund, President of WWF-Netherlands, speech, the Young Presidents' Organization, 6 May 1974

7 Diversification in a living system has adaptive value of course, but it also often seems to be the product of sheer exuberance and expressive fancy.

HOWARD L. PARSONS, *Marx and Engels on Ecology*, 1977

8 When a community or species has no known economic worth or other value to humanity, it is as dishonest and unwise to trump up weak resource values for it as it is unnecessary to abandon the effort to conserve it.

DAVID EHRENFELD, *The Arrogance of Humanism*, 1978

9 I suggest that as biological knowledge grows the ethic will shift fundamentally so that everywhere, for reasons that have to do with the very fiber of the brain, the fauna and flora of a country will be thought part of the national heritage as important as its art, its language, and that astonishing blend of achievement and farce that has always defined our species.

EDWARD O. WILSON, *Biophilia*, 1984

10 The value of biodiversity is more than the sum of its parts.

BRYAN G. NORTON, speech, National Forum on Biodiversity, Washington, D.C., 21 September 1986

11 Biological conservation, if it is to be successful, has to be spread effectively over the entire landscape.

D. H. M. CUMMING, speech, Conservation 2100 Symposium, Rockefeller University, New York City, October 1986

12 Wildlife resources extend from the wilderness to city centers, and each component of the landscape, and of man's activities, has some capacity to contribute to the conservation of biological resources and diversity.

D. H. M. CUMMING, speech, Conservation 2100 Symposium, Rockefeller University, New York City, October 1986

13 Poverty, ownership uncertainties, and the crushing necessity to replace useless with useful species defy the logic of conserving diversity for its own sake.

DAVID WESTERN, speech, Conservation 2100 Symposium, Rockefeller University, New York City, October 1986

14 Natural species are the library from which genetic engineers can work.

THOMAS E. LOVEJOY, *Time*, 13 October 1986

15 Relatively few benefits have flowed to the people who live closest to the more than 3,000 protected areas that have been established in tropical countries during the past 50

years. For this reason, the preservation of biodiversity is often thought of as something that poor people are asked to do to fulfill the wishes of rich people living in comfort thousands of miles away.

PETER H. RAVEN, *BioScience*, November 1986

16 In short, for every kind of organism that we lose because of our indifference or lack of attention, we deny to our children the ability to enrich and improve their lives by using those organisms as elements in their management of the global ecosystem.

PETER H. RAVEN, speech, National Audubon Society, Bellingham, Wash., 24 August 1987

17 Biotic diversity is not linked to the distribution of elephants, rhinos, and other so-called charismatic megaherbivores. The massive investment in conservation campaigns does more for the souls of the donors and the egos of the elephant experts than it does for biotic diversity, which is centered on less exciting communities of montane forests, Mediterranean heathlands, wetlands, lakes and rivers.

BRIAN J. HUNTLEY, in Edward O. Wilson, ed., *Biodiversity*, 1988

18 The love of diversity is now under a cloud, but it has not gone away—there would be no zoos, botanical gardens, or natural history museums if it had.

DAVID EHRENFELD, in David Western and Mary Pearl, eds., *Conservation for the 21st Century*, 1989

19 Thus, remarkably, we do not know the true number of species on earth even to the nearest order of magnitude. My own guess, based on the described fauna and flora and many discussions with entomologists and other specialists, is that the absolute number falls somewhere between five and thirty million.

EDWARD O. WILSON, in David Western and Mary Pearl, eds., *Conservation for the 21st Century* (1989)

20 We consider species to be like a brick in the foundation of a building. You can probably lose one or two or a dozen bricks and still have a standing house. But by the time you've lost 20 per cent of species, you're go-ing to destabilize the entire structure. That's the way ecosystems work.

DONALD FALK, *Christian Science Monitor*, 26 May 1989

21 Wilderness may temporarily dwindle, but wildness won't go away. A ghost wilderness hovers around the entire planet, the millions of tiny seeds of the original vegetation are hiding in the mud on the foot of an arctic tern, in the dry desert sands, or in the wind. These seeds are each uniquely adapted to a specific soil or circumstance; each has its own little form and fluff, ready to float, freeze, or be swallowed, always preserving the germ. Wilderness will inevitably return, but it will not be as fine a world as the one that was glistening in the early morning of the Holocene. Much life will be lost in the wake of human agency on Earth, that of the 20th and 21st centuries. Much is already lost.

GARY SNYDER, *Sierra*, September–October 1989

22 Biodiversity is the tool with which you play the game of promoting global stability. But it also consists of the organisms that give wonder and beauty and joy to the world, and that provide the context in which we evolved.

PETER H. RAVEN, quoted in *New York Times*, 18 December 1990

23 In terms of species richness and biological productivity, coral reefs are the tropical forests of the sea.

WORLD WILDLIFE FUND, *Focus*, January–February 1991

24 If you don't like diversity, drop dead.

BYRON KENNARD, February 1991

25 We must insist on diversity itself. We must relish the very process of generation, of a single organism becoming many, of destinies evolving in their eccentric pools. We must love the multiplicity of eyes that gaze back at us from fur, plumage, from cracked gray hide, and from scales. The wonder of them mirrors our own in this single water hole that is earth.

BRUCE BERGER, *American Way*, 1 February 1991

10 BIOTECHNOLOGY

1 I don't know what we have learned in two hundred years of biology, if we can have a Supreme Court that says there is no difference between the living and the non-living.

JONATHAN KING, criticizing the Supreme Court's ruling in *Diamond* v. *Chakrabarty*, which stated that genetically altered bacterium was patentable, "Life: Patent Pending," *Nova*, WGBH-TV, Boston, 28 February 1982

2 In the case of *Diamond* v. *Chakrabarty* [June 1980], the Supreme Court told us we could patent new life forms and have intellectual property in a gene. This may sound farreaching but it isn't really, and eighteen years of protection is, of course, merely the twinkling of an eye in the evolutionary scheme of biology.

DAVID PADWE, speech, Los Alamos National Laboratory, 9 March 1982

3 Biotechnology is biology for economic development.

CORNELL UNIVERSITY, Cornell Biotechnology Program brochure, March 1983

4 Our concern here is with momentum—the commercial and scientific momentum that builds around any new and dynamic technology. Our concern is that a certain kind of product momentum will be set in motion in the earliest stages of this technology that may be difficult to turn around should something go wrong; difficult to reverse because of huge capital investments, scientific careers on the line, and accrued political support.

JACK DOYLE, on biotechnology, testimony, Senate Environment and Public Works subcommittee, 27 September 1984

5 If almost any molecular geneticist can engineer new organisms in a modest laboratory, can we expect our regulatory programs to stay on top of releases?

JOHN D. DINGELL, U.S. Representative, hearing, House Energy and Commerce subcommittee, 11 December 1984

6 A corn plant with a single new gene isn't a kudzu vine. It's a corn plant with a single new gene. There is no more reason to fear it than there is to fear a corn breeder's new strain.

NINA FEDOROFF, testimony, House Energy and Commerce subcommittee, 11 December 1984

7 It would be a bleak world indeed that treated living things as no more than separable sequences of information available for disarticulation and recombination in any order that pleased human whim.

STEPHEN JAY GOULD, *Discover*, January 1985

8 Some critics fear that certain conjunctions might have potent and unanticipated effects—creating a resistant agent of disease or simply a new creature so hardy and fecund that . . . it spreads to engulf the earth in a geological millisecond. I am not persuaded by these excursions into science fiction, but the distant and deeper issue does merit discussion: What are the consequences, ethical, aesthetic, and practical, of altering life's fundamental geometry and permitting one species to design new creatures at will?

STEPHEN JAY GOULD, *Discover*, January 1985

9 It is a sad commentary on the nature of our political process that the governmental powers are more than willing to legitimize the full-scale application of this technology into the economic and social life of our society, even before citizens have had an oportunity to be fully informed of the many issues raised by this emerging technological revolution.

JEREMY RIFKIN, *Environmental Forum*, February 1985

10 I detect an atmosphere of hubris. That's when you laugh at the gods.

GEORGE E. BROWN, JR., on federal regulatory agency assurances of their competence to deal with biotechnology, hearing, U.S. House Science and Technology subcommittee, 17 April 1985

11 For a new technology characterized by a low probability of causing harm, the early stages of development need cause little worry. But as the technology becomes more widely used and moves in new directions, the likelihood of an undesirable consequence increases. . . . Genetic engineering appears to fit this pattern. . . . The very power, usefulness,

versatility, and applicability of genetic engineering make the issue of hazard especially relevant.

MARTIN ALEXANDER, *Issues in Science and Technology*, Spring 1985

12 Biotechnology is the ultimate in corporate vertical integration, where control begins with the gene and ends at the supermarket.

RICHARD NILSEN, Third World Biotechnology Conference, France, March 1987

13 Long and sad experience with the introduction of forms of life new to particular environments dictates great caution for any and all proposals for releasing organisms that are foreign, and hence unadapted, to the ecosystem.

EUGENE ODUM, *Conservation 90*, December 1990

14 Scientists have fused sheep and goat cells, creating the geep—a half sheep, half goat chimera. . . . Should biotechnology be allowed to use the environmental crisis as an excuse to play God, crossing human genes into animals, and animal genes into plants? . . . Cross-species genetic transfers may be the ultimate offense to the dignity and integrity of the biotic community. Prolonged and expanded use of these cross-species engineering feats could mean the end of the natural world as we currently know it.

ALEX ANTYPAS and JEANNE LAWSON, *The Green Lifestyle Handbook*, 1990

15 The final act of hubris is currently fomenting deep within the laboratories of genetic engineers. The ultimate deception—where new genes are added or substituted for old—was where we got into trouble with the microbial world in the first place. . . . Will these manipulations also generate reverberating and largely irreversible changes in the ecosystem? The answer is almost certainly yes.

MARC LAPPE, *Chemical Deception*, 1991

16 The granting of patent privileges over genetically engineered microorganisms, plants, and animals represents the culmination of a five-hundred-year movement to enclose the plan-

etary commons that began inauspiciously on the village green in small rural hamlets scattered throughout England and the European continent. Now even the building blocks of life itself have been enclosed, privatized, and reduced to marketable products.

JEREMY RIFKIN, *Biosphere Politics*, 1991

---

11 BIRDS
See also   139 WILDLIFE

---

1 A robin redbreast in a cage
  Puts all heaven in a rage.
    WILLIAM BLAKE (1757–1827), "Auguries of Innocence"

2 The sedge is withered from the lake,
  And no bird sings.
    JOHN KEATS (1795–1821), *La Belle Dame sans Merci*, 1819

3 Do you ne'er think what wondrous beings these?
  Do you ne'er think who made them, and who taught
  The dialect they speak, where melodies
  Alone are the interpreters of thought?
  Whose household words are songs in many keys,
  Sweeter than instrument of man e'er caught!
  Whose habitations in the tree-tops even
  Are half-way houses on the road to Heaven!
    HENRY WADSWORTH LONGFELLOW (1807–1882), "Birds of Killingworth"

4 You call them thieves and pillagers; but know
  They are the winged wardens of your farms,
  Who from the cornfields drive the insidious foe,
  And from your harvests keep a hundred harms;
  Even the blackest of them all, the crow,
  Renders good service as your man-at-arms,
  Crushing the beetle in his coat of mail,
  And crying havoc on the slug and snail.
    HENRY WADSWORTH LONGFELLOW (1807–1882), "Birds of Killingworth"

5 There are no more shadows across the land,
  and the birds in the sky—infinite dreams,
  white visions seeking shady places—will

soon have no more trees in which to build their nests.
VICTOR DE LAPRADE (1812–1887), *La mort d'un chêne*, 1844

6 Man feels himself an infinity above those creatures who stand, zoologically, only one step below him, but every human being looks up to the birds. They suit the fancy of us all. What they feel they can voice, as we try to; they court and nest, they battle with the elements, they are torn by two opposing impulses, a love of home and a passion for far places. Only with birds do we share so much emotion.
DONALD CULROSS PEATTIE, *Singing in the Wilderness*, 1935

7 When we who have a feeling for birds observe a mighty eagle, or the perfection of a tiny warbler, we see, not the inspiration of God filtered through human agency, but the very handiwork of the Creator Himself.
ROSALIE EDGE, "Good Companions in Conservation: Annals of an Implacable Widow," 1940s

8 The Lord did well when he put the loon and his music into this lonesome land.
ALDO LEOPOLD (1886–1948), *Round River*, 1953

9 God loved the birds and invented trees. Man loved the birds and invented cages.
JACQUES DEVAL (b.1894), *Afin de vivre bel et bien*

10 We are destroying half the basis of English poetry.
ALDOUS HUXLEY (1894–1963), on the decline of bird populations because of pesticides, quoted by Julian Huxley, letter, *New York Times*, 19 April 1964

11 If I had to choose, I would rather have birds than airplanes.
CHARLES A. LINDBERGH (1902–1974), *Reader's Digest*, July 1964

12 If you want to see birds, you must have birds in your heart.
JOHN BURROUGHS, *Outside*, December 1977

13 Birds seems to me to reflect some kind of life force.
ROGER TORY PETERSON, quoted in Frank Graham, Jr., *The Audubon Ark*, 1990

12 CHEMICALS
See also 99 PESTICIDES

1 [Its like] handing a loaded .45 automatic to a child and telling him to run out and play.
CARL BUCHEISTER, on the widespread use of chemicals, *Audubon*, July–August 1961

2 The chemicals to which life is asked to make its adjustment are no longer merely the calcium and silica and copper and all the rest of the minerals washed out of the rocks and carried in rivers to the sea; they are the synthetic creations of man's inventive mind, brewed in his laboratories, and having no counterparts in nature.
RACHEL CARSON, *Silent Spring*, 1962

3 For the first time in the history of the world, every human being is now subjected to contact with dangerous chemicals, from the moment of conception until death.
RACHEL CARSON, *Silent Spring*, 1962

4 If we are going to live so intimately with these chemicals—eating and drinking them, taking them into the very marrow of our bones—we had better know something about their nature and their power.
RACHEL CARSON, *Silent Spring*, 1962

5 As crude a weapon as the cave man's club, the chemical barrage has been hurled against the fabric of life.
RACHEL CARSON, *Silent Spring*, 1962

6 In this now universal contamination of the environment, chemicals are the sinister and little-recognized partners of radiation in changing the very nature of the world—the very nature of life.
RACHEL CARSON, *Silent Spring*, 1962

7 Over increasingly large areas of the United States, spring now comes unheralded by the return of the birds, and the early mornings are strangely silent where once they were filled with the beauty of bird song.
RACHEL CARSON, *Silent Spring*, 1962

8 When combined with the chemical industry's productive overcapacity, and the hustling salesmanship of a free enterprise system, this commitment threatens to poison the land-

scape and to make the farmer increasingly dependent and the consumer well nigh helpless.

ROLAND C. CLEMENT, speech, Natural Resources Conference of the Garden Club Federation of Pennsylvania, 10 March 1964

9 In other words, for a prudent toxicological policy, a chemical should be considered guilty until proven innocent.

UMBERTO SAFFIOTTI, proceedings, Eleventh Canadian Research Conference, 6–8 May 1976

10 The bottom line on carcinogenesis testing is this. You can drown an animal in a pool of some substance, suffocate an animal under a heap of it, or beat an animal to death with a sock full of it, but if it isn't carcinogenic, you can't give an animal cancer with it.

WILLIAM HINES and JUDITH RANDAL, quoted in Samuel S. Epstein, *The Politics of Cancer*, 1978

11 We need to develop a coherent system to know what's really important. This is to avoid the chemical-of-the-week syndrome, in which the *Washington Post* every Sunday produces an article about some new deadly chemical that we have never heard of.

WILLIAM DRAYTON, on chemical risks, quoted in *Conservation Foundation Letter*, February 1978

12 There are hundreds of highly dangerous "natural" chemicals, just as there are thousands of perfectly harmless "synthetics." Yet environmentalism has managed to establish the doctrine that everything in nature is "good," while things that are made in the laboratory hold the potential for destruction.

WILLIAM TUCKER, *Harper's*, August 1978

13 The assumption that these and a great many other technological innovations are required-for "progress" is too often made without any real justification. . . . It is paradoxical that those who talk most about progress are in fact almost always the enemies of change.

LIEBE F. CAVALIERI, on the argument that society is dependent on industrial chemicals for progress and prosperity, letter, *New York Times*, 8 August 1978

14 It is not clear society will lose all that much by some reduction in the number of chemicals introduced.

J. CLARENCE DAVIES, testimony, U.S. House Interstate and Foreign Commerce subcommittee, 22 August 1980

15 We're all living in a chemical soup.

LANCE A. WALLACE, *Newsweek*, 7 January 1985

16 There seems to be a feeling that anything that is natural must be good. Strychnine is natural.

ISAAC ASIMOV, *Isaac Asimov's Book of Science and Nature Quotations*, 1988

17 The child that I am carrying right now has probably and is currently receiving the heaviest loadings of toxic chemicals that it will receive in its lifetime.

KATE DAVIES, International Joint Commission Science Advisory Board meeting, 1989

18 With each species that we lose, we lose a notebook of genes—genes that are potentially valuable transferable resources. We should be looking at organisms not previously studied to see if they contain novel chemicals that are biologically active. Insects are the most versatile chemists on earth. . . . Every single new idea in chemistry has come not from the minds of chemists but from nature.

THOMAS EISNER, quoted in *New York Times*, 10 January 1989

19 Asbestos, EMFs, and CFCs have given us a degree of humility. When yesterday's "triumph of modern chemistry" turns out instead to be today's deadly threat to the global environment, it is legitimate to ask what else we don't know.

DENIS HAYES, speech, Museum of Natural History, New York City, 8 November 1989

20 The 1990s are the beginning of the end of the chemical era. Agrichemicals will shift from being the driving force to being the helping hand.

DAVE DYER, *Smithsonian*, April 1990

21 Nature never was "squeaky clean" with respect to hazardous chemicals and organisms.

LOUIS J. THIBODEAUX, *Environmental Science and Technology* 24, no. 4, April 1990

22 Americans did not fight and win the wars of the 20th century to make the world safe for green vegetables.
RICHARD DARMAN, lecture, Harvard University, 1 May 1990

23 There is a clear pattern of fraudulent misconduct in the dioxin science performed by the chemical industry and its indentured academics.
SAMUEL S. EPSTEIN, *Greenpeace News*, 29 November 1990

24 Fertilizer [should] be treated like a prescription drug, its use strictly limited and only by official permission.
ANONYMOUS EPA CHESAPEAKE BAY OFFICIAL, quoted in *Washington Post*, 26 November 1990

25 The question is not when or how the canal will leak, but rather that the chemicals that did leak for over 25 years have merely been contained, not removed. In 1980 they told us not to eat out of our gardens, drink the water, get pregnant or let our children play in the yard. Nothing has happened to make it OK to do any of those things in Love Canal today.
LOIS GIBBS, *E* magazine, January–February 1991

---

13 CITIES
See also   125 SUBURBS, 129 TOWNS, 132 URBAN ENVIRONMENT

---

1 A city, like a living thing, is a united and continuous whole.
PLUTARCH (around A.D. 50–120), *Moralia*

2 Let the river roll which way it will, cities will rise on its banks.
RALPH WALDO EMERSON (1803–1882), *Journals*

3 The gross heathenism of civilization has generally destroyed nature, and poetry, and all that is spiritual.
JOHN MUIR (1838–1914), letter to J. B. McChesney, 19 September 1871

4 The outcome of the cities will depend on the race between the automobile and the elevator, and anyone who bets on the elevator is crazy.
FRANK LLOYD WRIGHT (1867–1959), quoted on PBS, 27 May 1974

5 Modern nature worship is all upside down. Trees and fields ought to be the ordinary things; terraces and temples ought to be extraordinary. I am on the side of the man who lives in the country and wants to go to London.
G. K. CHESTERTON (1874–1936), *Alarms and Discussions*, 1910

6 When you get there, there is no there there.
GERTRUDE STEIN (1874–1946), on California cities such as Oakland, quoted in *The American Land*, 1979

7 A city that outdistances man's walking powers is a trap for man.
ARNOLD TOYNBEE (1889–1975), quoted in *The American Land*, 1979

8 With all history to contradict us, it is hardly worthwhile to speak of city life as entailing "spiritual loss," because it is out of touch with Nature. It is in touch with humanity, and humanity is Nature's heaviest asset.
AGNES REPPLIER, *Times and Tendencies*, 1931

9 Culture suggests agriculture, but civilization suggests the city. In one aspect civilization is the habit of civility; and civility is the refinement which townsmen, who made the word, thought possible only in the *civitas* or city. For in the city are gathered, rightly or wrongly, the wealth and brains produced in the countryside; in the city invention and industry multiply comforts, luxuries and leisure; in the city traders meet, and barter goods and ideas; in that cross-fertilization of minds at the crossroads of trade intelligence is sharpened and stimulated to creative power. In the city some men are set aside from the making of material things, and produce science and philosophy, literature and art. Civilization begins in the peasant's hut, but it comes to flower only in the towns.
WILL DURANT, *The Story of Civilization*, 1935

10 As a remedy to life in society, I would suggest the big city. Nowadays it is the only desert within our means.
ALBERT CAMUS (1913–1960), *Notebooks, 1935–1942*

11 Each generation writes its own biography in the cities it creates.
LEWIS MUMFORD, *The Culture of Cities*, 1938

12 In other times, when painters tried to paint a scene of awful desolation, they chose the desert or heath of barren rocks, and there would try to picture man in his great loneliness—the prophet in the desert. . . . But for a modern painter, the most desolate scene would be a street in almost any one of our great cities on a Sunday afternoon. . . . Nothing. Nothing at all. And this is what gives the scene its special quality of tragic loneliness, awful emptiness and utter desolation. Every modern city man is familiar with it.
THOMAS WOLFE (1900–1938), *You Can't Go Home Again*, 1940

13 No city should be too large for a man to walk out of in a morning.
CYRIL CONNOLLY (1903–1974), *The Unquiet Grave*, 1944

14 The city is the only place where true diversity can thrive and where specialization can reach its apogee.
E. M. FISHER, ed., *The Metropolis and Modern Life*, 1955

15 For [Europeans] a city is, above all, a past; to [Americans] it is mainly a future; what they like in the city is everything it has not yet become and everything it can be.
JEAN-PAUL SARTRE (1905–1980), *Literary and Philosophical Essays*, 1955

16 Cities were in many cases originally created for protection. This is about the only logic of urban growth which is no longer significant.
ROBERT MOSES (1888–1981), *Working for the People*, 1956

17 Big cities and countrysides can get along well together. Big cities need real countryside close by. And countryside—from man's point of view—needs big cities, with all their diverse opportunities and productivity, so human beings can be in a position to appreciate the rest of the natural world instead of to curse it.
JANE JACOBS, *The Death and Life of Great American Cities*, 1961

18 An Americancity is a place where the post office looks like the Parthenon, the home of the town's richest citizen is a replica of Blenheim Palace, and everybody else lives like a Texas rancher.
CONRAD KNICKERBOCKER, *Life*, 24 December 1965

19 Once we have decided on a city's optimum size, how do we prevent the uncontrolled growth that leads to many of today's urban problems? The answer is *not* to control individuals, but to design a mix of industrial, commercial, and other employment opportunities that keeps the population in a healthy equilibrium.
ATHELSTAN SPILHAUS, *Daedalus*, Fall 1967

20 Man has built and loved cities because in the urban form he constructs the superimage of his ideal self. The common denominator of cities, from Nineveh to New York, is a collective idol worship, praying for power over nature, destiny, knowledge, and wealth.
SIBYL MOHOLY-NAGY, *Matrix of Man*, 1968

21 On the city street . . . no one chooses to understand and to make it a garden. We have chosen to make it a parking lot instead. The practice persists for cities to subsidize the middle-income owners of automobiles with free parking facilities along the curbs of streets—*public* land, comprising anywhere from a quarter to a third of the total land area of a city.
CHARLES E. LITTLE, *A Town Is Saved*, 1973

22 There isn't anything we don't know about the modern city—its demography, its water table, its engineering design, its art, its slums, its economics, its politics. We just don't seem to know how to make it beautiful, accessible, solvent, safe and clean.
HARLAN CLEVELAND, *The National Observer*, 16 August 1975

23 On the one hand, we lament the city as being without nature. On the other hand, the nature we have in mind and about which we are

nostalgic is stripped of its most forbidding qualities: loneliness, unpredictability, and the terrors of the uninhabitable.
JOHN J. MCDERMOTT, *The Culture of Experience*, 1976

24 New York City has become strangled with cars: no crosstown trips at lunch time, no appointments before eleven or after three o'clock, no friendships except within walking distance.
ADA LOUISE HUXTABLE, 1969, quoted in Jacques Cousteau, *The Cousteau Almanac*, 1980

25 To drive a wide boulevard through a quarter of the old city became almost a symbolic act of modernity and independence.
ALBERT HOURANI, on post-colonial Arab societies, *A History of Arab Peoples*, 1991

26 The only sustainable city—and this, to me, is the indispensable ideal and goal—is a city in balance with its countryside: a city, that is, that would live off the *net* ecological income of its supporting region, paying as it goes all its ecological and human debts. . . . Some cities can never be sustainable, because they do not have a countryside around them, or near them, from which they can be sustained.
WENDELL BERRY, *Atlantic Monthly*, February 1991

14 CITIZEN ACTION
See also   103 POLITICS

1 It is they who get the men started. Their federated clubs are invaluable as local propagandists and ground breakers. If once women see the light, the militant kind will fight forever against all odds.
ROBERT S. YARD, on women in conservation, letter to R. L. Wilbur, 31 January 1929

2 Never doubt that a small group of thoughtful, committed citizens can change the world. Indeed, it's the only thing that ever has.
MARGARET MEAD (1901–1978), quoted in John M. Richardson, ed., *Making It Happen*, 1982

3 We are witnessing, I believe, an awakening in our society by individuals from all walks of life who are resisting—some intelligently, some otherwise—the processes of dehumanization which an advanced, highly technical society seems to impose on them. We are witnessing man's attempt to preserve or regain that which is so precious to him—self-respect and a degree of control over the decision-making in his affairs. . . . Let there be no doubt, there will be participation. The question is whether it will be constructive and useful or erratic and wasteful.
DONALD RUMSFELD, U.S. Representative, on proposed requirements for public hearings on highway projects, testimony, Federal Highway Administration hearing, 1968

4 We must maintain that which is not defiled, enhance that which is degraded, and restore that which has been destroyed. . . . None of this can be done if the people of this nation leave the decisions and efforts to government and industry alone.
EDMUND S. MUSKIE, U.S. Senator, speech, Consumer Federation of America, 30 January 1969

5 These middle class activists command informational and organizational skills that can be employed to challenge official explanations and alibis. Among the citizens groups are accountants, lawyers, teachers, business executives, farmers, scientists, and engineers. They are quite capable of dissecting agency budgets, of uncovering the fallacies of cost-benefit ratios, and of pointing out alternatives that government officials failed to explore. For these activists, public office holds no mystique; and they have no patience with the proposition that government knows best, that government must act as it does on information that the public cannot have.
LYNTON K. CALDWELL, *Environment: A Challenge for Modern Society*, 1970

6 The naiveté, enthusiasm and idealism of young people is not a thing to be scorned, for it is the raw material of constructive growth. We will stop the destruction of this planet even at the cost of our futures, careers and blood.
PENNFIELD JENSEN, quoted in *Conservation Foundation Letter*, January 1970

7 This new act is a Magna Carta for conservation, and for those concerned citizens who

want to contribute in the fight to save our environment. By requiring the government to report on the environmental effects of its actions before they are taken, and by requiring that information to be made public, the act opens the way for a concerned public to make its voice clearly heard.

> HENRY REUSS, U.S. Representative, on the National Environmental Policy Act, quoted in *Conservation Foundation Letter*, April 1970

8 Sue the Bastards!

> VICTOR J. YANNACONE, advice to citizen activists, speech, Michigan State University, 22 April 1970

9 Intense, incessant citizen pressure is the only thing that will save us. We must assume that we are surrounded by rapacious developers, callous industrialists, inept public agencies, and insensitive politicians, and our only salvation is in our own two hands.

> RICHARD L. OTTINGER, U.S. Representative, speech, Sarah Lawrence College, 22 April 1970

10 We learn, when we respect the dignity of the people, that they cannot be denied the elementary right to participate fully in the solutions to their own problems. Self-respect arises only out of people who play an active role in solving their own crises and who are not helpless, passive, puppet-like recipients of private or public services. . . . Denial of the opportunity for participation is the denial of human dignity and democracy.

> SAUL ALINSKY, *Rules for Radicals,* 1971

11 It is true that both the radical environmentalists and the traditional Conservationists have been largely occupied with other wars, and that the job of preserving the stream valley in suburbia or the vacant city lot has fallen to single individuals or small groups of individuals whose press clippings are scant and whose cause is therefore relatively unknown. The headline value in preserving twenty acres of municipal woodland through patient diplomacy cannot, of course, match the drama of a frontal assault on GM or an acrimonious, charge-slinging campaign to save a wilderness area from corporate exploiters. Still, the local landsaving effort is no less important for being small, no less beneficial for being benign.

> CHARLES E. LITTLE and JOHN G. MITCHELL, *Space for Survival,* 1971

12 The only real force with long-lasting effects are groups of people in their own communities, who have involved themselves in problems that affect their communities, and have pursued hard and diligently, and who then begin to see the power of persistent, well-informed local action. People only really become involved in problems that affect them close to home.

> JOSEPH SAX, quoted in *Conservation Foundation Letter*, September 1971

13 It has been proven that a little old lady in Kansas can bring the Interior Department to its knees.

> ANONYMOUS FEDERAL OFFICIAL, on the requirements of the National Environmental Policy Act, 1972

14 These insipid and multitudinous suits [against highways] . . . are being maliciously used to halt the projects that Congress has worked for years and years and years to accomplish.

> ROBERT E. JONES, U.S. Representative, closed meeting of U.S. House Public Works Committee, 3 February 1972

15 Citizen organizations are uniquely qualified. They are independent of both government and industry. They can objectively evaluate the performance of both government and industry. They can focus public attention on what is and what is not being done. They articulate the public's desire for a better environment, they attract press attention which, in turn, helps nurture the climate of public opinion necessary for action. They have power. . . . With their healthy skepticism, organized citizen groups have already demonstrated their great capacity to prod and stir government and industry to action.

> ENVIRONMENTAL PROTECTION AGENCY, pamphlet, November 1972

16 *Silent Spring* was really the beginning. It showed for the first time, and on a grand scale, that a meticulously researched and lucidly written account of a faulty technology

could arouse the public to demand a more rational approach to problems of the environment.

> KEVIN P. SHEA, *Environment*, January–February 1973

17 Ironically, the years when pollsters have been telling us of rising rates of alienation, cynicism, apathy, and dropping out have been the same years that have produced an unprecedented rise in the consumer movement, public interest law firms, whistleblowers, and environmentalists.

> NICHOLAS JOHNSON, *Access* (newsletter of the National Citizens Committee for Broadcasting), 13 September 1974

18 Get back in your kitchen, lady, and let me build my road!

> ANONYMOUS ENGINEER, to a housewife trying to stop a road in San Mateo County, California, *Ladies Home Journal*, April 1976

19 In the end, because of the peculiar site-specific nature of wilderness politics, whether such areas thought to be threatened are actually protected, will depend upon the strength, drive, and determination of local grassroots leaders.

> BROCK EVANS, *Idaho Law Review* 16, 1980

20 We've always felt that "public interest" law is little more than a clever disguise for political activism.

> WALL STREET JOURNAL, editorial, 8 September 1982

21 We must have a true participation of all of the society in the decision-making and more particularly in the allocation of resources. And why so? Because all of us are perfectly aware that there will never be sufficient resources for everything that we wish, but if the population participates in the decision making it will benefit those who need the most and it will express their thought about the allocation of resources and it will give us the certainty that that which is being done is the legitimate aspiration of the people.

> ARISTIDES MARQUES, testimony, World Commission on Environment and Development, Brasilia, 30 October 1985

22 It would be totally unhealthy, counterproductive, and damaging for technical issues to be dealt with in public and constantly exposed to criticism and statements by just anyone.

> ANONYMOUS FRENCH NUCLEAR POWER OFFICIAL, in the aftermath of the Chernobyl nuclear power accident, quoted in *Science*, 27 August 1986

23 You go into a community and they will vote 80 percent to 20 percent in favor of a tougher Clean Air Act, but if you ask them to devote 20 minutes a year to having their car emissions inspected, they will vote 80 to 20 against it. We are a long way in this country from taking individual responsibility for the environmental problem.

> WILLIAM D. RUCKELSHAUS, former EPA administrator, *New York Times*, 30 November 1988

24 Regrettably, democratic societies rarely respond until a crisis has erupted. The threats of a renewed cartel upswing in oil prices lie too far in the future to spur us to action today.

> JAMES R. SCHLESINGER, former U.S. Secretary of Energy, quoted in *New York Times*, 4 January 1989

25 The nuclear[-power] issue in France was never a political one. The left side of the political scene and the right side were both, for different reasons, convinced about the necessity of nuclear energy. No politician was inclined to take this as the way of winning a battle. Certainly the fact that [the U.S. has] a Federal-state system is not good for nuclear energy because there are several levels where people can oppose energy and can try to stop it—and can succeed. In my view, the political system in [the U.S.] is really devoted to defend the individual. When somebody complains, he can stop everything. If anybody can stop anything, you go quickly to an inability to do anything.

> REMY CARLE, assistant director general, Electricité de France, quoted in *New York Times*, 8 May 1989

26 If we don't absorb the energy of the citizens' groups, environmental protection will go no-

where. I've always said that there's a limit to what the government can do alone.

KOSUGI TAKASHI, *Japan Environment Monitor* 2, no. 5, 30 September 1989

27 Environmentalists must force the political system to assign high priority to distant but dire threats. We must draw a line in the political sand on this side of each irreversible threshold. The public intuitively understands this. Environmental victories are always carried on the shoulders of a mobilized public.

DENIS HAYES, speech, Museum of Natural History, New York City, 8 November 1989

28 Without strong, ongoing citizen advocacy for change, most policymakers will continue to support environmental deficit spending, just as they have budget deficit spending. That is to say, current policies encourage squandering the natural endowment of future generations, who will be faced with paying off our environmental debts (pollutants) with fewer capital resources (forests, topsoil, watersheds, extinct species, etc.).

CLAUDINE SCHNEIDER, U.S. Representative, in Jeremy Rifkin, ed., *Green Lifestyle Handbook*, 1990

29 Environmental democracy is responsible for essentially killing the nuclear power industry. The people said, We don't want this— loudly enough that the industry had to put so many controls on it that they priced it out of the market. The big upsurge in recyling is a result of environmental democracy, of public opposition to incinerators.

BARRY COMMONER, *Mother Earth News*, March–April 1990

30 A couple of years ago there was a huge groundswell in the movement, but now things have cooled off a bit. You don't see as many people coming to anti-nuke meetings as before. So things like this give one pause to wonder if the grass roots is really rooted well, or if it's all just a passing phase. If the grass roots doesn't stay the course with more conviction, I don't see how things are going to change.

HIKANE HAMADA, *Japan Environment Monitor* 3, no. 3, 30 June 1990

31 There isn't a government in the world that would have done anything for the environment if it weren't for the citizen groups.

KONRAD VON MOLTKE, discussion, World Wildlife Fund, 4 March 1991

15 CLIMATE

See also 57 GREENHOUSE EFFECT, 136 WEATHER

1 Today civilization seems to make great progress only where a stimulating climate exists.

ELLSWORTH HUNTINGTON, *Civilization and Climate*, 1915

2 Climate . . . is fundamental by reason of its vital influence upon the quantity and quality not only of man's food but of most of his other resources; it plays a large part in determining the distribution and virulence of the parasites which cause the majority of diseases; and through its effect upon human occupations, modes of life, and habits, it is one of the main determinants of culture.

ELLSWORTH HUNTINGTON, *Civilization and Climate*, 1915

3 It is clear that small changes in the past 10,000 years had very large ecological effects and they can happen bloody fast. The end of the ice age took less than a century—kapow! It's fast, and that worries me because we don't know but what in a few years we could have a significant change that would disrupt our entire climate.

REID A. BRYSON, *Wall Street Journal*, 31 December 1969

4 The elements of the climatic system are tightly coupled and the system is nonlinear (i.e., a small stimulus could cause a large response). Slight changes in one area can set off feedback mechanisms that could cause an entirely unexpected result.

STEPHEN H. SCHNEIDER, speech, American Association for the Advancement of Science, Washington, D.C., December 1972

5 What *has* happened *can* happen; climatic history can repeat itself.
> REID BRYSON, warning of major fluctuations in climate, quoted in Stephen H. Schneider, *The Genesis Strategy*, 1976

6 Any rapid change in a regional climate is more likely to produce detrimental effects that far outweigh the beneficial ones.
> C. F. BAES, JR., et al., *American Scientist*, May–June 1977

7 The famines ahead, wherever and whenever they occur, will assure that millions in the poorer, less developed countries will not survive to witness a "warmer earth."
> WILLIAM W. KELLOGG, in John Gribbin, ed., *Climatic Change*, 1978

8 We should accept the cyclic pattern of mother nature's moods. The desert is not the enemy.
> FAROUK EL-BAZ, on prolonged drought in sub-Saharan Africa, *Washington Post*, 10 November 1985

9 In the Old Testament book of Genesis, the prophet Joseph listened to an account of one of the Egyptian Pharaoh's dreams and warned that seven "fat years" would be followed by seven "lean years." He urged the Pharaoh to store grain as a hedge against the adversity to come. With his dream interpretation, Joseph became one of the first to write a scenario for variable climate—as well as a plan for dealing with it. This principle, dubbed "The Genesis Strategy" by climatologist Stephen Schneider, can help societies build a kind of safety margin into food reserves.
> FRANCESCA LYMAN, *The Greenhouse Trap*, 1990

---

16 COASTS
See also   48 ESTUARIES

---

1 When I have seen the hungry ocean gain
Advantage on the kingdom of the shore,
And the firm soil win of the watery main,
Increasing store with loss and loss with store. . .
> WILLIAM SHAKESPEARE (1564–1616), Sonnet 64

2 Once men could walk these roads
and hear no sound
Save the sad ocean beating on the shore.
> ANNIE ADAMS FIELDS, *The Singing Shepherd*, 1895

3 I hunger for the sea's edge, the limits of the land.
Where the wild old Atlantic is shouting on the sand.
> JOHN MASEFIELD (1878–1967), "A Wanderer's Song," 1902

4 It is the drawback of all sea-side places that half the landscape is unavailable for purposes of human locomotion, being covered by useless water.
> NORMAN DOUGLAS, *Alone*, 1921

5 Also alarming is the unstated, lingering doubt among all of us concerned with the proper management of the coastal zone that the problem is too complex, our scientific knowledge too limited, our institutions too inflexible, and our political will too weak in order to do the job that must be done. . . . Yet regardless of the problem's complexity, the continuing destruction of the coastal resource compels immediate corrective action.
> JOSEPH D. TYDINGS, U.S. Senator, speech, 16 April 1970

6 The tender ecology of the seashore is being invaded by a host of pollutants that directly threaten marine life.
> EDWARD WENK, JR., *The Politics of the Ocean*, 1972

7 [The coastal zone is] rich in a variety of natural, commercial, recreational, industrial and esthetic resources of immediate and potential value to the present and future well-being of the nation.
> COASTAL ZONE MANAGEMENT ACT of 1972

8 There should be public access (to shorelines and beaches) to the maximum extent compatible with the maintenance of natural systems.
> WILMA FREY, testimony, hearing of National Oceanic and Atmospheric Administration, Boston, 17 January 1974

9 Beaches can be crowded or lonely. Many Americans believe that the crowds are too dense; they argue that, where it is permissi-

ble, we should restrict beaches to two people per mile. More than that, they contend, spoils poetic communion. That is true for those two people.

CHARLES FRASER, testimony, U.S. House Committee on Interstate and Foreign Commerce, September 1974

10 The coastal zone is . . . the frontier of America's energy sufficiency.

WAYNE GIBBENS, testimony, U.S. House Committee on Commerce, September 1974

11 [Barrier islands constitute] a thin necklace on the edge of a vast continent.

EDWARD THOMPSON, JR., quoted in *Conservation Foundation Letter*, July 1976

12 In order to protect the Patuxent River, the county has decided to acquire 35 miles of shoreline. Accidentally, I found out I was going to be a baseball park. I'm also under the 100-year floodplain regulations. I'm in the watershed management plan. I'm in historic sites, and critical areas. If one of you guys doesn't get me, another will.

DIANE MCCLARY, on plans to acquire her property for coastal protection, testimony, Maryland Department of Natural Resources, 15 January 1977

13 [The coastal zone management program at least] has the virtue of being geographically specific, and dealing with land forms that have inherent values everybody understands. If that is being fouled up, what would you expect from some vague program that involves everybody planning their hearts out?

CHARLES E. LITTLE, quoted in *Conservation Foundation Letter*, February 1977

14 The seashore is a native place for the lives and minds of all living things and one of the natural environments that is essential to the livelihood and culture of human beings as well as other creatures that base their lives on the seashore environment. . . . Once we are deprived on this valuable natural inheritance by destruction or pollution, it cannot be recreated by human hands.

IRIHAMAKAN (the right of common shore), proclaimed in Japan, May 1976

15 [The National Floodplain Insurance Program] is saddled with $15 billion worth of structures built on barrier islands, mainland beaches, and other low-lying, high-hazard areas. Sooner or later, hurricanes are going to destroy these buildings.

TREVOR O'NEILL, quoted in *New York Times*, 13 September 1981

16 The coastal zone may be the single most important portion of our planet. The loss of its biodiversity may have repercussions far beyond our worst fears.

G. CARLETON RAY, in Edward O. Wilson, ed., *Biodiversity*, 1988

17 If we can't have clean beaches and an attractive coastline and an ocean that we can swim in, then what is life about anyway?

MICHAEL S. DUKAKIS, campaign speech, Linden, N.J., 29 May 1988

18 The sea that gives us life is the coral reef sea. The life proceeding from the tiny coral polyps flows into the life of the island people—in this is found the sacred universe.

UOZUMI KEI, representative, Women and the Sea Association, *Japan Environment Monitor* 2, no. 5, 30 September 1989

17 COMMON RESOURCES

See also   80 LIMITS, 86 NATURAL RESOURCES

1 Nature has poured forth all things for the common use of all men. And God has ordained that all things should be produced that there might be food in common for all, and that the earth should be the common possession of all. Nature created common rights, but usurpation has transformed them into private rights.

AMBROSE (339–397), bishop of Milan, *On the Duties of the Clergy*

2 The use of the sea and air is common to all; neither can a title to the ocean belong to any people or private persons, forasmuch as neither nature nor public use and custom permit any possession thereof.

ELIZABETH I of England (1533–1603), letter to Spanish ambassador, 1580

3 It will, perhaps, be objected to this, that if gathering the acorns or other fruits of the

earth, etc., makes a right to them, then any one may engross as much as he will. To which I answer, Not so. The same law of Nature that does by this means give us property, does also bound that property too. . . . But how far has [God] given it us—"to enjoy"? As much as any one can make use of to any advantage of life before it spoils, so much he may by his labour fix a property in. Whatever is beyond this is more than his share, and belongs to others. Nothing was made by God for man to spoil or destroy.

JOHN LOCKE (1632–1704), *Two Treatises on Government*, 1690

4 He that is nourished by the acorns he picked up under an oak, or the apples he gathered from the trees in the wood, has certainly appropriated them to himself. . . . And will anyone say he had no right to those acorns or apples he thus appropriated because he had not the consent of all mankind to make them his? Was it a robbery thus to assume to himself what belonged to all in common? If such a consent as that was necessary, man had starved, notwithstanding the plenty God had given him. We see in commons, which remain so by compact, that it is the taking any part of what is common, and removing it out of the state Nature leaves it in, which begins the property, without which the common is of no use. And the taking of this or that part does not depend on the express consent of all the commoners.

JOHN LOCKE (1632–1704), *Two Treatises on Government*, 1690

5 You forget that the fruits belong to all and that the land belongs to no one.

JEAN-JACQUES ROUSSEAU (1712–1778), *Discours sur l'origine et les fondements de l'inégalité parmi les hommes*, 1755

6 The air, the water and the ground are free gifts to man and no one has the power to portion them out in parcels. Man must drink and breathe and walk and therefore each man has a right to his share of each.

JAMES FENIMORE COOPER (1789–1851), *The Prairie*, 1827

7 Why are the cattle on a common so puny and stunted: Why is the common itself so bare-worn, and cropped so differently from the adjoining enclosures? . . . [I]f he puts more

cattle on a common, the food which they consume forms a deduction which is shared between all the cattle, as well that of others as his own, in proportion to their number, and only a small part of it is taken from his own cattle.

WILLIAM FORSTER LLOYD, lecture, Oxford University, 1833

8 The law locks up both man and woman
Who steals the goose from off the common,
But lets the greater felon loose
Who steals the common from the goose.

ANONYMOUS, cited by Edward Potts Cheyney, *Social and Industrial History of England*, 1901

9 We abuse land because we regard it as a commodity belonging to us. When we see land as a community to which we belong, we may begin to use it with love and respect.

ALDO LEOPOLD (1886–1948), *A Sand County Almanac*, 1949

10 The tragedy of the commons develops in this way. Picture a pasture open to all. . . . [T]he rational herdsman concludes that the only sensible course for him to pursue is to add another animal to his herd. And another; and another. . . . But this is the conclusion reached by each and every rational herdsman sharing a commons. Therein is the tragedy. Each man is locked into a system that compels him to increase his herd without limit—in a world that is limited.

GARRETT HARDIN, *Science*, 13 December 1968

11 Using the commons as a cesspool does not harm the general public under frontier conditions, because there is no public; the same behavior in a metropolis is unbearable.

GARRETT HARDIN, *Science*, 13 December 1968

12 After the design capacity of any facility has been reached, amenities diminish exponentially with arithmetic increases in the load. For example, when a 21st person enters an elevator designed to hold 20 persons, everyone in the elevator suffers a loss of comfort; and when a 22nd person enters, the percentage loss of amenity is much greater than the 4.8 percent increase in the number of passengers.

NEIL H. JACOBY, *Center* magazine, November–December 1970

13 Let us imagine a business which derives its profit from the exploitation of some natural resource which renews itself—a whale fishery, perhaps. When this business is being run responsibly, it makes a certain profit. For a limited period of time, until the resource is depleted, it can be run irresponsibly at a higher rate of profit. This profit can then be invested, and a regular dividend collected from the investment. [Thus, under appropriate circumstances] it pays for the businessman to kill his business.
DANIEL FIFE, *Environment*, April 1971

14 In a free market economy a consumer will purchase an automobile no matter how foul the atmosphere and no matter how many others are adversely affected by his addition to the number of cars on the road. And why should he not? According to his calculus his addition to the foulness of the atmosphere is minimal and his desire for the automobile is great. This is true of all these products. . . . The free market measures the value of the output to an individual consumer, but it takes no account of the damage done to all other inhabitants of the area.
EDWARD S. MASON, speech, Resources for the Future forum, Washington, D.C., 20 April 1971

15 The general economic analysis of a biological resource . . . suggests that overexploitation in the physical sense of reduced productivity may result from not one, but two social conditions: common-property competitive exploitation on the one hand, and private-property maximization of profits on the other.
COLIN W. CLARK, *Science*, 17 August 1973

16 The natural land ought everywhere to be regarded as a community rather than as a private resource.
LOUIS WASSERMAN, *Critics of Henry George*, 1979

17 The Earth is one but the world is not. We all depend on one biosphere for sustaining our lives. Yet each community, each country, strives for survival and prosperity with little regard for its impact on others.
WORLD COMMISSION ON ENVIRONMENT AND DEVELOPMENT, *Our Common Future*, 1987

18 Climate change is a Tragedy of the Commons writ large.
LESTER BROWN, *State of the World*, 1988

19 The tragedy of the commons is a collective trap that occurs because the costs and benefits apparent to the individual are inconsistent with the costs and benefits to the collective society.
ROBERT COSTANZA, *BioScience* 37, no. 6, June 1987

20 Social traps abound in environmental issues because of the abundance of imperfectly owned and common property resources. To turn these traps into trade-offs, we must calculate the long-term social cost of activities with environmental impacts and charge those costs to the responsible parties in the short run. . . . We must make protecting the environment as economically attractive to individuals in the short run as it is to society in the long run.
ROBERT COSTANZA, *BioScience*, 37, no. 6, June 1987

21 Under colonial rule, game was declared as common property, and whoever chose to kill an animal was entitled to its carcass. Such a legal arrangement gave rise to a so-called "tragedy of the commons," with hunters attempting to shoot as much as possible for themselves before someone else beat them to it.
MIKE T'SAS-ROLFES, on the extermination of African wildlife, *Endangered Wildlife*, June 1990

18 CONSERVATION
See also   19 CONSERVATION MOVEMENT, 40 ENERGY CONSERVATION

1 Willful waste brings woeful want.
ANONYMOUS PROVERB

2 In the end, we conserve only what we love. We will love only what we understand. We will understand only what we are taught.
BABA DIOUM, Senegalese poet

3 The land shall keep a sabbath unto the Lord. . . . In the seventh year shall be a sab-

bath of rest unto the land, a sabbath for the lord; thou shalt neither sow thy field, nor prune thy vineyard.

BIBLE, Leviticus 25:2–4

4 [Natural resource conservation is] the weightiest problem now before the nation. . . . [T]he enormous consumption of these resources, and the threat in imminent exhaustion of some of them, due to reckless and wasteful use, once more calls for common effort, common action.

THEODORE ROOSEVELT (1858–1919), U.S. governors conference, 13 May 1908

5 Conservation and rural-life policies are really two sides of the same policy; and down at bottom this policy rests upon the fundamental law that neither man nor nation can prosper unless, in dealing with the present, thought is steadily taken for the future.

THEODORE ROOSEVELT (1858–1919), The Outlook, 27 August 1910

6 The Universe requires an eternity . . .
Thus they say that the conservation of this world is a perpetual creation and that the verbs, "conserve" and "create," so much at odds here, are synonymous in heaven.

JORGE LUIS BORGES, Historia de la eternidad, 1936

7 Thou shalt inherit the holy earth as a faithful steward, conserving its resources and productivity from generation to generation. Thou shalt safeguard thy fields from soil erosion, thy living waters from drying up, thy forests from desolation, and protect the hills from overgrazing by thy herds, that their descendants may have abundance forever. If any shall fail in this stewardship of the land, thy fruitful fields shall become sterile stony ground and wasting gullies, and thy descendants shall decrease and live in poverty or perish from off the face of the earth.

WALTER C. LOWDERMILK, "The Eleventh Commandment," Jerusalem Radio, June 1939

8 I have come to realize that most of our wildlife conservation troubles are due to lack of organization. Wildlife interests remind me of an unorganized army, beaten in every battle, zealous and brave, but unable to combat the trained legions who are organized to get what they want.

J. N. DARLING, Current Biography, 1942

9 Conservation is a basis of permanent peace. Many different kinds of natural resources are being wasted; other kinds are being ignored; still other kinds can be put to more practical use for humanity if more is known about them. Some nations are deeply interested in the subject of conservation and use and other nations are not at all interested.

FRANKLIN D. ROOSEVELT (1882–1945), letter to Cordell Hull, 1944, quoted in Gifford Pinchot, Breaking New Ground, 1947

10 To preach conservation at such a time, when all our resources, national and otherwise are being sacrificed in unprecedented measure, might seem to some anomalous, even ironical. . . . But we firmly believe, and now are more acutely aware than ever, that conservation is basically related to the peace of the world and the future of the race.

JOHN DETWEILER, 1945, quoted in Wes Jackson, New Roots for Agriculture, 1983

11 [Theodore Roosevelt's] Administration originated, formulated, and laid before the American people and the world the Conservation idea—the greatest good for the greatest number for the longest time, the development and use of the earth and all its resources for the enduring good of men—both on a national and international scale. And not only the idea, but its practical and successful application in many fields.

GIFFORD PINCHOT (1865–1946), Breaking New Ground, 1947

12 The first great fact about conservation is that it stands for development. There has been a fundamental misconception that conservation means nothing but the husbanding of resources for future generations. There could be no more serious mistake. . . . The first principle of conservation is the use of the natural resources now existing on this continent for the benefit of the people who live here now.

GIFFORD PINCHOT (1865–1946), Breaking New Ground, 1947

13 Conservation is the application of common sense to the common problems for the com-

mon good. Since its objective is the ownership, control, development, processing, distribution, and use of the natural resources for
the benefit of the people, it is by its very nature the antithesis of monopoly. So long as
people are oppressed by the lack of such
ownership and control, so long will they continue to be cheated of their right to life, liberty, and the pursuit of happiness, cheated
out of their enjoyment of the earth and all
that it contains. It is obvious, therefore, that
the principles of Conservation must apply to
human beings as well as to natural resources.

The Conservation policy then has three
great purposes.

First: wisely to use, protect, preserve, and
renew the natural resources of the earth.

Second: to control the use of the natural resources and their products in the common interest, and to secure their distribution to the
people at fair and reasonable charges for
goods and services.

Third: to see to it that the rights of the people to govern themselves shall not be controlled by great monopolies through their
power over natural resources.

> GIFFORD PINCHOT (1865–1946), *Breaking New
> Ground*, 1947

14 Alaska was closed to development under the
guise of conservation. . . . The true meaning
of conservation is controlled use and wise
management. But in Alaska, conservation as
it is and has been practiced means paralysis. . . . This so-called conservation is actually a waste of the worst sort.

> ROBERT B. ATWOOD, 1953, quoted in John
> Hanrahan and Peter Gruenstein, *Lost Fron-
> tier: The Marketing of Alaska*, 1977

15 Conservation is a bird that flies faster than
the shot we aim at it.

> ALDO LEOPOLD (1886–1948), *Round River*,
> 1953

16 Conservation is a state of harmony between
men and land.

> ALDO LEOPOLD (1886–1948), *Round River*,
> 1953

17 To save every cog and wheel is the first pre-
caution of intelligent tinkering.

> ALDO LEOPOLD (1886–1948), *Round River*,
> 1953

18 The long fight to save wild beauty represents
democracy at its best. It requires citizens to
practice the hardest of virtues—self-restraint.

> EDWIN WAY TEALE, *Circle of the Seasons*, 1953

19 When I personally get to speculating about
this problem of conservation, and let my
mind run on into the future, I get into such an
intricate problem that I am forced back, willy-
nilly, to the immediate problem of the day,
and that is: What do we do now in order that
we may get to the next step?

> DWIGHT D. EISENHOWER (1890–1969), 1954,
> quoted in Samuel H. Ordway, Jr., *Prosper-
> ity Beyond Tomorrow*, 1955

20 What is commonly called "conservation" will
not work in the long run because it is not really conservation at all but rather, disguised
by its elaborate scheming, only a more
knowledgeable variation of the old idea of a
world for man's use only. That idea is unreal-
izable.

> JOSEPH WOOD KRUTCH, 1955, *A Krutch Omni-
> bus*, 1970

21 The conservation conscience can be dominant in American life from time to time and
place to place without representing a conviction on the part of the majority of the people.

> ANONYMOUS SPEAKER, North American Wild-
> life Conference, 1959

22 Conservation is to a democratic government
by free men as the roots of a tree are to its
leaves. We must be willing wisely to nurture
and use our resources if we are going to keep
visible the inner strengths of democracy.

> CLINTON P. ANDERSON, U.S. Senator, *Ameri-
> can Forests*, July 1963

23 The most unhappy thing about conservation
is that it is never permanent. Save a priceless
woodland or an irreplaceable mountain today, and tomorrow it is threatened from another quarter.

> HAL BORLAND, quoted in *New York Times
> Book Review*, 25 February 1964

24 Our conservation must not be just the classical conservation of protection and development, but a creative conservation of
restoration and innovation. Its concern is not
with nature alone, but with the total relation
between man and the world around him. Its

object is not just man's welfare, but the dignity of man's spirit.
LYNDON B. JOHNSON (1908–1973), special message to Congress on the conservation and restoration of natural beauty, 8 February 1965

25 Let man heal the hurt places and revere whatever is still miraculously pristine.
DAVID R. BROWER, in Eliot Porter, *Summer Island: Penobscot Country*, 1966

26 To the extent that we create or maintain beauty through an ordered diversity, we will also enhance the stability, health, and productivity of America.
RAYMOND F. DASMANN, speech, Columbus, Ohio, 1966

27 I don't think there is anything more important than conservation, with the exception of human survival, and the two are so closely interlaced that it is hard to separate one from the other.
CHARLES A. LINDBERGH (1902–1974), speech to Alaska Legislature, 1968

28 Multiple-purpose development is no longer good enough. All-purpose conservation must be our standard.
HUBERT H. HUMPHREY, speech, The Dalles, Oregon, 28 September 1968

29 The McCarthy era of the conservation movement.
FRANK GRAHAM, JR., on the late 1950s as a period when Rachel Carson's concerns about the misuse of pesticides were seen as subversive in some government and scientific circles, *Since Silent Spring*, 1970

30 The great question of the 70's is, shall we surrender to our surroundings, or shall we make our peace with nature and begin to make reparations for the damage we have done to our air, our land and our water? Restoring nature to its natural state is a cause beyond party and beyond factions. It has become a common cause of all the people of America.
RICHARD M. NIXON, state of the union message, 22 January 1970

31 There is no historical precedent for conservation of a major resource as it became obvious that the resource was being wiped out. The response to precipitous declines in buffalo in

the American West and blue whales in the oceans was to harvest both resources harder than ever, up to the point at which they were almost extinct—and it was no longer economically worthwhile to harvest them.
KENNETH E. F. WATT, in Clifton Fadiman and Jean White, eds., *Ecocide*, 1971

32 There is a widespread tendency to assume that the ultimate goal of conservation is to protect nature *against* man, whereas it should be the discovery and development of the potentialities that permit a creative harmonious interplay between man and nature.
RENE DUBOS, *American Scholar*, Spring 1971

33 Conservation is no longer for the birds.
LES LINE, *Audubon*, March 1971

34 It is only in a human services society which is labor intensive, rather than capital intensive, that the resources of the Earth will be conserved and human resources be expended for the benefit of human beings.
ARTHUR PEARL, *Social Policy*, September–October 1971

35 The word conservation can be used in many connections but I am going to use it in the context of the conservation of the environment. By this I mean the creation of a satisfactory state of existence for all living things on this earth. It includes the protection of the best of what we have inherited, the correction of the worst mistakes, and the considerate planning of future development.
PRINCE PHILIP, duke of Edinburgh, lecture, Cardiff Institute of Science and Technology, 23 November 1973

36 Marxism has not been an environmentalist's ideology. . . . One of its creeds is that man is master of his fate and, by the same token, of his apparently inexhaustible lands. State ownership does not guarantee conservation any more than in capitalist countries.
ANTHONY HUXLEY, *Plant and Planet*, 1975

37 Most conservation problems exist on particular pieces of ground, occupied or cared for by a particular group of people. Attempts to solve them at a global, or even national level often strike far from the mark.
RAYMOND F. DASMANN, speech, Kinshasa, Zaire, 19 September 1975

38 Industrial mankind can be likened to . . . irresponsible tenants in a rented house. . . . We've been burning up the furniture, woodwork and food supplies to keep the place warm because we've been too irresponsible and lazy to figure out how to work the central heating.
HENRY KING STANFORD, speech, December 1976

39 [Being ecologically conscious means] taking a judicious stock of the existing resources and advocating stringent measures so that they last longer.
HENRYK SKOLIMOWSKI, Ecologist Quarterly, Autumn 1978

40 Conservation is the religion of the future.
JANE FONDA, quoted in Life, December 1979

41 The preservationist often appears as nothing more than the voice of effete affluence, trying to save a disproportionate share of the public domain for his own minoritarian pleasures. . . . Is he a spokesman for minority rights, or diversity, seeking only a small share of our total natural resources? Or is he the prophet of a secular religion—the cult of nature—that he seeks to have Congress establish?
JOSEPH SAX, Mountains without Handrails, 1980

42 To fulfil human potential is to transcend our present condition, to fulfil the requirement of evolution, to adapt the idiom of frugality which is a precondition of inner beauty, and to assure our short-term and long-term survival.
HENRYK SKOLIMOWSKI, Eco-Philosophy, 1981

43 In losing stewardship we lose fellowship; we become outcasts from the great neighborhood of creation.
WENDELL BERRY, The Gift of Good Land, 1981

44 If one views conservation as saving for future generations, reclamation may be as important as preservation. If complete recovery is indeed possible, a distant future generation may not be able to distinguish the reclaimed area from a preserved one.
JOHN CAIRNS, ed., The Recovery Process of Damaged Ecosystems, 1981

45 Stereotypical female behavior and values—including nurture, prudence, the protection of life, a love of beauty—do lend themselves to conservation.
STEPHEN FOX, John Muir and His Legacy, 1981

46 It is, perhaps, odd that it would require a surgical operation to get into the heads of some people who fancy themselves conservative, an idea sympathetic to conservation and other environmental values. But there are many such people.
GEORGE F. WILL, Washington Post, 18 January 1981

47 There is something about conservation that has drawn special contempt from the [Reagan] Administration.
FEDERATION OF AMERICAN SCIENTISTS, National Council, Public Interest Report, April 1981

48 The ultimate choice is between conservation or conflict. Trees now or tanks later. The choice for governments is either to find the means by which to pay now to stop the destruction of the resource base, or to be prepared to pay later, possibly in blood.
PETER THACHER, speech at World Wildlife Fund/International Union for the Conservation of Nature, Tropical Forest campaign, Bali, 1982

49 Just as it was impossible to be half a Christian, so too was it impossible to be half a preservationist.
ALSTON CHASE, Playing God in Yellowstone, 1986

50 Roosevelt's brand of conservation set the course that others would follow for decades. Its focus was responsibility and restraint in managing natural resources, and its opponent within the camp was preservationism (led by John Muir), which favored protecting the earth from the hand of man. The tension between management and preservation is present to this day in both natural resource agencies and the environmental movement itself.
PETER BORELLI, Crossroads, 1988

51 The only way conservation can work is if it is seen as just part of the fabric of development—part of the fabric of growth of human society.
PETER SELIGMANN, quoted in Christian Science Monitor, 4 April 1988

52 The purpose of conservation is to preserve natural diversity: A fundamental problem and paradox of conservation is that Western men and women no longer value diversity, and because of their preoccupation with the general and the power that an understanding of general laws brings, we are committed to the kind of exploitative approach to nature that places diversity in jeopardy.

> DAVID EHRENFELD in David Western and Mary Pearl, eds., *Conservation for the 21st Century*, 1989

53 The most unhappy thing about conservation is that it is never permanent. If we save a priceless woodland today, it is threatened from another quarter tomorrow.

> MARJORIE STONEMAN DOUGLAS, quoted in Governor's Commission on the Future of Florida's Environment, *Facing Florida's Environmental Future*, April 1990

54 I've never been interested in just doing with less. I'm interested in doing *more* with less. We don't have to become vegetarians and ride bicycles to save the Earth.

> AMORY LOVINS, *Smithsonian*, April 1990

55 At one level, the environmentalists have swept away all opposition. The "conservation ethic" has become one of the fixed guiding stars of American politics—a "value question" that permits only one answer from anyone who hopes to be part of the public dialogue.

> DAVID S. BRODER, *Washington Post*, 22 April 1990

56 We need to look at the peaceful ideology of *chado* [the Way of Tea] to develop true humanity in the world and to live in harmony with nature. . . . Now is the time to unite and take up problems of environmental conservation.

> NAYA SOTAN, *Urasenke Newsletter*, Spring 1990

57 Conservation cannot be imposed from above. It must have the support of the people.

> MICHAEL WERIKHE, *E* magazine, July–August 1990

58 The things that conservation biologists are saying are enough to cause me to have a drinking problem: that we're going to lose one third of all species in the next 20 years, that the only large mammals left are those that we choose to allow to exist, that vertebrate evolution is at an end. At best the conservation movement has tapped on the brakes a little bit, to cause the flood of industrialism to eddy around a few places. Sometimes you just want to say, "Why bother?" But you *have* to bother, you have to fight.

> DAVE FOREMAN, *E* magazine, September–October 1990

59 The creative life of every person, Camus once said, is the attempt to recapture through the tortuous routes of art those several images in the presence of which his soul first opened. My heroes were not the great conservationists; I never heard of Aldo Leopold or John Muir until I was an adult. My idols were the scientific adventurers like William Beebe and the explorers of the living world whose work is encapsulated in the wonderful field guides I carried in my pack. The unique experience of my generation of tropical naturalists was the imposition of finiteness on our dreams of conquest that turned us at last into stewards. Our challenge now is to keep alive the fire of adventure in a circumscribed and carefully attended world.

> EDWARD O. WILSON, on the relationship of naturalists to conservation, *Orion*, Winter 1990

60 Conservation is sometimes perceived as stopping everything cold, as holding whooping cranes in higher esteem than people. It is up to science to spread the understanding that the choice is not between wild places or people, it is between a rich or an impoverished existence for Man.

> THOMAS E. LOVEJOY, quoted in Kathryn A.Kohm, ed., *Balancing on the Brink of Extinction*, 1991

19 CONSERVATION MOVEMENT

1 On its face the Conservation Movement is material, yet in truth there has never been in all human history a popular movement more

firmly grounded in ethics, in eternal verities, in the divinity of human rights!

W. J. McGee, *Proceedings of the Mississippi Valley Historical Association*, 1909–1910

2 Most of the conservation measures are so closely related to business that it is sometimes difficult for men to take a strong stand on the side of the public interest. But women can do it, and they should.

Rosalie Edge, *Independent Woman*, April 1946

3 Individual thinkers since the days of Ezekiel and Isaiah have asserted that the despoliation of land is not only inexpedient but wrong. Society, however, has not yet affirmed their belief. I regard the present conservation movement as the embryo of such an affirmation.

Aldo Leopold (1886–1948), *Round River*, 1953

4 The real father of conservation is considered to be John Muir, a California naturalist.

Time, 17 September 1965

5 The presumably radical ecotacticians of the 1970s are in large part the heirs of a conservationist history that, in a thousand variations, has peddled the proposition that "only man is vile." It is also clear, when conservation is transformed into a passion for population control, that some kinds of men are more vile than others.

Richard Neuhaus, *In Defense of People*, 1971

6 Is it love of beauty that moves us to the effort [of environmental protection], because we know beauty is denied to so many of our fellow men?

Frank Fraser Darling, *Wilderness and Plenty*, 1971

7 [Aldo Leopold was] the Moses of the New Conservation impulse of the 1960's and 1970's, who handed down the Tablets of the Law but did not live to enter the promised land.

Donald Fleming, *Perspectives in American History*, 1972

8 Today, 70 per cent of our population lives in the midst of traffic tangles, suffocating smog, poisoned water, deafening noise and terror-

izing crime. These problems are real, not illusory. Nevertheless, to many of our nation's 20 million blacks, the conservation movement has about as much appeal as a segregated bus.

Thomas Bradley, *Sierra Club Bulletin*, April 1972

9 The conservation movement is much the same as women's lib and all the rest of the elitist operations that have come into being since people got sick and tired of fighting for the rights of black people.

Richard H. Newhouse, speech, Woodstock, Ill., 15 November 1972

10 The conservationist movement set the value of what it sought to achieve in human terms. Its members measured their plans by asking what is good for man in the broadest and longest sense; what raises him from present poverty without condemning him to future need; what raises his spirit by bringing him into touch with natural harmony; what teaches natural economics by preserving the resources to make life fuller.

Roger Starr, *New York Times Magazine*, 19 August 1979

11 For all their conservative aspects, conservationists ultimately are more radical than any Marxists. Dissenting from both the capitalists and the communists, they declare that history is not a line but a circle; that meaning resides less in matter than in spirit, less in striving than in stasis, less in humans than in Nature, less indoors than outdoors.

Stephen Fox, *John Muir and His Legacy*, 1981

12 Conservation is often accused of being a plaything of the rich, an indulgence of wealthy people with nothing else on their minds. According to this view, affluent conservationists have cared more for birds and trees than for their less fortunate fellow human beings. A moot point; yet conservation leadership, especially in the modern period, has included very few individuals of great wealth. Rich people have often given money, but little else. Decision making, lobbying, and the grubby everyday work of public education have generally been carried out by people of moderate income. Wealthy conservationists have paid many bills but have not exerted

much direct influence on the course of the movement.

STEPHEN FOX, *John Muir and His Legacy*, 1981

13 On a practical level conservation has been sustained by this interplay between professionals and radical amateurs. Professionals keep the movement organized. Amateurs keep it honest. The ghosts of Muir and Pinchot still wrestle for control—in a fractious but symbiotic embrace.

STEPHEN FOX, *John Muir and His Legacy*, 1981

14 Thoreau served as prophet, Henry Adams as historian, Lewis Mumford as philsopher. The conservation movement, the most successful exercise in antimodernism, corresponded to the Russian Revolution. Muir was its Lenin. Pinchot was its Stalin.

STEPHEN FOX, *John Muir and His Legacy*, 1981

15 The early conservation movement had generated the first stages in shaping a "commons," a public domain of public ownership for public use and the public ownership of fish and wildlife as resources not subject to private appropriation. This sense of jointly held resources became extended in the later years to the concept of air, land, and water as an environment. Their significance as common resources shifted from a primary focus on commodities to become also meaningful as amenities that could enhance the quality of life.

SAMUEL P. HAYS, *Beauty, Health and Permanence*, 1987

20 CONSUMERISM
See also 3 AFFLUENCE, 79 LIFE-STYLE, 110 POVERTY

1 Consumption is the sole end and purpose of all production; and the interest of the producer ought to be attended to, only in so far as it may be necessary for promoting that of the consumer. The maxim is so perfectly self-evident, that it would be absurd to attempt to prove it.

ADAM SMITH (1723–1790), *The Wealth of Nations*, 1776

2 The genius of the American people is not to be found in self-denial, but in production for

use; not in saving but in spending and consuming. We are embarked upon an attempt, with the aid of science to make Nature yield the abundance necessary to support an expanding level of living, and any movement not in harmony with this basic drive is not likely to become popular.

CHARLES E. LIVELY, "Some Reflections on the Conservation Movement," 1953

3 When we depend less on industrially produced consumer goods, we can live in quiet places. Our bodies become vigorous; we discover the serenity of living with the rhythms of the earth. We cease oppressing one another.

ALICIA BAY LAUREL, *Living on the Earth*, 1971

4 As physical resources are everywhere limited, people satisfying their needs by means of a modest use of resources are obviously less likely to be at each other's throats than people depending upon a high rate of use. Equally, people who live in highly self-sufficient local communities are less likely to get involved in large-scale violence than people whose existence depends on world-wide systems of trade.

E. F. SCHUMACHER, *Small Is Beautiful*, 1973

5 An attitude to life which seeks fulfillment in the single-minded pursuit of wealth—in short, materialism—does not fit into this world, because it contains within itself no limiting principle, while the environment in which it is placed is strictly limited.

E. F. SCHUMACHER, *Small Is Beautiful*, 1973

6 The aim should be to obtain the maximum of well-being with the minimum of consumption. The cultivation and expansion of needs is the antithesis of wisdom. It is also the antithesis of freedom and peace.

E. F. SCHUMACHER, *Small Is Beautiful*, 1973

7 All of us have opted for environmental damage, albeit unwittingly, by voting for convenience with our dollars.

RUSSELL W. PETERSON, speech, American Association for the Advancement of Science, 30 January 1975

8 We are hooked like junkies, dependent on the drug of wasteful consumption.

RAYMOND F. DASMANN, quoted in *New York Times*, 1 December 1976

9 Confronted on the one hand with an old-fashioned, earth-bashing consumer, and on the other with a caring, Earth-loving "Guppie" (a Green yuppie), the choice is clear. We can't help but support the move toward thoughtful, reflective consumerism.

JONATHAN PORRITT, *One Earth*, Winter 1988

10 There is a massive problem here. With the breakdown of community at all levels, human beings have become more like what the traditional model of *Homo economicus* described. Shopping has become the great national pastime. The one place one can be most assured of a welcome is in a store. Status attaches to finding unusual goods and unusual prices.

HERMAN E. DALY and JOHN B. COBB, JR., *For the Common Good*, 1989

11 It's unjust that a few of the privileged continue to accumulate more goods than they need, devastating the available resources, when multitudes of people live in conditions of misery, at bare subsistence level. . . . And now it's the traumatic dimensions of ecological problems that teach us when greed and selfishness, individual and collective, have gone against the order of creation.

POPE JOHN PAUL II, "Peace with God the Creator, Peace with All of Creation," document issued to mark the Roman Catholic World Day of Peace, 1 January 1990

12 Materialism simply cannot survive the transition to a sustainable world.

LESTER BROWN, *State of the World*, 1990

13 We used to be hunter-gatherers, now we're shopper-borrowers.

ROBIN WILLIAMS, Earth Day special, ABC-TV, 22 April 1990

14 The power we can exercise outside the voting booth, not only by consuming less but by consuming products that are environmentally benign, is a giant just stretching its limbs.

EVAN EISENBERG, *New Republic*, 30 April 1990

15 The key to protecting the planet is to prevent a problem at the source, rather than tinkering with it after it is already created. In the consumer society, this means intervening early in the game in the decisions about what is produced and how it is produced. A society in which consumption is conscious and restrained requires that new and different decisions be made in corporate boardrooms as well as in national capitals, decisions that put the needs of the planet ahead of the profits of the corporation.

DEBRA LYNN DADD and ANDRE CAROTHERS, *Greenpeace*, May–June 1990

16 The selling of the environment may make the cholesterol craze look like a Sunday school picnic.

HUBERT HUMPHREY III, commenting on the phenomenon of "green consumerism," the marketing and advertising of environmentally friendly products, *Greenpeace*, May–June 1990

17 It's quite clear that consumers are now almost more aware of the packaging than the product.

JOHN ELKINGTON, quoted in *EcoSource*, June 1990

18 I worry about the growing trivialization of environmental issues. Television ads present simplistic views of environmental consequences. Products are marketed for their environmental value—biodegradability and ozone safety—frequently without justification. A spate of popular books exhort the public to save the planet through actions that are disproportionate to that goal. Legitimate public concern for the environment is being distorted by the hoopla.

ROBERT M. WHITE, *The Bridge*, Summer 1990

19 We cannot extend the orgies of the consumer society to the whole planet.

JOSE A. LUTZENBERGER, speech, Nature Conservancy, Washington, D.C., 15 November 1990

20 Moreover, there are myriad problems for which consumer action is not an effective instrument. Consumer power will have little effect on toxic dumps at military bases. Consumers cannot stop a freeway or build a public transportation system. Consumers will not safeguard national parks, or promote sustainable agriculture in the Horn of Africa. All these, and thousands of other environmental objectives can be achieved only through traditional environmental activism.

DENIS HAYES, *Issues in Science and Technology*, Winter 1990–1991

21 In theory, almost every American is pro-environment. But the ardent environmental attitudes that come out in opinion polls cool down significantly when you look at consumer behavior.

THOMAS MILLER, *American Demographics*, February 1991

22 Sometimes it seems like environmentalism's main accomplishment has been to transform a simple trip to the supermarket into an occasion for anguished self-criticism, and a shopping list into the measure of one's relationship with Mother Earth.

BILL GIFFORD, *City Paper* (Washington, D.C.), 1 March 1991

21 DAMS AND WATER PROJECTS
See also   119 RIVERS, 134 WATER

1 None shall cut off a stream of water.

PHILO OF ALEXANDRIA (c. 13 B.C.–c. A.D. 50), c. A.D., 20, quoted in Eusebius (c. A.D. 260–c. A.D. 339), *Preparation of the Gospel*

2 [The aqueducts of Rome] are a signal testimony to the greatness of the Roman Empire. . . . With so many indispensable structures for all these waters you are welcome to compare, if you will, the idle pyramids or all the useless, though famous, works of the Greeks.

FRONTINUS (c. A.D. 35–A.D. 103), *The Water Supply of Rome*, c. 100

3 I am one with thee, and who knows what may avail a crowbar against that Billerica dam?

HENRY DAVID THOREAU (1817–1862), on committing eco-sabotage, *A Week on the Concord and Merrimack Rivers*, 1849

4 These temple destroyers, devotees of ravaging commercialism, seem to have a perfect contempt for Nature, and instead of lifting their eyes to the God of the mountains, lift them to the Almighty Dollar. Dam Hetch Hetchy! As well dam for water tanks the people's cathedrals and churches, for no holier temple has ever been consecrated by the heart of man.

JOHN MUIR, (1838–1914), *Sierra Club Bulletin*, January 1908

5 [The Panama Canal] is the greatest liberty that man has taken with Nature.

JAMES BRYCE (1838–1922), *South America*, 1912

6 There is only so much water in the Colorado River but, though there is more money than water, there is only so much money too.

BERNARD DE VOTO (1897–1955), on proposals to dam the Colorado River, *Harper's*, September 1954

7 The greatest single weakness in the Federal Government's activities in the field of water resources development is the lack of cooperation and coordination of the Federal agencies with each other and with the States and local interests.

U.S. PRESIDENTIAL ADVISORY COMMITTEE ON WATER RESOURCES, report, 1956

8 If the dam is built, the amount of Federal money spent on construction in the five years preceding initial power production will . . . exceed the total amount spent for military construction in Alaska from 1950 to 1955. The whole job will pour a minimum of one and a third billion dollars into Alaska and probably a great deal more. As one legislator is said to have remarked privately, Rampart Dam will have served its purpose if it is blown up the day it is finished.

Recognition of Rampart as a sort of colossal make-work project—a Federal subsidy for the state economy—explains a great deal.

PAUL BROOKS, on the proposed Rampart Dam in Alaska, *Atlantic Monthly*, May 1965

9 I can find no truly independent review, appraisal, or check of the economic evaluation of a federal water project which confirms the benefit-cost ratio calculated by the construction agency.

HERBERT MARSHALL, *Water Research*, 1966

10 New reservoirs can therefore be developed as gathering grounds for people as well as water, for whether we accept the Freudian explanations the fact is clear that water attracts us, and on every scale from sea to garden

pools. In any landscape it is a magnet which draws us.
NAN FAIRBROTHER, *New Lives, New Landscapes*, 1970

11 In the view of conservationists, there is something special about dams, something . . . metaphysically sinister.
JOHN MCPHEE, *Encounters with the Archdruid*, 1971

12 I hate all dams, large and small. If you are against a dam, you are for a river.
DAVID R. BROWER, quoted in John McPhee, *Encounters with the Archdruid*, 1971

13 Should we also flood the Sistine Chapel so tourists can get near the ceiling?
DAVID R. BROWER, recalling a full-page ad against the U.S. Bureau of Reclamation's plans to dam the Grand Canyon, in John McPhee, *Encounters with the Archdruid*, 1971

14 The cost of building dams is always underestimated—
There's erosion of the delta that the river has created,
There's fertile soil below the dam that's likely to be looted,
And the tangled mat of forest that has got to be uprooted.—
        . . .
There's disappointing yield of fish, beyond the first explosion;
There's silting up, and drawing down, and watershed erosion.
Above the dam the water's lost by sheer evaporation;
Below, the river scours, and suffers dangerous alteration.
KENNETH E. BOULDING, "The Ballad of Ecological Awareness" in M. Taghi Farvar and John P. Milton, eds., *The Careless Technology*, 1972

15 The first thing they noticed was that the river was no longer there. Somebody had removed the Colorado River.
EDWARD ABBEY, *The Monkey Wrench Gang*, 1976

16 We must realize that the federal government's dam-building era is coming to an end. Most beneficial projects have been built. . . . I have stated many times that as President I will halt the construction of unnecessary dams by the Corps of Engineers.
JIMMY CARTER, campaign position paper, 1976

17 The first recorded civilization, that of the Sumerians, was thriving in the southern Tigris-Euphrates Valley by the fourth millenium B.C. Over the course of two thousand years, Sumerian irrigation practices ruined the soil so completely that it has not yet recovered. . . . Vast areas of southern Iraq today glisten like fields of freshly fallen snow.
ERIK P. ECKHOLM, *Losing Ground*, 1976

18 One of the main turning points in the spiritual life of the nation, perhaps the chief turning point, as far as the future was concerned. It marked the real closing of the concept of unlimited expansion, and insisted on the point that man was going to have to think of depriving himself rather than abusing his environment. But more than that, it marked the moment when the implicit religious attitudes of the people gained explicit status, and though by a kind of reflex America violated its conscience, dammed the Hetch Hetchy, opted for the norms of the past rather than those of the future, a blow that sent Muir to his grave, nevertheless the corner was in fact turned.
WILLIAM EVERSON, on the damming of Hetch Hetchy Valley, *Archtype West*, 1976

19 I personally don't believe that any of the projects ought to be built.
JIMMY CARTER, on thirty water resource projects he had put under review for environmental, safety, or economic analysis, news conference, 24 March 1977

20 Water projects don't create water, they move it around, and sometimes lose some in the process. We are coming to the end of the dam-building era in America.
CECIL D. ANDRUS, quoted in *New York Times Magazine*, 8 May 1977

21 Where you deliver water and how is a powerful tool.
PHILIP SCHMUCK, quoted in *Conservation Foundation Letter*, May 1979

22 Massive construction projects designed to bring more water to more acres of land have

caused desertification, air and water pollution, failure of the underground water system and destruction of fisheries and estuaries in the San Francisco Bay and Sacramento River delta.

BILL DEVALL and GEORGE SESSIONS, *Deep Ecology*, 1985

23 The whole state [of California] thrives, even survives, by moving water from where it is, and presumably isn't needed, to where it isn't, and presumably is needed. No other state has done as much to fructify its deserts, make over its flora and fauna, and rearrange the hydrology God gave it. No other place has put as many people where they probably have no business being.

MARC REISNER, *Cadillac Desert*, 1986

24 No one will ever know how many ill-conceived water projects *were* built by the Bureau [of Reclamation] and the [Army] Corps [of Engineers] simply because the one agency thought the other would build it first.

MARC REISNER, *Cadillac Desert*, 1986

25 When archaeologists from some other planet sift through the bleached bones of our civilization, they may well conclude that our temples were dams. Imponderably massive, constructed with exquisite care, our dams will outlast anything else we have built—skyscrapers, cathedrals, bridges, even nuclear power plants. When forests push through the rotting streets of New York and the Empire State Building is a crumbling hulk, Hoover Dam will sit astride the Colorado River much as it does today—intact, formidable, serene.

MARC REISNER, *Cadillac Desert*, 1986

26 For all their breathtaking immensity, dams are oddly vulnerable things. . . . The engineers who have built them have gone to great lengths to make them safe from earthquakes, landslides, and floods. But their ultimate vulnerability . . . is to silt. Every reservoir eventually silts up—it is only a matter of when.

MARC REISNER, *Cadillac Desert*, 1986

27 Free shackled rivers! . . . The finest fantasy of eco-warriors in the West is the destruction of [Glen Canyon] Dam and the liberation of the Colorado [River].

DAVE FOREMAN, 1981, quoted in Roderick F. Nash, *The Rights of Nature*, 1989

28 We don't need your electricity. Electricity won't give us food. . . . We need our forests to hunt and gather in. We don't want your dam. Everything you tell us is a lie.

ANONYMOUS KAYAPO (Brazilian Indian), quoted in Julian Burger, *The Gaia Atlas of First Peoples*, 1990

29 I've lived my life with the land that will be flooded. I despise a civilization and society that think nothing of destroying nature and driving out the people living there because they can make money doing it.

KAIZAWA, Ainu spokesman, against the Nibutani dam, *Japan Environment Monitor*, 4, no. 1, April 1991

30 Let us begin by saying that God, praised and high, created a remedy for every ill. Yet when man interferes, everything is spoiled. The great Nile River used to flood every year. This flooding cleansed the basic river channel, carrying away all of the pollutants that had accumulated and killing vegetation. When the flooding ended after construction of the High Dam, the responsibilities of obtaining pure water fit for human usage necessarily increased.

AFAF AL-DAHSHAN, *Akhir Sa'ah* (in Arabic), 20 March 1991, reprinted in English in *JPRS Report*, 11 June 1991

22 DEFORESTATION
See also 51 FORESTRY, 131 TROPICAL FORESTS

1 What now remains compared with what then existed is like the skeleton of a sick man, all the fat and soft earth having been wasted away, and only the bare framework of the land being left.

PLATO (c. 428–348 B.C.), on deforestation in Attica, *Critias*

2 Whenever there are men competent for the task, let them be given forest to cut down in order to improve our possessions.

CHARLEMAGNE (742–814), *Capitulare de Villis*

3 [Forests are "one of the bulwarks" of England but their "epidemical" destruction is in part caused by the desire of greedy men] utterly to extirpate, demolish, and raze, as it were, all those many goodly woods and forests, which our more prudent ancestors left standing for the ornament and service of their country.
JOHN EVELYN (1620–1706), *Sylva*, 1664

4 Woodman, spare that tree!
Touch not a single bough!
In youth it sheltered me,
And I'll protect it now.
GEORGE POPE MORRIS, "Woodman, Spare That Tree," 1830

5 Man makes war on the peaceful forests, and each day the shadows on the mountains retreat. Nothing will remain for us of the mystic refuges where we could garner thought and love.
VICTOR DE LAPRADE (1812–1887) *Le mort d'un chêne*, 1844

6 Naked lay, in sunshine glowing,
Hills that once had stood
Down their sides the shadows throwing
Of a mighty wood.
JOHN GREENLEAF WHITTIER (1807–1892), "The Fountain," 1860

7 The clearing of the woods has, in some cases, produced within two or three generations, effects as blasting as those generally ascribed to geological convulsions, and has laid waste the face of the earth more hopelessly than if it had been buried by a current of lava or a shower of volcanic sand.
GEORGE PERKINS MARSH (1801–1882), *Man and Nature*, 1864

8 The development of culture and of industry in general has ever evinced itself in such energetic destruction of forests that everything done by it conversely for their preservation and restoration appears infinitesimal.
KARL MARX (1818–1883), *Das Kapital*, 1867

9 We have now felled forest enough everywhere, in many districts far too much. Let us restore this one element of material life to its normal proportions, and devise means of maintaining the permanence of its relations to the fields, the meadows, and the pastures,

to the rain and the dews of heaven, to the springs and rivulets with which it waters the earth.
GEORGE PERKINS MARSH (1801–1882), *The Earth as Modified by Human Action*, 1874

10 Oh, I don't object, of course, to cutting wood from necessity, but why destroy the forests? The woods of Russia are trembling under the blows of the axe. Millions of trees have perished. The homes of the wild animals and birds have been desolated; the rivers are shrinking, and many beautiful landscapes are gone forever. And why? Because men are too lazy and stupid to stoop down and pick up their fuel from the ground.
ANTON CHEKHOV (1860–1904), *Uncle Vanya*, 1897

11 it wont be long now it wont be long man is making deserts on the earth it wont be long now before man will have used it up so that nothing but ants and centipedes and scorpions can find a living on it
DON MARQUIS, *the life and times of archie and mehitabel*, 1935

12 america was once a paradise of timberland and stream but it is dying because of the greed and money lust of a thousand little kings who slashed the timber all to hell and would not be controlled and changed the climate and stole the rainfall from posterity
DON MARQUIS, *the life and times of archie and mehitabel*, 1935

13 We now send food to peoples whose ancestors failed to realize that without soil and trees on the hillside the town in the valley dies, without recognizing that we ourselves are busily engaged in emulating the ancient error.
M. GRAHAM NETTING, quoted in *Conservation Foundation Letter*, 23 February 1968

14 Properly managed, forests can enrich human life in a variety of ways which are both material and psychological. Poorly managed, they can be a source for the disruption of the environment of an entire region. However, through the centuries we have seen a pattern repeated. The misuse of axe or saw, of fire or grazing, causes forest destruction. This leads to disruption of watersheds, to the erosion or loss of fertility of soils, to siltation and flooding in stream valleys, and to loss of the con-

tinued productivity of the land on which man must depend.

RAYMOND F. DASMANN, *Environmental Conservation*, 1976

15 Industry can buy 100 million board feet at one time. It can badger the Forest Service on the layout of the cut. It can take five years to get it out, and time the cuts to the market. It can build its mills where the big tracts are. It's a catered affair. You can understand why they clamor for more federal timber.

THOMAS J. BARLOW, quoted in *Conservation Foundation Letter*, July 1981

16 The rainforests are being destroyed not out of ignorance or stupidity but largely because of poverty and greed.

MICHAEL H. ROBINSON, *Saving the Tropical Forests*, 1988

17 Many of the forests of the world are being mowed down. . . . But the rest of the world isn't going to say, "Okay, we'll save our forests, but you Americans can keep driving all your cars!" There has to be give and take.

THOMAS R. PICKERING, U.S. ambassador to the United Nations, quoted in *Cosmopolitan*, September 1989

18 The practice of clearcutting is an ecologically illiterate exercise in economic opportunism, a form of slow-motion terrorism committed against those who need forest beauty now and forest products in the future.

DAVID R. BROWER, *For Earth's Sake*, 1990

19 Every day thousands of acres of tropical forests fall, victims of chainsaws, burning, and shortsighted government policies. In what amounts to a geological blink of the eye, we are witnessing the extinction of more species of plants and animals than all those that disappeared in the amount of time it took evolution to kill off the dinosaurs.

ROBERT REDFORD, in Scott Lewis, *The Rainforest Book*, 1990

20 The evolutionary idiocy of eliminating that diversity, and replacing it with short-lived monocultures of cash crops or grassland, exemplifies the arrogance of the West in its dealings with the natural world.

PRINCE PHILIP, duke of Edinburgh, speech, Royal Botanic Gardens, Kew, 6 February 1990

21 We, the richest nation in the world, are going to tell the dirt-poor people of Brazil and Indonesia and Zaire to be good environmentalists and not cut down their rainforests? Ha, We're showing them how.

ELLIOT A. NORSE, *Los Angeles Times*, 6 August 1990

23 DESERTS AND DESERTIFICATION

1 It is not by chance that several of the great religions of the world have been the products of the arid regions. The clear skies, the brilliant stars, the far-reaching visions, the wonderful colors of the rocks, have found expression in poetry and legend and man has been led to high things as he has wandered amid the exhilarating silence of the deserts.

RICHARD ELWOOD DODGE, *Journal of Geography* 8, 1910

2 I envy you [Americans] your deserts—not just because they are deserts, but because you can afford to keep them deserts.

DAVID BEN-GURION, speech, southern California, 1951

3 Life in a garden is relaxed, quiet, and sweet, like the life of Virgil's Tityrus, but survival in a howling desert demands action, the unceasing manipulation and mastery of the forces of nature, including, of course, human nature. Colonies established in the desert require aggressive, intellectual, controlled, and well-disciplined people.

LEO MARX, *A Machine in the Garden*, 1964

4 Although people may continue to live where they want, they must pay a price for their choice. In other parts of the country this price may be expressed in higher bills for fuel or in the cost of winter clothing; in the drylands it is the cost of water.

FRANK QUINN, *Geographical Review*, January 1968

5 The desert lies in wait for arable land and never lets go.

FERNAND BRAUDEL, *The Mediterranean*, 1972

6 Desertification breaks out, usually at times of drought stress, in areas of naturally vulnerable land subject to pressures of land use.

These degraded patches, like a skin disease, link up to carry the process over extended areas.
UNITED NATIONS CONFERENCE ON DESERTIFICATION, 1978

7 Here the land always makes a promise of aching beauty and the people always fail the land.
CHARLES BOWDEN, on the Sonoran Desert, *Blue Desert*, 1986

8 To really experience the desert you have to march right into its white bowl of sky and shape-contorting heat with your mind on your canteen as if it were your last gallon of gas and you were being chased by a carload of escaped murderers. You have to imagine what it would be like to drink blood from a lizard or, in the grip of dementia, claw barehanded through sand and rock for the vestigial moisture beneath a dry wash.
MARC REISNER, *Cadillac Desert*, 1986

9 Confronted by the desert, the first thing Americans want to do is change it. People say they "love" the desert, but few of them love it well enough to live there. I mean in the real desert, not in a make-believe city like Phoenix. . . . Most people "love" the desert by driving through it in air-conditioned cars, "experiencing" its grandeur.
MARC REISNER, *Cadillac Desert*, 1986

10 The desert makes you squint, and all its realities are stark. Much about nature comes clearer there. It throws its even pitiless light on self and soul both.
STEPHANIE MILLS, ed., *What Ever Happened to Ecology?*, 1989

11 Half the farming regions of humanity's first civilizations are now deserts.
PHIL HOLLIDAY, quoted in Stephanie Mills, ed., *In Praise of Nature*, 1990

12 We get rain because the Everglades are there. If we don't protect them, south Florida will become a desert.
MARJORIE STONEMAN DOUGLAS, *Countryside*, Winter 1990

13 Desertification is a mega-concept. It encompasses many processes such as wind and water erosion, soil salinization, overgrazing, water-logging and deforestation. It also has competing definitions, of which there are

more than a hundred. This perspective sees desertification as a process of change, rather than just the end result of that change.
MICHAEL GLANTZ, *Buzzworm*, January 1991

---

24 DEVELOPERS
See also   77 LAND USE

---

1 All this grand portion of our Union instead of being in a state of nature, is now more or less covered with villages, farms, and towns, where the din of hammers and machinery is constantly heard. . . . Whether these changes are for the better or worse, I shall not pretend to say.
JOHN JAMES AUDUBON (1785–1851), 1831, about Ohio, quoted in Wayne Hanley, *Natural History in America*, 1977

2 To clear, to till, and to transform the vast uninhabited continent which is his domain, the American requires the daily support of an energetic passion; that passion can only be the love of wealth; the passion for wealth is therefore not reprobated in America, and, provided it does not go beyond the bounds assigned to it for public security, it is held in good honor.
ALEXIS DE TOCQUEVILLE (1805–1859), *Democracy in America*, 1835

3 If people destroy something replaceable made by mankind, they are called vandals; If they destroy something irreplaceable made by God, they are called developers.
JOSEPH WOOD KRUTCH (1893–1970), quoted in *Mother Earth News*, March–April 1990

4 The machine running wild, the bulldozer on the rampage, the crane swinging aimlessly against the sky—these are signs of a people that is making things over without knowing why, or to what end. The physical and cultural environment has meaning only in so far as it bears the marks of what we are and what we aspire to be.
AUGUST HECKSCHER, *The Public Happiness*, 1962

5 It was the ancient mariner himself who shot the albatross and thus brought the necessity for using the bird as a neckpiece. Likewise, it was the developer, the subdivider, the housebuilder, who, because of his land

butchery, shoddy construction practice and general irresponsibility made it necessary in the first place to devise building codes, housing codes, zoning and subdivision regulations.

DENNIS O'HARROW, *American Society of Planning Officials Newsletter* 30, no. 1, 1964

6 Somehow I feel every road and oil well is an imposition, an intruder on the solitude which was once mine as I flew over it. Looking down on them from the air, those marks seem like a disease—a rash spreading slowly over the earth's surface.

CHARLES A. LINDBERGH (1902–1974), *Wartime Journals*, 1970

7 In one respect every natural area has a common uniqueness—it takes everyone forever to preserve it, but one person and one time to destroy it.

E. J. KOESTNER, quoted in *Reader's Digest*, August 1970

8 In America today you can murder land for private profit. You can leave the corpse for all to see, and nobody calls the cops.

PAUL BROOKS, *The Pursuit of Wilderness*, 1971

9 The plethora of small industries associated with development—engineering, real estate, construction, finance, architecture, etc.—have little experience in the kind of close teamwork that is desirable. Government programs, which are typically financed separately and mutually inconsistent, have further reduced coordination in the industry. The result is a hop-scotch of relatively small projects which are ill-conceived, ill-planned and ill-located.

JOSEPH E. HARING, testimony, U.S. Senate Public Works subcommmittee, 31 March 1971

10 [The] destruction value [of land can be] accurately measured on an economic scale, just as the "location value" of land is traditionally appraised, taxed, and used as a basis for trade. Every square foot of original natural topography, every cubic foot of soil, every spring, creek, pond, swamp or drainway, every bird and animal, every tree and shrub has value that can be measured. If the developer eliminates these things by "improving" through clearing, excavating, filling, dredg-

ing, refilling, regrading, covering with buildings and pavement, then he should pay to a public body of jurisdiction a destruction penalty equal to the appraised ecological loss incurred.

ROBERT W. RAMSEY, *Landscape Architecture*, April 1971

11 Suburbia is where the developer bulldozes out the trees, then names the streets after them.

BILL VAUGHN, quoted in Jon Winokur, *The Portable Curmudgeon*, 1987

12 Developers are not to be trusted. They're like crack addicts who scream for more when their supply is cut off.

ANTHONY DOWNS, on developers' reliance on bank lines of credit, *National Journal*, 3 November 1990

25 DRINKING WATER
See also 59 GROUNDWATER, 134 WATER

1 Don't say, I'll never drink of this water, how dirty soever it be.

ANONYMOUS

2 There are also kinds of water that cause death, as they run through harmful juices in the soil and become poisonous.

VITRUVIUS (1st century B.C.), *On Architecture*

3 He who drinks a tumbler of London water has literally in his stomach more animated beings than there are men, women, and children on the face of the globe.

SYDNEY SMITH (1771–1845), letter to Countess Grey, 19 November 1834

4 We are a water-drinking people, and we are allowing every brook to be defiled.

GEORGE BIRD GRINNELL, 1890 quoted in *Outdoor America*, February 1925

5 And if from man's vile arts I flee
And drink pure water from the pump,
I gulp down infusoria
And quarts of raw bacteria,
And hideous rotatoræ,
And wriggling polygastricæ,
And slimy diatomacæ,

And various animalculæ
Of middle, high and low degree.
WILLIAM JUNIPER, *The True Drunkard's Delight, 1933*

6 I would not drink water in Poughkeepsie.
FRANKLIN D. ROOSEVELT (1883–1945), 1938, quoted in Edgar B. Nixon, ed., *Franklin D. Roosevelt and Conservation, 1957*

7 I would rather be able to take my drinking water where I find it, like the fox or the Indian.
LOUIS J. HALLE, JR., *Spring in Washington, 1947*

8 We all drink somebody else's sewage.
KENNETH E. BOULDING, in Anne Chisholm, ed., *Philosophers of the Earth: Conversations with Ecologists, 1972*

9 Of all environmental ills, contaminated water is the most devastating in consequences. Each year 10 million deaths are directly attributable to waterborne intestinal diseases. One-third of humanity labors in a perpetual state of illness or debility as a result of impure water; another third is threatened by the release into water of chemical substances whose long-term effects are unknown.
PHILIP QUIGG, *Water: The Essential Resource, 1976*

10 Here is the recipe for the most popular drink in town. Start with raw branch water, as in bourbon-and-branch. Drop it through a funnellike device. Shake it up a bit. Strain it to remove large impurities, like fish and trees. Add some chlorine to kill the germs. Add some fluoride, so the drink's good for your teeth. Funnel some more. Add aluminum sulfate to settle the dirt. Add charcoal, if needed, to kill bad tastes. Let set several hours. Filter it and add some more chlorine. Let set some more. Pour into a glass and drink it neat.
JUDITH SERRIN, *Detroit Free Press*, 28 May 1978

11 It is time to realize that we should zone land from a hydrogeologic standpoint as well as from a political standpoint.
RONALD A. LANDON, on drinking-water contamination, speech, Fourth National Groundwater Quality Symposium, Minneapolis, 20 September 1978

12 In every glass of water we drink, some of the water has already passed through fishes, trees, bacteria, worms in the soil, and many other organisms, including people. . . . Living systems cleanse water and make it fit, among other things, for human consumption and for the needs of other species. Trout are even fussier in their needs than we are.
ELLIOT A. NORSE, in R. J. Hoage, ed., *Animal Extinctions, 1985*

13 If people in a Third World nation have no pure water for drinking, is it still all right to use First World water for swimming pools?
SARA EBENRECK, *Catholic World*, July–August 1990

---

26 EARTH
See also   54 GAIA HYPOTHESIS

---

1 The Earth is our Mother, and we are all her children.
HINDU PROVERB, quoted by Karam Singh, Assisi Declarations, World Wildlife Fund 25th Anniversary, 29 September 1986

2 Earth gives life and seeks the man who walks gently upon it.
HOPI LEGEND

3 Holy Mother Earth, the trees and all nature, are witnesses of your thoughts and deeds.
WINNEBAGO SAYING

4 O Lord, how manifold are thy works! in wisdom hast thou made them all: the earth is full of thy riches. So is this great and wide sea, wherein are things creeping innumerable, both small and great beasts.
BIBLE, Psalm 104:24–25

5 How the universe is like a bellows!
Empty, yet it gives a supply that never fails;
The more it is worked, the more it brings forth.
LAO-TSU (6th century B.C.), *Tao-te Ching*

6 The world is a sacred vessel,
Which must not be tampered with or grabbed after.
To tamper with it is to spoil it,
And to grasp it is to lose it.
LAO TSU (6th century B.C.), *Tao-te Ching*

7 All things come from earth, and to earth they all return.
> MENANDER (c. 342–c. 290 B.C.), *Monostikhoi*

8 Water rises in mist, freezes into hail, swells in waves, falls headlong in torrents; air becomes thick with clouds and rages with storms; but earth is kind and gentle and indulgent, ever a handmaid in the service of mortals, producing under our compulsion, or lavishing of her own accord, what scents and savours, what juices, what surfaces for the touch, what colours! how honestly she repays the interest lent her!
> PLINY THE ELDER (A.D. 23–79), *Natural History*, A.D. 77

9 What is the earth but a lump of clay surrounded by water?
> BHARTRHARI (c. 570–c. 651), *Vairagya-sataka*

10 Praise be, my Lord, for our sister, Mother Earth, Who sustains and governs us And brings forth diverse fruits with many-hued flowers and grass.
> FRANCIS OF ASSISI (c. 1181–1226), *Canticle of the Sun*, translated from the Italian by Matthew Arnold (1822–1888). Saint Francis was proclaimed patron saint of ecology in 1979.

11 This goodly frame, the earth, seems to me a sterile promontory; this most excellent canopy, the air, look you, this brave o'erhanging firmament, this majestical roof fretted with golden fire, why, it appears no other thing to me but a foul and pestilent congregation of vapors.
> WILLIAM SHAKESPEARE (1564–1616), *Hamlet* 2.2. 309–315

12 Heaven says nothing, and the whole earth grows rich beneath its silent rule.
> IHARA SAIKAKU (1642–1693), *Japanese Family Storehouse*

13 The earth belongs to the living, not to the dead.
> THOMAS JEFFERSON (1743–1826), letter to John W. Eppes, 24 June 1813

14 The poetry of earth is never dead.
> JOHN KEATS (1795–1821), "On the Grasshopper and Cricket," 1816

15 To make earth an object of huckstering—the earth which is our one and all, the first condition of our existence—was the last step toward making oneself an object of huckstering.
> FRIEDRICH ENGELS (1820–1895) *Outlines of a Critique of Political Economy*, quoted in Karl Marx, *The Economic and Philosophic Manuscripts of 1844*

16 This we know: the earth does not belong to man: man belongs to the earth. . . . All things are connected like the blood which unites one family. . . . Whatever befalls the earth, befalls the sons of the earth. Man did not weave the web of life: he is merely a strand in it. Whatever he does to the web, he does to himself.
> SEATTLE (Seathl), patriarch of the Duwamish and Squamish Indians of Puget Sound, letter to U.S. President Franklin Pierce, 1855

17 The earth is like the breasts of a woman: useful as well as pleasing.
> FRIEDRICH WILHELM NIETZSCHE (1844–1900), *Thus Spoke Zarathustra*, 1883–1892

18 Earth has no sorrow that earth cannot heal.
> JOHN MUIR, (1838–1914), 1892, in L. M. Wolfe, ed., *John Muir, John of the Mountains: The Unpublished Journals of John Muir*, 1938

19 This grand show is eternal. It is always sunrise somewhere; the dew is never all dried at once; a shower is forever falling; vapor is ever rising. Eternal sunrise, eternal sunset, eternal dawn and gloaming, on sea and continents and islands, each in its turn, as the round earth rolls.
> JOHN MUIR (1838–1914), 1913, in L. M. Wolfe, ed., *John Muir: John of the Mountains: The Unpublished Journals of John Muir*, 1938

20 O sweet spontaneous earth how often . . . has the naughty thumb of science prodded thy beauty. . . thou answerest them only with spring.
> E. E. CUMMINGS, *Tulips and Chimneys*, 1924

21 Do no dishonor to the earth, lest you dishonor the spirit of man.
> HENRY BESTON, *The Outermost House*, 1928

22 Only to the white man was nature a "wilderness" and only to him was the land "infested" with "wild" animals and "savage" people. To us it was tame. Earth was bountiful and we were surrounded with the blessings of the Great Mystery.

> LUTHER STANDING BEAR (1868–1939), *Land of the Spotted Eagle,* 1933

23 The people know the salt of the sea
and the strength of the winds
lashing the corners of the earth.
The people take the earth
as a tomb of rest and a cradle of hope.

> CARL SANDBURG (1878–1967), "The People, Yes," 1936

24 Earth is probably the lost paradise.

> FEDERICO GARCIA LORCA (1899–1936), "Mar"

25 It seems to me that the earth may be borrowed but not bought. It may be used but not owned. It gives in response to love and tending, offers its seasonal flowering and fruiting. But we are tenants and not possessors, lovers and not masters. Cross Creek belongs to the wind and the rain, to the sun and the seasons . . . and beyond all, to time.

> MARJORIE KINNON RAWLINGS (1896–1953), *Cross Creek,* 1942

26 The earth is not a perfect home for man. . . . Most soils are deficient in something, most climates call the tune on man's comfort and crop possibilities.

> ISAIAH BOWMAN, *Journal of Geography* 44, 1945

27 Once a photograph of the Earth, taken from the outside is available . . . a new idea as powerful as any other in history will be let loose.

> FRED HOYLE, 1948, quoted in Peter Borelli, ed., *Crossroads,* 1988

28 We must surround our people with the physical security, bodily vigor, and spiritual peace that come from close contact with earth and sky.

> CHARLES A. LINDBERGH (1902–1974), *Of Flight and Life,* 1948

29 Whether men use the advantages of the earth for good or evil ends is a question in social and political morality. Science leaves the field at this point with a single challenging conclusion: the earth is big enough and rich enough for us all if we learn how to live in peace.

> ISAIAH BOWMAN, *Journal of Geography,* 50, 1951

30 The supreme reality of our time is . . . the vulnerability of our planet.

> JOHN F. KENNEDY (1917–1963), speech, 28 June 1963

31 On Spaceship Earth there are no passengers; everybody is a member of the crew. We have moved into an age in which everybody's activities affect everybody else.

> MARSHALL MCLUHAN (1911–1980), *Understanding Media,* 1964

32 We travel together, passengers on a little space ship, dependent on its vulnerable reserves of air and soil; all committed for our safety to its security and peace; preserved from annihilation only by the care, the work, and, I will say, the love we give our fragile craft. We cannot maintain it half fortunate, half miserable, half confident, half despairing, half slave—to the ancient enemies of man—half free in a liberation of resources undreamed of until this day. No craft, no crew can travel safely with such vast contradictions. On their resolution depends the survival of us all.

> ADLAI STEVENSON (1900–1965), U.S. ambassador to the United Nations, last major speech, to the Economic and Social Council of the United Nations, Geneva, Switzerland, 9 July 1965

33 A tiny raft in the enormous, empty night.

> ARCHIBALD MACLEISH, quoted in *New York Times,* 19 April 1970

34 Now there is one outstanding important fact regarding Spaceship Earth, and that is that no instruction book came with it.

> R. BUCKMINSTER FULLER, quoted in *New York Times,* 8 August 1971

35 We haven't too much time left to ensure that the government of the earth, by the earth, for the earth, shall not perish from the people.

> C. P. SNOW and PHILIP SNOW, quoted in *Reader's Digest,* March 1972

36 The earth, seen wholly, is holy ground. There is no waste, only matter-energy, all transformable into life and life support.
RASA GUSTAITIS, *Wholly Round*, 1973

37 What is [the earth] *most* like? . . . It is *most* like a single cell.
LEWIS THOMAS, *The Lives of a Cell*, 1974

38 In the industrialized countries man behaves not as an ally of Nature but as her opponent. . . . Undoubtedly, an industrial society leads to material profits, but it also leads to the failure of mankind; for it impoverishes an irreplaceable asset: Nature. This Earth of ours is precious because it is not infinite but limited. We must love it, cherish it, and protect it, for our own good, for the good of our children, and for the good of our grandchildren.
MOBUTO SESE SEKO, President of Zaire, speech to IUCN 12th General Assembly, September 1975

39 Humanity is on the march, earth itself is left behind.
DAVID EHRENFELD, *The Arrogance of Humanism*, 1978

40 The concept of sovereignty cannot deny the physical and biological unity of the earth and its biosphere.
RUSSELL E. TRAIN, Conservation Foundation, *Conservation and Values*, 1978

41 The belief that we can manage the Earth and improve on Nature is probably the ultimate expression of human conceit, but it has deep roots in the past and is almost universal.
RENE DUBOS, *The Wooing of the Earth*, 1980

42 Let us open our eyes to the sacredness of Mother Earth, or our eyes will be opened for us.
GRANDFATHER DAVID MONONGYE, letter to the United Nations General Assembly, *New Age*, December 1982

43 With care, Mother Earth can remain a beneficent, stable, and comfortable protector for humankind and all of nature. It is a good thing this is so, for I am very sure that there is nowhere else in the universe we can realistically go if we don't like it here.
WALTER ORR ROBERTS, *Conservation Foundation Letter*, April 1983

44 Of all celestial bodies within reach or view . . . the most wonderful and marvellous and mysterious is turning out to be our own planet earth. It is the strangest of all places, and there is everything in the world to learn about it. It can keep us awake and jubilant with questions for millennia ahead, if we can learn not to meddle and not to destroy.
LEWIS THOMAS, *Late Night Thoughts on Listening to Mahler's Ninth*, 1984

45 Once we no longer live beneath our mother's heart, it is the earth with which we form the same dependent relationship, relying . . . on its cycles and elements, helpless without its protective embrace.
LOUISE ERDRICH, *New York Times*, 28 July 1985

46 The difference between our Ark and Noah's is that we cannot "disembark." Our Ark *is* the air, water and land, and all the species of plants and animals, including ourselves, are the crew.
LEE DURRELL, *Gaia State of the Ark Atlas*, 1986

47 Earth is a spacecraft in a deadly vacuum, with a life-support system as precious as is an astronaut's backpack.
JAMES C. FLETCHER, quoted in *Christian Science Monitor*, 31 March 1987

48 The earth will not continue to offer its harvest, except with faithful stewardship. We cannot say we love the land and then take steps to destroy it for use by future generations.
POPE JOHN PAUL II, homily, Monterey, California, 17 September 1987

49 Whilst we fight our wars of ideology on the face of this planet, we are losing our productive relationship with the planet itself.
DAVID BULL, World Commission on Environment and Development hearing, 23 September 1986, quoted in *Our Common Future*, 1987

50 The earth is a book in which we read not only
its history, but the history of the living things
it has borne.

>ISAAC ASIMOV, *Isaac Asimov's Book of Science
and Nature Quotations*, 1988

51 There is something fundamentally wrong in
treating the Earth as if it were a business in
liquidation.

>HERMAN E. DALY, *Science*, 17 June 1988

52 We have only one planet. If we screw it up,
we have no place to go.

>J. BENNETT JOHNSTON, U.S. Senator, *USA To-
day*, 23 August 1988

53 Let us remember as we chase our dreams into
the stars that our first responsibility is to our
Earth, to our children, to ourselves. Yes, let
us dream, let us pursue those dreams, but let
us also preserve the fragile world we inhabit.

>GEORGE BUSH, Global Change Conference,
1989

54 Molecules don't have passports. All the creatures on Earth are in this together. We need a
primary allegiance to the species and to
planet Earth.

>CARL SAGAN, quoted in Eknath Easwaran,
The Compassionate Universe, 1989

55 We've got to get the planet into intensive
care, [and] start to monitor its vital signs.

>JOHN EDDY, quoted in *Sierra*, July–August
1989

56 We talk about the spaceship Earth, but who is
monitoring the dials and turning the knobs?
No one; there are no dials to watch, only occasional alarms made by people peering out
the window, who call to us that they see species disappearing, an ozone hole in the upper
atmosphere, the climate change, the coasts of
all the world polluted. But because we have
never created the system of monitoring our
environment or devised the understanding
of nature's strange ecological systems, we are
still like the passengers in the cabin who
think they smell smoke or, misunderstanding how a plane flies, mistake light turbu-
lence for trouble. We need to instrument the
cockpit of the biosphere and to let up the win-

dow shade so that we begin to observe nature
as it is, not as we imagine it to be.

>DANIEL B. BOTKIN, *Discordant Harmonies*,
1990

57 To make peace with the planet, we must
make peace among the peoples who live in it.

>BARRY COMMONER, *Making Peace with the
Planet*, 1990

58 I'll admit I still get a tiny bit depressed when I
try to think about it from her [the Earth's]
point of view. Imagine spending 4 billion
years stocking the oceans with seafood, filling the ground with fossil fuels, and drilling
the bees in honey production—only to produce a race of bed-wetters!

>BARBARA EHRENREICH, *The Worst Years of Our
Lives*, 1990

59 Our children may save us if they are taught to
care properly for the planet; but if not, it may
be back to the Ice Age or the caves from
where we first emerged. Then we'll have to
view the universe above from a cold, dark
place. No more jet skis, nuclear weapons,
plastic crap, broken pay phones, drugs, cars,
waffle irons, or television. Come to think of
it, that might not be a bad idea.

>JIMMY BUFFET, *Mother Earth News*, March–
April 1990

60 We could have saved it, but we were too
damned cheap.

>KURT VONNEGUT, *Mother Earth News*, March–
April 1990

61 We live on a planet run by physical rules and
filled with life that is not only glorious but
stubborn.

>NEW YORKER, 18 June 1990

62 If we all treated others as we wish to be
treated ourselves, then decency and stability
would have to prevail.

>I suggest that we execute such a pact with
our planet.

>STEPHEN JAY GOULD, *Natural History*, Sep-
tember 1990

63 This planet is not private property.

>HAZEL HENDERSON, "Profit the Earth," PBS,
23 September 1990

64 "Flowers and trees," said he, "do not speak,
but they have hearts and spirits just like you

and me. They can feel your love, hear your heart's message. And 'we,' the guardians, were created to remind all things of their relationship, and to never, never forget Earth Mother. She is a living thing—very, very important in the Great Creation of the Great Spirit. Do you understand, Little Girl?"

TONY SHEARER, *The Praying Flute: Song of the Earth Mother*, 1991

27 EARTH DAY

1 We hope to involve an entire society in a rethinking of many of its basic assumptions.
DENIS HAYES, press conference, Washington, D.C., January 1970

2 "Earth Day" in America was one huge pantheistic feast.
JEAN-FRANÇOIS REVEL, *Without Marx or Jesus*, 1970

3 Earth Day is a commitment to make life better, not just bigger and faster; to provide real rather than rhetorical solutions. It is a day to re-examine the ethic of individual progress at mankind's expense. It is a day to challenge the corporate and governmental leaders who promise change, but who shortchange the necessary programs. It is a day for looking beyond tomorrow. April 22 seeks a future worth living. April 22 seeks a future.
ENVIRONMENTAL TEACH-IN, advertisement, *New York Times*, 18 January 1970

4 A disease has infected our country. It has brought smog to Yosemite, dumped garbage in the Hudson, sprayed DDT in our food, and left our cities in decay. Its carrier is man. The weak are already dying. Trees by the Pacific. Fish in our streams and lakes. Birds and crops and sheep. And people. On April 22 we start to reclaim the environment we have wrecked.
ENVIRONMENTAL TEACH-IN, advertisement, *New York Times*, 18 January 1970

5 Earth Day will have to be extended to Earth Year, Decade, Generation if the poisoning of water, air, and soil is to be halted or even appreciably slowed down. . . . This exercise is not to be confused with community paint-up, clean-up weeks coincident with the first nice days of spring.
ERIC SEVAREID, CBS Evening News, 22 April 1970

6 Twenty years after Earth Day, those of us who set out to change the world are poised on the threshold of utter failure. Measured on virtually any scale, the world is in worse shape today than it was 20 years ago.
DENIS HAYES, NRDC Marshall Lecture, Museum of Natural History, New York City, 8 November 1989

7 In fact, Earth Day 1990 should be a time to celebrate. Back in 1970 Commoner was not sure we would make it to 1990, so fragile did he conceive our ecosystem to be, and Dr. Paul Ehrlich was equally pessimistic. . . . Well, by 1975 Americans were as fat as ever. The famine never arrived. . . . Earth Day 1990 should be a festival in celebration of how Americans have dedicated themselves to conserving nature, preserving resources, and creating new ones.
R. EMMETT TYRRELL, JR., reprinted from *The American Spectator*, in *Utne Reader*, November–December 1989

8 Domestically, Earth Day is a reaffirmation of the values and social impulse that were expressed twenty years ago: a blossoming of environmentalism as a mass social movement. But beyond that, it is activism on a global scale. We have a world movement going on now.
PHILIP SHABECOFF, *Amicus Journal*, Spring 1990

9 But Earth Day—as was intended—demonstrated to the Washington Establishment and the public that there *was* an environmental movement. The principal and lasting effect was to make environmental concerns a permanent part of the political dialogue in this country.
GAYLORD NELSON, *Smithsonian*, April 1990

10 Yes, Virginia, there was an environmental movement before Earth Day, a long, slow revolution in values of which contemporary environmentalism is a consequence and a

continuation. We are still in transition from the notion of Man as master of Earth to the notion of Man as a part of it.
WALLACE STEGNER, *Smithsonian*, April 1990

11 For some people, Earth Day was payday.
NATIONAL INHOLDERS ASSOCIATION, advertisement, *Washington Post*, 4 June 1990

12 If Theodore Roosevelt's conservation ethic represented the first important era of U.S. environmental concern, then the decade of new laws following the original Earth Day was the second. Our challenge now is to move aggressively into a third era: a period when practical and economically sensible policies will provide more effective and efficient environmental protection and natural-resource management.
JOHN HEINZ, U.S. Senator, *Business Week*, 18 June 1990

13 Finally, Earth Day is an important day because it represents another step in our civilization, that is, a step toward making us more civilized. Ours is not the first environmental movement, but it is the first based on scientific investigation and reasoning rather than on naturalism. It juxtaposes two powerful forces: a faith in technology that became almost a religion during the past century and deeply ingrained feelings about nature that are apparently within us all. It is, therefore, a potentially profound development in the evolution of human culture.
WILLIAM H. GLAZER, *Environmental Science and Technology* 24, no. 4, April 1990

28 ECOLOGISTS

1 The rise of the ecologist exactly parallels the decline of the naturalist.
PAUL SEARS, *Charles Darwin: The Naturalist as a Cultural Force*, 1950

2 What do ecologists offer? No panaceas or quick returns, so much as a point of view which restrains, shows the consequences of different types of action, and possibly how mistakes in land-use can be rectified, and

why they were mistakes. Ecology is a science of identifying causes and consequences.
FRANK FRASER DARLING, speech, British Association, Aberdeen meeting, 29 August 1963

3 Over the long haul of life on this planet, it is the ecologists, and not the bookkeepers of business, who are the ultimate accountants.
STEWART L. UDALL, speech, Congress on Optimum Population and Environment, Chicago, 9 June 1970

4 Ecologists believe that a bird in the bush is worth two in the hand.
STANLEY C. PEARSON, quoted in *Peter's Quotations*, 1977

5 He is the latest *arriviste* in the world of aspiring expertise, and henceforth, by wide agreement, he is to perform the role of mediator between man and nature.
DONALD WORSTER, *Nature's Economy*, 1977

6 The ecologist is the most recent of science's prophets. He offers not only a credible explanation of the way nature works, but also something of a metaphysical insight, a set of ethical precepts—perhaps even a revolutionary program.
DONALD WORSTER, *Nature's Economy*, 1977

7 The science of ecology is no longer something of interest only to ecologists or a subject to be studied only for its intellectual fascination (although that still exists). Many of the major problems the world faces—pollution, overpopulation, the wise use of resources—are at heart ecological problems. Ecologists will help to find solutions to these problems, but so will everybody else.
RICHARD BREWER, *Principles of Ecology*, 1979

8 Ecologists and others interested in preserving wild species should not be required to solve all the problems of jobs, urbanization, and industries in order to advocate protection of other species.
BILL DEVALL and GEORGE SESSIONS, *Deep Ecology*, 1985

9 Shallow [ecologists] encourage the destructiveness and wastefulness of industrial society even as they seek to reform it. For example, deep ecologists argue that environ-

mental regulations based on emissions standards and tolerances represent licenses to pollute. Thus, NRDC, National Audubon, the National Wildlife Federation, and other such groups are considered shallow by most deeps.

PETER BORELLI, ed., *Crossroads*, 1988

10 Ecologists are aware that their view of ecosystem processes is warped by the length of the human lifetime, if not by the length of the research grant.

LAWRENCE R. POMEROY and JAMES ALBERTS, *Concepts of Ecosystem Ecology*, 1988

29 ECOLOGY

See also   36 ECOSYSTEMS, 65 HOLISM

1 Easy is everything to nature's majesty, who uses her strength sparingly, and dispenses it with caution and foresight for the commencement of her works by imperceptible additions, but hastens to decay with suddenness and in full career.

WILLIAM HARVEY (1578–1657), *Animal Generation*, 1651

2 Nature is one connected whole. At any given moment every part must be precisely what it is, because all other parts are what they are, and not a grain of sand could be moved from its place without changing something throughout all parts of the immeasurable whole.

JOHANN GOTTLIEB FICHTE (1762–1814), *Die Bestimmung des Menschen*, 1800

3 It is a legal maxim that "the law concerneth not itself with trifles," . . . but in the vocabulary of nature, little and great are terms of comparison only; she knows no trifles, and her laws are as inflexible in dealing with an atom as with a continent or a planet.

GEORGE PERKINS MARSH, *Man and Nature*, 1864

4 When we try to pick out anything by itself, we find that it is bound fast by a thousand invisible cords that cannot be broken to everything in the universe. I fancy I can hear a heart beating in every crystal, in every grain of sand and see a wise plan in the making

and shaping and placing of every one of them. All seems to be dancing in time to divine music.

JOHN MUIR (1838–1914), *Journal*, 27 July 1869

5 For in nature nothing takes place in isolation. Everything affects every other thing and *vice-versa*, and it is mostly because this all-sided motion and interaction is forgotten that our natural scientists are prevented from clearly seeing the simplest things.

FREDERICK ENGELS (1820–1895), *Dialectics of Nature*, 1895

6 All things by immortal power
  Near or far
  Hiddenly
To each other linked are,
That thou canst not stir a flower
Without troubling of a star.

FRANCIS THOMPSON (1859–1907), c. 1896

7 Ecology has arisen from the need to unite originally separate branches of science in a new and natural doctrine; it is characterized by the breadth of its aims, and its peculiar power and strength in its ability to unite knowledge of organic life with knowledge of its home, our earth. It assumes the solution of that most difficult as well as most fascinating problem which occupies the minds of philosophers and theologians alike— namely, the life history of the plant and animal worlds under the influences of space and time.

O. DRUDE, *Congress of Arts and Sciences*, vol. 4, Universal Exposition, Saint Louis, 1904

8 Nature as a whole is a progressive realization of purpose strictly comparable to the realization of purpose in any single plant or animal.

JOHN DEWEY (1859–1952), "The Influence of Darwinism on Philosophy," 1909

9 [Ecology is] the science of communities.

VICTOR E. SHELFORD, *Laboratory and Field Ecology*, 1929

10 Ecological concepts may be regarded as the epitome of scientific thinking.

G. T. RENNER, JR., *Journal of Geography* 30, 1931

11 A living organism . . . feeds upon negative entropy. . . . Thus the device by which an or-

ganism maintains itself stationary at a fairly high level of orderliness (= fairly low level of entropy) really consists in continually sucking orderliness from its environment.

ERWIN SCHRODINGER (1887–1961), *What Is Life?*, 1944

12 There is a body of knowledge, a point of view, which peculiarly implies all that is meant by conservation, and much more. Certainly it is the science of perspective. . . . It is the approach to biological knowledge which is called ecology.

PAUL SEARS, *Deserts on the March*, 1947

13 The God who planned the well-working machines which function as atom and solar system seems to have had no part in arranging the curiously inefficient society of plants and animals in which everything works against everything else.

JOSEPH WOOD KRUTCH, *The Twelve Seasons*, 1949

14 There is continuity in the life patterns of all organic forms. . . . ecology is but a new name for an old subject.

AMOS HAWLEY, *Human Ecology*, 1950

15 Ecology is an infant just learning to talk, and, like other infants, is grossed with its own coinage of big words. Its working days lie in the future. Ecology is destined to become the lore of Round River, a belated attempt to convert our collective knowledge of biotic materials into a collective wisdom of biotic navigation. This, in the last analysis, is conservation.

ALDO LEOPOLD (1886–1948), *Round River*, 1953

16 Instead of learning more and more about less and less, we must learn more and more about the whole biotic landscape.

ALDO LEOPOLD (1886–1946), *Round River*, 1953

17 Ecology is the physiology of community.

FRANK FRASER DARLING, speech, British Association, Aberdeen meeting, 29 August 1963

18 With remarkable suddenness it has mounted a powerful threat to established assumptions in society and in economics, religion, and the

humanities, as well as the other sciences and their ways of doing business.

PAUL SEARS, *BioScience* 14, no. 7, July 1964

19 Modern ecological studies leave no doubt that almost any disturbances of natural conditions are likely to have a large variety of indirect unfavorable effects because all components of nature are interrelated and interdependent.

RENÉ DUBOS, speech, Agriculture Department Graduate School, 1966

20 With laissez-faire and price atomic,
Ecology's Uneconomic,
But with another kind of logic
Economy's Unecologic.

KENNETH E. BOULDING, in Frank F. Darling and John P. Milton, eds., *Future Environments of North America*, 1966

21 The beauty of the idea [of ecology] was in its bigness and readiness to cross boundaries, looking into less well-understood fields than one's own and finding links, correlations, comparisons, contrasts, and differences of exquisitely fine scale and subtlety.

FRANK FRASER DARLING, *Daedalus*, Fall 1967

22 Ecology is the science that deals with the relations between all of the elements in an environment—the ecosystem. It rests upon all of the biological and physical sciences—botany, zoology, chemistry, physics, geology, soil science, meteorology, etc., with their innumerable ramifications—and when man is a part of the environment, the social sciences are also involved. Its distinguishing characteristic is that it uses these sciences in their relations to each other to determine what happens in a given environment, under both natural and modified conditions, and why it happens. In comprehensiveness and complexity, it is unique.

SAMUEL T. DANA, quoted in *Conservation Foundation Letter*, 23 February 1968

23 We may go down in history as an elegant technological society which underwent biological disintegration through lack of ecological understanding.

DAVID M. GATES, quoted in *This Week in Public Health*, 19 September 1968

24 The Earth is one ecological unit. The student of disease pandemics—cholera, plague, in-

fluenza—has long understood that the world is bound by bacterial bonds.

ABEL WOLMAN, *Foreign Affairs,* October 1968

25 Although ecology may be treated as a science, its greater and overriding wisdom is universal.

PAUL SHEPARD, introduction, in Paul Shepard and Daird McKinley, eds., *The Subversive Science,* 1969

26 The ideological status of ecology is that of a resistance movement. Its Rachel Carsons and Aldo Leopolds are subversive.

PAUL SHEPARD, introduction in Paul Shepard and Daird McKinley, eds., *The Subversive Science,* 1969

27 The Four Laws of Ecology . . . 1. Everything is connected to everything else, 2. Everything must go somewhere, 3. Nature knows best, 4. There is no such thing as a free lunch.

BARRY COMMONER, *The Closing Circle,* 1971

28 Ecological awareness leads to questioning of goals:
This threatens the performance of some old established roles.

KENNETH E. BOULDING, "The Ballad of Ecological Awareness," in M. Taghi Farvar and John P. Milton, eds., *The Careless Technology,* 1972

29 In ecology, as in economics, . . . every gain is won at some cost. . . . Because the global ecosystem is a connected whole, in which nothing can be gained or lost and which is not subject to over-all improvement, anything extracted from it by human effort must be replaced. Payment of this price cannot be avoided; it can only be delayed. The present environmental crisis is a warning that we have delayed nearly too long.

BARRY COMMONER, *The Closing Circle: Nature, Man, and Technology,* 1972

30 Its sensibility—wholistic, receptive, trustful, largely nontampering, deeply grounded in aesthetic intuition—is a radical deviation from traditional science. Ecology does not systematize by mathematical generalizations or materialist reductionism, but by the almost sensuous intuiting of natural harmonies on the largest scale. Its patterns are not those of numbers, but of unity in process.

THEODORE ROSZAK, *Where the Wasteland Ends,* 1972

31 But nowadays younger ecologists feel that if we are going to extend ecology as a hard science, we must make it predictive, so that we can tell in advance what the consequences for the environment will be when we add a pollutant or introduce a new species.

EDWARD O. WILSON, in Anne Chisholm, ed., *Philosophers of the Earth: Conversations with Ecologists,* 1972

32 Ecology . . . is a kind of extension of the Golden Rule. What have been held up to us in the past as moral truths, ecology is now telling us are facts of nature—not separate, isolated facts and phenomena but a remarkably complex web of interacting variables in which any happening, however minute, affects something or someone else.

EVELYN AMES, *New York Times,* 20 May 1972

33 One might say [ecology] is the creed, or code, of the earth, our home.

EVELYN AMES, *New York Times,* 20 May 1972

34 Ecology is neither an emotional state of mind nor a political point of view, although there are those who seek to use ecological ideas to whip up emotions and influence politics. Ecology is a science.

RAYMOND F. DASMANN, et al., *Ecological Principles for Economic Development,* 1973

35 Ecology challenges us to vigorous complexity, not passive simplicity.

JOSEPH W. MEEKER, *The Ecologist,* June 1973

36 Ecology is boring for the same reason that destruction is fun.

DON DELILLO, quoted in *New York Times,* 14 July 1974

37 There was the ecological vision.

FRANK FRASER DARLING, on Darwin's *The Origin of Species,* quoted in *Conservation Foundation Letter,* October 1975

38 The best that might be hoped for from the science of ecology, at present, is the more careful management of those resources, to preserve the biotic capital while maximizing

the income. That of course is a thoroughly sensible strategy in any household, the earth's included.

DONALD WORSTER, *Nature's Economy*, 1977

39 All creatures on the earth are related to one another essentially as producers and consumers; interdependence in such a world must mean sharing a common energy income. And as part of nature, man must be considered primarily as an economic animal—he is at one with all life in a push for greater productivity. Within the scope of recent ecology, there is little room for that arcadian sense of fellowship found in the science of Gilbert White, Thoreau, or Darwin.

DONALD WORSTER, *Nature's Economy*, 1977

40 In our present state of knowledge one cannot show that wolves, bears, tigers, eagles, green sea turtles, orioles, bullfrogs, monarch butterflies, olive baboons, red kangaroos, bottle-nosed dolphins, or a thousand other big species are really indispensable to their ecosystems. Indeed, the domino theory is just opposite the true metaphor of the web of nature. If one small strand goes, the whole does not fall, and in fact the survivors adjust to the break.

PAUL SHEPARD, *Thinking Animals*, 1978

41 The new understanding of life must be systemic and interconnected. It cannot be linear and hierarchical, for the reality of life on earth is a whole, a circle . . . in which everything has its part to play and can be respected and accorded dignity.

ELIZABETH DODSON GRAY, *Why the Green Nigger: Remything Creation*, 1979

42 Ecology is now fashionable, indeed faddish—and with this sleazy popularity has emerged a new type of environmentalist hype.

MURRAY BOOKCHIN, *The Ecology of Freedom*, 1982

43 The forests and the oceans are free private enterprise beyond the dreams of Milton Friedman, governed entirely and exclusively by the invisible hand of ecological interaction.

KENNETH E. BOULDING, speech, American Association for the Advancement of Science, 7 January 1982

44 If modern ecology was to show us how we could, following [Aldo] Leopold's advice, become biotic citizens, it needed to become a science that would demonstrate the proper role for humanity in nature.

ALSTON CHASE, *Playing God in Yellowstone*, 1986

45 While scientists [of ecology] moved ever more narrowly into the abstract realms of mathematical manipulation, environmentalists traveled more widely in search of a spiritual cosmology of nature. As scientists learned more and more about less and less, environmentalists were learning less and less about more and more.

ALSTON CHASE, *Playing God in Yellowstone*, 1986

46 The conflict between the image of science as objective and value-free and that of ecology as intrinsically value-laden and a guide to ethics for humans, animals, and even trees is difficult to reconcile.

ROBERT P. McINTOSH, *The Backround of Ecology*, 1987

47 Ecology was, and is, a science which does not fit readily into the familiar mold of science erected on the model of classical physics, and it deals with phenomena which frequently touch very close to the quick of human sensibilities, including aesthetics, morality, ethics, and, even worse in some minds, economics.

ROBERT P. McINTOSH, *The Backround of Ecology*, 1987

48 [Ecology] has not been able to deliver the facts, understanding, and predictions [needed for environmental reform].

TOM REGAN, quoted by Kristin Shrader-Frechetter, *The Environmental Professional 9*, no. 2, 1987

49 The essence of the human dilemma [is that] the energy evoked by the ecological vision has not been sufficient to offset the energies evoked by the industrial vision—even when its desolation becomes so obvious as it is at the present time.

THOMAS BERRY, *The Dream of the Earth*, 1988

50 Ecology and economy are becoming ever more interwoven—locally, regionally, na-

tionally, and globally—into a seamless net of causes and effects.

STEVEN H. ARNOLD, testimony, Joint Economic subcommittee, U.S. Congress, 13 June 1989

51 The term ecology comes from the Greek word *oikos*, and means "the household." Ecological responsibility, then, begins at home and expands to fill the entire planet.

JEREMY RIFKIN, introduction to *The Green Lifestyle Handbook*, 1990

52 A healthy ecology is the basis for a healthy economy.

CLAUDINE SCHNEIDER, U.S. Representative, in Jeremy Rifkin, ed., *The Green Lifestyle Handboook*, 1990

53 Many things in nature, from cells to ecosystems, tend to regulate themselves. While they do not, like a thermostat, regulate themselves exactly to human specifications, they do tend to keep themselves in a state of health that, in the long run, is better for the humans associated with them than a state of illness. What allows natural systems to regulate themselves is their wildness, the cleverness bred in them by natural selection.

EVAN EISENBERG, *New Republic*, 30 April 1990

54 The implications of this "Butterfly Effect" for ecology are profound. If a single flap of an insect's wings in China can lead to a torrential downpour in New York, then what might it do to the Greater Yellowstone Ecosystem? What can ecologists possibly know about all the forces impinging on, or about to impinge on, any piece of land? What can they safely ignore and what must they pay attention to? What distant, invisible, minuscule events may even now be happening that will change the organization of plant and animal life in our back yards? This is the predicament, and the challenge, presented by the science of chaos, and it is altering the imagination of ecologists dramatically.

DONALD WORSTER, on meteorologist Edward Lorenz's notion of the butterfly effect, *Environmental History Review* 14, nos. 1–2, Spring/Summer, 1990

55 Behind the persistent enthusiasm for ecology, I believe, lies the hope that this science

can offer a great deal more than a pile of data. It is supposed to offer a pathway to a kind of moral enlightenment that we can call, for the purposes of simplicity, "conservation."

DONALD WORSTER, *Environmental History Review* 14, nos. 1–2, Spring–Summer, 1990

56 In [Paul] Sears's day ecology was basically a study of equilibrium, harmony, and order; it had been so from its beginnings. Today, however, in many circles of scientific research, it has become a study of disturbance, disharmony, and chaos, and coincidentally or not, conservation is often not even a remote concern.

DONALD WORSTER, *Environmental History Review* 14, nos. 1–2, Spring–Summer 1990

---

30 ECONOMIC GROWTH

See also 32 ECONOMICS, GNP, 34 ECONOMICS, STEADY-STATE

---

1 What we call "progress" is the exchange of one nuisance for another nuisance.

HAVELOCK ELLIS (1859–1939), *Impressions and Comments*, 1924

2 Economic advance is not the same thing as human progress.

JOHN CLAPHAM, *A Concise Economic History of Britain*, 1957

3 We can have the social planning that erases grime and squalor and preserves and enhances beauty. A price in industrial efficiency may be necessary. Indeed it should be assumed. Economic development enables us to pay the price; it is why we have development. We do not have development in order to make our surroundings more hideous, our culture more meretricious or our lives less complete.

JOHN KENNETH GALBRAITH, *Science*, 10 July 1964

4 The entire history of American government policy, federal, state, and local, has been based upon the notion of growth indefinitely extended. Possible states of social or environmental stability are therefore automatically

viewed as something abnormal and threatening.

SANFORD S. FARNESS, in Frank F. Darling and John P. Milton, eds., *Future Environments of North America*, 1966

5 The chief sources of social welfare are not to be found in economic growth *per se*, but in a far more selective form of development which must include a radical reshaping of our physical environment with the needs of pleasant living, and not the needs of traffic or industry, foremost in mind.

E. J. MISHAN, *The Costs of Economic Growth*, 1969

6 The suggestion of curtailing growth is [considered] unthinkable. Greek rationalism, the Roman engineering mentality, the Biblical injunction to conquer and subdue nature, the post-Englightenment mystique about technical progress—all espouse development.

BARRY WEISBERG, *Ramparts*, January 1970

7 [There is no] fundamental contradiction between economic growth and the quality of life. The answer is not to abandon growth, but to redirect it.

RICHARD M. NIXON, State of the Union message, 22 January 1970

8 [Nixon] sounded about as convincing as a doctor telling a cancer patient not to worry about the growth of his tumor.

JOHN FISCHER, *Harper's*, April 1970

9 A rising GNP will enable the nation more easily to bear the costs of eliminating pollution.

NEIL H. JACOBY, *Center Magazine*, November–December 1970

10 For anyone to whom clean water is the only valuable product, there has been no economic growth since the time of Hiawatha.

COUNCIL OF ECONOMIC ADVISERS, annual report, 1971

11 Economic growth is a means, an instrumental goal, while environmental quality is an end in itself, an important component of the quality of existence. In assessing the instrumental goal of growth, we need to inquire: whether it is growth itself, or its particular forms, that get us into environmental trouble.

WALTER HELLER, paper for Senate Interior Committee, 1971

12 A point that's often made by developers is that we should grow more, because if we grow more we will broaden the tax base and the cost of living relative to our income will be less for all of us. . . . [But] I know of no data whatsoever which will support that contention, and in fact, there are lines of evidence suggesting that this is quite wrong, and the truth is the other way; the more you grow the greater the cost of living becomes relative to mean family income, and the people move backward.

KENNETH E. F. WATT, speech, California Tomorrow Plan conference, 13 April 1971

13 One principle that is an ecological upsetter
Is that if anything is good, then more of it is better,
And this misunderstanding sets us very, very wrong,
For no relation in the world is linear for long.

KENNETH E. BOULDING, "The Ballad of Ecological Awareness," in M. Taghi Farvar and John P. Milton, eds., *The Careless Technology*, 1972

14 I have said long ago that growth addiction was the creed of our times, but it was a surprise even to me that it had the intensity of a fanatical religion.

DENNIS GABOR, on those who attack reports on the limits to growth, *The Ecologist*, March 1972

15 Thus growth tends to threaten traditional middle-class values: it is felt to be disruptive and unpleasant precisely because it turns minority privileges into majority ones—because it means crowded roads, crowded beaches, and so on.

RUDOLF KLEIN, *Commentary*, June 1972

16 We can move away from the recent sterile argument of growth versus anti-growth, and resume the real argument. How do we use and direct our growth?

ANTHONY CROSLAND, *Sunday Times* (London), 26 June 1972

17 Many developmentalists believe that the progress of mankind depends on ceaseless technological improvement, measured by such elements as speed.

CHARLES A. LINDBERGH, *New York Times*, 27 July 1972

18 If we do not have the strength [to reduce greed and simplify our needs] could we perhaps stop applauding the type of economic "progress" which palpably lacks the basis of permanence and give what modest support we can to those who, unafraid of being denounced as cranks, work for non-violence: as conservationists, ecologists, protectors of wildlife, promoters of organic agriculture, distributists, cottage producers, and so forth?
E. F. SCHUMACHER, *Small Is Beautiful*, 1973

19 Not blind opposition to progress, but opposition to blind progress.
SIERRA CLUB, motto

20 The more we look at it the more it is apparent that economic growth is a device for providing us with the superfluous at the cost of the indispensible.
EDWARD GOLDSMITH, *The Ecologist*, February 1974

21 I want to make it clear, if there is ever a conflict [between environmental quality and economic growth] I will go for beauty, clean air, water, and landscape.
JIMMY CARTER, quoted in *New York Times*, 19 September 1976

22 Encouraging one kind of development over another is not "antigrowth"; rather, it is a statement of priorities and goals. Different growth patterns reflect different values. Some investment strategies create more jobs than others. Some create better jobs. Some produce more pollutants, disease, and environmental destruction. . . . What mix of industries and business enterprises is preferable? Who should decide? These are important questions for any society to consider.
RICHARD KAZIS and RICHARD L. GROSSMAN, *Fear at Work*, 1982

23 Deterioration of existing facilities and insufficient capacity to accommodate future growth can eventually constrain economic development. The nation's transportation network, water supply, and wastewater treatment facilities provide vital services for both industries and individuals; where capacity is inadequate to meet the needs of growth, that growth can be stunted.
U.S. CONGRESSIONAL BUDGET OFFICE, *Public Works Infrastructure*, April 1983

24 There is also a great consensus that the application of strict environmental standards is good for economic growth, as well as for the environment, and that they encourage innovation, promote inventiveness and efficiency, and generate employment.
STANLEY CLINTON-DAVIS, hearing, World Commission on Environment and Development, Oslo, 24–25 June 1985

25 Growth for the sake of growth is the ideology of the cancer cell. Cancer has no purpose but growth; but it does have another result—the death of the host.
EDWARD ABBEY, *One Life at a Time, Please*, 1988

26 The battle before us is a battle for organization of our planet [but we are battling only] in order to give us a fresh chance for development.
MICHEL ROCARD, French prime minister, *Audubon*, January 1990

27 President Bush today demonstrated a fundamental misunderstanding. . . . Limiting pollution does not mean limiting growth . . . It is time that the Bush Administration recognizes what our G-7 [Group of Seven] allies already know: energy efficiency and the creation and commercial exploitation of environmentally sound technologies such as solar power are the growth industries of the future.
MICHAEL BEAN, quoted in *Inside EPA*, 20 July 1990

28 We [in Czechoslovakia] didn't get into this [environmental] mess only because the Communists suffered excessively from a growth mentality. The West is little different on that score. The planned economy led to some awful distortions, but it did not invent unsustainable forestry, chemical agriculture, crowded cities, traffic jams, or industrial smog.
PETR PITHART, Czech government official, quoted in *Audubon*, January 1991

31 ECONOMICS
See also   35 ECONOMICS, VALUATION

1 The note of gloom and pessimism which distinguishes so much of the economic doctrine

of the nineteenth century is in no small measure the legacy of [Thomas Robert] Malthus.
ALEXANDER GRAY, *The Development of Economic Doctrine*, 1931

2 Economics can be seen as the ecology of man; ecology as the study of the economy of nature.
MARSTON BATES, *The Forest and the Sea*, 1960

3 Because we depend on so many detailed and subtle aspects of the environment, *any* change imposed on it for the sake of some economic benefit has a price. . . . Sooner or later, wittingly or unwittingly, we must pay for every intrusion on the natural environment.
BARRY COMMONER, *Science and Survival*, 1966

4 The quality of the human environment must enter as one necessary element into all economic planning. . . . An informed and alerted public opinion is essential for influencing governments, international organizations, private industry, etc. towards making rational planning for an improved physical and social environment an integral part of the planning for economic growth.
SVERKER ASTROM, at U.N. General Assembly, 3 December 1968

5 Racial injustice, war, urban blight, and environmental rape have a common denominator in our exploitative economic system.
CHANNING E. PHILLIPS, speech, Washington, D.C., 22 April 1970

6 There seems to be no reason to believe . . . that the employment-creating effects of restoring the environment will be any less than those involved in polluting the environment.
EDWARD S. MASON, speech, Resources for the Future forum, Washington, D.C., 20 April 1971

7 The elite's environmental deterioration is often the common man's improved standard of living.
ANTHONY DOWNS, *The Public Interest*, Summer 1972

8 Upper-class whites have . . . found it necessary to ask for government assistance to avoid the unpleasant externalities of the very system from which they themselves have already benefited so extensively.
PETER MARCUSE, in James N. Smith, *Environmental Quality and Social Justice in Urban America*, 1974

9 One man's conservation is all too frequently another man's unemployment.
MIKE MCCORMACK, quoted in *Time*, 12 December 1977

10 It seems anomalous that institutions bent on private greed need not apologize for their polluting activities, whereas agencies that are devoted to the protection of public health, under due process of law, must apologize in terms that it's good for the economy.
RALPH NADER, speech, Public Citizens Forum, Washington, D.C., 3 August 1978

11 Compensation for the damages caused by environmental pollution should be an integral part of a coherent and rational environmental protection policy.
WERNER PFENNIGSTORF, *American Bar Foundation Research Journal*, Spring 1979

12 All my life I've seen the lads leaving Ireland for the big smoke in London, Pittsburgh, Birmingham, and Chicago. It'd be better for Ireland if they stayed here and we imported the smoke.
ANONYMOUS IRISH POLITICIAN, quoted in *Conservation Foundation Letter*, August 1982

13 Neither of the dominant economic paradigms that guide human interactions—namely, capitalism and socialism (or whatever other labels we assign these two major sets of economic thought)—constructively addresses the necessity of our living in balance with the natural environment. Both paradigms encourage us to exploit and despoil the environment for short-term gains. As a result, our most fundamental arrangements for conducting human interactions largely ignore the human-environment relationship.
RICHARD S. BOOTH, quoted in Peter Borelli, ed., *Crossroads*, 1988

14 We have hitched our star so firmly to economic individualism, we have virtually lost the means to act for the common good.

JAMES FALLOWS, speech, Brigham Young University, Salt Lake City, Utah, March 1990

15 In the long run a healthy economy can only exist in symbiosis with a healthy ecology.

ROBERT COSTANZA and LISA WAINGER, *Washington Post*, 2 September 1990

16 We are making a mistake if we ask markets to do things they are not designed to do. Markets are only meant to allocate resources in the short-term, not to tell you how much is enough, or how to achieve integrity or justice. Markets are meant to be efficient, not sufficient; greedy, not fair. If they do something good for whales or wilderness or God or grandchildren, that's purely coincidental.

AMORY B. LOVINS, *Orion Nature Quarterly*, Winter 1990

17 The progress of civilization [can be charted] in terms of the internalization of costs formerly viewed as external.

HAROLD M. HUBBARD, *Scientific American*, April 1991

18 When prices reflect full costs, the market is an excellent system for strengthening the economy and for dealing with such serious issues as clean air, global climatic change and energy security.

HAROLD M. HUBBARD, *Scientific American*, April 1991

32 ECONOMICS, GNP
See also 30 ECONOMIC GROWTH, 34 ECONOMICS, STEADY-STATE

1 As every economist knows, calculations of GNP, especially in the poor countries, are largely exercises in the statistical imagination, and even if they were accurate, the GNP itself can be a very poor measure of welfare.

KENNETH E. BOULDING, *American Economic Review*, May 1966

2 The gross national product rises . . . when trailer courts, souvenir shops, sawmills, gas stations, and subdivisions spring up on private inholdings in 44 of the 66 natural areas of the National Park System . . . often strategically located for maximum ill effect on prime park scenes.

GEORGE B. HARTZOG, JR., speech, North American Wildlife and Natural Resources Conference, Houston, 1968

3 I look forward to the day when statisticians add up the national accounts to take account of the depreciation of the environment. When we learn to do this, we will discover that our gross national product has been deceiving us.

ARTHUR BURNS, testimony, U.S. Congress, Joint Economic Committee, February 1970

4 Does anyone really believe that the average person or family in the United States is two and a half times as contented or "fulfilled" as the average person or family in the United Kingdom?

EDWARD J. MISHAN, on aggregate and per capita measures of economic growth, *The Ecologist*, January 1971

5 The $100 to $200 added to the cost of the car [for air-pollution control] will appear in the price of the car and thus take its place in GNP even though the addition merely attempts to get us back to where we were in terms of air quality.

EDWARD S. MASON, speech, Resources for the Future forum, Washington, D.C., 20 April 1971

6 I don't pay much attention to gross product. In all our states this has been something sacred, but it's the devil. We must think instead in terms of the happiness of our people.

SICCO MANSHOLT, quoted in *Wall Street Journal*, 18 May 1972.

7 We devote more effort and resources to mining poorer mineral deposits and to cleaning up increased pollution, and we then count many of these extra expenses as an increase in GNP and congratulate ourselves on the extra growth! The problem with GNP is that it counts consumption of geological capital as current income.

HERMAN E. DALY, *Steady-State Economics*, 1977

33 ECONOMICS, INCENTIVES

1 [Emission charges or taxes levied on industry in lieu of regulatory restrictions are] licenses to pollute.
ANONYMOUS

2 In the case of the conservationists, the opposition [to pollutant emission charges] seems to reflect a puritanical ideal that common property resources should not be used for residual deposit at all. This is idealism run wild.
ALLEN V. KNEESE, speech, American Economic Association, December 1970

3 We must better understand how economic forces induce some forms of environmental degradation, and how we can create and change economic incentives to improve rather than degrade environmental quality. Economic incentives, such as the sulfur oxides charge and the lead tax, can create a strong impetus to reduce pollution levels. We must experiment with other economic incentives as a supplement to our regulatory efforts. Our goal must be to harness the powerful mechanisms of the marketplace, with its automatic incentives and restraints, to encourage improvement in the quality of life.
RICHARD M. NIXON, message on the environment, 8 February 1971

4 Whale populations grow at a very slow rate, something between 3% and 8% per annum. To the whaling companies, a 3%–8% return on capital "assets" (whales) can almost surely be improved upon by liquidating the assets and devoting the profits to some more productive alternative investment.
COLIN W. CLARK, on why some whaling nations deplete stocks, Animal Welfare Institute paper, April 1975

5 The key to progress is to ensure that consumers and producers realize the true environmental costs and benefits of their decisions. Incentive systems provide ways to do this.
JOHN HEINZ, U.S. Senator, *Business Week*, 18 June 1990

6 Contrary to the doomsayers, both past and present, people have a knack for innovating their way out of "crises"—if they have both

the permission and the incentive to do so. So we find that people developed petroleum as whale oil became scarce, the farmers turn to drip irrigation as water prices rise, and that drivers bought fuel-efficient cars when gas prices went up.
VIRGINIA I. POSTREL, speech, City Club of Cleveland, Ohio, 19 June 1990

7 Taxing products and activities that pollute, deplete, or otherwise degrade natural systems is a way of ensuring that environmental costs are taken into account in private decisions, such as whether to commute by car or via mass transit.
LESTER BROWN *State of the World*, 1991

34 ECONOMICS, STEADY-STATE
See also   30 ECONOMIC GROWTH,
32 ECONOMICS, GNP

1 The open economy, the "cowboy economy" . . . is characteristic of open societies. The closed economy of the future might similarly be called the "spaceman economy," in which the earth has become a single spaceship, without unlimited reservoirs of anything, either for extraction or for pollution. . . . The difference between the two types of economy becomes apparent in the attitudes towards consumption. In the cowboy economy, consumption is regarded as a good thing and production likewise: and the success of the economy is measured by the amount of the throughput from the "factors of production," a part of which, at any rate is extracted from the reservoirs of raw materials and noneconomic objects, and another part of which is output into the reservoirs of pollution. . . . By contrast, in the spaceman economy, throughput is by no means a desideratum, and is indeed to be regarded as something to be minimized rather than maximized.
KENNETH E. BOULDING, "The Economics of the Coming Spaceship Earth," 1966

2 The no-growth or slow-growth philosophy is a concept that could threaten our entire economic system. It would magnify, rather than alleviate, poverty and unemployment. And it is a direct contradiction to those fundamental

instincts which motivate people to compete, to acquire, and to improve their way of living.

ARIZONA PUBLIC SERVICE COMPANY, annual report, 1970

3 [Short of a clear threat of extinction] it is hard to believe that the public would accept the tight controls, lowered material living standards, and large income transfers required to create and manage the stationary state.

WALTER HELLER, Resources for the Future forum, Washington, D.C., 20 April 1971

4 We could regard the stationary state as a kind of maturity in which physical growth is no longer necessary and in which, therefore, human energies can be devoted to qualitative growth.

KENNETH E. BOULDING, Resources for the Future forum, 21 April 1971

5 Ecological humanism must create an economy in which economic and population growth is halted, technology is controlled, and gross inequalities of income are done away with.

VICTOR FURKISS, *The Future of Technological Civilization*, 1974

6 "Eternal Progress" is a nonsensical myth. What must be implemented is not a "steadily expanding economy," but a *zero-growth economy*, a stable economy. *Economic growth is not only unnecessary but ruinous.*

ALEKSANDR I. SOLZHENITSYN, letter to Soviet leaders, 1974

7 A limitation on growth as our society is currently structured would impose a crushing sentence on the presently disadvantaged. We still operate under the terms of a "trickle-down" philosophy, where the poor get a little something only when the rich get richer.

MAURICE BARBASH, letter, *New York Times*, 4 October 1974

8 The steady-state economy seeks to change institutions in such a way that people become autonomous and technology is not abandoned, but is demoted to its proper accommodating role. Growth economics gave technology free rein. Steady-state economics channels technical progress in the socially benign directions of small scale, decentralization, increased durability of products, and

increased long-run efficiency in the use of scarce resources.

HERMAN E. DALY, *Steady-State Economics*, 1977

9 A steady-state economy [is] an economy with constant stocks of people and artifacts, maintained at some desired, sufficient levels by low rates of maintenance "throughput," that is, by the lowest feasible flows of matter and energy from the first stage of production (depletion of low-entropy materials from the environment) to the last stage of consumption (pollution of the environment with high-entropy wastes and exotic materials).

HERMAN E. DALY, *Steady-State Economics*, 1977

---

35 ECONOMICS, VALUATION
See also 31 ECONOMICS

---

1 Entirely aside from the commercial value of the enormous production of life in the brackish waters of Everglades mangrove margins, and aside from the tourist and sportfishing dollars derived from the park's attractions, we are tampering with products of a kind as yet inadequately measured. . . . We haven't learned yet to assess accurately the benefits to man of the sight of an alligator sliding into dark waters, or of a horizon free of smokestacks and overpasses, or an evening sky glittering with the flash of white wings catching the last rays of daylight; but our inability to measure them makes those values no less real.

GEORGE B. HARTZOG, JR., speech, North American Wildlife and Natural Resources Conference, Houston, 1968

2 The trouble with the conservation organizations is that they are accustomed to dealing with cheap labor, the mighty hand of God.

VICTOR J. YANNACONE, JR., on the failure to attach economic values to natural resources, conference on law and the environment, Warrenton, Va., September 1969

3 They include the consistent overestimation of the economic benefits which are claimed for proposed projects, through the tacking on of secondary benefits. . . . They include the understatement of the cost of these projects, both construction and future operation and

maintenance costs. They include the neglect, indeed disdain, of the environmental disbenefits which appear as side effects to the manipulation of natural rivers.

WILLIAM PROXMIRE, U.S. Senator, on improper procedures used by the Army Corps of Engineers, speech, U.S. Senate, 18 March 1970

4 "Environment" and "safety" are fine objectives, but they have become sacred cows about which it is almost heresy to ask whether the return justifies the cost.

MILTON FRIEDMAN, *Newsweek,* 19 August 1974

5 What we are involved in is a simple but meaningful thing, the commandment that in civilized society thou shall not kill. The proponents of cost-benefit analysis would have us believe that it is all right to kill if killing is not too expensive.

JAMES SMITH, on the regulation of chemicals, testimony, Occupational Safety and Health Administration hearing, 1978, quoted in Samuel S. Epstein, *The Politics of Cancer,* 1978

6 We cannot substitute the sophisticated but mechanical business of piling numbers on either side of a balance for the agonizing process of making a fallible, inescapable, human judgment. For such judgments are at one and the same time the dilemma and the glory of any society that aspires to be just.

DOUGLAS M. COSTLE, speech, conference on cost-benefit analysis sponsored by the Conservation Foundation and the Illinois Institute of Natural Resources, Chicago, 15 October 1980

7 When Oscar Wilde said that people do not value sunsets because they cannot pay for them, he was touching, with the stiletto of his cynicism, a difficulty. It is the difficulty a commercial civilization comes to have in assigning values other than economic values— the difficulty it has doing justice to important intangibles.

GEORGE F. WILL, *Washington Post,* 18 January 1981

8 [Most people arguing for cost-benefit calculations and assuming the result would be re-

duced environmental control] could be in for a real surprise. . . . I wonder what the reaction would be if cost-benefit calculations showed that we should be spending more on pollution control, not less?

ROBERT T. STAFFORD, U.S. Senator, speech, Environmental Industry Council, 26 February 1981

9 Environmentalism that is careless about cost will be regressive in effect and will discredit itself by seeming to be a luxury of persons affluent and callous.

GEORGE F. WILL, *Newsweek,* 16 August 1982

10 How far would the right-to-life people have gotten if they had based their arguments on the economic value of the fetus in the womb.

DAVID EHRENFELD, on the impossibility and undesirability of trying to put an economic value on biological species, speech, National Forum on Biodiversity, Washington, D.C., 21 September 1986

11 By trying to value environmental services [in monetary terms], we are forced into a rational decision-making frame of mind.

DAVID PEARCE, ANIL MARKANDYA, and EDWARD B. BARBIER, *Blueprint for a Green Economy,* 1989

12 If you calculated the real cost of a can of aerosol hair spray [in terms of ozone layer damage], it would be $12,000–$13,000.

HAZEL HENDERSON, broadcast interview, "Profit the Earth," PBS, 23 September 1990

36 ECOSYSTEMS
See also   29 ECOLOGY

1 [An ecosystem is] a closely organized cooperative commonwealth of plants and animals.

WALTER P. TAYLOR, *Quarterly Review of Biology* 10, no. 3, September 1935

2 The habitat of an organism is the place where it lives, or the place where one would go to find it. The ecological niche, on the other hand, is the position or status of an organism within its community and ecosystem resulting from the organism's structural adapta-

tions, physiological responses and specific behavior (inherited and/or learned). The ecological niche of an organism depends not only on where it lives but also on what it does. By analogy, it may be said that the habitat is the organism's "address," and the niche is its "profession," biologically speaking.

WILLIAM E. ODUM, *Fundamentals of Ecology*, 1959

3 Environments are not passive wrappings, but are, rather, active processes which are invisible.

MARSHALL MCLUHAN, *The Medium Is the Massage*, 1967

4 I submit that an anarchist community would approximate a [normal] ecosystem; it would be diversified, balanced, and harmonious.

MURRAY BOOKCHIN, linking anarchism and ecology, *Post-Scarcity Anarchism*, 1971

5 On purely theoretical grounds it is self-evident that any economic system which is impelled, by its own requirements for stability, to grow by constantly increasing the rate at which it extracts wealth from the ecosystem must eventually drive the ecosystem to a state of collapse.

BARRY COMMONER, speech, Washington, D.C., 20 April 1971

6 To kill an ecosystem you must burn it up, plow it under, or poison it. Only at the level of its plant life, its microbes and its invertebrate fauna, is the natural system itself vulnerable.

PAUL SHEPARD, *Thinking Animals*, 1978

7 Both in biological and social ecosystems the ultimate effect of any specific change is often very hard to trace, simply because these are what I call "echo systems," in which an event or a decision echoes and re-echoes all over the system.

KENNETH E. BOULDING, speech, American Association for the Advancement of Science, Washington, D.C., 3 January 1982

8 The very concept of an ecosystem is based upon cybernetics systems theory which is an attempt to apply a machine model to natural organic processes.

BILL DEVALL and GEORGE SESSIONS, *Deep Ecology*, 1985

9 For their part, loving the *idea* of ecosystem, most environmentalists even so remained woefully ignorant about it. . . . they began to turn science into religion.

ALSTON CHASE, *Playing God in Yellowstone*, 1986

10 Any intact ecosystem—rainforest or desert or marshland—exhibits a complexity far beyond any supermachine, any metropolis, any whole civilization of human devising.

KIRKPATRICK SALE, *Harper's*, July 1990

11 To halt the decline of an ecosystem, it is necessary to "think like an ecosystem."

DOUGLAS P. WHEELER, *EPA Journal*, September–October 1990

12 The links between ecosystem and human health are many and obvious: the value of wetlands in filtering pollutants out of ground-water aquifers; the potential future medical use of different plants' genetic material; the human health effects of heavy metal accumulation in fish and shellfish. It is clear that healthy ecosystems provide the underpinnings for the long-term health of economies and societies.

F. HENRY HABICHT, *EPA Journal*, September–October 1990

13 Pick an area for each of our major ecosystems and reclaim the American wilderness—not in little pieces of a thousand acres, but in chunks of a million or ten million. Move out the people and cars. Reclaim the roads and plowed land.

DAVE FOREMAN, *Washington Post*, 20 March 1991

37 EDUCATION

1 Education is the instruction of the intellect in the laws of Nature, under which name I include not merely things and their forces but men and their ways, and the fashioning of the affections and of the will into an earnest and loving desire to move in harmony with these laws.

THOMAS H. HUXLEY (1825–1895), *Science and Education*, 1868

2 One of the penalties of an ecological education is that one lives alone in a world of wounds.

Much of the damage inflicted on land is quite invisible to laymen. An ecologist must either harden his shell and make believe that the consequences of science are none of his business, or he must be the doctor who sees the marks of death in a community that believes itself well and does not want to be told otherwise.

ALDO LEOPOLD (1886–1948), *Round River*, 1953

3 What conservation education must build is an ethical underpinning for land economics and a universal curiosity to understand the land mechanism. Conservation may then follow.

ALDO LEOPOLD (1886–1948), *Round River*, 1953

4 I am much more concerned with seeing the ecological point of view permeating society and education than with seeing the sole preparation of ecologists in the narrower sense, although these are terribly important people, too.

IAN MCHARG, in Frank F. Darling and John P. Milton, eds., *Future Environments of North America*, 1966

5 The conservationist's most important task, if we are to save the earth, is to educate.

PETER SCOTT, founder chairman of World Wildlife Federation, quoted in *Sunday Telegraph*, 6 November 1986

6 The ecologization of politics requires us to acknowledge the priority of universal human values and make ecology part of education and instruction from an early age, moulding a new, modern approach to nature and, at the same time, giving back to man a sense of being a part of nature. No moral improvement of society is possible without that.

MIKHAIL GORBACHEV, quoted in *Coalition for Education in the Outdoors* (CEO) *Newsletter*, Fall–Winter 1990

---

38 ENDANGERED SPECIES

See also   9 BIODIVERSITY, 139 WILDLIFE

---

1 When I hear of the destruction of a species I feel just as if all the works of some great writer had perished; as if we had lost all instead of part of Polybius or Livy.

THEODORE ROOSEVELT (1858–1919), letter to Frank M. Chapman, president of the Audubon Society, 6 February 1899

2 The beauty and genius of a work of art may be reconceived, though its first material expression be destroyed; a vanished harmony may yet again inspire the composer; but when the last individual of a race of living things breathes no more, another heaven and another earth must pass before such a one can be again.

WILLIAM BEEBE, *The Bird: Its Form and Function*, 1906

3 Extinction, n. The raw material out of which theology created the future state.

AMBROSE BIERCE (1842–c. 1914), *The Devil's Dictionary*, 1906

4 It is a century now since Darwin gave us the first glimpse of the origin of species. We know now what was unknown to all the preceding caravans of generations; that man is only a fellow-voyager with other creatures in the Odyssey of evolution, and that his captaincy of the adventuring ship conveys the power, but not necessarily the right, to discard at will among the crew. We should, in the century since Darwin, have achieved a sense of community with living things, and of wonder over the magnitude and duration of the biotic enterprise.

ALDO LEOPOLD (1886–1948), 1947, at the dedication of the monument to the passenger pigeon, Wyalusing State Park, Wisconsin Society for Ornithology

5   DEDICATED
TO THE LAST WISCONSIN
PASSENGER PIGEON
SHOT AT BABCOCK, SEPT. 1899
THIS SPECIES BECAME EXTINCT
THROUGH THE AVARICE AND
THOUGHTLESSNESS OF MAN.
Erected by
The Wisconsin Society for Ornithology
WISCONSIN SOCIETY FOR ORNITHOLOGY, 1947

6 We have no intention of campaigning against mousetraps or flypapers.

PRINCE PHILIP, DUKE OF EDINBURGH, asserting that the World Wildlife Fund did not seek to protect all species against everything, speech, November 1962

7 The California condor is America's rarest large bird. Only a concerted, cooperative effort by all the land agencies involved, state and federal, and the people of California, can

ensure the perpetuation of this great bird which has come down to us unchanged through eons of time. All it needs is elbow room and to be left alone. What space we leave or fail to leave for it will be a measure of the level of our civilization.

> CARL W. BUCHHEISTER, speech, 5 May 1965, quoted in David Phillips and Hugh Nash, *The Condor Question*, 1986

8 In our concern with the whooping crane we are at once symbolizing and concealing a far deeper anxiety—namely, the prospective total extermination of all species.

> LEWIS MUMFORD, in Frank F. Darling and John P. Milton, eds., *Future Environments of North America*, 1966

9 But man himself is the wild species that is threatened, and it's time we recognize where the threat comes from: not from our enemies but from ourselves.

> LEWIS MUMFORD, in Frank F. Darling and John P. Milton, eds., *Future Environments of North America*, 1966

10 While we indulge in worthy, earnest, but nevertheless limited enterprises such as saving the whooping cranes, we fail to notice our own growing eligibility for the title "endangered species."

> U.S. DEPARTMENT OF THE INTERIOR, *Conservation Yearbook*, 1968

11 The real importance of saving such things as condors is not so much that we need condors as that we need to save them. We need to exercise and develop the human attributes required in saving condors; for these are the attributes so necessary in working out our own survival.

> IAN MCMILLAN, quoted in *Landscape* 18, 1969

12 What can I do? The tigers in my coat were already dead. . . . If I don't buy the coats somebody else will.

> GINA LOLLOBRIGIDA, on her purchase of seven new fur coats, quoted in *Sports Illustrated*, 19 January 1970

13 Don't dismiss our extermination of passenger pigeons and Carolina parakeets by saying that extinction had always gone on. Evolution of new species used to occur too.

> DANIEL L. MCKINLEY, *New York Times*, 18 July 1971

14 One can easily imagine how much money and effort we would be willing to devote to preserve an animal species on the moon if the astronauts had found one. No species on earth is less precious. No effort should be spared to save unique and irreplaceable products of millions of years of evolution with which our small planet has been endowed.

> U THANT (1909–1974), speech, World Wildlife Fund 10th anniversary, 11 September 1971

15 We are masters of extermination, yet creation is beyond our powers.

> DAVID W. EHRENFELD, *Conserving Life on Earth*, 1972

16 The only animal whose disappearance may threaten the biological viability of man on earth are the bacteria normally inhabiting our bodies.

> EUGENE RABINOWITCH, *Times* (London), 29 April 1972

17 [The Convention on International Trade in Endangered Species is] the Magna Carta for wildlife . . . the single most important international conservation measure ever agreed upon.

> LEWIS REGENSTEIN, *The Politics of Extinction*, 1975

18 The ecological domino theory: first the dodo, then the passenger pigeon, then the brown pelican . . . and then man—the last endangered species.

> JOHN RODMAN, *Inquiry*, Spring 1976

19 Species are becoming extinct today before they are known to man. Usually we remain in eternal ignorance of what we have lost. Who on receiving a package would toss it out before looking inside? Yet that is what we are doing with our biological heritage.

> THOMAS E. LOVEJOY, *Smithsonian*, July 1976

20 I happen to think that people are more important than whooping cranes.

> BARRY COMMONER, quoted in *New York Times Magazine*, 7 November 1976

21 The evolution of a single species is a process which may take millions of years and which can never be duplicated.

> MICHAEL BERGER, speech, American Association for the Advancement of Science, 17 February 1978

22 By the time a species is as reduced in population as the California condor or the snail darter, it is doubtful that its ecological function is important to anything except itself—and, perhaps, to an ecosystem already on the verge of extinction.
CHARLES WARREN, speech, American Association for the Advancement of Science, 17 February 1978

23 In essence the process is tantamount to book burning, yet is even worse in that it involves books yet to be deciphered and yet to be read.
JAMES L. BUCKLEY, on allowing the extinction of species, National Public Radio, 2 March 1978

24 Man is incapable of making permanent changes in the cosmos. Except one. In only one way can man truly make his mark upon time and life and evolution: by exterminating any species of plant or animal. If he does that, if he eradicates or allows to fail any line of evolution through time, he will have permanently altered the life potential of the cosmos for as long as matter and energy are in balance.
ROGER CARAS, speech, Yale School of Forestry symposium, 10 April 1978

25 I submit that a nation which cannot afford to protect its endangered species has already overreached itself biologically.
THOMAS E. LOVEJOY, speech, Yale School of Forestry symposium, 10 April 1978

26 You ought to require that *elected* officials sign the death certificate before it is finally executed.
TOM GARRETT, on allowing the extinction of a species, testimony, U.S. Senate Environment and Public Works subcommittee, 13 April 1978

27 I have a picture of a snail darter. You cannot eat it. It is not much to look at. It is a slimy color.
JOHN DUNCAN, on the loss of 3,000 jobs due to the controversy over the minnow at Tellico Dam, testimony, U.S. House Subcommittee on Merchant Marine and Fisheries, May–June, 1978

28 It may seem curious to some that the survival of a relatively small number of three-inch fish among all the countless millions of species extant would require the permanent halting of a virtually completed dam for which Congress has expended more than $100 million.
WARREN E. BURGER, Chief Justice of the United States, in decision stopping construction of the Tellico Dam to protect the snail darter under the Endangered Species Act, *Tennessee Valley Authority* v. *Hill et al.*, 437 U.S. 153, 15 June 1978

29 There will be little sentiment to leave this dam standing before an empty reservoir, serving no purpose other than a conversation piece for incredulous tourists.
LEWIS F. POWELL, dissenting in the Supreme Court opinion halting construction of the almost-completed Tellico Dam to protect the endangered snail darter, *Tennessee Valley Authority* v. *Hill et al.*, 437 U.S. 153, 15 June 1978

30 Of what good is a snail darter? As practical men measure "good," probably none; but we simply don't know. What value would they have placed on the cowpox virus before Pasteur; or on penicillium molds (other than those inhabiting blue cheeses) before Fleming; or on wild rubber trees before Goodyear learned to vulcanize their sap? Yet the life of almost every American is profoundly different because of these species.
JAMES L. BUCKLEY, *Washington Post*, 4 September 1979

31 Perhaps even more shocking than the unprecedented wave of extinction is the cessation of significant evolution of new species of large plants and animals. Death is one thing—an end to birth is something else.
MICHAEL SOULÉ, *Conservation Biology*, 1980

32 Extinct is forever.
KURT BENIRSCHKE, *Christian Science Monitor*, 29 May 1980

33 Why do they prefer to tell stories about the possible medicinal benefits of the Houston toad rather than to offer moral reasons for supporting the Endangered Species Act? That law is plainly ideological; it is hardly to be excused on economic grounds.
MARK SAGOFF, on the reluctance of environmentalists to argue on openly ideological or political grounds for species protection, *Environmental Law* 12, 1982

34 Extinction is not something to contemplate; it is something to rebel against.
JONATHAN SCHELL, *The Fate of the Earth*, 1982

35 Extinction of a species does not simply mean the loss of one volume from the library of nature. It means the loss of a loose-leaf book whose individual pages, were the species to survive, would remain available in perpetuity for selective transfer and improvement of other species.
THOMAS EISNER, quoted in Earthscan briefing document no. 33, October 1982

36 The question of what to do about animal extinctions is even more difficult to answer than why we should be concerned in the first place.
DAVID CHALLINOR, in Robert J. Hoage, ed., *Animal Extinctions*, 1985

37 The [endangered species] policy remains mired in a philosophic dispute over what society really wants. That lack of direction led to a floundering of efforts: enough to keep most species hanging on, but not aggressive enough to make progress toward recovery. . . . The problem lies with Congress for not making clear what path endangered species policy should take: ethical protection or managed conservation.
LAURA L. MANNING, *The Dispute Processing Model of Public Policy Evolution*, 1986

38 From an evolutionary point of view, we perceive ourselves as sharing with other species a similar origin as well as an existential condition that includes the ever-present possibility of total extinction.
PAUL W. TAYLOR, *Respect for Nature*, 1986

39 Throughout the long history of life on our planet natural disasters ("disasters," that is, from the standpoint of some particular organism or group of organisms) have always taken their toll in the death of many creatures. Indeed, the very process of natural selection continually leads to the extinction of whole species. After such disasters a gradual readjustment always takes place so that a new set of relations among species-populations emerges.
PAUL W. TAYLOR, *Respect for Nature*, 1986

40 It's like having astronomy without knowing where the stars are.
EDWARD O. WILSON, on the loss of species before they can be discovered and evaluated, *Time*, 13 October 1986

41 No large wild terrestrial animal will persist long into the future unless cared for in some way by man.
WILLIAM G. CONWAY, quoted in *Science*, 28 November 1986

42 From the dawn of consciousness until August 6, 1945, man had to live with the prospects of his death as an individual; since that day when the first bomb outshone the sun over Hiroshima, mankind as a whole has had to live with the prospect of its extinction as a species.
ARTHUR KOESTLER, quoted in Frank Barnaby, *Gaia Peace Atlas*, 1988

43 American environmentalists showcased the rescue of the whooping crane from the brink of extinction as evidence of the new, ecological morality.
BRYAN G. NORTON, *Why Preserve Natural Variety*, 1988

44 Without firing a shot, we may be killing off one-fifth of all species on the planet within twenty years.
RUSSELL E. TRAIN, 1988, quoted in the annual report of the National Aquarium, Baltimore, 1988

45 We've got to save the irreplaceable living beings (which ultimately means saving their surroundings); . . . It's like rushing into the burning house to save the babies.
STEPHANIE MILLS, *What Ever Happened to Ecology?*, 1989

46 Habitat destruction in conjunction with climate change sets the stage for an even larger wave of extinction than previously imagined. . . . Small remnant populations of most species, surrounded by cities, roads, reservoirs, and farm land, would have little chance of reaching new habitat if climate change makes the old unsuitable. Few animals or plants would be able to cross Los Angeles on the way to the promised land.
ROBERT L. PETERS, in Dean E. Abrahamson, ed., *The Challenge of Global Warming*, 1989

47 The bad news is that a lot of species will have perished by the time the ark's gangplank is lowered.

MICHAEL SOULÉ, in David Western and Mary Pearl, eds., *Conservation for the 21st Century*, 1989

48 I estimate that the number of species requiring management (to a greater or lesser extent) by the year 2100 will be closer to 10,000. . . . How much, then, does it cost to manage one species? The National Audubon Society proposed spending $2 million per year for fifteen years to develop a sound management plan for the northern spotted owl. The California condor recovery plan costs more than $1 million annually. Globally, 10,000 such projects might therefore cost $10 billion annually. This is more, to be sure, than the $4 billion budget of the U.S. National Institutes of Health, but a little less than the gross national product of Bangladesh and far less than Americans spend on their pets annually.

DAVID S. WOODRUFF, in David Western and Mary Pearl, eds., *Conservation for the 21st Century*, 1989

49 If we were really serious about species conservation, we might launch a Species Defense Initiative (SDI, this use of the acronym replacing current misuse for the Strategic Defense [Star Wars] Initiative).

DAVID S. WOODRUFF, in David Western and Mary Pearl, eds., *Conservation for the 21st Century*, 1989

50 We've tried to play Noah. We'e found our Ark is too small. Now, we're playing God, deciding which species may live.

NORMAN MYERS, "Can the Elephant Be Saved?," WBGH-TV, Boston, 1990

51 There's an argument for species preservation that rarely enters the impassioned animals rights debate. Namely, that other creatures may be evolving toward sapience, too. In principle many if not most species ought to be "trying" to become intelligent, because as *Homo sapiens* has shown, intelligence is the most powerful of adaptive mechanisms. Dolphins, chimpanzees, and apes aren't merely creatures that right-thinking people shouldn't want killed; they are potentially like us.

GREGG EASTERBROOK, *New Republic*, 30 April 1990

52 Why is it that we can find domestic cattle everywhere in abundance, but the Black Rhino is an endangered species? Both animals have commercial value and both are easily tamed. Black Rhinos may cost more to keep, but they are also worth a lot more. The only reason why Black Rhinos are not farmed in the same way as any other species is because the government does not allow it. If people were allowed to own rhinos privately, and were allowed to use them for the production of any goods or services, rhinos would be no more endangered than cattle, goats, donkeys, ostriches and crocodiles.

MIKE T'SAS-ROLFES, *Endangered Wildlife*, June 1990

53 Contrary to what you may have heard, the rarest things in these parts are not spotted owls but open minds.

JOHN BALZAR, *Los Angeles Times*, 6 August 1990

54 Indeed, by attempting to preserve species living on the brink of extinction, we may be wasting time, effort and money on animals that will disappear over time, regardless of our efforts.

MICHAEL D. COPELAND, *Natural History*, September 1990

55 Endangered species are sensitive indicators of how we are treating the planet, and we should be listening carefully to their message.

DONALD A. FALK, E magazine, September 1990

56 Elephants still aren't out of the woods.

HUMANE SOCIETY, advertisement, *Mother Jones*, September–October 1990

57 Inevitably, most of the species being preserved have no current direct economic value, but they may have option values, existence values, and bequeathment values.

GORDON H. ORIANS, *Environment*, November 1990

58 All that lives beneath Earth's fragile canopy is, in some elemental fashion, related. Is born, moves, feeds, reproduces, dies. Tiger and turtle dove; each tiny flower and homely frog; the running child, father to the man, and, in ways as yet unknown, brother to the salamander. If mankind continues to allow

whole species to perish, when does their peril also become ours?
WORLD WILDLIFE FUND, in Kathryn A. Kohm, ed., *Balancing on the Brink of Extinction*, 1991

39 ENERGY
See also   40 ENERGY CONSERVATION, 41 ENERGY POLICY, 90 NUCLEAR ENERGY, 93 OIL AND GAS, 123 SOLAR ENERGY

1 The total energy of the universe is constant and the total entropy is continually increasing. [The two laws of thermodynamics.]
JAMES JOULE (1818–1889), quoted by Isaac Asimov, *Smithsonian*, August 1970

2 We have to make the momentous choice between brief greatness and longer continued mediocrity.
WILLIAM STANLEY JEVONS, on the adequacy of coal reserves, *The Coal Question*, 1865

3 Not only will atomic power be released, but someday we will harness the rise and fall of the tides and imprison the rays of the sun.
THOMAS A. EDISON (1847–1931), 22 August 1921

4 It can be predicted with all security that in fifty years light will cost one-fiftieth of its present price, and in all the big cities there will be no such thing as night.
J. B. S. HALDANE (1892–1964), quoted in *Le Figaro*, 3 February 1927

5 The preservation of a system of values requires a continuous supply of energy equal to the demands imposed by that system of values. . . . [C]onversely changes in amount and form of energy available give rise to conditions likely to result in changes of values.
FRED COTTRELL, *Energy and Society*, 1955

6 By 1980 all "power" (electric, atomic, solar) is likely to be virtually costless.
HENRY LUCE (1898–1967), *The Fabulous Future*, 1956

7 A few decades hence, energy may be free— just like the unmetered air.
JOHN VON NEUMANN, *"Can We Survive Technology?"* 1956

8 Since energy is an essential ingredient in all terrestrial activity, organic and inorganic, it follows that the history of the evolution of human culture must also be a history of man's increasing ability to control and manipulate energy.
M. KING HUBBERT, 1962, in Earl Ferguson Cook, *Man, Energy, Society*, 1976

9 Nations, like ecosystems, tend toward complexity, which, at its best, means efficiency in energy flow.
FRANK FRASER DARLING, *Daedalus*, Fall 1967

10 Given an infinite source of energy, population growth still produces an inescapable problem. The problem of the acquisition of energy is replaced by the problem of its dissipation.
GARRETT HARDIN, *Science*, 13 December 1968

11 On such a time scale [10,000 years] . . . the epoch of the fossil fuels can only be a transitory and ephemeral event—an event, nonetheless, which has exercised the most drastic influence experienced by the human species during its entire biological history.
M. KING HUBBERT, *Resources and Man*, 1969

12 It is evident that the fortunes of the world's human population, for better or for worse, are inextricably interrelated with the use that is made of energy resources.
M. KING HUBBERT, *Resources and Man*, 1969

13 [The people of this country] are going to have their electricity, and they are going to shut up about ecological conditions.
CRAIG HOSMER, U.S. Representative, hearing, Joint Committee on Atomic Energy, 23 April 1969

14 All power pollutes.
GARRETT DE BELL, *The Environmental Handbook*, 1970

15 The extension to the rest of the world of the U.S. per capita energy consumption level would exhaust all of the world's energy resources in the space of 40 years.
JOHN F. O'LEARY, speech, American Association for the Advancement of Science, 28 December 1971

16 It is not in the cards for America to continue a gluttonous way of life in a world where most

of the people live in a perpetual energy black-out. We are witness to the end of an era. As much as we hate to face up to it, the joy ride is really over.

S. DAVID FREEMAN, testimony, U.S. Congress, Joint Economic subcommittee, 19 November 1973

17 That isn't bad; that is good. That means we are the richest, strongest people in the world, and that we have the highest standard of living in the world. That is why we need so much energy, and may it always be that way.

RICHARD M. NIXON, on the fact that per capita energy consumption in the United States is far higher than elsewhere in the world, speech, 26 November 1973

18 [The U.S. needs a] much wider process of self-emancipation from dependence on foreign-controlled sources of energy. We can be grateful that we were kicked into such a beginning. If we quail at this minor inconvenience, it will be a bad omen . . . for it will mean that our addiction to the wastage of energy, particularly through the medium of the automobile, is so abject that we prefer to face the loss of a considerable portion of our independence of policy.

GEORGE F. KENNAN, New York Times, 2 December 1973

19 If people panic, the whole apparatus of environmental protection might be swept away. But if only meaningful, necessary, well-considered steps are taken, we can get over this emergency fairly fast and the environment won't suffer.

ELVIS STAHR, on the energy crisis, quoted in New York Times, 2 December 1973

20 If the energy crisis forces us to diminish automobile use in the cities, stops us from building highways and covering the country with concrete and asphalt, forces us to rehabilitate the railroads, causes us to invest in mass transportation and limits the waste of electrical energy, one can only assume that the Arab nations and the big oil companies have united to save the American Republic.

JOHN KENNETH GALBRAITH, quoted in Newsweek, 31 December 1973

21 Wonder if the extreme environmentalists who so sincerely stall energy expansion—

oblivious of the economic consequences—will discover the cost of going too far too fast. Wish they'd understand that within every person there lurks a consumer as well as an environmentalist.

MOBIL CORPORATION, advertisement, New York Times, 18 July 1974

22 The word "energy" incidentally equates with the Greek word for "challenge." I think there is much to learn in thinking of our federal energy problem in that light. Further, it is important for us to think of energy in terms of a gift of life.

THOMAS CARR, testimony, U.S. Senate Commerce Committee, September 1974

23 Operating in the American economy is a negative force which reinforces the energy-intensive economy: the desire to avoid economic crisis. This force generates the dominant policy of increasing supplies first and curtailing waste second.

RICHARD A. WALKER and DAVID B. LARGE, Ecology Law Quarterly 4, no. 4, 1975

24 When I talk about energy, I am talking about jobs. Our American economy runs on energy. No energy—no jobs.

GERALD R. FORD, address to the nation on energy policy, 27 May 1975

25 The future is not what it used to be.

KENNETH E. F. WATT et al., on energy-consumption trends, "The Long-Term Implications and Constraints of Alternate Energy Policies," January 1976

26 Since the energy needed today to produce a unit of GNP varies more than 100-fold depending on what good or service is being produced, and since GNP in turn hardly measures social welfare, why must energy and welfare march forever in lockstep?

AMORY B. LOVINS, on the presumed linkage between energy use and economic growth, Foreign Affairs, October 1976

27 There exists today a body of energy technologies that have certain specific features in common and that offer great technical, economic and political attractions, yet for which there is no generic term. For lack of a more satisfactory term, I shall call them "soft" technologies: a textural description, intended to mean

not vague, mushy, speculative or ephemeral, but rather flexible, resilient, sustainable and benign. . . . The distinction between hard and soft energy paths rests not on how much energy is used, but on the technical and sociopolitical *structure* of the energy system, thus focusing our attention on consequent and crucial political differences.

> AMORY B. LOVINS, *Foreign Affairs*, October 1976

28 Per-capita consumption of electrical energy in the United States in the early 1970s was twice that of the early 1960s. Has that recent doubling made much difference to welfare? Has it increased or decreased welfare? At the margin, it does not seem that our extra energy consumption is very productive of well-being.

> HERMAN E. DALY, *Steady-State Economics*, 1977

29 Alternative energy is a future idea whose time is past. Renewable energy is a future idea whose time has come.

> BILL PENDEN, quoted in *Atlas World Press Review*, April 1977

30 Considering the prices we've been paying, we haven't been wasteful [of energy] at all. We've simply been using it according to the way it's been valued in the marketplace.

> BERNARD GELB, quoted in *Newsweek*, 18 April 1977

31 We have declared to ourselves and the world our intent to control our use of energy and thereby to control our own destiny as a nation.

> JIMMY CARTER, on passage of the National Energy Act, October 1978

32 After all, if the country should not develop nuclear power, and if coal is too dirty, and if offshore oil development is too dangerous, and synthetic fuel development too hard on the environment, what shall we use to power the nation's economy? Red tape?

> MOBIL CORPORATION, advertisement, *Washington Post*, 4 November 1979

33 Giving society cheap, abundant energy at this point would be the equivalent of giving an idiot child a machine gun.

> PAUL R. EHRLICH, *Fortune*, 5 November 1979

34 Energy organizes society. With too little energy man is a slave to its production; with too much, he is a slave to its consumption. These two conditions summarize the history of social evolution.

> CHARLES J. RYAN, speech, American Association for the Advancement of Science, January 1979

35 The energy problem will provide the frame for a host of confrontations with ourselves about the limits within which we taste those experiences that deliver to us a sense of our human significance.

> EUGENE KENNEDY, *New York Times Magazine*, 2 December 1979

36 Energy is the power to do work. It is necessary to most of the dimensions of a broad, civilized niche [for individuals].

> PAUL COLINVAUX, *The Fates of Nations*, 1980

37 The most serious energy crisis in the world is the depletion of human energy—a depletion that comes about because the brain receives too few calories or too few proteins to think, and the body too few to act.

> RICHARD J. BARNET, *New Yorker*, 31 March 1980

38 We can have reasonable development of our energy resources and preserve our natural environment, if we are given an opportunity to phase in, with proper safeguards, the expansion being demanded by the nation.

> JAMES G. WATT, press conference on nomination to be Secretary of the Interior, 22 December 1980

39 The energy-land interrelationship resembles a cat's cradle: one string, an endless loop, which running from the fingers of one hand to another, crosses and recrosses upon itself, linking each finger with multiple connections.

> AMERICAN LAND FORUM, Spring 1981

40 There are limits [to energy resources] that can't be circumvented with any amount of technology and ingenuity.

> ALVIN M. WEINBERG, speech, American Association for the Advancement of Science, Washington, D.C., 3 January 1982

41 Aided by an Administration committed to a policy of "let the market do it," and abetted

by a decline in world oil prices resulting from conservation and a slow economy, Americans have largely consigned the energy crisis to sit alongside the Hula-Hoop and the Crockpot in the attic of yesterday's fads.

GRANT P. THOMPSON, *Conservation Foundation Letter*, July–August 1984

42 The faith in the infinite substitutability of nonrenewable resources is founded on the experience of a peculiar period in history, during which energy was extremely cheap. But now that that era is over, the cost of all resources will increase because of the increasing energy costs of extraction and processing. The falling price of natural resources during the first seventy years of this century was a one-time phenomenon upon which a faulty view of the future has been built.

HERMAN E. DALY and JOHN B. COBB, JR., *For the Common Good*, 1989

43 At the heart of modern society lies an economy driven by energy use. Unfortunately, the same energy that brings us comfort, convenience and prosperity also brings us pollution, impoverishment and global warming. Our challenge is to maximize the benefits gained from energy consumption while minimizing the costs incurred.

DOUGLAS FOY, *Power by Design: A New Approach to Investing in Energy Efficiency*, 1989

44 The balance between city and countryside is destroyed by industrial machinery, "cheap" productivity in field and forest, and "cheap" transportation. Rome destroyed the balance with slave labor; we have destroyed it with "cheap" fossil fuel.

WENDELL BERRY, *Atlantic Monthly*, February 1991

---

40 ENERGY CONSERVATION
See also   39 ENERGY, 41 ENERGY POLICY

---

1 Actually, the winter is only two and a half months long. So show that you are tough, that you are American—the same that built

the country—and don't destroy it. Love it, protect it, work for it, and don't foul things up.

ANNA LANSBURGH, Washington, D.C., resident who keeps her thermostat at 55°, quoted in *Washington Star-News*, 27 November 1973

2 As far as I'm concerned, any formula for fuel efficiency which leaves out speed is completely irrelevant for any policy determination. . . . The sedan chair would be the most efficient, I suspect, or possibly the wheelbarrow.

STEWART G. TIPTON, testimony, U.S. House Appropriations subcommittee, 5 March 1974

3 Availability of personal transportation will continue to be a jealously prized freedom in the American setting and an energy policy which involves a drastic curtailment of that freedom is not apt to have staying power.

PAUL W. McCRACKEN, on encouraging saving energy by switching to smaller cars, *Wall Street Journal*, 26 December 1974

4 You may well ask why we believe automobile manufacturers will voluntarily comply with our fuel economy goal when mandatory programs have been necessary for emissions, safety, damageability and noise. The crucial difference is that fuel economy has market value. The industry is going to sell cars that the public demands, and the public will demand more efficient cars.

JOHN W. BARNUM, testimony, U.S. Senate Commerce Committee, 12 March 1975

5 The record is clear that left to their own devices, the automobile manufacturers lack the wisdom or the will or both to switch decisively to the production of inexpensive, compact, energy-saving cars appropriate to our present needs.

DONALD E. WEEDEN, testimony, U.S. Senate Commerce Committee, 12 March 1975

6 [Energy] conservation alone is a slow walk down a dead-end street.

MELVIN LAIRD, quoted in *Time*, 10 October 1977

7 [The evidence] suggests that there is no definable limit to conservation, at least not until

we approach both thermodynamic limits and the exhaustion of our ingenuity to modify and refine tasks.

LEE SCHIPPER and JOEL DARMSTADTER, *Technology Review*, January 1978

8 The [automobile] mileage standards have no justification whatever. They are part of Washington's hare-brained and destructive attempts to ration energy by any means except price.

WALL STREET JOURNAL, editorial, 14 February 1980

9 At best, it means we will run out of energy a little more slowly.

RONALD REAGAN, quoted in *Science*, 28 November 1980

10 [One way I save energy] is by asking my servants not to turn on the self-cleaning oven until after seven in the morning.

BETSY BLOOMINGDALE, quoted in *Esquire*, January 1982

11 If we are willing to risk military engagement to ensure the supply of Persian Gulf oil, does it make sense to propose cuts in energy conservation programs that will help reduce our dependence on that oil?

JOHN HEINZ, U.S. Senator, speech, U.S. Senate, 10 June 1987

12 The law of conservation of energy tells us we can't get something for nothing, but we refuse to believe it.

ISAAC ASIMOV, *Isaac Asimov's Book of Science and Nature Quotations*, 1988

13 Minicars make miniprofits.

BARRY COMMONER, *Making Peace with the Planet*, 1990

14 Small steps . . . can, cumulatively, have profound impacts. For example, if everyone used the most efficient refrigerators, we could save an amount of energy equivalent to the generating capacity of 12 nuclear plants.

DENIS HAYES, *Environmental Science and Technology* 24, no. 4, April 1990

15 You don't need a chain saw to cut butter.

AMORY B. LOVINS, on energy conservation, quoted in *Smithsonian*, April 1990

16 To think that the technological genius of a nation capable of building a warplane invisible

to radar and a submarine silent as a winter's night cannot build efficient cars and buildings is an insult to America.

CURTIS MOORE and S. DAVID FREEMAN, *Washington Post*, 16 September 1990

17 Do I hear a criticism of the auto industry for advertising luxury cars to try to recapture some of the market? Are you discounting safety, discounting comfort simply to increase gas mileage? Why don't we all go to work in golf carts?

MICHAEL BILIRAKIS, against raising fuel-efficiency standards, hearing, U.S. House Energy and Commerce Committee, 19 September 1990

18 I don't want to drive to work in a breadbox every day.

JOE BARTON, against raising fuel-efficiency standards, hearing, House Energy and Commerce Committee, 19 September 1990

19 I think the reason we have done so badly in energy efficiency lies at the psychological level. It is very profound. We look at energy efficiency as an admission of failure, as totally un-American. Maybe it comes from having a huge frontier and our enormous wealth of resources. You know, when you go to Europe, you don't see products advertised as the cheapest, you see them advertised as the *best*. People there are very aware of the life-cycle cost, as opposed to the initial cost. These are things that are difficult to change.

JESSICA TUCHMAN MATTHEWS, *Orion*, Winter 1990

20 [Energy conservation is] simply a euphemism for reducing your standard of living.

HERB SCHMERTZ, quoted in *Washington Post*, 2 February 1991

41 ENERGY POLICY
See also 39 ENERGY, 40 ENERGY CONSERVATION, 90 NUCLEAR ENERGY, 93 OIL AND GAS, 123 SOLAR ENERGY

1 The energy policies adopted during the current decade will determine the range of social relationships a society will be able to enjoy by

the year 2000. A low energy policy allows for a wide choice of life styles and cultures. If, on the other hand, a society opts for high energy consumption, its social relations must be dictated by technocracy and will be equally distasteful whether labelled capitalist or socialist.

IVAN ILLICH, *Ecologist*, February 1974

2 We cannot continue to depend on the price and supply whims of others. The Congress cannot drift, dawdle and debate forever with America's future.

GERALD R. FORD, address to the nation on energy policy, 27 May 1975

3 The energy issue is a clinical case of interrelatedness. [It is] also a clinical case of how there can be so many interests in conflict over an issue as to cause paralysis. . . . One result of the complexity of the issue is that it is one on which people cannot even agree about the terms of the debate.

ELIZABETH DREW, *New Yorker*, 21 July 1975

4 Without a national energy policy to chart the course, there is really no way to measure the wisdom or fairness of the various individual decisions affecting the energy problem. . . . *Somebody* will have to make the hard choices about what level of energy consumption we can maintain, and which fuels, or combinations of fuels, we should rely upon. And equally important, *somebody* will have to undertake the massive, concerted effort necessary to convince a skeptical public of what is ahead, of what needs to be done, of what painful choices simply have to be made.

DAVID BAZELON, on the energy crisis, speech, Atomic Industrial Forum, January 1977

5 This difficult effort [to solve the energy crisis] will be the "moral equivalent of war," except we will be uniting our efforts to build and not to destroy.

JIMMY CARTER, address to the nation, 18 April 1977. The phrase "moral equivalent of war" comes from the title of a 1910 article by William James (1842–1910).

6 The notion of a one-to-one link between energy use and well-being is the most dangerous delusion in the energy-policy arena.

JOHN P. HOLDREN, quoted in *Conservation Foundation Letter*, March 1978

7 The problem isn't a shortage of fuel, it's a surplus of government.

RONALD REAGAN, quoted in *Newsweek*, 1 October 1979

8 We still construe energy policy as producing energy for however many people there are, not as producing fewer people so as to give each one as much energy as he or she needs.

KINGSLEY DAVIS, *Cry California*, Summer 1981

9 I think our policy is called aircraft carriers.

IRWIN STELTZER, on U.S. efforts to deal with the problem of large oil imports, quoted in *Wall Street Journal*, 19 June 1987

10 The drop in oil prices, while certainly a major factor, is not the sole culprit of our growing dependence on imported oil. Believing that the best energy policy is no energy policy, the Reagan Administration took a meat ax to America's domestic energy programs.

ROBERT C.BYRD, U.S. Senator, quoted in *Washington Post*, 26 August 1987

11 How can the present market, which determines the price of electricity, coal, and so on, possibly represent the true cost of these fuels or the energy produced from them if there is no charge for the environmental damage they do?

STEPHEN H. SCHNEIDER, *Global Warming: Are We Entering the Greenhouse Century?*, 1989

12 During my professional career, I have seen coal plants converted to oil for air quality, [then] oil plants converted to coal because of import concerns; nuclear plants first promoted by the Congress, then discouraged; . . . natural gas encouraged, then banned, then encouraged again as a generation fuel. . . . All of which has taught our industry the virtue of being nimble.

WILLIAM S. LEE, quoted in *Christian Science Monitor*, 8 August 1989

13 If we use resources productively and take to heart the lessons learned from coping with the energy crisis, we face a future confronted only, as Pogo once said, by insurmountable .

opportunities. The many crises facing us should be seen, then, not as threats, but as chances to remake the future so it serves all beings.

HUNTER LOVINS and AMORY B. LOVINS, *Utne Reader*, November–December 1989

14 [There is, in the debate on global warming] a little tendency by some of the faceless bureaucrats on the environmental side to try and create a policy in this country that cuts off our use of coal, oil, and natural gas.

JOHN H. SUNUNU, ABC News, 4 February 1990

15 At the root of our problem is America's addiction to cheap energy. It would be a sad commentary if our leaders found it easier to send Americans to fight in the desert than to impose gasoline and other energy taxes.

JAMES GUSTAVE SPETH, *Los Angeles Times*, 19 August 1990

16 That racket you hear from the Middle East is opportunity knocking. It's telling us that when it comes to energy policy, the moral equivalent of war is vastly preferable to the real thing.

CURTIS MOORE and S. DAVID FREEMAN, *Washington Post*, 16 September 1990

17 Since the election of Ronald Reagan, the nation has approached energy policy in the same ambivalent way it has approached sex education: some people think it is indispensable; others think it is none of the government's business.

MATTHEW L. WALD, *New York Times*, 17 February 1991

18 Energy policy will be and should be driven by environmental policy in the future.

TIMOTHY WIRTH, U.S. Senator, 20 February 1991

19 This plan is designed to keep the country powered, fueled and heated through the next several decades without suggesting that there are any bad habits that need to be changed. It's an instructive document, but it's not likely to prove to be a very realistic one.

WASHINGTON POST, on the Bush Administration energy strategy, 21 February 1991

42 ENGINEERS

1 The engineer is a man with the biggest blinkers on. Glaucoma is his by choice, a way of isolating most of the physical and biological world and seeing only big dam foolishness or a world of pipes.

IAN MCHARG, in Frank F. Darling and John P. Milton, eds., *Future Environments of North America*, 1966

2 In the automotive industry, our technology has advanced to the stage that our engineers can invent practically on demand. Almost any device we can dream up, the engineers can make.

DONALD FREY, Ford Motor Company vice-president, speech, Purdue University, 2 January 1966

3 I've often thought that if our zoning boards could be put in charge of botanists, of zoologists and geologists, and people who know about the earth, we would have much more wisdom in such planning than we have when we leave it to the engineers.

WILLIAM O. DOUGLAS (1898–1980), U.S. Supreme Court justice, remarks at a conference sponsored by the American Histadrut Cultural Exchange Institute, Harriman, New York, 17–19 February 1967

4 All engineering acts are violations of nature; when the deleterious results are sufficiently unacceptable to the public, society will react and readjustment will occur.

AUGUSTUS B. KINZEL, speech, University of Santa Clara, 16 April 1968

5 Sometimes it is suggested that since scientists and engineers have made the bombs, insecticides, and autos, they ought to be responsible for deciding how to deal with the resultant hazards. . . . This approach would . . . force us to rely on the moral and political wisdom of scientists and engineers, and there is no evidence that I know of that suggests they are better endowed in this respect than other people.

BARRY COMMONER, *Columbia Forum*, Spring 1968

6 In industry the most important wits are the engineers. So I must confess it is a total mystery to me that engineering is not the most encouraged, popular, prosperous and respected pro-

fession in the country. In my opinion, if we had our priorities right, it would be just that.

PRINCE PHILIP, duke of Edinburgh, *Men, Machines, and Sacred Cows*, 1984

7 Thousands of engineers can design bridges, calculate strains and stresses, and draw up specifications for machines, but the great engineer is the man who can tell whether the bridge or the machine should be built at all, where it should be built, and when.

EUGENE G. GRACE, quoted in *Isaac Asimov's Book of Science and Nature Quotations*, 1988

8 To conserve well is to engineer within the rules of natural changes, patterns, and ambiguities; to engineer well is to conserve, to maintain the dynamics of the living systems.

DANIEL B. BOTKIN, *Discordant Harmonies*, 1990

43 ENVIRONMENT

See also   44 ENVIRONMENTAL DEGRADATION, 45 ENVIRONMENTAL IMPACTS, 55 GLOBAL ENVIRONMENT, 67 HUMANKIND AND ENVIRONMENT, 71 INDOOR ENVIRONMENT, 132 URBAN ENVIRONMENT, 141 WORKPLACE ENVIRONMENT

1 You say the word "house" and it means so many different things to different people. One person sees it on an open road in the countryside; another sees a village. One thinks of a farm; another of a cliff dwelling in the urban landscape. Environment is a culture and culture is archetypal; it grows from deep within you, embodies long-lived feelings toward shelter, family, community, and self.

MOSHE SAFDIE, *Beyond Habitat*, 1970

2 We are finally coming to recognize that the natural environment is the exploited proletariat, the downtrodden nigger of everybody's industrial system. . . . Nature must also have its natural rights.

THEODORE ROSZAK, *Person/Planet*, 1978

3 The word *environment* does not mean something that surrounds us but an organism of all life within which we are fastened.

MOSE RICHARDS, quoted in Jacques-Yves Cousteau, *The Costeau Almanac*, 1980

4 Environment begins in the household economy.

TYLER MILLER, *Living in the Environment*, 1982

5 I think the environment should be put in the category of our national security. Defense of our resources is just as important as defense abroad. Otherwise what is there to defend?

ROBERT REDFORD, Yosemite National Park dedication, 1985

6 When we talk about the environment we are talking not about wilderness and forests, but about people and their lives. That's where our work is—with people.

FURUZOMO, Japanese environmentalist, *Environmental Action*, July–August 1986

7 What makes it so hard to organize the environment sensibly is that everything we touch is hooked up to everything else.

ISAAC ASIMOV, *Isaac Asimov's Book of Science and Nature Quotations*, 1988

8 International economic security is inconceivable unless related not only to disarmament but also to the elimination of the threat to the world's environment.

MIKHAIL GORBACHEV, speech, quoted in *Time*, 2 January 1989

9 And the word *Environment*. Such a bloodless word. A flat-footed word with a shrunken heart. A word increasingly disengaged from its association with the natural world. Urban planners, industrialists, economists, and developers use it. It's a lost word, really. A cold word, mechanistic, suited strangely to the coldness generally felt toward Nature. It's their word now. You don't mind giving it up. As for *Environmentalist*, that's one that can really bring on the yawns, for you've tamed and tidied it, neutered it quite nicely. An environmentalist must be calm, rational, reasonable, and willing to compromise, otherwise you won't listen to him. Still, his beliefs are *opinions* only, for this is the age of radical subjectivism.

JOY WILLIAMS, *Esquire*, February 1989

10 This is the first generation in the history of the world that finds that what people do to their natural environment is maybe more important than what the natural environment does to and for them. We also have some measuring sticks for change that we never

had before. And, as always happens with knowledge, as soon as you know something, you have some responsibility.

HARLAN CLEVELAND, quoted in *Christian Science Monitor*, 1 September 1989

11 The environment is too important to be left solely to the environmentalists.

HELMUT SIHLER, paper presented at the Industry Forum on Environment, Bergen, Norway, 10–11 May 1990

12 I believe the issue of the environment will cause as much acrimony and tension among nations in the future as capitalism versus communism has caused in recent decades.

GILBERT M. GROSVENOR, *Business Week*, 18 June 1990

13 The environment is one thing that's concrete. It's the food we eat, the water we drink, the air we breathe. Each person does all three of those things so they feel an immediate sense of investment in it.

MARC L. MIRINGOFF, *Christian Science Monitor*, 10 August 1990

14 The Environment: As I understand it, the environment is the entire system of energies we live within, suns, black holes, grass, ants, baby daughters, memories of our own childhood.

Nature: In my understanding, nature is a subset under the environment, part of the environment, the living system which has evolved on the surface of the Earth (including us).

WILLIAM KITTREDGE, *Northern Lights*, Autumn 1990

44 ENVIRONMENTAL DEGRADATION

See also   45 ENVIRONMENTAL IMPACTS, 67 HUMANKIND AND ENVIRONMENT, 104 POLLUTION

1 Thank God, they cannot cut down the clouds!

HENRY DAVID THOREAU (1817–1862)

2 They have poisoned the Thames and killed the fish in the river. A little further development of the same wisdom and science will complete the poisoning of the air, and kill the dwellers on the banks. . . . I almost think it is the destiny of science to exterminate the human race.

THOMAS LOVE PEACOCK (1785–1866), *Gryll Grange*, 1860

3 Man is everywhere a disturbing agent. Wherever he plants his foot, the harmonies of nature are turned to discords.

GEORGE PERKINS MARSH (1801–1882), *Man and Nature*, 1864

4 The earth is fast becoming an unfit home for its noblest inhabitant, and another era of equal human crime and human improvidence . . . would reduce it to such a condition of impoverished productiveness, of shattered surface, of climatic excess, as to threaten the deprivation, barbarism, and perhaps even extinction of the species.

GEORGE PERKINS MARSH (1801–1882), *Man and Nature*, 1864

5 Man, on the contrary, extends his action over vast spaces, his revolutions are swift and radical, and his devastations are, for an almost incalculable time after he has withdrawn the arm that gave the blow, irreparable.

GEORGE PERKINS MARSH, (1801–1882), *The Earth as Modified by Human Action*, 1874

6 There is as yet no social stigma in the possession of a gullied farm, a wrecked forest, or a polluted stream, provided the dividends suffice to send the youngsters to college. Whatever ails the land, the government will fix it.

ALDO LEOPOLD (1886–1948), *Round River*, 1953

7 It will be said of this generation that it found England a land of beauty and left it a land of beauty spots.

CYRIL JOAD, *The Observer*, 31 May 1953

8 For it is the nature of the problems of land and water that damage done to either is cumulative.

BERNARD DE VOTO (1897–1955), *Harper's*, August 1954

9 [We stand] today poised on a pinnacle of wealth and power, yet we live in a land of vanishing beauty, of increasing ugliness, of

shrinking open space and of an overall environment that is diminished daily by pollution and noise and blight. This, in brief, is the quiet conservation crisis.

STEWART L. UDALL, U.S. Secretary of the Interior, *The Quiet Crisis*, 1963

10 It is not to be wondered that the man who, when trying to wrest a living from nature after the fashion which three centuries of American history found good may explode in frustrated, uncomprehending outrage at the suggestion that he is selfishly exploitive. The pioneer with ax and gun and plow is still revered in American folklore; it is difficult for those who would emulate his psychology today to see themselves, at best, as anachronistic and, at worst, as destroyers of the national heritage.

LYNTON K. CALDWELL, in Frank F. Darling and John P. Milton, eds., *Future Environments of North America*, 1966

11 The American people today are involved in a warfare more deadly than the war in Vietnam, but few of them seem aware of it and even fewer of them are doing anything about it. This is a war that is being waged against the American environment, against our lands, air, and water, which are the basis of that environment.

NORMAN COUSINS, testimony, U.S. Senate Public Works subcommittee, June 1966

12 With the population explosion, the carcinoma of planless urbanism, the new geological deposits of sewage and garbage, surely no creature other than man has ever managed to foul its nest in such short order.

LYNN I. WHITE, JR., *Science*, 10 March 1967

13 Everywhere, societies seem willing to accept ugliness for the sake of increase in economic wealth. Whether natural or humanized, the landscape retains its beauty only in the areas that do not prove valuable for industrial and economic exploitation. The change from wilderness to dump heap symbolizes at present the course of technological civilization. Yet the material wealth we are creating will not be worth having if creation entails the raping

of nature and the destruction of environmental charm.

RENÉ DUBOS, speech, UNESCO biosphere conference, Paris, 1968

14 Affluent as it was for the majority, the society we have produced was not admirable. It might be better than others, but it was nowhere near what it should have been. It was, in fact, going rotten. The private gain had for so long triumphed over the public need that the cities had become unlivable, the country desecrated, the arteries choked, and pollution—of air, of water, yes, of spirit too—a daily, oppressive, fact. And who else but our generation (if not ourselves) had made it so?

MARYA MANNES, *Them*, 1968

15 The American environment represents a unit. Man has tied together its most remote parts in an intricate web. Decisions in Washington determine conditions of life everywhere. The environment is unified, but our treatment of it is fragmented by political subdivisions and the delegation of partial responsibility to thousands of separate agencies. In the face of this disunity we seem at times powerless to arrest environmental deterioration.

RAYMOND F. DASMANN, quoted in *Conservation Foundation Letter*, 23 February 1968

16 In the long view the progressive deterioration of our environment may cause more death and misery than any conceivable food-population gap.

PAUL R. EHRLICH, *The Population Bomb*, 1969

17 No other nation on Earth so swiftly wasted its birthright; no other, in time, made such an effort to save what was left.

WALLACE STEGNER, *The Sound of Mountain Water*, 1969

18 Industrial vomit . . . fills our skies and seas. Pesticides and herbicides filter into our foods. Twisted automobile carcasses, aluminum cans, non-returnable glass bottles and synthetic plastics form immense kitchen middens in our midst as more and more of our detritus resists decay. We do not even begin to know what to do with our radioactive

wastes—whether to pump them into the earth, shoot them into outer space, or pour them into the oceans. Our technological powers increase, but the side effects and potential hazards also escalate.

ALVIN TOFFLER, *Future Shock*, 1970.

19 We have come tardily to the tremendous task of cleaning up our environment. We should have moved with similar zeal at least a decade ago. But no purpose is served by post-mortems. With visionary zeal but the greatest realism, we must now address ourselves to the vast problems that confront us.

GERALD R. FORD, Earth Day address, Grand Rapids, Michigan, 22 April 1970

20 Environments which are being upset by smogs, pesticides, or strip mining are not destroyed thereby; they will become different by evolving in directions determined by these challenges. We may not like the consequences of these changes for ethical, esthetic, or economic reasons, but it is nevertheless certain that the disturbed environments will eventually achieve some new kind of biologic status, as has been the case in the past after all great ecological disasters.

RENE DUBOS, *A God Within*, 1972

21 What *is* certain is that our sudden, vast accelerations—in numbers, in the use of energy and new materials, in urbanization, in consumptive ideals, in consequent pollution—have set technological man on a course which could alter dangerously and perhaps irreversibly, the natural systems of his planet upon which his biological survival depends.

BARBARA WARD and RENÉ DUBOS, *Only One Earth*, 1972

22 The environmental crisis is the result of success—success in cutting down the mortality of infants (which has given us the population explosion), success in raising farm output sufficiently to prevent mass famine (which has given us contamination by pesticides and chemical fertilizers), success in getting people out of the noisome tenements of the 19th-century city and into the greenery and privacy of the single-family home in the suburbs (which has given us urban sprawl and

traffic jams). The environmental crisis, in other words, is largely the result of doing too much of the right sort of thing.

PETER F. DRUCKER, *Harper's*, January 1972

23 Doomsday is quite within our reach, if we will only stretch for it.

LOUDON WAINWRIGHT, *Life*, 28 January 1972

24 North American civilization is one of the ugliest to have emerged in human history, and it has engulfed the world. Asphalt and exhaust fumes clog the villages. . . . This great, though disastrous, culture can only change as we begin to stand off and see . . . the inveterate materialism which has become the model for cultures around the globe.

ARTHUR C. ERICKSON, speech, Simon Fraser University, 1973

25 Environmental degradation is not a distinctive characteristic of capitalism. Pollution is just as bad in Soviet Russia, and for the same nondialectical reasons: blind dedication to production at the expense of human amenities.

GLADWIN HILL, *Madman in a Lifeboat*, 1973

26 The distribution of the population, the size of the country it inhabits, the degree and kind of its industrialization, the flexibility of the ecological systems in which it lives and works, the nature of its social traditions and attitudes, all of these play a notable part in determining its degree of ecological destructiveness.

JOHN PASSMORE, *Man's Responsibility for Nature*, 1974

27 Ecological devastation is the excrement, so to speak, of man's power worship.

ERNEST BECKER, *Escape from Evil*, 1975

28 The family which takes its mauve and cerise, air-conditioned, power-steered and power-braked automobile out for a tour passes through cities that are badly paved, made hideous by litter, blighted buildings, billboards and posts for wires that should long since have been put underground. They pass on into a countryside that has been rendered largely invisible by commercial art. . . . They picnic on exquisitely packaged food from a

portable icebox by a polluted stream and go on to spend the night at a park which is a menace to public health and morals. Just before dozing off on an air mattress, beneath a nylon tent, amid the stench of decaying refuse, they may reflect vaguely on the curious unevenness of their blessings. Is this, indeed, the American genius?

JOHN KENNETH GALBRAITH, *The Affluent Society*, 1976

29 We're destroying the planet, there's not a damn thing that can be done about it. It's going to be very slow, drawn-out and ugly or so fast it doesn't make any difference.

KURT VONNEGUT, JR., *The Nation*, 13 May 1978

30 No people has inherited a more naturally beautiful land. . . . We are about to turn this beautiful inheritance into the biggest slum on the face of the earth.

PETER BLAKE, on Americans, *God's Own Junkyard*, 2d ed., 1979

31 The more you learn about what people have done and continue to do to the environment in the West, the less you can go around cheering, saying, "God, isn't that great country," which is the way I began.

WALLACE STEGNER, in Richard W. Etulain, *Conversations with Wallace Stegner on Western History and Literature*, 1983

32 We see an increasing number of so-called environmental refugees, particularly in Africa—hundreds of thousands of people trying to escape from an environment that can no longer sustain them.

PRINCE AGA KHAN, speech to Independent Commission on International Humanitarian Issues, 1985

33 It is quite true that if environmental pollution and degradation reach a certain point, or if damage to the Earth's biosphere goes beyond a certain limit, the physical conditions for our continued existence will be irreversibly undermined and we will be doomed to extinction.

PAUL W. TAYLOR, *Respect for Nature*, 1986

34 We approach the millennium in a world in which global interdependence is the central reality, but where absolute poverty and environmental degradation cloud our vision of a common future, and where a geopolitical climate dominated by nuclear terrorism and increasing militarization saps the idealism of the young and the will to dream in us all.

RALPH TORRIE, hearing, World Commission on Environment and Development, Ottawa, 26–27 May 1986

35 I think the whole question of air pollution, acid rain—we have created that. God, in His wisdom, created a balance in creation that we as human beings shortsightedly have upset very often.

ROGER J. MAHONY, Roman Catholic archbishop of Los Angeles, quoted in *USA Today*, 13 May 1987

36 We can break the mountains apart; we can drain the rivers and flood the valleys. We can turn the most luxuriant forests into throwaway paper products. We can tear apart the great grass cover of the western plains and pour toxic chemicals into the soil and pesticides onto the fields until the soil is dead and blows away in the wind. We can pollute the air with acids, the rivers with sewage, the seas with oil—all this in a kind of intoxication with our power for devastation at an order of magnitude beyond all reckoning.

THOMAS BERRY, *The Dream of Earth*, 1988

37 Until now, the environment has been large in proportion to the demands that we've put on it. Now our influences are large.

GEORGE M. WOODWELL, quoted in *Christian Science Monitor*, 25 July 1988

38 The roots of the problem of environmental degradation lie in Western culture's philosophy about nature. The culture simply does not place nature in a prominent place in its list of priorities. The dominant thinking in the West was articulated three centuries ago when philosophers postulated that human behavior focusing exclusively on the accumulation of money was somehow sane and rational.

RICK HILL, *Daybreak* (American Indian culture quarterly), Autumn 1988

39 No nation in the world has grappled so successfully with [environmental] issues [in the

past] as the United States. Without these accomplishments, where would we be today? We would be like Mexico City or Sao Paulo. [But] the problems hitting us now—problems like toxic wastes, acid rain and global warming—are hellishly more complex and difficult, not only technically but politically and economically.

RUSSELL TRAIN, *New York Times*, 30 November 1988

40 The earth is slowly dying, and the inconceivable—the end of life itself—is actually becoming conceivable.

QUEEN BEATRIX OF THE NETHERLANDS, Christmas message, December 1988

41 There is an old science experiment in which a frog is put into a pan of water, and the water is slowly heated to the boiling point. The frog sits there and boils because its nervous system will not react to the gradual increase. But if you boil the water first and then put the frog in, it immediately jumps out. We are at an environmental boiling point right now.

ALBERT GORE, JR., U.S. Senator, quoted in *Time*, 2 January 1989

42 [The Great Plains] are America's steppes, extending over much of 10 states—endlessly windswept, nearly treeless, semiarid, austerly beautiful, historically untenable, increasingly empty, and now facing ecological devastation.

FRANK J. POPPER and DEBORAH EPSTEIN POPPER, *Washington Post*, 6 August 1989

43 We [in Czechoslovakia] have laid waste to our soil and the rivers and the forests that our forefathers bequeathed to us, and we have the worst environment in the whole of Europe today.

VACLAV HAVEL, speech, Prague, 1 January 1990

44 I find it difficult to accept that it is the will of God that humanity should degrade, deface, desecrate, and ultimately perhaps destroy His Creation on Earth. Yet this is the course on which we are embarked.

RUSSELL E. TRAIN, speech, North American Conference on Religion and Ecology, Washington, D.C., 18 May 1990

45 This is a beautiful planet and not at all fragile. Earth can withstand significant volcanic

eruptions, tectonic cataclysms, and ice ages. But this canny, intelligent, prolific, and extremely self-centered human creature had proven himself capable of more destruction of life than Mother Nature herself. . . . We've got to be stopped.

MICHAEL L. FISCHER, *Harper's*, July 1990

45 ENVIRONMENTAL IMPACTS

See also 44 ENVIRONMENTAL DEGRADATION, 67 HUMANKIND AND ENVIRONMENT, 104 POLLUTION, 109 POPULATION IMPACTS, 128 TOURISM

1 I suspect that in the long run we are going to have to . . . make all of our agencies bring in some kind of ecological litmus test on every single decision they make.

ERNEST F. ROBERTS, JR., conference on law and the environment, Warrenton, Va., September 1969

2 The Congress authorizes and directs that, to the fullest extent possible: . . . all agencies of the federal government shall include in every recommendation or report on proposals for legislation and other major federal actions significantly affecting the quality of the human environment, a detailed statement by the responsible official on . . . the environmental impact of the proposed action.

U.S. NATIONAL ENVIRONMENTAL POLICY ACT, January 1970

3 It will be up to you, as part of the conservation conscience of America, to see that environmental impact studies are read and studied and talked about. There should be no shroud of secrecy around these reports.

RUSSELL E. TRAIN, speech to conservationists, Washington, D.C., March 1970

4 [Environmental-impact] statements on highways and sewage treatment plants seldom evaluate the resulting impact on urban growth patterns. These secondary or induced effects may, however, be more damaging than the primary effects. The second form of shortsightedness is the tendency to consider only changes in the physical environment and to ignore changes in the social environment. Yet impacts on population pat-

terns or community behavioral patterns may affect the quality of the human environment much more than impacts on air and solid waste.

U.S. ENVIRONMENTAL PROTECTION AGENCY, letter to Council on Environmental Quality, 21 December 1971

5 So cost-benefit analysis is nearly always sure,
To justify the building of a solid concrete fact,
While the Ecologic Truth is left behind in the Abstract.

KENNETH E. BOULDING, "The Ballad of Ecological Awareness," in M. Taghi Farvar and John P. Milton, eds., *The Careless Technology,* 1972

6 If we squeeze time . . . and compress the earth's four billion years into the six days of creation, the earth began only last Sunday at midnight, life arrived Tuesday noon, to grow, spread, diversify, and become ever more beautiful. Neanderthal man came 11 seconds before Saturday midnight, agriculture only 1½ seconds before midnight. The Industrial Revolution began its attack on the earth 1/40th of a second ago.

It is midnight now, and high time to slow the attack. So far almost all nations have been asking for more speed, believing that some kind of technological magic will stretch the earth. There is no such magic. We ought soon to learn to ask, before starting a vast new project, What will we gain if we don't build it? What will it cost the earth?

DAVID R. BROWER, ed., *Only a Little Planet,* 1972

7 NEPA [National Environmental Policy Act] only requires what should already be implicit in the notion of responsible decision-making. Decisions which ignore adverse environmental effects of proposed actions are excluding relevant costs and disadvantages which can only make them less than fully responsible choices.

TIMOTHY B. ATKESON, American Law Institute–American Bar Association seminar, 17 February 1972

8 The agencies must guard against a natural but unfortunate tendency to let the writing of impact statements become a form of bureaucratic gamesmanship, in which the newly acquired expertise is devoted not so much to the shaping of the project to meet the needs of the environment as to the shaping of the impact statement to meet the needs of the agency's preconceived program and the threat of judicial review.

ROGER C. CRAMTON, testimony, joint meeting of U.S. Senate Interior and Senate Public Works committees, 7 March 1972

9 The ecological integrity of the Florida Everglades has suffered, not from a single adverse decision, but from a multitude of small pin pricks. . . . One key to avoiding the problem of cumulative effects of small environmental decisions lies in a holistic view of the world around us.

WILLIAM E. ODUM, *BioScience,* October 1982

10 The astonishing thing about Grand Coulee [Dam]—about the whole era—was that people just went out and built it, built anything, without knowing exactly how to do it or whether it could even be done. There were no task forces, no special commissions, no proposed possible preliminary outlines of conceivable tentative recommendations. Tremendous environmental impacts, but no environmental impact statements.

MARC REISNER, *Cadillac Desert,* 1986

11 Of course, the "no-build" alternative is a required consideration of all federal Environmental Impact Statements nowadays, but we seldom accord it the seriousness it deserves.

TOM HORTON, *Bay Country,* 1987

12 People complained and pricked the consciences of others, the government acted, and, finally, companies themselves have learned it is better not to pollute . . . Today, no one is willing to propose a major industrial construction project in Brazil without including the costs of an environmental-impact study. Anyone who ignored it would be shunned by the others.

JESUS MARDEN DOS SANTOS, quoted in *World Press Review,* April 1987

13 Impact per person × Number of persons = Total Environmental Impact.

PAUL R. EHRLICH, on impact equation, *E* magazine, November–December 1990

14 A well-conceived EIA [environmental-impact assessment] can reveal the environmental limits to economic growth, just as there are

economic limits to the improvement of environmental quality. What is needed, therefore, is holistic systems design for renewable resource management.

M. K. MUTHOO, *Unasylva* 41, no. 163, 1990

15 Many of the problems with Japan's environmental policies, particularly their seemingly inequitable nature, stem from the closed and hegemonic nature of the decision-making process. . . . EIA in Japan has not changed the balance of power in this process and is thus seen as merely a form of project justification.

BRENDAN F. D. BARRETT and RIKI THERIVAL, *Environmental Policy and Impact Assessment in Japan*, 1991

46 ENVIRONMENTALISTS

See also 47 ENVIRONMENTAL MOVEMENT

1 Hungry? Out of Work? Eat an Environmentalist!

BUMPER STICKER

2 The cult of nature is a form of patronage by people who have declared their materialistic independence from nature and do not have to struggle with nature every day of their lives.

BROOKS ATKINSON, *Once Around the Sun*, 1951

3 The rapidly rising interest of students in environmental reform promises a brilliant harnessing of youthful idealism to the desperate cause of checking the world's physical deterioration. . . . The threat of self-extinction hangs over us all but, if the young and fresh take up the cause, there is hope for the physical environment; if they are joined by the rest of society, there is hope for the human climate as well.

NEW YORK TIMES, editorial, 7 December 1969

4 Ironically, today's ecology enthusiasts do not seem to like living things. Life must be limited, they say, else it will destroy itself. We must have a small population and a lot of space. People corrupt things. They breed, they eat, they shit, they need clothing, they need shelter, they need fuel. We must eliminate people; otherwise they'll *use* the earth.

ROBERT CHRISMAN, *Scanlan's*, 1970

5 Violence is morally wrong. . . . [N]onviolent action alone has seldom produced beneficial change on our planet.

PAUL WATSON and WARREN ROGERS, *Sea Shepherd: My Fight for Whales and Seals*, 1970

6 Anyone who proposes to cure the environment crisis undertakes thereby to change the course of history.

BARRY COMMONER, *The Closing Circle*, 1971

7 Folk singers are not going to solve the environmental crisis. They could not even build a sewage treatment plant.

PETER F. DRUCKER, speech, Claremont College, 13 April 1971

8 Folk singers aren't going to be much help when it comes down to the nitty gritty.

WILLIAM F. ROCKWELL, JR., speech, American Institute of Industrial Engineers, Pittsburgh, 1972

9 The first environmentalists were probably the scientists who, toward the end of World War II, sensed that the development of nuclear weapons posed a grave threat to the human race.

JOHN MADDOX, *Saturday Review of the Society*, 21 October 1972

10 While the environmentalists have received floods of publicity, they remain incomprehensible to the very men whose understanding would be most valuable: the executives, engineers and government officials who administer the American energy industries. . . . For the environmentalists, the quality of life is the most important thing, and the traditional yardsticks, such as GNP, provide only partial measures for it.

THE ECONOMIST, 7 July 1972

11 [It seems that] the average environmentalist has his heart in the hinterland and his head, if not buried, at least turned from the unpleasant business of human survival in urban America.

JAMES NOEL SMITH, *Environmental Quality and Social Justice in Urban America*, 1974

12 [The Mundeys and other Australian environmental leaders of the "green ban" movement] have effected one of those rare shifts in public thinking that occurs only a few times in a lifetime. Maybe they were madhatters and larrikins—a true Australian tradition—but, by

God, there's many a Sydney resident who will remember them with love.
MARION HARDMAN and PETER MANNING, *Green Bans: The Story of an Australian Phenomenon*, 1975

13 The environmental movement, because of its class origins, retains the vitality to enlist the energies of a large number of middle- and upper-class Americans in political action on issues which go far beyond their own narrow economic self-interests.
CARL POPE, *Sierra Club Bulletin*, April 1975

14 As far as I'm concerned, environmentalists and food-stamp cheaters are the same thing.
TOM HAGEDORN, *Washington Post Magazine*, 7 March 1976

15 Is the message of ecology a sermon on the virtues of poverty, to be heeded only by those who are still have-nots? Can middle-class environmentalists bring off a revolution against their own economic self-interest, or do they in reality mean to enact liberal, pragmatic reforms that will leave the base of the bourgeois culture intact?
DONALD WORSTER, *Nature's Economy*, 1977

16 If these do-gooders have their way, you'll need a permit to turn on a faucet in the bathroom.
JOHN B. BREAUX, U.S. Representative, quoted in *Outside*, December 1977

17 People who would starve to death if they couldn't drive their cars to the supermarket were opposing new road construction because "fossil fuels are disappearing" and "we aren't going to be using cars anymore."
WILLIAM TUCKER, *Harper's*, December 1977

18 The environmentalists in any given area seemed very easy to identify. They were, quite simply, members of the local aristocracy, often living at the end of long, winding country roads. They had learned the lessons of conspicuous consumption and had allowed a certain amount of genteel rusticity to enter their lives.
WILLIAM TUCKER, *Harper's*, December 1977

19 To say that one is an "environmentalist," or that one favors "no-growth," is to say that one has achieved enough well-being from the present system and that one is now content to let it remain as it is—or even retrogress a little—because one's material comfort under the present system has been more or less assured.
WILLIAM TUCKER, *Harper's*, December 1977

20 We sometimes overlook just how essential the cacophony of vigorous, aggressive, self-appointed spokesmen for nature really is, and will continue to be.
WILLIAM K. REILLY, in the Conservation Foundation's *Conservation and Values*, 1978

21 What is the real motive of the extreme environmentalists, who appear to be determined to accomplish their objectives at whatever cost to society? Is it to simply protect the environment? Is it to delay and deny energy development? Is it to weaken America?
JAMES G. WATT, quoted in *Denver Post*, 1978

22 This was the environmental movement, a concatenation of glorious amateurs, "aroused" citizens with a knack for talking about what they really didn't understand, vocationless aristocrats defending the imagined glories of the past, housewives with a flare for writing publicity releases, lawyers with a talent for histrionics, and "militant" scientists and academics with a willingness to shade the truth just a bit in pursuit of a "good cause."
WILLIAM TUCKER, *Harper's*, August 1978

23 The widespread anxiety [about environmental problems] leads me to remember the late Howard Hughes, crouched in a corner of a hotel room, worried about people meddling with nuclear energy and afraid of amoebas in his food.
LEWIS H. LAPHAM, quoted in *Environmental Action*, 21 October 1978

24 Those [environmentalists] whom I've had the good fortune to meet, all of them worthy and well-meaning people, have belonged almost invariably to the equestrian class.
LEWIS H. LAPHAM, *Harper's*, January 1979

25 [Environmentalists are] coercive utopians.
H. PETER METZGER, Public Service Company of Colorado official, June 1979

26 The backpack bund is *hostile* to people. It prefers (say) mosquitoes. And to protect such

pests, it is perfectly willing to arrange for untold millions of humans to suffer, go without employment, and even to freeze.

ALAN STRONG, *American Opinion*, December 1979

27 At bottom there is something cockeyed about the notion that people who travel in wilderness are an elite. To delight in clean air and water, to respond to natural beauty, to revel in the vigorous exercise of one's limbs and lungs—all this requires no knowledge of Proust or Schönberg. It demands only the possession of basic human equipment—senses and muscles. We are standing the concept of elitism on its head—not to mention admitting that Americans have all but lost an important link with the hardihood of their pioneer ancestors—when we say it is snotty to walk a wilderness mile.

DENNIS DRABELLE, *Washington Post*, 8 January 1980

28 From now on, our movement will need fewer rabble-rousers like me, and more technicians.

BROCK EVANS, quoted in *Conservation Foundation Letter*, January–February 1980

29 [The middle-class whites who make up a large part of the environmental movement bring to it] lessons learned from previous movements: a knowledge of how the system works, access to a certain amount of scientific expertise, an understanding of how to use the media, and an ability to raise enough funds to maintain viable, albeit lean, organizations.

ROBERT CAMERON MITCHELL, *Natural Resources Journal*, April 1980

30 We are in the hands of environmental extremists.

RONALD REAGAN, quoted in *Sierra*, 10 September 1980

31 Environmental extremists wouldn't let you build a house unless it looked like a bird's nest.

RONALD REAGAN, quoted in *Newsweek*, 3 November 1980

32 We have wished, we ecofreaks, for a disaster, or for dramatic social change to come and bomb us into the Stone Age, where we might

live like Indians in our valley, with our localism, our Appropriate Technology, our gardens, and our homemade religion, guilt-free at last.

STEWART BRAND, *Next*, November–December 1980

33 It is precisely the prejudices, guilt feelings, and class interests (conscious and unconscious) of the affluent, the elite, and the privileged which inspire studies like Global 2000.

HERMAN KAHN, *Policy Review*, Spring 1981

34 We have a young lady that is director now of the Environmental Protection Agency, and she is introducing as fast as she can common sense in an area that I think has been yielding to environmental extremists.

RONALD REAGAN, at a Republican fund-raising event in Santa Barbara, Calif., 27 August 1981

35 America's resources . . . should not be denied to the people by elitist groups.

JAMES G. WATT, quoted in *Nation's Business*, September 1981

36 Environmentalists, homosexuals, ecologists, and other ideological eunuchs.

ANONYMOUS ADMINISTRATION OFFICIAL, quoted by Associated Press, 8 October 1981

37 Environmentalists. That's a facade for liberal Democrats.

JAMES G. WATT, *Las Vegas Sun*, 13 October 1981

38 We still tend to become environmentalists by a sort of "cultural osmosis," soaking up environmentalist sentiments without much critical thought. That can get us into a lot of trouble.

RON ARNOLD, *At the Eye of the Storm*, 1982

39 It was always people who owned business plants, ski lodges, $15,000 Land Rovers, or $250,000 helicopters who called me an elitist because I wanted some place beautiful that I could *walk* into in my $8 shoes without running into all this expensive technology.

WILLIAM CHAPMAN, interview, 1982

40 The old saying was that it took three generations to make a gentleman, and I have the distinct impression that it now takes at least

two generations to make an environmentalist. It is usually the sons and daughters of people who have achieved complete material security who make the most strident environmentalists. In families where there is at least some memory of hard times—some generational recollection that economic security is not in the natural order of things—the impulse toward environmentalism usually does not run as strong.

WILLIAM TUCKER, *Progress and Privilege,* 1982

41 Environmentalists are self-motivated to thwart economic development through resource preservation because only they garner the benefits of extremist environmental protection and only they are isolated from the harmful consequences of sluggish economic activity. . . . [I]t can be safely asserted that environmental groups represent only a minority fringe of the American public.

REPUBLICAN STUDY COMMITTEE, U.S. House of Representatives, *The Spectre of Environmentalism,* 1982

42 You can't outrun an environmentalist to the left. . . . [T]hey will always stay ahead of you and demand more from you.

JAMES G. WATT, quoted in Ron Arnold, *At the Eye of the Storm,* 1982

43 [Environmentalists constitute] a left-wing cult which seeks to bring down the type of government I believe in.

JAMES G. WATT, quoted in *New York Times,* 15 April 1982

44 [Interior Secretary James G.] Watt is partly a cause and partly an effect of persons for whom environmentalism is political romanticism masquerading as science, a doctrine for putting sand in the gears of industrialism and for expressing root and branch rejection of America's commercial civilization. Their liking of chipmunks expresses primarily a dislike of human beings, creatures of nasty despoiling rationality. Such environmentalists value wilderness areas primarily as refuges from all reminders that they share the planet with other human beings.

GEORGE F. WILL, *Newsweek,* 16 August 1982

45 The environmentalists . . . thump about man's desecration of nature—because, they argue

implicitly, Man the Almighty is *outside* nature.

A. LAWRENCE CHICKERING, book review, *Wall Street Journal,* 17 September 1982

46 Millions of Americans have for years regarded environmentalists as a bunch of elitists who love deer and rabbits more than people, and whose ideals are out of touch with the real world. But those Americans now know that the environmental crisis is about people who can't drink their town's water, people who bleed, and bleed, and bleed during a simple operation because of dioxin contamination; people who suffer brown lung and black lung diseases and assorted outbreaks of cancer because of pollution at the work place and the homesite.

CARL T. ROWAN, *Washington Post,* 18 February 1983

47 I don't think they will be happy until the White House looks like a bird's nest.

RONALD REAGAN, on environmental "extremists," meeting with press, 11 March 1983

48 I would not have used the bird's nest analogy, but the president is close to correct. Indeed, in terms of environmental policy, the White House, the EPA, and the Department of [the] Interior are beginning to look like a dodo bird's nest: out of date, out of touch, and almost extinct.

GAYLORD NELSON, 11 March 1983

49 What I call "commercial" environmentalists are hard-core, left-wing radicals, manipulating the press. . . . They have a conspiracy of shared values. Their real objective is partisan politics to change the form of government.

JAMES G. WATT, quoted in *Washington Post,* 27 April 1983

50 Environmentalists are never against jobs as some opponents charge, but are certainly proponents of jobs which are ecologically benign.

BILL DEVALL and GEORGE SESSIONS, *Deep Ecology,* 1985

51 We're a nation of laws. Terrorism has no place in changing public policy.

JAY D. HAIR, on violence used as a tactic by the new environmentalists, *Esquire,* February 1987

52 Monkeywrenching is an American tradition. Look at the Boston Tea Party—it's celebrated on a postage stamp. Someday we'd like to see tree-spiking celebrated that way.
MIKE ROSELLE, quoted in *Utne Reader*, May–June 1987

53 We are neither [politically] left or right; we are in front.
RONNIE Z. HAWKINS, *Earth First!*, 21 June 1987

54 The environmentalists, God bless them, are doing a fine job—but black people have more to think about, and they don't see the same priorities. You have to give us our daily bread before you can move on to dessert. And I think the environmentalists were already working on dessert when the others were still on the soup course.
ED BRUSKE, on the defeat of the District of Columbia bottle bill, *Washington Post*, 8 November 1987

55 At first we were gonna try to work within the system. But the more we got involved in Earth First!, the more we began to question the assumptions of technological civilization and to realize it isn't reformable. I think of us as being on the *Titanic*. There are icebergs ahead and nobody's in the pilot cabin; everybody's arguing about rearranging the deck chairs. I just want to make sure there are some lifeboats outfitted, you see?
DAVE FOREMAN, quoted in Peter Borelli, ed., *Crossroads*, 1988

56 Some environmentalists have criticized the grass-roots toxics movement for being crude and selfish. We are sometimes called NIMBYs (Not In My Back Yard), as though it is a moral defect to fight for home, family, and children. But now, many of the *solutions* the grassroots toxics movement has promoted—waste reduction, recycling, reclamation, and reuse—have become the common wisdom.
LOIS MARIE GIBBS, in Peter Borelli, ed., *Crossroads*, 1988

57 I'd like to challenge the sincere and dedicated individuals who work for environmental causes to repudiate the more extreme and hostile voices in their movement and to try to work with us to raise the level of dialogue. . . . There are some people for whom a love of the works of nature seems to engender a corresponding hatred of the works of man. . . . These people need to realize that human technology and the products of our industry are what stand between us and the hostile elements, between us and constant hunger, between us and the ravages of disease and predation.
GEORGE M. KELLER, *Nation's Business*, 12 June 1988

58 If the environmental evangelists have any unique skill, it's the ability, with the blind cooperation of the press, to scare the daylights out of the public.
W. C. LOWREY, letter, *Wall Street Journal*, 1 September 1988

59 Our method of doing environmental protection really has depended on a crisis mentality. . . . The whole notion of crisis is a short-term orientation that worked in the past to environmentalists' advantage. But I'm not sure it does anymore. Sometimes the problems stretch out too long to be able to show real crisis.
ROBERT ROYCROFT, *Christian Science Monitor*, 14 September 1988

60 Environmentalists who are patiently, conventionally trying to turn public policy towards sustainability; social theorists and visionaries who dream of democratic, egalitarian, life-enhancing political forms, are working the decisive human angle of the ecological crisis. But in terms of triage, the most critical ecological work is species saving, ark building, habitat preservation.
STEPHANIE MILLS, *What Ever Happened to Ecology?*, 1989

61 The new environmentalists who believe in the rights of nature dismiss conservation and stewardship as ethically meaningless just as abolitionists scorned kindly slavery. What the deep ecologists call "reform environmentalism" or "shallow ecology" seems to them just a more efficient form of exploitation and oppression. It compares to feeding slaves well or to buying women new dresses while refusing them the right to vote. Real reform, the radical environmentalists agree with the abolitionists, depends on replacing the entire exploitative system with one premised on the rights of the oppressed minority.
RODERICK F. NASH, *The Rights of Nature*, 1989

62 The Green movement draws on the inspiration of Native American culture, the original Committees of Correspondence, Jeffersonian democracy, the abolitionists, the populists, the Socialist Party, the women's movement, the labor movement, the civil rights movement, and the social experiments of the '60s and '70s.
JAY WALLJASPER, *Utne Reader*, September–October 1989

63 Planetary corporations and the politicians in their thrall will not change a system that has been very, very good to them simply because we ask them to. They may adopt our rhetoric but not our values. All our leaders now call themselves environmentalists. But their brand of environmentalism poses very few challenges to the present system. Instead they propose to spruce up the planet with a few technical fixes or individual lifestyle changes: scrubbers on coal plants, eating "all-natural" cereals, and so on.
DAVID MORRIS, *Utne Reader*, November–December 1989

64 My definition of extremist: someone who disagrees with you too effectively.
DAVID R. BROWER, on environmental activism, *For Earth's Sake*, 1990

65 I find some people think of the environment in an airy-fairy way, as if we could go back to some kind of village life.
MARGARET THATCHER, *New Scientist*, 24 March 1990

66 I'm not an environmentalist. I'm an Earth warrior. I am the Earth defending itself. I'm trying to de-domesticize myself. I'm trying to feralize myself.
DARRYL CHERNEY, quoted in *Smithsonian*, April 1990

67 No compromise in defense of Mother Earth. It ain't junior high anymore. They don't just send you to the principal's office. Some of us are going to spend a lot of time in jail. Some of us are going to die.
DAVE FOREMAN, *Smithsonian*, April 1990

68 Some so-called "environmentalism" looks suspiciously like self-interest on the part of America's richest elites, protecting turfs from the upstart bourgeoisie through a kind of worldwide "snob zoning," most of it purchased at taxpayer and consumer expense.
WARREN BROOKES, *Washington Times*, 17 April 1990

69 One does not become an environmentalist until one achieves some kind of privilege and feels one has something worth protecting. Environmentalists are a privileged minority.
WILLIAM TUCKER, *Washington Times*, 20 April 1990

70 The politically energetic environmentalists on both sides of the Atlantic are articulate, convincing and influential out of proportion to their numbers. They are the representatives of that thin slice of the populace that can be described as the intelligentsia. . . . The priesthood of this political congregation comes from academe and assorted "public interest" enclaves.
WOODY WEST, *Washington Times*, 20 April 1990

71 Increasingly, we are all environmentalists. The President is an environmentalist. Republicans and Democrats are environmentalists. Jane Fonda and the National Association of Manufacturers, Magic Johnson and Danny Devito, Candace Bergen and The Golden Girls, Bugs Bunny and the cast of Cheers are all environmentalists.
RICHARD DARMAN, lecture, Harvard University, 1 May 1990

72 The academic Frederick Turner, on the one hand, reinvents the Great Chain of Being, at the top of which he places man himself. The activist Dave Foreman, on the other, wields the clever but utterly useless metaphor of man as global cancer. Both points of view—and these sentiments are pervasive among grass-roots environmental activists—are predicated on the faulty notion that man and nature are separate and antagonistic, because one or the other is fallen.
GEORGE G. HRUBY, *Harper's*, July 1990

73 Tenets: To promote ecological wisdom, grass-roots democracy, personal and social responsibility, nonviolence, decentralization of power, community-based economy, respect for diversity, and global responsibility.
GREEN PARTY (U.S.), *Los Angeles Times*, 6 August 1990

74 Celebrities are drawn to environmental causes like dolphins to tuna.
WALTER GOODMAN, *New York Times*, 7 October 1990

75 Environmentalists make terrible neighbors but great ancestors.
DAVID R. BROWER, quoted in *Orion*, Winter 1990

76 The real battle in the environmental world now is between animal rights people and mainline traditional conservationists.
LLOYD KIFF, *Los Angeles Times*, 16 December 1990

77 Monkey-wrenching as a philosophy is fine, but as a practice it sucks. We are a nation of laws, and we ought to stick with the law. . . . Like any other great social movement of our time, there's always the fringe that cannot be controlled and towards which [the opposition] always points. To the degree that people believe the most outrageous of their statements, they do harm the environmental movement.
T. H. WATKINS, *Washington Post*, 20 March 1991

78 They're winning. They've managed to capture the moral high ground with the general public.
JAMES A. McCLURE, quoted in *Washington Post*, 16 May 1991

47 ENVIRONMENTAL MOVEMENT
See also   19 CONSERVATION MOVEMENT, 46 ENVIRONMENTALISTS

1 We cannot be dilettante and lily-white in our work. Nice Nellie will never make it. . . . We cannot go on fiddling while the earth's wild places burn in the fires of our undisciplined technology.
DAVID R. BROWER, *New York Times*, 4 May 1969

2 It is absurd to regard the ecological battle as a mere skirmish or a spin-off from the main war. The ecological battle is one of the pieces of the revolutionary puzzle, and it is necessary to complete the picture.
JEAN-FRANÇOIS REVEL, *Without Marx or Jesus*, 1970

3 [Among the characteristics of the "revolutionary universe" in America are] a determination that the natural environment is more important than commercial profit . . . [and] a radical reappraisal of the goals of technology and its consequences.
JEAN-FRANÇOIS REVEL, *Without Marx or Jesus*, 1970

4 [A "new revolution" rising in America] offers the only escape for mankind today: the acceptance of technological civilization as a means and not as an end, and—since we cannot be saved either by the destruction of civilization or by its continuation—the development of the ability to reshape that civilization without annihilating it.
JEAN-FRANÇOIS REVEL, *Without Marx or Jesus*, 1970

5 The moral revolution, and the ecological revolution that is part of it . . . is not simply a transfer of power, but also a change in the goals for the sake of which power is exercised, and a new choice in the objects of love, hate, and respect.
JEAN-FRANÇOIS REVEL, *Without Marx or Jesus*, 1970

6 [Peoples' involvement with the environment will not be a] quieting force—stilling troubled campuses and healing the wounds of a divided nation. That is wishful thinking. There are fundamental value conflicts between those who seek a better world, and those who care only for size, speed, and profit.
DENIS HAYES, press conference, Washington, D.C., January 1970

7 [The environment movement will not] co-opt people from other pressing social concerns to march on pollution. It won't. For ecology is concerned with the total system—not just the way it disposes of its garbage. Our goal is not to clean the air while leaving slums and ghettos, nor is it to provide a healthy world for racial oppression and war. We wish to make the probability of life greater, and the quality of life higher. Those who share these goals

cannot be "co-opted"; they are our allies—
not our competitors.
DENIS HAYES, press conference, Washington, D.C., January 1970

8 This environment movement is one of the
subversive element's last steps. They've
gone after the military and the police and
now they're going after our parks and play-
grounds. . . . The real problem of pollution
of our environment is being distorted and ex-
aggerated by emotional declarations and by
intensive propaganda.
MRS. CLARENCE HOWARD, during debate at
Daughters of the American Revolution
Continental Congress, April 1970

9 Our goal is an environment of decency, quality, and mutual respect for all other human
creatures and for all other living creatures.
An environment without ugliness, without
ghettos, without discrimination, without
hunger, without poverty, and without war.
GAYLORD NELSON, U.S. Senator, speech,
University of Wisconsin, 21 April 1970

10 Until we have a leadership willing to make
the enormous changes—psychological, military, and bureaucratic—to end the existing
world system, a system of hatred, of anarchy,
of murder, of war and pollution, there is no
use talking about buying more wastebaskets
or spending a couple of hundred million dollars on the Missouri River. If we do not challenge these fundamental causes of peril, we
will be conned by the establishment while basic decisions are being made over which we
have very little control, though they endan-
ger everything on which our future and the
world's depend.
I. F. STONE, speech, Washington, D.C., 22
April 1970

11 I suggest that the rapid rise of ecology on the
nation's agenda of public business is a sign
more of sickness than of health, of regression
than of renewal, that it is diversionary, de-
ceptive and finally seductive of the radical
impulse to change.
RICHARD NEUHAUS, In Defense of People, 1971

12 My special plea is that we do not, out of a
combination of emotional zeal and ecological
ignorance, hastily substitute environmental
tragedy for existing environmental deteriora-

tion. Let's not replace known devils with in-
sufficiently understood unknown devils.
PHILIP HANDLER, speech, May 1971

13 The doomsday cause would be more telling if
it were more securely grounded in facts, better informed by a sense of history and an
awareness of economics, and less cataclysmic
in temper.
JOHN MADDOX, The Doomsday Syndrome, 1972

14 The ecological movement is not only middle-
class in character; more, it is a kind of Protes-
tant drive toward hygiene and cleanliness, in
which every home becomes a Howard
Johnson's replica; and in which cleanliness is
not only next to Godliness, but often indistin-
guishable.
IRVING HOROWITZ, Environmental Quality and
Social Responsibility, 1972

15 Extraordinary challenges, like war, have a
way of calling up extraordinary responses
and the ecological challenge is so deep-reach-
ing it needs to be met by a movement of religious force. The time for such a movement
seems ripe; it has a lot going for it.
EVELYN AMES, New York Times, 20 May 1972

16 Arguably, only when the majority of a population have achieved middle-class standards
of living will they also accept middle-class
standards of values—and be prepared to give
priority to, say, anti-pollution measures over
consumer durables.
RUDOLF KLEIN, Commentary, June 1972

17 Instead of alerting people to important problems, the "doomsday syndrome" may be as
much a hazard to human survival as any of
the environmental conundrums society has
created for itself.
JOHN MADDOX, Saturday Review of the Society,
21 October 1972

18 People are easily anesthetized by overstatement, and there is a danger that the environmental movement will fall flat on its face
when it is most needed, simply because it has
pitched its tale too strongly.
JOHN MADDOX, Saturday Review of the Society,
21 October 1972

19 The environmental movement is, you might
say, a movement of repressed Romantics.
CHARLES E. LITTLE, A Town Is Saved, 1973

20 Environmentalism must now balance its predictions of apocalypse with visions of a better
life. When it predicts disaster, it does the safe
thing; for if it is right, it can say "I told you
so," should there be anybody left to listen;
and if it is wrong, no one will care, or even
remember much of what the hullaballo was
all about.
CHARLES E. LITTLE, *A Town Is Saved*, 1973

21 On the whole one can say that in the ecological movement—or perhaps one should say
movements—the scientific aspects . . . have
merged in an extremely confused alliance
with a whole series of political motivations
and interests, which are partly manifest,
partly concealed. At a deeper level one can
identify a great number of sociopsychological
needs. These include: hopes of conversion
and redemption, delight in the collapse of
things, feelings of guilt and resignation, es-
capism and hostility to civilization.
HANS MAGNUS ENZENZBERGER, *New Left Review*, 1974

22 I would suggest that the idea that nature—
the presumed imperatives of nature—has a
role in determining public policy is classically
fascist. It was an articulated doctrine of the
Nazi Regime. It is an articulated doctrine of
much of what has been called Western conservatism and of "enlightened" imperialism.
It is a kind of social Darwinism—the application to social policies of the biological model
of evolution.
RICHARD NEUHAUS, in James N. Smith, *Environmental Quality and Social Justice in Urban
America*, 1974

23 There is not much of a difference qualitatively
between much of the doomsday rhetoric
which characterizes at least a large part of the
environmental movement and the doomsday
rhetoric on which the Pentagon depends.
RICHARD NEUHAUS, in James N. Smith, *Environmental Quality and Social Justice in Urban
America*, 1974

24 People realized that maybe we cannot overcome racism in America, and maybe we cannot reconstruct our cities, and maybe we

cannot end the war in Vietnam, but, damn it,
we can all collect bottles.
RICHARD NEUHAUS, in James N. Smith, *Environmental Quality and Social Justice in Urban
America*, 1974

25 Environmentalism, so far, has not been concerned with forging a compatible accommodation between man in nature and man as a
social and political animal. Indeed, much environmental thinking is distrustful of the essential nature of man.
JAMES NOEL SMITH, *Environmental Quality and
Social Justice in Urban America*, 1974

26 Most recent environmental legislation is
based upon the thesis that unless restricted
and prohibited by threat of fine, imprisonment, or social sanction, man will lay waste
the natural landscape and defile his own habitat. It could be argued, then, that instead of
being essentially romantic, environmental
thought is really much closer to classic conservatism in its distrust of human nature and
its adherence to a hierarchical ordering of
things, both in the natural and the social system.
JAMES NOEL SMITH, *Environmental Quality and
Social Justice in Urban America*, 1974

27 It seems to me that the power of the environmental movement represents, at least as
much as a concern with purity of air and water, a mature belief that we must move beyond consumption to find fulfillment. The
rediscovery of nature, of the interdependence, diversity and stability that characterize healthy natural systems, is a metaphor
with ethical implications for growing numbers of people, particularly the young.
WILLIAM K. REILLY, *Conservation Foundation
Letter*, November 1975

28 [Environmentalism is] a crusade to stop all
development in this country.
DONALD M. HODEL, quoted in *Wall Street
Journal*, 17 December 1975

29 The anti-growth movement and its accompa-
nying excessive concern with the environment not merely leads to a regressive change
in the distribution of resources in the commu-

nity, it also distracts attention from the real issues of choice that society has to face.

WILFRED BECKERMAN, *In Defense of Economic Growth*, 1976

30 Environmentalism . . . is one of the few big popular movements that continue to enlist volunteers, excite idealism, and evoke steadfast, unselfish commitment.

WILLIAM V. SHANNON, *New York Times*, 18 September 1976

31 One of the most important ethical issues raised anywhere in the past few decades has been whether nature has an order, a pattern, that we humans are bound to understand and respect and preserve. It is the essential question prompting the environmentalist movement in many countries.

DONALD WORSTER, *Nature's Economy*, 1977

32 Environment has become the Vietnam of the middle class.

PETER MENKE-GLUCKERT, quoted in *Time*, 25 April 1977

33 [The ecology movement] is not about small tactical gains here and there, but about remaking the unjust, parasitic, overexploited and shrinking world.

HENRYK SKOLIMOWSKI, *The Ecologist*, October 1977

34 The fact is that the environmentalists have won, and it has to be said that their achievements in a few short years have been massive. What they have achieved is an institutionalization of concern for the environment to every level of national life.

LLEWELLYN KING, *Power Engineering*, December 1977

35 The environmental vision is an artistocratic one, conjured at the point where an idyllic past blends nicely with an imaginary future.

WILLIAM TUCKER, *Harper's*, December 1977

36 What the industrial magnates and their minions never understood was that the spirit of the environmental movement was concern for the brotherhood of life. They saw it instead as pollution, an "energy crisis," poor techniques. Dirty air and water, and the poisoning of the environment by wastes and fertilizers and pesticides pre-empted, for them,

its real meaning. Political, economic, and ideological attention to the environment as an issue made pollution its cause, for that could be dealt with by the existing system.

PAUL SHEPARD, *Thinking Animals*, 1978

37 Many of the debates that characterize the environmental movement—perhaps any social movement—are on the surface "factual" or "technical" in nature. But closer inspection often reveals them to be debates over values. However, scientists are unsure over how to debate about values—indeed, how to measure or choose between values. So they use the language of facts and technology to express their ideological positions. (I should note that the term "ideology" is used neutrally here; we all act and speak out of ideological convictions.)

DAVID L. SILLS, speech, American Association for the Advancement of Science, 13 February 1978

38 The more I examine the environmental movement, the more it seems like a kind of secular religion, with a decidedly Puritan strain. Like all religious movements, it draws its strength from what we *don't* know. It tries to hide in the cracks of our understanding, instilling us with the fear of what we haven't yet been able to learn from nature. [I]t is only when some deeply conservative organization such as the Church or environmentalism has orchestrated such fears that these anxieties become institutionalized and *all* scientific advance comes under suspicion. Only then do ordinary human fears about newness and invention start to play a decisive role in history.

WILLIAM TUCKER, *Harper's*, August 1978

39 Certainly the presence of some sort of elite was the only stumbling block for many projects stopped at the local level back in the days before environmental quality became a more universal concern.

DEBORAH BALDWIN, *Environmental Action*, 21 October 1978

40 The last thing we need is simply another liberation movement—for animals, trees, flora, fauna, and rivers.

K. E. GOODPASTER and K. M. SAYRE, eds., *Ethics and Problems of the 21st Century*, 1979

41 [There has been a shift] from the ragged squad of citizens' militia to the disciplined platoons of lawyers, scientists, and civil servants who know how to translate passion into the tedious but essential minutiae of the statute books. This transition . . . inevitably entails a drop in emotional temperature. Yet such a cooling-off is part of the natural maturing process of any successful public movement.

DOUGLAS M. COSTLE, *EPA Journal*, November–December 1979

42 The enthusiasms of Earth Day 1970 have been "institutionalized" in legislation, regulation, litigation, political dynamics and new personal values, and woven into the fabric of national life.

GLADWIN HILL, *New York Times*, 30 December 1979

43 The tocsin that sounded for the environment a decade ago is "a bell that cannot be unrung."

GLADWIN HILL, *New York Times*, 30 December 1979

44 The aim of the Green Alternative is to overcome social conditions, in which the short-term emphasis on economic growth, which only benefits part of the entire population, takes precedence over the ecological, social and democratic needs for the life of humanity.

TAGES ZEITUNG, 15 January 1980

45 The best hope for the environmental movement's future would appear to lie in energetic reaffirmation of its common goals with consumers, workers, minorities, and small businesses.

RICHARD N. L. ANDREWS, *Natural Resources Journal*, April 1980

46 [The environmental movement, in both its philosophy and its methods] shares an essential goal with those working for social justice: to increase the accountability of large-scale economic and political institutions to democratic processes.

RICHARD N. L. ANDREWS, *Natural Resources Journal*, April 1980

47 Environmentalism finally attained maturity when it intersected with the heterogeneous social movements of the day. Reaching its crest at the end of a decade of social activism,

the environmental revolution borrowed from all the major movements and, at last and none too soon, took off on its own.

STEPHEN FOX, *John Muir and His Legacy*, 1981

48 In the late 1960s the ecological drift found expression in a new, all-inclusive label: "environmentalism." The term embodied the ecological imperative to study every problem in its context.

STEPHEN FOX, *John Muir and His Legacy*, 1981

49 Environmentalism itself, properly viewed, is not an obstructionist philosophy but rather an expression of purpose, yearning and rising expectations, another chapter in the saga of human progress.

SAMUEL C. FLORMAN, *New York Times*, 25 January 1981

50 We are beginning to ask the right questions, and this is one great achievement of the environmental movement, which has played an important part in our ways of looking at life and in our view of the world.

HAROLD GILLIAM, *Cry California*, Fall 1981

51 Environmentalism over the past two decades has taken on more and more of the concrete features we find in traditional faiths until today it displays most if not all the behaviors of a religion. I mean that environmentalism has acquired the outward forms of ritual and worship on a secular plane that standard religions possess.

RON ARNOLD, *At the Eye of the Storm*, 1982

52 All rhetoric about nonprofit goals and no financial gain [for environmentalism] simply serves to hide the fact that the movement is a serious and powerful competitor for economic resources in America today.

RON ARNOLD, *In the Eye of the Storm*, 1982

53 All of the characteristic fundamentalist beliefs are there: belief in the inherent sinfulness of man, his unrelenting hubris, and, the inevitability of his coming damnation and imminent extinction. One sees also the fundamentalist cast of mind—the sanctimoniousness, the extreme intolerance toward opposing views, the fire-and-brimstone rhetorical style, threatening the Apocalypse, promising it . . . reveling in it.

A. LAWRENCE CHICKERING, *Wall Street Journal*, 17 September 1982

54 I would argue that American environmentalism can be characterized most accurately as
utilitarian, focused by and large on problems
of concern to people's physical well-being
and their use of nature.
ZACH WILLEY, letter, *Wall Street Journal* 30
September 1982

55 The widespread expression of social values in
environmental action marks off the environmental era from the conservation years.
SAMUEL P. HAYS, *Environmental Review*, 1983

56 This juggernaut [environmentalism], fueled
by false information and special interest values, must be stopped before the world is led
too far along the road to disaster.
JULIAN L. SIMON, *Interaction*, 1983

57 I believe we are battling for the form of government under which we and future generations will live. . . . The battle's not over the
environment. If it was, they would be with
us. They want to control social behavior and
conduct.
JAMES G. WATT, quoted in *Washington Post*,
27 April 1983

58 It looks like we might possibly be reaching
the point of diminishing returns in our recent
efforts to do no harm to the moral, ethnic, religious, sexual, ideological, age-related, environmental and physical sensibilities of
America's men, women, children, animals,
forests, rivers and streams.
WALL STREET JOURNAL, editorial, 27 September 1983

59 The term "environmental" is a misnomer for
this movement, since it had many other attributes which are not communicated by that
concept, and which, indeed, are obliterated
by it. . . . *This was not just "environmentalism"—this was the voice of the apocalypse in new
secular attire.*
EDITH EFRON, *The Apocalyptics: Cancer and the
Big Lie*, 1984

60 [The environmental movement] is insatiable.
GEORGE F. WILL, "This Week with David
Brinkley," 26 August 1984

61 The environmental lobbies seem to have acquired many of the worst traits of the defense
lobby. In the same way that being pro-de-

fense is often an excuse to neglect cost overruns and badly built weapons, being pro-
environment is, increasingly, a license to
disregard the failure of anti-pollution programs.
JAMES BOVARD, *New York Times*, 10 July 1985

62 In surveying the state of environmentalism, I
am struck by its diversity. The organized
movement comprising national and international organizations—themselves as diverse
as the Natural Resources Defense Council
and Greenpeace—is but the most visible part
of a global awakening and transformation.
PETER BORELLI, *Crossroads*, 1988

63 I said they're spiking trees which shouldn't
be cut, by an industry that's only concerned
about the short run. The environmental
movement has gotten very drowsy, and I
think Earth First! is giving it CPR. I admire
people who put their bodies where their
mouth is.
DAVID R. BROWER, quoted in Peter Borelli,
ed., *Crossroads*, 1988

64 The well-to-do industrialized nations must
learn rapidly to do more with less, and . . .
poor developing countries must tackle poverty and environmental degradation together. Neither of these imperatives fits
easily with our national obstacles-be-damned
character, and both force American environmentalists to deal with issues outside their
traditional realm. Herein lies the challenge to
the environmental movement in the next decade.
JANET WELSH BROWN, in Peter Borelli, ed.,
Crossroads, 1988

65 The environmental movement has passed
from the Messianic phase to a more mature
phase. It's harder to tell the good guys from
the bad guys. When Martin Luther King, Jr.,
sat down at that diner in Tuscaloosa, the issue was as clear as the sky over Arizona.
Now civil rights issues include affirmative action, quotas, and so on. They're much more
complicated. The same is true of environmental questions.
DAVID SIVE, quoted in Peter Borelli, ed.,
Crossroads, 1988

66 Today the environmental movement has
never been stronger, but I sometimes worry

that the pendulum may swing back—if it hasn't already begun to. As America's finite resources and fossil fuels begin to run out, will ecologically aware legislators be able to resist the pressures of a voting public that may well be willing to exchange open space and free-flowing rivers, even the "Crown Jewels" of Alaska, for jobs and highways and gasoline? I hope so, but it saddens me to say: I wouldn't bet on it.

MORRIS K. UDALL, U.S. Representative, *Too Funny to Be President*, 1988

67 I am utterly convinced that most of the great environmental struggles will be either won or lost in the 1990's. And that by the next century it will be too late.

THOMAS E. LOVEJOY, quoted in Lester Brown, *State of the World*, 1989

68 Conservation, environmentalism, and the ecology movement were and are, like most movements, directed by male honchos.

STEPHANIE MILLS, *What Ever Happened to Ecology?*, 1989

69 Environmental threats now vie with nuclear war as the preeminent peril to our species. If the world is to avoid calamity, the environmental movement must take both the tiller and the laboring oar. We must provide the direction and the energy for change.

DENIS HAYES, speech, American Museum of Natural History, New York City, 8 November 1989

70 The inroads Greens have made into German politics are a populist reaction to what is basically an unlivable European environment. The only problem with the Greens is that their defense of the natural world started too late, only after they no longer had anything natural to defend.

JESSE HARDIN, quoted in Christopher Manes, *Green Rage*, 1990

71 Environmentalism may well be the template through which we may finally perceive how power works in our society.

CHRISTOPHER MANES, *Green Rage*, 1990

72 The humanized landscape of Europe has understandably led to a radical ecology movement with its own unique concerns and an ideological turn of mind that sometimes seems to stray from the tangible, earthy questions of ecology.

CHRISTOPHER MANES, *Green Rage*, 1990

73 The true test for American environmentalism is to achieve a better balance between fear of ecological catastrophe and trust in our political system.

BRUCE PIASECKI and PETER ASMUS, *In Search of Environmental Excellence*, 1990

74 Radical environmentalism emerges out of an ecological consciousness that comes from the heart—not the head—that has experienced the natural world.

RIK SCARCE, *Eco-Warriors*, 1990

75 Environmentalism began on the periphery of the economy, saving a bit of landscape here, bottling up some pollution there. The challenges ahead are such that it must spread as creed and code to permeate to the core of economic activity worldwide.

JAMES GUSTAVE SPETH, *Environmental Science and Technology* 24, no. 4, 1990

76 Pessimism is a hallmark of the environmental movement. The movement has grown and prospered by being ever ready to point out new crises just around the corner. Consequently, environmentalists are sometimes accused of being merchants of gloom and doom who push the prospect of imminent catastrophes to recruit members, raise money and increase their political clout. Since they deal with the future, most of these indictments remain to be proved. However, in the immediate past and present, environmentalists have been extraordinarily persuasive.

BILL GILBERT, *Smithsonian*, April 1990

77 Environmentalism or conservation or preservation, or whatever it should be called, is not a fact, and never has been. It is a job.

WALLACE STEGNER, *Smithsonian*, April 1990

78 Nearly every aspect of environmentalism . . . has demonstrated the same pattern: a charismatic and influential individual who discerns a problem and formulates a public concern; a group that forms itself around him or around his ideas, and exerts educational pressure on the public and political pressure on Congress; legislation that creates some new kind of reserve—national park, national

forest, national monument, national wildlife sanctuary or wilderness area; and finally, an increasingly specific body of regulatory law for the protection of what has been set aside.
WALLACE STEGNER, *Smithsonian*, April 1990

79 The environmental movement doesn't have many deserters and has a high level of recruitment. Eventually there will be open war.
PAUL WATSON, *Smithsonian*, April 1990

80 One big lesson I learned was that human flaws inside the movement can damage the cause more than the movement's opponents.
BYRON KENNARD, *Not Man Apart*, April–May 1990

81 [Member churches should] recognize that much of the cause of local and global environmental problems stems from an unwillingness of power elites—including power elites who are members of Christian congregations and power elites in the churches themselves—to talk with, listen to and to be involved with those most affected by environmental problems: the poor, the marginalized, women and indigenous peoples.
WORLD COUNCIL OF CHURCHES, recommendations of advisory group, May 1990

82 If green ideology is guilt transformed into politics, we might wonder why people adopt it. Partly, I think, green ideology appeals to many people's sense of frustration with modern life. Technology is too complicated, work too demanding, communication too instantaneous, information too abundant, the pace of life too fast. Stasis looks attractive, not only for nature but also for human beings.
VIRGINIA I. POSTREL, speech, City Club of Cleveland, Ohio, 19 June 1990

83 The environmental movement has been built on crisis. Around the turn of the century, Americans were terrified of the growing lumber shortage. A 1908 New York *Times* headline read: "Hickory Disappearing, Supply of Wood Nears End—Much Wasted and There's No Substitute." Actually, as prices rose, the railroads—the major consumers of wood—did find substitutes. And more efficient ways of using wood.
VIRGINIA I. POSTREL, speech, City Club of Cleveland, Ohio, 19 June 1990

84 We cannot govern by listening to the loudest voice on the extreme of an environmental movement. . . . I did not rely heavily on them for support in getting elected president of the United States and I'm not going to be persuaded that I can get some brownie points by appealing to one of these groups or another.
GEORGE BUSH, speech, international economic summit, Houston, Texas, 11 July 1990

85 Indeed, rather than becoming a part of nature . . . the actual goal of environmentalism is the opposite: to inculcate a new morality with respect to the natural world that is found nowhere else in nature. No other creature is obligated to protect other species—as the Bible says that Noah was once commanded to do, and as the Endangered Species Act of 1973 again seeks to accomplish.
ROBERT H. NELSON, *Policy Review*, Summer 1990

86 The national concern with pollution of all kinds—in the atmosphere, the sea, the slums, the movie theaters—trembles on the verge of acute hypochondria, and too many signs point unerringly in the direction of a desperate and intolerant wish to cleanse the world of its impurities.
LEWIS H. LAPHAM, *Harper's*, August 1990

87 The environmental movement is a good bridge between individual concerns and social ones.
MARC L. MIRINGOFF, *Christian Science Monitor*, 10 August 1990

88 Saving the earth has never seemed so important, or so confusing. Not only do we have to deal with holes in our ozone layer, toxic seepage in our homes, vanishing lemurs in our burning rain forests, and too damn many copies of *999 Simple Things You Can Do to Embrace the Planet*, we've also got to hack our way through a jungle of environmental organizations that's thick and getting thicker.
BILL GIFFORD, *Outside*, September 1990

89 There is no social or economic issue today that isn't also, by definition, an environmental one.
MIKE GUERRERO, *Buzzworm*, September 1990

90 The environmental movement isn't only about middle-class white people worrying about the preservation of trees and animals and pretty flowers. It's also about people of color preserving the integrity of their communities and the land where they work.

RICHARD MOORE, *Buzzworm*, September–October 1990

91 Environmentalism is no longer about wilderness protection; it's about saving the collective neck of humanity.

MICHAEL OPPENHEIMER, *New York Times Book Review*, 25 November 1990

92 [Unless the environmental movement considers the needs of the poor] environmentalism bodes well to become the imperialism of the 21st century.

THOMAS SPEAR, *Christian Science Monitor*, 30 November 1990

93 Absent is any single source of leadership. There is no jolly green giant emerging from a wetland who speaks for all.

PETER A. A. BERLE, *Audubon*, January 1991

94 The constant flogging of one or another environmental crisis eventually finds its way into the political system, whose solutions tend to be very expensive. If society is expected to accept these imposed costs, it deserves some reassurance that the policies are the result of real science and not just the half-developed theories of tendentious public-interest groups.

WALL STREET JOURNAL, editorial, 11 January 1991

95 Public hysteria is going to destroy industrial civilization. . . . The movement lost its vision. It became corrupted by a few leaders who had their own personal demons, and they set themselves up as gurus of an anti-human, quasi-religious philosophy.

RON ARNOLD, quoted in *Washington Post*, 16 May 1991

96 I'm suggesting a rebellion. . . . I think we ought to take up arms, put these people on notice that this is our livelihood, our jobs, and if we go down we're going to take someone with us.

ROBERT F. SMITH, against the old-growth forest preservationists, quoted in *Washington Post*, 16 May 1991

48 ESTUARIES
See also   16 COASTS

1 [Chesapeake Bay is] an immense outdoor protein factory.

H. L. MENCKEN (1880–1956), *Happy Days*, 1940

2 Estuaries are a happy land, rich in the nutrients of the continent itself, stirred by the forces of nature like the soup of a French chef; the home of myriad forms of life from bacteria and protozoans to grasses and mammals; the nursery, resting place, and refuge of countless species. . . . And estuaries are an unhappy land because of pollution, dredging, and filling, and all of the things that man does to alter and destroy them.

STANLEY A. CAIN, speech, 1966

3 San Francisco Bay is one of the world's great bays and the most significant open space within any major metropolitan area in the United States or abroad. As such, it is an amenity which must be guarded and restored. Its beauty enriches the lives of those who live around it and visit it. Its spaciousness keeps congesting cities at arm's length. It tempers the climate, provides a setting for recreation, and nourishes a rich marine life. All its values depend in some way on its size and natural character, as well as the quality and transparency of the air mass above it.

SIERRA CLUB, October 1966

4 [Estuaries have become] the septic tank of the megalopolis.

PAUL DE FALCO, JR., in *Estuaries*, 1967

5 Many estuaries produce more harvestable human food per acre than the best midwestern farmland.

STANLEY A. CAIN, testimony, U.S. House of Representatives Merchant Marine and Fisheries subcommittee, March 1967

6 [The estuary] is the point where man, the sea—his immemorial ally and adversary—and the land meet and challenge each other.

U.S. DEPARTMENT OF THE INTERIOR, National Estuarine Pollution Study, November 1969

7 If the Chesapeake Bay were located in Japan, they could manage its resources so it would be

capable of producing enough food to feed their entire country.

WILLIAM C. BAKER, quoting a group of Japanese scientists, quoted in *Conservation Foundation Letter,* March–April 1984

8 Broad, beautiful, productive, mysterious, polluted . . . how many are the adjectives we reach for in trying to describe our beloved Chesapeake. I would suggest a new one that may lend some perspective to most of the others. When you think of the bay, think THIN.

TOM HORTON, *Bay Country,* 1987

49 ETHICS
See also   117 RELIGION

1 In the relations of man with the animals, with the flowers, with the objects of creation, there is a great ethic, scarcely perceived as yet, which will at length break forth into the light and which will be the corollary and complement to human ethics.

VICTOR HUGO (1802–1885), *En voyage, Alpes et Pyrénées,* 1867

2 [In man's moral development, his "social instincts and sympathies" gradually extended beyond himself to his fellow men until they] became more tender and widely diffused, extending to men of all races, to the imbecile, maimed, and other useless members of society, and finally to the lower animals.

CHARLES DARWIN (1809–1882), *The Descent of Man,* 1871

3 Love the animals, love the plants, love everything. If you love everything, you will perceive the divine mystery in things. Once you perceive it, you will begin to comprehend it better every day. And you will come at last to love the whole world with an all-embracing love.

FYODOR DOSTOYEVSKY, *The Brothers Karamazov,* 1880

4 [The ethical person] shatters no ice crystal that sparkles in the sun, tears no leaf from its tree, breaks off no flower, and is careful not to crush any insect as he walks.

ALBERT SCHWEITZER (1875–1965), *Philosophy of Civilization: Civilization and Ethics,* 1923

5 The basis of any real morality must be the sense of kinship between all living beings.

HENRY SALT, *The Creed of Kinship,* 1935

6 All ethics so far evolved rest upon a single premise: that the individual is a member of a community of interdependent parts. His instincts prompt him to compete for his place in the community, but his ethics prompt him also to co-operate (perhaps in order that there may be a place to compete for).

The land ethic simply enlarges the boundaries of the community to include soils, waters, plants, and animals, or collectively: the land.

ALDO LEOPOLD (1886–1948), *A Sand County Almanac,* 1949

7 No important change in ethics was ever accomplished without an internal change in our intellectual emphasis, loyalties, affections, and convictions. The proof that conservation has not yet touched these foundations of conduct lies in the fact that philosophy and religion have not yet heard of it. In our attempt to make conservation easy, we have made it trivial.

ALDO LEOPOLD (1886–1948), *A Sand County Almanac,* 1949

8 Examine each [land-use] question in terms of what is ethically right, as well as what is economically expedient. A thing is right when it tends to preserve the integrity, stability, and beauty of the biotic community. It is wrong when it tends otherwise.

ALDO LEOPOLD (1886–1948), *A Sand County Almanac,* 1949

9 There is as yet no ethic dealing with man's relation to land and to the animals and plants which grow upon it. Land, like Odysseus' slave-girls, is still property. The land-relation is still strictly economic, entailing privileges but not obligations.

ALDO LEOPOLD (1886–1948), *A Sand County Almanac,* 1949

10 Ethics are possibly a kind of community instinct in-the-making.

ALDO LEOPOLD (1886–1948), *Round River,* 1953

11 Man's violence towards his surroundings is just as sinful as his violence towards his fellows.

DONALD E. ENGEL, *Zygon,* September 1970

12 [There is] a serious risk that preoccupation over dirty air, foul streams and poisoned estuaries may blind us to the dismal fact that for too many millions of our citizens, the threshold test of environment is adequate housing reasonably accessible to jobs. . . . [This] must surely be as legitimate an endeavor in an ethical society as resting places for terns.

RICHARD F. BABCOCK, testimony, U.S. Senate Interior Committee, 23 June 1971

13 Environmental leadership . . . must achieve new intensities of insight and action, enforcing the laws, passing new ones, and finding positive means to manage man's habitat. But in spirit it must rise to advance everyman's living condition, by showing the way to a prosperity that is at peace with natural and man-made systems. Let us attack the most degraded human environments hard, at home and abroad, without lessening our concern for the earth's wild treasures. Whatever our own missions may be, let our ecological view encompass rats and revolvers, paychecks and pollution. Conservation for the club alone has no place among us.

SYDNEY HOWE, Conservation Foundation Letter, December 1971

14 Man must feel the earth to know himself and recognize his values. . . . God made life simple. It is man who complicates it.

CHARLES A. LINDBERGH (1902–1974), Reader's Digest, July 1972

15 Do people have ethical obligations toward rocks? . . . To almost all Americans, still saturated with ideas historically dominant in Christianity . . . the question makes no sense at all. If the time comes when to any considerable group of us such a question is no longer ridiculous, we may be on the verge of a change of value structures that will make possible measures to cope with the growing ecologic crisis. One hopes that there is enough time left.

LYNN I. WHITE, JR., in Ian G. Barbour, ed., Western Man and Environmental Ethics, 1973

16 We do need a "new metaphysics" which is genuinely not anthropocentric. . . . The working out of such a metaphysics is, in my judgment, the most important task which lies ahead of philosophy . . . the emergence of new moral attitudes to nature is bound up then with the emergence of a more realistic philosophy of nature. This is the only adequate foundation for effective environmental concern.

JOHN PASSMORE, Man's Responsibility for Nature, 1974

17 Speciesism [comparable to racism and sexism] is the belief that we are entitled to treat members of another species in a way in which it would be wrong to treat members of our own.

PETER SINGER, Philosophic Exchange, Summer 1974

18 Far from being peripheral concerns, [values] are in fact dominant, driving variables in all human systems, whether technological or social. [But] values and insights are driven into hiding by our culture's insane commitment to objectification, to linear, reductionist, inductive, rationalistic, quantitative, logical, positivist forms of cognition—the whole Cartesian trip.

HAZEL HENDERSON, speech, World Future Society, June 1975

19 [T]he "environmental perspective" is deeply embedded in the social and political fabric of our existence. It has become a penetrating and pervasive feature of our daily lives, influencing our judgments, our moral positions, our systems of belief, and our everyday conduct. But, as with all fundamental social issues, the environmental perspective offers neither reconciliation nor peaceful resolution, but rather a set of tantalizing contractions or divergent patterns of belief and action which constantly defy solution yet persistently invite a striving for mediation.

T. O. RIORDAN, Environmentalism, 1976

20 It is intriguing to dwell on the possibility that the quest today for an environmental ethic is an effort to recover something that has been lost rather than to discover something new. Primitive man may well have possessed an ethic that extended well beyond his fellow men, one which embraced plants and animals, even mountains and rivers, all seen as members of his community and subject to

ethical restraints. It is possible that, under the pressures of individualism, competition, technology, nationalism, and capitalism, mankind gradually lost this broad ethical perspective. Today, under the countervailing pressures of internationalism, exhaustion of resources, revision of priorities, and a growing understanding of ecological reality, we may be recovering—or rediscovering—something our ancestors instinctively grasped.

RODERICK F. NASH, *Center,* November–December 1977

21 We must instill the morality and ethics of conservation in the fiber of contemporary consciousness.

ROGER CARAS, speech on protecting endangered wildlife, Yale School of Forestry symposium, 10 April 1978

22 The recognition of sanctity appears to be a necessary prerequisite for the preservation of life worth living in the long run.

HENRYK SKOLIMOWSKI, on the sanctity of life, *Ecologist Quarterly,* Autumn 1978

23 Humanistic value systems must be replaced by supra-humanistic values that bring all plant and animal life into the sphere of legal, moral and ethical consideration.

GREENPEACE, *Greenpeace Chronicles,* 1979

24 We must each find the answer, not only in our political, economic and social systems, but also in our own consciences.

ANTONY CHRISTIANARVIS, World Environment Day/International Year of the Child Poster Contest, Environment Liaison Centre, Nairobi, Kenya, 23 January 1979

25 Whatever the social distance separating birdwatchers and welfare mothers, in a vital sense they share a lot of common ground. At bottom, because the world is a single living body, the interests of the poor and the interests of the environment are the same. It's not an accident that most ecological enthusiasts are strong liberals, or that the voting record of the congressional black caucus on environmental issues looks much better than the record of congressmen from the rural West or the entire Deep South and the Southwest. Philosophically speaking, the spokesmen for the natural world and of the poor (two op-

pressed areas) are fighting for the freedom of self-determination.

PETER HEINEGG, *Environmental Ethics,* Winter 1979

26 A land ethic changes the role of *Homo sapiens* from conqueror of the land community to plain member and citizen of it. It implies respect for fellow-members *and also* respect for the community as such.

J. BAIRD CALLICOTT, *Matters of Life and Death,* 1980

27 [Saint] Francis [of Assisi] tried to depose man from his monarchy over creation and set up a democracy of all God's creatures.

GEORGE SESSIONS, essay, *Earth Day X Colloquium,* 1980

28 A fundamental difference appears between [Albert] Schweitzer's principle of Reverence for Life, which proclaims the intrinsic and sacred value of life itself—"A man is ethical only when life, as such, is sacred to him"—and the seeming worship of the ecological niche, which is but a worship of our physical resources.

HENRYK SKOLIMOWSKI, *Eco-Philosophy,* 1981

29 [It is argued that] the reason why we should take care of the ecological habitat is because it takes care of us. It would be counterproductive to destroy it, therefore we should preserve it. It is a principle of *good management* to take good care of our resources. So, in the final analysis, the ecological habitat becomes a *resource.* The ecological ethic is thus based on a calculus of optimization of our resources. It becomes an *instrumental* ethic: the ecological habitat is not a value in itself but only an instrument, a means of supporting us.

HENRYK SKOLIMOWSKI, *Eco-Philosophy,* 1981

30 Natural philosophy has brought into clear relief the following paradox of human existence. The drive toward perpetual expansion—or personal freedom—is basic to the human spirit. But to sustain it we need the most delicate, knowing stewardship of the living world that can be devised. Expansion and stewardship may appear at first to be conflicting goals, but they are not. The depth of the conservation ethic will be measured by the extent to which each of the two ap-

proaches to nature is used to reshape and re-inforce the other. The paradox can be resolved by changing its premises into forms more suited to ultimate survival, by which I mean protection of the human spirit.

EDWARD O. WILSON, *Biophilia*, 1984

31 All things in the biosphere have an equal right to live and blossom and to reach their own individual forms of unfolding and self-realization.

BILL DEVALL and GEORGE SESSIONS, *Deep Ecology*, 1985

32 Deep ecology goes beyond a limited piece-meal shallow approach to environmental problems and attempts to articulate a com-prehensive . . . philosophical worldview. . . . [Its] basic insight . . . of biocentric equality is that all things in the biosphere have an equal right to live and blossom and to reach their own individual forms of . . . self-realization.

BILL DEVALL and GEORGE SESSIONS, *Deep Ecology*, 1985

33 I will argue that, once we are willing to view the natural world from a standpoint that is not anthropocentric, the desirability of hu-man life is a claim that needs rational sub-stantiation. It cannot just be assumed with-out question. Indeed, to assume it without question is already to commit oneself to an anthropocentric point of view concerning the natural world and the place of humans in it, and this is to beg some of the most funda-mental issues of environmental ethics.

PAUL W. TAYLOR, *Respect for Nature*, 1986

34 While human ethics has to do with the moral relations holding among human beings themselves and environmental ethics with the moral relations between humans and the natural world, the ethics of the bioculture is concerned with the human treatment of ani-mals and plants in artificially created environ-ments that are completely under human control.

PAUL W. TAYLOR, *Respect for Nature*, 1986

35 [Environmental ethics] is made up of three components: a belief-system, an ultimate moral attitude, and a set of moral rules and standards. These elements stand in relation to each other in the same way that the three components of human ethics are interrelated. The belief-system supports and makes intelli-gible the adopting of the attitude, and the rules and standards give concrete expression to that attitude in practical life.

PAUL W. TAYLOR, *Respect for Nature*, 1986

36 If there is a just God, how humanity would writhe in its attempt to justify its treatment of animals.

ISAAC ASIMOV, *Isaac Asimov's Book of Science and Nature Quotations*, 1988

37 It is time for a new American hegemony based on moral, humane, and technical strengths, on a stewardship of earth and its people that takes advantage of American id-iosyncracies—our optimism, our generosity, our love of nature, our growing awareness of environmental threats, our strong indepen-dent sector, and our technological ingenuity.

CHARLES E. LITTLE, in Peter Borelli, ed., *Crossroads*, 1988

38 How far are we justified in rearranging the foundations of creation to better serve our own purposes? That depends on how closely our purposes mirror the creation's purposes. What are these purposes? Until we reflect more deeply and seriously on this ques-tion . . . , it seems that right action in the world is best approximated by some com-monsense rules: if it ain't broke, don't fix it; if you must tinker, save all the pieces; and, if you don't know where you're going, slow down.

HERMAN E. DALY and JOHN B. COBB, JR., *For the Common Good*, 1989

39 From the perspective of intellectual history, environmental ethics is revolutionary; it is ar-guably the most dramatic expansion of mo-rality in the course of human thought.

RODERICK F. NASH, *The Rights of Nature*, 1989

40 There are, then, two separate debates about environmental values. One debate is *intellec-tual*, the other is *strategic*. The first debate concerns the *correct moral stance* toward na-ture. The second debate concerns which moral stance, or rationale, is likely to be *effec-tive* in saving wild species and natural eco-systems.

BRYAN G. NORTON, *Conservation for the 21st Century*, 1989

41 There was an eighty-seven year hiatus from the Declaration of Independence to the Emancipation Proclamation and the freeing of American blacks from slavery. . . . The idea of an inalienable right of self-determination has moved with irresistible force to become what Jefferson claimed it was in 1776: a self-evident truth. . . . It is now nature's turn to be liberated.
    DONALD WORSTER, in Roderick F. Nash, *The Rights of Nature*, 1989

42 We are the generation that searched on Mars for evidence of life but couldn't rouse enough moral sense to stop the destruction of even the grandest manifestations of life on earth. In that sense we are like the Romans whose works of art, architecture and engineering inspire our awe but whose traffic in slaves and gladiatorial combat is mystifying and loathsome.
    ROGER PAYNE, in Anna Sequoia, *67 Ways to Save the Animals*, 1990

43 A century ago, the greatest dangers we faced arose from agents outside ourselves: microbes, flood and famine, wolves in the forest at night. Today the greatest dangers—war, pollution, starvation—have their source in our own motives and sentiments: greed and hostility, carelessness and arrogance, narcissism and nationalism. The study of values might once have been a matter of primarily individual concern and deliberation as to how best to lead the "good life." Today it is a matter of collective human survival.
    M. SCOTT PECK, in Hunter Lewis, *A Question of Values*, 1990

44 Without a global revolution in the sphere of human consciousness, nothing will change for the better in the sphere of our being as humans, and the catastrophe toward which this world is headed—be it ecological, social, demographic or a general breakdown of civilization—will be unavoidable.
    VACLAV HAVEL, address to U.S. Congress, 21 February 1990

45 In this setting of anxiety, two principles are essential. First, scientific knowledge and ecological expertise are vital if people are to understand *what* to do. But secondly and equally important are the moral and ethical aspects—the religious dimension—which help people understand *why* they should care for nature.
    PRINCE PHILIP, duke of Edinburgh, *WWF News*, July–August 1990

46 If we faced a truly either/or decision between the goods of a stable economy for the present generation and survival of conditions for life of future generations, how would ethics guide us?
    SARA EBENRECK, *Catholic World*, July–August 1990

50 FISHERIES

1 That fish which is bred in the dirt will always taste of the mud.
    WILLIAM CLOWES (1544–1604), *Treatise for the Artificial Cure of Struma*, 1602

2 [The Potomac River] aboundeth with all manner of fish. The Indians in one night will catch 30 sturgeons in a place where the river is not above 12 fathoms broad.
    HENRY FLEETE, journal, 1632

3 We must plant the sea and herd its animals . . . using the sea as farmers instead of hunters. That is what civilization is all about—farming replacing hunting. . . . [I]n the sea we act like barbarians.
    JACQUES COUSTEAU, interview, 17 July 1971

4 [Oil] drilling on Georges Bank at this time amounts to playing Russian roulette with our fishing resources.
    MILTON OLIVER, testimony, Bureau of Land Management hearing, 1976

5 Underfishing is a sin of omission, overfishing a crime against humanity.
    PEDRO OJEDA PAULLADA, quoted in *American Journal of International Law*, October 1983

6 Methods of fishing are becoming more and more efficient but the whole fishing industry is based on the exploitation of a wild population. This is almost a prehistoric concept on land, but it has never been questioned at sea.
    PRINCE PHILIP, duke of Edinburgh, *Men, Machines, and Sacred Cows*, 1984

7 The development of extensive mariculture will require the identification of marine property rights. . . . First, we can create private property in the sea as we have done on land. Second, we might create public property in the sea; governments would control the resource and could sell off parts as they see fit. Finally, common property can be created and the rights of use can be defined for equal users.
EDWARD D. GOLDBERG, *Environmental Science and Technology*, 24, no. 4, April 1990

8 Strains of fish that grow bigger faster and are resistant to diseases could spark a "blue revolution" in aquaculture in the way fertilizers, herbicides, and pesticides sparked a "green revolution" in agriculture.
GARETH L. FLETCHER, *New York Times*, 27 November 1990

9 Stripmining the seas.
EARTH FIRST, on drift-net fishing, which injures or kills many nontarget species, quoted on "Frontline," PBS, 22 May 1991

---

51 FORESTRY
See also 22 DEFORESTATION, 52 FORESTS, 131 TROPICAL FORESTS

---

1 Nothing is less known; nothing more neglected. The forest is a gift of nature which it is sufficient to accept just as it comes from her hands.
GEORGES-LOUIS LECLERC, COMTE DE BUFFON (1707–1788), *Histoire de l'Académie Royale des Sciences, Mémoires*, 1742

2 What will the axemen do, when they have cut their way from sea to sea?
JAMES FENIMORE COOPER (1789–1851), *The Pioneers*, 1823

3 We are, even now breaking up the floor and wainscotting and doors and window frames of our dwelling.
GEORGE PERKINS MARSH, on wasteful forestry practices, *Man and Nature*, 1864

4 These great bodies of reserved lands cannot be withdrawn from all occupation and use.

They must be made to perform their part in the economy of the Nation.
NATIONAL FOREST COMMISSION, report, 1 May 1897

5 Sequoias, kings of their race, growing close together like grass in a meadow, poised their brave domes and spires in the sky three hundred feet above the ferns and lilies that enameled the ground; towering serene through the long centuries, preaching God's forestry fresh from heaven.
JOHN MUIR (1838–1914), *Atlantic Monthly*, August 1897

6 Forestry is the preservation of forests by wise use.
THEODORE ROOSEVELT (1858–1919), first message to Congress, December 1901

7 The object of our forest policy is not to preserve the forests because they are beautiful—or because they are refuges for the wild creatures of the wilderness—but the making of prosperous homes—every other consideration becomes secondary.
GIFFORD PINCHOT (1865–1946), speech, 1903

8 Millions of board feet of prime timber are needlessly lost each year [in the parks because of] laws enacted to satisfy ill-advised pressure groups in search of a "worthy cause."
RAYONIER, INC., advertisement in *Time*, 1953

9 As we urbanize, the green leaf is becoming increasingly important to our content and well-being. The eastern forest of the United States, which has little or no timber value and a rapidly declining significance for fuel supplies, is approaching its zenith of service to mankind as the suburban forest, the pleasance of the people.
FRANK FRASER DARLING, *Daedalus*, Fall 1967

10 When there are homeless people in the world, there is no more a right to waste wood than there is a right to waste food when there are hungry people. Whether people like it or not, the old forest must make way for the new.
W. D. HAGENSTEIN, *Environmental Law*, Summer 1978

11 Loggers and environmentalists might seem to have little in common, but many share at least one thing: acceptance of the "either/or" fallacy: Either we have biological diversity or timber production.
ELLIOT NORSE, *Ancient Forests of the Pacific Northwest*, 1989

12 [The commercial lumber industry] didn't discover forestry, and practice tending forests and regrowing them, until after World War II. Companies only *harvested* prior to that. . . . We've made most of the mistakes. But the United States is large enough and has such a variety of forests and relatively low population pressures, that when we screwed up the East, the Great Lakes states and the South, we had the West to move to. With exceptions, such as the Tennessee Valley, we didn't denude cutover lands. We didn't eliminate the natural cover and degrade the soil. We harvested our interest, but we didn't bankrupt our principal.
STANLEY L. KRUGMAN, quoted in *Los Angeles Times*, 22 June 1989

13 Liquidating old-growth is not forestry, it is simply spending our inheritance. Nor is planting a monoculture . . . forestry; it is simply plantation management.
CHRIS MASER, *World Watch*, July–August 1990

14 Save a Logger—Eat a Spotted Owl.
ANONYMOUS, quoted in *Probe Post*, Spring 1990

15 Somehow we should have the wit and will to preserve our forest heritage and maintain a steady flow of lumber to our markets.
DANIEL J. EVANS, address, University of Washington, Seattle, 9 June 1990

16 Sustainable logging means jobs forever.
RHONA MAHONEY, *E* magazine, November–December 1990

17 We have now used taxpayers' dollars to build so many roads for loggers that their total length is equal to eight times the entire length of the whole Interstate Highway System. That just does not make sense.
ALBERT GORE, U.S. Senator, *Conservation 90* 8, no. 10, December 1990

52 FORESTS

See also 51 FORESTRY, 130 TREES, 131 TROPICAL FORESTS

1 The forest is the poor man's overcoat.
NEW ENGLAND PROVERB

2 Forests were the first temples of the Divinity, and it is in the forests that men have grasped the first idea of architecture.
FRANÇOIS-RENE DE CHATEAUBRIAND (1768–1848), *Génie du christianisme*, 1802

3 Who can describe the sentiment one feels when entering forests as old as the world, forests which alone provide an idea of the creation, as it left the hands of God?
FRANÇOIS-RENE DE CHATEAUBRIAND (1768–1848), *Voyage en Amérique*

4 No site in the forest is without significance, not a glade, not a thicket that does not provide analogies to the labyrinth of human thoughts. Who among those people with a cultivated spirit, or whose heart has been wounded, can walk in a forest without the forest speaking to him? . . . If one searched for the causes of that sensation, at once solemn, simple, gentle, mysterious, that seizes one, perhaps it would be found in the sublime and ingenious spectacle of all the creatures obeying their destinies, immutably docile.
HONORE DE BALZAC (1799–1850), *Le curé de village*, 1839

5 This is the forest primeval. The murmuring
   pines and the hemlocks . . .
Stand like Druids of old.
HENRY WADSWORTH LONGFELLOW (1807–1882), *Evangeline*, 1847

6 [Michael Astroff] says that forests are the ornaments of the earth, that they teach mankind to understand beauty and attune his mind to lofty sentiments. Forests temper a stern climate, and in countries where the climate is milder, less strength is wasted in the battle with nature, and the people are kind and gentle.
ANTON CHEKHOV (1860–1904), *Uncle Vanya*, 1897

7 When I cross those pleasant forests which I have saved from the axe, or hear the rustling

of the young trees, which I have set out with my own hands, I feel as if I had had some small share in improving the climate, and that if mankind is happy a thousand years from now I shall have been partly responsible in my small way for their happiness. When I plant a young birch tree and see it budding and swaying in the wind, my heart swells with pride.

ANTON CHEKHOV (1860–1904), *Uncle Vanya*, 1897

8 I . . . thanked the Author of my being for the gift of that wild forest, those green mansions where I had found so great a happiness!

WILLIAM HENRY HUDSON (1841–1922), *Green Mansions*, 1904

9 The forest stretched no living man knew how far. That was the dead, sealed world of the vegetable kingdom, an uncharted continent with interlocking trees, living, dead, half-dead, their roots in bogs and swamps, strangling each other in a slow agony that had lasted for centuries. The forest was suffocation, annihilation.

WILLA CATHER (1873–1947), *Shadows on the Rock*, 1931

10 Many of our greatest American thinkers, men of the caliber of Thomas Jefferson, Henry Thoreau, Mark Twain, William James, and John Muir, have found the forests an effective stimulus to original thought.

ROBERT MARSHALL, *The People's Forests*, 1933

11 [Forests are] the "lungs" of our land, purifying the air and giving fresh strength to our people.

FRANKLIN D. ROOSEVELT (1883–1945), speech, 29 January 1935

12 The potential output of the 9,000 million acres of world forest . . . indicate[s] that the forests can be made to produce about 50 times their present volume of end products and still remain a permanently self-renewing source for our raw-material supplies. Only forests—no other raw-material resource—can yield such returns. The forest can, and so must, end the chronic scarcities of material goods that have harassed man's existence since the beginning of history.

EGON GLESINGER, *The Coming Age of Wood*, 1949

13 Guéorgui loved the forest, this forest as old as a legend, gentle as a mother and stern as a father.

NICOLAÏ LEVKOV, *La terre pleure*, 1958

14 In Canada there is too much of everything. Too much rock, too much prairie, too much tundra, too much mountain, too much forest. Above all, too much forest. Even the man who passionately believes that he shall never see a poem as lovely as a tree will be disposed to give poetry another try after he has driven the Trans-Canada Highway.

EDWARD MCCOURT, *The Road Across Canada*, 1965

15 Old-growth forests remind me of an old folks home, just waiting to die.

ANONYMOUS REAGAN ADMINISTRATION OFFICIAL, 1984, quoted in Bill Devall and George Sessions, *Deep Ecology*, 1985

16 Humanity is cutting down its forests, apparently oblivious to the fact that we may not be able to live without them.

ISAAC ASIMOV, *Isaac Asimov's Book of Science and Nature Quotations*, 1988

17 I am trying to save the knowledge that the forests and this planet are alive, to give it back to you who have lost the understanding.

PAULINHO PAIAKAN, leader of the Kayapo of Brazil, in Julian Burger, *The Gaia Atlas of First Peoples*, 1990

18 There are no such things as natural landscapes in Amazonia, the forest has been moulded by native peoples. The monuments of their civilization are not cities and temples, but the natural environment itself.

DARRELL POSEY, in Julian Burger, *The Gaia Atlas of First Peoples*, 1990

19 At first, the people talking about ecology were only defending the fishes, the animals, the forest, and the river. They didn't realize that human beings were in the forest—and that these humans were the real ecologists, because they couldn't live without the forest and the forest couldn't be saved without them.

OSMARINO AMANCIO RODRIGUES, quoted in Andrew Revkin, *The Burning Season*, 1990

20 A well-tended garden is better than a neglected woodlot.

DIXIE LEE RAY, *Trashing the Planet*, 1990

53 FUTURE
See also 100 PLANNING, FORESIGHT

1 All the flowers of all the tomorrows are in the seeds of today.
CHINESE PROVERB

2 We have not inherited the world from our forefathers—we have borrowed it from our children.
KASHMIRI PROVERB

3 In our every deliberation, we must consider the impact of our decisions on the next seven generations.
IROQUOIS CONFEDERATION, 18th century, attributed

4 It has been my opinion, that he who receives an Estate from his ancestors is under some kind of obligation to transmit the same to their posterity.
BENJAMIN FRANKLIN (1706–1790), codicil to will, 1789

5 I hold that man is in the right who is most clearly in league with the future.
HENRIK IBSEN (1828–1906), letter to George Brandes, 3 January 1882

6 There is wide agreement that the state should protect the interests of the future in some degree against the effects of our irrational discounting, and of our preference for ourselves over our descendants. The whole movement for "conservation" in the United States is based upon this conviction. It is the clear duty of government which is the trustee for unborn generations as well as for its present citizens, to watch over and if need be, by legislative enactment, to defend exhaustible natural resources of the country from rash and reckless spoliation.
A. C. PIGOU, The Economics of Welfare, 1924

7 The wild things of this earth are not ours to do with as we please. They have been given to us in trust, and we must account for them to the generations which will come after us and audit our accounts.
WILLIAM T. HORNADAY (1854–1937), quoted in Kathryn A. Kohm, ed., Balancing on the Brink of Extinction, 1991

8 I believe that this generation may either be the last to exist or the first to have the vision, the daring and the greatness to say, "I will have nothing to do with the destruction of life; I will play no part in this devastation of the land; I am destined to live and work for peaceful construction for I am morally responsible for the world of today and the generations of tomorrow."
RICHARD ST. BARBE BAKER, The New Earth Charter, 1950

9 The earth we abuse and the living things we kill will, in the end, take their revenge; for in exploiting their presence we are diminishing our future.
MARYA MANNES, More in Anger, 1958

10 Man's autonomous decisions are the only factors that are capable of transforming the future. Otherwise, the future rolls on and we roll with it or roll under it, as the case may be.
LEWIS MUMFORD, in Frank F. Darling and John P. Milton, eds., Future Environments of North America, 1966

11 Although I'm sometimes pessimistic about man's future, I don't believe him to be innately evil. I'm more worried about his insatiable curiosity than I am about his poor character: his preoccupation with the moon is disturbing to me, particularly since his own rivers run dirty and his air is getting fouler every year.
E. B. WHITE, letter to Judith W. Preusser, 25 February 1966

12 Our ideals, laws and customs should be based on the proposition that each generation, in turn, becomes the custodian rather than the absolute owner of our resources—and each generation has the obligation to pass this inheritance on to the future.
CHARLES A. LINDBERGH (1902–1974), quoted in New York Times Magazine, 23 May 1971

13 I think the present ecological crisis is an eschatological crisis: a crisis about the future. Part of it is caused by the approach of the year 2000, which is a magic number; it's a millennial year, so everyone has started to worry about the way things are going. It's an apocalyptic sort of fear.
KENNETH E. BOULDING, in Anne Chisholm, Philosophers of the Earth: Conversations with Ecologists, 1972

14 Worse yet, will [men] not curse these future generations whose claims to life can be hon-

ored only by sacrificing present enjoyments; and will [men] not, if it comes to a choice, condemn them to nonexistence by choosing the present over the future?

ROBERT L. HEILBRONER, *An Inquiry into the Human Prospect,* 1974

15 If the human species is to survive, man must develop a *sense of identification with future generations* and be ready to trade benefits to the next generations for the benefits to himself.

MIHAJLO MESAROVIC and EDWARD PESTEL, speech, World Future Society, June 1975

16 The irony of the matter is that future generations do not have a vote. In effect, we hold their proxies.

CHARLES J. HITCH, Resources for the Future, annual report, 1976

17 The development of civilization, an exceptionally rapid event on the time scale of geological history, has radically changed the outlook for the further existence of the biosphere.

M. I. BUDYKO, *Climatic Changes,* American Geophysical Union, 1977

18 I think that some of the people who warn us about environmental crisis have got their perspectives wrong. Indeed, I think they are wrong to call it a crisis at all. A crisis is a situation that will pass; it can be resolved by temporary hardship, temporary adjustment, technological and political expedients. What we are experiencing is not a crisis: it is a climacteric. For the rest of man's history on earth, so far as one can foretell, he will have to live with problems of population, of resources, of pollution.

ERIC ASHBY, *Reconciling Man with Environment,* 1978

19 There must be a common denominator that gives priority to the needs and desires of this generation of people. Future generations will cope with future problems. . . . Protect if we can, alter if necessary, destroy if we must, but above all, may it never be said that we failed our obligation of meeting the needs and desires of our generation under the guise of planning for the future.

CALIFORNIA ASSOCIATION OF FOUR-WHEEL DRIVE CLUBS, quoted by Joseph Bodovitz in Conservation Foundation, *Conservation and Values,* 1978

20 It is my belief that the people who are alive today may be the last generation that can significantly alter the future of the world. By this I mean the long-term future, such as forever.

RAYMOND F. DASMANN, speech, 1979, quoted in Stephanie Mills, *What Ever Happened to Ecology?,* 1989

21 If present trends continue, the world in 2000 will be more crowded, more polluted, less stable ecologically and more vulnerable to disruption than the world we live in now.

COUNCIL ON ENVIRONMENTAL QUALITY, *Global 2000 Report,* 1980

22 Our obligation to provide future individuals with an environment consistent with ideals we know to be good is not, necessarily, an obligation to those individuals, but to the ideals themselves. It is an obligation to civilization to continue civilization: to pass on to future generations a heritage, natural and cultural, that can be valued and enjoyed without absurdity.

MARK SAGOFF, *Environmental Law* 12, 1982

23 What do you do when the past is no longer a guide to the future?

JESSE ANSUBEL, *Fortune,* 4 July 1988

24 People need to see the environment as a cause that is positive, hopeful and attractive. The costs that we bear to maintain the environment and improve it have to be seen as highly worthwhile investments in our future, as important as investments in education, science and defense.

WILLIAM K. REILLY, quoted in *New York Times,* 22 February 1989

25 We have, at most, ten years, to embark on some undertakings if we are to avoid crossing some dire environmental thresholds. Individually, each of us can do only a little. Together, we can save the world.

DENIS HAYES, speech, Museum of Natural History, New York City, 8 November 1989

26 There is a certain magic about the number 21 in our society, and perhaps the 21st century will be an age of maturity by comparison with the adolescent centuries of wild growth and disorder that have preceded it. If this is to happen, we must have very widespread images of the future that will lead us towards it.

KENNETH E. BOULDING, in Norman Myers, *Gaia Atlas of Future Worlds,* 1990

27　We believe the apocalypse is at hand, and the reasons for that belief are overwhelming: chemical and biological weapons, nuclear proliferation, deforestation, the greenhouse effect, ozone depletion, acid rain, the poisoning of our air and water, rising racism, massive species loss, toxic waste, the AIDS pandemic, the continuing population explosion, encroaching Big Brotherism, and at least a thousand points of blight. These aren't just conversation topics for yuppie cocktail parties; they're grade A, unadulterated harbingers of destruction, 100 percent bona fide specters of doom, and they're all proof that we don't need God to end it for us. The coming end will be a strictly do-it-yourself apocalypse.

DOOM (Society for Secular Armageddonism), telephone hot-line message, 1990

28　Eco-justice is nothing less than taking seriously the destiny of humanity and the planet on which we live. If there is a future, it will be Green.

PETRA K. KELLY, Fletcher Forum of World Affairs 14, no. 2, Summer 1990

29　Which is the better fate, to be remembered by those grandchildren we don't have or reviled by those we do?

DANIEL B. LUTEN, speech, population symposium, Washington, D.C., 20 April 1990

30　The idea of posterity . . . is . . . the hallmark of all great leaders, from Moses on down.

CHARLES E. LITTLE, Wilderness, Autumn 1990

31　The ultimate irony would be if the world would not end.

ANONYMOUS IRISH PRIEST, quoted by Eugene McCarthy in personal correspondance to the compiler, 31 December 1990

54 GAIA HYPOTHESIS
See also　26 EARTH, 49 ETHICS

1　The envelope of life, namely, the area of living matter. . . . The biosphere can be regarded as the area of the earth's crust occupied by transformers that convert cosmic radiation into effective terrestrial energy—electrical, chemical, mechanical, thermal, etc.

VLADIMIR VERNADSKY, 1911, quoted in James Lovelock, The Ages of Gaia, 1990

2　It is the contributions and activities of the plants, bacteria, algae, and the protozoans that carry weight. We vertebrates are the silverfish and cockroaches of this great house, living marginally, in the interstices, profiting from a structure built for and maintained by a different order of being.

FRED HAPGOOD, explaining the Gaia hypothesis, Atlantic Monthly, December 1977

3　This new interrelationship of Gaia with man is by no means fully established; we are not yet a truly collective species, corralled and tamed as an integral part of the biosphere, as we are as individual creatures. It may be that the destiny of mankind is to become tamed so that the fierce, destructive, and greedy forces of tribalism and nationalism are fused into a compulsive urge to belong to the commonwealth of all creatures which constitutes Gaia.

JAMES E. LOVELOCK, Gaia: A New Look at Life, 1979

4　The Gaia hypothesis, that Earth is a single huge organism intentionally creating an optimum environment for itself, has been made palatable; interesting science is coming of it.

RICHARD A. KERR, Science, 22 April 1988

5　The Gaialike feedback loop . . . would link the microscopic phytoplankton living near the sea surface and the reflectivity of stratus clouds and thus climate.

RICHARD A. KERR, Science, 22 April 1988

6　[The Gaia hypothesis holds that] the nonliving and the living represent a self-regulating system that keeps itself in a constant state.

JAMES E. LOVELOCK, Science, 22 April 1988

7　Our concept of the individual is totally warped. All of us are walking communities of microbes. Plants are sedentary communities. Every plant and animal on Earth today is a symbiont, living in close contact with others.

LYNN MARGULIS, on the Gaia hypothesis, Smithsonian, August 1989

8　Some of us still get all weepy when we think about the Gaia Hypothesis, the idea that the earth is a big furry goddess-creature who resembles everybody's mom in that she knows what's best for us. But if you look at the historical record—Krakatoa, Mt. Vesuvius, Hurricane Charley, poison ivy, and so forth down the ages—you have to ask yourself: Whose side is she on, anyway?

BARBARA EHRENREICH, *The Worst Years of Our Lives*, 1990

9 The Gaia Hypothesis is a whole range of things at once, hence the cloud of acrimony and enthusiasm which doggedly accompanies it. On the one hand, it's a serious and testable hypothesis in planetary astronomy; on the other hand (and this has not made the winning of scientific credibility any easier), it's a nucleus thrown into a culture desperate for alternative organizing metaphors through which to understand its relationship to nature.

YAAKOV GARB, in Stephanie Mills, ed., *In Praise of Nature*, 1990

10 The Gaia Hypothesis asserts that Earth's atmosphere is continuously interacting with geology (the lithosphere), Earth's cycling waters (the hydrosphere), and everything that lives (the biosphere). . . . The image is that the atmosphere is a circulatory system for life's biochemical interplay. If the atmosphere is part of a larger whole that has some of the qualities of an organism, one of those qualities we now must pray for is resilience.

STEPHANIE MILLS, ed., *In Praise of Nature*, 1990

11 The entire reach of the biospheric envelope is less than thirty to forty miles from ocean floor to outer space, a distance that, were it horizontal, could be traversed in under an hour by automobile. It is within this narrow vertical band that living creatures and the earth's geochemical processes interact to sustain each other.

JEREMY RIFKIN, *Biosphere Politics*, 1991

55 GLOBAL ENVIRONMENT
See also 43 ENVIRONMENT

1 We have today the knowledge and the tools to look at the whole earth, to look at everybody on it, to look at its resources, to look at the state of our technology, and to begin to deal with the whole problem. I think that the tenderness that lies in seeing the earth as small and lonely and blue is probably one of the most valuable things that we have now.

MARGARET MEAD (1901–1978), speech, New York City, 22 April 1970

2 It is scarcely surprising that the outcast majority of the earth who have to survive on an annual income that most poor Americans would scorn as a weekly wage, illiterate, and with a horizon of comprehension limited to their own village, will be unimpressed by any show of ecological caution on the part of their political leaders.

BRIAN JOHNSON, VISTA, January–February 1971

3 Space exploration has been midwife to the birth of a new global consciousness. Two decades ago, with my first serendipitous sighting of a satellite, I was one of the lucky few to be touched for a moment by this philosophy. The children of the future, however, will be raised with the benefits of these space-age lessons.

JACQUES COUSTEAU, *The Cousteau Almanac*, 1980

4 Think globally, but act locally.
RENÉ DUBOS, *Celebrations of Life*, 1981

5 The world's environmental problems are greater than the sum of those in each country. Certainly, they can no longer be dealt with purely on a nation-state basis. . . . The growing trend towards isolationism demonstrates that the current rhythm of history is out of harmony with human aspirations, even with its chances for survival.

The challenge ahead is for us to transcend the self-interests of our respective nation-states so as to embrace a broader self-interest—the survival of the human species in a threatened world.

TOM MCMILLAN, hearing, World Commission on Environment and Development, 26–27 May 1986

6 Today more than ever before life must be characterized by a sense of Universal responsibility, not only nation to nation and human to human, but also human to other forms of life.

DALAI LAMA, His Holiness Tenzin Gyatso, quoted in World Wildlife Fund Thailand, *A Cry from the Forest*, 1987

7 So far, this new world order has not had its adequate presentation. Yet when it comes, it will take the form of what we are designating as the ecological age. This age can provide the historical dynamism associated with the Marxist classless society, the age of plenty envisaged by the capitalist nations, and the millennial age of peace envisaged in the Apocalpyse of John the Divine. At present, however, we are in that phase of transition that must be described as the groping phase. We are like a musician who faintly hears a melody deep within the mind, but not clearly enough to play it through.
THOMAS BERRY, in Peter Borelli, ed., *Crossroads*, 1988

8 Every time some ecosystem is destroyed, it impacts people around the world. It may be indirect. What impact do all of our pollutants going into the air have on somebody in Africa, where there's no industry? . . . It doesn't have to be in your back yard to cause you to be dismayed about it.
GAYLORD NELSON, quoted in *USA Today*, 29 March 1989

9 In the not-distant future, there will be a new "sacred agenda" in international affairs: policies that enable rescue of the global environment. This task will one day join, and even supplant, preventing the world's incineration through nuclear war as the principal test of statecraft.
ALBERT GORE, speech, Global Change Conference, Smithsonian Institution and the National Academy of Sciences, 3 May 1989

10 The global environmental crisis will improve our lives by offering us a planet-wide crisis of the soul, an opportunity to mature as a species. We are, as these things go, a fairly adolescent creature, with prowess all out of proportion to our wisdom.
STEPHANIE MILLS, *Utne Reader*, November–December 1989

11 There is no such thing as a "national" environment. Our growing economic interdependence provides the context for global cooperation in dealing with the global ecosystem.
JOHN NAISBITT, *Utne Reader*, November–December 1989

12 World peace is threatened not only by the arms race, by regional conflicts and by injus-

tices between peoples and nations but also by the lack of necessary respect for nature, by the disordered exploitation of her resources and by the progressive deterioration in the quality of life. The ecological crisis has assumed such proportions as to be everyone's responsibility.
POPE JOHN PAUL II, World Day of Peace proclamation, 8 December 1989

13 The crisis of life grows ever greater and ever more insistent, like an environmental *Bolero*. This is a time for scientific and environmental statesmanship of the highest order. This is in many ways the moment in history for biologists. Daunting as the task may be, we should set our sights at the highest possible point.
THOMAS E. LOVEJOY, quoted in Terrell J. Minger, ed., *Greenhouse Glasnost*, 1990

14 The fact that so many people from all over the world are taking heed is proof that environment is the crisis of our time, and that it is playing the role of stress necessary to thrust us into a new and higher order of development. In a very real sense, our pathology is our opportunity.
YOWERI KAGUTA MUSEVENI, *Mother Earth News*, March–April 1990

15 Initially, your children may not know how successful World Environment Day was. But eventually, they'll find out for themselves.
CARLOS SALINAS DE GORTARI, speech on Mexico World Environment Day, 5 June 1990

16 The '90s, they tell us, is the decade of the environment. . . . [U]ntil this decade, environmental deprivation has always been local. . . . The thing that is different about the '90s . . . is the global character of environmental issues. For the first time we're really having global effects.
STEPHEN JAY GOULD, quoted in *Christian Science Monitor*, 8 June 1990

17 Without geographic knowledge, citizens cannot possibly understand that an ozone hole over Antarctica affects people in New York, or that the destruction of tropical forests in Brazil influences the climate of Chicago.
GILBERT M. GROSVENOR, *Business Week*, 18 June 1990

18 If there is any real hope for a transnational sense of the brotherhood of man, it may

come from an environmental disaster that makes us feel we're all on the same side, fighting a common foe.

JAMES FALLOWS, *The Atlantic,* July 1990

19 We should not put our country in the position of exercising environmental imperialism.

JAY VROOM, *E* magazine, July–August 1990

20 From Bangladesh to Haiti, we are confronted with an increasing number of ecological basket cases.

RUSSELL E. TRAIN, *The Bridge,* Summer 1990

21 The global environmental crisis we now face can be summarized in a single phrase: There are too many humans doing too many things stupidly.

DAVID WANN, *Buzzworm,* November 1990

22 Properly speaking, global thinking is not possible. Those who have "thought globally" (and among them the most successful have been imperial governments and multinational corporations) have done so by means of simplifications too extreme and oppressive to merit the name of thought. Global thinkers have been, and will be, dangerous people. National thinkers tend to be dangerous also; we now have national thinkers in the northeastern United States who look upon Kentucky as a garbage dump.

WENDELL BERRY, *The Atlantic,* February 1991

23 Global thinking can only be statistical. Its shallowness is exposed by the least intention to do something. Unless one is willing to be destructive on a very large scale, one cannot do something except locally, in a small place. Global thinking can only do to the globe what a space satellite does to it: reduce it, make a bauble of it. Look at one of those photographs of half the earth taken from outer space, and see if you recognize your neighborhood.

WENDELL BERRY, *The Atlantic,* February 1991

24 In order to make ecological good sense for the planet, you must make ecological good sense locally. You can't act locally by thinking globally. If you want to keep your local acts from destroying the globe, you must think locally.

WENDELL BERRY, *The Atlantic,* February 1991

25 We can't extend the model of Germany and the United States to the rest of the world. A

world with three billion or more private cars is unthinkable. So is a world with thousands of big chemical complexes and thousands of nuclear or coal-fired stations. So we must think of something else.

JOSE ANTONIO LUTZENBERGER, quoted in *New York Times,* 30 April 1991

26 Far more than half of this planet's human population already lives and thinks locally, and always has. Thinking locally has, over the ages, given us things like burning witches at the stake, segregation, apartheid, buying and selling slaves, family and tribal feuds, overgrazing, deforestation, and, yes, even regional pollution, which we now see has global consequences. Ideas must be judged on their intrinsic merits, not on attributes like concreteness or seals. I can't see how local foodlishness can be superior to national or international foolishness.

JEAN ANDERSON, letter to the editor, *The Atlantic,* May 1991

56 GOVERNMENT
See also   75 INTERNATIONAL GOVERNANCE, 103 POLITICS, 116 REGULATION

1 If . . . the machine of government . . . is of such a nature that it requires you to be the agent of injustice to another, then, I say, break the law.

HENRY DAVID THOREAU (1817–1862), *On the Duty of Civil Disobediance,* 1849

2 Our government . . . is like a rich and foolish spendthrift who has inherited a magnificent estate in perfect order, and then has left his fields and meadows, forests and parks, to be sold and plundered and wasted.

JOHN MUIR (1838–1914), *Atlantic Monthly,* August 1897

3 No more lawless or irresponsible Federal group than the Corps of Army Engineers has ever attempted to operate in the United States, either outside of or within the law. . . . For too many years the Corps of Army Engineers has been an insubordinate secret society whose slogan has been "One for all and all for one." Nothing could be worse for

the country than this wilful and expensive Corps of Army Engineers closely banded together in a self-serving clique in defiance of their superior officers and in contempt of the public welfare.

HAROLD L. ICKES (1874–1952), U.S. Secretary of the Interior, foreword to A. Maass, *Muddy Waters*, 1951

4 We can all see profit in conservation practice, but the profit accrues to society rather than to the individual. This, of course, explains the trend, at this moment, to wish the whole job on the government.

ALDO LEOPOLD (1886–1948), *Round River*, 1953

5 We have used legislative means to modify our economy many times, both by prohibition and by economic forces. . . . The largest and most expensive functions of government are carried out without free-market appraisal; there seems to be no reason why environmental quality should be an exception.

JOHN W. TUKEY, testimony, U.S. House Science and Aeronautics subcommittee, 1966

6 Despite stalemates and distractions that will come along the way, such as present limitations resulting from Vietnam, the major political concern of this country for the remainder of this century is likely to be how to utilize government as a tool in improving the quality of American life.

FRANK E. SMITH, North American Wildlife and Natural Resources Conference, Houston, March 1968

7 We have seen a change in basic approach from the day when government was a referee among competing resource users to a day when government must be a trustee of the environment for all the people.

LAURENCE ROCKEFELLER, speech, colloquium, U.S. Congress, 17 July 1968

8 The deep loss of popular belief that government is capable of protecting and advancing the public interest against this airborne epidemic and its corporate sources reflects a broader absence of confidence particularly among the young, that government can be honest and courageous enough to administer law for the people.

RALPH NADER, on air pollution, in John C. Esposito, *Vanishing Air*, 1970

9 It is the countinuing responsibility of the federal government to . . . assure for all Americans safe, healthful, productive, and esthetically and culturally pleasing surroundings.

NATIONAL ENVIRONMENTAL POLICY ACT (U.S.), January 1970

10 President Nixon deserves praise for giving an unprecedented emphasis to the environmental needs of the country. But if the country is really to "make peace with nature," as he wisely counsels, he will have to demand for the purpose, in far greater quantities than he has yet suggested, the chlorophyl of good green cash.

NEW YORK TIMES, editorial, 11 February 1970

11 I tell you this, that if we don't get our president's attention this planet may soon die. . . . He has our money and he has our power. He must use our money and power in order that the planet will not die. I am sorry he's a lawyer; I wish to God that he was a biologist. He said the other night that America has never lost a war, and he wasn't going to be the first American president to lose one. He may be the first American president to lose an entire planet.

KURT VONNEGUT, JR., on president Richard M. Nixon, speech, New York City, 22 April 1970

12 The men who cared so much for the future, who were so concerned about the establishment of rights against infringement by government or individual, these visionary men *forgot* to establish your right to breathe clean air or drink potable water.

VICTOR J. YANNACONE, speech, Michigan State University, 22 April 1970

13 A nation that is seriously and justifiably aroused over environmental disruption needs to believe that its government cares enough to make hard and politically difficult decisions in this area if the facts warrant them.

FORTUNE, on the pending decision whether to continue funding the SST airplane, January 1971

14 The National Park Service is entrenched as a large bureaucracy (excellent and honest people, in the main, comprise the bureau). What it gains in complexity it has lost in sensitivity and awareness and more sheets of paper

move over the desks than autumn leaves fall in Shenandoah!

ANSEL ADAMS, speech, University of California, Berkeley, 3 March 1975

15 If the United States government can be said to have any single solution for the energy crisis, it is that we will be saved by nuclear power.... [But] the entire nuclear program is headed for extinction.

BARRY COMMONER, New Yorker, 9 February 1976

16 The greatest pollution we have is the government itself.

ANONYMOUS, at Maryland Coastal Zone Management hearing, 15 January 1977

17 Without mega projects and war there is something of a void. How does the state justify its existence? . . . [M]aintenance of complex and subtle ecological balance affords little opportunity for visible achievement and thus a minimal base for government legitimacy.

DAVID W. ORR and STUART HILL, Western Political Quarterly, December 1978

18 OMB can kill this agency and you won't see any visible scars.

DOUGLAS M. COSTLE, EPA administrator, on the Office of Management and Budget's efforts to curb regulation by the Environmental Protection Agency, quoted in Environmental Science and Technology, February 1981

19 If we lose an excellent EPA, we will have lost something rare and very hard to recreate. And we will pay a very big bill in the future. Neither the economy nor the environment can afford a second-rate EPA.

WILLIAM DRAYTON, testimony, U.S. House Budget Committee, 16 March 1981

20 James G. Watt is the first chief conservation officer of the whole country to be an outspoken opponent of the environmental movement and will do a great deal of damage to our park plans and our environment.

GAYLORD NELSON, U.S. Senator, San Francisco Examiner/Chronicle, 5 April 1981

21 No other Secretary of the Interior, in recent times at least, has had a President who understands my department like Ronald Reagan does. He's a Westerner. Fifty per cent of his state is owned and managed by the federal government. When I said, "I want to do this, I want to do that," he replied, "Sic 'em."

JAMES G. WATT, U.S. Secretary of the Interior, quoted in The New Yorker, 4 May 1981

22 I'm out to make decisions and I will make them quickly. . . . I make lots of mistakes because I make a lot of decisions.

JAMES G. WATT, U.S. Secretary of the Interior, quoted in The New Yorker, 4 May 1981

23 It isn't the government's job to tell people what kind of air they should breathe. Each person should decide for himself. I may like carbon monoxide, you may prefer coal dust, your next-door neighbor might prefer to inhale sulphur fumes. By making clean air standards the same for everyone, we are only giving aid and comfort to the environmentalists.

ART BUCHWALD, quoted in Sierra, November–December 1981

24 EPA is being mugged in broad daylight.

MORRIS UDALL, U.S. Representative, on the Reagan Administration's proposed fiscal year 1983 budget for the Environmental Protection Agency, Washington Post, 5 February 1982

25 [The Corps of Engineers has] kind of a beaver mentality.

DAN QUAYLE, U.S. Senator, quoted in Washington Post, 2 April 1982

26 This is an unusual bureaucracy because we produce goods and services. It's like running a business.

JIM PERRY, supervisor, Santa Fe National Forest, on the U.S. Forest Service, quoted in Conservation Foundation Letter, June 1982

27 EPA must be non-confrontational in its approach, leading by action and encouragement. I assure you that, this will be my guiding credo.

ANNE M. GORSUCH, EPA director, EPA Journal, November–December 1982

28 Everybody here would acknowledge that we've got problems at EPA. A lot of us frankly have not been paying much attention to it in the last two years.

ANONYMOUS, SENIOR WHITE HOUSE AIDE, quoted in New York Times, 26 February 1983

29 It is difficult for me to understand how perfectly reasonable actions . . . could become
distorted and then be blown up into the fire-
storm that brought EPA virtually to a complete halt earlier this year.
> Anne M. Gorsuch, EPA director, on oppo-
> sition to her administration, U.S. House
> Energy and Commerce subcommittee, 28
> September 1983

30 Though personally honest, Mr. Watt has pre-
sided over the most destructive giveaways of
America's publicly owned natural resources
to private interests since Teapot Dome, and
proved himself the most dangerous Interior
Secretary in the department's history.
> John B. Oakes, New York Times, 18 October
> 1983

31 This system is designed to fail because it
avoids defining national goals and setting
priorities. Our Balkanized environmental de-
partments have lacked a sense of strategy as
well as leaders who press to win and to reward those who champion environmental
goals. We are lucky to have accomplished as
much as we have in curbing criteria air pollutants and controlling some water pollutants.
> William J. Futrell, on pollution control, in
> Peter Borelli, ed., Crossroads, 1988

32 What made Reagan the first overtly anticon-
servation president of this century was the
belief he shared with President Calvin
Coolidge, that "the business of government
is business."
> Stewart Udall, in Peter Borelli, ed., Cross-
> roads, 1988

33 Clean air is an area where the Federal government will wimp out with the slightest bit of
pressure.
> Patricia Schroeder, U.S. Representative,
> quoted in USA Today, 5 May 1988

34 In an Administration that believes in free-
market ideology, the guy who speaks for the
environment has got to do so very clearly, because there won't be anybody else delivering
the message.
> William K. Reilly, New York Times Maga-
> zine, 13 August 1989

35 Imperfect as they are, politicized, corrupted
by local pressures and cowed by local threats,
the federal bureaus are absolutely essential,
the only possible barrier to real disaster in the
arid and drought-threatened West where
they function. They represent the country's
effort, inadequate and faltering, to stand in
the way of that good old American spirit of
enterprise that according to myth won the
West, and according to history half ruined it.
> Wallace Stegner, Sierra, September–Octo-
> ber 1989

36 This Administration wants the United States
to be the world leader in addressing environmental problems and I want the Department
of Defense to be the federal leader in agency
environmental compliance and protection.
> Richard Cheney, U.S. Secretary of Defense,
> memorandum for secretaries of military
> departments, 10 October 1989

37 Ronald Reagan was the most antienviron-
mental head of state since Ivan the Terrible.
His Department of [the] Interior was controlled by people who regarded wilderness in
much the same way that Rome regarded
Carthage. The Council on Environmental
Quality was pillaged. The Department of Energy was placed in a state of intellectual re-
ceivership.
> Denis Hayes, speech, American Museum of
> Natural History, New York City, 8 Novem-
> ber 1989

38 The military has created "national sacrifice
zones" as testimonials to their complete disregard for America's environmental security.
> National Toxic Campaign Fund, Responsi-
> ble Citizens for Responsible Government,
> on hazardous waste sites at military bases,
> "Filthy Habit," 1990

39 For the past 20 years, EPA has been basically
a "reactive" agency. . . . the Agency has
made very little effort to anticipate environmental problems or to take preemptive actions that reduce the likelihood of an environmental problem occurring. . . . at EPA
there has been little correlation between the
relative resources dedicated to different environmental problems and the relative risks
posed by those problems.
> U.S. Environmental Protection Agency,
> Science Advisory Board, Reducing Risk,
> 1990

40 Unreasonable expectations about what the
EPA—which is slated to receive full Cabinet

status this year—could and should do inclined activists to blame the agency for all environmental imperfections. As a result, the environmental community has come to regard the EPA not as an ally—as, for example, the Commerce Department is regarded as an ally of the business community—but as a major federal enemy.

BILL GILBERT, *Smithsonian*, April 1990

41 As the years have passed, EPA has not delivered "fishable and swimmable water" by 1983, nor much of anything else by Congressional deadlines. EPA does not act like it is accountable to Congress or the public. It acts more like an assembly of people showing up for work and collecting pay checks.

MICHAEL MCCLOSKEY, *EPA Journal*, September–October 1990

57 GREENHOUSE EFFECT
See also 15 CLIMATE

1 We are embarked on the most colossal ecological experiment of all time; doubling the concentration in the atmosphere of an entire planet of one of its most important gases; and we really have little idea of what might happen.

PAUL A. COLINVAUX, on the buildup of carbon dioxide, *Why Big Fierce Animals Are Rare*, 1978

2 Carbon dioxide, until now an apparently innocuous trace gas in the atmosphere, may be moving rapidly toward a central role as a major threat to the present world order.

GEORGE M. WOODWELL, *Scientific American*, January 1978

3 The only practical strategy [to deal with global warming] is adjustment. Technology will help to ease that adjustment but the institutional rigidities of our advanced societies may correspondingly make the response to the changed climate stickier than in earlier, simpler ages.

CHARLES F. COOPER, *Foreign Affairs*, April 1978

4 A critical problem for humans, is to avoid arriving inadvertently at a critical threshold that might trigger an abrupt accelerated

warming of the climate. . . . Animals today are generally adapted to relatively cool conditions, as were faunas prior to the terminal Mesozoic extinctions. A sudden climatic warming could potentially impose on us conditions comparable to those that terminated a geologic age.

DEWEY M. MCLEAN, *Science*, 4 August 1978

5 It is the sense of the scientific community that carbon dioxide from unrestrained combustion of fossil fuels potentially is the most important environmental issue facing mankind.

U.S. DEPARTMENT OF ENERGY, report, 2 April 1979

6 The unthinkable is that we're distorting this atmospheric balance. We're shifting the chemical balance so that we have more poisons in the atmosphere—ozone and acid rain on ground level—while we're also changing the thermal climate of the earth through the greenhouse effect and—get this—simultaneously causing destruction of our primary filter of ultraviolet light. It's incredible. Talk about the national-debt crisis—we're piling up debts in the atmosphere, and the piper will want to be paid.

MICHAEL OPPENHEIMER, in Peter Borelli, ed., *Crossroads*, 1988

7 This is not a matter of Chicken Little telling us the sky is falling. The scientific evidence is telling us we have a problem, a serious problem.

JOHN CHAFFEE, in Peter Borelli, ed., *Crossroads*, 1988

8 It [the greenhouse effect] is so much more comprehensive, so much more dangerous, so much more revolutionary, so much more life-changing than anything else we have done, that it literally means everything as far as this Congress is concerned and as far as our lifestyles and our very economy is concerned.

J. BENNETT JOHNSON, U.S. Senator, quoted in *Los Angeles Times*, 1 September 1988

9 If we do nothing, warming could drive the sugar maple right out of Vermont, which would be a catastrophe for my state. . . . Congress can't seem to make up its mind about whether it wants a two-year budget, let alone focus on the effects of global warming

which may not occur for several decades. It is our job to worry about the long-term future of American agriculture and forestry.

PATRICK J. LEAHY, U.S. Senator, on the global warming trend, quoted in *Los Angeles Times*, 2 December 1988

10 As there are no quick fixes or easy solutions, we must gear up for the long hard job of figuring out how the earth system operates. . . . Even with great intensification of effort, I fear the greenhouse impacts may come largely as surprises.

WALLACE BROECKER, quoted in Dean E. Abrahamson, ed., *The Challenge of Global Warming*, 1989

11 The greenhouse effect is a more apt name than those who coined it imagined. The carbon dioxide and trace gases act like the panes of glass on a greenhouse—the analogy is accurate. But it's more than that. We have built a greenhouse, a human creation, where once there bloomed a sweet and wild garden.

BILL MCKIBBEN, *The End of Nature*, 1989

12 The Los Angelesization of the planet cannot take place, for in the greenhouse effect nature has her own negative feedback mechanisms for shutting down the furnace of industrial civilization.

WILLIAM IRWIN THOMPSON, quoted in Francesca Lyman, *The Greenhouse Trap*, 1990

13 Given the logarithmic dependence of warming on CO_2, the elimination of America's 20% contribution to CO_2 production will merely reduce warming by a fraction of a degree—a reduction that would be wiped out in a few years. Even with international co-operation, the draconian sacrifices that would be required of much of the world are unlikely to be made—and perhaps should not be made.

RICHARD LINDZEN, *Environmental Science and Technology*, April 1990

14 In my opinion, forecasts of "the end of the world" or "nothing to worry about" are the two least likely cases, with almost any scenario in between being more probable.

STEPHEN H. SCHNEIDER, *Environmental Science and Technology*, April 1990

15 There is perhaps no other issue which has such an ability to mobilise our common ef-

forts to a common purpose across all of the differences of wealth, belief, history, or experience which divide us.

PRINCE CHARLES, prince of Wales, Rainforest Harvest Conference, Royal Geographical Society, 17 May 1990

16 The danger is that so many things are changing at once. The concentrations of trace gases are increasing while the global temperature is rising and the ozone layer is thinning. It's like playing football when the size of the field, the shape of the ball, the number of players and the method of scoring change with every play.

IRVING MINTZER, quoted in *Washington Post*, 29 July 1990

17 [The effects of global warming] roughly translate into a change of temperature less than moving from Washington to Atlanta.

MICHAEL J. BOSKIN, quoted in *Greenpeace*, September–October 1990

18 This is not a disaster, it is merely a change. The area [Bangladesh] won't have disappeared, it will just be under water. Where you now have cows, you will have fish.

J. R. SPRADLEY, quoted in *Environmental Forum*, November–December 1990

19 The first proof of global warming may well come from the bleaching of the fragile and highly sensitive coral reef system.

ERNEST H. WILLIAMS, *BioScience*, February 1991

20 There is a selective use of facts. Nobody tells an untruth. But nobody tells the whole truth, either. It all depends on the ideological outlook. My nuclear friends are happy to promote the greenhouse effect. My natural gas friends are happy to promote the greenhouse effect. A lot of scientists promote the greenhouse effect because of increased funding.

S. FRED SINGER, quoted in *Washington Post*, 3 February 1991

58 GREEN REVOLUTION
See also 4 AGRICULTURE

1 [New crop seeds present] an opportunity where irrigation, fertilizer and peasant educa-

tion can produce miracles in the sight of the beholder. The farmer himself in one short season can see the beneficial results of that scientific agriculture which has seemed so often in the past to be a will o'the wisp tempting him to innovation without benefit.

ROBERT S. MCNAMARA, World Bank annual meeting, 1968

2 The revolution is green only because it is being viewed through green-colored glasses.

WILLIAM C. PADDOCK, *BioScience*, 15 August 1970

3 Thus, in providing the means to kill hunger, the Green Revolution will destroy many vested interests. It will force the reappraisal of the problem of landless peasants, of the unemployment of workers and of the alienation of the masses. And in the final analysis, it will precipitate a prodigious economic, social and political transformation in the developing countries.

EDMUNDO FLORES, Mexican development economist, 1972, quoted in Robert Katz, *A Giant in the Earth*, 1973

4 The truth is that, while the new wheat and rice varieties are excellent high yielders under certain specialized conditions (controlled irrigation, high fertilization), they have done little to overcome the biological limits of the average farm. The hungry nations of Asia, Africa and Latin America are hungry because they have a poor piece of agricultural real estate, and no one should delude them into believing that some sort of technological wizardry can nullify the consequences of too many people on too little arable land.

WILLIAM C. PADDOCK, *Washington Post*, 3 June 1973

5 There remains one vast incalculable—nature itself. One thing that has been harshly, even humiliatingly, made clear in the last two years is that, despite all-out technological progress, despite all the buoyant hopes invested not long ago in the so-called green revolution, harvests are still far too often at the mercy of the weather. In this respect at least, man has so far failed to master his natural environment.

ADDEKE H. BOERMA, director-general of U.N. Food and Agriculture Organization, 1 February 1973, quoted in *Conservation Foundation Letter*, October 1973

6 If the Green Revolution has created food for millions, it is because science has tamed nature.

NEW YORK TIMES, editorial, 29 August 1986

7 The "Green Revolution" of the last 20–30 years has achieved enormous increases in the yield of staple crops, such as wheat, rice and maize, making a dramatic impact on the Third World and keeping pace with population growth. The costs of those increases are now, however, becoming apparent: the cost of reduced stability and sustainability of production, of increased vulnerability to environmental shocks and stresses, and of growing social inequity.

GORDON R. CONWAY and EDWARD B. BARBIER, *After the Green Revolution*, 1990

8 Regarded by many as the most efficient form of agriculture in history, it is also becoming obvious that it is the least sustainable. While green revolution technology boosted production in a short time with the use of petrochemical fertilizers, pesticides, and high-yield monocultures, it did so at the expense of eroding and poisoning the soil base, undermining the genetic diversity of agricultural crops, and increasing the effect of global warming.

JEREMY RIFKIN, *Biosphere Politics*, 1991

59 GROUNDWATER
See also   25 DRINKING WATER, 134 WATER

1 Or the water of the garden
Will run off underground
So that thou wilt never
Be able to find it.

KORAN, Sura 18:41

2 Texas law continues to regard most groundwater as a mysterious blessing . . . legitimately subject to capture and use in unlimited quantities by any property owner who digs or drives a well.

JOHN GRAVES, *The Water Hustlers*, 1971

3 By the 1980s water declines should make serious inroads in irrigated agriculture; thirty or forty years hence this commerce of pumped water should be over. The humans of the High

Plains will be staring down tens of thousands of dry holes.
> CHARLES BOWDEN, *Killing the Hidden Waters,* 1977

4 Humans build their societies around consumption of fossil water long buried in the earth, and these societies, being based on temporary resources, face the problem of being temporary themselves.
> CHARLES BOWDEN, *Killing the Hidden Waters,* 1977

5 What are you going to do with all that water? Are you just going to leave it in the ground? . . . When we use it up, we'll just have to get more water from somewhere else.
> FELIX SPARKS, Colorado Water Conservation Board, on water withdrawals from the Ogallala aquifer, quoted in Marc Reisner, *Cadillac Desert,* 1986

6 Groundwater is the most mysterious part of our planet's hydrologic cycle. Many people imagine groundwater as pristine underground rivers that magically clean themselves of contaminants and supply us with an abundance of fresh, drinkable water. In the real world, underground rivers exist only infrequently.
> ANN MAEST, *Buzzworm,* January–February 1991

---

60 HAZARDOUS WASTES
See also   133 WASTE AND WASTES

---

1 Every individual and all of industry and even government itself . . . have contributed to this horrible mess.
> ROBERT A. ROLAND, president, Chemical Manufacturers Association, *Washington Post,* 21 April 1979

2 The Administration is moving away from doing things which protect the environment in favor of doing things which take care of the consequences of not doing the things which protect the environment.
> WILLIAM SANJOUR, EPA official, testimony, U.S. Senate Governmental Affairs subcommittee, 1 August 1979

3 We have found the sources of hazardous waste and they are us.
> U.S. ENVIRONMENTAL PROTECTION AGENCY, booklet, "Everybody's Problem: Hazardous Waste," 1980

4 Granted this is one of our most complex and acute environmental problems; but does it take 2,000 pages of regulations to attack it?
> NORMAN B. LIVERMORE, *Cry California,* Summer 1981

5 We have dug into this earth like a bacteria culture into soft living flesh, and we have spread, gnawing hungrily through link after link of the great chain, leaving our toxic waste everywhere around us.
> JOE PADDOCK, NANCY PADDOCK, and CAROL BLY, *Soil and Survival,* 1986

6 With apologies to Descartes, I say, "I am, therefore I pollute." This is the first law of hazardous waste. It is inescapable for food processors, chemical manufacturers, and all other manipulators and transformers of materials—in other words, for all human beings—because they generate hazardous waste. Human body waste was the first hazardous waste problem. It includes toxic chemicals (such as urea, ammonia, hydrogen sulfide, methane, nitrates, and possibly others) and toxic microorganisms.
> LOUIS J. THIBODEAUX, *Environmental Science and Technology,* April 1990

7 In an age marked by an overabundance of waste, regulation, and litigation, here is an industry [hazardous-waste cleanup] that thrives on all three.
> BRUCE STUTZ, *Harper's,* October 1990

8 The poor shall inherit the earth . . . and all the toxic waste thereof.
> GREENPEACE, slogan to support the Waste Trade Project, 1991

9 As long as there are poor and minority areas to dump on, corporate American won't be serious about finding alternatives to the way toxic materials are produced and managed.
> LEON WHITE, quoted in *Z* magazine, April 1991

61 HEALTH
See also   104 POLLUTION, 118 RISK

1 The best six doctors anywhere
And no one can deny it
Are sunshine, water, rest, and air
Exercise and diet.
These six will gladly you attend
If only you are willing
Your mind they'll ease
Your will they'll mend
And charge you not a shilling.
NURSERY RHYME, quoted by Wayne Fields, *What the River Knows*, 1990

2 'Tis a sordid profit that's accompanied by the destruction of Health.
BERNARDINO RAMAZZINI (1633–1714), *Treatise on the Diseases of Tradesmen*, 1705

3 A physician is obligated to consider more than a diseased organ, more even than the whole man—he must view the man in his world.
HARVEY CUSHING (1869–1939), c. 1930, quoted in René Dubos, *Man Adapting*, 1965

4 A community which ignores or repudiates its origins, in its present acts, is no more whole and healthy than a man who has lost his memory.
EDWARD HYAMS, *Soil and Civilization*, 1952

5 Filthy environments may make us mentally ill before they make us physically sick.
ATHELSTAN SPILHAUS, *Daedalus*, Fall 1967

6 The truly healthful environment is not merely safe but stimulating.
WILLIAM H. STEWART, *Environmental Science and Technology*, February 1968

7 [Rachel Carson] will have accomplished as real a service as any physician who devoted a lifetime to patients and she will have reached a practice encompassing everyone!
ANONYMOUS PHYSICIAN, quoted in Frank Graham, *Since Silent Spring*, 1970

8 Let us make no mistake—the benefits of a high-quality, cleaner environment will far outweigh the costs. Improved health and lowered medical bills will provide a funda-

mental measure of those benefits. . . . When we face the issues involved in the Clean Air Act, we are not dealing just with amenities or the elitist values of a few esthetes—we are dealing with the basic health protection of ourselves and our families.
RUSSELL E. TRAIN, EPA administrator, speech, National Press Club, 18 September 1973

9 Instead of calling it environment and conservation, let's call it public health once in a while. The word "environment" has all sorts of unfortunate connotations. Almost a defeatist attitude about it. When you're in the inner city or in any real hard crunch with a tough political problem—which all of these things are—it helps if you can relate the problem very flatly and specifically. Bad air and bad water is not what people like to push aside as the environment—it's public health!
ANGELA ROONEY, in James N. Smith, *Environmental Quality and Social Justice in Urban America*, 1974

10 Sure, cancer is a long and painful illness. But if you take the nitrites out of cured pork, you get botulism. That'll take you out fast and you'll have nothing to worry about.
EARL BUTZ, U.S. Secretary of Agriculture, 1975, quoted in *Isaac Asimov's Book of Science and Nature Quotations*, 1988

11 Cancer in the last quarter of the 20th century can be considered a social disease, a disease whose causation and control are rooted in the technology and economy of our society.
UMBERTO SAFFIOTTI, quoted in *Time*, 1975

12 Some carcinogens have always been with us, and the body's chief detoxifying organ, the liver, is to some extent equipped to deal with them. But it can be overtaxed. The benzpyrene found in cigarette smoke, for example, is produced by every fire, and the liver has enzymes to deal with it. But the liver can stand only so much benzpyrene or any other carcinogen, and what is a tolerable dose for one person may be fatal to another.
JUDITH RANDAL, *Washington Post*, 31 August 1975

13 [One of the basic prerequisites of health is that one] must not depart radically from the

pattern of personal behavior under which man evolved, for example, by smoking, over-eating, or sedentary living.

THOMAS MCKEOWN, "The Role of Medicine: Dream, Mirage, or Nemesis?," 1976

14 The contrast is startling between the runaway spending for health care and the resistance of most of American business to spending for environmental health protection.

PAUL G. ROGERS, speech, Third Annual Conference on Health Policy, 22 May 1978

15 It is extraordinary that we have just now be-come convinced of our bad health, our con-stant jeopardy of disease and death. . . . when the facts should be telling us the opposite. In a more rational world, you'd think we would be staging bicentennial cere-monies for the celebration of our general good shape. In the year 1976, out of a popula-tion of around 220 million, only 1.9 million died, or just under 1 percent, not at all a dis-couraging record once you accept the fact of mortality itself.

LEWIS THOMAS, The Medusa and the Snail, 1979

16 A prudent policy of cancer prevention re-quires protection of the most sensitive indi-viduals in the population.

UMBERTO SAFFIOTTI, quoted in Federal Regis-ter, 22 January 1980

17 [The United States has become] thoroughly persuaded of the teachings of Genesis—car-cinogenesis, teratogenesis, and mutagenesis.

ANONYMOUS BRITISH SCIENTIST, Royal Society of Medicine, The Chemical Industry and the Health of the Community, 1985

18 Well, it will cause an increase in skin cancer especially in light-skinned people. Dark-skinned people are so very nicely protected by melanin that they do not have as much to worry about. There is a kind of cosmic justice in this: the light-skinned people develop the chlorofluorocarbons, which then preferen-tially give skin cancer to light-skinned peo-ple: the dark-skinned people who had nothing to do with the invention are pro-tected.

CARL SAGAN, on the consequences of the thinning of the ozone layer, quoted in Anurdha Vittachi, Earth Conference One, 1989

19 The basic policy of the central government concerning Minamata disease victims is to wait for their death.

GOTO TAKANORI, Japan Times, 5 January 1989

20 Environmental illness is simply an incurable disease. There is no cure. It can only be pre-vented.

BARRY COMMONER, quoted in Mother Earth News, March–April 1990

21 A series of political actions has been taken under the wrong banner. Much environmen-tal legislation and regulation has been en-acted under the promise of protection, not of the physical environment, but of human health. The threat to health has been used over the past two decades for "selling" envi-ronmental legislation and regulation, often in ways or to a degree that contradicts scientific evidence. Health has been used as a surro-gate; the promoters of political action—legis-lators, environmentalists, and professional consumerists—have been right for the wrong reasons.

EDWARD J. BURGER, JR., Daedalus, Autumn 1990

62 HIGHWAYS
See also   8 AUTOMOBILES

1 The actual building of roads devoted to mo-tor cars is not for the near future, in spite of the many rumors to that effect.

HARPER'S WEEKLY, 2 August 1902

2 The craze is to build all the highways possible everywhere while billions may yet be bor-rowed from the unlucky future. The fashion is to barber and manicure wild America as smartly as the modern girl. . . . Motorway and solitude together constitute a contradic-tion.

R. S. YARD, Living Wilderness, September 1935

3 Our national flower is the concrete cloverleaf.

LEWIS MUMFORD, The Culture of Cities, 1938

4 The horizontal line of a new Freedom extend-ing from ocean to ocean.

FRANK LLOYD WRIGHT (1867–1959), An Auto-biography, 1943

5 The emphasis on superhighways—and on supercars which require them—takes on much of the lunatic quality of an arms race. As highways get bigger and better, they invite more cars, destroy what undeveloped and unschematized country (or central city) remains, and require still more highways in an unending spiral.

DAVID RIESMAN, *Annals of the American Academy of Political and Social Science*, November 1957

6 Perhaps our age will be known to the future historian as the age of the bulldozer and the exterminator; and in many parts of the country the building of a highway has about the same result upon vegetation and human structures as the passage of a tornado or the blast of an atom bomb.

LEWIS MUMFORD, *The Highway and the City*, 1963

7 No white men's roads through black men's homes.

SAMMIE A. ABBOTT, slogan used in fight against inner-city highway in Washington, D.C., 1965

8 [The interstate highway program has] sent great rivers of concrete creeping like lava through residential neighborhoods and commercial areas, dislocating families, schools, churches and businesses.

HOMER BIGART, *New York Times*, 13 November 1967

9 Of particular concern has been the damage done to the quiet beauty of many once remote and inaccessible areas, as well as the intrusion of the seemingly endless line of asphalt and concrete into the enclaves which many people have sought as surcease from the hustle and bustle of modern day life.

KENNETH B. KEATING, judge, New York Court of Appeals, on the "massive" highway construction program, 1968

10 The nation's highways sometimes seem to have a momentum of their own, spreading out in all directions no matter how many homes are displaced or scenic values destroyed. Now, however, it appears there's a chance that road-building may develop a somewhat better sense of direction. . . . It's high time more people realized that there's more to highway construction than building the swiftest route from here to there.

WALL STREET JOURNAL, editorial, 25 October 1968

11 It is in the cities that our world-renowned road building competence is meeting its sternest test. Our mastery of the engineering problems in moving automobiles over every conceivable terrain is unrivaled. But we have yet to reconcile it with the traditions, amenities and aspirations of city life. That is the roughest terrain of all.

JOHN W. GARDNER, letter to Federal Highway Administration, 20 November 1968

12 There are those who say the American Dream is a split-level in the suburbs with a half-acre, a guaranteed annual income, and membership in the Best Club. Others maintain it's just a matter of all the booze and broads you can handle. Not so. The American Dream is to drive from coast to coast without encountering a traffic light.

A. Q. MOWBRAY, *Road to Ruin*, 1969

13 O Almightly God, who has given us this earth and has appointed men to have domination over it; who has commanded us to make straight the highways, to lift up the valleys and to make the mountains low, we ask thy blessing upon these men who do just that. Fill them with a sense of accomplishment, not just for the roads built, but for the ways opened for the lengthening of visions, the broader hopes and the greater joys which make these highways a possibility for mankind. Bless these, our nation's road builders, and their friends. For the benefits we reap from their labors, we praise thee; may thy glory be revealed in us. Amen.

AMERICAN ROAD BUILDERS ASSOCIATION, official prayer, quoted by Helen Leavitt, *Superhighway—Superhoax*, 1970

14 Many people advocate mass transit for the other person so they themselves will be able to enjoy riding on congestion-free expressways.

ERIC SEVAREID, "Evening News," CBS-TV, 1970

15 That streak of road, fired like an arrow through the heart of the jungle, is being lethal to the old kingdom.

ANTHONY SMITH, on a highway into Brazil's Amazon rain forest, *Mato Grosso: The Last Virgin Land,* 1971

16 I want to find something that will shortstop all of these little pestiferous suits that are hamstringing the programs. . . . I like wildlife and fish life and animal life, but mainly the environment exists for human life, and we are improving the environment for human life.

JIM WRIGHT, U.S. Representative, on highway construction projects, closed meeting, U.S. House Public Works Committee, 3 February 1972

17 Freeways are now familiar phenomena across America, but in Los Angeles they have reached their highest stage of development, victors in a Darwinian struggle over various forms of trains, trolleys and traffic lights. Here, they are such a pervasive influence that they stand as the symbol of the city, sources of mythology, objects of esthetic appreciation and ecological anger, man-made monuments of such an elemental force that they might have heaved up out of the earth eons ago. The freeway is our Mother!

STEVEN V. ROBERTS, *New York Times Magazine,* 15 April 1973

18 We have a huge supply of lawyers, city planners, politicians, lobbyists and not-in-my-backyard suburbanites to make it legal and politically impossible to build new roads. We built them to cause development, they say, so we can stop development by not building them. Except that the development goes on anyway, and what we get is more traffic jams.

HENRY ALLEN, *Washington Post,* 21 October 1990

63 HISTORIC PRESERVATION

1 And they shall build the old wastes, they shall raise up the former desolations, and they shall repair the waste cities, the desolation of many generations.

BIBLE, Isaiah 61:4

2 Older buildings and neighborhoods are being conserved because we now know that they are integral threads in the unique fabric or sense of place in any community. Cared for and interwoven with new cultural threads, they can help effect positive changes and stimulate new growth in shabby or decayed areas.

CHARLES H. PAGE, *American Preservation,* October–November 1977

3 I cannot agree with those who say that the fine old buildings of our cities offensively represent elitist architecture, and elitist architecture is but a specialized means of communication "above and beyond the common use"; a set of symbols, idioms and concepts with which the rich and mighty spoke to themselves and the world, and thus are not worth saving.

JOE LOUIS MATTOX, *American Preservation,* February–March 1978

4 I believe that we are starting to realize that [these] man-made resources, such as the fine old homes, are just as much a part of our natural environment as our trees, streams, [etc.].

R. MARTIN WILLETT, *American Preservation,* February–March 1978

5 Not only do these buildings in their workmanship represent the lessons of the past and embody the precious features of our heritage, they serve as examples of quality for today.

WILLIAM J. BRENNAN, JR., U.S. Supreme Court justice, *Penn Central Transportation Co., et al.* v. *New York City,* 26 June 1978

6 Historic preservationists must make common cause with general environmentalists if we are to save the cultural as well as the physical environment—both as integral parts of our rich heritage. Such collaboration, hopefully wise, but necessarily aggressive, will do much constructively to influence our civilization for the future.

JANE HOLTZ KAY, *American Preservation,* October–November 1978

7 The style of the preservation movement is aggressive, underdog. There is a crisis mentality with lots of adrenalin to stop the bulldozer.

MARY MEANS, *American Preservation,* October–November 1978

8 A compact among generations is being violated. There is no law of supply and demand for real estate and parking lots that justifies

bulldozing the national patrimony. Once gone, it is lost. State volunteers and local cake sales cannot replace such an effort.

WASHINGTON POST, editorial, on cuts in funding for historic preservation, 11 April 1981

9 Actually, in view of what was happening to the built world in America, the movement appeared at the last possible moment, the fifty-ninth minute.

JAMES MARSTON FITCH, on the historic preservation movement in the United States, *American Heritage*, April 1987

---

64 HISTORY

See also 67 HUMANKIND AND ENVIRONMENT, 68 HUMANKIND AND NATURE

---

1 And I brought you into a plentiful country, to eat the fruit thereof and the goodness thereof; but when ye entered, ye defiled my land, and made mine heritage an abomination.

BIBLE, Jeremiah 2:7

2 History itself is an actual part of natural history, of nature's development into man. Natural science will in time include the science of man as the science of man will include natural science: there will be one science.

KARL MARX (1818–1883), c. 1845, quoted in Loyd D. Easton and Kurt H. Guddat, eds., *Writings of the Young Marx on Philosophy and Society*, 1967

3 Soil erosion, if not controlled, has demonstrated its ability to undermine nations and civilizations regardless of what may have been the social or economic conditions that set it going or stimulated its destructiveness.

WALTER CLAY LOWDERMILK, Smithsonian Institution annual report, 1943

4 [Man's] own past is full of clear and somber warnings—vanished civilizations buried, like dead flies in lacquer, beneath their own dust and mud.

PAUL SEARS, *Deserts on the March*, 1947

5 Throughout the history of the world, various nations have risen and fallen in accordance

with overexploitation and deterioration of their resource bases.

S. DILLON RIPLEY, secretary of the Smithsonian Institution, testimony, U.S. Senate Interior Committee, 27 April 1966

6 We sputter against The Polluted Environment—as if it was invented in the age of the automobile. We compare our smoggy air not with the odor of horsedung and the plague of flies and the smells of garbage and human excrement which filled cities in the past, but with the honeysuckle perfumes of some nonexistent City Beautiful. We forget that even if the water in many cities today is not as spring-pure nor as palatable as we would like, for most of history the water of the cities (and of the countryside) was undrinkable.

DANIEL J. BOORSTIN, *Newsweek*, 6 July 1970

7 Although the history of human effort contains numerous incidents of mankind's failure to live within physical limits, it is success in overcoming limits that forms the cultural tradition of many dominant people in today's world. Over the past three hundred years, mankind has compiled an impressive record of pushing back the apparent limits to population and economic growth by a series of spectacular technological advances.

DONELLA H. MEADOWS, et al., *The Limits to Growth*, 1972

8 As a historian, you have to be conscious of the fact that every civilization that has ever existed has ultimately collapsed.

HENRY A. KISSINGER, quoted in *New York Times*, 13 October 1974

9 The decline and fall of the Roman Empire evidently had an environmental dimension. . . . The Romans placed too great a demand upon the available natural resources . . . ecological failures interacted with social, political, and economic forces to assure that the vast entity called the Roman Empire would disappear or be changed beyond recognition.

J. DONALD HUGHES, *Ecology in Ancient Civilizations*, 1975

10 It has only been within the past 100 years or so that any major civilization has been able to reverse a trend of environmental degradation.

JAMES R. DUNN, quoted in *Conservation Foundation Letter*, November 1979

11 Behind all the great climactic struggles of history we will find symptoms of an expanding population. Whenever people have been ingenious so that the quality of their lives has improved they have let their numbers rise.
PAUL COLINVAUX, *The Fates of Nations*, 1980

12 History has been a long progression of changing ways of life and changing population, the one always chasing the other. War, trade, and empire are the results.
PAUL COLINVAUX, *The Fates of Nations*, 1980

13 Perhaps the hardest thing to grasp is the geological and historical uniqueness of the next few decades. There simply is no precedent for what is happening to the biological fabric of this planet. . . . There is no escaping the conclusion that in our lifetimes, this planet will see a suspension, if not an end, to many ecological and evolutionary processes which have been uninterrupted since the beginnings of paleontological time.
MICHAEL A. SOULE and BRUCE A. WILCOX, *Conservation Biology*, 1980

14 Certainly the ecology movement would have done better—and would do better in the future—if its partisans drew their image of time not from the romantic notion of history with its apocalyptic redemption, but from nature, where there is no apocalypse—just continual, and sometimes dramatic, adaptation and change. I still believe that industrial culture is not sustainable, and that it will in time change, and change dramatically; but the scale of time in which that change will happen is most likely to be larger and longer than an individual human life. There won't be a particular morning in which we rise and stretch and, glancing out the window, realize that it has happened. The rhythm of the apocalypse will be in geologic time, where a crisis can last 1,000 years and the moment of judgment can be played out in centuries.
ERIC ZENCEY, *North American Review*, June 1988

15 To give an accurate chronological account of human history in 30 minutes, one would have to spend 29 minutes and 51 seconds on gathering and hunting groups, a little more than 8 seconds describing settled agricultural societies, and a fraction of a second consider-

ing the problems of the modern industrial world. . . . Viewed over the long term, human history has been a story of rising numbers and greater pressures on the environment. In ancient times, those pressures occurred on a local scale, as in Mesopotamia and other areas. Now, with the creation of a global economy to exploit resources, humanity for the first time must contend with damage to the global mechanisms that make life on Earth possible—the ozone layer and the concentration of carbon dioxide in the atmosphere. Given the 2-million-year history of humans on Earth, it is still an open question whether the 10,000-year-old development of agriculture and settled societies and the more recent dependence on nonrenewable fossil fuels constitute an ecologically sustainable strategy.
CLIVE POINTING, *Environment*, November 1990

16 Life would be so much easier if we weren't always struggling to clean up our grandparents' messes!
BRIAN TOKAR, *Utne Reader*, November–December 1989

65 HOLISM
See also   29 ECOLOGY

1 When we try to pick out anything by itself, we find it hitched to everything else in the universe.
JOHN MUIR (1838–1914), *My First Summer in the Sierra*, 1911

2 The astronomer looks high, the geologist low. Who looks between on the surface of the earth? The farmer, I suppose, but too often he sees only grain, and of that only the mere bread-bushel-and-price side of it.
JOHN MUIR (1838–1914), 1870 or 1871, in L. M. Wolfe, ed., *John Muir; John of the Mountains: The Unpublished Journals of John Muir*, 1938

3 It would be fantastic . . . to make the mistake now of so expanding the scope of ecology that it would become all-embracing, so that the ecologist would bog down in a morass of

his own ignorance, and become the supreme irritating busybody.

FRANK FRASER DARLING, speech to the British Association, Aberdeen meeting, 29 August 1963

4 The befouling of the American environment by a fantastically productive economy results from a persistent fallacy that afflicts the American mind and misguides our energies. It is the fallacy of single-purpose planning, both public and private. Most engineers, developers, industrialists, and government officials are single-purpose planners.

HAROLD GILLIAM, *Daedalus*, Autumn 1967

5 Most of the scientists thus employed by industry are "positivists" whose vision is further restricted by what one ecologist has called "the tendency to fractionate, intensify, and barricade the subdisciplines." They do not try to interpret their fields in social terms. The complexities of population biology find no place in their circumscribed world. It is no wonder, then, that they have failed to uncover the damaging, ecosystemic effects of the persistent pesticides. And so, since they have failed to detect anything, they insist that what they have not seen does not exist. The glass of their knowledge does not take in the many interdependent strands which make up the web of nature.

FRANK GRAHAM, *Since Silent Spring*, 1970

6 Once having assigned a problem by default or otherwise to a set of experts, the discussion thereafter is strongly influenced by their particular disciplinary and methodological biases. Economists' use of cost-benefit analysis, for example, may cause distortions because of its inability to deal with incommensurable values, soft variables, holistic-ecological issues, questions of justice, and the interests of future generations. In such cases the demand for rigor can lead to rigor mortis.

DAVID W. ORR, *Journal of Politics*, November 1979

7 This, then, is the essential message of Eco-philosophy: we can affect every element of our social, individual, spiritual, ecological and political life, not separately, but by affecting them all at once. Moreover, unless we affect them all, none will be affected.

HENRYK SKOLIMOWSKI, *Eco-Philosophy*, 1981

8 A primary problem of American environmentalism is that its self-assigned tasks are complex almost beyond the capacity of single minds to grasp. To demand synthesis, to demand holistic thought in a world of specialists is to demand superbrains.

DANIEL B. LUTEN, *Landscape*, Spring 1981

9 Nobody knows how to put together a holistic system. In many cases you don't want to combine biological and social data. They're different and they operate on different time scales. You have to retain a respect for the different systems involved.

JOHN W. BENNETT, speech, American Association for the Advancement of Science, Washington, D.C., 3 January 1982

10 The problems of today do not come with a tag marked energy or economy or CO_2 or demography, nor with a label indicating a country or a region. The problems are multi-disciplinary and transnational or global.

PER LINDBLOM, hearing, World Commission on Environment and Development, Oslo, Norway, 24–25 June 1985

11 When you believe that, above all, the most indispensable thing is to view problems in terms of their interrelationships rather than in terms of the elements they're made up of, it means that you must first be very familiar with those elements. If not, you're just jabbering.

RENÉ DUBOS, in Gerard Piel and Osborn Segerberg, Jr., eds., *The World of René Dubos*, 1990

12 Now that we are effectively conducting a vast experiment with the planetary ecosystem itself, science must consider a more integrated view of the world. This needs a new breed of scientist, an interdisciplinary scientist. A good number of scientists believe they already qualify, but they are really multidisciplinary scientists. Worthy as this is, it is far from comprehending the world with its seamless webs of natural and social interactions. The interdisciplinarian appreciates that prime attention should be directed instead to the "grey" areas between disciplines.

NORMAN MYERS, *The Gaia Atlas of Future Worlds*, 1990

13 If the ultimate test of any body of scientific knowledge is its ability to predict events, then all the sciences and pseudosciences—physics, chemistry, climatology, economics, ecology—fail the test regularly. They all have been announcing laws, designing models, predicting what an individual atom or person is supposed to do; and now, increasingly, they are beginning to confess that the world never quite behaves the way it is supposed to do.

DONALD WORSTER, *Environmental History Review* 14, nos. 1–2, Spring–Summer 1990

66 HUMAN ADAPTATION
See also   68 HUMANKIND AND NATURE

1 [People] do not consider how admirable these things [the elements of nature] are in their own places, how excellent in their own natures, how beautifully adjusted to the rest of creation, and how much grace they contribute to the universe by their own contributions as to a commonwealth; and how serviceable they are even to ourselves, if we use them with a knowledge of their fit adaptations—so that even poisons, which are destructive when used injudiciously, become wholesome and medicinal when used in conformity with their qualities and design. . . . And thus divine providence admonishes us not foolishly to vituperate things, but to investigate their utility with care.

AUGUSTINE OF HIPPO (354–430), *City of God*, 10.22

2 How fleeting are the wishes and efforts of man! how short his time! and consequently how poor will be his results, compared with those accumulated by Nature during whole geological periods! Can we wonder, then, that Nature's productions should be far "truer" in character than man's productions; that they should be infinitely better adapted to the most complex conditions of life, and should plainly bear the stamp of far higher workmanship?

CHARLES DARWIN (1809–1882), *On the Origin of Species*, 1859

3 We can so far take a prophetic glance into futurity as to foretell that it will be the common and widely spread species, belonging to the larger and dominant groups within each class, which will ultimately prevail and procreate new and dominant species.

CHARLES DARWIN (1809–1882), *On the Origin of Species*, 1859

4 A human [is] not a fallen god, but a promoted reptile.

J. HOWARD MOORE, *The Universal Kinship*, 1906

5 We talk of our mastery of nature, which sounds very grand; but the fact is we respectfully adapt ourselves, first, to her ways.

CLARENCE DAY, *This Simian World*, 1920

6 People are inexterminable—like flies and bed bugs. There will always be some that survive in cracks and crevices—that's us.

ROBERT FROST (1874–1963), quoted in *The Observer*, 29 March 1959

7 Man's destiny is to be the sole agent for future evolution of this planet. He is the highest dominant type to be produced over two and a half billion years of the slow biological movement effected by the blind opportunistic workings of natural selection.

JULIAN HUXLEY, *The Humanist Frame*, 1961

8 Till now man has been up against Nature; from now on he will be up against his own nature.

DENNIS GABOR, *Inventing the Future*, 1963

9 We must face the fact that modern man has failed to build adequate cities. In the past his problems were simpler, and he solved them by trial and error. Now human forces and mechanical ones are mixed and man is confused. He tries and fails. We say he will become adapted. Yes, he is running the danger of becoming adapted, since adaptation is only meaningful if it means the welfare of man. Prisoners, too, become adapted to conditions! For man to adapt to our present cities would be a mistake, since he is the great prisoner. Not only is man unsafe in his prison, but he is facing a great crisis and heading for disaster.

CONSTANTINOS A. DOXIADIS, *Saturday Review*, 18 March 1967

10 The dangers posed by the increase in human population make it clear that the Darwinian

concept of adaptation cannot be used when the welfare of the human species is used as a criterion of adaptability. . . . Man can achieve some form of tolerance to environmental pollution, excessive environmental stimuli, crowded and competitive social contacts, the estrangement of life from the natural biological cycles, and other consequences of life in the urban and technological world. . . . But in many cases, it is achieved through organic and mental processes which may result in the chronic and degenerative disorders that so commonly spoil adult life and old age, even in the most prosperous countries.

RENÉ DUBOS, speech, UNESCO biosphere conference, Paris, 1968

11 Man will survive as a species for one reason: He can adapt to the destructive effects of our power-intoxicated technology and of our ungoverned population growth, to the dirt, pollution and noise of a New York or Tokyo. And that is the tragedy. It is not man the ecological crisis threatens to destroy but the quality of human life.

RENÉ DUBOS, quoted in *Life*, 28 July 1970

12 While there is no doubt that man can function and reproduce in a completely artificial environment, it is probable that alienation from nature will eventually rob him of some of his important biological attributes and most desirable ethical and aesthetic values.

RENÉ DUBOS, *The Ecologist*, October 1970

13 Compare these miraculous accomplishments [of nature] with creations of the intellect that is so worshiped by modern man: our population explosion, our genetic deficiencies, our nuclear weapons, the breaking-down environment with which life now intertwines. How can one avoid the conclusion that, to date, the mind of man has selected for life a negative evolution?

CHARLES A. LINDBERGH (1902–1974), *Reader's Digest*, November 1971

14 Nature—that is, biological evolution—has not fitted man to any specific environment. . . . Among the multitude of animals which scamper, fly, burrow, and swim around us, man is the only one who is not locked into his environment. His imagination, his reason, his emotional subtlety and toughness, make

it possible for him not to accept the environment but to change it. And that series of inventions by which man from age to age has remade his environment is a different kind of evolution—not biological, but cultural evolution. I call that brilliant sequence of cultural peaks *The Ascent of Man.*

JACOB BRONOWSKI, *The Ascent of Man*, 1973

15 Even without mutation, it is always possible that some hitherto obscure parasitic organism may escape its accustomed ecological niche and expose the dense human populations that have become so conspicuous a feature of the earth to some fresh and perchance devastating mortality.

WILLIAM H. MCNEILL, *Plagues and Peoples*, 1976

16 If we do not identify ourselves with the flow of evolution, then we are doomed, both conceptually and existentially. Our politics, in short, must coincide with the tactics and strategies of life at large.

HENRYK SKOLIMOWSKI, *The Ecologist*, October 1977

17 Natural selection over millions of years shaped our ancestors in ways that suited earlier environments. We do not know how well we are now suited biologically and behaviorally to the world our species has so rapidly made.

DAVID A. HAMBURG and SARAH SPAGHT BROWN, *Science*, 26 May 1978

18 What seems to be missing from the ecologists' dogma is the recognition that all forms of life, including man, must fight for survival, and if they survive they must forever keep changing to keep surviving. The animals on the savanna know this; mankind in a free society knows it; escape from this natural law comes only in a cage at the zoo or a regimented society. Neither man nor beast can escape this reality.

To be free means to survive. To survive means to adapt, to cope.

SAM WITCHEL, *New York Times*, 3 May 1979

19 Ecology mandates that all species be preserved in their present state and cancels completely the commandment of survival only for the fittest or that genetic change breeds

into the species those characteristics necessary to cope with the environment.

In fact, ecology apparently wishes to insure the survival of the least fit: evolution is heresy, natural selection is Original Sin.
SAM WITCHEL, *New York Times*, 3 May 1979

20 Man can be adapted to anything—to the dirt and noise of New York City—and that is what is tragic. As we can accept worse and worse conditions, we don't realize that there is something worse than extinction—the progressive degradation of human life.
RENE DUBOS, *Man Adapting*, 1980

21 [With a] planet dying faster than at its natural rate . . . [the] accelerated and pathological entropy would break the natural evolutionary continuum. The ultimate purpose and significance of the entire creative process would then be lost—to man and all.
MICHAEL W. FOX, *Returning to Eden*, 1980

22 On an island near Japan, biologists introduced freshly dug sweet potatoes as a new food to some monkeys. The monkeys were reluctant to eat the dirty potatoes, as all their other food could be eaten without preparation. Eventually, one eighteen-month old female carried some potatoes down to a stream and washed them before feeding. She then taught this behavior to her mother and playmates who taught it to their mothers. The only adults to adopt the behavior were those who were taught by their children. Suddenly, however, a critical threshold was passed (perhaps the hundredth monkey learned it) and the behavior became universal, even among monkeys who had not observed the washing. The phenomenon could be extrapolated to people; when enough of us come to hold something to be true, it becomes true for most everyone. We even have a name for it; we call it, "An idea whose time has come."
LESTER MILBRATH, drawing on Lyall Watson's *Lifetide* (1980), which explains "the hundredth monkey phenomenon," *Envisioning a Sustainable Society*, 1989

23 The human being is a weed species.
S. DILLON RIPLEY, quoted in Roger Stone, *The Sanderling*, 1989

24 People living in an environment like Tokyo will, if they continue in the direction society seems to be taking them, cease to be human and turn into robots.
VICTOR MONTOMBRI, Indonesian environmentalist, quoted in *Japan Environmental Monitor* 2, no. 5, 31 October 1989

25 Nature has had this tendency toward increasingly more complex ways of passing on information from the big bang all the way up. Humankind is what nature has been trying, all these millenia, "to be."
FREDERICK TURNER, *Harper's*, April 1990

26 Der Mench gewöhnt sich an alles.
(People can get used to anything)
HANNE SIMONSEN, on environmental conditions in East Germany, *Tomorrow* 1, no. 1, 1991

67 HUMANKIND AND ENVIRONMENT
See also   44 ENVIRONMENTAL DEGRADATION, 45 ENVIRONMENTAL IMPACTS, 64 HISTORY

1 Hurt not the earth, neither the sea, nor the trees.
BIBLE, Revelation 7:3

2 As for those who would take the whole world
To tinker it as they see fit,
I observe that they never succeed:
For the world is a sacred vessel
Not made to be altered by man.
The tinker will spoil it;
Usurpers will lose it.
LAO-TZU (6th century B.C.), quoted in Stephen Fox, *John Muir and His Legacy*, 1981

3 The first and greatest knowledge, and also common to all men, is the division and order of our environment.
POLYBIUS (c. 200–c. 118 B.C.), *Histories*, 130 B.C.

4 It is He who has
Made the earth manageable

For you, so traverse
Ye through its tracts
And enjoy of the sustenance
Which He furnishes . . .
KORAN, sura 67.15

5 No man is an island, entire of itself; every man is a piece of the continent, a part of the main.
JOHN DONNE (1572–1631), *Devotions upon Emergent Occasions*, 1624

6 Thus is Man that great and true Amphibian whose nature is disposed to live . . . in divided and distinguished worlds.
THOMAS BROWNE (1605–1682), *Religio Medici*, 1642

7 While the earth was left to its natural fertility and covered with immense forests, whose trees were never mutilated by the axe, it would present on every side both sustenance and shelter for every species of animal. Men, dispersed up and down among the rest, would observe and imitate their industry, and thus attain even to the instinct of the beasts, with the advantage that, whereas every species of brutes was confined to one particular instinct, man, who perhaps has not any one peculiar to himself, would appropriate them all.
JEAN-JACQUES ROUSSEAU (1712–1778), *Discours sur l'origine et les fondements de l'inégalité*, 1755

8 Men are like plants; the goodness and flavour of the fruit proceeds from the peculiar soil and exposition in which they grow.
J. HECTOR ST. JOHN DE CREVECOEUR (1735–1813), *Letters from an American Farmer*, 1782

9 Yes, gentlemen, give me the map of any country, its configuration, its climate, its waters, its winds, and the whole of its physical geography; give me its natural productions, its flora, its zoology, &c., and I pledge myself to tell you, *à priori*, what will be the quality of man in that country, and what part its inhabitants will act in history.
VICTOR COUSIN (1792–1867), *Introduction to the History of Philosophy*, 1832

10 It is not the tropics with their luxuriant vegetation, but the temperate zone, that is the mother-country of capital. It is not the mere fertility of the soil, but the differentiation of the soil, the variety of its natural products, the changes of the seasons, which form the physical basis for the social division of labour, and which, by changes in the natural surroundings, spur man on to the multiplication of his wants, his capabilities, his means and modes of labour.
KARL MARX (1818–1883), *Das Kapital*, 1867

11 Man has too long forgotten that the earth was given to him for usufruct alone, not for consumption, still less for profligate waste.
GEORGE P. MARSH, *The Earth as Modified by Human Action*, 1874

12 A grateful environment is a substitute for happiness. It can quicken us from without as a fixed hope and affection, or the consciousness of a right life, can quicken us from within.
GEORGE SANTAYANA (1863–1952), *The Sense of Beauty*, 1896

13 We all dwell in a house of one room—the world with the firmament for its roof—and are sailing the celestial spaces without leaving any track.
JOHN MUIR (1838–1914), quoted in L. M. Wolfe, ed., *John Muir, John of the Mountains: The Unpublished Journals of John Muir*, 1938

14 Man has been endowed with reason, with the power to create, so that he can add to what he's been given. But up to now he hasn't been a creator, only a destroyer. Forests keep disappearing, rivers dry up, wild life's become extinct, the climate's ruined and the land grows poorer and uglier every day.
ANTON CHEKHOV (1860–1904), *Uncle Vanya*, 1897

15 Man is a product of the earth's surface. This means not merely that he is a child of the earth, dust of her dust; but that the earth has mothered him, fed him, set him tasks, directed his thoughts, confronted him with difficulties that have strengthened his body and sharpened his wits, given him his problem of navigation or irrigation, and at the same time whispered hints for their solutions.
ELLEN CHURCHILL SEMPLE, *Influences of Geographic Environment*, 1911

16 We have changed our environment more quickly than we know how to change ourselves.
WALTER LIPPMANN, *Drift and Mastery*, 1914

17 The civilization under which people are restricted and controlled by a material environment from which they cannot escape, and under which they cannot utilize human thought and intellectual power to change environment and improve conditions, is the civilization of a lazy and nonprogressive people. It is a truly materialistic civilization.
HU SHIH (1891–1962), *La jeunesse nouvelle*, April 1919

18 Creation destroys as it goes, throws down one tree for the rise of another. But ideal mankind would abolish death, multiply itself million upon million, rear up city upon city, save every parasite alive, until the accumulation of mere existence is swollen to a horror.
D. H. LAWRENCE (1885–1930), *St. Mawr*, 1925

19 In the last analysis, it is probable that certain regions and peoples are advanced mainly because of the highly favorable environments in which the race has evolved: that their initiative, energy, and intelligence are products of underlying environmental factors operating upon these people for long ages. It is the old question of race versus place; and the geographer will hold that the *masterful race is the product of the place that nourished it*. And so our cycle returns upon itself—the *place makes the race and then the race progressively remakes the place*.
R. H. WHITBECK, *Annals of the Association of American Geographers* 16, 1926

20 Human institutions originate from specific needs of man in his environmental relations. Man's religious institutions arise from emotional urges which drive him to compensate for the inadequacies of his environment and the unsatiated desires of his experience.
G. T. RENNER, JR., *Annals of the Association of American Geographers* 17, 1927

21 It is not necessarily those lands which are the most fertile or most favoured in climate that seem to me the happiest, but those in which a long struggle of adaptation between man and his environment has brought out the best qualities of both.
T. S. ELIOT (1888–1965), "After Strange Gods," 1934

22 Breed, crowd, encroach, expand, expunge yourself, die out, *homo* called *sapiens*.
EDNA ST. VINCENT MILLAY (1892–1950), *Wine from These Grapes*, 1934

23 The geographic environment is a mould into which the human race has been poured, and the history of the race has been shaped by that mould.
A. E. PARKINS, *Journal of Geography* 33, 1934

24 The environment of solitude [is] a human need rather than a luxury or plaything.
ROBERT S. YARD, *Living Wilderness*, September 1935

25 After all anybody is as their land and air is. Anybody is as the sky is low or high, the air heavy or clear and anybody is as there is wind or no wind there. It is that which makes them and the arts they make and the work they do and the way they eat and the way they drink and the way they learn and everything.
GERTRUDE STEIN (1874–1946), *An American and France*, 1936

26 It is not merely soil, nor plant, nor animal, nor weather which we need to know better, but chiefly man himself.
PAUL SEARS, *Deserts on the March*, 1947

27 The more we get out of the world the less we leave, and in the long run we shall have to pay our debts at a time that may be very inconvenient for our own survival.
NORBERT WIENER, *The Human Use of Human Beings*, 1954

28 How can the spirit of the earth like the White man? . . . Everywhere the White man has touched, it is sore.
WINTU INDIAN, quoted in Dorothy Lee, *Freedom and Culture*, 1959

29 Man's unique reward, however, is that while animals survive by adjusting themselves to their background, man survives by adjusting his background to himself.
AYN RAND, *For the New Intellectual*, 1961

30 Never have people been more the masters of their environment. Yet never has a people felt more deceived and disappointed. For never has a people expected so much more than the world could offer.

DANIEL J. BOORSTIN, *The Image*, 1962

31 We stand now where two roads diverge. But unlike the roads in Robert Frost's familiar poem, they are not equally fair. The road we have long been traveling is deceptively easy, a smooth superhighway on which we progress at great speed, but at its end lies disaster. The other fork of the road—the one "less traveled by"—offers our last, our only chance to reach a destination that assures the preservation of our earth.

The choice, after all, is ours to make.

RACHEL CARSON, *Silent Spring*, 1962

32 Are we faced with the proposition that civilisation is a contradiction in terms; that civilisation carries its own seeds of decay because ecologically retrogressive processes once begun cannot be checked?

FRANK FRASER DARLING, speech, British Association, Aberdeen meeting, 29 August 1963

33 Never before has man had such capacity to control his own environment, to end thirst and hunger, to conquer poverty and disease, to banish illiteracy and massive human misery. We have the power to make this the best generation of mankind in the history of the world—or to make it the last.

JOHN F. KENNEDY (1917–1963), speech, United Nations General Assembly, New York City, 20 September 1963

34 Since the individual's desire to dominate his environment is not a desirable trait in a society which every day grows more and more confining, the average man must take to daydreaming.

GORE VIDAL, *Esquire*, December 1963

35 [Our environment is] largely the sum of the unplanned, uncoordinated, and often cross-purpose pursuits of individuals, corporations, and government agencies, all seeking their own objectives, and seldom with regard for the cumulative consequences of their actions.

LYNTON K. CALDWELL, in Frank F. Darling and John P. Milton, eds., *Future Environments of North America*, 1966

36 We have been massively intervening in the environment without being aware of many of the harmful consequences of our acts until they have been performed and the effects—which are difficult to understand and sometimes irreversible—are upon us. Like the sorcerer's apprentice, we are acting upon dangerously incomplete knowledge. We are, in effect, conducting a huge experiment *on ourselves*.

BARRY COMMONER, *Science and Survival*, 1966

37 We presume to change the natural environment for all the living creatures on this earth. Do we, who are transients on this earth, and not overly wise, really believe we have the right to upset the order of nature, an order established by a power higher than man?

HYMAN G. RICKOVER, speech, Royal National Foundation, Athens, 1966

38 To sustain an environment suitable for man, we must fight on a thousand battlegrounds. Despite all of our wealth and knowledge, we cannot create a redwood forest, a wild river, or a gleaming seashore.

LYNDON B. JOHNSON (1908–1973), message to Congress, 23 February 1966

39 Every modification of the physical environment brings about a series of changes, sometimes beneficial, sometimes adverse, often unforeseen. This does not mean that man should forego modifying the environment. It does mean, however, that we should make every reasonable effort to understand the results of our action, to minimize the detrimental impact of our actions upon the environment, and to take advantage of opportunities for positive benefits.

CONSERVATION FOUNDATION, testimony, Senate Commerce Committee, 27 July 1966

40 The emergence in widespread practice of the Baconian creed that scientific knowledge means technological power over nature . . . [and] its acceptance as a normal pattern of action may mark the greatest event in human history since the invention of agriculture.

LYNN I. WHITE, JR., *Science*, 10 March 1967

41 What does the concept of "environment" mean? Does it refer to the natural world alone

or does it include everything that affects the physical and mental health of man? What are the criteria for a good quality environment? Who should decide this and who should bear the costs involved? What is an appropriate division of responsibilities between the private and public sectors for environmental quality management?

> HENRY JACKSON, U.S. Senator, colloquium on the environment, U.S. Congress, 17 July 1968

42 The battle for the quality of the American environment is a battle against neglect, mismanagement, poor planning and a piecemeal approach to problems of natural resources.

> RICHARD M. NIXON, radio address, 18 October 1968

43 Change the environment; do not try to change man.

> R. BUCKMINSTER FULLER, *Design Science*, 1969

44 [Consider] the profound and striking similarities between ecological systems and the activities of man: between predators and land speculators; between animal-population growth and economic growth; between plant dispersal and the diffusion of people, ideas and money.

> CRAWFORD S. HOLLINGS, quoted in *Time*, 15 August 1969

45 We are none of us good enough for the world we have.

> EDWARD ABBEY, *Appalachian Wilderness*, 1970

46 Mankind has an incestuous relationship with Mother Earth.

> ANONYMOUS GRAFFITO, 1970

47 After all, for thousands of years mankind has lived . . . by drinking contaminated water, and he has survived the resulting dysentery and typhoid epidemics. Suffering apparently is not enough to move one to fight for a better environment. Malaria has never caused a revolution. In order to fight, one must be able to see a clear relationship between nature, technology, economic power, and political power. One must also be able to rise to the belief that nature belongs to every man.

> JEAN-FRANÇOIS REVEL, *Without Marx or Jesus*, 1970

48 As we constantly become more and more nearly lords of creation, there is nothing so much to be feared as ourselves, yet we know so little about fearsome us.

> HOWARD ZAHNISER, quoted in Stephen Fox, *John Muir and His Legacy*, 1970

49 Someone has said: "We don't know who discovered water but we're sure it wasn't a fish." Unfortunately, man in relation to his environment is in the same state of unawareness.

> HARLEY PARKER, Arts-canada, April 1970

50 We shall never understand the natural environment until we can see it as a living organism.

> PAUL BROOKS, *The Pursuit of Wilderness*, 1971

51 Reclamation is the father of putting water to work for man—irrigation, hydropower, flood control, recreation. Let's *use* our environment. Nature changes the environment every day of our lives—why shouldn't *we* change it?

> FLOYD DOMINY, quoted in John McPhee, *Encounters with the Archdruid*, 1971

52 The word nature . . . applies not only to undisturbed wilderness, but also to fields, meadows, forests, and waterways, which have been so managed as to bring out characteristics that were inherent in the place—in the *genius loci*.

> RENÉ DUBOS, *American Scholar*, Spring 1971

53 If we go on the way we have, the fault is our greed [and] if we are not willing [to change], we will disappear from the face of the globe, to be replaced by the insect.

> JACQUES COUSTEAU, interview, 17 July 1971

54 Clearly, the real environmental struggle has begun. It is a struggle with ourselves, as a people who have always *known* that more is better and that another clean environment lies beyond the next rise. It is a struggle that may wax and wane in public interest but will not go away, for its ingredients are founded in practice and habit.

> SYDNEY HOWE, *Conservation Foundation Letter*, December 1971

55 We have met the enemy, and it is us.

> WALT KELLY, *Pogo*, 1972

56 The enormous power and capricious behavior of the environment has amazed and terrified man throughout the ages. Its vast and destructive powers have launched him on a relentless search for an effective method to harness its overwhelming forces. Once achieved, this ability to control and manipulate the environment will provide him with a means to wreak untold and indiscriminate damage upon his fellow human beings.
   CLAIBORNE PELL, U.S. Senator, speech, U.S. Senate, 17 March 1972

57 My preference for change through minute particulars [rather than a grand blueprint] is simply that this is the way societies have, with great benefit to the common man, adapted themselves for centuries to the consequences of their own impact on the environment.
   ERIC ASHBY, The Ecologist, April 1972

58 And what is environment but the whole outside of ourselves? Everything and everybody "around" and, by implication, what was around in the past and will be in the future as a result of what we are and do. All other people, living, dead, unborn; all other living beings; plants, rocks, water, dirt; all things present in natural form or made by us into something else: these are our environment. Each one of us is the inside of it; the earth—and space—are our outer body.
   EVELYN AMES, New York Times, 20 May 1972

59 Infinity is ended, and mankind is in a box;
   The era of expanding man is running out of rocks;
   A self-sustaining Spaceship Earth is shortly in the offing
   And man must be its crew—or else the box will be his coffin!
   KENNETH E. BOULDING, "The Ballad of Ecological Awareness" in M. Taghi Farvar and John P. Milton, eds., The Careless Technology, 1972

60 The crux of the matter is not only whether the human species will survive, but even more whether it can survive without falling into a state of worthless existence.
   CLUB OF ROME EXECUTIVE COMMITTEE, in Donella H. Meadows et al., The Limits to Growth, 1972

61 Ecology provides us the reasons for disaster, but not a life-affirming motive for changing our ways. It is therefore an incomplete idea. A Romantic view of nature provides a life-affirming motive for a faithful stewardship of the ecosphere, but no substantive reasons as an imperative. It is therefore also an incomplete idea.
   CHARLES E. LITTLE, A Town Is Saved, 1973

62 We have forgotten how to be good guests, how to walk lightly on the earth as its other creatures do.
   BARBARA WARD, Only One Earth, 1972

63 It is quite obvious that the human race has made a queer mess of life on this planet. But as a people we probably harbor seeds of goodness that have lain for a long time waiting to sprout when the conditions are right. Man's curiosity, his relentlessness, his inventiveness, his ingenuity have led him into deep trouble. We can only hope that these same traits will enable him to claw his way out.
   E. B. WHITE, Letter to Mr. Nadeau, 30 March 1973, in Letters of E. B. White, 1976

64 We will look upon the earth and her sister planets as being with us, not for us. One does not rape a sister.
   MARY DALY, Beyond God the Father, 1973

65 The landscape of earth is dotted and smeared with masses of apparently identical individual animals. . . . What if God has the same affectionate disregard for us that we have for barnacles? I don't know if each barnacle larva is of itself unique and special, or if we the people are essentially as interchangeable as bricks.
   ANNIE DILLARD, Pilgrim at Tinker Creek, 1974

66 The new fact, however, is that the right to a good environment has come to be regarded as a natural right of man for which the community is responsible. . . . There will be popular resentment against control measures that appear unfair, elitist, or wasteful. But this will not make people forget that they are entitled to a good environment. There has never been a lasting retreat from the recognition of a natural right of man.
   RENÉ DUBOS, Saturday Review/World, 24 August 1974

67 The environment is not just one more factor to be considered along with dozens of others

in making social and economic decisions. The environment is not a crisis or a problem at all. Rather, it is the context in which all crises and problems have to be analyzed and judged.

WILLIAM V. SHANNON, *New York Times*, 29 September 1974

68 It is not absurd to class the ecological role of humankind in its relationship to other life forms . . . as an acute epidemic disease.

WILLIAM H. MCNEILL, on the similarity between man upsetting the balance of nature and a disease upsetting the natural balance in a host's body, *Plagues and Peoples*, 1976

69 The emergence of intelligence, I am convinced, tends to unbalance the ecology. In other words, intelligence is the great polluter. It is not until a creature begins to manage its environment that nature is thrown into disorder.

CLIFFORD D. SIMAK, *Shakespear's Planet*, 1976

70 Man has probably always worried about his environment because he was once totally dependent on it.

ANTHONY C. FISHER and FREDERICK M. PETERSON, *Journal of Economic Literature*, March 1976

71 The modern urban-industrial society is based on a series of radical disconnections between body and soul, husband and wife, marriage and community, community and earth. At each of these points of disconnection the collaboration of corporation, government, and experts sets up a profit-making enterprise that results in the further dismemberment and impoverishment of the Creation.

WENDELL BERRY, *The Unsettling of America*, 1977

72 Man is the original and basic pollutant.

J. O'M. BOCKRIS, *Environmental Chemistry*, 1977

73 DDT and plutonium are exotic materials that we have been pushed into using by the demands for more food and more energy for more people. These two substances did not even exist until the 1940s. The biosphere evolved over billions of years without ever having had any evolutionary experience with DDT or plutonium. Consequently, the biosphere is totally unadapted to these substances, and their large-scale, or even small-scale, introduction cannot fail to be disruptive.

HERMAN E. DALY, *Steady-State Economics*, 1977

74 The laws of thermodynamics restrict all technologies, man's as well as nature's, and apply to all economic systems whether capitalist, communist, socialist, or fascist. We do not create or destroy (produce or consume) anything in a physical sense—we merely transform or rearrange. And the inevitable cost of arranging greater order in one part of the system (the human economy) is creating a more than offsetting amount of disorder elsewhere (the natural environment).

HERMAN E. DALY, *Steady-State Economics*, 1977

75 Man is an open system. What was man three months ago is now environment; what was environment yesterday is man today. Man and environment are so totally interdependent it is hard to say where one begins and the other ends. This total interdependence has not diminished and will not in the future, regardless of technology.

HERMAN E. DALY, *Steady-State Economics*, 1977

76 We may be perfectly sure of where we are in relation to the supermarket and the next coffee break, but I doubt that any of us knows where he is in relation to the stars and to the solstices.

N. SCOTT MOMADAY, *Americans and the Land*, 1977

77 Perhaps we are all unredeemably "edge" creatures, never wholly at home either in the dark humid forest or the big open-sky country of the grassland, always struggling to convert both into a Kentucky idyll of shady oak groves dappled across a pastoral meadow. But then we also know that we are animals of remarkable adaptability—when and where we have to be.

DONALD WORSTER, *Nature's Economy*, 1977

78 There are two tragedies to be avoided. One is the very real possibility that we will wantonly destroy our life support system. The other is the almost equally grim prospect that we will jettison the open society and much of our

western heritage in the name of survival. Our argument is that neither of these outcomes is necessary.

DAVID W. ORR and STUART HILL, *Western Political Quarterly*, December 1978

79 In losing stewardship we lose fellowship; we become outcasts from the great neighborhood of creation.

WENDELL BERRY, *Sierra*, 1979

80 By our ravenous use of fossil [fuels] . . . we not only prolonged human corruption but also began undoing what evolution had done in getting the atmosphere ready for animals (including man) to breathe, and ready to sustain the kind of climate in which present species (including ourselves) had been evolved.

WILLIAM R. CATTON, JR., *Overshoot: The Ecological Basis of Revolutionary Change*, 1980

81 The protection of the environment, of course, is intimately connected to the quest for happiness. When we perceive our oneness with humanity, it is easy to perceive humanity's oneness with the environment. Even the salinity of our bodies is a legacy of our marine origins, as the first living cell took shape from ocean waters. Safeguarding the environment, then, is a way of extending ourselves in every way possible—by knowledge, by love, by sharing, by creation. We can find happiness in protecting the world around us not only because we cherish it for its awesome beauty, power, mystery, but because we cherish our fellow humans, those who live today and those who will live tomorrow, living beings who, like ourselves, will increasingly depend on the environment, for happiness and even for life itself.

JACQUES COUSTEAU, *The Cousteau Almanac*, 1980

82 Human life cannot be nurtured, nursed, and sustained unless we nurse and sustain the ecological habitat within the womb of which we all reside.

HENRYK SKOLIMOWSKI, *Eco-Philosophy*, 1981

83 Ecological Humanism offers an authentic alternative to industrial society. It holds that: *The coming age is to be seen as the age of stewardship:* we are here not to govern and exploit, but to maintain and creatively transform, and to carry on the touch of evolution.

HENRYK SKOLIMOWSKI, *Eco-Philosophy*, 1981

84 If it is true that the environment is the infrastructure of all life and all activity on the planet; if it is true . . . that unless we maintain the productive capacity of the world's ecosystems, the existence of sustained development is not possible; if it is true, as we firmly believe, that many of the social and economic problems afflicting us derive from the degradation of the environment, the obvious conclusion is that under no circumstances and under no pretext can we relax our vigilance in the face of the demands of a rational, vitally necessary environmental policy.

MAGARINOS DE MELLO, speech, United Nations Environment Program, Nairobi, 26 May 1981

85 Things that have a dignity, I believe, are in general the things that help us to define our relationship with one another. The environment we share has such a dignity. The way we use and the way we preserve our common natural heritage helps to define our relation or association with each other. It also helps to define our association with generations in the future and in the past.

MARK SAGOFF, *Environmental Law* 12, 1982

86 From the biological point of view, rationality is merely one of the possible evolutionary strategies for competing in the struggle for existence. We professors undoubtedly tend to overrate it. After all, if rationality were such a successful attribute, why is it that only one rational species has ever evolved? (If that many.)

JACK HIRSHLEIFER, speech, American Association for the Advancement of Science, Washington, D.C., 3 January 1982

87 It is so easy to pontificate about the needs of people; to decide in the abstract what is good for them and then to design an environment which in practice turns out to be much less acceptable than supposed. This is not necessarily due to the cussedness of people, it is just as likely to be due to a lack of understanding of human behaviour.

PRINCE PHILIP, duke of Edinburgh, *Men, Machines, and Sacred Cows*, 1984

88 In our own beginnings, we are formed out of the body's interior landscape. For a short while, our mothers' bodies are the boundaries and personal geography which are all

that we know of the world. . . . Once we no longer live beneath our mother's heart, it is the earth with which we form the same dependent relationship, relying . . . on its cycles and elements, helpless without its protective embrace.

LOUISE ERDRICH, *New York Times*, 28 July 1985

89 Generally speaking, it seems clear that without meeting the basic needs of human beings, concern for the environment has to be secondary. Man has to survive, answer, and attend first to his basic survival needs—food, housing, sanitation—and then to the environment.

WALTER PINTO COSTA, hearing, World Commission on Environment and Development, São Paulo, 28–29 October 1985

90 We are like goldfish who have been living in an aquarium for as long as we can remember; and being clever goldfish, we have discovered how to manipulate the controls of the aquarium: put more oxygen in the water, get rid of the pesky turtle we never liked anyway, triple the supply of goldfish food. Only once we realize we're partly running the aquarium, it scares some of us. What if we make a mistake, and wreck the aquarium entirely? We couldn't live outside it.

NOEL PERRIN, in Daniel Halpern, *On Nature*, 1986

91 You're pretty well off. You expect to be better off soon. You do. What does this mean? More software, more scampi, more square footage? You have created an ecological crisis. The earth is infinitely variable and alive, and you are killing it. It seems safer this way. But you are not safe. You want to find wholeness and happiness in a land increasingly damaged and betrayed, and you never will. More than material matters. You must change your ways.

JOY WILLIAMS, *Esquire*, February 1989

92 We are living in an historic transitional period in which awareness of the conflict between human activities and environmental constraints is literally exploding. . . . Never before in our history have we had so much knowledge, technology and resources. Never before have we had such great capacities. The time and the opportunity have come to break out of the negative trends of the past.

GRO HARLEM BRUNDTLAND, Prime Minister of Norway, speech, National Press Club, Washington, D.C., 5 May 1989

93 If a society forgets or no longer cares where it lives, then anyone with the political power and the will to do so can manipulate the landscape to conform to certain social ideals or nostalgic visions. People may hardly notice that anything has happened, or assume that whatever happens—a mountain stripped of timber and eroding into its creeks—is for the common good. The more superficial—or artificial—becomes a society's knowledge of the real dimensions of the land it occupies, the more vulnerable the land is to exploitation, to manipulation for short-term gain.

BARRY LOPEZ, *Orion Nature Quarterly*, Autumn 1989

94 We in America have as much reason as the Soviet Union to engage in a *perestroika* of our own—to open to public discussion the serious conflict between our unexamined capitalist ideology and the failed effort to resolve the environmental crisis—as a prelude to radical (in the sense of getting at the root of the problem) remedial action.

BARRY COMMONER, *Making Peace with the Planet*, 1990

95 The environment is all just a matter of *attitude*. In fact, you can think of your attitude as your "inner environment," which can be as fresh and green and perky as you like, even when the Great Lakes turn to solid waste and the Himalayas are placed on smog alert.

BARBARA EHRENREICH, *The Worst Years of Our Lives*, 1990

96 But the most liberating thing I've learned in Environmental Grief Counseling is when to let go, say good-bye, and stand on your own two feet. I mean, human beings have been clinging to the environment for aeons now, creeping around on the rocks, eating the berries, filling their tires with the air.

This is *dependency*, and dependency is a form of *addiction*. What the human race needs is a heavy-duty twelve-step program to wake us up to the fact that the environment is just a

crutch—a great big security blanket that we can finally set aside.
BARBARA EHRENREICH, *The Worst Years of Our Lives*, 1990

97 Always my life comes up against the fact that it does not flourish or wane separate from worldwide experience but is, in fact, wired, like a neuron in the brain, to all other circuits of life on earth.
JOHN NICHOLS, *The Sky's the Limit*, 1990

98 [Unconstrained individualism is] the pursuit of an environment that maximizes one's own well-being, without regard to the collective results of such behavior.
ANTHONY DOWNS, *Synergy/Planning*, July 1990

99 Let me warn you about a species potentially more dangerous than the fire ant, one that originated in Africa and has spread to all of the continents—yes, even Antarctica. While many insects produce toxins that they inject by means of a bite or sting, this critter produces several toxins that it sprays indiscriminately throughout its environment. It forms huge colonies and, as with the fire ant, colony size has been rapidly increasing. . . . They are capable of killing baby birds, fawns, children, one another, you name it. They reproduce at a phenomenal rate, and neither scientists nor politicians have found an effective way to control them.
JOY FATOOH, *Smithsonian*, September 1990

100 Other animals simply adapt to their environment. Our intelligence seems to have outpaced our sense of place in the universe, and the result is that we're enormously dangerous.
PETER MATTHIESSEN, quoted in *Sports Illustrated*, 3 December 1990

101 When we think about our relationship to the environment, we should know where we are, where we come from, and then agree to live intentionally in those places in a way that will allow people to remember us well. It is when we reaffirm that compact between ourselves and our progeny that duty is born.
DAN KEMMIS, quoted in *Harper's*, February 1991

68 HUMANKIND AND NATURE
See also   66 HUMAN ADAPTATION

1 Thou shalt be in league with the stones of the field; and the beasts of the field shall be at peace with thee.
BIBLE, Job 5:23

2 Live in accordance with nature.
GREEK (STOIC) MAXIM

3 I am a lover of knowledge, and the men who dwell in the city are my teachers, and not the trees or the country.
SOCRATES (c. 470–399 B.C.), quoted in Plato, *Phaedrus* 10

4 The goal of life is living in agreement with Nature.
ZENO THE STOIC (c. 335–c. 263 B.C.), quoted in Diogenes Laertius, *Lives of Eminent Philosophers*

5 We are wise because we follow nature as the best of guides, and obey her as a goddess.
CICERO (106–43 B.C.), *De senectute*, 45–44 B.C.

6 Nature has given us life, at interest, like money, no day being fixed for its return.
CICERO (106–43 B.C.), *Tusculanae disputationes*, 44 B.C.

7 So the Creator made man all things, as a sort of driver and pilot, to drive and steer the things on earth, and charged him with the care of animals and plants, like a governor subordinate to the chief and great King.
PHILO OF ALEXANDRIA (c. 20 B.C.–A.D. 40), *On the Creation*

8 True wisdom consists in not departing from nature and in molding our conduct according to her laws and model.
SENECA (4 B.C.–A.D. 65), *Moral Essays*

9 It is far from easy to determine whether she [Nature] has proved to man a kind parent or a merciless stepmother.
PLINY THE ELDER (A.D. 23–79), *Natural History*

10 Never does Nature say one thing and Wisdom another.
JUVENAL (about A.D. 55–about A.D. 127), *Satires*

11 All that thy seasons, O Nature, bring
      is fruit for me!
   All things come from thee, subsist in
      thee, go back to thee.
   MARCUS AURELIUS (121–180), *Meditations*

12 Go, my sons, buy stout shoes, climb the
   mountains, search . . . the deep recesses of
   the earth. . . . In this way and in no other will
   you arrive at a knowledge of the nature and
   properties of things.
   SEVERINUS, 7th century

13 The sky and the earth and the waters and the
   things that are in them, the fishes, and the
   birds and the trees are not evil. All these are
   good; it is evil men who make this evil world.
   AUGUSTINE OF HIPPO (354–430), *Sermones ad
   Populum*

14 Now birds and trees perform their books of
   wonder, passersby hear wondrous news and
   are less sad.
   LOUISE LABÉ (c. 1524–1566), Sonnet 15

15 Sweet are the uses of adversity;
   Which, like the toad, ugly and venomous,
   Wears yet a precious jewel in his head:
   And this our life exempt from public haunt
   Finds tongues in trees, books in running
      brooks,
   Sermons in stones and good in every thing.
   WILLIAM SHAKESPEARE (1564–1616), *As You
   Like It*, 2.1.16–17, 1599

16 One touch of nature makes the whole world
   kin.
   WILLIAM SHAKESPEARE (1564–1616), *Troilus
   and Cressida*, 3.3.175, 1601–1602

17 There are in nature certain fountains of justice, whence all civil laws are derived but as
   streams.
   FRANCIS BACON (1561–1626), *The Advancement of Learning*, 1605

18 In nature's infinite book of secrecy
   A little I can read.
   WILLIAM SHAKESPEARE (1564–1616), *Antony
   and Cleopatra*, 1.2.9, 1606–1607

19 About nature consult nature herself.
   FRANCIS BACON (1561–1626), *De Augmentis
   Scientiarum*, 1623

20 The insufferable arrogance of human beings
   to think that Nature was made solely for their

benefit, as if it was conceivable that the sun
had been set afire merely to ripen men's apples and head their cabbages.
SAVINIEN DE CYRANO DE BERGERAC (1619–
1655), *États et empires de la lune*, 1656

21 Accuse not Nature, she hath done her part;
   Do thou but thine.
   JOHN MILTON (1608–1674), *Paradise Lost*, 1667

22 What is man in nature? Nothing in relation to
   the infinite, everything in relation to nothing,
   a mean between nothing and everything.
   BLAISE PASCAL (1623–1662), *Pensées*, 1670

23 It were happy if we studied nature more in
   natural things, and acted according to nature,
   whose rules are few, plain, and most reasonable.
   WILLIAM PENN (1644–1718), *Some Fruits of
   Solitude*, 1693

24 Nature will always maintain her rights, and
   prevail in the end over any abstract reasoning
   whatsoever.
   DAVID HUME (1711–1776), *Essays Moral and
   Political*, 1741

25 Deviation from Nature is deviation from happiness.
   SAMUEL JOHNSON (1709–1784), *Rasselas*, 1759

26 Nature's instructions are always slow, those
   of men are generally premature.
   JEAN-JACQUES ROUSSEAU (1712–1778), *Émile*,
   1762

27 It is in man's heart that the life of nature's
   spectacle exists; to see it, one must feel it.
   JEAN-JACQUES ROUSSEAU (1712–1778), *Émile*,
   1762

28 Men argue, nature acts.
   VOLTAIRE (1694–1778), *Philosophical Dictionary*, 1764

29 Gie me ae spark o' Nature's fire,
   That's a' the learning I desire.
   ROBERT BURNS (1759–1796), "Epistle to John
   Lapraik No. 1," 1786

30 We may regard it as a favour that nature has
   extended to us, that besides giving us what is
   useful it has dispensed beauty and charms in
   such abundance, and for this we may love it,
   just as we view it with respect because of its
   immensity, and feel ourselves ennobled by

such contemplation—just as if nature had erected and decorated its splendid stage with this precise purpose in its mind.

IMMANUEL KANT (1724–1804), *The Critique of Judgment*, 1790

31 So far from making man, regarded as one of the many animal species, an ultimate end, nature has no more exempted him from its destructive than from its productive forces, nor has it made the smallest exception to its subjection of everything to a mechanism of forces devoid of an end.

IMMANUEL KANT (1724–1804), *The Critique of Judgment*, 1790

32 There is not a sprig of grass that shoots uninteresting to me, nor any thing that moves.

THOMAS JEFFERSON (1743–1826), letter to Martha Jefferson Randolph, 23 December 1790

33 Nature goes forward in her never-ending course, and cares nothing for the race of man that is ever passing before her. . . . When man turns to reflection and resigns himself to the inevitable . . . then the eternal, unchangeable order of Nature has a comforting and peaceful influence.

WILHELM VON HUMBOLDT (1767–1859), letter

34 Kings, aristocrats, and tyrants, whoever they may be, are slaves in rebellion against the sovereign of the earth, which is mankind, and against the legislator of the universe, which is nature.

MAXIMILIEN ROBESPIERRE (1758–1794), on the Declaration of the Rights of Man and of the Citizen, 1789

35 Nature never did betray
The heart that loved her.

WILLIAM WORDSWORTH (1770–1850), "Lines Composed a Few Miles Above Tintern Abbey," 1798

36 I must confess that I am not romance-hit about nature. The earth, the sea, and sky (when all is said) is but as a house to dwell in.

CHARLES LAMB (1775–1834), letter to Thomas Manning, 28 November 1800

37 Nature appears to make use of mankind for her projects without caring for the instruments she uses, somewhat like tyrants who destroy those who have been of service to them.

SEBASTIEN CHAMFORT (1741–1794), *Maximes et pensées*, 1803

38 Go forth, under the open sky, and list
To Nature's teachings.

WILLIAM CULLEN BRYANT (1794–1878), "Thanatopsis," 1817, 1821

39 To him who in the love of nature holds
Communion with her visible forms, she speaks
A various language; for his gayer hours
She has a voice of gladness, and a smile
And eloquence of beauty, and she glides
Into his darker musings, with a mild
And healing sympathy that steals away
Their sharpness ere he is aware.

WILLIAM CULLEN BRYANT (1794–1878), "Thanatopsis," 1817, 1821

40 [My] edication has been altogether in the woods; the only book I read, or care about reading, is the one which God has opened before all his creatures in the noble forests, broad lakes, rolling rivers, blue skies, and the winds, and tempests, and sunshine, and other glorious marvels of the land! This book I can read, and I find it full of wisdom and knowledge.

JAMES FENIMORE COOPER (1789–1851), *The Last of the Mohicans*, 1826

41 Boundless Nature, where shall I grasp thee?

JOHANN WOLFGANG VON GOETHE (1749–1832), *Faust*, 1832

42 Nature is medicinal and restores their tone. The tradesman, the attorney, comes out of the din and craft of the street and sees the sky and the woods, and is a man again. In their eternal calm, he finds himself. The health of the eye seems to demand a horizon. We are never tired, so long as we can see far enough.

RALPH WALDO EMERSON (1803–1882), *Nature*, 1836

43 Neither does the wisest man extort her [nature's] secret and lose his curiosity by finding out all her perfection.

RALPH WALDO EMERSON (1803–1882), *Nature*, 1836

44 The sky is the daily bread of the eyes.

RALPH WALDO EMERSON (1803–1882), entry written 25 May 1843, *Journals*, 1909–1914

45 Nature hates calculators.
    RALPH WALDO EMERSON (1803–1882), *Essays,
    Second Series*, 1844

46 Beneficent Nature, how often does the heart
    of man, crushed beneath the weight of his
    sins or his sorrows, rise in reproach against
    thine unchanged serenity!
    MARIA McINTOSH (1803–1878), *Two Lives*,
    1846

47 It is the marriage of the soul with Nature that
    makes the intellect fruitful, and gives birth to
    imagination.
    HENRY DAVID THOREAU (1817–1862), *Journal*,
    21 August 1851

48 Say what some poets will, Nature is not so
    much her own ever-sweet interpreter, as the
    mere supplier of that cunning alphabet,
    whereby selecting and combining as he
    pleases, each man reads his own peculiar les-
    son according to his own peculiar mind and
    mood.
    HERMAN MELVILLE (1819–1891), *Pierre*, 1852

49 This is a delicious evening, when the whole
    body is one sense, and imbibes delight
    through every pore. I go and come with a
    strange liberty in Nature, a part of herself.
    HENRY DAVID THOREAU (1817–1862), *Walden*,
    1854

50 It appears to be a law that you cannot have a
    deep sympathy with both man and nature.
    HENRY DAVID THOREAU (1817–1862), *Walden*,
    1854

51 We must go out and re-ally ourselves to Na-
    ture every day. We must take root, send out
    some little fibre at least, even every winter
    day.
    HENRY DAVID THOREAU (1817–1862), *Journal:
    Winter*

52 Now I see the secret of the making of the best
    persons. It is to grow in the open air, and to
    eat and sleep with the earth.
    WALT WHITMAN (1819–1892), *Leaves of Grass*,
    1855–1892

53 Nature . . . cares nothing for appearances,
    except in so far as they are useful to any be-
    ing. She can act on every internal organ, on
    every shade of constitutional difference, on
    the whole machinery of life. Man selects only
    for his own good: Nature only for that of the
    being which she tends.
    CHARLES DARWIN (1809–1882), *On the Origin
    of Species*, 1859

54 Nature tells every secret once.
    RALPH WALDO EMERSON (1803–1882), *The
    Conduct of Life*, 1860

55 Nature is profoundly imperturbable. We may
    adjust the beating of our hearts to her pendu-
    lum if we will and can, but we may be very
    sure that she will not change the pendulum's
    rate of going because our hearts are palpitat-
    ing.
    OLIVER WENDELL HOLMES, SR. (1809–1894),
    speech to the Massachusetts Medical Soci-
    ety, Boston, 30 May 1860

56 Nature is not a temple but a workshop in
    which man is the laborer.
    IVAN TURGENEV (1818–1883), *Smoke*, 1867

57 Nature has made up her mind that what can-
    not defend itself shall not be defended.
    RALPH WALDO EMERSON (1803–1882), *Society
    and Solitude*, 1870

58 Nature, in her most dazzling aspects or stu-
    pendous parts, is but the background and
    theatre of the tragedy of man.
    JOHN MORLEY (1838–1923), *Critical Miscella-
    nies*, 1871–1908

59 Inebriate of air am I,
    And débauchée of dew,
    Reeling, through endless summer days,
    From inns of molten blue.
    EMILY DICKINSON (1830–1886), *Poems*

60 How strange that Nature does not knock,
    and yet does not intrude!
    EMILY DICKINSON (1830–1886), letter to Mrs.
    J. S. Cooper, 1880

61 After you have exhausted what there is in
    business, politics, conviviality, and so on—
    have found that none of these finally satisfy,
    or permanently wear—what remains? Nature
    remains.
    WALT WHITMAN (1819–1892), *Specimen Days*,
    1882

62 There is no better way of loving nature than
    through art.
    OSCAR WILDE (1854–1900), quoted in Lead-
    ville (Colo.) *Herald*, 13 April 1882

63 Nature has had her day; she has finally and totally exhausted the patience of all sensitive minds by the loathsome monotony of her landscapes and skies.

J. K. HUYSMANS (1848–1907), À rebours, 1884

64 One goes to Nature only for hints and half-truths. Her facts are crude until you have absorbed them or translated them. . . . It is not so much what we see as what the thing seen suggests.

JOHN BURROUGHS (1837–1921), Signs and Seasons, 1886

65 Most people are on the world, not in it—have no conscious sympathy or relationship to anything about them—undiffused, separate, and rigidly alone like marbles of polished stone, touching but separate.

JOHN MUIR (1838–1914), 1890, in L. M. Wolfe, ed., John Muir, John of the Mountains: The Unpublished Journals of John Muir, 1938

66 Nature . . . has almost as many ways as a woman, and is to be lived with, not merely looked at.

FRANCIS THOMPSON (1859–1907), letter to Mrs. Alice Meynell, September 1893

67 He who makes two blades of grass grow where one grew before is the benefactor of mankind, but he who obscurely worked to find the laws of such growth is the intellectual superior as well as the greater benefactor of mankind.

HENRY A. ROWLAND, (1848–1901), quoted in D. S. Greenberg, The Politics of Pure Science, 1967

68 The more men know about nature, and the more they rely upon nature, the more agnostic and hopeless they become.

O. A. CURTIS, The Christian Faith, 1905

69 Let me enjoy the earth no less
Because the all-enacting Might
That fashioned forth its loveliness
Had other aims than my delight.

THOMAS HARDY (1840–1928), Time's Laughingstocks and Other Verses, 1909

70 For what is Nature? Nature is no great mother who has borne us. She is our creation. It is in our brain that she quickens to life. Things are because we see them, and

what we see, and how we see it, depends on the Arts that have influenced us. . . . [Nature] has no suggestions of her own.

OSCAR WILDE (1854–1900), The Decay of Lying, 1909

71 I only went out for a walk and finally concluded to stay out till sundown, for going out, I found, was really going in.

JOHN MUIR (1838–1914), 1913, in L. M. Wolfe, ed., John Muir, John of the Mountains: The Unpublished Journals of John Muir, 1938

72 There is an eagle in me and a mockingbird . . . and the eagle flies among the Rocky Mountains of my dreams and fights among the Sierra crags of what I want . . . and the mockingbird warbles in the early forenoon before the dew is gone, warbles in the underbrush of my Chattanoogas of hope, gushes over the blue Ozark foothills of my wishes— and I got the eagle and the mockingbird from the wilderness.

CARL SANDBURG (1878–1967), Cornhuskers, 1918

73 There is no need for man and no demand for man, in nature; it is complete without him.

WILLIAM GRAHAM SUMNER (1840–1910), The Forgotten Man and Other Essays, 1918

74 Nature is like a beautiful woman that may be as delightfully and as truly known at a certain distance as upon a closer view; as to knowing her through and through, that is nonsense in both cases, and might not reward our pains.

GEORGE SANTAYANA (1863–1952), Character and Opinion in the United States, 1921

75 What better comfort have we, or what other
Profit in living
Than to feed, sobered by the truth of Nature,
Awhile upon her bounty and her beauty,
And hand her torch of gladness to the ages
Following after?

GEORGE SANTAYANA (1863–1952), "Ode"

76 Nature: The Unseen Intelligence which loved us into being, and is disposing of us by the same token.

ELBERT HUBBARD (1856–1915), The Roycroft Dictionary and Book of Epigrams, 1923

77 Man is the only creature in the animal kingdom that sits in judgment on the work of the

Creator and finds it bad—including himself and Nature.

ELBERT HUBBARD (1856–1915), *The Notebook of Elbert Hubbard*, 1927

78 All the secrets of nature lie in the open and strike our eyes each day without our paying attention.

ANDRE GIDE (1869–1951), *Nouvelles nourritures*, 1935

79 Nature is proving that she can't be beaten—not by the likes of us. She's taking the world away from the intellectuals and giving it back to the apes.

ROBERT E. SHERWOOD (1896–1955), *The Petrified Forest*, 1935

80 Go often to collect your thoughts in nature! . . . Then you will be in a position to understand the works of men.

GONZAGUE DE REYNOLD (1880–1970), *Cités et paysages suisses*, 1937

81 A man and what he loves and builds have but a day and then disappear; nature cares not—and renews the annual round untired. It is the old law, sad but not bitter. Only when man destroys the life and beauty of nature, there is the outrage.

GEORGE MACAULAY TREVELYAN (1876–1962), *Grey of Fallodon*, 1937

82 A wrong attitude towards nature implies, somewhere, a wrong attitude towards God, and that the consequence is an inevitable doom. For a long enough time we have believed in nothing but the values arising in a mechanised, commercialised, urbanised way of life: it would be as well for us to face the permanent conditions upon which God allows us to live upon this planet.

T. S. ELIOT (1888–1965), *Christianity and Culture*, 1939

83 The love of Tao is the love of nature. There is an endless strength when we "lie back upon nature" and hush our hearts.

ALAN DEVOE, *Audubon*, November–December 1946

84 There are some who can live without wild things, and some who cannot.

ALDO LEOPOLD (1886–1948), *A Sand County Almanac*, 1949

85 Nature herself vindicates democracy. For nature plants gifts and graces where least expected, and under circumstances that defy all the little artifices of man.

FELIX FRANKFURTER (1882–1965), U.S. Supreme Court justice, speech, Aaronsburg, Pa., 23 October 1949

86 Your salvation is in your own hands. . . . Nature is indifferent to the survival of the human species, including Americans. She does not weep over those who fall by the way.

ADLAI E. STEVENSON (1900–1965), speech, 29 September 1952

87 The world began without man, and it will complete itself without him.

CLAUDE LÉVI-STRAUSS, *Tristes Tropiques*, 1955

88 The natural world, actually, is the test by which each man proves himself: I see, I feel, I love, I use, I alter, I appropriate, therefore I am.

WALLACE STEGNER, *This Is Dinosaur*, 1955

89 Nature, contended John Donne in the seventeenth century, is the common law by which God governs us.

LOREN EISELEY, *The Firmament of Time*, 1960

90 I have no patience with people who say they love nature and go out to look at a field on Sunday afternoon. Our families, the way we live with our fellowmen, are part of nature, too.

THORNTON WILDER (1897–1975), quoted in *New York Times Magazine*, 15 April 1962

91 What is this wildness Thoreau is talking about? . . . [It is] something more nearly akin to Bernard Shaw's Life Force—it is that something prehuman that generated humanity.

JOSEPH WOOD KRUTCH (1893–1970), *Saturday Review*, 8 June 1963

92 There may yet be, in the untrammeled tenth of America, enough nature, unsecond-guessed by technological arrogance, to build a good future on.

DAVID R. BROWER, in Eliot Porter, *Summer Island: Penobscot Country*, 1966

93 Man's chief goal in life is still to become and stay human, and defend his achievements against the encroachment of nature.

ERIC HOFFER, *The Temper of Our Time*, 1967

94 Nature thrives on patience; man on impatience.
PAUL BOESE, quoted in *Reader's Digest*, September 1968

95 Clearly the problem of man and nature is not one of providing a decorative background for the human play, or even ameliorating the grim city: it is the necessity of sustaining nature as source of life, milieu, teacher, sanctum, challenge and, most of all, of rediscovering nature's corollary of the unknown in the self, the source of meaning.
IAN MCHARG, *Design with Nature*, 1969

96 But it is illusion to think that there is anything fragile about the life of the earth; surely this is the toughest membrane imaginable in the universe, opaque to probability, impermeable to death. We are the delicate part, transient and vulnerable as cilia. Nor is it a new thing for man to invent an existence that he imagines to be above the rest of life; this has been his most consistent intellectual exertion down the millennia. As illusion, it has never worked out to his satisfaction in the past, any more than it does today. Man is embedded in nature.
LEWIS THOMAS, *The Lives of a Cell: Notes of a Biology Watcher*, 1971

97 In the eyes of Nature we are just another species in trouble.
LIONEL TIGER and ROBIN FOX, *The Imperial Animal*, 1971

98 Nature composes some of her loveliest poems for the microscope and telescope.
THEODORE ROSZAK, *Where the Wasteland Ends*, 1972

99 Every human has a fundamental right to an environment of quality that permits a life of dignity and well-being.
UNITED NATIONS CONFERENCE ON THE HUMAN ENVIRONMENT, Stockholm, 1972

100 The Edenic myth has dominated our public and private responses to landscape and is the tap that plunges down through the ages to the very beginnings of sentient man.
CHARLES E. LITTLE, *A Town Is Saved*, 1973

101 Within the limits of the physical laws of nature, we are still masters of our individual and collective destiny, for good or ill.
E. F. SCHUMACHER, *Small Is Beautiful*, 1973

102 Man has sufficient objective reasons to cling to the safe-keeping of the wild world. But nature will only be saved after all by our hearts.
JEAN DORST, *L'univers de la vie*, 1976

103 Every generation . . . writes its own description of the natural order, which generally reveals as much about human society and its changing concerns as it does about nature. And these descriptions linger on in bits and pieces, often creating incongruous or incompatible juxtapositions.
DONALD WORSTER, *Nature's Economy*, 1977

104 A margin of life is developed by Nature for all living things—including man. All life forms obey Nature's demands—except man, who has found ways of ignoring them.
EUGENE M. POIROT, *Our Margin of Life*, 1978

105 The overwhelming tragedy of planet Earth is man's contempt for nature.
ROBERT VAN DEN BOSCH, *The Pesticide Conspiracy*, 1978

106 Nature is trying very hard to make us succeed, but nature does not depend on us. We are not the only experiment.
R. BUCKMINSTER FULLER, quoted in *Minneapolis Tribune*, 30 April 1978

107 Nature, in the form of Sierra Club pantheism, was practically *invented* in the San Francisco Bay area.
GENE LYONS, *Harper's*, July 1978

108 I am not one of those supreme optimists who think all of the world's ills and especially this growing divide between man and nature, can be cured by a return to a quasi-agricultural, ecologically "caring" society.
JOHN FOWLES, *The Tree*, 1979

109 You cannot separate man and nature. So, the environmentalist's job is to make 'em compatible.
WALTER J. HICKEL, quoted in *The American Land*, 1979

110 The only solid piece of scientific truth about which I feel totally confident is that we are profoundly ignorant about nature. . . . It is this sudden confrontation with the depth and scope of ignorance that represents the most significant contribution of twentieth-century science to the human intellect.

LEWIS THOMAS, *The Medusa and the Snail,* 1979

111 Rather than anthropomorphizing animals, man more often has chosen to sanctify himself while animalizing himself.

MARGUERITE YOURCENAR, *Les yeux ouverts,* 1980

112 The outdoors is what you have to pass through to get from your apartment into a taxicab.

FRAN LEBOWITZ, *Washington Post Book World,* 30 August 1981

113 Love nature like a neighbor or relative.

JOHN CARMODY, *Ecology and Religion: Toward a New Christian Theology of Nature,* 1983

114 Righteous management would also be consistent with Taoist philosophy and ways of life wherein human activities fit in and flow with the larger cycles of Nature rather than attempt to modify Nature on a large scale to fit grandiose human projects and whims.

BILL DEVALL and GEORGE SESSIONS, *Deep Ecology,* 1985

115 There are many ways of seeing the biosphere. Each of us is a unique lens, a lens ground and coated by nature and nurture. And our responses to nature—to the world— are as diverse as our personalities, though each of us, at different times, may be awed, horrified, dazzled, or just amused by nature.

MICHAEL E.SOULE, National Forum on Biodiversity, Washington, D.C., 21 September 1986

116 In our minds, nature suffers from a terrible case of acne, or even skin cancer—but our faith in its essential strength remains, for the damage always seems local.

BILL MCKIBBEN, *The End of Nature,* 1989

117 Human happiness, and certainly human fecundity, are not as important as a wild and healthy planet. I know social scientists who remind me that people are part of nature, but

it isn't true. Somewhere along the line—at about a billion years ago, maybe half that—we quit the contract and became a cancer. We have become a plague upon ourselves and upon the Earth. It is cosmically unlikely that the developed world will choose to end its orgy of fossil-energy consumption, and the Third World its suicidal consumption of landscape. Until such time as Homo sapiens should decide to rejoin nature, some of us can only hope for the right virus to come along.

DAVID M. GRABER, *Los Angeles Times,* 22 October 1989

118 When Indians referred to animals as "people"—just a different sort of person from Man—they were not being quaint. Nature to them was a community of such "people" for whom they had a great deal of genuine regard and with whom they had a contractual relationship to protect one another's interests and to fulfill their mutual needs. Man and Nature, in short, was jointed by compact— not by ethical ties—a compact predicated on mutual esteem. This was the essence of the traditional land relationship.

ANONYMOUS, quoted in Julian Burger, *The Gaia Atlas of First Peoples,* 1990

119 A concern with nature is not merely a scientific curiosity, but a subject that pervades philosophy, theology, aesthetics, and psychology. There are deep reasons that we desire a balance and harmony in the structure of the biological world and that we seek to find that structural balance, just as our ancestors desired and sought that kind of balance in the physical world.

DANIEL B. BOTKIN, *Discordant Harmonies,* 1990

120 It is not true that "Nature knows best," It often creates ecosystems that are inefficient, wasteful and destructive. [It] is to be seen . . . as a garden to be cultivated for the development of its own potentialities for the human adventure.

RENÉ DUBOS, quoted in Gerald Piel and Osborn Segerberg, Jr., *The World of René Dubos,* 1990

121 The new, environmental-age Nature bears little resemblance to previous versions. She is

a slight, frail being, prone to vapors, fainting fits and many other debilitating ailments. The new Nature is not so intimidating, does not have the sort of grandeur that the old one did, but she is still very beautiful, though now somewhat in the style of an anorexic fashion model. Also she is very good—much better than the old one—for people. In fact, there is a widespread conviction that frequent congress with Nature is the ultimate therapy for mortal bodies and souls; thus, natural foods, fibers, medicines, exercises and gardens.

BILL GILBERT, *Smithsonian*, April 1990

122 It's easy for *homo sapiens* to imagine nature metaphysically pure, since we sit at the pinnacle of the food chain.

GREGG EASTERBROOK, *New Republic*, 30 April 1990

123 Nature and art are what the world is about. Nature is the universe and art is the human response. There's nothing else. Within all those interlocked realms is all passion and future.

MICHAEL TOBIAS, quoted in *Washington Post*, 22 February 1991

69 HUNTING
See also   7 ANIMAL RIGHTS

1 Hunting is one of those sensual pleasures which greatly excites the body and says nothing to the soul; it is an ardent desire to pursue some animal, and a cruel satisfaction to kill it; it is an amusement which renders the body robust and alert, and which lets the soul lie fallow and without culture.

FREDERICK II (Frederick the Great), King of Prussia (1712–1786), *Anti-Machiavel*, 1740

2 There is a passion for hunting something deeply implanted in the human breast.

CHARLES DICKENS (1812–1870), *Oliver Twist*, 1837–1839

3 Oh, horrible vulturism of earth! from which not the mightiest whale is free.

HERMAN MELVILLE (1819–1891), *Moby-Dick*, 1851

4 Man pursues his victims with reckless destructiveness; and while the sacrifice of life by the lower animals is limited by the cravings of appetite, he unsparingly persecutes, even to extirpation, thousands of organic forms which he can not consume.

GEORGE PERKINS MARSH, *The Earth as Modified by Human Action*, 1874

5 The terrible destructiveness of man is remarkably exemplified in the chase of large mammalia and birds, for single products, attended with the entire waste of enormous quantities of flesh and of other parts of the animal which are capable of valuable uses. The wild cattle of South America are slaughtered by millions, for their hides and horns; the buffalo of North America, for his skin or his tongue; the elephant, the walrus, and the narwhal, for their tusks; the cetacea, and some other marine animals, for their whalebone and oil; the ostrich and other large birds, for their plumage.... What a vast amount of human nutriment, of bone, and of other animal products valuable in the arts, is thus recklessly squandered!

GEORGE PERKINS MARSH, *The Earth as Modified by Human Action*, 1874

6 I could almost wish that the shooters of the birds, the taxidermists who prepare their skins, and the fashionable wearers of their feathers might share the penalty which was visited upon the Ancient Mariner who shot the Albatross.

JOHN GREENLEAF WHITTIER (1807–1892), 1886, quoted in Frank Graham, Jr., *The Audubon Ark*, 1990

7 The English country gentleman galloping after a fox—the unspeakable in full pursuit of the uneatable.

OSCAR WILDE (1854–1900), *A Woman of No Importance*, 1893

8 The older I grow the less I care to shoot anything except "varmints." I am still something of a hunter, although a lover of wild animals first.

THEODORE ROOSEVELT (1853–1919), 1897, quoted in Frank Graham, Jr., *Man's Dominion*, 1971

9 Bang! Now the animal
Is dead and dumb and done.

Nevermore to peep again, creep again, leap
again,
Eat or sleep or drink again, oh, what fun!
WALTER DE LA MARE (1873–1956), "Hi!," c.
1910

10 Making some bird or beast go lame the rest of
its life is a sore thing on one's conscience, at
least nothing to boast of, and it has no religion in it.
JOHN MUIR (1838–1914), 1913, in L. M.
Wolfe, ed., John Muir, John of the Mountains:
The Unpublished Journals of John Muir, 1938

11 The most appreciated, enjoyable occupation
for the normal man has always been hunting.
This is what kings and nobles have preferred
to do. . . . But it happens that the other social
classes have done or wanted to do the same
thing.
JOSÉ ORTEGA Y GASSET (1883–1955), Meditations on Hunting, 1943

12 When man hunts he succeeds in diverting
himself and in distracting himself from being
a man. And this is the superlative diversion:
it is the fundamental diversion.
JOSÉ ORTEGA Y GASSET (1883–1955), Meditations on Hunting, 1943

13 By hunting, man succeeds, in effect, in annihilating all historical evolution, in separating
himself from the present and in renewing the
primitive situation.
JOSÉ ORTEGA Y GASSET (1883–1955), Meditations on Hunting, 1943

14 One does not hunt in order to kill; on the contrary, one kills in order to have hunted.
JOSÉ ORTEGA Y GASSET (1883–1955), Meditations on Hunting, 1943

15 The passenger pigeon and other game species would still be plentiful if firearms had remained on the technological level of the 17th
and the 18th centuries.
S. V. CIRIACY-WANTRUP, Resource Conservation, 1952

16 You did not kill the fish only to keep alive and
to sell for food, he thought. You killed him
for pride and because you are a fisherman.
You loved him when he was alive and you
loved him after. If you love him, it is not a sin
to kill him. Or is it more?
ERNEST HEMINGWAY (1899–1961), The Old
Man and the Sea, 1952

17 Every ground is a hunting ground, whether it
lies between you and the curbstone, or in
those illimitable woods where rolls the Oregon. The final test of the hunter is whether he
is keen to go hunting in a vacant lot.
ALDO LEOPOLD (1886–1948), Round River,
1953

18 It is chiefly through the instinct to kill that
man achieves intimacy with the life of nature.
KENNETH CLARK, quoted in The Faber Book of
Aphorisms, 1964

19 Every living creature (often including the red-
skinned race of his own species) was fair
game to the gunner.
FRANK GRAHAM, JR., Man's Dominion: The
Story of Conservation in America, 1971

20 I am under the impression, too, that notwithstanding the vaunted "harmony" between
the American Plains Indians and Nature,
once they had equipped themselves with ri-
fles their pursuit of the buffalo expanded to
fill the technological potential.
CHRISTOPHER D. STONE, 45 Southern California
Law Review 450, 1972

21 Toward the end . . . it became fashionable for
wealthy hunters of big game and titled visitors to "kill the last buffalo."
CY MARTIN, The Saga of the Buffalo, 1973

22 Photography as a substitute for hunting is a
mockery.
PAUL SHEPARD, The Tender Carnivore and the
Sacred Game, 1973

23 The real immorality of the hunting movement is not its willingness to kill, per se, but
its unwillingness to respect the biological and
esthetic integrity of the natural world. In its
selective, self-serving attitudes toward wildlife, in its eagerness to manipulate the environment for the sole sake of its sport, the
hunting movement displays an ultimate in-
sensitivity to all lower life forms; it exemplifies the belief that the only legitimate
function of our planet and its organic community is to satisfy the wishes of mankind,
no matter what form these wishes may take.
This is the same inglorious ethic that guides
the conscience of a strip miner or real estate
speculator.
JACK E. HOPE, Smithsonian, January 1974

24 Surely no one is insensitive to the current run of press photos of dead or injured, oil-covered wildlife, but the question may be asked as to how horrified these same people are at the carnage visited each year upon countless numbers of these creatures by hunters.

JAMES J. REYNOLDS, president, American Institute of Merchant Shipping, letter, *Washington Post*, 1 January 1977

25 In the long run we are likelier to be kept sane by the example of those among us who can join the hunt and tolerate the ambiguity of things than by the childlike visions of half-informed Jeremiahs preaching the omnivorous guilt of others.

GENE LYONS, *Harper's*, July 1978

26 Most hunters do not really know why they hunt, and some probably would not want to know if it ever occurred to them to wonder.

JOHN G. MITCHELL, *The Hunt*, 1980

27 Hunting, by an outside species that does not form an integral part of an ecosystem, removes the food supply of predators, parasites, scavengers, and all other organisms that are in turn affected by these species.

RAYMOND F. DASMANN, *Wildlife Biology*, 1981

28 One way to get to know a good deal about wildlife is to hunt it. Obviously that's one of the reasons why hunters and fishermen have very often been close to the conservation movement. They've been saving ducks and duck habitats because they want to shoot ducks, but at least they've been saving them from other kinds of things which would have done them in. Hunters know ducks.

WALLACE STEGNER, in Richard W. Etulain, ed., *Conversations with Wallace Stegner on Western History and Literature*, 1983

29 Support the right to arm bears.

BUMPER STICKER

30 The days a man spends fishing or spends hunting should not be deducted from the time that he's on earth. In other words, if I fish today, that should be added to the amount of time I get to live. That's the way I look at recreation. That's why I'll be a big conservation, environmental President, because I plan to fish and hunt as much as I possibly can.

GEORGE BUSH, quoted in *Los Angeles Times*, 30 December 1988

31 They have managed wildfowl to such an extent that the reasoning has become, If it weren't for hunters, ducks would disappear. Duck stamps and licensing fees support the whole rickety duck-management system. Yes! If it weren't for the people who killed them, wild ducks wouldn't exist! Managers are managing all wild creatures, not just those that fly. They track and tape and tag and band. They relocate, restock, and reintroduce. They cull and control. It's hard to keep it all straight. Protect or poison? Extirpate or just mostly eliminate. Sometimes even the stewards get mixed up.

JOY WILLIAMS, *Esquire*, February 1989

32 The sports-hunting Establishment—the numerous private and public agencies, industries and lobbies whose life depends upon the killing of our native fauna for pleasure—is the most pampered, privileged, subsidized recreational group in existence. Nevertheless, it has a paranoiac fear of even the mildest criticism.

BIL GILBERT, quoted in Anna Sequoia, *67 Ways to Save the Animals*, 1990

33 Hunting is a human, animal and ecological tragedy. The hunting issue divides families and communities. And it takes its toll on the only legacy we can really leave our children—wildlife and the environment.

LUKE DOMMER, quoted in *E* magazine, May–June 1990

34 In the fall, [hunting is] what I want to do. It would be unnatural and dishonest to sit on my hands; I'm a hunter, a predator (in the fall). . . . To not pursue the thing one wants would be a waste of one's life.

RICK BASS, *Esquire*, October 1990

35 *Sportsman's conservation* is a contradiction in terms (We protect things now so that we can kill them later) and is broadly interpreted (Don't kill them all, just kill most of them).

JOY WILLIAMS, *Esquire*, October 1990

36 More sentimental drivel has been written about bird shooting than any other type of hunting. It's a soul-wrenching pursuit, apparently, the execution of birds in flight.

JOY WILLIAMS, *Esquire*, October 1990

37 This [Ortega y Gasset's defense of hunting] is the sort of intellectual blather that the "thinking" hunter holds dear.
JOY WILLIAMS, *Esquire*, October 1990

38 It's time to stop actively supporting and passively allowing hunting, and time to stigmatize it. It's time to stop being conned and cowed by hunters, time to stop pampering and coddling them, time to get them off the government's duck-and-deer dole, time to stop thinking of wild animals as "resources" and "game," and start thinking of them as sentient beings that deserve our wonder and respect, time to stop allowing hunting to be creditable by calling it "sport" and "recreation." Hunters make wildlife *dead, dead, dead*. It's time to wake up to this indisputable fact. As for the hunters, it's long past checkout time.
JOY WILLIAMS, *Esquire*, October 1990

39 There's really no excuse anymore for the old form of hunting where we go out and kill an animal for fun. That seems to me to be a very crass and primitive form of expression of the hunting urge when we're capable of transforming it into abstract hunting. That is why I personally find people who go out hunting for fun, killing animals, to me are backward human beings because they haven't moved on past that stage.
Having said all that, we also developed the ability to make symbolic equations. That means today, when we don't need to hunt for food, we can still satisfy hunting urges by using symbolic equivalents. I can hunt for the perfect book; a doctor can hunt for the perfect cure. We all have our hunts, but they're symbolic hunts.
DESMOND MORRIS, *Washington Post*, 2 December 1990

40 Whether hunting is right or wrong, a spiritual experience, or an outlet for the killer instinct, one thing it is *not* is a sport. Sport is when individuals or teams compete against each other *under equal circumstances* to determine who is better at a given game or endeavor. Hunting will be a sport when deer, elk, bears, and ducks are endowed with human intelligence and given 12-gauge shotguns. Bet we'd see a lot fewer drunk yahoos (live ones, anyway) in the woods if *that* happened.
R. LERNER, letter, *Sierra*, March–April 1991

70 INDIGENOUS PEOPLE

1 These people are wild in the same way as we say that fruits are wild, when nature has produced them by herself and in her ordinary way; whereas, in fact, it is those that we have artificially modified, and removed from the common order, that we ought rather to call wild. In the former, the true, most useful, and natural virtues and properties are alive and vigorous; in the latter we have bastardized them, and adapted them only to the gratification of our corrupt taste.
MICHEL DE MONTAIGNE (1533–1592), on the natives in Brazil, "On Cannibals," *Essays* 1.31, 1578–1580

2 Lo, the poor Indian! whose untutor'd mind
Sees God in clouds, or hears him in the wind;
His soul proud Science never taught to stray
Far as the solar walk or milky way.
ALEXANDER POPE (1688–1744), *Essay on Man*, 1733–1734

3 The Indian . . . stands free and unconstrained in Nature, is her inhabitant and not her guest, and wears her easily and gracefully. But the civilized man has the habits of the house. His house is a prison.
HENRY DAVID THOREAU (1817–1862), *Journal*, entry dated 26 April 1841

4 Our God is the same God. This earth is precious to Him. Even the white man cannot be exempt from the common destiny. We may be brothers after all. We shall see.
SEATTLE (Seathl), patriarch of the Duwamish and Squamish Indians of Puget Sound, letter to U.S. President Franklin Pierce, 1855

5 Indians walk softly and hurt the landscape hardly more than the birds and squirrels, and their brush and bark huts last hardly longer than those of wood rats, while their more enduring monuments . . . vanish in a few centuries.
How different are most of those of the white man . . . roads blasted in the solid rock, wild streams dammed and tamed and turned out of their channels and led along

the sides of cañons and valleys to work in mines like slaves. . . . Long will it be ere these marks are effaced, though Nature is doing what she can . . . patiently trying to heal every raw scar.

JOHN MUIR (1838–1914), 16 June 1869, *My First Summer in the Sierras*, 1911

6 Indians and animals know better how to live than white man; nobody can be in good health if he does not have all the time fresh air, sunshine, and good water.

FLYING HAWK, Oglala Sioux chief (1852–1931), c. 1930

7 The most common trait of all primitive peoples is a reverence for the lifegiving earth, and the native American shared this elemental ethic: the land was alive to his loving touch, and he, its son, was brother to all creatures. . . . During the long Indian tenure the land remained undefiled save for scars no deeper than the scratches of cornfield clearings or the farming canals of the Hohokams on the Arizona desert.

STEWART L. UDALL, *The Quiet Crisis*, 1963

8 Today the conservation movement finds itself turning back to ancient Indian land ideas, to the Indian understanding that we are not outside of nature, but part of it.

STEWART L. UDALL, *The Quiet Crisis*, 1963

9 We [must] preserve the diverse habitats which diverse peoples need for their survival. To be sure, the restricted and specialized habitats of civilization give the greatest opportunities for what we . . . are pleased to call intelligence. But we have now learnt that intelligence is of many kinds. . . . And its diversity, if lost, cannot easily be recovered.

C. D. DARLINGTON, *The Evolution of Man and Society*, 1969

10 Something true and clear, massively unsentimental, runs through all their works, and this is, at bottom, the relationship between men and nature that they embody and reveal. In this they occupy a clear position in relation to the fundamental problem of human life: how to get along—which means in the end how to live and die—with the natural world and its laws.

VINCENT SCULLY, *Pueblo, Mountain, Village, Dance*, 1975

11 While some cultures wait till the last moment to modify consumption of resources, we Eskimos and Indians have routinely conserved as a matter of life-style.

THERESA J. PEDERSON, testimony, U.S. House Interior subcommittee, 25 April 1977

12 What is most disturbing about the ecologists' order of importance is the absolute disregard for aboriginal man. If the disappearance of animal species in the wild is tantamount to sin, why do so few mourn the passing of aboriginal man in our century?

Does it help the planet to keep tribes in man's pristine state or should they not have the "benefits" of civilization? Then why must wild animals be preserved only in their pure wild environment? Is this their special state of grace?

SAM WITCHEL, *New York Times*, 3 May 1979

13 Strictly speaking, living above subsistence level is doing avoidable harm to the planet and to traditional peoples.

STEPHANIE MILLS, *What Ever Happened to Ecology?*, 1989

14 Indigenous peoples are on the front line of the ecological crisis. They are the first victims, yet they may also be humanity's hope for the future.

JULIAN BURGER, *The Gaia Atlas of First Peoples*, 1990

15 What modern civilization has gained in knowledge, it has perhaps lost in sagacity. The indigenous peoples of the world retain our collective evolutionary experience and insights which have slipped our grasp. Yet these hold critical lessons for our future. Indigenous peoples are thus indispensible partners as we try to make a successful transition to a more secure and sustainable future on our precious planet.

MAURICE STRONG, quoted in Julian Burger, *The Gaia Atlas of First Peoples*, 1990

16 Native Americans maintained a careful balance with their environment, not because of technological primitivism but because of complex social laws that regulated greed, wealth, and power. Material equality was the cornerstone of most tribes' social philosophy. They recognized that preserving their envi-

ronment derived from social control rooted in social justice.

CARL GAWBOY, *Harper's,* July 1990

17 With the world becoming more crowded and technological advances making it smaller, indigenous populations will not be able to insulate themselves from culture change indefinitely.

H. J. VAN WAGENINGEN, commenting on Conoco's oil exploration in Ecuador's rain forest, *Environmental Forum,* September–October, 1990

71 INDOOR ENVIRONMENT

See also   6 AIR POLLUTION

1 Odds me, I marvel what pleasure or felicity they have in taking this roguish tobacco! it's good for nothing but to choke a man, and fill him full of smoke and embers.

BEN JONSON, *Every Man in His Humour,* 1598

2 A custom lothsome to the eye, hateful to the nose, harmful to the braine, dangerous to the lungs, and in the blacke stinking fume thereof, neerest resembling the horrible Stigian smoke of the pit that is bottomelesse.

JAMES I, king of England, (r. 1603–1625), on smoking, *A Counterblaste to Tobacco,* 1604

3 Smoking is a shocking thing—blowing smoke out of our mouths into other people's mouths, eyes and noses, and having the same thing done to us.

SAMUEL JOHNSON (1709–1784), quoted in James Boswell's *Tour of the Hebrides,* 19 August 1773

4 Pernicious weed! whose scent the fair annoys,
Unfriendly to society's chief joys.

WILLIAM COWPER (1731–1800), on smoking, "Conversation," 1781

5 A house of today is still almost as ill-ventilated, badly heated by wasteful fires, clumsily arranged and furnished as the house of 1858.

H. G. WELLS (1866–1946), *First and Last Things,* 1908

6 I prefer houses to the open air. In a house we all feel of the proper proportions. Everything is subordinated to us, fashioned for our use and our pleasure. Egotism itself, which is so necessary to a proper sense of human dignity, is entirely the result of indoor life. Out of doors one becomes abstract and impersonal. One's individuality absolutely leaves one. And then Nature is so indifferent, so unappreciative. Whenever I am walking in the park here I always feel that I am no more to her than the cattle that browse on the slope, or the burdock that blooms in the ditch.

OSCAR WILDE (1854–1900), *The Decay of Lying,* 1909

7 Fresh air and innocence are good if you don't take too much of them—but I always remember that most of the achievements and pleasures of life are in bad air.

OLIVER WENDELL HOLMES, JR. (1841–1935), U.S. Supreme Court justice, *Collected Legal Papers,* 1921

8 Gentlemen know that fresh air should be kept in its proper place—out of doors—and that, God having given us indoors and out-of-doors, we should not attempt to do away with this distinction.

ROSE MACAULAY (1889–1958), *Crewe Train,* 1926

9 We read of industrial vapors, automobile and jet-plane exhausts that contaminate the air. We never hear of the millions of *human* exhausts expelling tobacco smoke.

HARRY SWARTZ, quoted in *Reader's Digest,* November 1972

10 [Indoor air pollution] particularly threatens the young, the old, and the ill, because they are both more susceptible to the effects of pollution and more likely to be indoors.

LAURENCE S. KIRSCH, 6 *Harvard Environmental Law Review* 339, 1982

11 As national trends accelerate towards the reduction of ventilation and infiltration rates in buildings, coupled with an increased use of synthetic chemicals in the indoor environment, a new phenomenon has arisen: the "sick building" syndrome. Traditional approaches to environmental health developed

for the outdoor air, or for the industrial occupational setting, are inadequate to deal with this problem.

JAMES L. REPACE, *Environment International,* 1982

12 We face a public health threat which, if it had a single cause or a single set of symptoms, would be considered an epidemic of major proportions.

ALAN FOX, testimony on indoor air pollution, U.S. House Science and Technology subcommittee, 19 March 1985

13 It's only a matter of time before homeowners who want to sell their houses will have to get an EPA-approved "air-quality" test of their home, and spend thousands to "mitigate" any "problems" before they can sell.

WARREN T. BROOKS, quoted in *Environmental Forum,* July–August 1990

14 Mother Nature Says: "Clean Up Your Room"

ANONYMOUS T-SHIRT SLOGAN

72 INDUSTRY
See also 30 ECONOMIC GROWTH,
116 REGULATION

1 The question is not whether we can build a car that won't pollute the air; the question is whether we can overcome the resistance of the auto industry and the oil industry to get it built.

RALPH NADER, quoted in *New York Times Magazine,* 29 October 1967

2 The threats . . . that an industry will close down if required to institute pollution controls, putting employees out of work, are nothing but blackmail. . . . If the polluters knew the government would actually close them down for noncompliance with pollution control laws, the offending companies would begin installation of control equipment tomorrow morning at 7 a.m.

HERBERT P. READ, *Business Week,* 8 November 1969

3 Rarely revealed publicly, but still operational, are corporate rationalizations that air

pollution is the "price of progress" and the "smell of the payroll."

RALPH NADER, in John C. Esposito, *Vanishing Air,* 1970

4 Many corporate hardliners believe the "ecology thing" will blow over.

RALPH NADER, in John C. Esposito, *Vanishing Air,* 1970

5 Why these corporations are so shortsighted in this important public relations field I cannot understand, but instead of volunteering to join in smoke abatement they are resisting it. I have about reached the conclusion that, while large industry is important, fresh air and clean water are more important, and the day may well come when we have to lay that kind of a hand on the table and see who is bluffing.

BARRY M. GOLDWATER, letter to the editor, *Saturday Review,* 7 March 1970

6 The time has come to housebreak industry. The time has come to establish, once and for all time, as a fundamental principle of American justice, that industry owes the American people the cleanest air and the cleanest water that the existing state of the art in pollution control can secure.

VICTOR J. YANNACONE, speech, Michigan State University, 22 April 1970

7 The threat of companies closing down and moving away from Birmingham is nothing more than economic blackmail. . . . It is cheaper to frighten people with job loss and economic calamity than to make prompt, effective remedies to stop pollution.

UNITED STEELWORKERS OF AMERICA, District 36, press release, 21 April 1971

8 [An] insidious . . . trap would be to let antipollution become our new multibillion-dollar business: to let the pollution go on merrily in all its present forms, and superimpose a new multibillion-dollar business of antipollution on top of it. And in these days of conglomerates, it would be the same business. One branch of it would be polluting, the other branch of it antipolluting.

GEORGE WALD, speech, Harvard University, 21 April 1970

9 There is nothing in the theory of free-enterprise capitalism that says it operates better in filth than in a clean environment.
  GLADWIN HILL, *Madman in a Lifeboat*, 1973

10 When corporations produce their goods they use the cheapest and fastest methods available and leave behind vast quantities of waste. Then corporations dump the wastes in the poorest and most powerless parts of town. And when they earn their profits, the corporations divide them up among company executives and investors, leaving behind poor people who cannot afford medical care or food or decent homes.
  DANIEL ZWERDLING, *The Progressive*, February 1973

11 As I read and listen to advertisements, it is my very strong impression that there is a well-organized campaign afoot to propagandize the public into believing that our environmental concerns have been overstated and oversold and are the cause of major economic and energy problems. This is hot air—pure and simple.
  RUSSELL E. TRAIN, speech, National Press Club, 18 September 1973

12 What is good for General Motors is not necessarily good for the country.
  J. HERBERT HOLLOMAN, *Coastal Zone Management*, September 1974

13 One can almost admire the enterprise and clever salesmanship of the petrochemical industry. Somehow it has managed to convince the farmer that he should give up the free solar energy that drives the natural cycles and, instead, buy the needed energy—in the form of fertilizer and fuel—from the petrochemical industry. Not content with that commercial coup, these industrial giants have completed their conquest of the farmer by going into competition with what the farmer produces. They have introduced into the market a series of competing synthetics: synthetic fiber, which competes with cotton and wool; detergents, which compete with soap made of natural oils and fat; plastics, which compete with wood; and pesticides that compete with birds and ladybugs, which used to be free.

The giant corporations have made a colony out of rural America.
  BARRY COMMONER, in Wendell Berry, *The Unsettling of America*, 1978

14 And American industry fought every inch of the way against every environmental health requirement. Every dollar invested to reduce deadly coke oven emissions, to control arsenic and lead from copper smelters, to block unnecessary radiation exposures, to capture chemical plants' carcinogenic discharges, to curb toxic sulfates and nitrate particles from coal combustion, has come only after protracted political and legal struggles.
  PAUL G. ROGERS, U.S. Representative, speech, Third Annual Conference on Health Policy, 22 May 1978

15 It seems anomalous that institutions bent on private greed need not apologize for their polluting activities, whereas agencies that are devoted to the protection of public health, under due process of law, must apologize in terms that it's good for the economy.
  RALPH NADER, speech, Public Citizens Forum, 3 August 1978

16 All they have to do is fudge on a few figures, or lose a few animals.
  JACQUELINE M. WARREN, on chemical companies testing their own products, quoted in *Conservation Foundation Letter*, November 1978

17 Criminal liability makes each plant manager more responsible for his company's behavior, while standard regulatory machinery tends to take responsibility away from him. . . . Sending a few executives to jail will work wonders.
  WILLIAM GREIDER, *Washington Post*, 5 August 1979

18 He sincerely believes that he is standing between this country and disaster. His beliefs are close to those of corporate America's, because he believes that America would be better off if the companies were unshackled to do what they want.
  ANONYMOUS FRIEND OF JAMES G. WATT, quoted in *The New Yorker*, 4 May 1981

19 [To demonstrate environmental responsibility, the Valdez principles ask corporations to]

publicly affirm [their] belief that corporations and their stockholders have a direct responsibility for the environment . . . and [to] seek profits only in a manner that leaves the Earth healthy and safe.

COALITION FOR ENVIRONMENTALLY RESPONSIBLE ECONOMIES, Valdez Principles, September 1989

20 The coal industry actually produced studies showing that acid rain is good for the environment. The nuclear industry's reports showed that operating a reactor is safer than operating a health food store.

DENIS HAYES, speech, American Museum of Natural History, New York City, 8 November 1989

21 Ecological metaphors like string shopping bags or planting trees can be used to get rid of personal guilt. They don't provide solutions, and, in some cases, they interfere with the solutions. That's my position. Look, the problem is not in your head or my head. It's in the corporate boardrooms. That's where pollution begins.

BARRY COMMONER, Mother Earth News, March–April 1990

22 In our economic system, that decision process is totally under private control. A corporation's legal obligation is not to the nation but to its stockholders. Its decisions are made in the private interest, and that interest is maximizing profit.

So we now have to confront the clash between our economic ideology, which is capitalism, and the new idea that social interest in environmental quality must now intrude into this private province.

The scientific definition of socialism is social ownership and control of the means of production. What is important here is social control, not of every single piece of production but of the crucial ones. Clearly, society has to say, Build cars that do not produce smog. But it doesn't have to say how to make the wheels.

BARRY COMMONER, Mother Earth News, March–April 1990

23 Make environmental considerations and concerns part of any decisions you make, right from the beginning. Don't think of it as something extra you throw in the pot.

RICHARD E. CLARK, Business Week, 18 June 1990

24 Corporations that think they can drag their heels indefinitely on environmental problems should be advised: Society won't tolerate it, and DuPont and other companies with real sensitivity and environmental commitment will be there to supply your customers after you're gone.

E. S. WOOLARD, Business Week, 18 June 1990

25 It is a spiritual act to try to shut down DuPont.

RANDALL HAYES, quoted by Virginia Postrel, speech, City Club of Cleveland, Ohio, 19 June 1990

26 I think the enlightened corporations are recognizing that this is a long term interest, and it will not go away if they ignore it. People who make corporate decisions live on this planet, too, and would like to see it remain habitable.

KAREN FLORINI, E magazine, July–August 1990

27 As the damages mount with each new outrage, oil company officials are beginning to sound like problem drinkers who continue making promises they can't keep. How many more times are we going to allow these companies to throw up on our living room rug before we draw the line? Oil-hauling, like alcoholism, is a form of addictive behavior that is inevitably destructive.

GAR SMITH, E magazine, July–August 1990

28 Listen up, Exxon. Before you destroy the Arctic National Wildlife Refuge in your search for oil, why not subsidize your executives to go sit on a rock on the tundra and simply observe for a few weeks? Let them know what they do.

JIM NOLLMAN, E magazine, July–August 1990

29 Being dirty has lots of costs: being greener than the competition may have many advantages.

FRANCES CAIRNCROSS, The Economist, 8 September 1990

30 What a fortune awaits the company that de-vises—say—a way of transporting individu-als rapidly, safely and quietly, without emitting nasty fumes, in a container that melts back undetectably into the earth as soon as it reaches the end of its long life! The great engineering projects of the next century will be not the civil engineering of dams or bridges, but the bio-engineering of sewage works and waste tips. The star scientists will be those who find cheaper ways to dispose of plastics or to clean up contaminated soil. For far-sighted companies, the environment may turn out to be the biggest opportunity for en-terprise and invention the industrial world has seen.
>   FRANCES CAIRNCROSS, *The Economist*, 8 Sep-tember 1990

31 Greenwash was the term used by many activ-ists during Earth Week to describe corporate advertisements of environmental achieve-ments. For businesses concerned with their impact on the planet, however, the current environmental awareness at the corporate level represents a real commitment. As more and more companies begin to realize their contribution to environmental problems, they are using their ingenuity to solve and prevent them.
>   LEE M. THOMAS, *Environmental Forum*, Sep-tember–October 1990

32 The smart ones are going green, the dumb ones are not, and the foolish ones are pre-tending.
>   DAVID KRENTZ, on corporate environmental policy, quoted in *Globe and Mail* (Toronto), 13 October 1990

33 Exxon didn't really need to make five billion dollars in profit last year, when they could have spent a little bit more money in double-bottoming their tankers.
>   DAVID R. BROWER, *Orion*, Winter 1990

34 [The worldwide environmental movement is] not being led by business, and it should be, because businesses are really just your wealthy neighbors, and neighbors are sup-posed to help each other. Business knows how to sell. We can help make environmental issues sexy, and once we have people's atten-tion, we can start sharing crucial information. There's no use just telling people what's wrong—you have to help them figure out what to do about it.
>   ANITA RODDICK, *Orion*, Winter 1990

35 The multinational corporation seeks to be ev-erywhere, simultaneously—to assume un-challenged commercial control over the entirety of the global commons.
>   JEREMY RIFKIN, *Biosphere Politics*, 1991

---

73 INSECTS
See also   99 PESTICIDES, 139 WILDLIFE

---

1 Indeed what reason may not goe to Schoole to the wisedome of Bees, Aunts, and Spi-ders? what wise hand teacheth them to doe what reason cannot teach us? ruder heads stand amazed at those prodigious pieces of nature Whales, Elephants, Dromidaries and Camels; these I confesse, are the Colossus and Majestick pieces of her hand; but in these narrow Engines there is more curious Mathe-maticks, and the civilitie of these little Citi-zens, more neatly set forth the wisedome of their Maker.
>   THOMAS BROWNE (1605–1682), *Religio Medici*, 1642

2 As a thinker and planner the ant is the equal of any savage race of men; as a self-educated specialist in several arts she is the superior of any savage race of men; and in one or two high mental qualities she is above the reach of any man, savage or civilized.
>   MARK TWAIN (Samuel Langhorne Clemens, 1835–1910), *What Is Man?*, 1906

3 The planet drifts to random insect doom.
>   WILLIAM C. BURROUGHS, *The Naked Lunch*, 1959

4 Who has decided . . . that the supreme value is a world without insects, even though it be also a sterile world ungraced by the curving wing of a bird in flight? The decision is that of the authoritarian temporarily entrusted with power.
>   RACHEL CARSON (1907–1964), *Silent Spring*, 1962

5 [God has] an inordinate fondness for beetles.
J. B. S. HALDANE (1892–1964), when asked what his knowledge of biology had taught about the Creator, quoted in G. Evelyn Hutchinson, *The Enchanted Voyage*, 1962

6 It is a mistake of arrogance to mistake size for significance.
HELLSTROM CHRONICLES, 1971

7 Only two species are definitely on the increase, man and insects. Man because he's the only species with the ability to radically change the earth, and the insect because he's the only creature that can adapt to whatever changes man can make.
HELLSTROM CHRONICLES, 1971

8 Where there is no intelligence, there is no stupidity.
HELLSTROM CHRONICLES, 1971

9 Ants are so much like human beings as to be an embarrassment. They farm fungi, raise aphids as livestock, launch armies into war, use chemical sprays to alarm and confuse enemies, capture slaves, engage in child labor, exchange information ceaselessly. They do everything but watch television.
LEWIS THOMAS, *The Lives of a Cell*, 1974

10 Because butterflies are both so conspicuous and so fragile, the size and well-being of their populations serve as excellent monitors of environmental change and of rises in pollution levels.
ROBERT M. PYLE, quoted in *New York Times*, 2 March 1975

74 INTERNATIONAL DEVELOPMENT
See also 45 ENVIRONMENTAL IMPACTS, 58 GREEN REVOLUTION, 107 POPULATION, 126 SUSTAINABLE DEVELOPMENT

1 In a culture in which men's orientation toward nature is essentially one of fatalism and resignation their orientation toward government is likely to be much the same.
SIDNEY VERBA, in Sidney Verba and Lucian W. Pye, eds., *Political Culture and Political Development*, 1965

2 We must beware of the voices that are urging the Third World to settle for stunted development in the name of the environment.
EDMUND S. MUSKIE, U.S. Senator, speech, Conference on International Organization and the Human Environment, New York City, 21 May 1971

3 Development will conquer the diseases of the poor,
By spraying all the houses and by putting in the sewer.
And we'll know we have success in our developmental pitch,
When everybody dies from the diseases of the rich.
KENNETH E. BOULDING, "The Ballad of Ecological Awareness" in M. Taghi Farvar and John P. Milton, eds., *The Careless Technology*, 1972

4 [The poor] need [and] . . . we also need: a *different* kind of technology, a technology with a human face, which, instead of making human hands and brains redundant, helps them to become far more productive than they have ever been before.
E. F. SCHUMACHER, *Small Is Beautiful*, 1973

5 Our task is not to create an idyllic environment peopled by the poor. Our task is to create a decent environment peopled by the proud.
ROBERT S. MCNAMARA, quoted in *Reader's Digest*, March 1973

6 I don't know about all this talk about the environment. What we want is our share of the pollution.
GENERAL EMILIO GARRASTAZU MEDICI of Brazil, attributed, quoted in James Noel Smith, ed., *Environmental Quality and Social Justice in Urban America*, 1974

7 Unchecked, disregarded, left to grow and fester, there is here enough explosive material to produce in the world at large the pattern of a bitter class conflict, finding to an increasing degree a racial bias, erupting in guerrilla warfare and threatening ultimately the security even of the comfortable West.
BARBARA WARD, on the migration of the unskilled poor to the fringes of developing cities, *The Home of Man*, 1976

8 The very inability of some poor nations to achieve "development" may prove a blessing

in disguise, enabling them to avoid that economic "cannibalism" by which nations devour their own prosperity.

DENIS GOULET, *The Uncertain Promise*, 1977

9 Development is a means of exchanging the indispensable for the superfluous.

THE ECOLOGIST, November 1977

10 Material prosperity will never be within their grasp, but what they can develop is another type of prosperity—probably a more satisfying, certainly a more durable one, based on a more subtle exploitation of the vast capital that Nature has put at our disposal.

THE ECOLOGIST, November 1977

11 Constraints are set by political and economic, not ecological or physical, factors.

WILLIAM W. MURDOCH, on the fact that poorer countries are not close to the limit of their biological and physical resources, speech, American Association for the Advancement of Science, Washington, D.C., 3 January 1982

12 The most pressing problem of cultural adjustment is that too few African rural men regard agriculture as the key to development and village income. Growing food is often still seen as the woman's task. . . . The key to a prosperous and stable village-based African agricultural future lies in male cultural adaptation. Can these rural people leap over the long centuries this process took elsewhere?

RICHARD CRITCHFIELD, *Foreign Affairs*, Autumn 1982

13 Residents discovered that the benefits that followed being linked to the world—such as more education and health care, more efficient marketing of local products, some electricity, a few phones—have been accompanied by a series of disasters. The province was opened to the disintegrating elements of contemporary life: deforestation and pollution, the dying out of fish and fauna, the land being bought up by speculators or by the German and American hippies who have also introduced their drug culture to the area. . . . But the greatest worry is for the young. The road that allows so many strangers—

and strange things—into Talamanca is the same road that the young take to leave in droves.

ARIEL DORFMAN, on Cordillera de Talamanca, Costa Rica, *Grassroots Development* 8, 1984

14 Conscious, critical and active people are a prerequisite for progress.

OLOF PALME, Prime Minister of Sweden, speech, Nicaragua, 1984

15 I believe that the creative capacity of human beings is at the heart of the development process. What makes development happen is our ability to imagine, theorize, conceptualize, experiment, invent, articulate, organize, manage, solve problems, and do a hundred other things, with our minds and hands that contribute to the progress of the individual and of humankind. Natural resources, climate, geography, history, market size, governmental policies, and many other factors influence the direction and pace of progress. But the engine is human creative capacity.

LAWRENCE E. HARRISON, *Underdevelopment Is a State of Mind*, 1985

16 Underdevelopment is not just a collection of statistical indices which enable a socioeconomic picture to be drawn. It is also a state of mind, a way of expression, a form of outlook, and a collective personality marked by chronic infirmities and forms of maladjustment.

AUGUSTO SALAZAR BONDY, quoted in Lawrence E. Harrison, *Underdevelopment Is a State of Mind*, 1985

17 Government-to-government assistance is only as good as the recipient government. . . . Hunger is not caused by scarcity of land, nor scarcity of food, it's caused by a scarcity of democracy.

FRANCES MOORE LAPPE, *Rain*, July–August 1985

18 We have discovered that "the environment" is not a sectoral discipline at all. It is the very glue that holds development together. It is the sum of all resources, goods, and services that the earth and is its regions have to offer,

and therefore the very capital invested in development.

UNITED NATIONS DEVELOPMENT PROGRAM (Technical Advisory Division), "Comprehensive Development Strategies," 5 May 1986

19 [The foreign environmental professional] hasn't had starving children in the household. You have to have people who appreciate the need for a clearing to plant rice, even if they know it will make a hole in a monkey habitat.

CHUCK KLEYMEYER, quoted in *Conservation Foundation Letter*, January–February 1987

20 [Development must focus on] human potential and the sustainable management, restoration, and enhancement of ecosystems on which all economic systems rely.

HAZEL HENDERSON, *Futures Research Quarterly*, Autumn 1987

21 The Third World is littered with the rusting good intentions of projects that did not achieve social and economic success; environmental problems are now building even more impressive monuments to failure in the form of sediment-choked reservoirs and desertified landscapes.

WALTER REID, *Bankrolling Successes*, 1988

22 Our moral responsibility is to help spare the world from being destroyed, due to nuclear war, due to inequality between North and South, due to injustice in the development of a country and due to the destruction of the environment.

SOEHARTO, President of Indonesia, speech, 16 August 1988

23 Eco-development . . . means raising Third World living standards in ways that maintain natural systems and redeveloping richer countries to be more ecologically sound.

PETER BERG, quoted in Stephanie Mills, ed., *In Praise of Nature*, 1990

24 The concept of development in a developing country is not necessarily the same as that understood by one belonging to a "developed" country. In a developing country the idea of development is closely linked with the wish for freedom—freedom to run one's own affairs the way one knows and believes,

based on familiar traditions and ways of life. Freedom is in fact development, whether material progress and wealth are realized to the extent expected or not.

FRANCIS BUGOTU, in Julian Burger, *The Gaia Atlas of First Peoples*, 1990

25 We divide the world into the developed countries and the developing countries. I would rather call them "misdeveloped" countries.

JOSE A. LUTZENBERGER, Brazilian minister of the environment, speech, Nature Conservancy, Washington, D.C., 15 November 1990

26 An indigenous leader once told the story of an elephant and a duck who was sitting on her eggs. He likened the elephant to environmentalists (in this case, "green capitalists") and the duck to indigenous peoples. The duck was killed by an encroaching colonist, leaving her eggs unattended. The kind-hearted elephant decided to do his friend the duck a favour. He sat on the eggs.

ANDREW GRAY, *The Ecologist*, November–December 1990

27 One of the greatest ironies facing conservationists the world over is that while developing countries harbor much of the earth's most biologically rich habitats, they are least equipped financially to protect them.

KATHRYN S. FULLER, *Focus*, November–December 1990

28 By disregarding the effects of growth on the environment, the wealthy countries have used the equivalent of steroids to put on industrial muscle. That dependency is now threatening their very existence. Theirs is, therefore, a rehabilitation problem. They face the daunting task of recovering from a dangerous addiction. And we all know bad habits are hard to break.

The South is in a very different situation. Ours is a muscular deficiency. We need to put on some muscle, but we must choose whether we want to do it the easy way or the hard way. The easy way would be to set environmental concerns aside and focus on development à la the United States or Europe. Any such development would be artificial

and—as we have seen in Eastern Europe—could even be deadly in the long run.
RICARDO BAYON, *Tomorrow* 1, no. 1, 1991

29 You need free trade just as you need clean air to breathe.
HELMUT KOHL, German Chancellor, *Los Angeles Times*, 18 July 1991

75 INTERNATIONAL GOVERNANCE

1 When Kansas and Colorado have a quarrel over the water in the Arkansas River they don't call out the National Guard in each state and go to war over it. They bring a suit in the Supreme Court of the United States and abide by the decision. There isn't a reason in the world why we cannot do that internationally.
HARRY S. TRUMAN (1884–1972), speech, Kansas City, April 1945

2 Management of the world's resources in a logical and beneficial manner is completely possible in the present state of art and science. The constraints lie in public apathy, lack of political will, lack of funds and lack of a proper managerial structure and competence.
ABEL WOLMAN, *Foreign Affairs*, October 1968

3 The ultimate challenge of the exploited ocean is . . . political. What is "conquered" by technology must be governed, and in this respect an ocean subjected is no different from a nation subdued. This will be true of the coastal ocean and the high seas. The incentives to rational ocean government and use are considerable. So are the obstacles: the passions of exploitation, the abuses of one-eyed technology, the tensions of the cold war, the nagging distrust between poor nations and rich, and, not least of all, human carelessness. Yet one thing stands on the side of protected and peaceful oceans—our enduring and universal affection for them.
WESLEY MARX, *The Frail Ocean*, 1969

4 By approaching the ocean merely as a resource we foster conflict and eventual disaster. By approaching the ocean as an environment we can begin to meet the ultimate challenge: governing its anxious and ambitious exploiters.
WESLEY MARX, *The Frail Ocean*, 1969

5 Could there, one wonders, be any undertaking better designed to meet [the world's] needs, to relieve the great convulsions of anxiety and ingrained hostility that now rack international society, than a major international effort to restore the hope, the beauty and the salubriousness of the natural environment in which man has his being?
GEORGE F. KENNAN, *Foreign Affairs*, April 1970

6 [The United States and Soviet Union need environmental cooperation in] the great international media of human activity: the high seas, the stratosphere, outer space, perhaps also the Arctic and Antarctic.
GEORGE F. KENNAN, *Foreign Affairs*, April 1970

7 I would hope that in saving ourselves by preserving our environment we might also find a new solidarity and a new spirit among the governments and peoples of the earth.
U THANT (1909–1974), speech, University of Texas, 14 May 1970

8 [The wealthy and the impoverished may] operate in such disparate spheres that joint action [on environmental pollution] must await some great, perhaps catastrophic, change or event which submerges normal differences in some overriding common urgency.
EDWARD K. HAMILTON, unpublished paper, 1971

9 The controversy over the law of the sea has finally been understood as one of the basic chapters of the struggle against underdevelopment and against the hegemony of certain powers that would confine the sovereignty and jurisdiction of other states to narrow limits while remaining free themselves to exploit the natural resources of distant seas.
MIGUEL ANGEL DE LA FLOR VALLE, speech, United Nations 27th General Assembly, 1972

10 The protection of the vast international commons—the oceans and the atmosphere beyond national jurisdiction—will engender growing and continuing costs. Perhaps these

might best be met by some form of international toll or levy based on the use of the commons by aircraft and ships—in effect, an "ocean toll-booth" system.

MAURICE F. STRONG, *Foreign Affairs*, July 1973

11 It is the expropriation of the rights of posterity. It is the biggest smash-and-grab since the European powers, at the Berlin Conference of 1885, carved up Black Africa.

LORD RITCHIE-CALDER, in opposition to the plan to allow coastal nations to establish "exclusive economic zones" out to 200 miles—rather than set up an international ocean regime to govern these rich expanses, *Center* magazine, November–December 1974

12 It is no use having arrogant demands by one group of countries, or refusals to share by others. Resources are not infinite.

MOSTAFA K. TOLBA, quoted in *Los Angeles Times*, 6 February 1977

13 Everyone is going to act in their so-called waters the way they want. So instead of having one law of the sea, we are going to have a hundred laws of the sea.

JACQUES COUSTEAU, on the new 200-mile fishing limits, quoted in *Los Angeles Herald-Examiner*, 28 November 1977

14 In the matter of making strange bedfellows, ecology may outdistance politics.

DOUGLAS M. COSTLE, on United States-Soviet environmental cooperation, *Annals of the American Academy of Political and Social Science*, July 1979

15 We lack sufficiently developed international institutions for resolving problems that are here and now. Our international institutions often appear terribly sluggish in trying to cope with these [transnational] concerns. It took six years really to debate and discuss and get to the point where last year we could sign an international convention for the first time to deal with transboundary air pollution.

DOUGLAS M. COSTLE, *EPA Journal*, November–December 1980

16 The key factor in human salvation can now only be political will. Global efforts must be fully mobilized to confront the possibility of total biological disaster. A whole new concept of obligation and duty needs to be blueprinted on an international scale.

DANIEL ARAP MOI, President of Kenya, opening speech of the UNEP Conference, Nairobi, May 1982

17 The deliberate across-the-board abandonment of U.S. leadership on environmental, resource, and related global issues is of grave concern to us all. During the past two and a half years we have stood almost alone among nations in our refusal to cooperate with international efforts.

JIMMY CARTER, on Reagan Administration policies, Global Tomorrow Coalition conference, Washington, D.C., 2 June 1983

18 [A joint U.S.-Soviet global climate program] has all the potential to be very popular in all circles of society, including scientists, general media, politicians, etc., because its only aim is to save the future of mankind.

V. A. TROITSKAYA, Soviet scientist, testimony, U.S. House Science and Technology subcommittee, 29 July 1987

19 This is perhaps the most historically significant international environmental agreement. For the first time, the international community has initiated controls on production of an economically valuable commodity before there was tangible evidence of danger.

RICHARD E. BENEDICK, on the just-signed 24-nation pact to reduce the release of chemicals that can harm the earth's ozone shield, quoted in *New York Times*, 17 September 1987

20 No country is likely to radically solve the energy problem on its own, any more than develop the riches of the world's oceans. Only joint action can weaken and remove the global danger of an ecological seizure.

MIKHAIL S. GORBACHEV, quoted in *Los Angeles Times*, 5 November 1987

21 When we talk about preservation of the environment, it is related to many other things. Ultimately the decision must come from the human heart, so I think the key point is to have a genuine sense of universal responsibility.

DALAI LAMA (Tenzin Gyatso) and GALEN ROWELL, *My Tibet*, 1990

22 Life itself urgently requires pooling of the efforts of the world community in the interest

of a joint and effective solution to environmental problems.

GEORGII S. GOLITSYN, Soviet scientist, quoted in Robert Minger, ed., *Greenhouse Glasnost*, 1990

23 It is impossible not to acknowledge that the Soviet Union joined in active international cooperation in the ecological sphere remarkably late. . . . Thus we must make up for our negligence and make an extraordinary effort to restore trust in the USSR as a partner in environmental cooperation. . . . It is as if we are catching up with a train that has already attained considerable velocity.

EDWARD SHEVARDNADZE, quoted in Eric Green, *Ecology and Perestroika*, 1990

24 If this new wave of multilateralism prevails, what can people expect from global institutions for environmental management, or "international governance" as some have called it? Innovative approaches are necessary and possible in three areas: transnational environmental standard setting, transnational environmental licensing, and transnational environmental auditing.

PETER H. SAND, *Environment*, November 1990

25 Dictatorships and societies that support an affluent few at the expense of many in poverty have not been good stewards of the Earth.

PETER A. A. BERLE, *Audubon*, January 1991

---

76 LAND
See also   77 LAND USE, 111 PUBLIC LANDS

---

1 The land is mine: for ye are strangers and sojourners with me.

BIBLE, Leviticus 25:23

2 Since the land is the parent, let the citizens take care of her more carefully than children do their mother.

PLATO (428–348), *Laws*

3 Better be poor on land than rich on water.

DIOGENIANUS (2d century A.D.), *Adagia*, c. A.D. 125

4 Now would I give a thousand furlongs of sea for an acre of barren ground; long heath, brown furze, any thing.

WILLIAM SHAKESPEARE (1564–1616), *The Tempest*, 1.1.69, 1611–1612

5 This I dare boldly affirm . . . every man should have as much as he could make use of, would hold still in the world, without straitening anybody, since there is land enough in the world to suffice double the inhabitants, had not the invention of money, and the tacit agreement of men to put a value on it, introduced (by consent) larger possessions and a right to them.

JOHN LOCKE (1632–1704), *Two Treatises on Government*, 1690

6 Ill fares the land, to hastening ills a prey,
Where wealth accumulates, and men decay.

OLIVER GOLDSMITH (1730–1774), *The Deserted Village*, 1770

7 The small landholders are the most precious part of a state.

THOMAS JEFFERSON (1743–1826), letter to Rev. James Madison, 1785

8 Whenever there are in any country uncultivated lands and unemployed poor, it is clear that the laws of property have been so far extended as to violate natural right. The earth is given as a common stock for man to labor and live on.

THOMAS JEFFERSON (1743–1826), letter to Rev. James Madison, 28 October 1785

9 I think our governments will remain virtuous for many centuries; as long as they are chiefly agricultural; and this will be as long as there shall be vacant lands in any part of America. When they get piled upon one another in large cities, as in Europe, they will become corrupt as in Europe.

THOMAS JEFFERSON (1743–1826), letter to James Madison, 20 December 1787

10 My reason teaches me that the land cannot be sold, the Great Spirit gave it to his children to live upon, and cultivate; as far as is necessary for their subsistence, they have the right to the soil. . . . Nothing can be sold, but such things as can be carried away.

BLACK HAWK (1767–1838), c. 1834, quoted in Georgiana C. Nammack, *Fraud, Politics, and the Dispossession of the Indians*, 1969

11 You ask me to plow the ground. Shall I take a knife and tear my mother's breast? Then when I die she will not take me to her bosom to rest.

You ask me to dig for stone. Shall I dig under her skin for her bones? Then when I die I cannot enter her body to be born again.

You ask me to cut grass and make hay and sell it and be rich like the white men. But how dare I cut off my mother's hair?

SMOHALLA, Nez Percé Indian, quoted in T. C. McLuhan, *Touch the Earth*, 1972

12 The earth is the first condition of our existence. To make it an object of trade was the last step towards making human beings an object of trade. To buy and sell land is an immorality surpassed only by the immorality of selling oneself into slavery.

FRIEDRICH ENGELS (1820–1895), *Outlines of a Critique of Political Economy*, 1844

13 No man made the land. It is the original inheritance of the whole species. Its appropriation is wholly a question of general expediency. When private property in land is not expedient, it is unjust.

JOHN STUART MILL (1806–1873), *Principles of Political Economy*, 1848

14 Laws change; people die; the land remains.

ABRAHAM LINCOLN (1809–1865), quoted in Charles Bowden, *Blue Desert*, 1986

15 The land, the earth God gave to man for his home . . . should never be the possession of any man, corporation, (or) society . . . any more than the air or water.

ABRAHAM LINCOLN (1809–1865), quoted in Peter Blake, *God's Own Junkyard*, 1964

16 No land is bad, but land is worse. If a man owns land, the land owns him. Now let him leave home, if he dare.

RALPH WALDO EMERSON (1803–1882), *The Conduct of Life*, 1860

17 The equal right of all men to the use of land is as clear as their equal right to breathe the air—it is a right proclaimed by the fact of their existence. For we cannot suppose that some men have a right to be in this world, and others no right.

HENRY GEORGE (1839–1897), *Progress and Poverty*, 1879

18 This, then, is the remedy for the unjust and unequal distribution of wealth apparent in modern civilization, and for all the evils which flow from it: We must make land common property.

HENRY GEORGE (1839–1897), *Progress and Poverty*, 1879

19 The most valuable lands on the globe, the lands which yield the highest rent, are not lands of surpassing natural fertility, but lands to which a surpassing utility has been given by the increase of population.

HENRY GEORGE (1839–1897), *Progress and Poverty*, 1879

20 The land is like a woman's breast: useful as well as pleasing.

FRIEDRICH NIETZSCHE (1844–1900), *Thus Spake Zarathustra*, 1883–1892

21 Land ought not to be a commodity, because like air and water it is necessary to human existence; and all men have by birthright equal rights to its use.

PHILLIPS THOMPSON, *The Politics of Labour*, 1887

22 It is not the most beautiful lands, nor those where life is the most agreeable, that seize the heart more, but those where the terrain is the plainest, the most humble, the nearest to man, and speaks to him in a language both intimate and familiar.

ROMAIN ROLLAND (1866–1944), *Jean-Christophe*, 1905–1912

23 LAND, n. A part of the earth's surface, considered as property. The theory that land is property subject to private ownership and control is the foundation of modern society. . . . Carried to its logical conclusion, it means that some have the right to prevent others from living; for the right to own implies the right exclusively to occupy.

AMBROSE BIERCE (1842–c. 1914), *The Enlarged Devil's Dictionary*, 1906

24 He who has known how to love the land has loved eternity.

STEFAN ZEROMSKI (1864–1925), Polish author

25 Bring out your social remedies! They will fail, they will fail, every one, until each man has his feet somewhere upon the soil.

DAVID GRAYSON (Ray Stannard Baker, 1870–1946), *Adventures in Contentment*, 1907

26 What we mean by land in practical life is something which . . . consists very largely of the accumulated result of human effort.
  PHILIP H. WICKSTEED (1844–1927), attributed

27 The land belongs to the future . . . that's the way it seems to me. How many names on the county clerk's plat will be there in fifty years? I might as well try to will the sunset over there to my brother's children. We come and go, but the land is always here. And the people who love it and understand it are the people who own it—for a little while.
  WILLA CATHER (1873–1947), O Pioneers!, 1913

28 [Elsewhere, their culture had] stood on three legs—land, water, and timber [but on the Plains] civilization was left on one leg—land. It is small wonder that it toppled over in temporary failure.
  WALTER PRESCOTT WEBB, on American pioneers and the Great Plains "dust bowl," The Great Plains, 1931

29 Obligation to the land is fundamentally a matter of faith, and coöperation has the quality of spiritual fellowship.
  PAUL SEARS, Deserts on the March, 1947

30 The ground is holy. . . . Keep it, guard it, care for it, for it keeps men, guards men, cares for men. Destroy it and man is destroyed.
  ALAN PATON (1903–1988), Cry the Beloved Country, 1948

31 The art of land doctoring is being practiced with vigor, but the science of land health is yet to be born.
  ALDO LEOPOLD (1886–1948), A Sand County Almanac, 1949

32 Having to squeeze the last drop of utility out of the land has the same desperate finality as having to chop up the furniture to keep warm.
  ALDO LEOPOLD (1886–1948), A Sand County Almanac, 1949

33 Land, then, is not merely soil; it is a fountain of energy flowing through a circuit of soils, plants, and animals. Food chains are the living channels which conduct energy upward; death and decay return it to the soil. The circuit is not closed; some energy is dissipated in decay, some is added by absorption from the air, some is stored in soils, peats, and long-lived forests; but it is a sustained circuit, like a slowly augmented revolving fund of life.
  ALDO LEOPOLD (1886–1948), A Sand County Almanac, 1949

34 We shall never achieve harmony with land, any more than we shall achieve justice or liberty for people. In these higher aspirations the important thing is not to achieve, but to strive. It is only in mechanical enterprises that we can expect that early or complete fruition of effort which we call "success."
  ALDO LEOPOLD (1886–1948), Round River, 1953

35 The land was ours before . . . we were her people.
  ROBERT FROST (1874–1963), speech, inauguration of John F. Kennedy, 20 January 1961

36 A land ethic for tomorrow should be as honest as Thoreau's Walden, and as comprehensive as the sensitive science of ecology. It should stress the oneness of our resources and the live-and-help-live logic of the great chain of life. If, in our haste to "progress," the economics of ecology are disregarded by citizens and policy makers alike, the result will be an ugly America.
  STEWART L. UDALL, The Quiet Crisis, 1963

37 We have been the most prodigal of people with land, and for years we wasted it with impunity. There was so much of it, and no matter how we fouled it, there was always more over the next hill, or so it seemed.
  WILLIAM H. WHYTE, The Last Landscape, 1968

38 Every time we have objected to the use of the land as a commodity, we have been told that progress is necessary to American life. Now the laugh is ours.
  VINE DELORIA, We Talk, You Listen, 1970

39 Study how a society uses its land, and you can come to pretty reliable conclusions as to what its future will be. . . . [The] destinies of most of man's empires and civilizations were determined largely by the way the land was used.
  E. F. SCHUMACHER, Small Is Beautiful, 1973

40 Planner A: "One often hears the argument that public land ownership is communistic."

Planner B: "But there are societies which believed that God said land should be held in a common trust for the people."

Planner C: "God was a communist."

ANONYMOUS, at Public Land Ownership Conference, York University, Toronto, 13 November 1975

41 The manners and mores of society are the determining factors. In Holland, for example, it's accepted that land is a scarce commodity. It's ingrained in the national consciousness that you don't fool around with it.

R. W. G. BRYANT, speech, Public Land Ownership Conference, York University, Toronto, 13 November 1975

42 The exploiter typically serves an institution or organization; the nurturer serves land, household, community, place. The exploiter thinks in terms of numbers, quantities, "hard facts"; the nurturer in terms of character, condition, quality, kind.

WENDELL BERRY, The Unsettling of America, 1977

43 Grab this land! Take it, hold it, my brothers, make it, my brothers, shake it, squeeze it, turn it, twist it, beat it, kick it, kiss it, whip it, stomp it, dig it, plow it, seed it, reap it, rent it, buy it, sell it, own it, build it, multiply it, and pass it on—can you hear me? Pass it on!

TONI MORRISON, Song of Solomon, 1977

44 Land is immortal, for it harbors the mysteries of creation.

ANWAR EL-SADAT (1918–1981), President of Egypt, In Search of Identity, 1978

45 The size of the parcel of land matters less than the relationship of the people to it.

FRANCES MOORE LAPPE and JOSEPH COLLINS, Food First, 1979

46 [A]n owner of land has no absolute and unlimited right to change the essential natural character of his land so as to use it for a purpose for which it was unsuited in its natural state and which injures the rights of others.

FLORIDA SUPREME COURT, Graham v. Estuaries Properties, Inc., 1981

47 The difference between Indians and Europeans was not that one had property and the other had none; rather, it was that they loved property differently.

WILLIAM CRONON, Changes in the Land, 1983

48 One of the nicest things about American independence, which was born of free land, as far as I can determine—was born of free land from the very first settlement—is that you can tell the world to kiss your behind and go off. That is freedom; it is also irresponsibility, social irresponsibility. When the world tightens in around you, you can't do that anymore, and it probably means a lot more unhappiness for people of that stamp.

WALLACE STEGNER, quoted in Richard W. Etulain, ed., Conversations with Wallace Stegner on Western History and Literature, 1983

49 People are joined to the land by work. Land, work, people, and community are all comprehended in the idea of culture.

WENDELL BERRY, Sierra, September–October 1983

50 At a certain level of insight our relationship to land comes clear in the mind. We then know our connectedness—and indebtedness—in our bones; our ethical responsibility to the land then moves beyond the level of abstract idea to become a deep, emotionally based imperative. That is what land stewardship is about.

JOE PADDOCK, NANCY PADDOCK, and CAROL BLY, Soil and Survival, 1986

51 I think it is inappropriate to call land a "resource" because that term is tied so closely to economics. We can call gold or chrome or coal a resource, but land and people transcend a one-dimensional economic consideration.

WES JACKSON, American Land Forum, Summer 1986

52 In European countries, the political power to enact laws that require ethical behavior towards the land has come out of an aesthetic appreciation of the landscape. England's green and pleasant land is sung in every English public school, and Britain has made the protection of the green and pleasant land into law.

CHARLES E. LITTLE, American Land Forum, Summer 1986

53 Our world has fallen into a state of chaos because man, led astray by an embarrassment of knowledge, has engaged in futile labors. The road back to the land, back to the bosom of a pure, innocent nature still remains open to us all.

MASANOBU FUKUOKA, *The Natural Way of Farming*, 1987

54 For a variety of historical and cultural reasons, anyone who proposes a new land ethics runs the risk of being viewed, not primarily as an environmental messiah, but as an anti-Christ threatening the two religions of capitalism and democracy.

KRISTIN SHRADER-FRECHETTE, *Environmental Professional*, September 1987

55 The land is like poetry: it is inexplicably coherent, it is transcendent in its meaning, and it has the power to elevate a consideration of human life.

BARRY LOPEZ, quoted in Stephen Trimble, ed., *Words from the Land*, 1988

56 Too many people brings suffering to the land, and the land returns its suffering to the people.

O. SOEMARWOTO, Indonesian ecologist, in Julian Burger, *The Gaia Atlas of First Peoples*, 1990

77 LAND USE

See also   24 DEVELOPERS, 101 PLANNING, LAND USE, 142 ZONING

1 Woe unto them that join house to house, that lay field to field; till there be no place, that they may be placed alone in the midst of the earth!

BIBLE, Isaiah 5:8

2 As the man is worth, his land is worth.

R. C. TRENCH, *On the Lessons in Proverbs*, 1853

3 Something there is that doesn't love a wall.

ROBERT FROST, (1874–1963), "Mending Wall," *North of Boston*, 1914

4 But restriction imposed to protect public health, safety, or morals from dangers threatened is not a taking. . . . The property so restricted remains in the possession of the owner. The state does not appropriate it or make any use of it. The state merely prevents the owner from making a use which interferes with paramount right of the public.

LOUIS BRANDEIS (1856–1941), U.S. Supreme Court justice, dissent, *Pennsylvania Coal* v. *Mahon*, 1922

5 In the United States, there is more space where nobody is than where anybody is. That is what makes American what it is.

GERTRUDE STEIN (1874–1946), *The Geographical History of America*, 1936

6 Only in one area—in the determination of land-use patterns—need there be any curtailment of laissez-faire. But land use has never been determined solely by the market mechanism anyway; government has always intervened to some extent, in order to prevent a state of total anarchy.

EDMUND K. FALTERMAYER, *Redoing America*, 1968

7 Land should be used to encourage democratic choice and diversity—for places to live, work and play—and when market forces are inadequate, public expenditures should be used to encourage such diversity. We should enunciate a policy of future growth, to assure that the land is there and properly planned for decent urban growth. Among other things, this means that green spaces should be planned into future growth.

ROBERT C. WEAVER, U.S. Housing and Urban Development Secretary, on a national urban land policy to guide both public and private action, colloquium, U.S. Congress, 1968

8 In most states, there is no single focus for guiding rational development, because conservation, economic promotion, pollution control, tourism, highways and community planning are considered separately. Funds for land acquisition are hard to come by. Legal control over land use is complex and ineffectual. Ambitious and overlapping jurisdiction between local, state and federal government creates serious problems.

EDWARD WENK, JR., *Our Nation and the Sea*, January 1969

9 Firm public control of land usage under a long-range metropolitan plan is one reason

why such cities as London hold a strong attraction for their residents as well as for millions of foreign visitors.

NEIL H. JACOBY, *Center* magazine, November–December 1970

10 But the chaos in land-use planning is not the result of uncontrolled individual enterprise. It is a result of a combination of controls and lack of controls, of over-planning and anti-planning, enterprise and anti-enterprise, all in absolute disarray. I doubt that even the most intransigent disciple of anarchy ever wished for or intended the litter that prevails in the area of local land-use regulation.

RICHARD F. BABCOCK, *The Zoning Game*, 1971

11 This country is in the midst of a revolution in the way we regulate the use of our land. It is a peaceful revolution, conducted entirely within the law. It is a quiet revolution, and its supporters include both conservatives and liberals. It is a disorganized revolution, with no central cadre of leaders, but it is a revolution nonetheless.

The ancien régime being overthrown is the feudal system under which the entire pattern of land development has been controlled by thousands of individual local governments, each seeking to maximize its tax base and minimize its social problems, and caring less what happens to all the others.

The tools of the revolution are new laws taking a wide variety of forms but each sharing a common theme—the need to provide some degree of state or regional participation in the major decisions that affect the use of our increasingly limited supply of land.

FRED BOSSELMAN and DAVID CALLIES, "The Quiet Revolution in Land Use Control," Council on Environmental Quality, 1971

12 If the James G. Blaine Society [an Oregon group] had its way, travel brochures describing the state of Oregon would read: "Oregon—small, crowded, polluted. Freeways lousy. Economy failing. Crime rate and cost of living soaring. Natives hostile. State flower: poison ivy. State song: *Raindrops Keep Fallin' on My Head*."

All of which is a pack of lies, except that there really are some hostile natives—the Blaine Society—who would like to build barbed-wire fences along the state borders,

keep tourists and industry out and let Oregon go its own lovely way.

SPORTS ILLUSTRATED, 18 January 1971

13 As a nation, we still subscribe the the old "pioneer land ethic," which holds that the owner of the land has the God-given right to do with it as he damned pleases. And our real estate taxing and zoning system, as administered and misadministered by some 10,000 local jurisdictions, inevitably rewards "the highest and best use of the land." That means the most profitable use unless an incensed citizenry (which is not always a choir of angels, either) has smarter lawyers on its side.

WASHINGTON POST, editorial, 20 November 1971

14 The region should be comprehensible as a system of opportunities and constraints for all prospective land uses. Certain land uses in conflict with intrinsic suitability shall be defined as non-conforming uses.

IAN MCHARG, *Ecological Planning Study for Wilmington and Dover*, April 1972

15 What we will not countenance, then, under any guise, is community efforts at immunization or exclusion. But, far from being exclusionary, the present amendments merely seek, by the implementation of sequential development and timed growth, to provide a balanced cohesive community dedicated to the efficient utilization of land. . . . In sum, Ramapo asks not that it be left alone, but only that it be allowed to prevent the kind of deterioration that has transformed well-ordered and thriving residential communities into blighted ghettos with attendant hazards to health, security and social stability. . . . We only require that communities confront the challenge of population growth with open doors.

NEW YORK STATE COURT OF APPEALS, *Golden v. Planning Board of the Town of Ramapo*, 3 May 1972

16 [Since] all environmental problems are outgrowths of land-use patterns . . . it is essential that we develop a framework within which the myriad proposals to use or consume natural resources can be balanced against one another and measured against the demands they collectively impose upon the environment. We need a focal point upon

which we can compare alternative proposals to achieve our goals. That focal point should be the use of land.

HENRY M. JACKSON (1912–1983), U.S. Senator, quoted in *Conservation Foundation Letter*, August 1972

17 There is a growing consensus that control over land use is probably the most important single factor in improving the quality of the environment in the United States.

COUNCIL ON ENVIRONMENTAL QUALITY, *Environmental Quality*, 1973

18 Owners expect less of land that physically cannot be developed (quicksand, for example). What is needed is a comparable modification of expectations for land that should not be developed. Land whose development would be hazardous may be the place to begin. Surely it should be possible to develop a national consensus that profits from the residential development of a floodway are the moral equivalent of profits from selling tainted meat.

WILLIAM K. REILLY, ed., *The Use of Land*, 1973

19 Laws to regulate the use of land should recognize at least three objectives: First, land is a precious and scarce resource and should not be wasted. Second, when and as used, it should be used to satisfy the most or more pressing needs of society. Third, it should be utilized for the benefit and advantage of all people as distinct from any special class or group.

BERNARD H. SIEGAN, *Baltimore Sunday Sun*, 11 March 1973

20 There is no need for people or their governments to accept a future of blanketing urbanization in which people and communities lose their identity. Nor is there need to put up with suburban barriers to the mobility of people of modest means or dark skins. Nor is there need to accept endless development along our hills, valleys, forests, farms and horizons.

VERNON E. JORDAN, JR., speech, Washington, D.C., 24 May 1973

21 Much of the urban growth experience in the U.S. over the past quarter century has consisted of people running away—from other people in the older cities, now even from the suburbs to the mountains and the seas. Now

it is dawning on us that there is not really any place to run to. It may be time to try to reinvigorate our processes for getting along with each other. . . . Clustering, greenbelts, public services and facilities in vacation communities, new communities with a full mix of uses, more inclusive decision-making processes, impact analyses—all of these involve higher levels of social interaction and cooperation than we have usually achieved. There is no hiding on two-acre lots.

WILLIAM K. REILLY, speech, Washington, D.C., 24 May 1973

22 It is a profound mistake to think of land only in terms of its money values and, however natural it may be for individuals to do this, the nation or state should never do so. It should instead act always to preserve, foster, and cause to be developed to the maximum of its capacity not the monetary, but the real and physical value of every acre of its soil, both rural and urban. This is its educative, esthetic, and, in the fullest and widest sense of the meaning, productive, creative and enduring worth.

HYMAN G. RICKOVER, testimony, U.S. House Appropriations subcommittee, 19 June 1973

23 The U.S. policy of land use mainly for economic gain, with one exceptional aspect, characterizes our decision-making process, and constitutes one of the few remaining opportunities for complete scoundrels to enrich themselves with impunity at the public expense. The blessed though paltry exception to this policy is a national penchant for parks and open space.

CHARLES E. LITTLE, in James N. Smith, *Environmental Quality and Social Justice in Urban America*, 1974

24 We have come to expect more from land-use controls than we ever did before. This means that even within a single city, land-use decisions now must involve at least the environmental health and transportation planners, a host of public works and social agencies, the housing authority, the civil rights commission, and the energy producers, in addition to the planners, zoners, real estate men and homeowners.

BRUCE D. MCDOWELL, speech, American Association for the Advancement of Science, San Francisco, February 1974

25 Civilization follows the sewers. Sewers are the most effective planning mechanism we have, but we have not used them.
ROYCE HANSON, quoted in *Management and Control of Growth*, vol. 3, 1975

26 All too often, the construction of new sewers and treatment plants serves to, in effect, subsidize the development of floodplains, wetlands, prime agricultural land, and important wildlife habitat.
LOUIS S. CLAPPER, testimony, U.S. Senate Environment and Public Works subcommittee, 21 June 1977

27 From North Africa and Asia Minor to Greece and Spain, this planet is replete with examples of the catastrophic effect of imposing intensive land use for short-term gain on vulnerable landscapes.
GEORGE V. BURGER, in Howard P. Brokaw, ed., *Wildlife in America*, 1978

28 Presumably only a desperate person would take a job as an auto mechanic without some knowledge of automobile systems. However, people are constantly accepting employment or civic responsibilities involving land use without studying the relevant laws.
VAWTER PARKER, *Sierra*, September–October 1983

29 We have come to accept with enthusiasm the unprofessional, unappreciative, unskillful butchery of the land that goes under the name of planning.
WILLIAM L. PEREIRA, quoted in *Time*, 25 November 1985

30 The requirement to maintain species richness sets the most stringent limits on many forms of land use.
GORDON H. ORIANS, *Environment*, November 1990

---

78 LAW
See also 56 GOVERNMENT,
116 REGULATION

---

1 A court of equity is the *only* place to take effective action against polluters. Only in a courtroom can a scientist present his evidence, free from harassment by politicians. And only in a courtroom can bureaucratic hogwash be tested in the crucible of cross-examination.
VICTOR J. YANNACONE, JR., *New Republic*, 13 January 1968

2 And now when we look to the law for answers to many of our social and environmental problems, we do find that the law itself is the cause of many of those problems.
It is "the law" which zones the housing patterns which led to building too many highways for too many autos.
It is "the law" which expropriates public property for private profit.
It is "the law" which permits environmental degradation.
VICTOR J. YANNACONE, speech, Michigan State University, 22 April 1970

3 No lawsuit will, *ultimately*, win any conservation issue. We must never forget that Congress or the state legislatures can always overrule hard-won court victories.
JAMES MOORMAN, *Sierra Club Bulletin*, January 1972

4 Discovering a workable definition of environmental law is a little bit like the search for truth: the closer you get, the more elusive it becomes.
WILLIAM H. ROGERS, *Environmental Law*, 1977

5 I doubt very much that there has ever been such an outpouring of new legislation on any one subject as that enacted during the seventies to deal with environmental problems. . . . It is quite certain that at the time of original legislative consideration, the full implications of this regulatory complex for American society were seldom recognized by the Congress, business, or many others for that matter.
RUSSELL E. TRAIN, in Conservation Foundation, *Conservation and Values*, 1978

6 [The Endangered Species Act was] a determined attempt to keep the concept of the biblical ark afloat. Along the way, it is true that a lot of species have fallen off the ark. Some have been even been unwittingly crowded off by man himself; never before, however, has any species been intentionally thrown overboard.
MICHAEL BEAN, testimony, U.S. Senate Environment and Public Works subcommittee, 13 April 1978

7 When they voted for the [Endangered Species] act, congressmen thought they were voting to protect warm and cuddly animals, or bold and beautiful things like the bald eagle, and not little slimy, scaly things and invertebrates.

ANONYMOUS CONGRESSIONAL STAFF MEMBER, quoted in *New York Times*, 23 April 1978

8 Environmental legislation is not an instrument of economic policy, although economic consequences result from its implementation. [It] is an instrument of *social* policy with its main emphasis directed towards protection of workers, consumers, and other victims of pollution.

NICHOLAS A. ASHFORD, speech, International Conference on Public Control of Environmental Health Hazards, June 1978

9 It is a shame to refer to the Superfund as "environmental legislation" when in fact it is really disaster relief.

WILLIAM SANJOUR, testimony on the hazardous waste cleanup program, U.S. Senate Governmental Affairs subcommittee, 1 August 1979

10 The Endangered Species Act . . . recognizes values, be they ethical or aesthetic, that transcend the purely practical and admit to an awe in the face of the diversity of creation.

JAMES L. BUCKLEY, *Washington Post*, 4 September 1979

11 The people have a right to clean air, pure water, productive soils and to the conservation of the natural, scenic, historic, recreational, esthetic and economic values of the environment. America's natural resources are the common property of all the people, including generations yet to come. As trustee of these resources, the United States Government shall conserve and maintain them for the benefit of all people.

NATIONAL WILDLIFE FEDERATION, proposed environmental quality amendment to the Constitution, 1987

12 The legal victories won in the late sixties and early seventies formed the foundation on which the modern environmental movement is built.

JOHN ADAMS, in Peter Borelli, ed., *Crossroads*, 1988

13 In no other political and social movement has litigation played so important and dominant a role. Not even close.

DAVID SIVE, quoted in Peter Borelli, ed., *Crossroads*, 1988

14 Add the assets of all the environmental groups and the total would be equal to the assets of a fourth- or fifth-rate oil company you never heard of. Environmentalists can play the political game now: lobbying, publicity, publishing. But they didn't have that power until they started suing.

RICK SUTHERLAND, quoted in Peter Borelli, ed., *Crossroads*, 1988

15 Many environmental lawyers argue that the environmental law business is not so innovative as it was, that pure litigation is getting rare. It is, they say, being replaced by a complicated hybrid of lobbying, negotiation, compromise, and gentle persuasion.

TOM TURNER, in Peter Borelli, ed., *Crossroads*, 1988

16 Never before had American law demonstrated a concern for such an extended group. Utility to humankind was not a criterion for the 1973 lists; in fact, most of the creatures included could not be used or harvested in any way; many were almost completely unknown. But they were protected simply because they were part of what the ecologists and ecotheologians, in their separate ways, thought of as creation.

RODERICK F. NASH, on the Endangered Species Act, *The Rights of Nature*, 1989

17 [Public service] means protecting public health against environmental contamination. And that means strong laws on air and water pollution, toxic waste and drinking water. It means RCRA, and Superfund, the Clean Water Act, the Clean Air Act. It means raising the consciousness of the American people on the emerging challenge of global warming. It means saying no to those who seek private exceptions to pollution-control policies.

EDMUND S. MUSKIE, former U.S. Senator and Secretary of State, speech, 6 January 1989

18 Environmental law has come to be a bore . . . if the idea is to "teach" the "law" that we find in the "books." There is too much junk there, too many details. . . . Project this pic-

ture a bit and what you have for the future . . . is a bunch of lawyers who don't really know anything worth knowing.

JIM KRIER, quoted in *Environmental Law Reporter*, June 1989

19 Environmental law has largely become pollution law, and pollution law has failed to open new legal vistas or to engage environmental issues deeply.

JOSEPH SAX, *Environmental Law Reporter*, June 1989

20 There is a basic flaw embedded in the U.S. environmental laws: they activate the regulatory system only after a pollutant has contaminated the environment—when it is too late. This fault has spread through the system of environmental regulation, creating practices that seem reasonable and safe from criticism, but which on analysis can often be seen to violate, at their best, common sense and, at their worst, social mores and the public interest.

BARRY COMMONER, *Making Peace with the Planet*, 1990

21 With the possible exception of the abolitionists, no reform group in our history has used federal law so effectively—or created more of it—than environmentalists have.

BIL GILBERT, *Smithsonian*, April 1990

22 After about 90 days at EPA, I decided the laws we were expected to administer were poorly conceived and in many instances unworkable. Congress mandated that we do the impossible—create a permanently perfect environment.

WILLIAM RUCKELSHAUS, *Smithsonian*, April 1990

23 Nobody's told me the difference between a red squirrel, a black one or a brown one.

Do we have to save every subspecies? Do we have to save [an endangered species] in every locality where it exists?

MANUEL LUJAN, U.S. Secretary of the Interior, on the extreme mandate of the Endangered Species Act, *Washington Post*, 12 May 1990

24 Our legislators are playing doctor. If they write a prescription, I hope the laws retain flexibility to change when the real doctors find a better formula.

J. W. CHUCKMAN, senior economist, Imperial Oil, on the Clean Air Act, speech, Society of Management Accountants, Toronto, 17 May 1990

25 We must say boldly . . . that the right to a healthy environment is as inalienable as the right to free speech and freedom of worship.

JAY HAIR, *Earth Ethics*, Summer 1990

26 The case before this court [involving discharges of oil into a river] presents another chapter in the never-ending American environmental tragedy. A recalcitrant company in the private sector of the economy combined with the lethargic enforcement of the applicable statutes and regulations . . . have caused a continuing, if not constant . . . pollution.

NICHOLAS POLITAN, *Christian Science Monitor*, 10 August 1990

27 The Clean Air Act is the first opportunity this body [Congress] has had, Mr. President, since the fall of the Berlin Wall, to reflect whether or not we are going to be willing to register that this is a different world.

TIMOTHY WIRTH, U.S. Senator, *NRDC Newsline*, August–September 1990

28 The law is no panacea for anything, let alone the enormous and complex problems of environmental degradation. It cannot single-handedly take on the economic forces which have produced industrial fall-out so severe that life expectancy has been reduced in parts of East Europe; and which have produced such overconsumption elsewhere that the global commons have been hideously fouled. Nor can it withstand the social and economic pressures that are eroding the resource base in many developing countries. But it can help.

DANIEL NELSON, *Panos*, September 1990

29 EPA's legislative structure can be likened to an archeological dig. Each layer of legislation represents a set of political and technical judgments that often do not bear any relationship to other layers.

AL ALM, *EPA Journal*, September–October 1990

30 Spread this gospel across the land and there
will be no buildings ever. This is the "green
revolution." Its purpose, stripped of the
cover of protecting human rights, is to destroy capitalism, and put the nation into the
poverty that will result from a government
dedicated to the proposition that "nature is
good, but man is evil."
  EVERETT DEJAGER, against the proposed National Wildlife Federation environmental
  quality constitutional amendment, letter,
  Cincinnati Enquirer, 21 November 1990

79 LIFE-STYLE
See also 3 AFFLUENCE, 20 CONSUMERISM,
110 POVERTY

1 Live simply so others may simply live.
  BUMPER STICKER

2 I would rather sit on a pumpkin, and have it
all to myself, than to be crowded on a velvet
cushion.
  HENRY DAVID THOREAU (1817–1862), *Walden*,
  1854

3 The point is not that any particular style of
living is better than the others, but rather that
there is value—possibly very great value—to
the ability of each individual to have a wide
choice of life-styles.
  EZRA GLASER, in S. Fred Singer, ed., *Is There
  An Optimum Level of Population?*, 1971

4 Most new efforts at environmental control
will directly impact the number one polluter—the citizen himself. We will be attempting to make changes in his life-style, to alter
his way of living so that his ecology can continue to accommodate him. More and more
of the public is getting off the environmental
bandwagon as this changing emphasis takes
place. There is great resistance to such direct
impact; there is a defensiveness which makes
each individual in his own mind an exception
to whatever must be done.
  DIARMUID F. O'SCANNLAIN, testimony, U.S.
  Senate Public Works subcommittee, 25
  February 1974

5 Voluntary simplicity of living has been advo-
cated and practiced by the founders of most
of the great religions—Jesus, Buddha. Lao
Tse, Moses and Mohammed—also by many

saints and wise men such as St. Francis, John
Woolman, the Hindu rishis, the Hebrew
prophets, the Moslem sufis: by many artists
and scientists; and by such great modern
leaders as Lenin and Gandhi. It has been followed also by members of military armies
and monastic orders—organizations which
have had great and prolonged influence on
the world.
  RICHARD GREGG, *Manas*, 4 September 1974

6 We have six per cent of the world's population, and we consume thirty per cent of its
oil. Sooner or later, the rest of the world will
hate us for using so much oil. The American
way of life has to go through a major change.
The most important thing now is to get
started.
  ANONYMOUS U.S. REPRESENTATIVE, quoted in
  New Yorker, 21 July 1975

7 Reinhabitation means learning to live-in-
place in an area that has been disrupted and
injured through past exploitation. It involves
becoming native to a place through becoming
aware of the particular ecological relationships that operate within and around it.
  Living-in-place means following the necessities and pleasures of life as they are
uniquely presented by a particular site, and
evolving ways to ensure long-term occu-
pancy of that site.
  PETER BERG and RAYMOND F. DASMANN, after-
  word, Planet Drum Foundation, *Reinhabit-
  ing a Separate Country*, 1977

8 To live we must daily break the body and
shed the blood of Creation. When we do this
lovingly, knowingly, skillfully, reverently, it
is a sacrament. When we do it greedily, clumsily, ignorantly, destructively, it is a desecration. By such desecration we condemn
ourselves to spiritual and moral loneliness,
and others to want.
  WENDELL BERRY, *Sierra*, November–December 1979

9 The tastes of future individuals will depend
not only on what is advertised but on what is
available. People may come to think that a
gondola cruise along an artificial river is a
wilderness experience if there is simply nothing to compare it with.
  MARK SAGOFF, *Environmental Law* 12, 1982

10 Is it the way we live or eat, is it environmental
exposures, hot tub baths, drug abuse, pro-

miscuous sex, the high incidence of venereal disease? There are lots of things in today's life-style that are suspect.

ROBERT L. DIXON, on the occurrence of reproductive failures, quoted in *Conservation Foundation Letter*, May–June 1984

11 Be a half-assed crusader, a part-time fanatic. Don't worry too much about the fate of the world. Saving the world is only a hobby. Get out there and enjoy the world, your girlfriend, your boyfriend, husbands, wives; climb mountains, run rivers, get drunk, do whatever you want to do while you can, before it's too late.

EDWARD ABBEY (1927–1989), shortly before his death, quoted in *The Green Lifestyle Handbook*, 1989

12 Ectopia must be created on the material plane. No amount of Aquarian Age wishing will make it so. Lifestyle and livelihood are pivotal moral issues.

STEPHANIE MILLS, *What Ever Happened to Ecology*, 1989

13 The environmental movement as a whole is increasingly coming to realize that we can no longer make major gains by forcing people to put widgets on smokestacks or plants. Most of the easy sources to control already have controls. To get significant reductions now means changing a number of behaviors and on such a scale that we can't do it without controlling legislation.

ALEX CRISTOFARO, quoted in *New York Times*, 3 April 1989

14 Modern society will find no solution to the ecological problem unless it reviews its own lifestyle. In many areas of the world today, society is given to instant gratification and consumerism while remaining indifferent to the damage these cause.

POPE JOHN PAUL II, 8 December 1989

15 Many ordinary human beings would like a cleaner world. They are prepared to make sacrifices—*tradeoffs* is a better word—to get one. But ordinary human beings will not adopt the Buddha's life without desire.

VIRGINIA I. POSTREL, *Reason*, April 1990

16 To slow economy and society to the approved *adagio*, the greens have some fairly straightforward prescriptions: Restrict trade to the local area. Eliminate markets where possible. End specialization. Anchor individuals in their "bioregions," local areas defined by their environmental characteristics. Shrink the population. Make life simple again, small, self-contained.

VIRGINIA I. POSTREL, speech, City Club of Cleveland, Ohio, 19 June 1990

80 LIMITS
See also   17 COMMON RESOURCES

1 The limit of successful agriculture without irrigation has been set at 20 inches [annual rainfall]. . . . Many droughts will occur; many seasons in a long series will be fruitless; and it may be doubted whether [dryland] agriculture will prove remunerative.

JOHN WESLEY POWELL (1834–1902), recommending against development of the West because of the limits of natural resources, *Report on the Lands of the Arid Regions of the United States*, 1879

2 The notion of an absolute limit to natural resource availability is untenable when the definition of resources changes drastically and unpredictably over time.

H. J. BARNETT and C. MORSE, *Scarcity and Growth*, 1963

3 Humanity's mastery of vast, inanimate, inexhaustible energy sources and the accelerated doing more with less of sea, air, and space technology has proven Malthus to be wrong. Comprehensive physical and economic success for humanity may now be accomplished in one-fourth of a century.

R. BUCKMINSTER FULLER, *Comprehensive Design Strategy*, 1967

4 It would be tragic [to] conclude that the problem of expanding human populations versus finite resources can be solved merely by increasing the efficiency of utilization of the resources. Ultimately, such a one-sided approach would reduce men everywhere to the role of pitiful scavengers, constantly combing the litter of a ravaged biosphere in search of scraps overlooked in prior searches by vast hordes of fellow scavengers.

KENNETH E. F. WATT, *Ecology and Resource Management*, 1968

5 For some time, and indefinitely into the future, additional numbers of people can be accommodated only by a more intensive use of land and consumption of a larger share of the earth's resources.

This prognosis implies less room for other forms of life. Sooner or later, we must decide how much life to displace. Population will increase whether we decide to eliminate all other natural life or whether we try to preserve a biosphere that still provides us with most of our major needs. At the current rate of population increase such a biosphere may not last for more than 100 years.

MAN'S IMPACT ON THE GLOBAL ENVIRONMENT, report of the Study of Critical Environmental Problems, 1970

6 We live in . . . a tight ecological system. . . . If Homo sapiens insists on constant growth, within this system's inelastic walls, something has to pop, or smother.

JOHN FISCHER, Harper's, April 1970

7 There are no substantial limits in sight either in raw materials or in energy that alterations in the price structure, product substitution, anticipated gains in technology and pollution control cannot be expected to solve.

FRANK W. NOTESTEIN, Family Planning Perspectives, June 1970

8 Many leaders now use the rhetoric of "spaceship earth," but are they really prepared to accept the political and economic costs of self-denial that this rhetoric implies?

RICHARD N. GARDNER, remark at conference, Aspen Institute on Man and Science, 1971

9 When all resources are running out, will man, the pinnacle of biological evolution, really behave in a more rational fashion than the sharks? What is the evidence?

KENNETH E. F. WATT, in Clifton Fadiman and Jean White, eds., Ecocide, 1971

10 A French riddle for children illustrates another aspect of exponential growth—the apparent suddenness with which it approaches a fixed limit. Suppose you own a pond on which a water lily is growing. The lily plant doubles in size each day. If the lily were allowed to grow unchecked, it would completely cover the pond in 30 days, choking off the other forms of life in the water. For a long time the lily plant seems small, and so you decide not to worry about cutting it back until it covers half the pond. On what day will that be? On the twenty-ninth day, of course. You have one day to save your pond.

DONELLA H. MEADOWS et al., The Limits to Growth, 1972

11 [At the optimum level] individuals in the population . . . will show abundant individual growth and health not limited by shortages of any essential requirements. Such an optimum density can only be maintained by strong limitations on growth imposed by the behavior of the species concerned (self-limitation) or by removal of individuals . . . through predation.

RAYMOND F. DASMANN, JOHN P. MILTON, and PETER H. FREEMAN, Ecological Principles for Economic Development, 1973

12 Other peoples have accepted a dictatorship as their resources were depleted, hoping that a strong leader could regain for them a lost standard of living.

VERNON GILL CARTER and TOM DALE, Topsoil and Civilization, revised edition, 1974

13 It may be amusing to note, at such a depressing juncture, that both economists and ecologists have always agreed with Barry Commoner's proposition: There is no such thing as a free lunch. Now, the dismal second law of thermodynamics is forcing both groups into recognizing an even more dismal proposition: Each lunch costs more than the last.

HAZEL HENDERSON, in James N. Smith, Environmental Quality and Social Justice in Urban America, 1974

14 In a situation of ecological scarcity . . . the individualistic basis of society, the concept of inalienable rights, the purely self-defined pursuit of happiness, liberty as maximum freedom of action, and laissez-faire itself all require abandonment or major modification if we wish to avoid inexorable environmental degradation and perhaps extinction as a civilization. We must thus question whether democracy as we know it can survive.

WILLIAM OPHULS, in Stuart S. Nagel, ed., Environmental Politics, 1974

15 It makes little sense to attempt to establish an upper limit for a human population since

man is capable, to a degree far exceeding all other species, of changing both himself and his social and natural environment. Since man is able to adjust to as well as change the social and physical conditions under which he lives, any view that regards these conditions as inflexible constraints on an upper population limit is too simplistic.

A. BERRY CRAWFORD and A. BRUCE BISHOP, speech, American Association for the Advancement of Science, San Francisco, 1 March 1974

16 If the optimists are right in supposing that we can adjust to ecological scarcity with economics and technology, this effort will have, as we say, "side effects." For the collision with physical limits can be forestalled only by moving toward some kind of steady-state economy—characterized by the most scrupulous husbanding of resources, by extreme vigilance against the ever-present possibility of disaster should breakdown occur, and therefore, by tight controls on human behavior.

WILLIAM OPHULS, *Harper's*, April 1974

17 The future austerity will be perennial, and it will become progressively more severe. . . . Within each of the beleaguered "developed" countries there will be a bitter struggle for the control of their diminished resources. . . . [and] a new way of life—a severely regimented way—will have to be imposed by a ruthless authoritarian government.

ARNOLD TOYNBEE (1889–1975), *The Observer* (London), 14 April 1974

18 All rational observers agree that no physical quantity can grow exponentially forever. This is true, for example, of population, the production of energy and other raw materials, and the generation of wastes.

JOHN P. HOLDREN and PAUL R. EHRLICH, *American Scientist*, May–June 1974

19 It should not be surprising that, when limits do appear, they will appear suddenly. Such behavior is typical of exponential growth. If 20 doublings are possible before a limit is reached in an exponentially growing process (characterized by a fixed doubling time if the growth rate is constant), then the system will be less than half "loaded" for the first 19 dou-

blings—or for 95% of the elapsed time between initiation of growth and exceeding the limit. Clearly, a long history of exponential growth does not imply a long future.

JOHN P. HOLDREN and PAUL R. EHRLICH, *American Scientist*, May–June 1974

20 [While technology probably can find enough raw materials and even energy] other resources cannot be stretched much further. These resources provide space privacy, some taste of adventure for the young, and the right to sometimes do as you please. These resources will have to be rationed. To do this there will be more government and more bureaucracy.

PAUL COLINVAUX, *Yale Review*, Spring 1975

21 The high degree of emphasis on physical limits . . . is diverting our attention from social limits that may be the most fundamental and intractable.

JAY W. FORRESTER, speech, World Future Society, June 1975

22 We need, however, to shift the emphasis toward ecological adaptation, that is, to accept natural limits to the size and dominion of the human household, to concentrate on moral growth and qualitative improvement rather than on the quantitative imperialist expansion of man's dominion. The human adaptation needed is primarily a change of heart, followed by a shift to an economy that does not depend so much on continuous growth.

HERMAN E. DALY, *Steady-State Economics*, 1977

23 Population cannot grow forever, per-capita consumption cannot grow forever, the relevant time period cannot be shortened forever, and technology cannot reduce material and energy intensity forever. Nevertheless, there are short- and middle-run trade-offs among the four elements.

HERMAN E. DALY, on defining energy requirements, *Steady-State Economics*, 1977

24 Developed initially as a concept for describing the growth and dynamics of species populations, carry capacity was defined as a limit on the number of species that could be maintained within an ecosystem or habitat. . . . [T]he concept of carrying capacity needs

to be broadened to include interactions that occur between human and natural systems.

A. BERRY CRAWFORD and A. BRUCE BISHOP, Carrying Capacity and Planning, in Dean F. Peterson and A. Berry Crawford, eds., *Values and Choices in Development of the Colorado River Basin*, 1978

25 Alaska is our last frontier. The Canadians have one; so do the Russians, the Brazilians, and the Australians. The world has two, in the oceans and in the Antarctic, but we're running low on frontiers. And we better not run out. The frontier, in reality and in fantasy, has been too important for us all.

JEFFREY KNIGHT, *Not Man Apart*, Mid-May–June 1978

26 Limits to growth? What limits? The only limits are in some people's imagination and vision. How ridiculous to emphasize limits at this very moment when we are expanding into a limitless Universe of limitless resources, limitless space, limitless potentials, limitless growth.

F. M. ESFANDIARY, *Futurist*, June 1978

27 Our growing inability to maintain the physical infrastructure of our industrial society constitutes in itself yet another limit to growth.

EDWARD GOLDSMITH, *Ecology Quarterly*, Autumn 1978

28 America's gradual and grudging acceptance of a sense of national and individual limits during the '80's may arise not so much from a sense of renewed virtue as from exhaustion and desperation at discovering that, although learning to make sacrifices may be unpleasant, trying to be happy without giving something up for others is impossible.

EUGENE KENNEDY, *New York Times Magazine*, 2 December 1979

29 We cannot live without limits, and intelligent people realize this; but we must define these limits before they are thrust upon us. And to do so requires a sense of ethics, and leaders who can act out of principle, rather than organizing adversarially to defend some particular set of interests.

MICHAEL MACCOBY, quoted in *New York Times*, 30 December 1979

30 There are, in short, *social* limits to growth, and the dangers of exceeding these limits are, it is my conviction, more ominous than are the well-publicised dangers of exceeding material limits.

LORD ERIC ASHBY, *Environmental Science and Technology*, October 1980

31 The major constraint upon the human capacity to enjoy unlimited minerals, energy, and other raw materials at acceptable prices is knowledge. And the source of knowledge is the human mind. Ultimately, then, the key constraint is human imagination acting together with educated skills. This is why an increase of human beings, along with causing an additional consumption of resources, constitutes a crucial addition to the stock of natural resources.

JULIAN L. SIMON, *The Ultimate Resource*, 1981

32 Each major conflict over the allocation of resources will raise this question; it will force us to choose between our private interests and our shared values; it will require us to respond either as consumers or as citizens. . . . The conflict between these two approaches to problem solving *is* the environmental conflict.

MARK SAGOFF, *Environmental Law* 12, 1982

33 There is one important difference, however, between the biologists and economists on scarcity. In modern textbook economics we attribute scarcity mainly to the non-satiability of human wants rather than to sheer population pressure on resources.

JACK HIRSHLEIFER, speech, American Association for the Advancement of Science, Washington, D.C., 7 January 1982

34 The limits we are beginning to confront today are not primarily physical. They are limits of political and social will and of adequate institutional means to assure careful use of the earth's resources and equitable distribution of benefits and costs resulting from their use.

MAURICE F. STRONG, Royal Swedish Academy of Sciences conference, Rattvik, Sweden, November 1982

35 As any wildlife biologist knows, once a species reproduces itself beyond the carrying capacity of its habitat, natural checks and balances come into play. . . . The human spe-

cies is governed by this same natural law. And there are signs in many parts of the world today—Ethiopia is only one of many places, a tip of the iceberg—that we *Homo sapiens* are beginning to exceed the carrying capacity of the planet.

RUSSELL PETERSON, quoted in Peter Borelli, ed., *Crossroads*, 1988

36 Bioregionalism is a clumsy term, but a good conversation starter. The word connotes a concern with the vitality of the entire fabric of life in realms not determined by man, but by nature. Bioregionalism is crafting a way of life that can be sustained within the boundaries and limits suggested by place.

STEPHANIE MILLS, *What Ever Happened to Ecology?*, 1989

37 Every ideology has a primary value or set of values at its core—liberty, equality, order, virtue, salvation. For greens, the core value is stasis, "substainability" as they put it. The ideal is of an earth that doesn't change, that shows little or no effects of human activity. Greens take as their model of the ideal society the notion of an ecosystem that has reached an unchanging climax stage. "Limits to growth," is as much a description of how things *should* be as it is of how they *are*.

VIRGINIA I. POSTREL, speech, City Club of Cleveland, Ohio, 19 June 1990

38 As we've learned in the century since the closing of the frontier in America, this is a country that gets depressed and frustrated when there's no more excess capacity.

HENRY ALLEN, *Washington Post*, 21 October 1990

39 Sustainable development assumes that economic growth is essential to environmental solutions. Thus it leaves behind sterile growth/no growth debates. It also implies that there are limits to economic growth. The general view today, however, is that these are not the absolute limits whose existence was so hotly debated in the 1970s. Nor are the limits likely to be imposed by a dwindling, finite supply of resources. Instead, the limiting factor is likely to be the ability of the biosphere to absorb the effects of human activities.

JESSICA MATTHEWS, *Washington Post*, 1 January 1991

40 Americans, a people of plenty, are loath to learn this lesson: Scarcity can be an improving experience. Just as recessions wring inefficiencies from the economy, increased competition for a scarce resource encourages economic rationality.

GEORGE F. WILL, *Washington Post*, 28 March 1991

---

81 MINING

1 I have very large ideas of the mineral wealth of our Nation. I believe it practically inexhaustible. It abounds all over the western country, from the Rocky Mountains to the Pacific, and its development has scarcely commenced. . . . Tell the miners from me, that I shall promote their interests to the utmost of my ability; because their prosperity is the prosperity of the Nation, and we shall prove in a very few years that we are indeed the *treasury of the world*.

ABRAHAM LINCOLN (1809–1865), message for the miners of the West, 14 April 1865

2 This [mining] pit . . . seemed . . . to have the evil air of a gluttonous beast crouching there to devour the earth.

EMILE ZOLA (1840–1902), *Germinal*, 1885

3 Coal has always cursed the land in which it lies. When men begin to wrest it from the earth it leaves a legacy of foul streams, hideous slag heaps and polluted air. It peoples this transformed land with blind and crippled men and with widows and orphans. It is an extractive industry which takes all away and retores nothing. It mars but never beautifies. It corrupts but never purifies.

HARRY M. CAUDILL, *Night Comes to the Cumberlands*, 1962

4 Mining is like a search-and-destroy mission.

STEWART L. UDALL, *1976—Agenda for Tomorrow*, 1968

5 When you create a mine, there are two things you can't avoid: a hole in the ground and a dump for waste rock.

CHARLES PARK, quoted in John McPhee, *Encounters with the Archdruid*, 1971

6 [The strip miners] know that an outraged public will sooner or later clamp down and put a stop to this assault on the environment, so they are making a killing while they can get away with it.
KEN HECHLER, U.S. Representative, *Not Man Apart*, July 1971

7 Strip mining is like taking seven or eight stiff drinks: you are riding high as long as the coal lasts, but the hangover comes when the coal is gone, the land is gone, the jobs are gone, and the bitter truth of the morning after leaves a barren landscape and a mouth full of ashes.
KEN HECHLER, U.S. Representative, *Not Man Apart*, July 1971

8 It's hard not to chuckle. The white man is doing to other white men what the white man once did to the Indian.
DEWITT DILLON, Crow Indian, on strip mining, quoted in *Newsweek*, 9 October 1972

9 Here then is the terrible dilemma. The lands we shred for needed minerals are the same lands that feed, clothe and shelter us. When we dig, we shrink our farms. There is no land to spare.
HENRY M. CAUDILL, *Atlantic Monthly*, September 1973

10 Coal mining, in short, can do grave damage to the web of life on the face of the earth. But it is the men who go down into the pits who are most directly victimized. . . . Coal company stockholders along with power consumers enjoying their air-conditioned comfort have received a large and shameful subsidy in the form of the ruined health and early deaths of the miners.
S. DAVID FREEMAN, *Energy: The New Era*, 1974

11 "Reclamation" is the one-word answer to the problems posed by strip-mining. But as an environmentalist points out, " 'Reclamation' is without question the slipperiest word in the lexicon of strip mining." Too often in the past reclamation has meant simply smoothing out the overturned earth or planting a few seeds and hoping something would take root and grow. The failure to reclaim strip-mined land is an ugly fact beyond dispute.
S. DAVID FREEMAN, *Energy: The New Era*, 1974

12 There is an old saying that nobody knows the reserves of an oilfield until the last barrel has been pumped out and the same is true of mines.
TREVOR SYKES, *The Money Miners—The Great Australian Mining Boom*, 1979

13 That's what mining is all about—writing finis to finite resources.
STEPHANIE MILLS, *What Ever Happened to Ecology?*, 1989

14 When a person dies, we bury the body in the land and it turns into earth. So we can't leave our land; it would be like leaving our dead, our bodies. Because the earth is our mother. The liver of the earth is coal; the lung is uranium. Earthquakes and tornadoes are her breath. Now she's in pain. When the government takes her organs, she dies. The government only wants money. It doesn't think of her children: we people and the four-legged people who talk.
NAVAJO INDIAN, quoted in Julian Burger, *The Gaia Atlas of First Peoples*, 1990

82 MOUNTAINS

1 There are four rules for living in the mountains: let there be no formation in trees, no arrangement of rocks, no sumptuousness in the living house, and no contrivance in the human heart.
CHINESE PROVERB, in Lin Yutang, *The Widsom of China and India*, 1942

2 Have We not made
The earth as a wide
Expanse . . .
And the mountains as pegs?
KORAN, sura 78:6,7

3 On the mountains is freedom! The breath of decay never sullies the pure blowing air; nature is perfect, wherever we stray, if man did not come in to deform it with care!
FRIEDRICH VON SCHILLER (1759–1805), *The Bride of Messina*, 1803

4 Mountains are earth's undecaying monuments.
NATHANIEL HAWTHORNE (1804–1864), *The Notch of the White Mountains*, 1868

5 I have a low opinion of books; they are but piles of stones set up to show travelers where other minds have been, or at best signal smokes to call attention. . . . One day's exposure to mountains is better than a cartload of books.

> JOHN MUIR (1838–1914), 1872, in L. M. Wolfe, ed., *John Muir, John of the Mountains: Unpublished Journals of John Muir*, 1938

6 The mountains are fountains of men as well as of rivers, of glaciers, of fertile soil. The great poets, philosophers, prophets, able men whose thoughts and deeds have moved the world, have come down from the mountains—mountain-dwellers who have grown strong there with the forest trees in Nature's work-shops.

> JOHN MUIR (1838–1914), 1888, *Steep Trails*, 1918

7 A Californian whom I had recently the pleasure of meeting observed that if the philosophers had lived among your mountains, their systems would have been different from what they are. Certainly very different from what those systems are which the European genteel tradition has handed down since Socrates; for these systems are egotistical; directly or indirectly they are anthropocentric, and inspired by the conceited notion that man, or human reason, or the human distinction between good and evil, is the center and pivot of the universe. That is what the mountains and the woods should make you at last ashamed to assert.

> GEORGE SANTAYANA (1863–1952), speech, University of California, Berkeley, 1911

8 That wonderful world of high mountains, dazzling in their rock and ice, acts as a catalyst. It suggests the infinite but it is not the infinite. The heights only give us what we ourselves bring to them.

> LUCIEN DEVIES, preface to Maurice Herzog, *Annapurna*, 1952

9 Not to have known—as most men have not—either the mountain or the desert is not to have known one's self.

> JOSEPH WOOD KRUTCH (1893–1970), *The Desert Year*, 1952

10 The smaller we come to feel ourselves compared to the mountain, the nearer we come to participating in its greatness. I do not know why this is so.

> ARNE NAESS, in Michael Tobias, ed., *The Mountain Spirit*, 1979

11 [The Denver area is] the first alpine megalopolis.

> EVAN VLACHOS, quoted in *Conservation Foundation Letter*, May 1979

83 NATIONAL PARKS
See also   98 PARKS

1 [Yellowstone National Park] is just a howling wilderness of three thousand square miles, full of all imaginable freaks of a fiery nature.

> RUDYARD KIPLING (1865–1936), *From Sea to Sea*, 1899

2 The National Parks do not suffice as a means of perpetuating the larger carnivores; witness the precarious status of the grizzly bear, and the fact that the park system is already wolfless. Neither do they suffice for mountain sheep; most sheep herds are shrinking.

> ALDO LEOPOLD (1886–1948), *A Sand County Almanac*, 1949

3 In the first 10 months of 1953, forty-three million people had visited the parks. All except a handful of them seem to assume that a park ranger, a road, a comfort station, and a fire truck are just like the waterfalls, provided by nature at no expense.

> BERNARD DE VOTO (1897–1955), *Harper's*, February 1954

4 The progressive impairment of the parks by budgetary bloodletting is a national disgrace.

> BERNARD DE VOTO (1897–1955), *Harper's*, August 1954

5 The one overriding principle of the conservation movement is that no work of man (save the bare minimum of roads, trails, and necessary public facilities in access areas) should intrude into the wonder places of the National Park System.

> STEWART L. UDALL, 1960, quoted in *Current Biography*, 1961

6 National parks and reserves are an integral aspect of intelligent use of natural resources. It is the course of wisdom to set aside an am-

ple portion of our natural resources as national parks and reserves, thus ensuring that future generations may know the majesty of the earth as we know it today.

JOHN F. KENNEDY (1917–1963), speech, First World Conference on National Parks, Seattle, 23 June 1962

7 Why is the Park Service generally so anxious to accommodate that other crowd, the indolent millions born on wheels and suckled on gasoline, who expect and demand paved highways to lead them in comfort, ease and safety into every nook and corner of the national parks?

EDWARD ABBEY, *Desert Solitaire*, 1971

8 Let the people walk. Or ride horses, bicycles, mules, wild pigs—anything—but keep the automobiles and the motorcycles and all their motorized relatives out. We have agreed not to drive our automobiles into cathedrals, concert halls, art museums, legislative assemblies, private bedrooms and other sanctums of our culture; we should treat our national parks with the same deference, for they, too, are holy places.

EDWARD ABBEY, *Desert Solitaire*, 1971

9 The concern I have [is that] we're going to begin to discriminate against the elderly, the traveling families who have only a very limited time and modest budgets to visit the parks, and probably narrow the constituency of the parks to only those such as back packers and others who are able to spend the time and have the inclination to camp in the wilderness.

ROGERS C. B. MORTON, U.S. Secretary of the Interior, in response to recommendations that auto traffic and other types of development in National Parks be banned, quoted by United Press International, 17 September 1972

10 Ninety-five percent of your constituents and mine, . . . will never see Yosemite or Yellowstone or the Grand Canyon. . . . If we are going to treat all of the people equitably, if we are going to have a continuing constituency for national parks, then we are going to have to provide for the people in our most populous urban areas an outdoor recreation opportunity comparable to that we have

provided for those already located near some of our great parks.

JOHN F. SEIBERLING, U.S. Representative, speech, U.S. House of Representatives, 9 December 1974

11 In the planning and management of all parks, . . . we must be guided by the unifying management principle that protection of ecological health and historic integrity is our first consideration and priority; that these resources are conserved for the benefit and inspiration of the people through the understanding, appreciation and enjoyment of the values being preserved.

GARY EVERHARDT, National Park Service policy manual, June 1975

12 When California became a state, there were two million acres of coastal redwoods, all publicly owned. Someone then could have signed a piece of paper, establishing out of that acreage a big Redwood National Park for all t.me, and this would have been accomplished at no extra cost. But this year alone, we're going to pay $400 million to get for the American people a puny, inadequate Redwood National Park. That's a pretty good argument for doing now what needs to be done in Alaska, while all of these lands are in public ownership. Simply by signing a piece of paper, the President and the Congress can save what needs to be saved.

MORRIS UDALL, U.S. Representative, speech at the Conservation Foundation, *Conservation and Values*, 1 December 1978

13 People used to come for the beauty and serenity. Those who come now don't mind the crowds; in fact they like them. . . . They come for the action.

BRIAN HARRY, quoted in Joseph Sax, *Mountains without Handrails*, 1980

14 I will err on the side of public use versus preservation. We will use the budget system to be the excuse to make major policy decisions.

JAMES G. WATT, U.S. Secretary of the Interior, on management of the national parks, speech, conference of National Park concessioners, 28 March 1981

15 National parks are the best idea we ever had. Absolutely American, absolutely democratic, they reflect us at our best rather than our worst.

WALLACE STEGNER, *Wilderness*, Spring 1983

16 Most of the parks were set apart at a time in our nation's history when we hadn't even invented the word ecosystem. The park philosophy, as articulated in legislation and in policy, strives to create a situation where natural processes are left alone. You run into a situation in which you're going against the very tenets for which the parks were created, and yet, on the other hand, you can have species slipping away. It's an issue we're ill-prepared to grapple with.

JOHN VARLEY, on whether park administration should include active intervention into natural processes, *New York Times*, 3 February 1987

17 I've been through legislation creating a dozen national parks, and there's always the same pattern. When you first propose a park, and you visit the area and present the case to the local people, they threaten to hang you. You go back in five years and they think it's the greatest thing that ever happened.

MORRIS UDALL, *Too Funny to Be President*, 1988

18 We think that it's our responsibility to provide accommodations for various people. Not everybody wants to sleep in a sleeping bag on the ground. Some like tents; some like camper cars; some like a motel kind of accommodation. Our job is to provide a variety of accommodations.

WILLIAM PENN MOTT, director, U.S. National Park Service, disagreeing with environmentalist proposals that hotels and concessions be removed from national parks, quoted in *USA Today*, 25 August 1988

84 NATIONAL SECURITY

1 There is need of wider recognition that government has as much a duty to protect the land, the air, the water, the natural environment against technological damage, as it has to protect the country against foreign enemies and the individual against criminals.

HYMAN G. RICKOVER, speech, Royal National Foundation, Athens, 1966

2 If the scientists are to be believed, we can do ourselves in as thoroughly by failing to control the atmosphere as by failing to control nuclear weapons. In such a world, a rational diplo-

macy might regard the balance of nature as being—for the present, at least—as important as the balance of power. . . . The problems posed by power do not begin to compare in significance or urgency to the problems of survival. . . . If we can say with any assurance that nationalism transcends ideology, we can say with complete assurance that breathing transcends both.

RICHARD ROVERE, *New Yorker*, 24 February 1968

3 Ally and adversary, we all share the pain and the danger of the environmental crisis. A wall may keep freedom out and people in—but no wall could be high enough to keep the smog out of Potsdam or inside West Berlin.

EDMUND S. MUSKIE, U.S. Senator, speech, Conference on International Organization and the Human Environment, New York City, 21 May 1971

4 The purpose of national security deliberations should not be to maximize military strength but to maximize national security. . . . [T]he threats to security may now arise less from the relationship of nation to nation and more from the relationship of man to nature.

LESTER BROWN, "Redefining National Security," Worldwatch Paper 14, 1977

5 We need a wider definition of national security. . . . The destruction of the planet's environment is making the world a less stable place, politically, economically, and militarily.

GRO HARLEM BRUNDTLAND, Prime Minister of Norway, *Ms.*, January 1988

6 There are many signs that the next general international crisis is going to be about the environment. There have been warnings about environmental abuse for decades, but concerns were separated from high politics and security. Now convergence has begun.

FLORA LEWIS, *New York Times*, 27 July 1988

7 Unlike military security, environmental security nurtures more stable and cooperative relationships among nations.

MICHAEL G. RENNER, *World Watch*, November–December 1989

8 Governments preoccupied with security threats of military origin have ignored the perils of environmental degradation. But national security is a meaningless concept if it does not

include the preservation of livable conditions within a country—or on the planet as a whole. . . . [E]nvironmental degradation imperils nations' most fundamental aspect of security by undermining the natural support systems on which all of human activity depends.

MICHAEL G. RENNER, Worldwatch Paper 89, May 1989.

9 If a nation's environmental foundations are depleted, its economy will steadily decline, its social fabric deteriorate, and its political structure become destabilized. The outcome is all too likely to be conflict, whether in the form of internal disorder or hostilities with other nations.

NORMAN MYERS, The Gaia Atlas of Future Worlds, 1990

85 NATURAL DISASTERS

1 Diseased nature oftentimes breaks forth
In strange eruptions; oft the teeming earth
Is with a kind of colic pinch'd and vex'd
By the imprisoning of unruly wind
Within her womb; which, for enlargement striving,
Shakes the old beldame earth and topples down
Steeples and moss-grown towers.

WILLIAM SHAKESPEARE (1564–1616), Henry IV, Part 1, 3.1.27, 1598

2 In the West, our desire to conquer nature often means simply that we diminish the probability of small inconveniences at the cost of increasing the probability of very large disasters.

KENNETH E. BOULDING, Human Values on the Spaceship Earth, 1966

3 Nature destroys—and pollutes—segments of itself, sporadically and violently, with man often a major victim in these upheavals. Earthquakes, volcanic eruptions, tidal waves, floods, epidemics are examples.

GLENN T. SEABORG, speech, Argonne National Laboratory, 1969

4 Many people remain confident that history [in the form of a severe flood] will not be repeated. The feverish activity associated with rebuilding all that has been lost supports this contention. In the very best pioneering spirit,

flood victims everywhere appear determined to restore every lost bridge, every damaged house and trailer, every waterlogged business, to its "right" place on the flood plain. Their faith in themselves and nature appears limitless.

FRANKLIN S. ADAMS, Bulletin of the Atomic Scientists, 4 April 1973

5 Unfortunately, since disaster relief in the United States is a strange combination of humanitarian impulses and political machinations, all with an unwieldy administrative structure, there has been no comprehensive evaluation of the total cost of such an approach. For example, some South Dakota counties have been declared disaster areas for four years in a row. When can taxpayers in the rest of the country indicate to these people that perhaps Mother Nature is trying to tell them something.

ROBERT D. MIEWALD, speech, American Association for the Advancement of Science, 21 February 1977

6 We hear daily of so-called natural disasters, such as the drought in Ethiopia and the Sahel countries, but the fact is that proper concern for the conservation of nature and natural resources over the years might have limited the severity of the drought and its tragic consequences.

PRINCE PHILIP, Duke of Edinburgh, speech to International Union for the Conservation of Nature, General Assembly, Madrid, November 1984

7 Famine and flood are two faces of the same coin, the result of destruction of the environment by man, and not by natural phenomena, as is often heard.

ANDERS WIJKMAN, speech to the International Union for the Conservation of Nature General Assembly, Madrid, November 1984

86 NATURAL RESOURCES
See also   3 AFFLUENCE,
17 COMMON RESOURCES,
32 ECONOMICS, GNP, 64 HISTORY,
80 LIMITS, 100 PLANNING, FORESIGHT

1 No arbitrary regulation, no act of the legislature, can add anything to the capital of the

country; it can only force it into artificial channels.

J. R. McCulloch (1789–1864), *Principles of Political Economy*, 1825

2 Among the lucky circumstances that favored the establishment and assured the maintenance of a democratic republic in the United States the most important was the choice of the land itself in which the Americans live. Their fathers gave them a love of equality and liberty but it was God who, by handing a limitless continent over to them, gave them the means of long remaining equal and free.

Alexis de Tocqueville (1805–1859), *Democracy in America*, 1835

3 The materials of wealth are in the earth, in the seas, and in their natural and unaided productions.

Daniel Webster (1782–1852), remarks in the U.S. Senate, 12 March 1838

4 I recognize the right and duty of this generation to develop and use our natural resources, but I do not recognize the right to waste them, or to rob by wasteful use, the generations that come after us.

Theodore Roosevelt (1858–1919), speech, Washington, D.C., 1900

5 But there must be the look ahead, there must be a realization of the fact that to waste, to destroy, our natural resources, to skin and exhaust the land instead of using it so as to increase its usefulness, will result in undermining in the days of our children the very prosperity which we ought by right to hand down to them amplified and developed.

Theodore Roosevelt (1858–1919), seventh annual message, 3 December 1907

6 There is delight in the hardy life of the open. There are no words that can tell the hidden spirit of the wilderness, that can reveal its mystery, its melancholy, and its charm. The nation behaves well if it treats the natural resources as assets which it must turn over to the next generation, increased and not impaired in value. Conservation means development as much as it does protection.

Theodore Roosevelt (1858–1919), speech to Colorado Live Stock Association, Denver, 29 August 1910

7 As a people, we have the problem of making our forests outlast this generation, our iron outlast this century, and our coal the next; not merely as a matter of convenience or comfort, but as a matter of stern national necessity.

William Howard Taft (1857–1930), quoted in Paolo E. Coletta, *The Presidency of William Howard Taft*, 1973

8 We think of our land and water and human resources not as static and sterile possessions but as life-giving assets to be directed by wise provision for future days. We seek to use our natural resources not as a thing apart but as something that is interwoven with industry, labor, finance, taxation, agriculture, homes, recreation, good citizenship. The results of this interweaving will have a greater influence on the future American standard of living than all the rest of our economics put together.

Franklin D. Roosevelt (1883–1945), message to Congress, 24 January 1935

9 We are being made aware that the organisation of society on the principle of private profit, as well as public destruction, is leading both to the deformation of humanity by unregulated industrialism, and to the exhaustion of natural resources, and that a good deal of our material progress is a progress for which succeeding generations may have to pay dearly.

T. S. Eliot (1888–1965), *Christianity and Culture*, 1939

10 The American Colossus was fiercely intent on appropriating and exploiting the riches of the richest of all continents—grasping with both hands, reaping where he had not sown, wasting what he thought would last forever. New railroads were opening new territory. The exploiters were pushing farther and farther into the wilderness. The man who could get his hands on the biggest slice of natural resources was the best citizen. Wealth and virtue were supposed to trot in double harness.

Gifford Pinchot (1865–1946), *Breaking New Ground*, 1947

11 The earth and its resources belong of right to its people. Without natural resources life it-

self is impossible. From birth to death, natural resources, transformed for human use, feed, clothe, shelter, and transport us. Upon them we depend for every material necessity, comfort, convenience, and protection in our lives. Without abundant resources prosperity is out of reach.

> GIFFORD PINCHOT (1865–1946), *Breaking New Grand,* 1947

12 National life everywhere is built on the foundation of natural resources. Throughout human history the exhaustion of these resources and the need for new supplies have been among the greatest causes of war.

> GIFFORD PINCHOT (1865–1946), *Breaking New Ground,* 1947

13 The rightful use and purpose of our natural resources [is] to make all the people strong and well, able and wise, well-taught, well-fed . . . full of knowledge and initiative, with equal opportunity for all and special privilege for none.

> GIFFORD PINCHOT (1865–1946), quoted in Peter Borelli, ed., *Crossroads,* 1988

14 We Americans think we are pretty good! We want to build a house, we cut down some trees. We want to build a fire, we dig a little coal. But when we run out of all these things, then we will find out just how good we really are.

> WILL ROGERS (1879–1935), quoted in Francesca Lyman, *The Greenhouse Trap,* 1990

15 Industrialism is the systematic exploitation of wasting assets . . . progress is merely an acceleration in the rate of that exploitation. Such prosperity as we have known up to the present is the consequence of rapidly spending the planet's irreplaceable capital.

> ALDOUS HUXLEY (1894–1963), *Themes and Variations,* 1950

16 The fat years of the U.S. have ended.

> TIME, concurring with the Paley Commission report's warning of natural resource depletion, 30 June 1952

17 We may not appreciate the fact; but a fact nevertheless it remains: we are living in a Golden Age, the most gilded Golden Age of human history—not only of past history, but of future history. For, as Sir Charles Darwin

and many others before him have pointed out, we are living like drunken sailors, like the irresponsible heirs of a millionaire uncle. At an ever accelerating rate we are now squandering the capital of metallic ores and fossil fuels accumulated in the earth's crust during hundreds of millions of years. How long can this spending spree go on? Estimates vary. But all are agreed that within a few centuries or at most a few millennia, Man will have run through his capital and will be compelled to live, for the remaining nine thousand nine hundred and seventy or eighty centuries of his career as Homo sapiens, strictly on income.

> ALDOUS HUXLEY (1894–1963), *Collected Essays,* 1959

18 As we peer into society's future, we—and I, and our government—must avoid the impulse to live only for today, plundering for our own ease and convenience, the precious resources of tomorrow. We cannot mortgage the material assets of our grandchildren without risking the loss also of their political and spiritual heritage. We want democracy to survive for all generations to come, not to become the insolvent phantom of tomorrow.

> DWIGHT D. EISENHOWER (1890–1969), parting words from the Oval Office, 1961, quoted by Susan Eisenhower, *Washington Post,* 14 October 1990

19 The further you go from a mature society back toward the frontier, the less acceptable is the ecologic viewpoint of how to plan resource use.

> STARKER LEOPOLD, in Frank F. Darling and John P. Milton, eds. *Future Environments of North America,* 1966

20 America achieved world leadership as an industrial power at the cost of haphazard and wasteful exploitation of unparalleled natural resources. Virgin forests fell to the ax . . . the plow and strip mining tore our fertile soil . . . rivers and harbors were given over entirely to commerce . . . the odor of pollution in our air and water was welcomed by most as the "smell of prosperity."

> HUBERT H. HUMPHREY (1911–1978), speech, The Dalles, Oregon, 1968

21 We are driving through the earth's resources at a rate comparable to a man's driving an au-

tomobile a hundred and twenty-eight miles per hour . . . and we are accelerating.
JOHN MCPHEE, *Encounters with the Archdruid*, 1971

22 Few people value individual freedom more than I, but with respect to the use of our resources I have to say, reluctantly, that government must step in and . . . monitor and guide how we use our environment. Individual volunteer action is grand—it should be encouraged—but it is not sufficient to meet national needs.
ALDEN WHITMAN, *New York Times Magazine*, 23 May 1971

23 The world is finite, resources are scarce,
Things are bad and will be worse.
Coal is burned and gas exploded
Forests cut and soils eroded.
Wells are dry and airs polluted
Dust is blowing, trees uprooted.
Oil is going, ores depleted.
Drains receive what is excreted.
KENNETH E. BOULDING, "A Conservationist's Lament," in Anne Chisholm, *Philosophers of the Earth: Conversations with Ecologists*, 1972

24 Earth provides enough to satisfy every man's need, but not every man's greed.
MOHANDAS K. GANDHI (1869–1948), quoted in E. F. Schumacher, *Small Is Beautiful*, 1973

25 There is really no reason why we should not think of the productivity of natural resources as increasing more or less exponentially over time.
ROBERT SOLOW, in defense of economic growth, quoted in Andrew Weintraub et al., *The Economic Growth Controversy*, 1973

26 The Americans attributed their good fortune, not to their unprecedented blessing of excess resource, but to the moral worth of their American ways.
PAUL COLINVAUX, *The Fates of Nations*, 1980

27 The United States must overcome the materialistic fallacy: the illusion that resources and capital are essentially things, which can run out, rather than products of the human will and imagination which in freedom are inexhaustible. Because economies are governed by thoughts, they reflect not the laws of matter but the laws of the mind.
GEORGE GILDER, *Wealth and Poverty*, 1981

28 Capitalist democracies or socialist ones, monarchies, centrally controlled economies and even dictatorships can, in principle, provide resilient societies. But to do so, they must be characterized by distributive justice and efficient utilization of the nation's heritage from nature.
WALTER ORR ROBERTS and EDWARD J. FRIEDMAN, *Living with the Changed World Climate*, 1982

29 You see, in the end, copper and oil come out of our minds. That's really where they are.
JULIAN L. SIMON, *The Ultimate Resource*, 1982

30 The metaphor of the Earth as just natural resources to be exploited and consumed by humans remains the dominant image embedded in the psyches of modern [resource conservation and development] managers.
BILL DEVALL and GEORGE SESSIONS, *Deep Ecology*, 1985

31 In an industrial era, the power, the influence, and the security of a nation depend on assured supplies of food, energy, and mineral raw materials and on possession of an industrial structure capable of converting mineral raw materials into essential manufactured goods. Despite this, in the United States there is no commitment to maintaining a strong domestic mineral base.
EUGENE CAMERON, *The Mineral Problems of the U.S.*, 1986

32 Although governments, environmentalists, and the aid agencies kept their eye on the environmental ball during the 1970s and the early 1980s, recent events have starkly demonstrated that they were *watching the wrong ball*. While the world was worrying about the environmental impacts of investments, controlling pollution, and conserving resources, we collectively failed to notice the dramatic decline in what had complacently been called "renewable resources."
DAVID RUNNALS, testimony, World Commission on Environment and Development, Ottawa, Canada, 26–27 May 1986

33 The more complex the society, the greater the demand for minerals and the more intricate the interrelationships between minerals, other resources, and social, political, and eco-

nomic systems. Minerals are critical to national well-being and security.

> ANN DORR, *Minerals: Foundations of Society*, 1987

34 I'm concerned mostly, I think, about the obscene avariciousness with which we [in Western countries] consume resources. [It is] a reflection of our culture, which tells me that there's something wrong spiritually with us—that, at least in American society, we *consume* material culture, use it up, spend it, waste it.

> MICHAEL HOOVER, quoted in *Christian Science Monitor*, 25 July 1988

35 We are committed to protecting and enhancing the nation's valuable resources, as well as proceeding with their environmentally sound development. We can do both; we do not have to choose between them.

> MANUAL LUJAN, U.S. Secretary of the Interior designate, testimony, Senate confirmation hearing, Washington D.C., 26 January 1989

36 Just recognizing that natural resources are assets means that all of the dichotomy between environmental protection and economic growth disappears. The question of whether a country can afford to protect its resources is then seen as stupid: It cannot afford not to.

> ROBERT REPETTO, quoted in *New York Times*, 29 June 1989

37 The white man's advanced technological capacity has occurred as a result of his lack of regard for the spiritual path and for the way of all living things. The white man's desire for material possessions and power has blinded him to the pain he has caused Mother Earth by his quest for what he calls natural resources.

> THOMAS BANYACYA, in Julian Burger, *The Gaia Atlas of First Peoples*, 1990

38 It is easy for Americans to criticize Brazil's record on the environment, since they already live in a rich, industrialized country. But the U.S. achieved this status largely by doing just what Brazil is condemned for: ruthlessly exploiting natural resources—including cutting down most of its native for-

ests. Even more galling, the U.S. continues to be a major degrader of the planet.

> HAROLDO MATTOS DE LEMOS, Brazilian development official, *Fletcher Forum of World Affairs* 14, no. 2, Summer 1990

39 In nature, as in business, we cannot afford to squander our capital if we expect to prosper. Simple common sense dictates that we husband our capital and utilize the dividends it provides.

> CHARLES DE HAES, World Wildlife Fund International annual report, 1991

87 NATURE

See also   43 ENVIRONMENT,
68 HUMANKIND AND NATURE,
88 NATURE, CONTROL OF

1 Nature is a hanging judge.

> ANONYMOUS

2 All things in nature work silently. They come into being and possess nothing. They fulfill their function and make no claim. All things alike do their work, and then we see them subside. When they have reached their bloom, each returns to its origin. . . . This reversion is an eternal law. To know that law is wisdom.

> LAO-TSU (6th century B.C.)

3 Nature is not benevolent; with ruthless indifference she makes all things serve their purpose.

> LAO-TSU (6th century B.C.), *The Way of Virtue*, c. 550 B.C.

4 There is no birth in mortal things, and no end in ruinous death. There is only mingling and interchange of parts, and it is this that we call "nature."

> EMPEDOCLES (c. 490–430 B.C.), fragment 8, in Philip Wheelwright, *The Presocratics*, 1966

5 In all things of nature there is something of the marvelous.

> ARISTOTLE (384–322 B.C.), *On the Parts of Animals*

6 If one way be better than another, that you may be sure is Nature's way.

> ARISTOTLE (384–322 B.C.), *Nichomachean Ethics*

7 Nature does nothing in vain.

> PROVERB, cited by Aristotle (384–322 B.C.), *Politics*, and by Sir Thomas Browne (1605–1682), *Religio Medici*, 1642, where he calls it the only undisputed axiom in philosophy. William Harvey (1578–1657) expanded the proverb: "Nature does nothing in vain, nor works in any round-about way when a shorter path lies open to her," *Animal Generation*, 1651.

8 All things come from earth, and to earth they all return.

> MENANDER (342–292 B.C.), *Moyostikhoi*

9 Nature resolves everything into its component elements, but annihilates nothing.

> LUCRETIUS (c. 100–c. 55 B.C.), *De rerum natura*, 57 B.C.

10 It is undeniable that every organic whole must have an ultimate ideal of perfection. As in vines or in cattle we see that, unless obstructed by some force, nature progresses on a certain path of her own to her goal of full development.

> CICERO (106–43 B.C.), *On the Nature of the Gods*, c. 45 B.C.

11 It is a joy to contemplate Cytorus asurge with box-trees and the firwoods of Narycus, a joy also to see fields indebted to no drag-hoes or human care.

> VIRGIL (70–19 B.C.), *Georgics*, book 2

12 May the countryside and the gliding valley streams content me. Lost to fame, let me love river and woodland.

> VIRGIL (70–19 B.C.), *Georgics*, book 2

13 Drive out nature with a pitchfork, and she will always come back.

> HORACE (65–8 B.C.), *Epistles* 1.10.24

14 Nature is the nature of all things that are; things that are have a union with all things from the beginning.

> MARCUS AURELIUS (A.D. 121–180), *Meditations*, about A.D. 170

15 The evidence of nature is worth more than the arguments of learning.

> AMBROSE of Milan (339–397)

16 If something is said about nature, then it is already no longer nature.

> CH'ENG HAO (1032–1085), "Contemplating the Flowers in the Gardens of the South"

17 God and nature and any other agent make what is best in the whole, but not what is best in every single part, except in order to the whole. . . . And the whole itself, which is the universe of creatures, is better and more perfect if some things in it can fail in goodness, and do sometimes fail, God not preventing this.

> THOMAS AQUINAS (1225–1274), *Summa theologica*, 1266–1273

18 Nature is the art of God.

> DANTE ALIGHIERI (1265–1321), *De monarchia*, 1313

19 Nature, the vicaire of the almyghty lorde.

> GEOFFREY CHAUCER (c. 1342–1400), *The Parliament of Fowls*, 1380–1386

20 Necessity is the mistress and guardian of Nature. Necessity is the theme and artificer of nature, the bridle, the eternal law.

> LEONARDO DA VINCI (1452–1519), *Notebooks*, 1508–1518

21 Nature never breaks her own laws.

> LEONARDO DA VINCI (1452–1519), Notebooks, 1508–1518

22 Nature abhors a vacuum.

> LATIN PROVERB, cited by François Rabelais (c. 1483–1553), in *Gargantua*, 1534

23 We should . . . follow the wisdom of nature, which, as it takes very great care not to have produced anything superfluous or useless, often prefers to endow one thing with many effects.

> NICOLAUS COPERNICUS (1473–1543), *De revolutionibus*, 1543

24 Nature is a gentle guide, but not more sweet and gentle than prudent and just.

> MICHEL DE MONTAIGNE (1533–1592), *Essays*, 1588

25 Nothing in nature is unserviceable,
No, not even inutility itself.

> JOHN MARSTON (1576–1634), *Sophonisba*, 1606

26 Nature uses as little as possible of anything.

> JOHANNES KEPLER (1571–1630), *Astronomia nova*, 1609

27 Nature hath no gaole, though shee hath laws.

> JOHN DONNE (1572–1631), *The Progresse of the Soule*, 1612

28 Nature itself cannot err.
    THOMAS HOBBES (1588–1679), *Leviathan*, 1651

29 Green is the prime color of the world, and
    that from which its loveliness arises.
    PEDRO CALDERON DE LA BARCA (1600–1681),
    The Scarf and the Flower

30 Nature is an infinite sphere of which the cen-
    ter is everywhere, the circumference no-
    where.
    BLAISE PASCAL (1623–1662), *Pensées*, 1670

31 The whole visible world is but an impercepti-
    ble speck in the ample bosom of nature.
    BLAISE PASCAL (1623–1662), *Pensées*, 1670

32 The perfections of Nature show that she is
    the image of God; her defects show that she is
    only his image.
    BLAISE PASCAL (1632–1662), *Pensées*, 1670

33 Nature has no goal in view, and final causes
    are only human imaginings.
    BENEDICT SPINOZA (1632–1677), *Ethics*, 1677

34 The beauty, symmetry, regularity and order
    seen in the universe are the effects of a blind,
    unintelligent nature.
    PIERRE BAYLE (1647–1706), *Pensées diverses*,
    1680

35 Nature is a good housewife. She always
    makes use of what is cheapest, let the differ-
    ence be never so slight, and yet her frugality
    goes with an extraordinary magnificence,
    shining through all her works. That is to say,
    she is magnificence in design but frugal in ex-
    ecution—and what could be more praisewor-
    thy than a great design achieved at small
    expense?
    BERNARD DE FONTENELLE (1657–1757), *Entre-
    tiens sur la pluralité des mondes*, 1686

36 The philosophers say that Nature does noth-
    ing in vain, and more is in vain when less will
    serve; for Nature is pleased with simplicity,
    and affects not the pomp of superfluous
    causes.
    ISAAC NEWTON (1642–1727), *Principia*, 1687

37 The book of nature is a fine and large piece of
    tapestry rolled up, which we are not able to
    see all at once, but must be content to wait for
    the discovery of its beauty and symmetry lit-
    tle by little, as it gradually comes to be more
    unfolded.
    ROBERT BOYLE (1627–1691), *The Christian Vir-
    tuoso*, 1690

38 Nature, like Liberty, is but restrained
    By the same Laws which first herself or-
    dained.
    ALEXANDER POPE (1688–1744), *An Essay on
    Criticism*, 1711

39 That sort of beauty which is called natural, as
    of vines, plants, trees, etc., consists of a very
    complicated harmony; and all the natural mo-
    tions, and tendencies, and figures of bodies
    in the universe are done according to pro-
    portion, and therein is their beauty.
    JONATHAN EDWARDS (1703–1758), "Notes on
    the Mind," c. 1718

40 All Nature wears one universal grin.
    HENRY FIELDING (1707–1754), *Tom Thumb the
    Great*, 1730

41 Oh Nature! All sufficient! over all!
    Inrich me with the knowledge of thy works!
    Snatch me to heaven; thy rolling wonders
        there,
    World beyond world, in infinite extent,
    Profusely scattered o'er the blue immense
    Shew me; their motions, periods and their
        laws
    Give me to scan.
    JAMES THOMSON (1700–1748), "Autumn,"
    1730

42 Chase nature away, and it returns at a gallop.
    P. N. DESTOUCHES (1680–1754), *Le glorieux*,
    1732

43 All nature is but art, unknown to thee;
    All chance, direction, which thou canst not
        see;
    All discord, harmony not understood;
    All partial evil, universal good.
    ALEXANDER POPE (1688–1744), *An Essay on
    Man*, 1733–1734

44 Nature does not proceed by leaps.
    CARL VON LINNÉ (1707–1778), *Philosophia bo-
    tanica*, 1751

45 The volume of nature is the book of knowl-
    edge.
    OLIVER GOLDSMITH (1730–1774), *The Citizen of
    the World*, 1762

46 Nature is inexhaustible.
VOLTAIRE (1694–1778), *Sur l'ingratitude,* c. 1775

47 All the work of the crystallographers serves only to demonstrate that there is only variety everywhere where they suppose uniformity . . . that in nature there is nothing absolute, nothing perfectly regular.
GEORGES-LOUIS LECLERC DE BUFFON (1707–1778), *Histoire naturelle des minéraux,* 1788

48 Nature, who is a great economist, converts the recreation of one animal to the support of another.
GILBERT WHITE (1720–1793), *The Natural History of Selborne,* 1789

49 Nature is for us nothing but existence in all its freedom.
JOHANN FRIEDRICH VON SCHILLER (1759–1805), *Simple and Sentimental Poetry,* 1795–1796

50 Never, no never, did nature say one thing and wisdom say another
EDMUND BURKE (1729–1797), *Letters on a Regicide Peace,* 1797

51 In nature there is nothing melancholy.
SAMUEL TAYLOR COLERIDGE (1772–1834), "The Nightingale," 1798

52 The nearer we get to any natural object the more incomprehensible it becomes. A grain of sand is undoubtedly not what I take it to be.
GEORG C. LICHTENBERG, *Reflections,* 1799

53 Nature . . . is a great organ, on which our Lord God plays, and the Devil blows the bellows.
JOHANN WOLFGANG VON GOETHE (1749–1832), *Faust,* 1808–1832

54 Individuality seems to be Nature's whole aim—and she cares nothing for individuals.
JOHANN WOLFGANG VON GOETHE (1749–1832), *Maxims and Reflections*

55 Nature has an etiquette all her own.
LUDWIG VAN BEETHOVEN (1770–1827), letter to Breitkopf and Haertel, 17 September 1812

56 There is a pleasure in the pathless woods,
There is a rapture on the lonely shore,
There is society where none intrudes,
By the deep sea, and music in its roar:
I love not man the less, but Nature more.
GEORGE GORDON, LORD BYRON (1788–1824), *Childe Harold's Pilgrimage,* 1812–1818

57 "In the inside of Nature"—
O you Philistines—
Nature has neither kernel
Nor shell.
JOHANN WOLFGANG VON GOETHE (1749–1832), *Allerdings. Dem Physiker,* 1819–1820

58 The first steps in Agriculture, Astronomy, Zoölogy (those first steps which the farmer, the hunter, and the sailor take), teach that Nature's dice are always loaded; that in her heaps and rubbish are concealed sure and useful results.
RALPH WALDO EMERSON (1803–1882), *Nature,* 1836

59 The perpetual admonition of nature to us is, "The world is new, untried. Do not believe the past. I give you the universe a virgin today."
RALPH WALDO EMERSON (1803–1882), speech, Dartmouth College, 24 January 1838

60 Nature will bear the closest inspection. She invites us to lay our eye level with her smallest leaf, and take an insect view of it plain.
HENRY DAVID THOREAU, (1817–1862), *Journal,* entry dated 22 October 1839

61 There are no fixtures in nature. The universe is fluid and volatile.
RALPH WALDO EMERSON (1803–1882), *Circles,* 1841

62 Nature hates monopolies and exceptions.
RALPH WALDO EMERSON (1803–1882), *Compensation,* 1841

63 Nature provides exceptions to every rule.
MARGARET FULLER (1810–1850), in *The Dial,* July 1843

64 Nature, as we know her, is no saint.
RALPH WALDO EMERSON (1803–1882), *Essays, Second Series,* 1844

65 Nature is not what you think! She is not a mould, or an image without a soul. She has a

soul, she has freedom, she has love, and she can speak.

FYODOR TYUCHEV (1803–1873), *Nature Is Not What You Think*

66 Nature as a whole possesses a store of force which cannot in any way be either increased or diminished. . . . [T]herefore, the quantity of force in Nature is just as eternal and unalterable as the quantity of matter.

HERMANN VON HELMHOLTZ (1821–1894), *Über die Erhaltung der Kraft*, 1847

67 Nature, even when she is scant and thin outwardly, satisfies us still by the assurance of a certain generosity at the roots.

HENRY DAVID THOREAU (1817–1862), *A Week on the Concord and Merrimack Rivers*, 1849

68 Nature admits no lie.

THOMAS CARLYLE (1795–1881), *Latter Day Pamphlets*, 1850

69 Nature red in tooth and claw.

ALFRED, LORD TENNYSON (1809–1892), *In Memoriam*, 1850

70 What nature does generally, is sure to be more or less beautiful; what she does rarely, will either be *very* beautiful, or absolutely ugly.

JOHN RUSKIN (1819–1900), *Lectures on Architecture and Painting*, 1853

71 The cow crunching with depressed head surpasses any statue,
And a mouse is miracle enough to stagger sextillions of infidels.

WALT WHITMAN (1819–1892), *Leaves of Grass*, 1855–1891

72 Nature is full of genius, full of the divinity; so that not a snowflake escapes its fashioning hand.

HENRY DAVID THOREAU (1817–1862), *Journal*, entry dated 5 January 1856

73 I [Nature] am called a mother, but I am a grave.

ALFRED DE VIGNY (1797–1863), *La maison du berger*, 1864

74 The chess-board is the world; the pieces are the phenomena of the universe; the rules of the game are what we call laws of Nature.

THOMAS H. HUXLEY (1825–1895), "A Liberal Education," 1868

75 The eye of the trilobite [a prehistoric marine arthropod] tells us that the sun shone on the old beach where he lived; for there is nothing in nature without a purpose, and when so complicated an organ was made to receive the light, there must have been light to enter it.

LOUIS AGASSIZ (1807–1873), *Geological Sketches*, 1870

76 The study of Nature is intercourse with the Highest Mind. You should never trifle with Nature.

LOUIS AGASSIZ (1807–1873)

77 Nature is entirely indifferent to any reform. She perpetuates a fault as persistently as a virtue.

CHARLES DUDLEY WARNER (1829–1900), *Backlog Studies*, 1873

78 Nature means the sum of all phenomena, together with the causes which produce them; including not only all that happens, but all that is capable of happening.

JOHN STUART MILL (1806–1873), *Three Essays on Religion*, 1874

79 The world is charged with the grandeur of God.
It will flame out, like shining from shook foil;
It gathers to a greatness, like the ooze of oil
Crushed.

GERARD MANLEY HOPKINS (1844–1889), "God's Grandeur," 1877

80 Glory be to God for dappled things—
For skies of couple-colour as a brinded cow;
For rose-moles in all stipple upon trout that swim;
Fresh-firecoal chestnut-falls; finches' wings;
Landscape plotted and pieced—fold, fallow, and plough;
And áll trádes, their gear and tackle and trim.

All things counter, original, spare, strange;
Whatever is fickle, freckled (who knows how?)
With swift, show; sweet, sour; adazzle, dim;
He fathers-forth whose beauty is past change:
Praise him.

GERARD MANLEY HOPKINS (1844–1889), "Pied Beauty," 1877

81 Nothing is so beautiful as spring—
   When weeds, in wheels, shoot long and
   lovely and lush. . .

   What is all this juice and all this joy?
   A strain of the earth's sweet being in the
      beginning
   In Eden Garden.—Have, get, before it cloy . . .
      GERARD MANLEY HOPKINS (1844–1889),
      "Spring," 1877

82 My own experience is that the more we study
   Art, the less we care for Nature. What Art really reveals to us is Nature's lack of design,
   her curious crudities, her extraordinary monotony, her absolutely unfinished conditions. Nature has good intentions, of course,
   but, as Aristotle once said, she cannot carry
   them out.
      OSCAR WILDE (1854–1900), Nineteenth Cen-
      tury, January 1899

83 In nature there are neither rewards nor pun-
   ishments—there are consequences.
      ROBERT G. INGERSOLL (1833–1899), Some Rea-
      sons Why, 1896

84 The anthropomorphic notion of a deliberate
   architect and ruler of the world has gone forever from this field; the "eternal iron laws of
   nature" have taken its place.
      ERNEST HAECKEL (1834–1919), The Riddle of the
      Universe, 1901

85 There are no square-edged inflexible lines in
   Nature. We seek to establish a narrow line
   between ourselves and the feathery zeros we
   dare to call angels, but ask a partition barrier
   of infinite width to show the rest of creation
   its proper place.
      JOHN MUIR (1838–1914), quoted in Edwin
      Way Teale, The Wilderness World of John
      Muir, 1954

86 Nature is so uncomfortable. Grass is hard
   and lumpy and damp, and full of dreadful insects.
      OSCAR WILDE (1854–1900), The Decay of Ly-
      ing, 1909

87 There is hardly any such thing in Nature as a
   mere droop of weakness. Rigidity yielding a
   little, like justice swayed by mercy, is the
   whole beauty of the earth.
      G. K. CHESTERTON (1874–1936), Alarms and
      Discussions, 1910

88 Nature teaches more than she preaches.
   There are no sermons in stones. It is easier to
   get a spark out of a stone than a moral.
      JOHN BURROUGHS (1837–1921), Time and
      Change, 1912

89 Nature, in her indifference, makes no distinction between good and evil.
      ANATOLE FRANCE (1844–1924), Crainquebille,
      1916

90 Nature aborts all her works to make room for
   more. She never finishes anything nor permits anything to become perfect.
      MICHAEL J. DEE, Conclusions, 1917

91 Nature's way of dealing with unhealthy conditions is unfortunately not one that compels
   us to conduct a solvent hygiene on a cash basis. She demoralizes us with long credits and
   reckless overdrafts, and then pulls us up cru-
   elly with catastrophic bankruptcies.
      GEORGE BERNARD SHAW (1856–1950), Heart-
      break House, 1919

92 There can be nothing dead or mechanical in
   Nature. . . . [L]ife and feeling . . . must exist
   in everything. . . . A mountain, a tree, a
   river, the fish in the river, drops of water,
   rain, a plant, fire—each separately must possess a mind of its own.
      PETER D. OUSPENSKY, Tertium Organum, 1920

93 [Nature is] a conjugation of the verb to eat, in
   the active and passive
      WILLIAM RALPH INGE (1860–1954), Outspoken
      Essays, 1922

94 [Nature is] a structure of evolving processes.
   The reality is the process.
      ALFRED NORTH WHITEHEAD (1861–1947), Sci-
      ence and the Modern World, 1925

95 The three great elemental sounds in nature
   are the sound of rain, the sound of wind in a
   primeval wood, and the sound of outer ocean
   on a beach.
      HENRY BESTON, The Outermost House, 1928

96 Into every empty corner, into all forgotten
   things and nooks, Nature struggles to pour
   life, pouring life into the dead, life into life itself.
      HENRY BESTON, The Outermost House, 1928

97 Nature, in her blind thirst for life, has filled every possible cranny of the rotting earth with some sort of fantastic creature.
JOSEPH WOOD KRUTCH (1893–1970), *The Modern Temper*, 1929

98 Nature, [the biologist] might say, is wholly indifferent to the outcries of the individual; this vast process of which each of us is so insignificant a part, keeps going because there is in all the parts a superabundant urging to go on. There is no economy in it and no human order. Man, for example, has far more sexual desire than is needed for the rational propagation of the species.
WALTER LIPPMAN (1889–1974), *A Preface to Morals*, 1929

99 There is little rugged individualism in nature.
WALTER P. TAYLOR, *Quarterly Review of Biology*, September 1935

100 Nature, often as she hugs the old, seems seldom or never to revert to a past once abandoned. Evolution can scrap but not revive.
CHARLES SHERRINGTON, *Man on His Nature*, 1940

101 Adapt or perish, now as ever, is Nature's inexorable imperative.
H. G. WELLS (1866–1946), *Mind at the End of Its Tether*, 1945

102 It is only now and then, in a jungle, or amidst the towering white menace of a burnt or burning Australian forest, that Nature strips the moral veils from vegetation and we apprehend its stark ferocity.
H. G. WELLS (1866–1946), *The Happy Turning*, 1946

103 Nature may be a thing of beauty and is indeed a symphony, but above and below and within its own immutable essences, its distances, its apparent quietness and changelessness, it is an active, purposeful, coordinated machine.
FAIRFIELD OSBORN, *Our Plundered Planet*, 1948

104 The famous balance of nature is the most extraordinary of all cybernetic systems. Left to itself, it is always self-regulated.
JOSEPH WOOD KRUTCH (1893–1970), *Saturday Review*, 8 June 1963

105 Nature has . . . some sort of arithmetical-geometrical coordinate system. . . . [It] must be a real beauty, because in chemistry we find that the associations are always in beautiful whole numbers—there are no fractions.
R. BUCKMINSTER FULLER (1895–1983), quoted in *New Yorker*, 8 January 1966

106 All of us understand the put-and-take of checking accounts, but few understand the careful accounts of deposits and withdrawals that nature keeps.
ALFRED BESTER, *Holiday*, June 1966

107 [Nature] can refuse to speak but she cannot give a wrong answer.
CHARLES B. HUGGINS, *National Observer*, 21 November 1966

108 What nature delivers to us is never stale. Because what nature creates has eternity in it.
ISAAC BASHEVIS SINGER, quoted in *New York Times Magazine*, 26 November 1978

109 Usefulness is about as close to a "common goal" of nature as I can guess at.
LEWIS THOMAS, *The Medusa and the Snail*, 1979

110 Nature is what she is—amoral and persistent.
STEPHEN JAY GOULD, *New York Times*, 6 May 1979

111 The reality is that you've got to have mass production and mass slaughter, or the whole thing is going to pot. Life and death are the stock in trade of nature. There's no use sobbing about it, because we're all a part of it. It is not a matter of an animal being killed. The issue is *when* it's going to be killed. . . . Nature deals in unlimited time. And the whole thing is eminently respectable.
DURWARD L. ALLEN, quoted in John G. Mitchell, *The Hunt*, 1980

112 The word [Nature] comes from the Latin, to be born, which is fundamental enough, and puts it under the heading of abiding mystery.
JOHN HAY, in David Halpern, ed., *On Nature*, 1986

113 So what I'm going to call nature is everything on this planet that is at least partially

under the control of some other will than ours. Pure nature is of course what exists entirely without our will. In terms of landscape, there isn't much of it.

NOEL PERRIN, in Daniel Halpern, ed., *On Nature*, 1986

114 There is nothing in nature that can't be taken as a sign of both mortality and invigoration.

GRETEL EHRLICH, in Stephen Trimble, ed., *Words from the Land*, 1988

115 Nature bats last.

BUMPER STICKER, 1989

116 Wildness is . . . everywhere: ineradicable populations of fungi, moss, mold, yeasts, and such, that surround and inhabit us. Deer mice on the back porch, deer bounding across the freeway, pigeons in the park. Spiders in the corners.

GARY SNYDER, *Sierra*, September–October 1989

117 There are many themes in nature's symphony, each with its own pace and rhythm. We are forced to choose among these, which we have barely begun to hear and understand.

DANIEL B. BOTKIN, *Discordant Harmonies*, 1990

118 Nature is not a pretty, manicured place maintained for human beings. It is a dynamic continuum, often a violent one.

DAVE FOREMAN, *Harper's*, April 1990

---

88 NATURE, CONTROL OF
See also   68 HUMANKIND AND NATURE, 87 NATURE

---

1 And let them have dominion over the fish of the sea, and over the fowl of the air, and over the cattle, and over all the earth, and over every creeping thing that creepeth upon the earth.

BIBLE, Genesis 1:26

2 You glorify Nature and meditate on her:
Why not domesticate her and regulate her?
You depend on things and marvel at them:

Why not unfold your own ability and transform them?

HSUN-TZU (c. 298–c. 230 B.C.), quoted in Wing-Tsit Chan, *The Chinese Mind*, 1967

3 Never can custom conquer nature; for she is ever unconquered.

CICERO (106–43 B.C.), *Tusculanae disputationes*, 44 B.C.

4 Let us give Nature a chance; she knows her business better than we do.

MICHEL DE MONTAIGNE (1533–1592), *Essays*, 1588

5 Follow the order of nature, for God's sake! Follow it! It will lead who follows; and those who will not, it will drag along anyway.

MICHEL DE MONTAIGNE (1533–1592), *Essays*, 1588

6 Nature is not governed except by obeying her.

FRANCIS BACON (1561–1626), *Novum organum*, 1620

7 [My discoveries] have satisfied me that it is possible to reach knowledge that will be of much utility in this life; and that instead of the speculative philosophy now taught in the schools we can find a practical one, by which, knowing the nature and behavior of fire, water, air, stars, the heavens, and all the other bodies which surround us, as well as we now understand the different skills of our workers, we can employ these entities for all the purposes for which they are suited, and so make ourselves masters and possessors of nature.

RENÉ DESCARTES (1596–1650), *Discourse on Method*, 1637

8 Few enjoyments are given us from the open and liberal hand of nature; but by art, labour, and industry, we can extract them in great abundance. Hence the ideas of property become necessary in all civil society.

DAVID HUME (1711–1776), *An Enquiry Concerning the Principles of Morals*, 1751

9 I'm truly sorry man's dominion
Has broken Nature's social union.

ROBERT BURNS (1759–1796), *To a Mouse*, 1785

10 To nature's great command
All human laws are frail and weak.

GEORGE CRABBE (1754–1832), *The Hall of Justice*, 1807

11 The question before the human race is, whether the God of nature shall govern the world by his own laws, or whether priests and kings shall rule it by fictitious miracles?
JOHN ADAMS (1735–1826), letter to Thomas Jefferson, 20 June 1815

12 Nature, with equal mind,
   Sees all her sons at play;
   Sees man control the wind,
   The wind sweep man away;
   Allows the proudly-riding and the foundering bark.
MATTHEW ARNOLD (1822–1888), *Empedocles on Etna*, 1852

13 Nature cares nothing for logic, our human logic: she has her own, which we do not recognize and do not acknowledge until we are crushed under its wheel.
IVAN TURGENEV (1818–1883), *Smoke*, 1867

14 The scheme of nature regarded in its whole extent cannot have had, for its sole or even principal object, the good of human or other sentient beings. What good it brings to them is mostly the result of their own exertions. Whatsoever in nature gives indication of beneficent design proves this beneficence to be armed only with limited power; and the duty of man is to co-operate with the beneficent powers, not by imitating but by perpetually striving to amend the course of nature—and bringing that part of it over which we can exercise control more nearly into conformity with a high standard of justice and goodness.
JOHN STUART MILL (1809–1873), *Nature*, 1874

15 What would become of the garden if the gardener treated all the weeds and slugs and birds and trespassers as he would like to be treated, if he were in their place?
THOMAS H. HUXLEY (1825–1895), *Evolution and Ethics*, 1893

16 Let us not, however, flatter ourselves overmuch on account of our human conquests over nature. For each such conquest takes its revenge on us. Each [has] . . . unforeseen effects which only too often cancel out the [intended consequences].
FRIEDRICH ENGELS (1820–1895), *Dialectics of Nature*, 1895

17 It is in the measure that man has learned to change nature that his intelligence has increased.
FRIEDRICH ENGELS (1820–1895), *Dialectics of Nature*, 1895

18 [For the] moral equivalent of war . . . instead of military conscription, a conscription of the whole youthful population to form for a certain number of years a part of the army enlisted against *Nature* . . . [to do] their own part in the immemorial human warfare against nature . . . .
WILLIAM JAMES (1842–1919), *International Conciliation*, February 1910

19 The mastery of nature is vainly believed to be an adequate substitute for self-mastery.
REINHOLD NIEBUHR (1892–1971), quoted in *Christian Century*, 22 April 1926

20 The principal task of civilization, its actual *raison d'être*, is to defend us against nature.
SIGMUND FREUD (1856–1939), *The Future of an Illusion*, 1927

21 Here's good advice for practice: go into partnership with nature; she does more than half the work and asks none of the fee.
MARTIN H. FISCHER (1879–1962), quoted in Howard Fabing and Ray Marr, *Fischerisms*, 1930

22 Nature is not to be conquered on her own terms. She is not conciliated by cleverness or industry. . . . She is a very businesslike old lady, who plays no favorites. Man is welcome to outnumber and dominate other forms of life, provided he can maintain order among the relentless forces whose balanced operation he has disturbed.
PAUL SEARS, *Deserts on the March*, 1947

23 It is simply that in all life on earth as in all good agriculture there are no short-cuts that by-pass Nature and the nature of man himself and animals, trees, rocks and streams. Every attempt at a formula, a short-cut, a panacea, always ends in negation and destruction.
LOUIS BROMFIELD, *Malabar Farm*, 1948

24 The tide of the earth's population is rising, the reservoir of the earth's living resources is falling. . . . There is only one solution: Man must recognize the necessity of cooperating with nature. He must temper his demands

and use and conserve the natural living resources of this earth in a manner that alone can provide for the continuation of his civilization. The final answer is to be found only through comprehension of the enduring processes of nature. The time for defiance is at an end.

FAIRFIELD OSBORN, *Our Plundered Planet*, 1948

25 In remaking the world in the likeness of a steam-heated, air-conditioned metropolis of apartment buildings we have violated one of our essential attributes—our kinship with nature.

ROSS PARMENTER, *The Plant in My Window*, 1949

26 Amid the turmoil of conflicting ideas in which we live . . . there seems to be one proposition commanding nearly universal assent: *The control man has secured over nature has far outrun his control over himself.*

ERNEST JONES, *The Life and Work of Sigmund Freud*, 1953

27 We must not wait for favors from Nature; our task is to wrest them from her.

IVAN MICHURIN, slogan of the Lysenkoist school, from *Short Dictionary of Philosophy* (Moscow), 1955

28 Man masters nature not by force but by understanding. That is why science has succeeded where magic failed: because it has looked for no spell to cast on nature.

JACOB BRONOWSKI, *Science and Human Values*, 1956

29 Man has always frustrated nature, from the time he invented the first tool, and will continue to do so until on his last day on earth he lays down his latest invention.

FREDERICK E. FLYNN, speech, Catholic Physicians Guild of Southern California, 1960

30 The "control of nature" is a phrase conceived in arrogance, born of the Neanderthal age of biology and the convenience of man.

RACHEL CARSON (1907–1964), *Silent Spring*, 1962

31 Because of the true man's totality and centrality, he has the almost divine function of guardianship over the world of nature. Once this role is ignored or misused, he is in danger of being shown ultimately by nature who, in reality, is the conqueror, and who the conquered.

JOSEPH EPES BROWN, *The Spiritual Legacy of the American Indian*, 1964

32 Our power to disturb or alter the ponderous forces and rhythms of nature by man-induced manipulations has increased to the point where mistakes or unknown effects may be profound and irreversible.

U.S. HOUSE SCIENCE AND AERONAUTICS SUBCOMMITTEE, report, November 1966

33 The one consistently natural thing is to try by intelligence and imagination to improve on nature.

BRIGID BROPHY, *The Burglar*, 1967

34 It was through the Second World War that most of us suddenly appreciated for the first time the power of man's concentrated efforts to understand and control the forces of nature. We were appalled by what we saw.

VANNEVAR BUSH (1890–1974), *Science Is Not Enough*, 1967

35 You could cover the whole world with asphalt, but sooner or later green grass would break through.

ILYA EHRENBURG (1891–1967), *New York Times Book Review*, 22 October 1967

36 It is not really necessary to destroy nature in order to gain God's favor or even his undivided attention.

IAN MCHARG, *The Fitness of Man's Environment*, 1968

37 We manipulate nature as if we were stuffing an Alsatian goose. We create new forms of energy; we make new elements; we kill crops; we wash brains. I can hear them in the dark sharpening their lasers.

ERWIN CHARGAFF, *Forum*, Summer 1969

38 The Judeo-Christian idea of man dominating nature must be replaced by the goal of living in harmony with nature.

PAUL EHRLICH, *Audubon*, May 1970

39 We have broken out of the circle of life, converting its endless cycles into man-made, linear events.

BARRY COMMONER, *The Closing Circle*, 1971

40 Nature is going to compel posterity to revert to a stable state on the material plane and to turn to the realm of the spirit for satisfying man's hunger for infinity.

ARNOLD TOYNBEE (1889–1975), *The Observer,* 11 June 1972

41 Just as nature has not been capable by itself of giving full expression to the potential diversity of our globe, likewise it is not capable of maintaining manmade environments in a healthy state. Now that so much of the world has been humanized, environmental health depends to a very large extent on human care.

RENÉ DUBOS, lecture, U.S. Department of Agriculture, 29 December 1972

42 [Industrial change] has come so suddenly that we hardly noticed the fact that we were very rapidly using up a certain kind of irreplaceable capital asset, namely the *tolerance margins* which benign nature always provides.

E. F. SCHUMACHER, *Small Is Beautiful,* 1973

43 Homo sap, that creature who believes his purpose is to control and conquer Nature, is just now beginning to remember the obvious—that he is a part of Nature himself.

He has fought his way to the top of the planetary spinal cord, inflicting damage every step of the way. Now, bewildered, he looks around: *What am I doing here?*

Assuming responsibility, answers a still, small voice all around him.

PAUL WILLIAMS, *Das Energi,* 1973

44 The crisis of ecology, the threat of atomic war, and the disruption of the patterns of human life by advanced technology . . . [have resulted in the fact that] the lullaby of scientific progress, the dream of manipulating nature to suit our egoistic purposes, is ended.

JACOB NEEDLEMAN, *A Sense of the Cosmos,* 1975

45 I would feel more optimistic about a bright future for man if he spent less time proving that he can outwit Nature and more time tasting her sweetness and respecting her seniority.

E. B. WHITE, *Essays of E. B. White,* 1977

46 We cannot criticize the hierarchy of male over female without ultimately criticizing and overcoming the hierarchy of human over nature.

ROSEMARY R. REUTHER, *Sexism and God-Talk: Towards a Feminist Theology,* 1983

47 Man is part of nature, and in struggling against nature, we are fighting ourselves. . . . We've lost the psychological connection that would let us know the natural world's attitude toward us. Maybe we're not as smart as we think we are when we laugh at the pagans who drew no distinction between animate and inanimate objects.

S. P. ZALYGIN, *Los Angeles Times,* 22 June 1987

48 I believe that without recognizing it we have already stepped over the threshold . . . that we are at the end of nature.

BILL MCKIBBEN, *The End of Nature,* 1989

49 For 200 years we've been conquering Nature. Now we're beating it to death.

TOM MCMILLAN, quoted in Francesca Lyman, *The Greenhouse Trap,* 1990

50 Our environmental problems originate in the hubris of imagining ourselves as the central nervous system or the brain of nature. We're not the brain, we are a cancer on nature.

DAVE FOREMAN, *Harper's,* April 1990

51 Nature provides a free lunch, but only if we control our appetites.

WILLIAM RUCKELSHAUS, *Business Week,* 18 June 1990

52 Consider that the drive to "control" or dominate nature is by no means universal within human culture (it is more or less a Western concept) and that, where it has occurred, it has often brought with it the baggage of war, colonialism, and oppression of every kind.

JOHN SANBONMATSU, letter to the editor, *New York Times Magazine,* 11 November 1990

53 Does the wanton subjugation of nature by our species have a causal connection with the wanton subjugation of women by men?

DAVID QUAMMEN, *Outside,* April 1991

89 NOISE

1 I do not like noise unless I make it myself.
FRENCH PROVERB

2 I have often lamented that we cannot close our ears with as much ease as we can our eyes.
RICHARD STEELE (1672–1729), *The Spectator*, 1711–1712

3 But, hark! there is the whistle of the locomotive—the long shriek, harsh, above all other harshness, for the space of a mile cannot mollify it into harmony. It tells a story of busy men, citizens, from the hot street, who have come to spend a day in a country village, men of business; in short of all unquietness; and no wonder that it gives such a startling shriek, since it brings the noisy world into the midst of our slumbrous peace.
NATHANIEL HAWTHORNE (1804–1864), *American Notebooks*, 1844

4 Noise is the most impertinent of all forms of interruption.
ARTHUR SCHOPENHAUER (1788–1860), *Studies in Pessimism*, 1851

5 There are people, it is true—nay, a great many people—who smile at such things, because they are not sensitive to noise; but they are just the very people who are also not sensitive to argument, or thought, or poetry, or art, in a word, to any kind of intellectual influence.
ARTHUR SCHOPENHAUER (1788–1860), *Studies in Pessimism*, 1851

6 Noise: A stench in the ear.
AMBROSE BIERCE (1842–c. 1914), *The Devil's Dictionary*, 1906

7 The day will come when man will have to fight merciless noise as the worst enemy of his health.
ROBERT KOCH (1843–1910)

8 Air- and sound-conditioned houses may be the next luxury, when luxury is resumed, to the profit of our inventors and engineers, who, having devoted one century to creating pandemonium, may spend the next century in abating it.
WILLIAM H. LLOYD, *University of Pennsylvania Law Review* 82, 1934

9 Noise is any undesired sound. Noise is sound at the wrong time and in the wrong place.
N. W. McLACHLAN, *Noise*, 1935

10 The multiple and insidious ill effects of noise constitute an inadequately recognized, baneful influence on lives of millions of persons throughout the country.
C. P. McCORD et al., *Journal of the American Medical Association*, 7 May 1938

11 One of the greatest sounds of them all—and to me it is a sound—is utter, complete silence.
ANDRE KOSTELANETZ, *New York Journal-American*, 8 February 1955

12 Whether or not they realize it, the American people are waging unremitting war against themselves. The weapons are tranquilty-smashers, and are fitted out with decibel warheads. They penetrate all known cranial barriers and the innermost core of an individual's privacy, impeding the processes of sequential thought, breaking down the sensibilities, and unhinging the capacity for serenity. The noise level is rising and the level of common sanity is falling.
NORMAN COUSINS, *Saturday Review*, 8 December 1962

13 The locomotive, associated with fire, smoke, speed, iron, and noise, is the leading symbol of the new industrial power. It appears in the woods, suddenly shattering the harmony of the green hollow, like a presentiment of history bearing down on the American asylum.
LEO MARX, *The Machine in the Garden*, 1964

14 Sonic booms are an environmental annoyance like pollution of air or water. Americans will have to learn to live with them.
HENNING VON GIERKE, *New York Times*, 11 November 1965

15 But Nature, it now has been discovered, is building up a permanent defense against the nerve-dissolving, killing hubbub by gradually causing the ears of the city dweller to go deaf. It appears that the only adaptation the human ear knows to the constant pounding and thrumming it receives is by eliminating *all* sound stimuli. It is, without doubt, better to be stone-deaf than raving mad.
ROBERT RIENOW and LEONA TRAIN RIENOW, *Moment in the Sun*, 1967

16 In all probability the noise level will grow not only in urban centers, but with increasing

population and the proliferation of machines, noise will invade the few remaining havens of silence in the world. A century from now, when a man wants to escape to a quiet spot, there may be no place left to go.

LEO L. BERANEK, *UNESCO Courier*, July 1967

17 What was once critically described as "the busy hum of traffic" has now turned into an unbearable din for many city dwellers. The crescendo of noise—whether it comes from truck or jackhammer, siren or airplane—is more than an irritating nuisance. It intrudes on privacy, shatters serenity, and can inflict pain. We dare not be complacent about this ever-mounting volume of noise.

LYNDON B. JOHNSON (1908–1973), message to Congress, 8 March 1968

18 The best way of eliminating the threat of sonic boom for once and all in this country would be to have supersonic military planes fly across this capital city for two or three days and nights—when Congress is in session. I am confident that the great SST debate would come to an abrupt and decisive halt.

WILBUR H. FERRY, speech, National Conference on Noise, 14 June 1968

19 The Preamble of the Constitution of the United States sets forth as one of its purposes the insuring of "domestic tranquility." More and more today, as the sound effects of modern life bombard Americans, there is a need to promote "domestic tranquility" by reducing noise.

THOMAS KUCHEL U.S. Senator, speech, U.S. Senate, 11 July 1968

20 There is no free society without silence, without the internal and external space of solitude in which individual freedom can develop.

HERBERT MARCUSE (1898–1979), quoted in *New York Times Magazine*, 27 October 1968

21 The key to tomorrow's noise is quantum, a dramatic jump in noise sources, noise intensities, and human sensitivity. At the same time, there will be a decrease in our ability to escape.

ROBERT ALEX BARON, *The Tyranny of Noise*, 1970

22 A fearful thing happened to us on the way to the 1970s: we became trapped in a dangerous web of noise. Whether it comes in loud, sudden blasts or as a steady high level of sound, noise is loaded with threats to the health of us all. And, ever-increasing, it must now be recognized as a plague that has reached epidemic proportions.

JAMES STEWART-GORDON, *Reader's Digest*, February 1970

23 One man's noise may be another man's music.

MALCOLM F. BALDWIN and DAN H. STODDARD, *The Off-Road Vehicle and Environmental Quality*, 1973

24 Privacy, space and quietness may not be essential for survival, but they are needs deeply rooted in human nature, and the demand for them increases with prosperity.

RENE DUBOS, *Saturday Review/World*, 24 August 1974

25 In this universe full of noise and fury, it is the noise of some that provokes the fury of others.

ANTOINE BLONDIN, *Quat'saisons*, 1975

26 [In a quiet park, the intrusion of sound such as airplane noise] is, in essence, an act of robbery, a theft of those sounds which naturally belong in these environments.

DAVID F. HALES, quoted in *EPA Journal*, October 1979

27 Were it not for airplane noise, the quiet in some sections of [Grand Teton National Park] would be so profound that scientists could not register the sound levels. . . . Even the sounds of snow falling from the trees could be heard.

DAVID F. HALES, quoted in *EPA Journal*, October 1979

28 They say we're born with two inherent fears. The fear of loud noise, and the fear of falling. You can't ever really get used to loud noise. The ears are tied directly to the unconscious mind, and you can't consciously block a reaction in the unconscious.

CHARLES L. ELKINS, quoted in *Conservation Foundation Letter*, June 1980

29 Unhealthy noise shall include, but not be limited to, that noise created by a dog barking for 15 continuous minutes.

SMITHTOWN (N.Y.) TOWN BOARD, amendment to noise ordinance, quoted in *New York Times*, 23 August 1984

90 NUCLEAR ENERGY
See also   113 RADIATION

1 The greatest task of contemporary physics is to extract from the atom its latent energy—to tear open a plug so that energy should well up with all its might. Then it will become possible to replace coal and petrol by atomic energy which will become our basic fuel and motive power.
LEV DAVIDOVICH TROTSKY (1879–1940), speech, 1 March 1926

2 There is not the slightest indication that [nuclear] energy will ever be obtainable. It would mean that the atom would have to be shattered at will.
ALBERT EINSTEIN (1879–1955), 1932, quoted by John W. Finney, in Ruth Bloch, ed., *Hiroshima Plus 20*, 1965

3 The energy produced by the atom is a very poor kind of thing. Anyone who expects a source of power from the transformation of these atoms is talking moonshine.
ERNEST RUTHERFORD (1871–1937), after splitting the atom for the first time, September 1933, quoted in *Physics Today*, October 1970

4 The release of atomic energy constitutes a new force too revolutionary to consider in the framework of old ideas.
HARRY S. TRUMAN (1882–1974), message to Congress, 3 October 1945

5 Since I do not foresee that atomic energy is to be a great boon for a long time, I have to say that for the present it is a menace. Perhaps it is well that it should be. It may intimidate the human race into bringing order into its international affairs, which, without the pressure of fear, it would not do.
ALBERT EINSTEIN (1879–1955), *Atlantic Monthly*, November 1945

6 The unleashed power of the atom has changed everything save our modes of thinking, and we thus drift toward unparalleled catastrophes.
ALBERT EINSTEIN (1879–1955), quoted in *New York Times Magazine*, 2 August 1964

7 The physicists have known sin; and this is a knowledge which they cannot lose.
J. ROBERT OPPENHEIMER (1904–1967), 25 November 1947, quoted in *Skeptic*, July–August 1976

8 As human beings, our greatness lies not so much in being able to remake the world—that is the myth of the "atomic age"—as in being able to remake ourselves.
MAHATMA GANDHI (1869–1948), quoted in Ekrath Easwaran, *The Compassionate Universe*, 1989

9 I do not hesitate to forecast that atomic batteries will be commonplace long before 1980. . . . [I]t can be taken for granted that before 1980 ships, aircraft, locomotives and even automobiles will be atomically fuelled.
DAVID SARNOFF (1891–1971), *The Fabulous Future: America in 1980*, 1956

10 The supreme conservation achievement of this century. The atomic physicists who uncovered the edge of an infinite dynamo brought fire, like the gods of Greek mythology, from seemingly inert elements, and allayed our fears of fuel shortage once and for all.
STEWART L. UDALL, *The Quiet Crisis*, 1963

11 It would avoid ugly slag heaps, high stacks, and barge traffic. It would not pollute the atmosphere.
CLINTON ANDERSON, U.S. Senator, Sierra Club Wilderness Conference, 1965

12 Once we talked about making the deserts of the world blossom like the rose with atomic energy.
V. L. PARSEGIAN, *Bulletin of Atomic Scientists*, October 1971

13 We nuclear people have made a Faustian bargain with society. On the one hand, we offer—in the catalytic burner—an inexhaustible source of energy. . . . But the price that we demand of society for this magical energy source is both a vigilance and a longevity of our social institutions that we are quite unaccustomed to.
ALVIN M. WEINBERG, *Science*, 7 July 1972

14 [For nuclear plants to work as planned] requires a social commitment, and perhaps even a stability of the society, over very long times to maintain the expertise, the quality assurance, the vigilance that will keep us out of trouble. Most of us in the nuclear business believe such commitment is realistic because there are at least partial precedents for such technological demands: for example, the dikes of Holland require a very long social

commitment if they are to be kept in proper repair. Yet this is a debatable point.

ALVIN M. WEINBERG, *American Scientist*, January–February 1973

15 If so unforgiving a technology as large-scale nuclear fission energy production is adopted, it will impose a burden of continuous monitoring and sophisticated management of a dangerous material, essentially forever.

ALLEN V. KNEESE, *Resources*, September 1973

16 It is my belief that benefit-cost analysis cannot answer the most important policy questions associated with the desirability of developing a large-scale, fission-based economy. To expect it to do so is to ask it to bear a burden it cannot sustain. This is so because the questions are of a deep *ethical* character.

ALLEN V. KNEESE, *Resources*, September 1973

17 The decisive conflict of today is not between capitalists and communists, not between rich and poor, but between the mass producers of plutonium and us who merely wish to survive.

HANNES ALFVEN, Pugwash Conference, 1974

18 Our experience indicates that rather than sustaining a high degree of esprit, vigilance, and meticulous attention to detail, our governmental bureaucracies instead become careless, rigid, defensive and, less frequently, corrupt. A basic question, then, is whether we want to entrust so demanding and unrelenting a technology as plutonium recycle to [such] institutions.

NATURAL RESOURCES DEFENSE COUNCIL, "The Plutonium Decision," September 1974

19 A coal-fired power plant kills more people every few days than a nuclear power plant will in its 30 or so years of existence.

BERNARD COHEN, *Bulletin of Atomic Scientists*, October 1974

20 The uniquely unforgiving [nuclear technology was] designed by geniuses and is being run by idiots.

HENRY KENDALL, Critical Mass convention, November 1974

21 The response to nuclear power will be the garrison state.

DEAN E. ABRAHAMSON, testimony, Minnesota Pollution Control Agency, 12 December 1974

22 "Atoms for peace" and "atoms for war" are Siamese twins.

HANNES ALFVEN, October 1975, quoted in *Skeptic*, July–August 1976

23 A nuclear energy system meshes, most naturally, with a tightly organized, centralized industrial and political system, with all the potential for coercive and authoritarian tendencies which these systems have historically demonstrated. Adding all the necessary nuclear safeguard and security "solutions" together does not present a picture of the kind of peaceful, stable, and democratic world that I and, I think, most others would like to see.

GEORGE E. BROWN, JR., speech, American Association for the Advancement of Science, 20 February 1976

24 [Whether it is possible to produce nuclear power safely] is a technical question, and the answer to it may well be *yes*. But the real question we face is whether nuclear power can be produced safely *while maximizing profit*. The answer to that question is *no*.

GEORGE WALD, *New York Times*, 29 February 1976

25 On January 15, 1919, an "incredible" 15-foot wave of molasses killed 21 people and demolished a two-block area of Boston immediately after the rivets began popping from a tank holding 2.2 million gallons of the sticky goo. Damage was $2 million. Even the Atomic Energy Commission might have said, when the 21 victims were born, that the odds were EXCEEDINGLY REMOTE that they would die in a molasses tidal-wave.

COMMITTEE FOR NUCLEAR RESPONSIBILITY, "Common Sense about Nuclear Electricity," 1976

26 Nuclear power represents a kind of thermodynamic overkill. The use of nuclear radiation for the relatively mild task of producing steam (for electricity) violates the familiar caution against attacking a fly with a cannon.

BARRY COMMONER, *The Poverty of Power*, 1976

27 Once nuclear energy is about to become a charity ward of the public sector, then I think people will vote with their pocketbooks and it will go under, leaving us with a great radioactive white elephant.

BARRY COMMONER, *Skeptic*, July–August 1976

28 Those who hope to keep our type of society intact and essentially unchanged while introducing so bizarre and dangerous a technology as atomic energy are flying in the face of ecological wisdom.
GARRETT HARDIN, *Skeptic*, July–August 1976

29 If it is really true that the danger of nuclear accidents is less than the danger from lightning, then private insurers, always interested in making money, should leap at the chance of writing nuclear accident insurance.
GARRETT HARDIN, *Skeptic*, July–August 1976

30 A nuclear power plant is infinitely safer than eating, because 300 people choke to death on food every year.
DIXY LEE RAY, Governor of Washington, 1977, quoted in G. Barry Golson, ed., *The Playboy Interview*, 1981

31 [The plants and wastes remained] a brontosaurus that has had its spinal cord cut but is so big and has so many ganglia near the tail that it can keep thrashing around for years not knowing it's dead.
AMORY LOVINS, on the decline of the nuclear industry, quoted in *Boston Globe*, 8 October 1978

32 What will it take to get on with splitting atoms instead of hairs?
MOBIL CORPORATION, advertisement, 1 March 1979

33 The only accident [at the Three Mile Island nuclear power plant] is that this thing leaked out. You could have avoided this whole [public issue] by not saying anything.
CRAIG FAUST, April 1979, quoted in Linda Botts, ed., *Loose Talk*, 1980

34 I would not call [Three Mile Island] an accident. I would call it a malfunction. . . . It just so happens that the antinuclear movement, lacking a real accident, has latched onto this one, promoting it into something that it isn't.
EDWARD TELLER, August 1979, quoted in G. Barry Golson, ed., *The Playboy Interview*, 1981

35 In the nuclear industry . . . no acts of God can be permitted.
HANNES ALFVÉN, quoted in Linda Botts, ed., *Loose Talk*, 1980

36 The public knows what the facts are and if they had to choose between nuclear reactors and candles, they would choose candles.
RALPH NADER, quoted in Linda Botts, ed., *Loose Talk*, 1980

37 Capitalist isotopes and Marxist isotopes visit each other amicably in the skeletons of our children.
JEAN ROSTAND (1894–1980), *Inquiétudes d'un biologiste*, 1967

38 All the waste in a year from a nuclear power plant can be stored under a desk.
RONALD REAGAN, quoted in the *Burlington [Vermont] Free Press*, 15 February 1980

39 The country from which America borrowed the Marquis de Lafayette, and which spread the concepts of liberty, equality, and fraternity, is once more in a position to teach us a lesson. The French are proceeding, literally, full steam ahead with their nuclear energy program. . . . In looking at our nuclear mess, we can only say "vive la France!"
MOBIL CORPORATION, advertisement, *New York Times*, 13 March 1980

40 [Nuclear energy] must not be thwarted by a tiny minority opposed to economic growth which often finds friendly ears in regulatory agencies for its obstructionist campaigns.
RONALD REAGAN, *Sierra*, 10 September 1980

41 Nuclear power is the cleanest, the most efficient and the most economical energy source, with no environmental problems.
RONALD REAGAN, *Sierra*, 10 September 1980

42 The emotional campaign against nuclear power plants not only exaggerates the hazards of using such power to generate electricity, but is equally irrational in its advocacy of solar power as a substitute.
RONALD REAGAN, *Sierra*, 10 September 1980

43 The days when environmentalists and nonukers could menace the nuclear power industry seem to be finished. Unfortunately, it's not a simple obituary. The harassment—legal and otherwise—visited by the Abalones, Clamshells and Commoners has made a once attractive energy source into an expen-

sive, scary and over-regulated white elephant.
> WALL STREET JOURNAL, editorial, 22 Septem-
> ber 1981

44 [A] nuclear war could alleviate some of the
factors leading to today's ecological disturbances that are due to current high-popula-
tion concentrations and heavy industrial
production.
> ANONYMOUS official of the U.S. Office of
> Civil Defense, quoted in Jonathan Schell,
> The Fate of the Earth, 1982

45 From a strictly ecological viewpoint, nuclear
power is almost certainly the most benign of
all the main available or prospective energy
supply technologies.
> IAN BARBOUR et al., Energy and American Val-
> ues, 1982

46 The nuclear peril is usually seen in isolation
from the threats to other forms of life and
their ecosystems, but in fact it should be seen
at the very center of the ecological crisis.
> JONATHAN SCHELL, The Fate of the Earth, 1982

47 The prime cause of the accident was an extremely improbable combination of violations
of instructions in operating rules committed
by the staff of the unit.
> USSR STATE COMMITTEE, report on Cherno-
> byl nuclear plant accident, 1986

48 We can expect to see another serious [nu-
clear] accident in this country during the next
20 years.
> JAMES ASSELTINE, Nuclear Regulatory Com-
> missioner, testimony, U.S. House Com-
> mittee on Energy and Commerce, May
> 1986

49 Nuclear power must be got rid of.
> INGVAR CARLSSON, Prime Minister of Swe-
> den, assessing the Chernobyl nuclear plant
> accident, quoted in New York Times, 18 Au-
> gust 1986

50 For us the lessons from Chernobyl are clear.
The Faustian bargain of nuclear energy has
been lost.
> PETER JANKOWITSCH, Austrian Minister of
> Foreign Affairs, speech, Vienna, 24 Sep-
> tember 1986

51 This is basically a hazardous technology if not
properly operated. This means you have to

have discipline in the control room, detailed
procedures and a knowledgeable staff that
doesn't go by-passing a safety system in the
dark of the night to run a test. . . . We need to
focus on these operating details, the training
of operators, and make sure we don't have
anything that comes close [to Chernobyl].
> HAROLD DENTON, quoted in Los Angeles
> Times, 27 April 1987

52 Nuclear energy is not inherently good or inherently bad. It's how civilization uses it. In
the long term, we have to develop reactors
which are inherently safe and which do not
depend on human beings for their safety.
. . . [But] the likelihood of another major accident somewhere in the world in the next 10
years is not less than 25 per cent. Or that in
the United States the probability of a core
meltdown within the next 20 years is about 50
per cent.
> ROBERT P. GALE, quoted in Los Angeles Times,
> 27 June 1987

53 The nuclear-waste issue is probably the
toughest issue we deal with in the Department of Energy. I feel we will get to a permanent waste repository for both defense and
commercial waste. . . . [The] solution will be
deep geologic storage for nuclear waste. The
experts have looked at this for years. Deep
geologic burial of nuclear waste is the right
way to go. Japan is doing it; Sweden is doing
it; France is doing it. And we ought to do it.
> JOHN S. HERRINGTON, quoted in USA Today,
> 29 October 1987

54 It was not until 1901 that humanity knew that
nuclear energy existed. It is understandable
now—but useless to wish that we still lived in
the ignorance of 1900.
> ISAAC ASIMOV, Isaac Asimov's Book of Science
> and Nature Quotations, 1988

55 Unless we realize that the technologies we
are dealing with are of international consequence, that the technologies are very serious, we are headed down a very dangerous
and possibly disastrous path.
> ROBERT P. GALE, on nuclear power-plant ac-
> cidents, such as the one in 1986 at Cherno-
> byl in the U.S.S.R., after which he assisted
> the victims, quoted in USA Today, 27 April
> 1988

56 I'm deeply convinced nuclear energy should be developed, but it must be absolutely safe. My proposal is to put nuclear reactors underground.

ANDREI D. SAKHAROV, quoted in *USA Today*, 8 November 1988

57 Political times change. Constituencies change. Party control in given areas of the country change. People see this as consistent not just from a states' rights standpoint, but from the standpoint of electric-power production and energy policy, too. Here we have two huge plants [Seabrook and Shoreham] ready to operate, and we're looking at power outages in the Northeast, and everyone agrees on one thing: It's silly not to operate them.

FRANK M. CUSHING, quoted in *New York Times*, 21 November 1988

58 The fact that every year there is waste being produced that will take the next three ice ages, and beyond, to become harmless is something that has deeply impressed the imagination.

CRISPIN TICKELL, British ambassador to the United Nations, on radioactive waste produced by nuclear power plants, quoted in *Time*, 2 January 1989

59 Coal versus nuclear is not a Hobson's choice. It's a false choice. We must not solve global warming by creating a nuclear garrison state. We must not approach problems with such singleminded tunnel vision.

DENIS HAYES, speech, Museum of Natural History, New York City, 8 November 1989

60 It is easier to develop the safety systems than to do the cleanup after an accident, even if it is less tragic than the Chernobyl one.

N. I. RYZHKOV, Soviet Prime Minister, interview with *Moskovskaya Pravda*, 26 April 1990, quoted in *JPRS Report*, 5 July 1990

61 What Chernobyl fundamentally exposes, to the chagrin of the international nuclear industry, is that trying to control a chain reaction in unstable atoms of highly enriched uranium is an extremely foolhardy way to boil water.

ANDRE CAROTHERS, *Greenpeace*, January–February 1991

62 The lesson that Wall Street learned from Three Mile Island was that a group of feder-

ally licensed operators—not appreciably better or worse than any other crew—could convert a \$2 billion asset into a \$1 billion cleanup job in about 90 minutes.

PETER BRADFORD, quoted in *Washington Post*, 3 February 1991

63 Nuclear waste is the West's dirtiest laundry.

JANE KRAMER, *New Yorker*, 18 March 1991

64 Safety is the foundation of nuclear power. I believe that feeling anxiety is part of safety.

NASU SHO, president of the Tokyo Electric Power Company, quoted in *Mainichi Shimbun*, 7 April 1991

91 OCEAN POLLUTION
See also   92 OCEANS, 94 OIL SPILLS

1 The sea, the ever renewing sea!

PAUL VALERY (1871–1945), *Charmes*, 1922

2 It is a curious situation that the sea, from which life first arose, should now be threatened by the activities of one form of that life. But the sea, though changed in a sinister way, will continue to exist; the threat is rather to life itself.

RACHEL CARSON (1907–1964), *The Sea Around Us*, 1951

3 The sea is earth's primal antiseptic, taking its rot and ordure and debris at the littoral and destroying their infection.

CURTIS BOK, 1957, quoted in Roger Stone, *The Sanderling*, 1990

4 If we enter the sea in full force with all our technology without first understanding and taking account of the environmental implications, we will wreak the same tragic destruction on this fragile resource as we have on land.

GAYLORD NELSON, U.S. Senator, speech, 11 August 1970

5 The sea is the universal sewer.

JACQUES COUSTEAU, testimony, U.S. House Science and Astronautics Committee, 28 January 1971

6 To what degree and how often do we have to bruise this delicate living surface of the oceans with oil and other pollutants before

the whole system collapses or is destructively and irreversibly diminished?

NOEL MOSTERT, *Supership*, 1974

7 That the very seas should be considered a wasting asset must surely be the essential nightmare of the whole business of the despoliation of this planet which daily is perpetrated before our eyes, about our ears, and inside our nostrils. It is simply that the salt seas are for almost all of us the perpetual assurance of an accessible freshness and cleanness; and, I suppose, there is in this as well the remnant of an atavistic instinct defensive of our remote origin, a much-needed conviction of their inviolability, that whatsoever other havoc we wreak, however deeply we pile the ashes, the seas still will rise and fall and safely breathe in their depths.

NOEL MOSTERT, *Supership*, 1974

8 We see great damage to specific areas of the seas. They are disease spots like a black spot on the lung.

ARVID PARDO, on pollution of the oceans, especially places like the coastal wetlands, estuaries, and continental shelf, *Bill Moyers' Journal*, 8 May 1975

9 Only when we fully perceive that there is no fundamental difference between the various bodies of water on our planet, beyond the fact that the ocean is the largest of all lakes, can we begin to realize that the ocean has something else in common with all other bodies of water: it is vulnerable. In the long run the ocean can be affected by the continued discharge of all modern man's toxic waste. . . . A dead ocean means a dead planet.

THOR HEYERDAHL, *Saturday Review*, 25 November 1975

10 The issue is really whether we are going to recognize that the oceans, like the land, are not limitless, self-healing, and invulnerable to humanity's harmful activities.

ELIZABETH KAPLAN, testimony, joint hearing of U.S. House Merchant Marine and Fisheries subcommittees, 20 February 1980

11 The sea has always been regarded by coastal and seafaring people as the ideal place for dumping their waste and this is, of course, a very reasonable and proper attitude. Almost everything put into the sea is either diluted . . . or broken down or stored harmlessly on the seabed. . . . Not the least of the attractions of the sea as a dumping ground has been the lack of administrative controls.

JOHN DUNSTER, quoted in E. Pike and V. Cooper, paper, Seminar on Preventing Water Pollution, Blackpool, England, 23 June 1987

12 It is a sign of our power, and our criminal folly, that we can pollute the vast ocean and are doing so.

ISAAC ASIMOV, *Isaac Asimov's Book of Science and Nature Quotations*, 1988

13 There's no mystery to marine pollution. The worst problem today is the huge quantity of raw sewage and industrial effluent spewed into the sea, with no thought to consequences, from coastal cities all over the world.

STJEPAN KECKES, *United Nations Environment Program News*, April 1988

14 The ocean is tired. It's throwing back at us what we're throwing in there.

FRANK LAUTENBERG, U.S. Senator, on recent cases of dumped waste washing ashore at beaches, quoted in *USA Today*, 11 August 1988

15 Plastic that finds its way into the waters anywhere around our coast is automatically taken up into the north equatorial current, then, like a stunned commuter on the Circle Line, it is doomed to revolve forever.

ROBERT FANNIN, *The Independent*, 28 September 1990

92 OCEANS

See also   91 OCEAN POLLUTION

1 Roll on, thou deep and dark blue ocean—roll!
Ten thousand fleets sweep over thee in vain;
Man marks the earth with ruin—his control
Stops with the shore.

GEORGE GORDON, LORD BYRON (1788–1824), *Childe Harold's Pilgrimage*, 1812

2 For as this appalling ocean surrounds the verdant land, so in the soul of man there lies one insular Tahiti, full of peace and joy, but

encompassed by all the horrors of the half
known life.

HERMAN MELVILLE (1819–1891), *Moby-Dick,*
1851

3 There is, one knows not what sweet mystery
about this sea, whose gently awful stirrings
seem to speak of some hidden soul beneath; . . . And meet it is, that over these sea
pastures, wide-rolling watery prairies and
Potters' Fields of all four continents, the
waves should rise and fall, and ebb and flow
unceasingly; for here, millions of mixed
shades and shadows, drowned dreams, som-
nambulisms, reveries; all that we call lives
and souls, lie dreaming, dreaming, still; toss-
ing like slumberers in their beds; the ever-
rolling waves but made so by their rest-
lessness.

HERMAN MELVILLE (1819–1891), *Moby-Dick,*
1851

4 And I have asked to be
Where no storms come,
Where the green swell is in the havens
dumb,
And out of the swing of the sea.

GERARD MANLEY HOPKINS (1844–1889),
"Heaven-Haven," 1865

5 The ocean: A body of water occupying about
two-thirds of a world made for man—who
has no gills.

AMBROSE BIERCE (1842–1914?), *The Devil's
Dictionary,* 1906

6 [Man] cannot control or change the ocean as,
in his brief tenancy of earth, he has subdued
and plundered the continents.

RACHEL CARSON (1907–1964), *The Sea Around
Us,* 1951

7 In its mysterious past [the sea] encompasses
all the dim origins of life and receives in the
end, after, it may be, many transmutations,
the dead husks of that same life. For all at last
returns to the sea—to Oceanus, the ocean
river, like the ever-flowing stream of time,
the beginning and the end.

RACHEL CARSON (1907–1964), *The Sea Around
Us,* 1951

8 Probably this is the best, and possibly the
last, opportunity to channel, as a matter of
right, large amounts of the earth's common
wealth to developing nations. Who can foresee the embittering consequences of failure?

If grasped, who could price its contribution
to the right ordering of life on the planet
Earth?

A. BARTON LEWIS and MIRIAM L. LEVERING,
"Ocean Resources and the Ocean Environment," Sierra Club, 1974

9 Natural systems, including the oceans, are
incredibly resistant. . . . Regeneration is a
special property of water and it is exercised
on an inconceivably massive and majestic
scale by the oceans, the healers and cleansers
of the whole terrestrial globe. But the system
is nonetheless an organic system. As such it
is still capable of death.

BARBARA WARD, in Robert M. Hallman, *Towards an Environmentally Sound Law of the
Sea,* 1974

10 We have always depended upon the sea for a
great variety of substances, oils, fats, furs,
fertilizers, to name only a few apart from
food, but the flora and fauna of the oceans are
the reverse cornucopia which could provide
us in the future with substitute sources for all
sorts of items, including chemicals and plastics. We have hardly begun to explore the potential variety of the oceans' plants and their
yields, or the many by-products of the sea's
creatures.

NOËL MOSTERT, *Audubon,* May 1975

11 From his contact with the marine environment, man should derive fear and respect; he
should be taught the complexity and oneness
of the biosphere, the vital importance of conservation, and maintenance and rational use
of the oceanic ecosystem in which (although
it is not his natural environent) he has arro-
gated the right to intervene.

BERNARD SALVAT, speech, International Conference on Marine Parks and Reserves,
Tokyo, 14 May 1975

12 Life originated in the sea, and about eighty
percent of it is still there.

ISAAC ASIMOV, *Isaac Asimov's Book of Science
and Nature Quotations,* 1988

13 The oceans are the planet's last great living
wilderness, man's only remaining frontier on
earth, and perhaps his last chance to prove
himself a rational species.

JOHN L. CULLINEY, *Wilderness Conservation,*
September–October 1990

93 OIL AND GAS
See also   94 OIL SPILLS

1 Your motto is Service. Back on the farm, when I heard that the bull was "servicing" the cows, I looked behind the barn. And, gentlemen, what that bull was doing to the cow is exactly what you people have been doing to the public all these years.
WILL ROGERS (1879–1935), speaking to the board of directors of Standard Oil Company, quoted in Morris K. Udall, *Too Funny to Be President*, 1988

2 The better you live, the more oil you use.
ESSO COMPANY, advertisement, *New Yorker*, 1949

3 The best thing that could happen to the American people would be a chronic shortage of gasoline.
R. C. PEALE, in Frank F. Darling and John P. Milton, eds., *Future Environments of North America*, 1966

4 The 55-gallon oil drum is the new state flower of Alaska.
E. L. HARDIN, quoted in *Ramparts*, January 1970

5 By 1980 we will be self-sufficient and will not need to rely on foreign enemies . . . uh, energy.
RICHARD M. NIXON, responding to the current gasoline shortage, 1973

6 In strategic, geopolitical, and survival terms, probably what we should do with the North Slope oil is to leave it right where it is for now. The tundra is the only suitable storage facility we have. If oil is valuable now, think what it will be in 20 or 50 years. The real national interest is to hold on to our own reserves as long as we can.
ANONYMOUS OIL COMPANY EXECUTIVE, quoted in *Audubon*, May 1975

7 [Gasoline] has less than a generation of useful life left to it. If we can learn how to manage its death, we will have learned how to begin.
FREDERICK C. THAYER, speech, World Future Society, Washington, D.C., 2 June 1975

8 The best thing you can do for your country is to junk your present car, buy the biggest new car you can afford, and then don't drive it.
ANONYMOUS, on what to do in the face of the recession and oil shortage of 1974, quoted in Herman E. Daly, *Steady-State Economics*, 1977

9 Who knows what a moose thinks, anyway, when he approaches the [Alaska oil] pipeline?
ANONYMOUS ALASKA OIL PIPELINE OFFICIAL, 1976, quoted in John Hanrahan and Peter Gruenstein, *Lost Frontier: The Marketing of Alaska*, 1977

10 When the world was made, a greater wisdom than ours put billions of barrels of oil on that North Slope, seeing that as its highest and best use.
PAUL HARVEY, radio commentary, quoted in *Conservation Foundation Letter*, June 1978

11 The white market [of gasoline rationing coupons that can be bought and sold] will be the classic, wide-open, unregulated bazaar of the economists' dreams.
DAVID A. STOCKMAN, U.S. Representative, letter to colleagues in U.S. Congress, 8 May 1979

12 Buy the shore of Gitche Gumee,
Buy the shining offshore leases,
Buy the shining mining leases,
Giving me the credit due me,
and you'll be as rich as Croesus,
Richer far than old King Croesus.
Though the Congress may beshrew me,
Pick my policies to pieces,
Reagan's will is working through me,
Not to mention Edwin Meese's.
FELICIA LAMPORT, *New York Times*, 23 October 1983

13 The bottom of the oil barrel is now visible.
CHRISTOPHER FLAVIN, Worldwatch Paper 66, July 1985

14 The faster we drill for oil, the more oil we waste and the sooner we run out.
CARRYING CAPACITY, INC., *Beyond Oil: The Threat to Food and Fuel in the Coming Decades*, 1986

15 Our economic and energy security is inextricably tied to the fates and fortunes of our domestic petroleum industry through this century.
JOHN S. HERRINGTON, U.S. Secretary of Energy, quoted in *Christian Science Monitor*, 18 March 1987

16 In its rush to be chief advocate for the oil companies, the Reagan Administration has lost all credibility when it comes to the Arctic Refuge. Its agenda is clear: oil at any cost. But the American public will not stand for it.

GEORGE T. FRAMPTON, JR., Wilderness Society president, criticizing the Reagan Administration's plans for opening Alaska's Arctic National Wildlife Refuge for oil and gas exploration, quoted in *New York Times*, 21 April 1987

17 How does it ensure our long-term national security to use up America's last crude-oil reserves, especially at a time when cheap foreign supplies are available?

WILLIAM S. CURTISS, *Los Angeles Times*, 2 June 1987

18 If sanity prevails and we are able to show what professional environmentalists can do—and by that I mean oil men.

FRANK E. MOSIER, president of Standard Oil, predicting success at the Arctic National Wildlife Refuge, *Washington Post*, 20 June 1987

19 I think we can compatibly have off-shore [oil-drilling] leasing. Right now we're sitting fat, dumb and happy in the United States; [we've] got energy prices down; you have what appears to be a glut of energy. [But] we are becoming more and more dependent on foreign oil, and that is not good national-security policy.

GEORGE BUSH, quoted in *Washington Post*, 6 June 1988

20 It's easier, and thus "more fun," to use oil for almost everything. Raking leaves, for instance. By 1987 Americans alone had paid more than a hundred million dollars to buy electric leaf blowers—machines that blow leaves around a yard, thereby replacing the rake.

BILL McKIBBEN, *The End of Nature*, 1989

21 I'm determined to be an environmentalist. I *am* one, and I'm concerned that we not do irreparable damage to the environment. On the other hand, I remember some of the same arguments being made against the Alaska [oil] pipeline. And we have some radical national-security interests at stake here, and I'm one who believes we can find the balance between environmental interests and national-security interests that dictate prudent development of our domestic oil and gas resources.

GEORGE BUSH, quoted in *New York Times*, 26 January 1989

22 Crude Addiction.

NATIONAL WILDLIFE FEDERATION, on U.S. dependance on oil imports, *Conservation 90*, 15 October 1990.

23 If we're willing to risk American lives to protect a source of foreign imports, we certainly ought to be able to risk environmental consequences to develop [domestic sources].

TED STEVENS, U.S. Senator, *Washington Post*, 21 August 1990

24 Breaking America's oil addiction would not lead to a future of sackcloth and ashes.

COLMAN McCARTHY, *Washington Post*, 12 October 1990

25 Not only is the world addicted to cheap oil, but the largest liquor store is in a very dangerous neighborhood.

CHRISTOPHER FLAVIN, Worldwatch Paper 100, December 1990

26 If America remains addicted to oil, Saddam Hussein will not be the last oil dictator, and this will not be the last oil war.

MIKE CLARK, *Friends of the Earth*, Winter 1991

27 The U.S. went to war for oil and was victorious. Full stop. No further action on the energy front will be forthcoming. For future security and energy supply, it almost makes you wish the war had been lost.

ROD McQUEEN, *Financial Post*, 6 March 1991

28 Who goes there to enjoy the wilderness? The very, very wealthy. The people from Delaware. And where did they get their money? From the oil industry.

TED STEVENS, U.S. Senator (Alaska), in favor of oil exploration, rather than wilderness designation, for part of the Alaska National Wildlife Refuge, testimony, Senate Environment and Public Works subcommittee, 19 April 1991

29 A reduction of petroleum dependency is a much more intelligent and practical national-security policy than the buildup of a gas-guzzling war machine to coerce access to cheap oil.

RICHARD J. BARNET, *New Yorker*, 29 April 1991

94 OIL SPILLS
See also   91 OCEAN POLLUTION

1 Every tanker, however well managed, drops some of its oil into the sea in some form or another; badly managed ships are ceaseless polluters and, like garden snails, can often be followed by the long iridescent trail of their waste.
   NOEL MOSTERT, *Supership*, 1974

2 Yet now the speed limits are back where they were, the thirsty quest for North Sea oil presses, and the folly of basing one's technology on oil is forgotten. North Sea oil has been grasped at as an answer when it should properly have remained a question.
   ALASTAIR REID, on British policy in the aftermath of the energy crisis, *New Yorker*, 7 October 1974

3 It's ironic that the Americans now turn their attention to the oceans as an alternative food supply while simultaneously we rush ahead with this oil development that can cancel out any future gain from the very fertile and shallow continental shelf waters of Alaska.
   TOM CASEY, manager of Alaskan fish marketing association, quoted in John Hanrahan and Peter Gruenstein, *Lost Frontier: The Marketing of Alaska*, 1977

4 Without meaning to ignore the ugliness of any oil spill, I suggest that the Argo Merchant and Olympic Games incidents add up to a minuscule spill when considered as part of the tremendous flow of oil continually entering this country to heat our homes, operate our plants, run our cars and buses, etc.
   JAMES J. REYNOLDS, president, American Institute of Merchant Shipping, letter, *Washington Post*, 1 January 1977

5 An oil spill is so appalling that it beggars meaningful response. It makes for a desperate feeling. You want to battle it and not stand idly by as the ugly, reeking muck fouls the beaches, the meeting ground of earth and sea. And the miserable, defenseless birds, shrouded in stinging crude oil, innocent victims, become the totems of the entropy battle.
   STEPHANIE MILLS, *What Ever Happened to Ecology?*, 1989

6 I've never seen such a goddamned mess in my life.
   STEVE COWPER, on *Exxon Valdez* oil spill, 24 March 1989, quoted in Art Davidson, *In the Wake of the Exxon Valdez*, 1990

7 The only cry [from environmentalists] now is: "No more Alaskan oil." That's all very well, but which of the alternatives do you like? Do you like importing oil? Do you like nuclear power? Do you like coal?
   JOHN CHUBB, on *Exxon Valdez* oil spill, quoted in *Christian Science Monitor*, 11 April 1989

8 We should come down hard on the [oil] industry's laxness. But if we don't produce oil here, we'll produce it somewhere else, ship it to the U.S., and face the same risks.
   WALTER HICKEL, on *Exxon Valdez* oil spill, quoted in *USA Today*, 10 May 1989

9 Conceptually, what Exxon did was reposition a natural contaminant from inside a rock formation to the surface of a water body, where natural forces (wave action, bacteria, sunlight) immediately began acting in opposition to the intrusion.
   GREG EASTERBROOK, *Newsweek*, 24 July 1989

10 The Alaska oil spill by Exxon was like the drunken dad getting drunk one night and coming home, saying, "Oh, I'm sorry." The only way that the cycle is broken is to have a family conference—we're not going to allow this anymore—the game is up.
   KATHERINE BURTON, quoted in Francesca Lyman, *The Greenhouse Trap*, 1990

11 It wasn't his [the captain of the *Exxon Valdez*] driving that caused the Alaskan oil spill. It was yours.
   GREENPEACE advertisement, *New York Times*, 25 February 1990

95 OPEN SPACE
See also   98 PARKS, 101 PLANNING, LAND USE, 114 RECREATION, 132 URBAN ENVIRONMENT

1 The towns of to-day can only increase in density at the expense of the open spaces which are the lungs of a city.

We must increase the open spaces and diminish the distances to be covered. Therefore, the centre of the city must be constructed vertically.

LE CORBUSIER (1887–1965), *The City of Tomorrow and Its Planning*, 1929

2 One item that will require big public money is open space. If [suburban] sprawl is to be effectively contained, and if future development is to take a more compact form than at present, there must be an abundance of public parks, beaches, bicycle paths, and riding trails. Privately owned green spaces—e.g., farms and golf courses—could be protected from the bulldozer without dispossessing the present owners.

EDMUND K. FALTERMAYER, *Fortune*, March 1969

3 It may not be crowding *per se* that degrades us, but a lack of relief from crowding—a lack of open space, a lack of green, of nature going its own way.

CHARLES E. LITTLE and JOHN G. MITCHELL, *Space for Survival*, 1971

4 Let us accept the conceit of a green world—in which different emotional and intellectual responses are available—as fundamental to the human condition, a requirement of a civilized being; and ask that these availabilities be extended to an ever-growing number of citizens. . . . National, regional and local parks together must form so massive an area of open space that no man is deprived of its advantages.

WILLIAM M. ROTH, speech, Conservation Foundation symposium, Washington, D.C., 1971

5 Although urban open space is usually thought of as providing recreation, it serves many other purposes as well. Open space can provide beauty, privacy, and variety; moderate temperature; and create a sense of spaciousness and scale. It can protect a water supply; provide a noise and safety buffer zone around an airport; or substitute for development on unsuitable soils, in flood plains, or in earthquake zones.

COUNCIL ON ENVIRONMENTAL QUALITY, *Environmental Quality*, 1973

6 The logic of history requires gardens in our cities, a pastoral landscape aesthetic in our suburbs, and unadulterated wilderness for retreat.

CHARLES E. LITTLE, *A Town Is Saved*, 1973

7 I have pictures of the prairie. You would say, "That isn't a picture of anything—just space." That was our environment—space. We learned to love it just as the Swiss love the Alps. This open prairie.

PATRICIA D. DUNCAN, *Tallgrass Prairie*, 1978

8 I think a current understanding about urban behavior tells us that it's important that people get out and be able to get away from the concrete jungles and the dense environment where they live for their own mental well-being. If they don't do this, the costs in human loss and human sickness will be far greater than what we would be expending for these kinds of releases and open spaces.

BARRY GOLDWATER, U.S. Senator, testimony, U.S. House Interior subcommittee, 20 March 1981

9 I am one of those people who deeply resents not having been born in the 19th century, when there were still open places to explore.

BRUCE BABBITT, former Governor of Arizona, quoted in *Los Angeles Times*, 3 March 1987

10 Open space . . . can no longer be considered a given, it must be planned for as a basic infrastructure need as essential as roads, sewers and schools.

HELEN FRENSKE, testimony, Greenway Council, Hudson River Valley, 12 February 1990

11 [Presidential adviser John Sununu's] idea of open space was a K Mart parking lot.

PATRICK JACKSON, quoted in *New York Times*, 14 May 1990

96 OUTER SPACE

1 Who would therefore looke dangerously up at Planets, that might safely look downe at Plants?

JOHN GERARD (1545–1612), *Herball*, 1597

2 How strange and wonderful is our home, our earth, with its swirling vaporous atmosphere, its flowing and frozen climbing crea-

tures, the croaking things with wings that hang onrocks and soar through fog, the furry grass, the scaly seas . . . how utterly rich and wild. . . . Yet some among us have the nerve, the insolence, the brass, the gall to whine about the limitations of our earthbound fate and yearn for some more perfect world beyond the sky.

EDWARD ABBEY, *Appalachian Wilderness*, 1970

3 There's nothing in the entire remainder of the solar system as precious as one acre on the Earth.

GEORGE WALD, speech, Harvard University, 21 April 1970

4 There are no "limits to growth." . . . Even if the Earth's resources prove ultimately to be finite, those of the solar system and the great galaxy beyond are, for all practical purposes, infinite.

ADRIAN BERRY, *The Next Ten Thousand Years*, 1974

5 The very idea of Space Colonies carries to a logical—and horrifying—conclusion processes of dehumanization and depersonalization that have already gone much too far on the Earth. In a way, we're gotten ready for Space Platforms by a systematic degradation of human ways of life on the Earth.

GEORGE WALD, *CoEvolution Quarterly*, Spring 1976

6 There are untold resources awaiting man in the Arctic, to say nothing of the oceans, the Antarctic and the great jungles of the Southern Hemisphere. . . . It is the energy industry that more than any other factor in modern civilization has freed man from slavery, poverty, and ignorance. . . . In terms of future centuries, I might be worried if this was the only planet we could see, the only star in the sky. We'll soon discover that the planets out there are made up of copper, iron ore, phosphorus, and so on—they will all be available for humans to use. Yes, we'll be mining in space. I see no limits on man. The only limits are those we place on ourselves.

WALTER J. HICKEL, speech, Los Angeles, 21 October 1976

7 People in space are diminished people, out of their ancient, inherited, and supremely beau-

tiful context. And like anything ripped from context, there is no point to them.

DAVID EHRENFELD, *The Arrogance of Humanism*, 1978

8 One can find some irony in the fact that we are spending enormous amounts of money to discover evidence of life in outer space while at the same time some of us are content to watch countless numbers of species, about which we know nothing, disappear from the face of the earth.

MICHAEL BEAN, legal brief for environmental organizations, *Tennessee Valley Authority* v. *Hill et al.* (Telleco Dam snail darter case), January 1978

9 As frontiers on this planet shrink, the search for space turns both inward to the mind and outward to the stars.

RODERICK NASH, in *The American Land*, 1979

10 The prospect of expanding life into the heavens may sound too remote to be relevant to today's environmental debates. Hardly. It's far more meaningful than such details as unburned hydrocarbon gram levels or delayed Subtitle D regulations. This prospect gives us reason to believe that humankind can take a constructive place in the larger natural scheme.

GREGG EASTERBROOK, *New Republic*, 30 April 1990

11 A millimeter-sized particle can enter the body of an astronaut as a hole the size of a hypodermic needle and leave as a hole the size of a football.

ROBERT BRACHER, quoted in *San Francisco Examiner*, 17 March 1991

12 Within a few years, astronauts are likely to face what scientists call "a significant risk" of being hit by a droplet of urine at more than 30,000 mph. At such a speed, they estimate, the impact of a cubic centimeter of urine would be equivalent to a car travelling at 110 mph.

STEVE CONNOR, quoted in *San Francisco Examiner*, 17 March 1991.

97 OZONE LAYER

1 We [the U.S.] once led the way in attacking such problems as acid rain, ozone depletion,

water pollution and toxic wastes. Now our leaders speak and the world laughs. What is their answer to ozone depletion? Hats and sunglasses.

> PATRICIA SCHROEDER, U.S. Representative, quoted in *Ms.*, February 1988

2 Damage already done to the ozone layer will be with us, our children and our grandchildren throughout the 21st century.

> MARGARET THATCHER, quoted in *Washington Post*, 8 October 1988

3 There was no moment when I yelled "Eureka!" I just came home one night and told my wife, "The work is going very well, but it looks like the end of the world."

> SHERWOOD ROWLAND, on his discovery that CFCs damage the ozone layer, quoted in Eknath Easwaran, *The Compassionate Universe*, 1989

4 My feeling is we overestimate our ability to predict [great changes in the earth's environment]. Many of the things that are going to happen to the planet will be surprises, like the ozone hole over Antarctica. Therefore, we should be much more careful about what we are doing and much more observant of how the system works.

> WALLACE S. BROECKER, quoted in *New York Times*, 17 January 1989

5 The disintegrating ozone layer and warming atmosphere are making it intolerable to think of industrial growth as progress; now it appears to us as aggression against the human condition.

> IVAN ILLICH, *New Perspectives Quarterly*, Spring 1989

6 If companies don't reclaim the CFCs in their equipment, they are doing to the atmosphere what Exxon did to the Arctic.

> CARMELO J. SCUDERI, quoted in H. Patricia Hynes, *Earth Right*, 1990

7 Because life as we know it would not have developed on Earth without an ozone layer, the continuing manufacture of substances that destroy it is highly alarming.

> SHERWOOD ROWLAND, quoted in *Business Week*, 18 June 1990

8 Which would you rather have, a spot on your tie or a hole in the ozone?

> DAVID DONIGER, on the ban of ozone depleting chemicals, including dry-cleaning solvents, by the year 2000, *NRDC Newsline*, July–August 1990

98 PARKS

See also   83 NATIONAL PARKS, 95 OPEN SPACE, 114 RECREATION

1 The parks are the lungs of London.

> WILLIAM PITT (1708–1778), attributed by William Windham, 1808

2 . . . those vegetable puncheons
Called parks, where there is neither fruit nor flower
Enough to gratify a bee's slight munchings.
But after all it is the only "bower"
. . . where the fashionable fair
Can forma slight acquaintance with fresh air.

> GEORGE GORDON, LORD BYRON (1788–1824), *Don Juan*, 1819–1824

3 We want a ground to which people may easily go after their day's work is done, and where they may stroll for an hour, seeing, hearing, and feeling nothing of the bustle and jar of the streets, where they shall, in effect, find the city put far away from them. . . . Practically, what we most want is a simple, broad, open space of clean greensward, with sufficient play of surface and a sufficient number of trees about it to supply a variety of light and shade. . . . We want depth of wood enough about it not only for comfort in hot weather, but to completely shut out the city from our landscapes.

> FREDERICK LAW OLMSTED (1822–1903), *Public Parks and the Enlargement of Towns*, 1870

4 We should undertake nothing in a park which involves the treating of the public as prisoners or wild beasts.

> FREDERICK LAW OLMSTED (1822–1903), *Journal of Social Science*, November 1871

5 Parks have plainly not come as the direct result of any of the great inventions or discoveries of the century. They are not, with us,

simply an improvement on what we had before, growing out of a general advance of the arts applicable to them. . . . It would seem rather to have been a common spontaneous movement of that sort which we conveniently refer to the "Genius of Civilization."

> FREDERICK LAW OLMSTED (1822–1903), 1880, in Frederick Law Olmsted and Theodora Kimball, *Forty Years of Landscape Architecture*, 1928

6 Parks [in cities] are but pavement disguised with a growth of grass.

> GEORGE GISSING (1857–1903), *The Private Papers of Henry Ryecroft*, 1903

7 The creation of the mental domain of phantasy has a complete counterpart in the establishment of "reservations" and "natureparks." . . . The "reservation" is to maintain the old condition of things which has been regretfully sacrificed to necessity everywhere else; there everything may grow and spread as it pleases, including what is useless and even what is harmful. The mental realm of phantasy is also such a reservation reclaimed from the encroaches of the reality-principle.

> SIGMUND FREUD (1856–1939), *General Introduction to Psychoanalysis*, 1920

8 The silence of a shut park does not sound like the country silence: it is tense and confined.

> ELIZABETH BOWEN (1899–1973), *The Death of the Heart*, 1938

9 In terms of quantity of space, the city park is a joke. It would have to cover thousands of square miles to provide a truly natural amount of wandering space for the huge city population it serves. The best that can be said for it is that it is decidedly better than nothing.

> DESMOND MORRIS, *The Human Zoo*, 1969

10 One might consider an ideal series of parks as you might a great water system, using the metaphor of green water in massive lakes emptying into larger rivers and small creeks, rushing narrowly over waterfalls and flowing placidly and broadly through the flat countryside in a continuous sequence of parklands. Then it curls around and through cities in man-determined forms, held back by res-

ervoirs, channeled over aqueducts and finally rising—as in Rome, in fountains, small ones in dusty corners and large, baroque ones in mighty plazas. Thus, the fields and trees of parks should be, as water, not scattered oases such as Yosemite, but a weaving, interconnected green mass that changes in size and purpose, but always inter-penetrates forcibly but gently the urban, suburban, and rural scene.

> WILLIAM M. ROTH, speech, Conservation Foundation symposium, Washington, D.C., 1971

11 [P]arks are at the center of a community's character; they reflect and strengthen the sense of place and identity that make cities fit places for people.

> CONSERVATION FOUNDATION, *National Parks for the Future*, 1972

12 Park and open-space efforts can be described as an institutional reflection of the principal means by which urban man has historically engaged in the Edenic search. He has, since the beginnings of civilization, sought gardens in his cities, a pastoral landscape outside of his cities, and wilderness for retreat away from his cities. Baghdad boasted a thousand gardens; Alexander set aside one quarter of his north African city as a park; . . . wilderness served as retreat for Jesus of Nazareth, as it did later for the Waldensians and the Franciscans; and meditation in the wilderness is a common theme in Far Eastern cultures. Thus, there is good evidence that a propensity for greenery as a substitute Eden in urban civilizations is not a peculiarity of any single race, religion, or national culture.

> CHARLES E. LITTLE, in James N. Smith, *Environmental Quality and Social Justice in Urban America*, 1974

13 We [Eskimos and Indians] have never invented nor needed to conceive of the idea of parks and preserves. It is this conceptual problem that is the source of misunderstanding which makes our approach to nature so essentially different. Now that Americans have recognized a measure of importance to wilderness, they are panic-struck about this and have delivered this panic to our doorsteps. Now we are forced to help them quell that panic and bring relief. It is certainly

within our altruistic nature to help, but I wonder if their relief requires our death.
THERESA J. PEDERSON, testimony, U.S. House Interior subcommittee, 25 April 1977

14 Tranquilized wilderness—nicely purged of scorpions, ticks, poisonous reptiles, and lethal microorganisms, thank you—has become the biggest theme park of all.
GENE LYONS, *Harper's*, July 1978

15 For many of their keenest supporters, parks are still viewed as the living embodiment of romantic values.
E. MAX NICHOLSON, quoted in *The American Land*, 1979

16 The preservationist is not an elitist who wants to exclude others, notwithstanding popular opinion to the contrary; he is a moralist who wants to convert them. He is concerned about what other people do in the parks not because he is unaware of the diversity of taste in the society, but because he views certain kinds of activity as calculated to undermine the attitudes he believes the parks can, and should, encourage.
JOSEPH SAX, *Mountains without Handrails*, 1980

17 As long as you're on the side of parks, you're on the side of the angels.
ROBERT MOSES, (1888–1981), *New York Times*, 30 July 1981

18 What was a visit [to a park] like 25 years ago, and what is it like now? . . . There is no way to increase the number of quality parks. People go to the parks for quiet, solitude, and the feeling of space.
GARRETT HARDIN, speech, American Association for the Advancement of Science, Washington, D.C., 3 January 1982

19 Designating parks—a static solution to a dynamic problem—is no longer enough to avert mass extinction.
EDWARD C. WOLF, in Lester Brown, *State of the World*, 1988

20 A nature preserve surrounded by police with weapons seems to violate the idea of the preserve and to require funds that would seem impossible to obtain.
DANIEL B. BOTKIN, *Discordant Harmonies*, 1990

99 PESTICIDES
See also   12 CHEMICALS

1 A spray like DDT makes people think of a continent arranged like a manicured garden, but you can't kick nature around that way.
RICHARD H. POUGH, quoted in *New Yorker*, 26 May 1945

2 Under the philosophy that now seems to guide our destinies, nothing must get in the way of the man with the spray gun.
RACHEL CARSON (1907–1964), *Silent Spring*, 1962

3 If Darwin were alive today the insect world would delight and astound him with its impressive verification of his theories of the survival of the fittest. Under the stress of intensive chemical spraying the weaker members of the insect populations are being weeded out. . . . Only the strong and fit remain to defy our efforts to control them.
RACHEL CARSON (1907–1964), *Silent Spring*, 1962

4 [We should] require public justification of any tax-supported [pesticide] control program and insist that this justification contain a clear description of the purposes of the control program, the methods by which it is to be conducted, the hazards inherent in it, and the economic or social gains that justify both costs and hazards.
ROBERT L. RUDD, *Pesticides and the Living Landscape*, 1964

5 I submit that the campaign of false fear against the use of modern pesticides has, is, and will cause deaths and sufferings greater than those of World War II. It has been over 12 years since a major new insecticide has been brought to market and this is due to unnecessary controversy.
LOUIS A. McLEAN, *BioScience*, September 1967

6 The worst residue problem we have to face today is the residue of public opinion left by Rachel Carson's *Silent Spring*.
JAMIE L. WHITTEN, U.S. Representative, testimony, U.S. House Appropriations subcommittee, 1968

7 We cannot say that the continued use of herbicides, insecticides, and other biocides will

lead to the eventual extermination of man. Neither, however, can we afford to rest easily. With uncontrolled use of poisons which have received little or no ecological testing, the future of man on earth cannot be considered secure.

RAYMOND F. DASMANN, "Vital Issues," April 1969

8 "Natural controls" are not automatically "safe controls." Many, in fact, are far from "natural." It would be disastrous to unleash these control agents, as we did the synthetic chemical pesticides, without knowing exactly what we were doing.

FRANK GRAHAM, *Since Silent Spring*, 1970

9 DDT is one of the safest pesticides being used.

JAMES M. BROWN, National Cotton Council of America, letter, *American Way*, June 1970

10 DDT, because it is a name popularly known to most segments of the public, has been the first target. Once that is accomplished, the so-called ecologists will work on hydrocarbons, then organo-phosphates, carbamates, weed killers and, perhaps, even fertilizers will come under the assault of their barrage of misinformation.

NORMAN BORLAUG, *U.S. News and World Report*, 1 November 1971

11 The poisoned mouse eliminates the useful
   owl and vulture,
But the growing world economy insists on
   monoculture.
O! Science may be phony but the social system's phonier,
And so spread on, insecticide, and sulphate
   of ammonia.

KENNETH E. BOULDING, "The Ballad of Ecological Awareness" in M. Taghi Farvar and John P. Milton, eds., *The Careless Technology*, 1972

12 By undiscriminating use of strong insecticide
Our temporary gain is lost when all our
   friends have died.

KENNETH E. BOULDING, "The Ballad of Ecological Awareness" in M. Taghi Farvar and John P. Milton, eds., *The Careless Technology*, 1972

13 The atomic bomb of the insect world.

JAMES WHORTON, on DDT, *Before Silent Spring*, 1974

14 There can certainly be no letup by man in his fight against insidious, fecund adversaries; it is a fight for our own survival. But man's manipulations in this field must be increasingly careful and precise.

ANTHONY HUXLEY, on agricultural pests, *Plant and Planet*, 1975

15 A virtual army of insecticide salesmen have in some parts of the country, not all, practically replaced the traditional dependence of the farmer on his university, their researchers, and the Extension Service, for their advice. A highly efficient pest control advisory system is needed, independent of insecticide salesmen and the insecticide industry.

CARL B. HUFFAKER, speech, U.S. Environmental Protection Agency seminar on integrated pest management, 16 March 1977

16 The greatest absurdity in contemporary pest control is the dominant role of the pesticide salesman who simultaneously acts as diagnostician, therapist, nostrum prescriber, and pill peddler. It is difficult to imagine any situation where society entrusts so great a responsibility to such poorly qualified persons.

ROBERT VAN DEN BOSCH, *The Pesticide Conspiracy*, 1978

17 Integrated pest management can cut pesticide requirements by half or more while providing adequate protection for crops.

WORLD RESOURCES INSTITUTE, *World Resources Report*, 1988–1989

18 To the average British farmer, organic farming is about as relevant as cavier and a flight on Concorde.

OLIVER WALSTON, *The Observer*, 15 January 1989

100 PLANNING, FORESIGHT
See also   53 FUTURE

1 No Amount of Planning Will Ever Replace Dumb Luck

ANONYMOUS, OFFICE SIGN

2 Where there is no vision, the people perish.
BIBLE, Proverbs 29:18

3 If you plan for a year, plant rice. If you plan for ten years, plant trees. If you plan for 100 years, educate your children.
CHINESE PROVERB

4 Plans are the dreams of the wise.
GERMAN PROVERB

5 Who plans the planners?
JUVENAL (A.D. 60–c. 130), paraphrased in *Saturday Review*, 26 July 1975. The original is "Who will guard the guards?"

6 Make no little plans, they have no power to stir men's souls.
DANIEL H. BURNHAM (1846–1912), quoted in Charles Moore, *Daniel H. Burnham*, 1921

7 Man has lost the capacity to foresee and to forestall. He will end by destroying the earth.
ALBERT SCHWEITZER (1875–1965), quoted in James Brabazon, *Albert Schweitzer*, 1975

8 We of the genus *Homo* ride the logs that float down the Round River, and by a little judicious "burling" we have learned to guide their direction and speed. This feat entitles us to the specific appellation *sapiens*. The technique of burling is called economics, the remembering of old routes is called history, the selection of new ones is called statesmanship, the conversation about oncoming riffles and rapids is called politics. Some of the crew aspire to burl not only their own logs, but the whole flotilla as well. This collective bargaining with nature is called national planning.
ALDO LEOPOLD (1886–1948), *Round River*, 1953

9 As we watch the sun go down, evening after evening, through the smog across the poisoned waters of our native earth, we must ask ourselves seriously whether we really wish some future universal historian on another planet to say about us: "With all their genius and with all their skill, they ran out of foresight and air and food and water and ideas," or, "They went on playing politics until their world collapsed around them."
U THANT (1909–1974), speech, 1970

10 Also there was considerable distrust of planning in any form. Planning was something the government was going to do to you. The

way people in democracies think of the government as something different from themselves is a real handicap. And, of course, sometimes the government confirms their opinion, unfortunately.
LEWIS MUMFORD, in Anne Chisholm, *Philosophers of the Earth: Conversations with Ecologists*, 1972

11 To the extent that the complex interaction of economic, ecological, social, and political factors makes prediction hazardous, the best prophets are those who allow for uncertainty: who do not sell the future like a patent medicine but persuade mankind to make continual running adjustments to what, after all, is a continually changing future.
RUDOLF KLEIN, *Commentary*, June 1972

12 We look to government to weigh the immediate against the distant, but our government is desperately short of people with the training and the vision to make such judgments.
ANTHONY LEWIS, *New York Times*, 13 January 1975

13 Truly long-range planning is no longer a luxury but a critical necessity [but a formidable obstacle to managing problems created by technology is] the pervasive tendency to discount the future.
HAROLD A. LINSTONE, speech, World Future Society, June 1975

14 Maybe we need to sit down quietly and make a list of our social goals, and of the industries and public services that should be enlarged, encouraged, or modified in order to reach these goals. . . . If long-term needs are not fed into the planning process now, more large cars, more nuclear and coal-burning power plants, more highways, more defense weapons and more consumption for the short term may result. We will follow the natural process of going in known directions because they are familiar—even if such actions are unwise and short-sighted.
JOANNA UNDERWOOD, *New York Times*, 7 June 1975

15 To preplan too thoroughly is to kill life.
PAUL GOODMAN (1911–1972), in Taylor Stoehr, ed., *Drawing the Line*, 1977

16 A planner can neither improve things nor make them much worse.
GEORGE KONRAD, *The City Builder*, 1977

17 We must re-myth our world! Lewis Mumford
   has observed that humanity dreams itself
   into existence. Our old dream has become a
   nightmare; we must dream a better dream.
      ELIZABETH DODSON GRAY, *Green Paradise Lost*,
      1979

18 At its best, Muddling Through recognizes
   that we are not really all that good at divining
   long-term, comprehensive solutions to problems—there are too many variables and im-
   ponderables involved. Instead we make
   admittedly incomplete, imperfect decisions,
   followed up by almost constant, incremental
   midcourse corrections. It is essentially how
   we run this country, for all our talk about
   long-range planning.
      TOM HORTON, *Bay Country*, 1987

19 Prophets, false or true, are inevitably odd-
   balls. There's not much need for prophets
   who are in synch with their society.
      BILL MCKIBBEN, *The End of Nature*, 1989

20 If we can't predict next year's economy, what
   is the point in trying to anticipate the fate of
   nature a century hence?
      DAVID WESTERN, *Conservation for the 21st Cen-
      tury*, 1989

21 The ability to anticipate and prevent environmental damage will require that the ecological dimensions of policy be considered at the
   same time as economic, trade, energy, agricultural and other dimensions.
      GRO HARLEM BRUNDTLAND, Prime Minister of
      Norway, *Ms.*, January 1988

22 What America does not do well is anticipate
   and avoid problems. Unfortunately, many
   environmental phenomena involve thresholds that, when passed, cause damage that is
   essentially irreversible. If we wait until the
   damage occurs and then respond, it will be
   too late.
      DENIS HAYES, speech, Museum of Natural
      History, New York City, 8 November 1989

101 PLANNING, LAND USE
See also   77 LAND USE, 95 OPEN SPACE

1 Town planning has now become a sort of
   dumping ground for every difficult and unre-
   solved problem such as the birth-rate, the so-

cial equilibrium, alcoholism, crime, the
morale of the great city, civic affairs and so
forth.
   LE CORBUSIER (1887–1965), *The City of Tomorrow and Its Planning*, 1929

2 Planning has become a fetish which in too
   many instances is carried to extremes, with
   little or no consideration given to the consti-
   tutionally ordained rights of property owners, or to the possible lack of judgment and
   vision of the temporary planners.
      JOHN BELL, chief justice, Supreme Court of
      Pennsylvania, *Valley Hills Civic Association
      v. Board of Adjustment of Tredyffrin Township*,
      1964

3 The planner really is not sure what he is or
   what he wants to be. Unlike his brothers in
   medicine, law, and engineering, he not only
   does not have a defined status, he is not himself able to provide a definition. Is he a sociol-
   ogist, an architect, a geographer, a landscape
   architect, a land economist? Or, more accurately, is each of these a "planner" because
   he deals with design or with land values, demography, or social ecology?
      RICHARD F. BABCOCK, *The Zoning Game*, 1966

4 Planners! No matter how you fudge it
   A Plan's no good without a budget,
   And budgets don't grow very well
   Without the power to tax or sell.
      KENNETH E. BOULDING, in Frank F. Darling
      and John P. Milton, eds., *Future Environ-
      ments of North America*, 1966

5 It is ironic that this [urban] disorganization
   and sprawl should have been co-terminous
   with the very period in which urban planning has bloomed, in the number of practitio-
   ners, in the amount of funds expended and
   in the powers and means of control available.
   It is not unfair, therefore, to question
   whether planning is not partially a cause for
   our present troubles, rather than merely a response to them.
      JERRY LLOYD, quoted in Richard F. Babcock,
      The Zoning Game, 1966

6 A city does not hire a planner until it decides
   it does not want anyone else in the city.
      WILLIAM WHEATON, quoted in Richard F.
      Babcock, *The Zoning Game*, 1966

7 Planning is an attempt to improve the making of decisions. Without it, in many bur-

geoning regional areas in this country with governmental and quasi-public agencies under severe and mounting pressures from population growth and financial stringency, the policy-formulating process may well become what one of my friends calls an exercise in pure and applied chaos.

COLEMAN WOODBURY, in Frank F. Darling and John P. Milton, eds., *Future Environments of North America*, 1966

8 The rapid and extreme growth which overruns communities leaves little time for these communities to plan effectively for that growth. We get little planning, very little citizen participation in the planning process, and a total failure to implement or administer planning with proper police power regulations. . . . We are developing "spread city"—it is neither city, suburban or rural, it is just an amorphous spread.

ROBERT H. FREILICH, testimony, U.S. Congressional Joint Economic subcommittee, 13 May 1971

9 The essential need is not for an ecological movement, but rather a movement that once and for all recognizes the need for planning. . . . And this means getting beyond the present consumerist stage, in which a box of low-enzyme soap suds is equated with ecological reform. The historic animosity for planning in America, the irrational linkage of any attempt at the regulation of people with a communist conspiracy, or at the very least, an affront on the free enterprise system has resulted in the special American problem of overdevelopment.

LOUIS HOROWITZ, in Ravindra S. Khare et al., eds., *Environmental Quality and Social Responsibility*, 1972

10 We've developed some linear cities in this country, and they look like hell. I think we will have to allow for a more disorderly, humanistic, organic process.

WILLIAM K. REILLY, speech, American Association for the Advancement of Science, San Francisco, February 1974

11 The planner's first consideration in formulating strategies for managing change should be that of insuring that serious carrying capacity failures or breakdowns do not occur. This will involve guarding against resource short-ages and depletions; wasteful and extravagent consumption; the unwarranted siting and distribution of population, commercial, and industrial centers; congestion and inefficiency in transportation and other distribution and delivery systems; pollution levels that virtually eliminate the capacity of environmental media to safely assimilate additional pollutants; and the lack or inability of institutional means to augment, mobilize, and redirect resources on short notice and to prevent sporadic shortfalls from reaching crisis proportions.

A. BERRY CRAWFORD and A. BRUCE BISHOP, speech, American Association for the Advancement of Science, 1 March 1974

12 If the planners really get hold of us so that they can stamp out all individual liberty and do what they like with our land, they might decide that whole counties full of inferior farms should be put back into forest.

PAUL COLINVAUX, *Why Big Fierce Animals Are Rare*, 1978

---

102 PLANTS

See also   139 WILDLIFE

---

1 Plants are created for the sake of animals, and the animals for the sake of men; the tame for our use and provision; the wild, at least for the greater part, for our provision also, or for some other advantageous purpose, as furnishing us with clothes, and the like.

ARISTOTLE, (384–322 B.C.), *Politics*

2 O, mickle is the powerful grace that lies
in herbs, plant, stones, and their true qualities:
For nought so vile that on the earth doth live
But to the earth some special good doth give.

WILLIAM SHAKESPEARE (1564–1616), *Romeo and Juliet*, 2.3.15, 1595. "Mickle" means "much."

3 Plants are the young of the world, vessels of health and vigor; but they grope ever upward towards consciousness; the trees are imperfect men, and seem to bemoan their imprisonment, rooted in the ground.

RALPH WALDO EMERSON (1803–1882), *Essays, Second Series*, 1844

4 They tell us that plants are not like man immortal, but are perishable—soul-less. I think
that this is something that we know exactly
nothing about.
  JOHN MUIR (1838–1914), *Journal* (autumn
  1867) John Muir Papers, Yosemite National
  Park

5 When I discovered a new plant, I sat down
beside it for a minute or a day, to make its
acquaintance and hear what it had to
tell. . . . I asked the boulders I met, whence
they came and whither they were going.
  JOHN MUIR (1838–1914), *Overland Monthly*,
  August 1873

6 What is a weed? A plant whose virtues have
not yet been discovered.
  RALPH WALDO EMERSON (1803–1882), *Fortune
  of the Republic*, 1878

7 The unlimited capacity of the plant world to
sustain man at his highest is a region as yet
unexplored by modern science.
  MOHANDAS K. GANDHI (1869–1948), quoted
  in Anthony Huxley, *Plant and Planet*, 1975

8 The earth's vegetation is part of a web of life
in which there are intimate and essential relations between plants and the earth, between
plants and other plants, between plants and
animals. Sometimes we have no choice but to
disturb these relationships, but we should do
so thoughtfully, with full awareness that
what we do may have consequences remote
in time and place.
  RACHEL CARSON (1907–1964), *Silent Spring*,
  1962

9 A root, a stem, a leaf, some means of capturing sunlight and air and making food—in
sum, a plant. The green substance of this
earth, the chlorophyll, is all summed up in
the plants. Without them we perish, all of us
who are flesh and blood.
  HAL BORLAND, *Our Natural World*, 1969

10 [Plants should be regarded as] jewels in the
devalued currency of our world environment.
  UBERTO TOSCO, *The World of Wildflowers and
  Trees*, 1973

11 The tallgrass prairie dazzles the eye with an
unending array of blooming plants, and this
spectacle, with some seventeen new species

coming into bloom each week, lasts from
March until October. The tallgrasses themselves, big bluestem, indiangrass, switch-
grass, and cordgrass, to name the common
ones, are the most powerful, the most expan-
sive, the most majestic of all the prairie
plants; they are the redwoods of the prairie.
  PATRICIA D. DUNCAN, *Tallgrass Prairie*, 1978

12 [Plants] are superb opportunists, making the
most of different combinations of water, air,
soil, and climate. Their grip on the planet,
their capacities for colonization, and their integration with the environment are due to an
astounding diversification and variety.
  ANTHONY HUXLEY, *Plant and Planet*, 1975

13 If man wholly or partly destroys himself, the
probability is that most natural vegetable life
will survive. Plants are essentially resilient.
. . . The potential revenge of the vegetable
kingdom would cover and disintegrate our
cities as it has in the past choked the once-
splendid towns and temples of Central
America and Asia, forcing apart our fabrica-
tions with the inexorable penetration and
swelling of their roots.
  ANTHONY HUXLEY, *Plant and Planet*, 1975

14 There are no idealists in the plant world and
no compassion. The rose and the morning
glory know no mercy. Bindweed, the morning glory, will quickly choke its competitors
to death, and the fencerow rose will just as
quietly crowd out any other plant that tried to
share its roothold. Idealism and mercy are
human terms and human concepts.
  HAL BORLAND, *Book of Days*, 22 July 1976

15 I do not know of a flowering plant that tastes
good and is poisonous. Nature is not out to
get you.
  EUELL GIBBONS, quoted in *Newsweek*, 12 January 1976

16 There is *no* plant that is unimportant. The
genetic information contained in the germ
plasm of each species is unique and cannot be
reproduced once the last living tissue is gone.
  EDWARD S. AYENSU, quoted in *Washington
  Post Magazine*, 22 January 1978

17 You may not ever travel to Maine to see the
Furbish lousewort. But the weeds in any
patch of natural vegetation issue the same

challenge. We have survived, say the weeds, since the Cretaceous. Man is a mere novice in evolution compared with us. He hasn't yet learnt the secret of the weeds: how to create fail-safe communities.

ERIC ASHBY, *Environmental Science and Technology*, October 1980

18 When I got to be 70, I thought, I'm going to take time to do what I really yearn to do, and that is work with native plants, wildflowers and trees, and encourage their use in the nation's landscape so they won't just be something of the past but will be passed on to our grandchildren.

LADY BIRD JOHNSON, quoted in *Good Housekeeping*, February 1988

19 Flowers in a city are like lipstick on a woman—it just makes you look better to have a little color.

LADY BIRD JOHNSON, quoted in *Time*, 9 May 1988

20 Dandelions are the supreme symbol of the failure of human control, a yellow flag of mockery, and every time we burn that flag, back it comes, stronger than ever. No plant or animal is as obstinately perverse in its flaunting of human wishes.

DAVID EHRENFELD, *Orion*, Winter 1990

21 Since you're human,
don't forget:
it's not people who give
pure, sweet water to plants—
it's the black-wet-bland soil
does that.
Since you're human. . .

MAKOTO OOKA, quoted in *Japan Environment Monitor*, no. 1, 30 April 1991

103 POLITICS
See also   14 CITIZEN ACTION,
56 GOVERNMENT

1 Government is nothing but the balance of the natural elements of a country.

JOSE MARTI (1853–1895), *Our America*, 1891

2 You can't be suspicious of a tree, or accuse a bird or a squirrel of subversion or challenge the ideology of a violet.

HAL BORLAND, *Sundial of the Seasons*, 1964

3 The urbanists say—understandably—that before we can achieve ecological solutions, we must first find solutions to the problems of men. However, to wait for the advent of social nirvana while mankind's habitat is destroyed is no solution either. This is not a world which will permit us the luxury of solving our problems one at a time.

ALAN GUSSOW, *Open Space Action*, May–June 1969

4 We've got a program to invent a new name for ecology, so we can keep it alive after it's been talked to death. We're thinking of calling it politics.

HARVEY WHEELER, quoted in *Newsweek*, 26 January 1970

5 Unanimity raises the danger of a new kind of pollution—a form of pollution that may be the greatest threat of all—political pollution. It could undermine all the concern that has been focused and mobilized in this new movement. When you find Nixon, Rockefeller, and Reagan on your side, you know you're in trouble.

RICHARD L. OTTINGER, U.S. Representative, speech, Sarah Lawrence College, 22 April 1970

6 It's a characteristic of environmental problems that, because they affect such large masses of people, their real threshing-ground is the arena of legislation and politics. So their solution inevitably depends heavily on the extent to which the enthusiasm of Earth Day can be annealed into the energies of many election days.

GLADWIN HILL, *New York Times*, 26 April 1970

7 The common justification of the environmentalists' technique of deliberate exaggeration is the claim that it is necessary to stir people up to get things done. But Aesop knew what happened to shepherd boys who cried wolf too often. People are easily anesthetized by overstatement, and there is a danger that the environmental movement will fall flat on its face when it is most needed, simply because it has pitched its tale too strongly.

JOHN MADDOX, *The Doomsday Syndrome*, 1972

8 Environment is one-tenth science and nine-tenths politics.
   ANONYMOUS BRITISH DELEGATE, U.N. Conference on Human Environment, Stockholm, June 1972

9 One question, then, is whether we can find a peacetime equivalent of war; that is, something short of disaster which can serve as an incentive to take difficult action for the common good. The new issues—food, raw materials, energy—have brought us to a new kind of politics: a politics of what might be called resource constraints. . . . There is already some serious questioning about whether a democratic society can do so.
   ELIZABETH DREW, New Yorker, 21 July 1975

10 Americans have always achieved marvels of engineering—in water storage, in highway building, in automobiles, in skyscrapers, in airplanes. . . . [D]espite occasional droughts, despite hit lists, despite environmental objections, the West will grow and water will be found to make the growth possible. The only real issue . . . is how and where it will grow, and that depends on two things: politicians and power.
   A. LICHTENSTEIN, San Francisco Sunday Examiner and Chronicle, 3 September 1978

11 Conservatism has been ill-served by the propensity of its leading spokesmen for gratuitous scorn of almost any concern over the degradation of the natural environment.
   R. V. YOUNG, JR., Environmental Ethics, Autumn 1979

12 We already have a fundamental and long-standing mechanism for weighing the benefits and costs of decisions—the democratic and representative political process. It involves collective choice with a capacity for self-correction over time.
   RICHARD N. L. ANDREWS, speech, Chicago, 15 October 1980

13 The politics of the future will be genetic politics, in which the human species—through its actions, its public and private institutions—will manage extinction and survival.
   WALT ANDERSON, Cry California, Summer 1981

14 There are some poeple who will never be brought around to my philosophy. And I pray I never yield to their positions. They are wrong.
   JAMES G. WATT, quoted in Time, 23 August 1982

15 [Vice President George Bush's] fingerprints are all over this [Reagan] administration's anti-environmental record.
   EDWARD J. MARKEY, U.S. Representative, letter, Washington Post, 8 September 1988

16 I would be a Republican president in the Teddy Roosevelt tradition. A conservationist. An environmentalist.
   GEORGE BUSH, campaign statement, Sierra, November–December 1988

17 While one can argue that politics is not the concern of conservationists, the reality is that resource scarcity is often the source of instability. Resources are a political issue, just as politics is a resource issue.
   DAVID WESTERN, Conservation for the 21st Century, 1989

18 All our leaders now call themselves environmentalists. But their brand of environmentalism poses very few challenges to the present system. Instead they propose to spruce up the planet with a few technical fixes or individual lifestyle changes: scrubbers on coal plants, eating "all-natural" cereals, and so on.
   IVAN ILLICH, New Perspectives Quarterly, Spring 1989

19 Japan's green movement is beginning to take a new direction. People now realize that opening one's own shell is opening the world, and that being able to open the world is dependent upon whether or not one can open oneself. Here, in particular, is where we find participation in the green movement by people involved in spiritualism and shamanism.
   OE MASANORI, Japan Environment Monitor 2, no. 10, 31 March 1989

20 There is in fact a "hard path" and a "soft path" in environmental politics. The soft path is the easy one; it accepts the private corporate governance of production decisions and seeks only to regulate the resultant environmental impact. (And free to do so, the corpo-

rations have invariably chosen the "hard" technologies, which are so impervious to environmental control.) In environmental politics, the hard path is the difficult one; it would confront the real source of environmental degradation—the technological choice—and debate who should govern it, and for what purpose. The hard political path is the only workable route to the soft environmental path.

BARRY COMMONER, *Making Peace with the Planet*, 1990

21 Unfortunately, the primary cost of environmental politics is that it has built itself on an adversarial basis. Using fear, simplification, an antiscience viewpoint, and a focus on the environment above all other issues, it pits the environment against other needs—exactly the opposite of what needs to be done.

PAUL L. BUSCH, *Environmental Science and Technology*, April 1990

22 When the media all jump feet first, on cue, into the coordinated manipulation of public opinion, as with this week of environmental "concern," they are doing something rather different from just covering the news. And one result is the reduction of complex issues to a pudding of trendy simplifications and synthetic anxiety and indignation.

GEORGE F. WILL, *Washington Post*, 19 April 1990

23 Environmental politics, at least at the national level, is in as sad a shape as the environment itself. I wish it was a Republican phenomenon, but sadly it is not. It's a bipartisan environmental disaster.

JIM HIGHTOWER, former Texas agriculture commissioner, speech, conference hosted by *Utne Reader*, Minneapolis, May 1990

24 We have a fundamental problem. We haven't come up with political institutions that take the long view of serious problems. The car is a major cause of the deficit and of global warming and air pollution. Any serious attempt to deal with these problems will be painful. Trouble is, we just don't have the political mechanisms to impose pain on citizens in a democratic society.

MICHAEL WALSH, *Greenpeace*, May–June 1990

25 Twenty years ago it might have been a triumph to have a governor unafraid to call himself an environmentalist. In 1990, that's the minimum qualification for the job.

JOHN K. VAN DE KAMP, *EcoSource*, June 1990

26 Farmland preservationists felt compelled to provide a crisis scenario and searched for shocking statistics because anything less would not move the sluggish political system. This inability of the political system to respond to problems in the making remains one of the troubling lessons of the farmland preservation experience.

TIM LEHMAN, *Environmental History Review*, Spring–Summer 1990

27 Conservation must replace consumption as the driving force of our economy. We can only take and use what we really need; ecological green politics is about "enough," not "more and more."

PETRA K. KELLY, *Fletcher Forum of World Affairs* 14, no. 2, Summer 1990

28 Rather than rational policy analysis, the making of natural resource and environmental policy in the United States has become an exercise in theological controversy.

ROBERT H. NELSON, *Policy Review*, Summer 1990

29 Traditionally we have thought of the political spectrum as ranging from the left to right, relating to ideas about the centralization of power in the state versus the delegation of such power to the individual. . . . [The] political spectrum is now defined by environmental protection at one end and economic development at the other. There is, I believe, much truth to this view. The green parties of Europe are in the vanguard. As yet, in the United States this separation has not taken place as both political parties color themselves pale green.

ROBERT M. WHITE, *The Bridge*, Summer 1990

30 EPA is caught in the middle of endless cross fire between complaining industries and environmentalists.

MICHAEL MCCLOSKEY, *EPA Journal*, September–October 1990

31 Our increasingly complex environmental problems seem to be stuck in a traffic jam, with everyone honking horns from all sides.

FRANK POPOFF, *EPA Journal*, September–October 1990

32 The ecology movement is being poisoned by becoming part of politics. Once it goes into the political system, ecology becomes the enemy of other parties, instead of inspiring them from the outside as we do [now].

JACQUES COUSTEAU, *Christian Science Monitor,* 10 October 1990

33 The conservation movement has been too genteel. We have to learn from some of the junkyard dog tactics of other [political action committees]—that you define yourself by who you support and who you oppose.

BRUCE A. BABBITT, quoted in *Washington Post,* 10 February 1991

34 Green politics must put itself to the vote in the USA and become a political factor in all elections at all levels. Greens must field credible and competent candidates. There is a desperate need to expose the long-term societal failures of Democrats and Republicans alike in the USA. They have brought us to the brink of disaster. Greens must offer a clear and credible political alternative to American voters.

PETRA K. KELLY, *Greenpeace,* July–August 1991

104 POLLUTION

See also   6 AIR POLLUTION, 91 OCEAN POLLUTION, 105 POLLUTION CONTROL, 106 POLLUTION PREVENTION, 135 WATER POLLUTION

1 Here in the United States we turn our rivers and streams into sewers and dumping-grounds, we pollute the air, we destroy forests, and exterminate fishes, birds, and mammals—not to speak of vulgarizing charming landscapes with hideous advertisements. But at last it looks as if our people were awakening.

THEODORE ROOSEVELT (1858–1919), *The Outlook,* 25 January 1913

2 I think the whole vast subject of pollution, of which this gypsy moth business is just a small part, is of the utmost interest and concern to everybody. It starts in the kitchen and extends to Jupiter and Mars. Always some special group or interest is represented, never the earth itself.

E. B. WHITE (1899–1985), 1958, quoted in Frank Graham, Jr., *Since Silent Spring,* 1970

3 In the last few decades entire new categories of waste have come to plague and menace the American scene. . . . Pollution is growing at a rapid rate. . . . Pollution destroys beauty and menaces health. It cuts down on efficiency, reduces property values and raises taxes. . . . A prime national goal must be an environment that is pleasing to the senses and healthy to live in.

LYNDON B. JOHNSON (1908–1973), special message to Congress on conservation and restoration of natural beauty, 8 February 1965.

4 The environment is a complex, subtly balanced system, and it is this integrated whole which received the impact of all the separate insults inflicted by the pollutants. Never before in the history of this planet has its thin life-supporting surface been subjected to such diverse, novel, and potent agents. I believe the cumulative effects of these pollutants, their interactions and amplifications, can be fatal to the complex fabric of the biosphere.

BARRY COMMONER, *Science and Survival,* 1966

5 Pollution is the undesirable change in the physical, chemical or biological characteristics of our air, land, and water that may or will harmfully affect human life or that of other desirable species, our industrial processes, living conditions, or cultural assets; or that may or will waste or deteriorate our raw material resources.

NATIONAL ACADEMY OF SCIENCES, National Research Council, *Waste Management and Control,* 1966

6 The air and water grow heavier with the debris of our spectacular civilization.

LYNDON B. JOHNSON (1908–1973), message to Congress, 30 January 1967

7 Unfortunately, these separate insults to the system do not impinge on one individual one at a time; they occur all at once. While the individual may be able to adapt to slightly polluted water, or air, or food, he probably cannot adapt to the collective onset of all of

them. And if he is subjected at the same time to slum housing, crowding, noise, and other urban environmental stresses, he will find life altogether unbearable.

WILBUR COHEN, colloquium, U.S. Congress, 1968

8 Practical problems that persist and accumulate in cities are symptoms of arrested development. The point is seldom admitted. It has become conventional, for instance, to blame congested and excessive automobile traffic, air pollution, water pollution and noise upon "rapid technological progress." But the automobiles, the fumes, the sewage and the noise are not new, and the persistently unsolved problems they afford only demonstrate lack of progress. Many evils conventionally blamed upon progress are, rather, evils of stagnation.

JANE JACOBS, The Economy of Cities, 1969

9 A new generation is being raised—with DDT in their fat, carbon monoxide in their systems and lead in their bones. That is technological man.

BARRY COMMONER, quoted in New York Times, 3 August 1969

10 The environment must be perceived as a single, interrelated system. . . . A single source may pollute the air with smoke and chemicals, the land with solid wastes, and a river or lake with chemical and other wastes. . . . Similarly, some pollutants—chemicals, radiation, pesticides—appear in all media.

ASH COUNCIL (Federal Advisory Council on Executive Reorganization), Reorganization Plan no. 3, 1970

11 Pollution is a crime compounded of ignorance and avarice.

LORD RITCHIE-CALDER, Foreign Affairs, January 1970

12 A circular future means that we cannot escape from whatever it is that we do here and now. Life is not linear, it is round. If we pollute the Earth and others do the same, the pollution will come up over the horizon one day and destroy us.

ALAN GUSSOW, speech, New York City, 22 April 1970

13 In boundless gratitude for all this wealth, O gods of plenty, profit, and convenience, we lay at your feet a hundred billion cans of beer and bottles of Coke, sixty billion plastic containers and paper wrappings, ninety billion tons of raw sewage, and enough lethal chemicals in air and water to kill legions of animals and to invade our lungs with deadly gases and our blood with deadly poisons.

MARYA MANNES, speech, New York City, 22 April 1970

14 Pollution can be said to be the result of multiplying three factors: population size, per capita consumption, and an "environmental impact" index that measures, in part, how wisely we apply the technology that goes with consumption.

PAUL EHRLICH and JOHN HOLDREN, Saturday Review, 4 July 1970

15 It is a sick society that can beat and murder black people in the streets, butcher thousands of people in Vietnam, spend billions of dollars on arms to destroy mankind, and then come to the conclusion that pollution is America's number one problem.

ANONYMOUS BLACK PANTHER, quoted in Norman J. Faramelli, New World Outlook, 1972

16 Pollution will do for the study of ecology what cancer did for molecular biology.

EDWARD O. WILSON, in Anne Chisholm, Philosophers of the Earth: Conversations with Ecologists, 1972

17 Instead of worrying about deadlines for man's extinction, we should give immediate thought to a closer danger: adaptation. The horror is not only that we are killing the land and possibly ourselves, but that we calmly adapt to it, often without even a fight. . . . Because adaptation to pollution is made in small fits, we see each giving-in as only a minor loss.

COLMAN MCCARTHY, quoted in Reader's Digest, August 1972

18 The classical definition of dirt is "matter in the wrong place"; pollution is simply the process of putting matter in such a place in quantities that are too large.

JOHN PASSMORE, Man's Responsibility for Nature, 1974

19 Pollution is so bad in New York that I saw the Statue of Liberty holding her nose.

JACKIE "MOMS" MABLEY, quoted in Black Star, May 1976

20 If the appropriate sanitation services are not provided, the counterpart of increasing opulence will be deepening filth.

JOHN KENNETH GALBRAITH, *The Affluent Society*, 1976

21 As in a quiet backwater, pollution collects in the stratosphere and no rain washes it away.

LOUISE YOUNG, *Earth's Aura*, 1977

22 Mother Nature herself is a polluter. . . . Studies of radiation effects almost uniformly conclude that man-made emissions are dwarfed by those produced by Sol. . . . [N]atural pollution has long been the dirty little secret of environmentalism.

WALL STREET JOURNAL, editorial, 3 August 1978

23 If present trends continue, the world in 2000 will be less crowded (though more populated), less polluted, more stable ecologically, and less vulnerable to resource-supply disruption than the world we live in now.

JULIAN SIMON and HERMANN KAHN, *The Resourceful Earth*, 1984

24 Pollution doesn't carry a passport.

THOMAS MCMILLAN, Canadian environment minister, quoted in *Christian Science Monitor*, 10 July 1987

25 From the beginning, the impacts of population and consumption have been ignored. . . . [T]here is no consensus that they are problems, let alone problems in need of solution. So Congress focused on the obvious . . . pollution, which is the least important of the three causes of ecosystem degradation.

ARNOLD REITZE, *Columbia Journal of Environmental Law* 14, no. 1, 1989

26 The solution to pollution is local self-reliance.

DAVID MORRIS, *Utne Reader*, November–December 1989

27 Now your way of life is no longer working, and so you are interested in our way. But if we tell you our way, then it will be polluted, we will have no medicine, and we will be destroyed as well as you.

BUFFALO TIGER, Miccasukee Indian, quoted in Julian Burger, *The Gaia Atlas of First Peoples*, 1990

28 In our country the infernal hell that Dante describes has already appeared on Kiev's Kreshchatik Street, in Yerevan, Alma-Ata, and Frunze—in the majority of republican capitals and in many regional and industrial centers, on the Ring Road and Gorky Street in Moscow. . . . Mother Nature has become tired, is grasping for breath, and with her the people are too. Good can turn into evil.

FEDOR MORGUN, former Soviet environment official, quoted in Eric Green, *Ecology and Perestroika*, 1990

29 When our pollution laws were crafted, they made certain assumptions which have subsequently proven to be partial or even incorrect: First, that pollution-related illnesses were primarily acute. Second, that pollution was essentially local. Third, that pollution tended to be concentrated and came out of smokestacks and pipes. And fourth, when a pollutant moved from one medium to another, we sometimes allowed ourselves to believe we had eliminated it.

WILLIAM K. REILLY, speech, Natural Resources Defense Council, Washington, D.C., 1990

30 The policy of using the environment as a treatment works is known as "dilute" and "disperse." Almost every other developed country now seems to regard it as a nineteenth century anachronism which should be abandonned. . . . Dilute and disperse means out of sight, out of mind. In general, we pollute, others receive. It is part of the story behind Britain's grimy reputation as "Dirty Man of Europe."

CHRIS ROSE, *The Dirty Man of Europe*, 1990

31 And what about the pulp mills creating the paper upon which this chipper little article is printed?

JOHN NICHOLS, *Buzzworm*, September–October 1990

32 From the standpoint of pollution, the market will be no kinder than the old command system. Profit is the top priority, and the environment is considered an investment with no return.

SPARTAK G. AKHMETOV, on the Russian new market system, *New York Times*, 11 November 1990

33 The greed of the rich is often the root cause of serious pollution problems. In such cases we can only pray "God do not forgive them, for they know what they do."

MONKO SWAMINATHAN, *New York Times,* 29 November 1990

105 POLLUTION CONTROL

1 Smoke and noise—so easy to overcome—will [by 1976] be held in decent check by legislation.

MORRIS L. ERNST, *Utopia 1976,* 1955

2 I disagree that our environment is being so increasingly polluted because of a technology gap; rather, it is because of a management gap. It is just unreasonable to accept as fact that those technicians who have contrived to make our increasingly complex industrial technology economical cannot also devise means to deal with solid, gaseous, or liquid pollutants in the wastes from their processes. . . . The major sources of polluted waters, ugly refuse heaps, and for a substantial part of the pollution in the atmosphere, are in the management offices of industrial and municipal plants of all descriptions. It simply is so much cheaper and so much less trouble to dump stuff or vent stuff than it is to take care of it, that production management will dump and vent just so long as it can get away with doing it.

BERTRAM C. RAYNES, Rand Development Corporation official, testimony, U.S. House Science and Astronautics subcommittee, 1966

3 Recommendations that children not run to and from school and that events be suspended are not a substitute for reducing pollution.

U.S. SENATE PUBLIC WORKS COMMITTEE, on the inadequacy of local government air-pollution-alert strategies, report, 1970.

4 The 1970's absolutely must be the years when America pays its debt to the past by reclaiming the purity of its air, its waters, and our living environment. It is literally now or never.

RICHARD M. NIXON, 1 January 1970

5 Now, let us say we have a plant that pollutes. The plant produces shirts. We are all paying part of the cost of production in the price we are paying for the shirt. We are also paying part of the cost of production in having our shirt dirtied by the smoke which that plant puts out. If we pay a higher price for the shirt to cover the cost of avoiding pollution, we are reducing the cost we are paying in other forms. The tendency to say that pollution control will make the cost of living higher is wrong. It will make total cost of living lower by making the cost of the things we buy higher but by making the costs imposed on us involuntarily lower.

MILTON FRIEDMAN, on the costs of pollution control, *Chicago Tribune,* 12 April 1970

6 Union Carbide is only the latest in a long line of major companies that have cried wolf at government proposals for pollution control—threatening plant shutdowns and job losses—only to find out later that pollution control wasn't so bad after all. True, there are some major shutdowns being planned, but these can be attributed as easily to the weak economy as to calls for pollution control.

AIR AND WATER NEWS, 12 April 1971

7 When we try to solve environmental problems more quickly than our technology permits, not only do we raise costs suddenly and sharply, but we increase the number of false steps that we take along the way.

MAURICE STANS, Secretary of Commerce, *Reader's Digest,* January 1972

8 [Tall smokestacks used to disperse pollutants are] manifestations of the out-of-sight, out-of-mind mentality of earlier times.

EDMUND S. MUSKIE, U.S. Senator, *Wall Street Journal,* 28 June 1973

9 When someone is chronically ill, the cost of pollution to him is almost infinite.

ANONYMOUS U.S. CONGRESSIONAL STAFF MEMBER, quoted in *Conservation Foundation Letter,* May 1974

10 Decades ago, American companies began developing a new industry based on providing cool air to consumers. We call it the air-conditioning industry. The manufacture of equipment to provide cool air has become a major source of profits, dividends, and jobs. Never

have I heard any industrial leader, economist, or banker refer to the air-conditioning industry as nonproductive. . . . And yet now, when a new industry—formed to manufacture, operate, and maintain equipment to produce *clean* air comes along, it is termed "nonproductive."

RUSSELL PETERSON, speech, United Auto Workers conference, May 1976

11 My experience as an ex-administrator of many of these programs confirms that by far the most difficult areas in which to apply environmental regulation effectively are those where the regulation in question directly affects the individual citizen. . . . One may speculate from this phenomenon that Americans are all for cleaning up pollution as long as someone else does the cleaning up, although I think this is an oversimplification. As good an explanation as any probably lies in the plain cussedness of human nature.

RUSSELL E. TRAIN, The Conservation Foundation, *Conservation and Values*, 1978

12 Pollution controls solve no problem. They only alter the problem, shifting it from one form to another, contrary to this immutable law of nature: the form of matter may be changed, but matter does not disappear. . . . [I]t is apparent that conventional controls, at some point, create more pollution than they remove and consume resources out of proportion to the benefits derived. . . . What emerges is an environmental paradox. It takes resources to remove pollution; pollution removal generates residue; it takes more resources to dispose of this residue and disposal of residue also produces pollution.

JOSEPH LING, former 3M official, quoted in M. G. Royston, *Pollution Prevention Pays*, 1979

13 The inherent complexities of air pollution control make it easy for an opponent to propose language changes which—seemingly innocuous on their face—in fact weaken the law to a serious degree. Lawyers are paid fortunes in Washington for such "creative draftsmanship."

DOUGLAS M. COSTLE, EPA administrator, speech, Air Pollution Control Association, 23 June 1980

14 [The Clean Water Act of 1972] was characterized by a pork-barrel approach, infatuation

with "best available-technology" and utopian standards (zero discharge of pollutants).

JAMES BOVARD, *New York Times*, 10 July 1985

15 We have found that, just as neglect of pollution controls means dirtier air, emphasis on controls can mean cleaner air. Americans are suffering from a man-made phenomenon that can be controlled. We have developed the technologies of control. We have the resources to apply those technologies. All we lack is the political will to do so.

GEORGE MITCHELL, U.S. Senator, quoted in *Washington Post*, 7 October 1988

16 It is the vagueness of Britain's traditional approach to pollution control—sprinkled with concepts such as the Victorian principle of "best practicable means," only now replaced by the equally antediluvian "best available technique not entailing excessive cost"— which has proved a recipe for fudge and smudge, a quagmire of intellectual fuzziness and a licence for administrative laxity, which has allowed the progressive deterioration of the UK environment.

CHRIS ROSE, *The Dirty Man of Europe*, 1990

106 POLLUTION PREVENTION
See also   115 RECYCLING

1 It is much easier to remove the olive from a martini than it is to remove the vermouth, once it has been added. . . . We must rely on prevention rather than decontamination.

IVAN L. BENNETT, JR., testimony, U.S. Senate Public Works subcommittee, 8 February 1967

2 Placing the cost of prevention on industry leads to corporate incentives that chose the most efficient technologies for the original design of industrial plants and consumer products.

RALPH NADER, in John C. Esposito, *Vanishing Air*, 1970

3 If we limit our efforts to the correction of environmental defects, we shall increasingly behave like hunted beasts taking shelter behind an endless succession of protective devices, each more complex and more costly, less dependable and less comfortable than its

predecessors. Today we develop afterburners for automobiles to protect us from air pollution and complicated sewage treatments to purify grossly contaminated water; tomorrow we shall turn to gas masks and to filters on our water faucets. Although technological fixes have transient usefulness, they complicate life and eventually decrease its quality. The ecological crisis will continue to increase in severity if we do not develop positive values integrating human nature and external nature.

RENÉ DUBOS, *A God Within*, 1972

4 Environmental policy is not fully accomplished by warding off imminent hazards and the elimination of damage which has occurred. Precautionary environmental policy requires furthermore that natural resources are protected and demands on them are made with care.

GERMAN FEDERAL REPUBLIC, *Vorsorgeprinzip* (precautionary principle), 1976

5 Conservation is prosaic, even boring. By the same token, "source reduction" or waste minimization isn't an issue that can fire peoples' hearts.

ROBERT STOBAUGH and DANIEL YERGIN, *Energy Future*, 1982

6 But your heart is disposed toward plastic. Someone, no doubt the plastics industry, told you it was convenient. This same industry is now looking into recycling in an attempt to get the critics of their nefarious, multifarious products off their backs. That should make you feel better, because *recycling* has become an honorable word, no longer merely the hobby of Volvo owners. The fact is that people in plastics are born obscurants. Recycling (practically impossible) won't solve the plastic glut, only reduction of production will, and the plastics industry isn't looking into that, you can be sure.

JOY WILLIAMS, *Esquire*, February 1989

7 Pollution often disappears when we switch to renewable resources.

DAVID MORRIS, *Utne Reader*, November–December 1989

8 Wisdom holds that an ounce of prevention is worth a pound of cure. That advice should serve as a cornerstone of our nation's waste

prevention policy in an age of budget constraint.

JAY D. HAIR, quoted in EPA, *Paying for Progress*, 1990

9 What's happening in this country is that there are now new grass-roots environmental organizations that have adopted the philosophy of prevention rather than control. The future of environmental improvement involves prevention, and there are some very serious consequences of making that shift.

BARRY COMMONER, *Orion Nature Quarterly*, Winter 1990

10 [The only real successes have occurred] when the relevant technologies of production have been changed to eliminate a pollutant.

BARRY COMMONER, *Amicus Journal*, Spring 1990

11 What do people mean by environmental protection in our country? Usually, some kind of resuscitation. That's like reducing the entire field of medical science to an ambulance service. Certainly we must improve our dust-scrubbing filters and gas-filtering equipment and treat waste water. But that's not the main thing. The main thing is to develop an attitude of resource husbandry.

NIKOLAI VORONTSOV, Soviet environment official, quoted in *Surviving Together*, Spring 1990

12 Pollution prevention is really a metaphor for restructuring and redesigning global industry. . . . It is best seen as a technical route to industry restructuring, modernizing, rejuvenation, energy conservation, productivity improvement, technological innovation and improved competitiveness.

JOEL HIRSCHHORN, background paper, World Resources Institute symposium, June 1990

13 Pollution prevention is not anti-industry or anti-growth, rather it is a path to achieve environmental objectives and improved industrial efficiency. But a new technical path implies changes that will ultimately produce winners and losers in industry. Companies that use pollution prevention as a catalyst to trigger more comprehensive technological and managerial innovations and improvements will be the winners.

JOEL HIRSCHHORN, background paper, World Resources Institute symposium, June 1990

14 The pivotal strategy for this pivotal era is pollution prevention. Pollution prevention means using materials, processes, practices, or products that reduce or eliminate pollutants.
WILLIAM K. REILLY, *Business Week*, 18 June 1990

15 We have a data base with a thousand examples of companies doing pollution prevention that pays—but we could clearly do the opposite and collect examples of where it doesn't pay.
J. CLARENCE DAVIES, quoted in *The Economist*, 8 September 1990

107 POPULATION
See also   108 POPULATION CONTROL, 109 POPULATION IMPACTS

1 And God said unto them, Be fruitful, and multiply, and replenish the earth, and subdue it.
BIBLE, Genesis 1:28

2 Man pairs and breeds at all seasons.
ARISTOTLE (384–322 B.C.), *History of Animals*

3 After performing the most exact calculation possible . . . I have found that there is scarcely one tenth as many people on the earth as in ancient times. What is surprising is that the population of the earth decreases every day, and if this continues, in another ten centuries the earth will be nothing but a desert.
CHARLES-LOUIS DE MONTESQUIEU (1689–1755), *Persian Letters*, 1721

4 Men multiply like mice in a barn if they have unlimited means of subsistence.
RICHARD CANTILLON (1680?–1734), *Essai sur la nature du commerce en générale*, 1755

5 [T]he population is constant in size and will remain so right up to the end of mankind.
ENCYCLOPÉDIE, 1756

6 Under a perfect government, the inconveniencies of having a family would be so intirely removed, children would be so well taken care of, and every thing become so favourable to populousness, that though some

stickly seasons or dreadful plagues in particular climates might cut off multitudes, yet in general, mankind would encrease so prodigiously, that the earth would at last be overstocked, and become unable to support its numerous inhabitants.
ROBERT WALLACE, *Various Prospects of Mankind, Nature, and Providence*, 1761

7 The power of population is indefinitely greater than the power in the earth to produce subsistence for man. Population, when unchecked, increases in a geometrical ratio. Subsistence only increases in an arithmetical ratio. A slight acquaintance with numbers will show the immensity of the first power in comparison of the second.
THOMAS ROBERT MALTHUS (1766–1834), *An Essay on the Principle of Population*, 1798

8 Increasing population is the most certain possible sign of the happiness and prosperity of a state: but the actual population may be only a sign of the happiness that is past.
THOMAS ROBERT MALTHUS (1766–1834), quoted in Robbins, *The Theory of Economic Development*

9 Misery, up to the extreme point of famine and pestilence, instead of checking, tends to increase population.
SAMUEL LAING (1812–1897), *National Distress*, 1844

10 It is vain to say, that all mouths which the increase of mankind calls into existence, bring with them hands. The new mouths require as much food as the old ones, and the hands do not produce as much.
JOHN STUART MILL (1806–1873), *Principles of Political Economy*, 1848

11 There is no exception to the rule that every organic being naturally increases at so high a rate, that, if not destroyed, the earth would soon be covered by the progeny of a single pair. Even slow-breeding man has doubled in twenty-five years, and at this rate, in less than a thousand years, there would literally not be standing-room for his progeny.
CHARLES DARWIN (1809–1882), *The Origin of Species*, 1859

12 Each organic being is striving to increase in a geometrical ratio . . . each at some period of

its life, during some season of the year, during each generation or at intervals, has to struggle for life and to suffer great destruction. . . . The vigorous, the healthy, and the happy survive and multiply.

CHARLES DARWIN (1809–1882), *On the Origin of Species*, 1859

13 The political problem of problems is how to deal with overpopulation, and it faces us on all sides.

THOMAS H. HUXLEY (1825–1895), *Government*, 1890

14 Malthusian, *adj.* Pertaining to Malthus and his doctrines. Malthus believed in artificially limiting population, but found that it could not be done by talking.

AMBROSE BIERCE (1842–1914?), *The Devil's Dictionary*, 1906

15 Why should the greatest *number* be preferred? Why not the greatest good of the most intelligent and most highly developed? The greatest good of a minority of our generation may be the greatest good of the greatest number in the long run.

OLIVER WENDELL HOLMES, JR. (1841–1935), c. 1910, quoted in Sheldon M. Novick, *Honorable Justice*, 1989

16 Behind all war has been the pressure of population . . . let countries become overpopulated and war is inevitable. It follows as daylight follows the sunrise.

MARGARET SANGER (1879–1966), *Women and the New Race*, 1920

17 Over-population . . . is a mechanism which has created conditions favourable to the survival of the unfit and the elimination of the fit.

WILLIAM RALPH INGE (1860–1954), *Outspoken Essays*, 1922

18 The command "Be fruitful and multiply" was promulgated, according to our authorities, when the population of the world consisted of two people.

WILLIAM RALPH INGE (1860–1954), *More Lay Thoughts of a Dean*, 1931

19 The bird of war is not the eagle but the stork.

CHARLES F. POTTER, attributed, 1931

20 Today the problem is how to get a people to abstain from not reproducing itself.

GUNNAR MYRDAL, on the falling birth rate of industrialized countries, *Population: A Problem for Democracy*, 1940

21 There is an old saying here that a man must do three things during life: plant trees, write books and have sons. I wish they would plant more trees and write more books.

LUIS MUÑOZ MARIN, quoted in *Time*, 23 June 1958

22 It surely must be a confession of complete failure on the part of our civilization and the Western way of life if in fact we admit that we want fewer people in this world.

LORD WALSTON, speech, House of Lords, 6 June 1962

23 We have been God-like in our planned breeding of our domesticated plants and animals, but we have been rabbit-like in our unplanned breeding of ourselves.

ARNOLD TOYNBEE (1889–1975), *National Observer*, 10 June 1963

24 Instead of needing lots of children, we need high-quality children.

MARGARET MEAD (1901–1978), *New York Times*, 30 October 1966

25 Those who warn of a population explosion picture a world of too many people and not enough food—sort of like the average cocktail party.

BILL VAUGHAN, quoted in *Reader's Digest*, September 1967

26 A cancer is an uncontrolled multiplication of cells; the population explosion is an uncontrolled multiplication of people.

PAUL R. EHRLICH, *The Population Bomb*, 1968

27 One of the most ominous facts of the current situation, is that roughly 40% of the population of the undeveloped world is made up of people *under 15 years old*. As that mass of young people moves into its reproductive years during the next decade, we're going to see the greatest baby boom of all time. Those youngsters are the reason for all the ominous predictions for the year 2000. They are the gunpowder for the population explosion.

PAUL R. EHRLICH, *The Population Bomb*, 1968

28 The only possible solution to [the population] question is one which envisages the social and economic progress both of individuals and of the whole of human society, and which respects and promotes true human values.

POPE PAUL VI (1897–1978), encyclical letter *Humanae Vitae*, 1968

29 It is my observation that the disadvantages of a larger population are seen most vividly by those who were born in an earlier era. Often the current inhabitants see nothing wrong with many of the changes that the older citizens decry.

ANSLEY J. COALE, speech, Population Society of America, June 1968

30 [Nations concerned with the population explosion are] tired, frightened civilizations, huddled behind the walls of ancient cities, deploring the barbarian hordes outside the gates. . . . [They] look at a baby and see only a mouth to be fed. They do not see the hands, which will be more than capable of feeding the mouth.

GERSH I. BUDKER, Soviet nuclear physicist, quoted in *Fortune*, August 1968

31 The skeptics . . . who doubted whether an agrarian, underdeveloped, conservative and "religion-ridden" society could become aware of its excessive fertility have been silenced.

S. CHANDRASEKHAR, Indian Minister for Health and Family Planning, on rising concern over India's population explosion, *Foreign Affairs*, October 1968

32 It is clear that we will greatly increase human misery if we do not, during the immediate future, assume that the world available to the terrestrial human population is finite. "Space" is no escape.

GARRETT HARDIN, *Science*, 13 December 1968

33 It now appears that the period of rapid population and industrial growth that has prevailed during the last few centuries, instead of being the normal order of things and capable of continuance into the indefinite future, is actually one of the most abnormal phases of human history.

M. KING HUBBERT, *Resources and Man*, 1969

34 To get land's fruit in quantity takes jolts of labour even more, hence food will grow like

one, two, three . . . while numbers grow like one, two, four . . .

ANONYMOUS, "Song of Malthus: A Ballad on Diminishing Returns," quoted in Paul A. Samuelson, *Economics*, 1970

35 Always and everywhere we come back to the problem of population—more people to make more mistakes, more people to be the victims of the mistakes of others, more people to suffer Hell upon Earth.

LORD RITCHIE-CALDER, *Foreign Affairs*, January 1970

36 The psychic rewards of parenthood seem especially important to persons who are deprived of either the satisfactions which come from steady employment or those which come from adequate social and recreational contacts.

POPULATION REFERENCE BUREAU, *Population Bulletin*, February 1970

37 The goal of nature is zero population growth, and only man violates that goal.

JOHN F. EISENBERG, quoted in *New York Times*, 22 March 1970

38 Mankind is like cancer cells that don't know when to stop multiplying. I published my first despairing paper on the population explosion 21 years ago and I'm getting a little tired of the subject.

LAMONT COLE, speech, Kearney (Nebraska) State College, 22 April 1970

39 This is a veritable calamity. Our situation will be similar to that of a rower who finds himself carried two meters backward by the current every time he advances one meter.

HABIB BOURGUIBA, President of Tunisia, on his country's 3 percent population growth rate, speech, 9 January 1971

40 We will be thrown on the cemetery of history.

STEFAN CARDINAL WYSZYNSKI, primate of Poland, on declining birth rates, speech, 22 March 1971

41 The growth of population has a great deal of momentum,
Neither spirals, interruptus, or safer still, absentum
Can do much about the kids who are already on the scene,

Who will still be in the labor force in twenty-seventeen.
So there isn't very much that the developed world can do
To help that poor old woman in the very crowded shoe.
KENNETH E. BOULDING, "The Ballad of Ecological Awareness" in M. Taghi Farvar and John P. Milton, eds., *The Careless Technology*, 1972

42 No fundamental human value would be endangered by a leveling off of demographic growth.
DONELLA H. MEADOWS et al., *The Limits to Growth*, 1972

43 They shout and scream about "standing room only." But we believe in reincarnation, my friend, so don't worry. We'll be back.
KARAN SINGH, speech, U.N. Conference on Population, August 1974

44 It seems to be harder and harder to keep a crisis going, even when a lot of people have a vested interest in stirring up public fears. The latest crisis to face the risk of public boredom is the population crisis, which once had even higher billing than the energy crisis, the ozone crisis, the law of the seas crisis, or what have you.
WALL STREET JOURNAL, editorial, 24 October 1975

45 The overpopulation worries and alarmist exhortations of the 1960s and 1970s may well be regarded as an amusing episode in human history.
HERMAN KAHN, *The Next 200 Years*, 1976

46 We all worry about the population explosion—but we don't worry about it at the right time.
ARTHUR HOPPE, attributed

47 Malthus has been buried many times, and Malthusian scarcity with him. But as Garrett Hardin remarked, anyone who has to be re-buried so often cannot be entirely dead.
HERMAN E. DALY, *Steady-State Economics*, 1977

48 To think that it is possible to lock the large and crowded countries of the world inside their boundaries and let them suffocate by their mounting population pressures is unrealistic. [They] . . . may develop the motiva-

tion to break out of their boundaries, as well as the political and military muscle to do it.
EMILIO CASETTI, *The Economist*, 22 April 1978

49 Rapid population increase in a traditional agricultural economy with little change in technology and productivity tends to be accompanied by diminishing returns rather than economies of scale. Moreover, the rapid population growth that characterizes the [less-developed countries] is occurring at a time when the population is already large in relation to resources, and before critical cultural changes of the type experienced in the Western more-developed countries, such as the Renaissance, the Reformation, and the emergence of science and advanced technology. Furthermore, population growth in the LDC's . . . is occurring while the great masses of population remain illiterate, unskilled, bogged down in poverty and, often, in despair.
PHILIP M. HAUSER, *World Population and Development*, 1979

50 I thought . . . what business do I have trying to help arrange it that fewer human beings will be born, each one of whom might be a Mozart or a Michelangelo or an Einstein—or simply a joy to his or her family and community, and a person who will enjoy life?
JULIAN L. SIMON, *The Ultimate Resource*, 1981

51 I personally give zero weight to the notion that more births among today's poor and downtrodden masses will increase the probability of another Einstein or Mozart (or Hitler or Caligula?).
HERMAN E. DALY, *Bulletin of Atomic Scientists*, January 1982

52 England now has 11 times as large a population as it had in Shakespeare's day. But not even an economist would maintain that there are 11 Shakespeares in England now. I doubt there is even one. You can't solve problems just by breeding babies.
GARRETT HARDIN, speech, American Association for the Advancement of Science, Washington, D.C., 3 January 1982

53 Life can't be good unless you're alive.
JULIAN L. SIMON, speech, American Association for the Advancement of Science, Washington, D.C., 3 January 1982

54 The purpose of population is not ultimately peopling earth. It is to fill heaven.
   GRAHAM LEONARD, Church of England Synod, church and bomb debate, 10 February 1983

55 Civilization's problems would not all be solved if growth of the human population were halted humanely by limiting births. They would not necessarily be solved if the world population were ultimately reduced to a more or less permanently sustainable size. Society might still be plagued by racism, sexism, religious prejudice, gross economic inequity, threats of war, and serious environmental deterioration. But without population control, none of these problems can be solved; halting growth and then moving toward lower numbers simply would give humanity an opportunity to grapple with them. The old saying still holds: *Whatever your cause, it's a lost cause without population control.*
   PAUL R. EHRLICH, quoted in Robert Redford, *Greenhouse Glasnost,* 1990

108 POPULATION CONTROL
See also   107 POPULATION,
109 POPULATION IMPACTS

1 [The earth] scarcely can provide for our needs; as our demands grow greater, our complaints against nature's inadequacy are heard by all. The scourges of pestilence, famine, wars, and earthquakes have come to be regarded as a blessing to overcrowded nations, since they serve to prune away the luxuriant growth of the human race.
   TERTULLIAN (c. 155–c. 220), *De anima*

2 But when the dreadful time should at last come, when our globe, by the most diligent culture, could not produce what was sufficient to nourish its numerous inhabitants, what happy expedient could then be found out to remedy so great an evil?
   In such a cruel necessity, must there be a law to restrain marriage? Must multitudes of women be shut up in cloisters like the ancient vestals or modern nuns? To keep a balance between the two sexes, must a proportionable number of men be debarred from marriage? Shall the Utopians . . . appoint a certain number of infants to be exposed to death as soon as they are born, determining the proportion according to the exigencies of the state; and pointing out the particular victims by lot, or according to some established rule? Or, must they shorten the period of human life by a law. . . . Or what other method should they devise (for an expedient would be absolutely necessary) to restrain the number of citizens within reasonable bounds?
   ROBERT WALLACE, *Various Prospects of Mankind, Nature, and Providence,* 1761

3 It is a truth which admits not a doubt, that the comforts and well-being of the poor cannot be permanently secured without some regard on their part, or some effort on the part of the legislature, to regulate the increase of their numbers, and to render less frequent among them early and improvident marriages.
   DAVID RICARDO (1772–1823), *Principles of Political Economy and Taxation,* 1817

4 The friends of humanity cannot but wish that in all countries the labouring classes should have a taste for comforts and enjoyments, and that they should be stimulated by all legal means in their exertions to procure them. There cannot be a better security against a superabundant population.
   DAVID RICARDO (1772–1823), *Principles of Political Economy and Taxation,* 1817

5 As prosperity increases so do the pleasures which compete with marriage, while the feeling towards children takes on a new character of refinement, and both these facts tend to diminish the desire to beget, and to bear children.
   L. BRENTANO (1844–1931), *Economic Journal,* 1910

6 If people waited to know one another before they married, the world wouldn't be so grossly over-populated as it is now.
   W. SOMERSET MAUGHAM (1874–1965), *Mrs. Dot,* 1912

7 A society which practices death control must at the same time practice birth control.
   JOHN ROCK, *The Time Has Come,* 1963

8 A system of marketable licences to have children is the only [technique] which will combine the minimum of social control . . . with a maximum of individual liberty and ethical choice.

KENNETH E. BOULDING, *The Meaning of the 20th Century*, 1965

9 Let us in all our lands—including this land—face forthrightly the multiplying problems of our multiplying populations and seek the answers to this most profound challenge to the future of all the world. Let us act on the fact that less than five dollars invested in population control is worth a hundred dollars invested in economic growth.

LYNDON B. JOHNSON (1908–1973), speech, San Francisco, 25 June 1965

10 Only man is capable of choosing deliberately to limit his populations. He has shown the ability to make this choice at many times in the past and in many places.

RAYMOND F. DASMANN, unpublished paper, Conservation Foundation, 1966

11 To me, having a baby inside me is the only time I'm really alive. I know I can make something, do something, no matter what color my skin is, and what names people call me. When the baby gets born I see him, and he's full of life, or she is; and I think to myself that it doesn't make any difference what happens later, at least now we've got a chance, or the baby does. You can see the little one grow and get larger and start doing things, and you feel there must be some hope, some chance that things will get better. . . . If we didn't have that, what would be the difference from death?

ANONYMOUS WOMAN, quoted in Robert Coles, *Children of Crisis*, 1967

12 The [Catholic] Church doesn't say breed, breed, breed. The Church endorses celibacy, continence, and the so-called rhythm method. . . . Actually, the Church is the greatest believer in birth control. . . . If everyone observed what the Church says on sex and control there would be a lot less population.

MONSIGNOR LUIGI LIGUTTI, Vatican Council, quoted in Robert Rienow and Leona Train Rienow, *Moment in the Sun*, 1967

13 It is not licit, even for the gravest reasons, to do evil so that good may follow therefrom,

even when the intention is to safeguard or promote individual, family, or social well-being.

POPE PAUL VI, in forbidding contraception other than the rhythm method, encyclical *Humanae Vitae*, August 1968

14 The population problem cannot be solved in a technical way, any more than can the problem of winning the game of tick-tack-toe.

GARRETT HARDIN, *Science*, 13 December 1968

15 Hundreds of millions for death control. Scarcely one percent for fertility control.

ROBERT S. MCNAMARA, speech, Notre Dame University, 1969

16 We do know this: There has never been a people on the face of this earth that, having acquired a literacy, education and a fair level of living, did not decrease their birth rates. We have yet to discover whether it is possible for a people mired in illiteracy and poverty, isolated as a subcultural group and living in a traditional type of society, whether such a people can decrease their birth rate.

PHILIP HAUSER, speech, First National Congress on Optimum Population and Environment, June 1970

17 Quite without outside interference, time and human nature will probably take care of the population problem. It has taken us barely a century to come down from the twelve-child family to the three-child family.

HENRY C. WALLICH, *Newsweek*, 29 June 1970

18 People are everywhere. Some people say there are too many of us, but no one wants to leave.

CHARLES SCHULZ, *Peanuts*, 23 January 1971

19 One of the best things people could do for their descendants would be to sharply limit the number of them.

OLIN MILLER, *Reader's Digest*, November 1971

20 In practice, the case for limiting population . . . rests much more on value judgments about what makes for a tolerable life-style than on psuedo-scientific predictions.

RUDOLF KLEIN, *Commentary*, June 1972

21 Development is the best contraceptive.

ANONYMOUS slogan at World Population Conference, Bucharest, 1974

22 In Africa we cannot afford to look upon our growing population as a problem. We have to face up to the challenge of engaging our young, expectant peoples in the struggle to achieve the most rapid development possible. . . . It seems almost sinister that there is so much money available to *control* life and hardly any to *promote* it.

MAAZA BEKELE, former Ethiopian official, in *Unesco Courier*, July–August 1974

23 Metaphorically each rich nation can be seen as a lifeboat full of comparatively rich people. In the ocean outside each lifeboat swim the poor of the world, who would like to get in, or at least share some of the wealth. . . . We have several options: we may be tempted to live by the Christian ideal of being "our brother's keeper," or by the Marxist ideal of "to each according to his needs." Since the needs of all in the water are the same, and since they can all be seen as "our brothers," we could take them all into our boat, making a total of 150 in a boat designed for 60. The boat swamps, everyone drowns. Complete justice, complete catastrophe. . . . The harsh ethics of the lifeboat become even harsher when we consider the reproductive differences between the rich nations and the poor nations.

GARRETT HARDIN, *Psychology Today*, September 1974

24 Some . . . feel that the population explosion in some parts of the world may have pushed the search for answers beyond the framework of traditional liberal values. Several people I talked to mentioned China. Though I am sure these people view China's repressive society as intolerable, they still look at China's improving living standards and rapidly declining birth rate and find repression an acceptable alternative to the degradation and death of millions.

WADE GREENE, *New York Times Magazine*, 5 January 1975

25 It would seem that the fundamentally most sensible adjustment to make . . . is to recognize that population and per-capita consumption must eventually be stabilized and that technological change should be relied on only for buying time—both time to make the adjustment to stable consumption levels and

time in the sense of the life span of the stable system itself.

HERMAN E. DALY, *Steady-State Economics*, 1977

26 Cancer in its many forms is undoubtedly a natural disease. It is probably one of nature's many ways of eliminating sexually effete individuals who would otherwise, in nature's view, compete for available food resources without advantage to the species as a whole.

F. J. C. ROE, quoted in Samuel S. Epstein, *The Politics of Cancer*, 1978

27 China is the world's foremost example of what happens with a population explosion. . . . [Producing enough food] has taken a very large toll. It has wiped out obesity, household pets, birds, private ownership of automobiles . . . and most importantly, freedom. It is a sheer fact that the Chinese had to choose between starvation and regimentation. They chose regimentation.

R. T. RAVENHOLT, quoted in *Conservation Foundation Letter*, February 1979

28 Men are quite hopeless when it comes to the whole field, what with their machismo, ingrained attitudes, and so forth. . . . Where the women are slaves of their husbands, there is very little chance of a successful program.

MARSHALL GREEN, on population-control programs, quoted in *Conservation Foundation Letter*, March 1979

29 If a man is hungry and asks you for bread, and you offer him the Pill, can you be surprised that he spits in your eye?

BARBARA WARD (1914–1981), quoted in *Financial Times*, 28 September 1990

30 How can we help a foreign country to escape overpopulation? Clearly, the worst thing we can do is send food. . . . Atomic bombs would be kinder. For a few moments the misery would be acute, but it would soon come to an end for most of the people, leaving a very few survivors to suffer thereafter.

GARRETT HARDIN, quoted in Peter Borelli, ed., *Crossroads*, 1988

31 Having children is a privilege rather than a duty. The community may not have to deny that privilege to any couple who truly desires

to exercise it. But by the same token, those who choose not to exercise that privilege deserve the respect and appreciation of all.

HERMAN E. DALY and JOHN B. COBB, JR., *For the Common Good*, 1989

32 The world population crisis, which is the ultimate outcome of the exploitation of poor nations by rich ones, ought to be remedied by returning to the poor countries enough of the wealth taken from them to give their peoples both the reason and the resources voluntarily to limit their own fertility.

BARRY COMMONER, *Making Peace with the Planet*, 1990

33 Population is a political issue, not an ecological issue. At this moment we produce twice as much food as needed to give every person on Earth a physiologically adequate diet. The real problem is poverty. Excess population is a symptom of poverty, not the other way around.

BARRY COMMONER *Mother Earth News*, March–April 1990

109 POPULATION IMPACTS
See also 107 POPULATION,
108 POPULATION CONTROL

1 In ancient times, people were few but wealthy and without strife. . . . The life of a nation depends upon having enough food, not upon the number of people.

HAN-FEI-TZU (d. 233 B.C.), *Fecundity and Prosperity*

2 Fewness of people, is real poverty.

SIR WILLIAM PETTY (1623–1687), "A Treatise of Taxes and Contributions," 1662

3 The most decisive mark of the prosperity of any country is the increase of the number of inhabitants.

ADAM SMITH (1723–1790), *The Wealth of Nations*, 1776

4 [Poverty] . . . seems even to be favourable to generation.

ADAM SMITH (1723–1790), *The Wealth of Nations*, 1776

5 With a population pressing against the means of subsistence, the only remedies are either a reduction of people, or a more rapid accumulation of capital.

DAVID RICARDO (1772–1823), *Principles of Political Economy and Taxation*, 1817

6 From high real wages, or the power of commanding a large portion of the necessaries of life, two very different results may follow; one, that of a rapid increase of population, in which case the high wages are chiefly spent in the maintenance of large and frequent families: and the other, that of a decided improvement in the modes of subsistence and the conveniences and comforts enjoyed, without a proportionate acceleration in the rate of increase.

THOMAS ROBERT MALTHUS (1766–1834), *Principles of Political Economy*, 1820

7 The limitation of the number of births, by raising wages, will accomplish every thing which we desire, without trouble and without interference.

JAMES MILL (1773–1836), *Elements of Political Economy*, 1821

8 In the common for man . . . the tickets for admission being so readily procurable, it cannot happen otherwise, than that the common . . . must be constantly stocked to the extreme point of saturation.

WILLIAM FORSTER LLOYD, lecture, Oxford University, 1833

9 But it is some hardship to be born into the world and to find all nature's gifts previously engrossed, and no place left for the newcomer.

JOHN STUART MILL (1806–1873), *Principles of Political Economy*, 1848

10 It is scarcely necessary to remark that a stationary condition of capital and population implies no stationary state of human improvement. There would be as much scope as ever for all kinds of mental culture, and moral and social progress; as much room for improving the Art of Living and much more likelihood of its being improved.

JOHN STUART MILL (1806–1873), *Principles of Political Economy*, 1848

11 Each successive addition to the population brings a consumer and a producer.
   HENRY CHARLES CAREY (1793–1879), *Harmony of Interests*, 1851

12 Both the jayhawk and the man eat chickens, but the more jayhawks, the fewer chickens, while the more men, the more chickens.
   HENRY GEORGE (1839–1897), quoted in Julian Simon, *The Ultimate Resource*, 1981

13 In their original form human societies bore no resemblance to the hive or the ant heap; they were merely packs. Civilization is, among other things, the process by which primitive packs are transformed into an analogue, crude and mechanical, of the social insects' organic communities. At the present time the pressures of over-population and technological change are accelerating this process. The termitary has come to seem a realizable and even, in some eyes, a desirable ideal.
   ALDOUS HUXLEY (1894–1963), *Brave New World Revisited*, 1958

14 It is obvious that the best qualities in man must atrophy in a standing-room-only environment.
   STEWART L. UDALL, *The Quiet Crisis*, 1963

15 If the world's population were to maintain its present growth rate for 6,000 years (about the period of recorded history), it would end in a mass of human flesh the periphery of which would be expanding at the speed of light.
   PHILIP M. HAUSER, speech, Albert Einstein College of Medicine commencement, New York City, June 1963

16 Unfortunately for his reputation, Malthus was living in a time when the set point (carrying capacity of the environment) was drifting upward, *but he didn't know it.* . . . History mocked him.
   GARRETT HARDIN, ed., *Population, Evolution, and Birth Control*, 1964

17 If the full development of human possibilities are the overriding aims of our evolution, then any overpopulation which brings malnutrition and misery, or which erodes the world's material resources or its resources of beauty or intellectual satisfaction are evil.
   JULIAN HUXLEY, *Essays of a Humanist*, 1964

18 People minus Space equals Poverty.
   MARYA MANNES, *Life*, 12 June 1964

19 We come inevitably to the fundamental question: What are people for? What is living for? If the answer is a life of dignity, decency and opportunity, then every increase in population means a decrease in all three. The crowd is a threat to every single being.
   MARYA MANNES, *Life*, 12 June 1964

20 Population growth in the United States is not now a serious threat to our material affluence. It is a threat to the quality of our lives and the beauty and esthetic character of our country. In this sense it threatens a better America.
   DUDLEY KIRK, speech, North American Wildlife and Natural Resources Conference, San Francisco, 15 March 1967

21 The problem is no longer that with every pair of hands that comes into the world there comes a hungry stomach. Rather it is that, attached to those hands are sharp elbows.
   PAUL A. SAMUELSON, *Newsweek*, 12 June 1967

22 The first biological lesson of history is that life is competition. Competition is not only the life of trade, it is the trade of life—peaceful when food abounds, violent when the mouths outrun the food.
   WILL DURANT and ARIEL DURANT, *The Lessons of History*, 1968

23 Population impaction, poverty itself, is a form of pollution as well as a source of ugliness, as important as water, air, noise and other kinds of pollution.
   ORVILLE FREEMAN, colloquium, U.S. Congress, 1968

24 In nature no animal, plant or bacterial population has ever maintained a logarithmic phase of growth for very long. The major factors that slow this rate of growth are exhaustion of food supply, accumulation of toxic products, decimation through disease, or the effects of some outside lethal agent which kills a high proportion of the population. Any one or all of these factors will force the population back into a lag phase. I leave it to your

imagination which of these factors might apply to the human population.

WILLIAM D. MCELROY, speech, meeting of American Institute of Biological Sciences, Columbus, Ohio, 1968

25 We must establish as a principle of national policy that the relationship between our population and our finite resources is a major concern of the federal government. No comprehensive policy for our environment can fail to include recognition of the hazards of irresponsible population growth. The federal government has for too long resisted involvement in this central issue.

STEWART L. UDALL, colloquium, U.S. Congress, 1968

26 Freedom to breed will bring ruin to all.

GARRETT HARDIN, *Science*, 13 December 1968

27 The preservation of a stable population with an optimum density not only avoids war, famine, and pestilence: it preserves the whole habitat.

C. D. DARLINGTON, *The Evolution of Man and Society*, 1969

28 To see that limits do exist, one need only consider that if the present world population were to be doubled but 15 more times, there would be one man for each square meter on all of the land areas of the earth, including Antarctica, Greenland, and the Sahara Desert. And at the present rate of growth, this would require but 525 more years.

M. KING HUBBERT, *Resources and Man*, 1969

29 The critical issue is whether social institutions will plan for their arrival and be able to accommodate them in a humane and intelligent way . . . Are our cities prepared for such an influx? The chaotic history of urban growth suggests that they are not and that many of their existing problems will be severely aggravated by a dramatic increase in numbers.

RICHARD M. NIXON, on the anticipated arrival of the next 100 million Americans in 30 to 35 years, 18 July 1969

30 Even with the population explosion a simple sum shows that the whole population of the world (3 billion) could be housed in Britain (60 million acres) at the medium density of 50 people per acre.

NAN FAIRBROTHER, *New Lives, New Landscapes*, 1970

31 It is important to recognize that "the population problem" is more than a numbers game—it is an extremely complex relationship between numbers of people, the age structure and growth of their populations, their present and future demands on a limited environment, and their future aspirations. The control of population is a complex social phenomenon that requires more than simplistic technological developments.

RICHARD S. MILLER, speech, First National Congress on Optimum Population and Environment, Chicago, 1970

32 Studies on rats show physical and psychological changes that are attributable to the process of crowding. These include cannibalism, failure to care for young, overaggressive defense of territory, changes in the adrenal glands and in the liver, hyperactive nerves, highly irregular reproductive activity, and finally, premature death. Social scientists are finding that Americans are beginning to show signs of increasing isolation from one another. The result is increasing dehumanization—particularly in the large urban centers.

THEODORE FOIN, JR., speech, University of California, Davis, 22 April 1970

33 How is it that the evolution of man-made ecosystems has not produced its own fail-safe stabilisers, such as natural ecosystems possess? I think it may be because the need for stabilisers in man-made systems is comparatively recent. In the days before mass aggregation into cities and mass transport and mass communication, *space* was the great stabiliser.

ERIC ASHBY, *Environmental Science and Technology*, October 1980

34 Population is pollution spelled inside out.

DAVID R. BROWER, quoted in John McPhee, *Encounters with the Archdruid*, 1971

35 To determine the optimum size of the human population we need to decide first what feature of human life we wish to optimize. In the

abstract, the choice might be made from among a wide range of conditions of value to human beings and involve the most complex moral, social and political questions. However, in the reality of present circumstances this choice is very considerably simplified, for the current condition of the human population is such that one value dominates all others—the survival of human society.

BARRY COMMONER, in S. Fred Singer, ed., *Is There an Optimum Level of Population?*, 1971

36 An area must be considered overpopulated if it can only be supported by the rapid consumption of nonrenewable resources. It must also be considered overpopulated if the activities of the population are leading to a steady deterioration of the environment.

PAUL EHRLICH and ANNE EHRLICH, *Population, Resources, Environment*, 1972

37 If the present growth trends in world population, industrialization, pollution, food production, and resource depletion continue unchanged, the limits to growth on this planet will be reached sometime within the next one hundred years. The most probable result will be a rather sudden and uncontrollable decline in both population and industrial capacity.

DONELLA H. MEADOWS et al., *The Limits to Growth*, 1972

38 There is hardly any social problem confronting this nation whose solution would be easier if our population were larger. Even now, the dreams of too many Americans are not being realized; others are being fulfilled at too high a cost.

PRESIDENT'S COMMISSION ON POPULATION GROWTH AND THE AMERICAN FUTURE, *Population and the American Future*, March 1972

39 No quantity of atomic bombs could stem the tide of billions . . . who will some day leave the poor southern part of the world to erupt into the relatively accessible spaces of the rich Northern Hemisphere looking for survival.

HOUARI BOUMÉDIENNE (1927–1978), President of Algeria, quoted in *Washington Post*, 17 July 1977

40 [If the United States tries to accommodate] an army of illegal immigrants [it will] become

sucked into a commons that globalizes poverty.

GARRETT HARDIN, *World Issues*, February–March 1978

41 Ecology's first social law may be written: *"All poverty is caused by the continued growth of population."*

PAUL COLINVAUX, *The Fates of Nations*, 1980

42 By far the worst prospect we have to face is that the freest of us will lose our liberty from a remorseless and gentle jostling of crowds of people.

PAUL COLINVAUX, *The Fates of Nations*, 1980

43 Rising numbers [of people] must always soak up spare resources by sharing them out among the extra people. One consequence of this is that poverty always persists.

PAUL COLINVAUX, *The Fates of Nations*, 1980

44 The larger the population, the smaller the fraction that can enjoy wilderness.

GARRETT HARDIN, speech, American Association for the Advancement of Science, Washington, D.C., 3 January 1982

45 Overly rapid population growth strains virtually every component of a developing society. . . . And it perpetuates a culture of poverty.

ROBERT S. MCNAMARA, lecture, Washington, D.C., 1 November 1985

46 How do you get a living out of the earth and support a population in a way that is ethically acceptable? How do you provide for a world of 8 billion people without a total, absolute technological domination of nature? Have the environmentalists, the feminists, or the social justice people shown us how we can support this world's population at anything remotely like an American standard of living at the same time that we develop and maximize a land ethic? That is the critical question.

DONALD WORSTER, *American Land Forum*, Summer 1986

47 Current population levels are undermining the biological basis for our future. There is not a single important problem facing the

planet that could not be more easily solved with a population of under 5 billion.

DENIS HAYES, speech, Museum of Natural History, New York City, 8 November 1989

48 We must recognize that 10 billion lives are better than five billion lives—as long as they are not all lived simultaneously! We should strive to maximize the cumulative number of lives ever to be lived over time at a per-capita standard of resource consumption sufficient for a good life. But if we have too many people and too much consumption at any one time, we will erode the Earth's long-run carrying capacity and therefore reduce the population and standard of consumption in all future time periods. We will thus reduce the cumulative total of lives ever to be lived at a decent level of consumption.

HERMAN E. DALY, *EPA Journal*, July–August 1990

49 Julian Simon's affirmations [that population growth does not threaten resources] are based on the premise that human ingenuity is limitless. That premise is the product of something for which the Greeks had a name. It is *hubris*, pride. One of the main theses of Greek mythology is that hubris results in disaster.

JOSEPH H. DEIBERT, letter, *New York Times Magazine*, 23 December 1990

110 POVERTY

See also   3 AFFLUENCE, 20 CONSUMERISM, 79 LIFE-STYLE

1 The rich may produce a better, or a more sumptuous meal; but his feelings can never be like those of the poor woodsman. Poor I ought not to call him, for nature and industry bountifully supply all his wants; the woods and rivers produce his chief dainties, and his toils are his pleasures.

JOHN JAMES AUDUBON (1785–1851), *Ornithological Biography, or An Account of the Habits of the Birds of the United States*, 1839

2 It is especially hard to take at face value the protestations that concern for the underprivileged should have precedence over concern for the environment. Why does it have to be

the either-or? Aren't the lungs of the poor as badly affected as those of the rich by the polluted air they breathe? More so, one would think, since more of them are concentrated for more of the time in the industrialized central cities. Are the children of the poor not entitled to relax at clean public beaches and to bathe in unpolluted water, especially since, unlike those of the rich, they are not likely either to have their own pools or be sent away for the summer? Do the poor have some immunity to fish contaminated by pesticides, or to other chemically poisoned food, which their affluent brothers do not enjoy?

NEW YORK TIMES, editorial, 22 April 1971

3 It is the rich alone, at present, who are able to opt out of any environment that is sinking in the scale of amenity: not the working man, and certainly not the poor, who have no choice at all.

E. J. MISHAN, *Public Interest*, Summer 1971

4 Those who cry that the ecological crisis is diverting us from a war on poverty, . . . fail to recognize that a genuinely ecological strategy is the only fundamental anti-poverty approach possible in the present and future world.

ARTHUR PEARL, *Social Policy*, September–October 1971

5 Let us recognize that of all segments of society the poor are the least responsible for pollution in the sense that materially they consume the least. Conversely, the poor are the chief sufferers from pollution in the sense that they have the least means of insulating themselves from pollution effects.

JOSEPH L. FISHER, Resources for the Future, annual report, 1972

6 The poor have, up to now, been forced to trade their amenities, health, safety, and even their lives for their small piece of the economic pie. Unless we squarely face these arbitrary, socially determined distribution patterns and endeavor to change those that are unjust, the poor will likely pay just as heavily for the piecemeal, uncoordinated, and often conflicting environmental policies now being implemented.

HAZEL HENDERSON, in James N. Smith, *Environmental Quality and Social Justice in Urban America*, 1974

7 When I am hungry, date palm gives me food. When my belly is full, behold, the tree is beautiful.
    ANONYMOUS JORDANIAN BEDOUIN, quoted by Guy Mountfort, 1978

8 One of the greatest challenges will be to meet the energy needs of the poor without repeating the mistakes of the rich.
    CHRISTOPHER FLAVIN, in Lester Brown, *State of the World*, 1988

9 Poverty is the ultimate form of pollution in a world out of balance with people's needs and its own future.
    BELLA ABZUG, Centre for Our Common Future, *Network '92*, October 1990

111 PUBLIC LANDS
See also   76 LAND

1 The vast and unmanageable extent which the accession of Louisiana will give to the United States; the consequent dispersion of our population; and the destruction of that balance which is so important to maintain between the Eastern and Western States, threatens, at no very distant day, the subversion of our Union.
    ROGER GRISWOLD (1762–1812), U.S. Representative, on the Louisiana Purchase, 1803

2 What do we want with this worthless area, this region of savages and wild beasts, or shifting sands and whirlwinds of dust, of cactus and prairie dogs? To what use could we ever hope to put these great deserts and endless mountain ranges?
    DANIEL WEBSTER (1782–1852), on the public lands of the West, quoted in *U.S. News and World Report*, 8 March 1982

3 Seward's Folly.
    ANONYMOUS, name applied to Alaska when Secretary of State William H. Seward signed a treaty for its purchase from Russia for $7.2 million, 1867

4 Alaska, with the Aleutian Islands, is an inhospitable, wretched, God-forsaken region, worth nothing, but a positive injury and incumbrance as a colony of the United States.

. . . Of what possible commercial importance can this territory be to us?
    ORANGE FERRISS, U.S. Representative, 1868

5 The possession of the country is of no value. . . . [It] will be a source of weakness instead of power, and a constant annual expense for which there will be no adequate return. . . . [It has] no capacity as an agricultural country . . . no value as a mineral country. . . . [Its] timber . . . [is] generally of a poor quality and growing upon inaccessible mountains. . . . [The] fisheries [are] of doubtful value . . .
    U.S. HOUSE OF REPRESENTATIVES FOREIGN RELATIONS COMMITTEE, minority report on the purchase of Alaska, 1868

6 To grab this vast treasure has stirred the pirate blood in many of our money kings till they would make any endeavor, legal or illegal, to obtain it.
    JOHN L. MATHEWS, 1909, on the natural resources of Alaska, quoted in David D. Anderson, ed., *Sunshine and Smoke*, 1971

7 Everyone gambled in that illimitable American resource—land. . . . The greatest stake in the speculative saturnalia was our almost incalculable public domain—an unpeopled stage of empire billowing from the westernmost settlements toward the sunset.
    MARQUIS JAMES, on the period around 1835, *The Life of Andrew Jackson*, 1938

8 The administration of the public-land laws by the General Land Office of the Interior Department is one of the great scandals of American history. At a time when, in the West, the penalty for stealing a horse was death—death without benefit of law—stealing the public land in open defiance of law was generally regarded with tolerance or even with approval. It cast no shadow on the reputation of the thief.
    GIFFORD PINCHOT (1865–1946), *Breaking New Ground*, 1947

9 Federal ownership or control of land is a form of communism.
    ANONYMOUS SPOKESMAN, Stockgrower's Association, quoted by Bernard De Voto, *Harper's*, July 1948

10 Sensation! In Nevada, perceive, socialism has ceased to creep; it has broken into a gallop

and will ride us down. The audience, its fear of Big Government aroused, is to envisage six-gun bureaucrats wrenching the state away from its citizens. The basic reason why 87 percent of Nevada is in public ownership is that more than 70 percent of it is land which the government proved unable to give away. . . . It is the very dregs of the public domain, waterless and sterile.

BERNARD DE VOTO (1897–1955), on a U.S. Chamber of Commerce lament that the federal government owns 87 percent of all the land in Nevada, *Harper's*, July 1953

11 To apply the economic efficiency concept to publicly owned resources is to substitute market-place decision-making for the democratic political process. Acting through its elected representatives, the citizens of this country have made it quite clear that long-term, environmental, public, intangible values should be paramount in the handling of our federal natural resources.

CHARLES H. STODDARD, *What's Ahead for Our Public Lands?*, 1971

12 The public lands have always been the arena where Americans fought for their dreams. The dream of wealth, the dream of home, the dreams of peace and escape chase each other across the history of these lands like streaks of light across the Western sky. They are now, as they have always been, inseparable from our national destiny. What we do with them tells a great deal about what we are, what we care about and what will become of us. . . . After a century and a half of carelessness and conflict, the land still retains its capacity to inspire and to console. It is a kind of drawing account for the spirit.

DONALD JACKSON, *Life*, 8 January 1971

13 [The public lands represent] in a sense, the breathing space of the nation.

RICHARD M. NIXON, environmental message, 8 February 1971

14 This is the single most important land-use decision in the lifetime of most of the people in this room. In terms of acreage involved, there's nothing that compares with it. No other single conservation decision in history is of its magnitude, except the action of President Theodore Roosevelt in establishing the

national forests at a time when they were seriously threatened.

MORRIS UDALL, on the Alaska lands bill, 1 December 1978

15 Throughout its first century, the social, political, and economic life of the United States was dominated by questions surrounding the public domain. . . . Land was merely a means of implementing revenue, states' rights, or social policy.

SAMUEL T. DANA and SALLY FAIRFAX, *Forest and Range Policy*, 1980

16 I have come to you today to ask you to join me in this second American Revolution. If the western states are ever to assume our rightful place, equal with the other states of the Union, we must throw off the shackles in which the federal government now holds the destiny of the West—ownership of the public domain.

ORRIN HATCH, U.S. Senator, quoted in *Cry California*, Summer 1980

17 This vast brokerage operation [federal government land disposal] was carried out under a set of uncoordinated, often contested, and certainly controversial sequence of acts, mandates, and proclamations.

PETER WOLF, *Land in America*, 1981

18 The only land policy questions debated with fervor in the early years of Congress had to do with who got what, and how much of it, and at what price. The notion that the federal lands should be entirely disposed of continued right through the last major national purchase, the acquisition of Alaska from Russia in 1867.

PETER WOLF, *Land in America*, 1981

19 Allow me to conclude by expressing my deepest concern that the environment of the West will be damaged by crisis-oriented, unreasonable programs to develop the energy potential of the West.

JAMES G. WATT, U.S. Secretary of the Interior designate, statement, Senate Energy and Natural Resources Committee, 7 January 1981

20 I do not see the need now for massive transfers of land. The Sagebrush Rebellion [against federal control of, and controls on,

so much public land] is caused by the arrogant attitude of certain bureaucrats. Good management will defuse the Sagebrush Rebellion.

> JAMES G. WATT, U.S. Secretary of the Interior designate, testimony, Senate Energy and Natural Resources Committee, 7 January 1981

21 I believe there is a life hereafter, and we are to be here to follow the teachings of Jesus Christ. One of the charges He's given us is to occupy the land until He returns. We don't know when He is coming, so we have a stewardship responsibility . . . to see that people are provided for until He does come and a new order is put in place.

> JAMES G. WATT, U.S. Secretary of the Interior, quoted in *New Yorker*, 4 May 1981

22 [Reagan Interior Secretary James G.] Watt's strident demand to "open up" public lands of marginal value is the best indication of how desperate an economy based on nonrenewable resources can become.

> WESLEY MARX, *Cry California*, Summer 1981

23 The public outcry over Eisenhower Administration policies [to dispose of federal lands] helped raise the level of consciousness in the Congress and set the stage for two decades of environmental legislation.

> MICHAEL S. HAMILTON, *Not Man Apart*, January 1982

24 The scandals of the 19th Century involved large private interests exploiting public land. Today, the reverse is true. Powerful public agencies exploit little property owners. Many in Washington will argue that the ends justify the means, but to us it looks no prettier.

> WALL STREET JOURNAL, editorial, 25 May 1982

25 I fear the states as potential owners of all this public land because I don't trust them not to be manipulated by the élites which run local government.

> WALLACE STEGNER, in Richard W. Etulain, *Conversations with Wallace Stegner on Western History and Literature*, 1983

26 The American people want to preserve their American heritage, and they have the quaint belief that public lands belong to them as much as to the people of the state where the lands are located.

> JOHN F. SEIBERLING, U.S. Representative, quoted in *New York Times*, 15 July 1984

27 [The public lands] are indeed the safety valve that they were once called; but the safety valve is there not to keep city mechanics from revolutionary unrest by providing them with land where they can make farms. This safety valve is a safety valve of the spirit, the most precious antidote to the spiritual demoralization that immersion in our industrial culture is likely to breed.

> WALLACE STEGNER, *Sierra*, September–October 1989

28 It's government land, but we don't think they should take it away after we pioneered it. We don't go back [east] and tell them to take down all those tall buildings.

> GENE GRIFFIN, on proposals to designate large wilderness areas in Utah, quoted in *Washington Post*, 23 April 1991

112 QUALITY OF LIFE

See also   79 LIFE-STYLE

1 We face the question whether a still higher "standard of living" is worth its cost in things natural, wild, and free. For us of the minority, the opportunity to see geese is more important than television, and the chance to find a pasqueflower is a right as inalienable as free speech.

> ALDO LEOPOLD (1886–1948), *A Sand County Almanac*, 1949

2 The major opportunity for the intensification of consciousness lies in nature. Any infringement in the opportunity for free contact with the natural scene diminishes the quality of our lives. Once we lose touch with nature, our society loses its values, its purpose.

> DANIEL B. LUTEN, *Sierra Club Bulletin*, December 1964

3 There are certain intangible aspects of living which cannot be adequately measured. It is those intangible features that provide the

quality of life which in turn maintain the moral, spiritual and philosophic vitality of a nation. . . . Rather than leaving the assessment of those intangible aspects which are embodied in sites of national interest to federal agencies like the Federal Power Commission or the Department of Interior, I would prefer to see them evaluated by individuals and organizations whose experience has given them a keener appreciation and broader perspective of those things to be preserved in order that all Americans might enjoy a finer quality of life.

CHARLES R. ROSS, quoted in *Conservation Foundation Letter*, 30 September 1966

4 If we are really serious about ensuring a living environment for every American—and we can afford to do no less—we need to make a clear declaration of national policy for the American environment. . . . Environmental quality must now become a top priority objective of American society. Governments at all levels must now assume a new positive role as trustees of the environment for all the people. The passive role of referee between special interest competitors for natural resources is no longer enough.

HUBERT H. HUMPHREY (1911–1978), U.S. Vice President, speech, The Dalles, Oregon, 1968

5 Our problem isn't one of numbers but of the quality of human lives. What we need to do is to produce that size of population in which human beings can most fulfill their potentialities, and from that point of view, in my opinion we are already overpopulated, not just in places like India and China and Puerto Rico, but here and in Western Europe, and with that overpopulation in our Western world there has gone, I think, a signal deterioration in our culture all through the last century.

GEORGE WALD, First National Congress on Optimum Population and Environment, Chicago, 1970

6 What is required are not only new methods and programs for preventing and controlling pollution, but new ideas and values directed to a future made safe for man. In such a future, the good life would be measured more in terms of an improvement in human rela-

tionships than in any increase of the gross national product. Satisfactions would be reckoned more in terms of the full creative and moral development of the individual than in the pleasures made possible by generating vast quantities of electric power.

NORMAN COUSINS, *Saturday Review*, 20 June 1970

7 The physical environment of large American cities has not degenerated *absolutely in an overall sense*, but probably has been improving. People easily forget the amenities taken for granted today that were lacking half a century ago. Examples are air-conditioned offices, restaurants and homes; thermostatically controlled electric and gas heat; underground utility wires and poles; paved boulevards and auto freeways. These have widely replaced the crowded slums, the filth of unpaved streets, the drafty cold water flats and belching chimneys of winter and the streaming miseries of unrefrigerated summers.

NEIL H. JACOBY, in Clifton Fadiman and Jean White, eds., *Ecocide*, 1971

8 The end purpose of economic development, in fact of virtually every worthwhile human endeavor, is to improve the total quality of life. And the quality of a man's life can only be measured in personal terms—in his own view of his net worth, his personal satisfactions and his sense of well-being.

AUBREY J. WAGNER, testimony, U.S. Senate Public Works subcommittee, 5 March 1971

9 The physical improvement of the quality of life will mean precious little if it assists only the precious few.

IRVING HOROWITZ, *Environmental Quality and Social Responsibility*, 1972

10 There is every reason to suppose that the stable society would provide us with satisfactions that would more than compensate for those which, with the passing of the industrial state, it will become increasingly necessary to forego.

EDWARD GOLDSMITH et al., "Blueprint for Survival," *The Ecologist*, January 1972

11 I become more and more doubtful that the superiority in science and technology of Eu-

ropean man is leading him to a better life than that achieved by other peoples.

CHARLES A. LINDBERGH (1902–1974), quoted in Wayne S. Cole, *Charles A. Lindbergh and the Battle against American Intervention in World War II,* 1974

12 A sophisticated and ecologically sound technology, using solar power and other renewable resources, could bring us a life of simple sufficiency that would yet allow the full expression of the human potential. Having chosen such a life, rather than having had it forced on us, we might find it had its own richness.

WILLIAM OPHULS, in Stuart S. Nagel, ed., *Environmental Politics,* 1974

13 The carrying capacity concept recognizes that in order to improve the "quality of life" relative to both natural and human environments, the pattern and level of production and consumption activities must be compatible with the capabilities of the natural environment, as well as with social preferences.

A. BERRY CRAWFORD and A. BRUCE BISHOP, paper, American Association for the Advancement of Science, San Francisco, 1 March 1974

14 The good life is balanced with some civilization, some wildness, some downtown and some Walden. We all need a change of scene, but some of our frantic escape from the city derives from the one-sidedness of the city. Recognizing the universal need for naturalness in our lives, we can build and care for more harmonious landscapes across the whole continuum.

NICHOLAS HELBURN, *Professional Geographer* 29, 1977

15 It's improving the quality of life. I think [historic] preservation could be articulated as a central strategy of that.

JOHN SOWER, *American Preservation,* October–November 1978

16 The conservationist movement set the value of what it sought to achieve in human terms. Its members measured their plans by asking what is good for a man in the broadest and longest sense; what raises him from present poverty without condemning him to future need; what raises his spirit by bringing him

into touch with natural harmony; what teaches natural economics by preserving the resources to make life fuller.

ROGER STARR, *New York Times Magazine,* 19 August 1979

17 Quality of life as a product of a person's interaction with his environment does not stand a chance in the sterile geometric spaces of modern architecture. Life does not like to be boxed. Life likes more amorphous, varied spaces. Our biological heritage is more attuned to nooks and crannies, the irregular and the round than to linear geometry.

HENRYK SKOLIMOWSKI, *Eco-Philosophy,* 1981

18 The question is: What will be the irrecoverable cost to precious intangibles—our capacity for awe; our moral imagination; our sense of nature, including human nature, as a realm of values—when we regard the world around and within us just as raw material in the service of our (by then necessarily) vagrant passions and imperious appetites?

GEORGE F. WILL, *Washington Post,* 18 January 1981

19 [Deep ecology means] appreciating *life quality* (dwelling in situations of inherent value) rather than adhering to an increasingly higher standard of living. There will be a profound awareness of the difference between big and great.

ARNE NAESS, quoted in Bill Sessions and Dave Devall, *Deep Ecology,* 1985

20 In 1974, the term "quality of life" was just beginning to appear in the technical language. It achieved a peak during the Carter administration and has not been in use much since then. It has become somewhat of a cliché. Quality of life values were heavily debated and studied because they reflected a new concern for how we thought and felt about the physical and psychological basis of our life styles across the country. The environment was the chief focus of attention, but the concept also spread elsewhere.

KENNETH E. BOULDING, in George L. Peterson, *Amenity Resource Valuation,* 1988

21 Whatever Quality of Life is, it must be by its very nature personal, individually defined, and based in the direct experience of human beings. . . . Quality is all around us and we

have only to reach out for it, or perhaps more precisely reach inward for it.
DONELLA H. MEADOWS, speech, Washington, D.C., January 1988

22 At best, societies and economies are devoted to the measurable components of human welfare. But by definition anything measurable is quantity, not quality.
DONELLA H. MEADOWS, speech, Washington, D.C., January 1988

23 "Simple in means, rich in ends" is the nutshell version of both deep ecology and voluntary simplicity. The richness lies in the empowerment and flourishing of the self in sustainable communities.
STEPHANIE MILLS, In Praise of Nature, 1990

24 To me, a minimum quality of life is a wood thrush.
BARBARA A. DOWELL, quoted in New York Times Magazine, 2 September 1990

25 Environmental protection may be to the next 50 years what the rise of the welfare state has been in the past 50: a drag on growth, true, but also a huge and hard-to-quantify source of increased human wellbeing.
FRANCES CAIRNCROSS, The Economist, 8 September 1990

26 What kind of Poland will be of the future? . . . We must find a way for the poorest people in Poland [in the Green Lungs Region of northeast Poland] to build a better life-quality.
ANDRZEJ KASSENBERG, Polish ecologist, remarks at World Wildlife Fund, Washington, D.C., 22 July 1991

113 RADIATION
See also   90 NUCLEAR ENERGY

1 I like people. I like animals, too—whales and quail, dinosaurs and dodos. But I like human beings especially, and I am unhappy that the pool of human germ plasm, which determines the nature of the human race, is deteriorating.
LINUS C. PAULING, on the effects of radioactive fallout on heredity, 1959, quoted in New York Times, 13 October 1962

2 Tomorrow we will have rain, and the rain falling on the garden will carry its cargo of debris from old explosions in distant places. Whether the amount of this freight is great or small, whether it is measurable by the farmer or can only be guessed at, one thing is certain: the character of rain has changed, the joy of watching it soak the waiting earth has been diminished, and the whole meaning and worth of gardens has been called into question.
E. B. WHITE (1899–1985), "Sootfall and Fallout," early 1960s, quoted in Bill McKibben, The End of Nature, 1989

3 I fear that when the history of this century is written, that the greatest debacle of our nation will be . . . our creation of vast armadas of plutonium, whose safe containment will represent a major precondition for human survival, not for a few decades or hundreds of years, but for thousands of years more than human civilization has so far existed.
JAMES D. WATSON, 1974, quoted in Herman E. Daly, Steady-State Economics, 1978

4 If our tongues were as sensitive as these radiation detectors, we could easily taste one drop of vermouth in five carloads of gin.
DIXY LEE RAY, 1976, in support of nuclear energy, quoted in Esther Stineman, American Political Women, 1980

5 Radiation need not be feared, but it must be respected.
KARL MORGAN, quoted in Peter Pringle and James Spigelman, The Nuclear Barons, 1981

6 The instinctive human fear of radioactivity is not irrational, as the nuclear advocates assert; it is also so universal and so enduring that it is a political fact of life.
PETER PRINGLE and JAMES SPIGELMAN, The Nuclear Barons, 1981

7 Hell no, we won't glow.
ANONYMOUS antinuclear slogan, 1982

8 There is no way I can justify my failure to help sound an alarm over these activities many years sooner than I did. I feel that at least several hundred scientists trained in the biomedical aspect of atomic energy, myself definitely included, are candidates for Nuremberg-type trials for crimes against hu-

manity for our gross negligence and responsibility. Now that we know the hazard of low-dose radiation, the crime is not experimentation—it's murder.

JOHN GOFMAN, health physicist, quoted in Responsible Citizens for Responsible Government, "Filthy Habit," 1990

9 If only radiation were red then these people would know what they are living in.

ANONYMOUS SOVIET PHYSICIAN, commenting on the 30-kilometer zone around the Chernobyl reactor, *Greenpeace,* January–February 1991

10 Reckoning with these truths and uncertainties has left the region [around Chernobyl] crippled environmentally, economically, and psychologically.

FELICITY BARRINGER, on the aftermath of the Chernobyl nuclear accident, *New York Times Magazine,* 14 April 1991

114 RECREATION
See also 83 NATIONAL PARKS, 95 OPEN SPACE, 98 PARKS, 128 TOURISM

1 The idle ways of the beach.

LADY KII, 8th century, untitled poem

2 The bow cannot possibly stand always bent, nor can human nature or human frailty subsist without some lawful recreation.

MIGUEL DE CERVANTES SAAVEDRA (1547–1616), *Don Quixote*

3 If bread is the first necessity of life, recreation is a close second.

EDWARD BELLAMY (1850–1898), *Looking Backward,* 1888

4 Quality as well as quantity must enter into any evaluation of competing types of recreation, because one really deep experience may be worth an infinite number of ordinary experiences.

ROBERT MARSHALL, *Arctic Village,* 1931

5 One should get away once in a while as far as possible from human contacts. To contemplate nature, magnificently garbed as it is in this country, is to restore peace to the mind.

HAROLD L. ICKES (1874–1952), U.S. Secretary of the Interior, on visiting Yosemite National Park, 1934, Harold L. Ickes Papers

6 Recreational development is a job not of building roads into lovely country, but of building receptivity into the still unlovely human mind.

ALDO LEOPOLD (1886–1948), *A Sand County Almanac,* 1949

7 Barring love and war, few enterprises are undertaken with such abandon, or by such diverse individuals, or with so paradoxical a mixture of appetite and altruism, as that group of avocations known as outdoor recreation.

ALDO LEOPOLD (1886–1948), *A Sand County Almanac,* 1949

8 Recreation is valuable in proportion to the intensity of its experiences, and to the degree to which it *differs from* and *contrasts with* workaday life.

ALDO LEOPOLD (1886–1948), *A Sand County Almanac,* 1949

9 Do human beings need outdoor recreation? What values are there for modern man in the world of nature outside the cities? These questions cannot be answered scientifically, because of the irrational nature of play as it comes to us from our remote ancestors, and because man is the most adaptable of animals. If the rat and the sparrow can learn to live for endless generations in the cities, why cannot man? The scientist cannot give us answers, but the prophets and poets can.

ROGER REVELLE, *Daedalus,* Fall 1967

10 Outdoor recreation may be alleged to have great psychic benefits, though demonstrating its dimensions or comparing it with television or people-watching on crowded streets is another matter.

AARON WILDAVSKY, *Daedalus,* Fall 1967

11 The purchase of this beautiful outdoor recreation land is not just an exercise in esthetics. . . . Recreation park land builds part of the real sinew of the American people; it enhances the quality of our national life. As our cities become more congested, the lack of such wholesome recreation facilities will only exacerbate the problems of crime, delinquency, and misuse of leisure time.

MARK HATFIELD, U.S. Senator, 19 September 1969, quoted in *Conservation Foundation Letter,* October 1969

12 The time has come to make more rational use of our enormous wealth of real property, giving a new priority to our newly urgent concern with public recreation.

RICHARD M. NIXON, environmental message, 10 February 1970

13 [A 1970 study of recreation problems in urban areas of California showed] an inverse relationship between family income and desire for recreation. For example, in families with an annual income under $2,000, the desire to participate in outdoor activities was almost double that of families with an income above $9,000.

COUNCIL ON ENVIRONMENTAL QUALITY, annual report, 1971

14 What has become patently clear since the riots of 1967 is that special programs, portable pools and playground equipment will never heal the recreational sores of the nation's ghettos unless a third dimension is also provided. And that dimension is open space. Without space, how can the programs be effective, or the equipment truly enjoyed? Yet in almost every city studied, decision-makers have ignored this fundamental need, as if ghetto children were somehow allergic to green grass simply because they were raised on concrete. . . . For the majority of ghetto youngsters, outdoor recreation still remains two-dimensional—without vistas, without reference to nature, a stand-in-line affair that begins on the front stoop and winds its way to the fireplug on the corner.

CHARLES E. LITTLE and JOHN G. MITCHELL, Space for Survival, 1971

15 Attitudes toward nature and recreational preferences seem purely matters of private taste. The auto tourist sees himself as every bit as virtuous as the backpacker.

JOSEPH SAX, Mountains without Handrails, 1980

16 The modern urban-industrial world—like the feudal world—offers adventure and freedom to a certain elite, the aristocracy of our time. . . . But most, the overwhelming majority, seem condemned to the role of spectators, servitors, dependent consumers. . . . But one exception remains to the iron rule of oligarchy. At least in America one relic of our

ancient and rightful liberty has survived. And that is—a walk into the Big Woods; a journey on foot into the uninhabited interior; a voyage down the river of no return. Hunters, fishermen, hikers, climbers, white-water boatmen, red-rock explorers know what I mean. In America at least this kind of experience remains open and available to all, democratic.

EDWARD ABBEY, Down the River, 1982

17 [We need] a Prairie Fire of concern and investment, community by community, that can keep our outdoors great.

LAMAR ALEXANDER, Governor of Tennessee, in Americans Outdoors: The Legacy, the Challenge, 1987

115 RECYCLING
See also 106 POLLUTION PREVENTION, 124 SOLID WASTES, 133 WASTE AND WASTES

1 Recyclers do it more than once.
BUMPER STICKER

2 Waste Is a Terrible Thing to Mind—Recycle
BUMPER STICKER

3 Some economists maintain that total recycling is too expensive, but neither they nor anyone else knows the staggering cost of present waste mismanagement. Other economists, with commendable confidence in the abilities of scientists and engineers, say "why worry to recycle"—we can invent substitutes for anything we may run out of. But recycling conserves not only what we ordinarily think of as natural resources, but also the one God-given resource that we cannot reinvent once we destroy it—our natural environment.

ATHELSTAN SPILHAUS, Daedalus, Autumn 1967

4 In recent years we've come to appreciate the interdependence of air, water and waste pollution control, and realized they are a systems problem. Goods are not consumed. They are used. Substances remain intact and the only place they can go is back into the environment. . . . The only way to take the burden off the environment is to recycle them. Treating just changes the form, so they are hopefully less harmful, but it doesn't elimi-

nate them. . . . It's no longer a situation where ad hoc controls can do the job. We must look at it in terms of systems analysis.

ALLEN V. KNEESE, North American Wildlife and Natural Resources Conference, Houston, 1968

5 What poor as well as rich families leave on the sidewalks these days for the Sanitation Department to cart away looks to me like the stuff people used to load on moving vans, not on dump trucks. I see lamps, umbrellas, TV sets, playpens, baby carriages, bicycles, tables, refrigerators—all cut down in the prime of life. We have been educated to use; we shall now have to be reeducated to reuse, restore, renew and conserve.

SAM LEVINSON, *New York Sunday News*, 28 November 1971

6 It's time we stopped turning up our noses at the nation's garbage dumps and started appreciating them for what they really are—the municipal mines, forests, oil wells and energy sources of the future!

MAX SPENDLOVE, quoted in *National Civic Review*, February 1972

7 Our country has developed and evolved marvelous systems for exploiting raw materials for the benefit of the consumer, for getting them out of the earth, processing them, marketing them, distributing them, making people aware of them and how to get them. We have not closed the circle, though, with regard to what we do with the materials that are discarded, the valuable ones and the ones that are not so valuable. We're still very primitive in that regard.

THOMAS F. WILLIAMS, quoted in *Conservation Foundation Letter*, April 1973

8 Without concerted efforts to reduce, recycle, and reuse more industrial waste, the quantities produced will overwhelm even the best treatment and disposal systems.

SANDRA POSTEL, *Worldwatch Paper 79*, 1987

9 Perhaps no American behavior is more ripe for change than recycling. Sending our natural resources on a one-way trip from the mine to the dump is spherically senseless: it makes no sense no matter how you look at it. We throw away valuable resources, eliminate jobs, waste embedded energy, and destroy the environment—all because people don't put glass in one container and aluminum in another.

DENIS HAYES, speech, Museum of Natural History, New York City, 8 November 1989

10 Recycling is a good thing to do. It makes people feel good to do it. The thing I want to emphasize is the vast difference between recycling for the purpose of feeling good and recycling for the purpose of solving the trash problem.

BARRY COMMONER, *Orion Nature Quarterly*, Winter 1990

11 But, of course, glass—like other forms of packaging—is convenient. Getting people to recycle it is a way of reminding them of the evils of materialism and the folly of convenience.

VIRGINIA I. POSTREL, speech, City Club of Cleveland, Ohio, 19 June 1990

12 If you are not recycling, you're throwing it all away.

ENVIRONMENTAL DEFENSE FUND, advertisement, *Environment*, November 1990

13 Recycling legitimizes making more.

HELEN CALDICOTT, National Public Radio, 15 May 1991

---

116 REGULATION
See also   56 GOVERNMENT, 72 INDUSTRY

---

1 The more laws and restrictions there are,
The poorer people become,
The sharper men's weapons,
The more trouble in the land.
The more ingenious and clever men are,
The more strange things happen.
The more rules and regulations,
The more thieves and robbers.

LAO-TZU (6th century B.C.), *Tao Te Ching* 57

2 Property, like liberty, though immune from destruction . . . is not immune from regulation . . . for the common good. What the regulation should be, every generation must work out for itself.

BENJAMIN CARDOZO (1870–1938), U.S. Supreme Court justice, *Helvering et al* v. *Davis*, 1937

3 Predictions of technological impossibility or infeasibility are not sufficient as reasons to avoid tough standards and deadlines, and thus to compromise the public health. The urgency of the problem requires that the industry consider not only the improvement of existing technology, but also alternatives to the internal combustion engine and new forms of transportation. Detroit has told the nation that Americans cannot live without the automobile. This legislation would tell Detroit that if that is the case, they must make an automobile with which Americans can live.

EDMUND S. MUSKIE, U.S. Senator, speech, U.S. Senate, September 1970

4 The secretive dialogue between the control agency and the polluter must become a thing of the past.

SYDNEY HOWE, testimony, U.S. Senate Public Works subcommittee, 1971

5 [The public] certainly never intended to give a handful of bureaucrats such immense powers. If the EPA's conception of its mission is permitted to stand, it will be the single most powerful branch of government, having far greater direct control over our individual lives than Congress, or the Executive, or state and local government. . . . nor are the American people likely to permit it to endure. Clean air is a good thing—but so is liberty, and so is democracy, and so are many other things.

IRVING KRISTOL, on the Environmental Protection Agency, *Wall Street Journal*, 16 December 1974

6 Questions involving the environment are particularly prone to uncertainty. Undoubtedly, certainty is the scientific ideal. . . . But certainty in the complexities of environmental medicine may be achievable only after the fact. . . . Where a statute is precautionary in nature, the evidence difficult to come by, uncertain, or conflicting because it is on the frontiers of scientific knowledge, the regulations designed to protect the public health, and the decision that of an expert administrator, we will not demand rigorous step-by-step proof of cause and effect.

J. SKELLY WRIGHT, U.S. appellate judge, *Ethyl Corp.* v. *Environmental Protection Agency*, 19 March 1976

7 One of the most distressing aspects of the job of Administrator of EPA has been the recurring need to make regulatory decisions which cannot be deferred, on a scientific basis which can charitably be described as barely adequate. Time and again we must extrapolate from fragmentary scientific data. . . . Only the course of future events will tell us for certain whether these extrapolations were justified.

RUSSELL E. TRAIN, testimony, U.S. Senate Public Works subcommittee, 18 January 1977

8 We have seen a spate of regulations and there are more in the offing. Each one of them, it seems to me, is very well intentioned. Each of them seemingly is designed to protect us from some hazard, small or large, and perhaps one could live with any one of them. The sum of them constitutes a failure of nerve, a desire to stop our technological progress.

PHILIP HANDLER, "In Search of the Real America," PBS, 1 June 1978

9 There seems to be no limit to what the federal government is willing to do to indulge the fanatical concerns about what we eat, drink, and breathe.

WILLIAM TUCKER, *Harper's*, August 1978

10 There's a tremendous emotional head of steam behind this antigovernment and anti-regulation phenomenon.

DOUGLAS M. COSTLE, EPA administrator, speech, Public Citizens Forum, Washington, D.C., 3 August 1978

11 [The major benefits of regulation may derive from] a restructuring of the nature of industrial production and earlier anticipation of avoidable problems, such as the hazardous waste disposal at Love Canal.

NICHOLAS A. ASHFORD, *New York Times*, 15 June 1980

12 The EPA has rules that would practically shut down the economy if they were put into effect.

DAVID A. STOCKMAN, Reagan administration budget director, *Science*, 28 November 1980

13 The real cost of regulations is likely to be far less than the hidden public subsidy to polluters—a subsidy which distorts the market-

place and which regulations should be designed to remove.
MALCOLM F. BALDWIN, *Environment*, April 1981

14 There is no doubt that regulation can impede and even prevent the introduction of new industrial products and processes. That is often the purpose of regulation: to force improvements and the consideration of alternatives, and to prevent some dangerous products from reaching the market.
RICHARD KAZIS and RICHARD L. GROSSMAN, *Fear at Work*, 1982

15 We can preserve everything, we can clean up everything. But then we have to be prepared to deal with no autos, no microchips, no dry-cleaning solvents.
ANNE M. GORSUCH, EPA administrator, quoted in *New York Times*, 28 September 1983

16 Government's view of the economy could be summed up in a few short phrases: If it moves, tax it. If it keeps moving, regulate it. And if it stops moving, subsidize it.
RONALD REAGAN, remarks at White House Conference on Small Business, 15 August 1986

17 Without any divine guidance or highly visible leadership, we just started identifying problems and fussing around with them and coming up with a program which typically was a regulatory program. By and large, given the agenda of the time, we did pretty damn well.
RUSSELL E. TRAIN, *Amicus Journal*, Summer 1987

18 At that rate it will take 1,820 years to do something about the remaining chemicals on the list, almost as long as since when Christ walked on Earth.
GERRY E. SIKORSKI, U.S. Representative, on the slow pace of regulation of 650 targeted highly toxic chemicals, 1984, quoted in Michael H. Brown, *The Toxic Cloud: The Poisoning of America's Air*, 1988

19 I don't care if the law's in effect or not. I just ain't gonna use a goddam TED [turtle extrusion device]. I been shrimpin' since 1972, and

I don't want a bunch of Washington politicians tellin' me how to catch shrimp.
JIMMY ("Like hell I'm gonna tell you my last name"), quoted in *Striking Back*, newsletter of the Reptile Defense Fund, 1989

20 We are realizing that conventional end-of-pipe regulations will in the long run do little more than move pollution around. We have also recognized that we need to use new mechanisms to achieve environmental quality, such as market incentives, technology transfer, and information.
ALVIN L. ALM, *Environmental Science and Technology* 24, no. 4, April 1990

21 I reject the extremist environmentalists who would burden our economy with mindless regulation.
GEORGE BUSH, on proposed new Clean-air Act, April 1990

22 In 1972, there were fewer than 500 pages of federal environmental regulations; today there are more than 10,000. . . . The increase in the amount of state environmental legislation and regulation has been much greater.
CLAYTON F. CALLIS, *Environmental Science and Technology* 24, no. 4, April 1990

23 If society had not mandated controls on automobiles and industry in 1970, emissions would be 130–315% higher today.
ANTHONY D. CORTESE, *Environmental Science and Technology* 24, no. 4, April 1990

117 RELIGION
See also 49 ETHICS, 68 HUMANKIND AND NATURE

1 What else is nature but God?
SENECA THE YOUNGER (4 B.C.–A.D. 65), *De beneficiis*

2 Those honor Nature well, who teach that she can speak on everything, even on theology.
BLAISE PASCAL (1623–1662), *Pensées*, 1670

3 Such is the artificial contrivance of this mighty machine of nature that, whilst its motions and various phenomena strike on our

senses, the hand which actuates the whole is itself unperceivable to men of flesh and blood.

GEORGE BERKELEY (1685–1753), *Principles of Human Knowledge*, 1710

4 All are but parts of one stupendous whole, Whose body nature is, and God the soul.

ALEXANDER POPE (1688–1744), *An Essay on Man*, 1733

5 The fruitfulness of Nature is without limits, since it is nothing but the exercise of the divine omnipotence.

IMMANUEL KANT (1724–1804), *Allgemeine Naturgeschichte*, 1755

6 All false religion is in conflict with nature.

JEAN-JACQUES ROUSSEAU (1712–1778), *La nouvelle Héloise*, 1761

7 Everything is perfect coming from the hands of the Creator; everything degenerates in the hands of man.

JEAN-JACQUES ROUSSEAU (1712–1778), *Émile*, 1762

8 The forces of nature move in numbered squadrons, with measured step, and on a predetermined plan, as if under the command of a presiding intelligence.

JAMES McCOSH, *The Method of Divine Government*, 1850

9 Blessed are they who never read a newspaper, for they shall see Nature, and, through her, God.

HENRY DAVID THOREAU (1817–1862), *Essays and Other Writings*, 1906

10 What I call God,
And fools call Nature.

ROBERT BROWNING, (1821–1889), *The Ring and the Book*, 1868–1869

11 The anthropomorphic notion of a deliberate architect and ruler of the world has gone forever from this field; the "eternal iron laws of nature" have taken its place.

ERNEST HAECKEL (1834–1919), *The Riddle of the Universe*, 1901

12 The more men know about nature, and the more they rely upon nature, the more agnostic and hopeless they become.

O. A. CURTIS, *The Christian Faith*, 1905

13 Nature . . . is God's daughter.

FRANCIS THOMPSON (1859–1907), *Nature's Immortality*, 1910

14 Every walk to the woods is a religious rite, every bath in the stream is a saving ordinance. Communion service is at all hours, and the bread and wine are from the heart and marrow of Mother Earth. There are no heretics in Nature's church; all are believers, all are communicants. The beauty of natural religion is that you have it all the time; you do not have to seek it afar off in myths and legends, in catacombs, in garbled texts, in miracles of dead saints or wine-bibbing friars. It is of to-day; it is now and here; it is everywhere.

JOHN BURROUGHS, *Accepting the Universe*, 1920

15 There is no religion healthier for a man's spiritual and physical well-being than the pagan worship of the woodsman.

IRVIN S. COBB, *Izaak Walton League Monthly*, February 1923

16 If, then, I call God nature, it is for greater simplicity, and because it irritates the theologians.

ANDRE GIDE (1869–1951), *Les nouvelles nourritures*, 1935

17 All devotees of nature and the outdoors are prophets and promulgators of a kind of gospel. . . . They are communicants of a common faith.

ALAN DEVOE, *Audubon*, November–December 1946

18 When the first peeper is heard in the spring on that day something older than any Christian God has risen. The earth is alive again.

JOSEPH WOOD KRUTCH (1893–1970), *The Twelve Seasons*, 1949

19 I think that the man who just likes to look at geysers has as much right to do so as the one who likes to look at a geyser and see God.

BERNARD DE VOTO (1897–1955), letter to Newton Drury, 3 February 1949

20 I do not think it is important whether a man enters religion by the front door or the back door as long as he enters. . . . If to find God by the garden path is the back door, then by all means go down the garden path.

LIN YUTANG, *On the Wisdom of America*, 1950

21 "Nature" has silently displaced God as the ultimate basis to which all other things are referred.
   WALTER MOBERLY, *The Crisis in the University*, 1951

22 Nature, as a whole and in all its elements, enunciates something that may be regarded as an indirect self-communication of God to all those ready to receive it.
   MARTIN BUBER (1878–1965), *At the Turning*, 1952

23 The basic tenets of all great religions, the distilled spiritual wisdom of humanity, coincide closely with what science reveals in nature. The universe is based on order, not on chaos and chance.
   GEORGE RUSSELL HARRISON, *What Man May Be*, 1956

24 One may point to nature and say, "There *is* a God," but one cannot point to nature and say "*There* God is."
   CARL MICHAELSON, in Paul Ramsey, ed., *Faith and Ethics*, 1957

25 Does morality bid man live according to nature? Hardly, nature is neither kind nor cruel, neither benevolent or malevolent. Nature is blind, irrational, capricious. This is why it is blasphemous to identify God and nature.
   FREDERICK E. FLYNN, speech, Catholic Physicians' Guild of Southern California, 1960

26 This is what I have learnt from my contact with the earth—the diaphany of the divine at the heart of a glowing universe, the divine radiating from the depths of matter a-flame.
   PIERRE TEILHARD DE CHARDIN (1881–1955), *Letters from a Traveller*, 1962

27 The laws of nature are written deep in the folds and faults of the earth. By encouraging men to learn those laws one can lead them further to a knowledge of the author of all laws.
   JOHN JOSEPH LYNCH, quoted in *New York Times*, 5 December 1963

28 The more our knowledge of the natural has grown, the more we have lost our former capacity to respond to supernatural reality transcendent to nature.
   WILLIAM G. POLLARD, *Space Age Christianity*, 1963

29 I believe in God, only I spell it Nature.
   FRANK LLOYD WRIGHT (1867–1959), quoted, 14 August 1966

30 Both our present science and our present technology are so tinctured with orthodox Christian arrogance toward nature that no solution for our ecologic crisis can be expected from them alone.
   LYNN I. WHITE, JR., *Science*, 10 March 1967

31 The victory of Christianity over paganism was the greatest psychic revolution in the history of our culture. By destroying pagan animism, Christianity made it possible to exploit nature in a mood of indifference to the feelings of natural objects.
   LYNN I. WHITE, JR., *Science*, 10 March 1967

32 Christianity is the most anthropocentric religion the world has ever seen.
   LYNN I. WHITE, JR., *Science*, 10 March 1967

33 We are in a kind of religion, an ethic with regard to terrain, and this religion is closest to the Buddhist, I suppose. We can take some cues from other religions. There is something else to do than bang your way forward.
   DAVID R. BROWER, quoted in Stephen Fox, *John Muir and His Legacy*, 1970

34 Religion cannot be kept within the bounds of sermons and scriptures. It is a force in itself and it calls for the integration of lands and peoples in harmonious unity. The lands [of the planet] wait for those who can discern their rhythms. The peculiar genius of each continent, each river valley, the rugged mountains, the placid lakes, all call for relief from the constant burden of exploitation.
   VINE DELORIA, *God Is Red*, 1973

35 Since the roots of our [environmental] trouble are so largely religious, the remedy must also be essentially religious.
   LYNN I. WHITE, JR., in Ian G. Barbour, ed. *Western Man and Environmental Ethics*, 1973

36 For Christians, nature cannot be fully nature except through man. There is no "democracy" of all creatures; a single human soul is worth more than the entire material creation. Just as man is here to serve God, so nature is here to serve man.
   R. V. YOUNG, *National Review*, 20 December 1974

37 The ecology movement, as many have noted, often takes on the quality of a religious awakening; in this respect it is only an overt example of our age's insistence on substituting science for traditional religions.
DONALD WORSTER, *Nature's Economy*, 1977

38 [Interior Secretary James G.] Watt seems to think he has divine sanction for his efforts to turn our natural resources over to concessioners and developers. He has been quoted . . . as saying, "My responsibility is to follow the Scriptures, which call upon us to occupy the land until Jesus returns."
SIERRA CLUB, *Sierra*, July–August 1981

39 Christianity, along with agriculture and artifice, wrenched man from his niche and made him sometime master of the earth.
JOHN R. STILGOE, *Common Landscape of America, 1580 to 1845*, 1982

40 Most people in deep ecology have had the feeling . . . that they are connected with something greater than their ego, greater than their name, their family, their special attributes as an individual—a feeling that is often called oceanic because many have it on the ocean. Without that identification, one is not easily drawn to become involved in deep ecology. . . . The main point is that deep ecology has a religious component, fundamental intuitions that everyone must cultivate if he or she is to have a life based on values and not function like a computer.
ARNE NAESS, quoted in Bill Devall and George Sessions, *Deep Ecology*, 1985

41 The encounter of God and man in nature is thus conceived in Judaism as a seamless webb with man as the leader and custodian of the natural world. . . . Man was given dominion over nature, but was commanded to behave towards the rest of creation with justice and compassion. Man lives, always, in tension between his power and the limits set by his conscience.
ARTHUR HERTZBERG, *Assisi Declarations*, World Wildlife Fund 25th anniversary, 29 September 1986

42 Unity, trusteeship and accountability, that is *tawheed,khalifa* and *akhrah*, the three central concepts of Islam, are also the pillars of the environmental ethics of Islam. They constitute the basic values taught by the Qur'an.
ABDULLAH OMAR NASEEF, *Assisi Declarations*, World Wildlife Fund 25th anniversary, 29 September 1986

43 The Quran states that human beings are God's vicegerents on Earth. It is therefore incumbent upon them to care for and to protect the natural environment which God has created and sustained and which reveals at every turn the glory of His creative power.
SEYYED HOSSEIN NASR, *Mother Earth News*, March–April 1990

44 Anthropocentrism is simply irrational. And yet this is the thrust of much of our traditional religious thought and teaching, particularly in the West.
RUSSELL E. TRAIN, speech, North American Conference on Religion and Ecology, Washington, D.C., 18 May 1990

45 . . . I have been puzzled—to say the least—by what seems to me to be the almost total obliviousness of organized religion toward the environment. It has been nothing less than extraordinary.
RUSSELL E. TRAIN, speech, North American Conference on Religion and Ecology, Washington, D.C., 18 May 1990

46 The natural world feeds not only our bodies but also our souls. We lose even the sacraments as we lose the natural world. If the water is polluted it cannot properly be used for Baptism since it is a sign of death rather than of life. If our bread is denatured or contaminated with chemicals, it is to that extent inappropriate for celebration of the Eucharist.
THOMAS BERRY, *Catholic World*, July–August 1990

118 RISK
See also   61 HEALTH, 116 REGULATION

1 Risk varies inversely with knowledge.
IRVING FISHER, *The Theory of Interest*, 1930

2 Our whole way of life today is dedicated to the *removal of risk*. Cradle to grave we are

supported, insulated, and isolated from the risks of life—and if we fall, our government stands ready with Bandaids of every size.

SHIRLEY TEMPLE BLACK, speech, Kiwanis International Convention, Texas, June 1967

3 When some high-sounding institute states that a compound is harmless or a process free of risk, it is wise to know whence the institute or the scientists who work there obtain their financial support.

LANCET, editorial on the "medical-industrial complex," 1973

4 Should we forbid international travel, given the certain knowledge that our quarantine procedures are quite unable to hinder the importation of exotic diseases?

JOSHUA LEDERBERG, arguing that the benefits of genetic engineering greatly outweigh the "speculative hazards," Prism, November 1975

5 It is obvious that many projects justified by cost-benefit analysis do result in the predictable loss of life. This is true for any projects that increase air or ground traffic, radiation exposure, or air pollution, for example. What allows cost-benefit analysts to "justify" such projects? It is essentially the fact that we never know in advance the identities of the specific people who will be killed. The result is that we never have to compensate anyone for his certain loss of life but instead we must compensate everyone for the additional risk to which he is exposed as a result of the project.

HERMAN E. DALY, Steady-State Economics, 1977

6 If all these foods and drinks we've been swallowing for centuries were as dangerous as they say, we'd all be dead, but we're not.

DAVID BRINKLEY, radio commentary, 23 May 1978

7 It is illogical to conclude that, since we are already subjected to many risks, a few more will not matter. It would seem to me that the public should be encouraged by scientists to consider carefully what they put into their bodies, intentionally or otherwise.

LIEBE F. CAVALIERI, letter, New York Times, 8 August 1978

8 The desire to build a risk-free society has always been a sign of decadence. It has meant that the nation has given up, that it no longer believes in its destiny, that it has ceased to aspire to greatness, and has retired from history to pet itself.

HENRY FAIRLIE, quoted in Congressional Record, 1 August 1979

9 Factual information must be available to citizens who increasingly make decisions in their own communities as to which degree of which risks they want to take and which measures they are willing to take to lower the risks.

THOMAS F. WILLIAMS, quoted in Conservation Foundation Letter, November 1981

10 Today's world is one in which the age-old risks of humankind—the drought, floods, communicable diseases—are less of a problem than ever before. They have been replaced by risks of humanity's own making—the unintended side-effects of beneficial technologies and the intended effects of the technologies of war. Society must hope that the world's ability to assess and manage risks will keep pace with its ability to create them.

J. CLARENCE DAVIES, quoted in Conservation Foundation, State of the Environment: An Assessment at Mid-Decade, 1984

11 How does the risk of 100 people contracting lung cancer compare with the risk of 50 deformed births, or the risk of 1,000 injuries resulting from automobile accidents to the risk of two fish species becoming extinct? But these are exactly the types of risks that somehow must be compared when setting priorities.

J. CLARENCE DAVIES, quoted in Conservation Foundation, State of the Environment: An Assessment at Mid-Decade, 1984

12 An unfamiliar, involuntary risk, such as living near a hazardous waste site, is perceived as more risky than a familiar, voluntarily accepted one, such as skiing.

COUNCIL ON ENVIRONMENTAL QUALITY, Risk Analysis, 1989

13 It is the safest of times, it is the riskiest of times. . . . What the Dickens is going on here?
DENTON MORRISON, on chemicals, technology, and risk, quoted in National Academy of Sciences, *Improving Risk Communication,* 1989

14 We must articulate these concerns, the trade-offs and the risk assessment that are involved in a way that the public can understand. . . . Americans should keep food-safety issues in perspective. Our food supply is safer than that of any other country in the world. Whether it is as safe as we would like it is a debatable question.
CLAYTON K. YEUTTER, U.S. Secretary of Agriculture, on the public's concern about food safety, pesticides, etc., quoted in *USA Today,* 4 April 1989

15 [If we] take an absolutist point of view [in pursuing zero risk, in a few years] there will be nothing on our tables [considered safe].
D. ALLAN BROMLEY, speech, annual meeting of American Industrial Health Council, 28 November 1990

119 RIVERS
See also 21 DAMS AND WATER PROJECTS

1 The flow of the river is ceaseless and its water is never the same. The bubbles that float in the pools, now vanishing, now forming, are not of long duration: so in the world are man and his dwellings. . . . [People] die in the morning, they are born in the evening, like foam on the water.
KAMO CHOMEI (1153–1216), *Hojo-ki* (An account of my hut), 1212

2 And an ingenious Spaniard says, that rivers and the inhabitants of the watery element were made for wise men to contemplate, and fools to pass by without consideration.
IZAAK WALTON (1593–1683)

3 The life in us is like the water in the river. It may rise this year higher than man has ever known it, and flood the parched uplands; even this may be the eventful year, which

will drown out all our muskrats. It was not always dry land where we dwell. I see far inland the banks where the stream anciently washed, before science began to record its freshets.
HENRY DAVID THOREAU (1817–1862), *Walden,* 1854

4 [The Grand Canyon] is, of course, altogether valueless. It can be approached only from the south, and after entering it there is nothing to do but leave. Ours has been the first, and will doubtless be the last, to visit this profitless locality. It seems intended by nature that the Colorado River, along the greater portion of its lonely and majestic way, shall be forever unvisited and undisturbed.
LIEUTENANT JOSEPH C. IVES, report to Congress on the Colorado River, 1861

5 For real company and friendship, there is nothing outside of the animal kingdom that is comparable to a river.
HENRY VAN DYKE (1852–1933), *Little Rivers,* 1895

6 The river has taught me to listen; you will learn from it, too. The river knows everything; one can learn everything from it. You have already learned from the river that it is good to strive downwards, to sink, to seek the depths.
HERMAN HESSE (1877–1962), *Siddharta,* 1922

7 I've known rivers:
  I've known rivers ancient as the world and older than the flow of human blood in human veins.
My soul has grown deep like the rivers.
LANGSTON HUGHES (1902–1967), "The Negro Speaks of Rivers," 1926

8 And how should a beautiful, ignorant stream of water know it heads for an early release— out across the desert, running toward the Gulf, below sea level, to murmur its lullaby, and see the Imperial Valley rise out of burning sand with cotton blossoms, wheat, watermelons, roses, how should it know?
CARL SANDBURG (1878–1967), *Good Morning America,* 1928

9 A river is more than an amenity . . . it is a treasure. It offers a necessity of life that must

be rationed among those who have power
over it.

OLIVER WENDELL HOLMES, JR. (1841–1935),
U.S. Supreme Court justice, *New Jersey* v.
New York, 4 May 1931

10 A river seems a magic thing. A magic, moving, living part of the very earth itself—for it
is from the soil, both from its depth and from
its surface, that a river has its beginning.

LAURA GILPIN, *The Rio Grande*, 1949

11 Hills may exalt the spirit; rivers cleanse and
soothe it. Seas and forests awe men by their
vastness; rivers are informal and companion-
able. One part of a woodland is pretty much
like the rest of it; dozens of mountains resem-
ble each other; no single acre of ocean, lake or
pond differs perceptibly from the remainder.
No one has ever seen two rivers that were
identical for a furlong. No one ever will.

FREDERIC F. VAN DE WATER, *In Defense of
Worms*, 1949

12 The life of every river sings its own song, but
in most the song is long marred by the discords of misuse.

ALDO LEOPOLD (1886–1948), *Sand County Almanac*, 1949

13 No one has the right to use America's rivers
and America's waterways, that belong to all
the people, as a sewer. The banks of a river
may belong to one man or one industry or
one State, but the waters which flow between
the banks should belong to all the people.

LYNDON B. JOHNSON (1908–1973), signing the
Clean Water Act of 1965

14 The river called. The call is the thundering
rumble of distant rapids, the intimate roar of
white water . . . a primeval summons to pri-
mordial values.

JOHN J. CRAIGHEAD, *Naturalist*, Autumn 1965

15 Some day our rivers will be equally as important as pleasure ways as our roadways are at
present. Some day they will become the most
important and the most beautiful highways
that we have, and especially if they are kept
in this primitive way.

JENS JENSEN, in Duke Frederick et al., eds.,
Destroy to Create, 1972

16 The real question is whether the [Hudson]
river's national importance shall be sacrificed

to these enterprises which would change the
shoreline, lower high peaks, destroy groves
of trees. . . . The Hudson answers a spiritual
need more necessary to the nation's health
than all the commercial products it can provide, than all the money it can earn.

CARL CARMER, quoted in *Harper's*, December
1977

17 Cleaning up a river is a cause worth fighting
for . . . . We had allowed some people to
make good profit along the Hudson and then
go somewhere else to enjoy clear water.

PETER SEEGER, quoted in *The Cousteau Almanac*, 1980

18 Rivers have what man most respects and
longs for in his own life and thought—a capacity for renewal and replenishment, continual energy, creativity, cleansing.

JOHN M. KAUFFMANN, *EPA Journal*. May 1981

19 One could almost say, then, that the history
of the Colorado River contains a metaphor for
our time. One could say that the age of great
expectations was inaugurated at Hoover
Dam—a fifty-year flowering of hopes when
all things appeared possible. And one could
say that amid the salt-encrusted sands of the
river's dried-up delta, we began to founder
on the Era of Limits.

MARC REISNER, *Cadillac Desert*, 1986

20 We grow up hearing so often that a straight
line is the shortest distance between two
points that we end up thinking it is also the
best way to get there. A river knows better—it
has to do with how it dissipates the energy of
its flow most efficiently; and how, in its
bends, the sediment deposited soon turns
into marshes and swampy islands, harboring
all manner of interesting life, imparting
charm and character to the whole waterway.
I would defy you to find a river on this planet
that prefers to run straight, unless it has been
taught so by the U.S. Army Corps of Engineers.

TOM HORTON, *Bay Country*, 1987

21 The Niagara is more than a river—it is a lesson in what happens when neighbors dump
garbage on one another's front lawn.

THOMAS MCMILLAN, Canadian Minister of
the Environment, quoted in *U.S. News and
World Report*, 16 February 1987

22 The [Hudson] river and its valley, are neither our enemy to be conquered, nor our servant to be controlled, nor our mistress to be seduced. The river is a pervasive presence beyond all these. It is the ultimate psychic as well as the physical context out of which we emerge into being and by which we are nourished, guided, healed, and fulfilled.

> THOMAS BERRY, in Peter Borelli, ed., *Crossroads*, 1988

23 Unfortunately, our rivers carry the waste into the bay like veins into a heart.

> PATRICK NOONAN, quoted in *Countryside*, Winter 1990

24 [A Montana statute] holds that a river has a right to overwhelm its banks and inundate its floodplain. Well, that's interesting, because it's not a right that *we* assign to the river. The river has earned it through centuries of deluging and shaping the floodplain, and the floodplain has a right to its rampaging river. They've earned their rights through a kind of reciprocal action.

> DAN KEMMIS, quoted in *Harper's*, February 1991

---

120 RURAL AREAS
See also   129 TOWNS

---

1 Forget six countries overhung with smoke,
Forget the snorting steam and piston stroke,
Forget the spreading of the hideous town;
Think rather of the pack-horse on the down,
And dream of London, small, and white, and clean.

> WILLIAM MORRIS (1834–1896), introduction to *The Earthy Paradise*, 1868

2 There is much confusion between land and country. Land is the place where corn, gullies, and mortgages grow. Country is the personality of land, the collective harmony of its soil, life, and weather. Country knows no mortgages, no alphabetical agencies, no tobacco road; it is calmly aloof to these petty exigencies of its alleged owners.

> ALDO LEOPOLD (1886–1948), *Round River*, 1953

3 In country, as in people, a plain exterior often conceals hidden riches, to perceive which requires much living in and with.

> ALDO LEOPOLD (1886–1948), *Round River*, 1953

4 The soft veil of nostalgia that hangs over our urbanized landscape is largely a vestige of the once dominant image of an undefiled, green republic, a quiet land of forests, villages, and farms dedicated to the pursuit of happiness.

> LEO MARX, *The Machine in the Garden*, 1964

5 Now [in the mid-20th century] the great world is invading the land, transforming the sensory texture of rural life—the way it looks and sounds—and threatening, in fact, to impose a new and more complete dominion over it.

> LEO MARX, *The Machine in the Garden*, 1964

6 Ironically, rural America has become viewed by a growing number of Americans as having a higher [quality of life] not because of what it has, but rather because of what it does not have!

> DON A. DILLMAN, *Annals of the American Academy of Political and Social Science*, January 1977

7 It needs so little to keep this precious heritage of a rural life on a scale that can be measured almost by our hands, so simple a decision as to stop the developers from moving in. There are some things more important than profits for realtors. Just pass a law—a Town and Country Planning Act, as it is called in Britain—and you will not have to go to England to find the stone walls and the hedges, the cows and the ducks, the hay and the corn, that bring the country to the very gates of the great cities.

> HENRY FAIRLEE, *National Parks and Conservation*, February 1978

8 Despite all our efforts, there is a steady, perceptible degradation of the countryside—an erosion of the distinctive qualities that differentiate one place from another. As they confront piecemeal urbanization, people all over the country are asking, how can we save our special places?

> WILLIAM K. REILLY, speech, Commonwealth Club, San Francisco, 1987

9 For the first time in U.S. history, rural and agriculture are no longer synonymous.

> RONALD D. KNUTSON, *Options in Developing a New National Rural Policy*, 1989

121 SCIENCE
See also   29 ECOLOGY

1 Why does not science, instead of troubling itself about sunspots, which nobody ever saw, or, if they did, ought not to speak about?—why does not science busy itself with drainage and sanitary engineering? Why does it not clean the streets and free the rivers from pollution? Why, in England there is scarcely a river which at some point is not polluted; and the flowers are all withering on the banks!
OSCAR WILDE (1854–1900), quoted in *Philadelphia Press*, 17 January 1882

2 Science has the power to illuminate, but not to solve, the deeper problems of mankind. For always after knowledge come choice and action, both of them intensely personal and individual.
PAUL SEARS, *Deserts on the March*, 1947

3 Science knows little about home range: how big it is at various seasons, what food and cover it must include, when and how it is defended against trespass and whether ownership is an individual, family, or group affair. These are fundamentals of animal economics, or ecology.
ALDO LEOPOLD (1886–1948), *A Sand County Almanac*, 1949

4 We are in a fever of almost hysterical emphasis on science as a material weapon; on increasing economic wealth, ability, invention, as a weapon. . . . Our civilization needs to adopt the mountaineer pace, somewhat slower, but steady and upward.
OLAUS J. MURIE, manuscript, 21 March 1958, Wilderness Society papers

5 The further I go, the more I am convinced that the only true science—the only one we can acquire in this ocean of weakness and ignorance—is the vision that begins to take shape under and through the multiplicity of things.
PIERRE TEILHARD DE CHARDIN (1881–1955), *Letters from a Traveller*, 1962

6 Science is triumphant with far-ranging success, but its triumph is somehow clouded by growing difficulties in providing for the simple necessities of human life on the earth.
BARRY COMMONER, *Science and Survival*, 1966

7 Science has, as its whole purpose, the rendering of the physical world understandable and beautiful. Without this you have only tables and statistics. The measure of our success is our ability to live with this knowledge effectively, actively and eventually with delight.
J. ROBERT OPPENHEIMER, *Look*, 1966

8 When the mad professor of fiction blows up his laboratory and then himself, that's okay, but when scientists and decision-makers act out of ignorance and pretend it is knowledge, they are using the biosphere, the living space, as an experimental laboratory, and the whole world is put at its hazard.
LORD RITCHIE-CALDER, in Clifton Fadiman and Jean White, eds., *Ecocide*, 1971

9 Conventional science is often as barren as its counterparts in the humanities and social sciences, and its effects have often been disruptive of healthy relationships between humanity and nature. But with care and good judgment, scientific knowledge of natural systems and processes can be pried loose from the narrow specializations where it is now confined, making it available for integration with other forms of knowledge.
JOSEPH MEEKER, *Cry California*, Summer 1981

10 It is possible to have a very good understanding of the overall behavior of a system *without* having a complete understanding of its microscopic workings. For example, we can predict quite well what the annual rainfall in Washington, D.C., will be this year, even though we have no idea whether it will rain exactly three weeks from today. We know unequivocally that smoking causes cancer, even though we don't know the detailed chemical mechanisms involved.
ROY R. GOULD, testimony, U.S. Senate Environment and Public Works Committee, 25 May 1982

11 All the sciences are fragmentary and incomplete in relation to basic rules and norms, so it's very shallow to think that science can

solve our problems. Without basic norms, there is no science.

ARNE NAESS, quoted in Bill Devall and George Sessions, *Deep Ecology*, 1985

12 Compared to the [scientific] professions that are taken more seriously, a naturalist is rather a dabbler. Naturalists are wanderers and wonderers, and perhaps there is not time for that in the highly paced world in which we live.

ANN ZURNGER, quoted in Daniel Halpern, *On Nature*, 1986

13 The saddest aspect of life right now is that science gathers knowledge faster than society gathers wisdom.

ISAAC ASIMOV, *Isaac Asimov's Book of Science and Nature Quotations*, 1988

14 There is a tension between the scientific culture of caution and reticence and the media's penchant for drama, dread, and debate that keeps the show lively and the audience tuning in. . . . [T]here is a growing mismatch between the complex nature of reality and the way such problems are usually reported in the popular media or perceived by the public.

STEPHEN H. SCHNEIDER, *Global Warming: Are We Entering the Greenhouse Century?*, 1989

15 As a scientist and engineer I find profoundly disturbing [the] great license taken with scientific facts and their interpretation in cases where scientific uncertainty prevents categorical answers.

ROBERT M. WHITE, *The Bridge*, Summer 1990

16 The entire scientific community is in its infancy in determining interactions among forms of pollution. Knowledge about the current state of the environment, exposure levels, and future trends is primitive at best.

AL ALM, *EPA Journal*, September–October 1990

---

122 SOIL

1 Stop treating soil like dirt.
BUMPER STICKER

2 The whole black earth is oppressed beneath the storm . . . all the rivers flow in flood, and many hillsides are furrowed deeply by the torrents, and they rush to the purple sea from the mountains, roaring mightily, and the fields of men are wasted.

HOMER, *Iliad*, c. 750 B.C.

3 Not every soil can bear all things.
VIRGIL (70–19 B.C.), *Georgics*, 36–29 B.C.

4 In fact in regard to one of nature's elements [soil] we have no gratitude. For what luxuries and for what outrageous uses does she not subserve mankind? She is flung into the sea, or dug away to allow us to let in the channels. Water, iron, wood, fire, stone, growing crops, are employed to torture her at all hours, and much more to make her minister to our luxuries than our sustenance. Yet in order to make the sufferings inflicted on her surface and mere outer skin seem endurable, we probe her entrails, digging into her veins of gold and silver and mines of copper and lead; we actually drive shafts down into the depth to search for gems and certain tiny stones; we drag out her entrails, we seek a jewel merely to be worn upon a finger!

PLINY THE ELDER (A.D. 23–79), *Natural History*

5 On fat land grow the foulest weeds.
WILLIAM LANGLAND (c. 1330–c. 1400), *Piers Plowman*

6 Most subject is the fattest soil to weeds.
WILLIAM SHAKESPEARE (1564–1616), *Henry IV, Part 2*, 4.4.54, 1598

7 The earth's a thief,
that feeds and breathes by a composture stolen
From general excrement.
WILLIAM SHAKESPEARE (1564–1616), *Timon of Athens*, 4.3.438, 1607

8 As sickly plants betray a niggard earth,
Whose barren bosom starves her gen'rous birth.
THOMAS GRAY (1716–1771), *The Alliance of Education and Government*, c. 1748

9 While the farmer holds the title to the land, actually, it belongs to all the people because civilization itself rests upon the soil.
THOMAS JEFFERSON (1743–1826), quoted in *Des Moines Register*, 8 July 1979

10 The limitation to production from the properties of the soil, is not like the obstacle op-

posed by a wall, which stands immovable in one particular spot, and offers no hindrance to motion short of stopping it entirely. We may rather compare it to a highly elastic and extensible band, which is hardly ever so violently stretched that it could not possibly be stretched any more, yet the pressure of which is felt long before the final limit is reached, and felt more severely the nearer that limit is approached.

JOHN STUART MILL (1806–1873), *Principles of Political Economy*, 1848

11 By avarice and selfishness, and a grovelling habit, from which none of us is free, of regarding the soil as property, or the means of acquiring property chiefly, the landscape is deformed, husbandry is degraded with us, and the farmer leads the meanest of lives. He knows Nature but as a robber.

HENRY DAVID THOREAU (1817–1862), *Walden*, 1854

12 Behold this compost! behold it well!
Perhaps every mite has once form'd part of a
    sick person—yet behold!
The grass of spring covers the prairies,
The bean bursts noiselessly through the
    mould. . . .
Out of its little hill faithfully rise the potato's
    dark green leaves,
Out of its hill rises the yellow maize-stalk, the
    lilacs bloom in the dooryards,
The summer growth is innocent and disdain-
    ful above all those strata of sour dead.

WALT WHITMAN (1819–1892), "This Compost," 1855

13 The plow is one of the most ancient and most valuable of man's inventions; but long before he existed the land was in fact regularly plowed, and still continues to be thus plowed by earthworms. It may be doubted whether there are many other animals which have played so important a part in the history of the world, as have these lowly organized creatures.

CHARLES DARWIN, (1809–1882), *The Formation of Vegetable Mold, through the Action of Worms*, 1881

14 When the soil is gone, men must go; and the process does not take long.

THEODORE ROOSEVELT (1858–1919), message to conservationists, 8 December 1908

15 As the day wore on Father fell into dumb, despairing rage. His rigid face and smoldering eyes, his grim lips, terrified us all. It seemed to him (as to us), that the entire farm was about to take flight and the bitterest part of the tragic circumstance lay in the reflection that our loss (which was much greater than any of our neighbors) was due to the extra care with which we had pulverized the ground.

HAMLIN GARLAND (1860–1940), *Son of the Middle Border*, 1917

16 The Chinese are the greatest individualists on earth. They cut their forests, silted up their streams, and destroyed millions of acres of their land by erosion gullies. Thus, they became increasingly subject to flood and drought. Their soil, exposed without cover to high winds, blew around in raging dust storms. The Chinaman's individualistic treatment of the land has exposed the Chinese again and again to famine.

They have been there a long time. Destructive as they have been, we in the United States, during the past mere 150 years, have handled our land in a way that indicates even more destructive possibilities. Over large areas we are even worse than the Chinese, because we made no real effort to restore to the soil the fertility which has been removed.

HENRY A. WALLACE (1888–1965), U.S. Secretary of Agriculture, *New Frontiers*, 1934

17 There was nothing sound in the situation in the past, when, spurred by ruinously low prices, farmers have been compelled to mine their soil of its fertility by overintensive cultivation. . . . Dust storms and mud-laden streams have been symbols of this exploitation. . . . Real damage to the consumer does not result from moderate increases in food prices, but from collapse of farm income so drastic as to compel ruthless depletion of soil. That is the real menace to the nation's future food supply.

FRANKLIN D. ROOSEVELT (1883–1945), statement on agricultural policy, October 1935

18 The nation that destroys its soil destroys itself.

FRANKLIN D. ROOSEVELT, letter to the governors, 26 February 1937

19 Little by little the sky was darkened by the mixing dust, and the wind felt over the earth,

loosened the dust, and carried it away. . . . The finest dust did not settle back to earth now, but disappeared into the darkening sky . . . . The corn fought the wind with its weakened leaves until the roots were freed by the prying wind and then each stalk settled wearily sideways toward the earth.

JOHN STEINBECK (1902–1968), *The Grapes of Wrath*, 1939

20 We all got to figure. There's some way to stop this. It's not like lightning or earthquakes. We've got a bad thing made by men, and by God that's something we can change.

JOHN STEINBECK (1902–1968), on the dust bowl, *The Grapes of Wrath*, 1939

21 You have stirred the soil with your plow, my friend.
It will never be the same again.

MARTHA OSTENSO, "O River, Remember," 1943

22 This nation and civilization is founded upon nine inches of topsoil and when that is gone there will no longer be any nation or any civilization.

HUGH BENNETT, quoted in Paul B. Sears, *Deserts on the March*, 1947

23 The soil is the source of life, creativity, culture, and real independence.

DAVID BEN-GURION (1886–1973), *Hazon VeDerek*, 1951

24 The continents themselves dissolve and pass to the sea, in grain after grain of eroded land.

RACHEL CARSON (1907–1964), *The Sea around Us*, 1951

25 Everything that man has ever done in his relationship with soil is significant for what he now does, and agricultural man can no more safely ignore his past than architectural man can ignore the Gothic cathedrals or the Baroque palaces, or a mathematician afford to know nothing of Newton. Man, being an organism living on organisms, his works have organic attributes, and the work man does grows out of the work he has done in the past.

EDWARD HYAMS, *Soil and Civilization*, 1952

26 The Mediterranean soil too is responsible for the poverty it inflicts on its peoples. . . . The thin layers of topsoil . . . are enabled to survive only by man's constant effort. Given these conditions, if the peasants' vigilance should be distracted during long periods of unrest, not only the peasantry but also the productive soil will be destroyed. . . . In the Mediterranean the soil dies if it is not protected by crops: the desert lies in wait for arable land and never lets go.

FERNAND BRAUDEL, *The Mediterranean*, 1972

27 The earth has roots, and the roots belong to the soil. If you cut a hole in the soil you have damaged the earth. You must therefore be certain it is necessary.

TAOS INDIAN, quoted in Nancy Wood, ed., *Hollering Sun*, 1972

28 [There are] millions of acres of farm and ranch land with soils so prone to blowing or water erosion that they should never be used for crops. We do not want to risk starting another Dust Bowl.

EARL L. BUTZ, U.S. Secretary of Agriculture, 5 October 1973

29 Man has always found it difficult to appreciate the delicacy of quality and texture of soil, and to realize that it is not inexhaustible, and that some processes are virtually irreversible.

ANTHONY HUXLEY, *Plant and Planet*, 1975

30 Apparently, neither the hard-bought and soon-forgotten lesson of the Dust Bowl, nor the unregulated forces of the free market, is sufficient to safeguard the soil.

ERIK P. ECKHOLM, *Losing Ground*, 1976

31 The state has a vital interest in protecting its soil as the greatest of its natural resources, and it has a right to do so.

IOWA SUPREME COURT, *Woodbury Soil Conservation District* v. *Ortner*, 30 May 1979

32 If soil conservation cannot be made to work effectively in the United States, with all the advantages of research, extension, and conservation services, plus wealthy, educated farmers on good land with gentle climates—if with all these benefits conservation is not successful—then what hope is there for struggling countries that have few, if none, of these advantages?

NORMAN W. HUDSON, *Journal of Soil and Water Conservation*, November–December 1983

33 Soil appeals to my senses. I like to dig in it and work it with my hands. I enjoy doing the soil texture feel test with my fingers or kneading a clay soil, which is a short step from ceramics or sculpture.

HANS JENNY, *Journal of Soil and Water Conservation*, May–June, 1984

34 How about the enlightened Moses who led the Israelites to the Promised Land? It was "a good land, a land of brooks of water, . . .; a land of wheat and barley and vines and fig trees and pomegrantes, a land of olive oil and honey.", . . . Three thousand years later, bedrock is exposed throughout the uplands with the soil now in the narrow valleys or at the sea. Civilizations that are fountains of knowledge do not necessarily exercise wisdom.

WES JACKSON, *New Roots for Agriculture*, 1985

35 The plowshare may well have destroyed more options for future generations than the sword.

WES JACKSON, quoted in *Atlantic Monthly*, November 1989

36 Let me ask you this–why are there only 8 inches of top-soil left in America, when there once were some 18 inches at the time of the Declaration of Independence in 1776? Where goes our sacred earth?

HOBART KEITH, Oglala Sioux, quoted in Julian Burger, *The Gaia Atlas of First Peoples*, 1990

123 SOLAR ENERGY

1 I have no doubt that we will be successful in harnessing the sun's energy. . . . If sunbeams were weapons of war, we would have had solar energy centuries ago.

SIR GEORGE PORTER, quoted in *The Observer*, 26 August 1973

2 Solar energy could perhaps do more to improve the material well-being of mankind without increasing his tensions than any other good available to man.

WILLIAM E. HERONEMUS, *Center Report*, February 1975

3 Solar energy is a paradox. It is available everywhere, but weak. It is enduring, but varies with weather, time of day, location, and season. It is free, but expensive to collect.

MANSON BENEDICT, *Technology Review*, May 1976

4 Modern industry runs on the scarcest of the available forms of low entropy. Traditional technology (windmills, waterwheels, etc.) runs on the more abundant solar source. How ironic, therefore, to be told by technological optimists that modern technology is freeing man from dependence on resources. The very opposite is true.

HERMAN E. DALY, *Steady-State Economics*, 1977

5 Another example of the misuse of cost-benefit analysis (or even straight economic calculation) comes in the dollar comparisons of solar-energy costs with the cost of energy from fossil fuels. At the current margin, fossil fuels are cheaper for most uses. Do we then conclude that solar energy is uneconomic? Not unless a good move in checkers is also a good move in chess. Different rules of the game are involved. Living off temporary geological capital is just a different ballgame from living off permanent solar income. The latter game accepts permanence and ecological discipline as rules of the game; the former does not.

HERMAN E. DALY, *Steady-State Economics*, 1977

6 Sunlight leaves an earth unravished, husbanded, renewed. It leaves a people unmutated, convivial, even illuminated. Above all, it respects the limits that are always with us on a little planet: the delicate fragility of life, the imperfection of human societies, and the frailty of the human design. We can still choose to live lightly, to live with light, and so choose life itself—by capturing the Hope left waiting at the bottom of Pandora's box.

AMORY B. LOVINS, *Soft Energy Paths*, 1977

7 I have a strong conviction now that [solar energy's] diffuseness—the difficulty there is in collecting enough energy to really damage something—may, in fact, be its main blessing.

THEODORE B. TAYLOR, symposium, Washington, D.C., 2 February 1977

8 Sunlight, in its many guises, is the force that has shaped and driven the miraculous living

fabric of this planet for billions of years. It embodies the best engineering, the widest safety margins, and the greatest design experience we know. It provides amply for our needs, yet limits our greed. . . . It is safe, eternal, universal, and free. It falls justly and equitably on South and North, East and West. It increases autonomy, fosters diversity, and does not hurt the balance of payments. Its quality is constant and very high.

THEODORE B. TAYLOR, *Skeptic*, March–April 1977

9 When you install some kind of solar heater, you are actually buying your own small utility company. Not just 10 shares—the whole thing. You are the chairman of the board and sole stockholder, and you receive monthly dividend checks in the form of savings on your *other* utility bill. These "dividends" are recession-proof, inflation-proof, strike-proof, pollution-proof, terrorism-proof, computer-error-proof . . . and, most important, *tax free.*

ANDREW TOBIAS, *New York Magazine*, 31 May 1977

10 Development of solar energy is an obsession with me.

JOSE LOPEZ PORTILLO, President of Mexico, quoted in *Los Angeles Herald-Examiner,* 31 October 1977

11 But right now, the new Washington-proclaimed sun worship is no more than a diversion from the real energy problem.

MOBIL CORPORATION, advertisement, *New York Times,* 4 May 1978

12 The use of solar energy has not been opened up because the oil industry does not own the sun.

RALPH NADER, quoted in Linda Botts, ed., *Loose Talk,* 1980

13 It would be wonderful eventually, but the technology is such that right now, to equal the power output we are getting from nuclear generators, we would have to cover an area equal to the entire state of New York with mirrors. I don't think the environmentalists would hold still for that.

RONALD REAGAN, quoted in *Field and Stream,* October 1980

14 The rising cost of energy will literally cannibalize the economic system that it's supposed to support. This is intolerable and we need to undertake a solar transition for that sake alone.

BARRY COMMONER, *Multinational Monitor,* January–February 1989

15 For solar advocates, the Reagan years were like Dunkirk without the boats.

DENIS HAYES, speech, Museum of Natural History, New York City, 8 November 1989

16 Environmentalists have long been fond of saying that the sun is the only safe nuclear reactor, situated as it is some ninety-three million miles away.

STEPHANIE MILLS, ed., *In Praise of Nature,* 1990

17 We owe our lives to the sun. . . . How is it, then, that we feel no gratitude?

LEWIS THOMAS, *Earth Ethics,* Summer 1990

124 SOLID WASTES
See also   115 RECYCLING, 133 WASTE AND WASTES

1 Take your refuse elsewhere or you will be fined.

ANCIENT ROMAN SIGNPOST, quoted by Institute for Solid Wastes and American Public Works Association, *Municipal Refuse Disposal,* 1970

2 Feudal lords shifted their headquarters from one castle to another, to get away, it has been said, from the accumulated filth.

PAUL B. SEARS, *Deserts on the March,* 1947

3 One person's trash basket is another's living space.

NATIONAL ACADEMY OF SCIENCES, "Waste Management and Control," 1965

4 [The nation's solid wastes] result in scenic blights, create serious hazards to the public health, including pollution of air and water resources, accident hazards, and increases in rodent and insect vectors of disease, have an adverse effect on land values, create public nuisances, otherwise interfere with community life and development.

SOLID WASTE DISPOSAL ACT (U.S.), 1965

5 Any material becomes a "waste" when its owner or producer no longer considers it of sufficient value to retain. Any suggestion

that he should thereafter invest more money in it, for the sake of disposal or any other financially unrewarding goal, is likely to be considered absurd.

PERCY H. McGAUHEY, testimony, U.S. House Interstate and Foreign Commerce subcommittee, 29 June 1965

6 Wastes management is worth whatever it costs within the framework of honest engineering and sound public health practice; . . . the cost is the price man must pay for the benefits of a modern urban-industrial-agricultural society.

PERCY H. McGAUHEY, testimony, U.S. House Interstate and Foreign Commerce subcommittee, 29 June 1965

7 We live in an environment whose principal product is garbage. The shined shoe in such a society is a hypocritical statement because it promotes the lie that we can thrive on garbage without being dirtied by it.

RUSSELL BAKER, New York Times, 22 February 1968

8 Skepticism must pale in the light of archeological fact: Of seven cities that have thrived at the site of Troy, each of the last six was erected on the refuse of its predecessor. America so far has avoided burial by garbage only by methodically building on top of it.

FRANK TRIPPETT, Look, 4 November 1969

9 And Man created the plastic bag and the tin and aluminum can and the cellophane wrapper and the paper plate, and this was good because Man could then take his automobile and buy all his food in one place and He could save that which was good to eat in the refrigerator and throw away that which had no further use. And soon the earth was covered with plastic bags and aluminum cans and paper plates and disposable bottles and there was nowhere to sit down or walk, and Man shook his head and cried: "Look at this Godawful mess."

ART BUCHWALD, 1970

10 We are itinerant polluters of our countryside, shedding litter like loose hairs wherever we go.

NAN FAIRBROTHER, New Lives, New Landscapes, 1970

11 Nowhere is the fragmentation and disorganization of local government more clearly visible than in the area of management of solid wastes.

HANS FEIBUSCH, speech, conference, Newton, Massachusetts, 1 June 1972

12 It is in the final analysis the public who must realize that the products they consume produce the wastes they deplore.

ECKARDT C. BECK, speech, National Solid Waste Management Association conference, Chicago, 3 October 1979

13 Maybe we're becoming a veneer of civilization—a thin layer of something good on top of trash.

GARRETT HARDIN, speech, American Association for the Advancement of Science, Washington, D.C., 3 January 1982

14 People are only aware of garbage when it piles up on the street.

NORMAN STEISEL, former New York City sanitation commissioner, quoted in USA Today, 7 July 1988

15 [Where the environment is concerned,] it's very difficult to get things done with finality. I've heard that garbage thrown into the Arctic waters takes a year to circumnavigate the pole and it's in your front yard again.

WILLIAM K. REILLY, quoted in Washington Post, 28 April 1989

16 Some of our landfills are now richer in resources than some of our mines.

DENIS HAYES, speech, Museum of Natural History, New York City, 8 November 1989

17 Source reduction is to garbage what preventive medicine is to health.

WILLIAM RATHJE, Atlantic Monthly, December 1989

18 U.S. consumers and industry dispose of enough aluminum to rebuild the commercial air fleet every three months; enough iron and steel to continuously supply all automakers; enough glass to fill New York's World Trade Center every two weeks.

ENVIRONMENTAL DEFENSE FUND advertisement, Christian Science Monitor, 1990

19 If the rest of the world aspires to our way of life . . . we'll bury ourselves in waste.

JOEL HIRSCHHORN, quoted in Center for Investigative Reporting and Bill Moyers, Global Dumping Ground, 1990

20 Philosophically, a landfill is only a temporary solution—you're digging a hole and filling it up.
DARYL DITZ, *Smithsonian*, April 1990

21 We need to look at waste as a great economic and environmental opportunity.
JIM HIGHTOWER, Texas commissioner of agriculture, *Smithsonian*, April 1990

22 During the last century we have made the error of overestimating the ability of nature to digest the waste of the industrial society. It is a relatively small error, because we have developed, or have the potential to develop, the technologies to solve these problems. We are not confronted with unsolvable problems; our fate is in our hands.
BERNHARD ULRICH, *Environmental Science and Technology* 24, no. 4, April 1990

23 Remember the *Mobro*? Three years ago, that ill-fated scow left Islip, Long Island, carrying some 3,000 tons of garbage and sailed into symbolhood.
RICHARD WOLKOMIR, *Smithsonian*, 1990 April

24 Except in a few densely populated cities, it's nutty to maintain that a country as vast as America is "running out" of space for landfills. There is room to landfill our trash until the Lord's return. What we are running out of is willingness to tolerate landfills. That's as it should be.
GREGG EASTERBROOK, *New Republic*, 30 April 1990

25 The most daunting obstacle is the popular state of mind that places blame for the garbage crisis on others and denies personal responsibility.
EDGAR BERKEY, *Christian Science Monitor*, 23 July 1990

26   The ABCs of Waste Disposal

NIMBY . . . Not in My Back Yard
NIMFYE . . . Not in My Front Yard Either
PIITBY . . . Put It In Their Back Yard
NIMEY . . . Not In My Election Year
NIMTOO . . . Not In My Term Of Office
LULU . . . Locally Unavailable Land Use
NOPE . . . Not On Planet Earth
WALL POSTER, seen at Environmental Protection Agency, reported in *Oceanus*, Summer 1990

27 Everyone wants you to pick up the garbage and no one wants you to put it down!
WILLIAM RUCKELSHAUS, quoted in *The Bridge*, Summer 1990

28 Dig a trench through a landfill and you will see layers of phone books like geographical strata or layers of cake. . . . During a recent landfill dig in Phoenix, I found newspapers dating from 1952 that looked so fresh you might read one over breakfast.
WILLIAM RATHJE, *The Economist*, 8 September 1990

29 With disposable diapers, the first lesson a child learns is that when you make a mess, you throw it into the garbage and it goes away. That message is fundamentally wrong.
PATRICIA GREENSTREET, *New York Times Magazine*, 23 September 1990

30 The packaging for a microwavable "microwave" dinner is programmed for a shelf life of maybe six months, a cook time of two minutes and a landfill dead-time of centuries.
DAVID WANN, *Buzzworm*, November 1990

31 Everybody used to believe in the Trash Fairy—put your trash on the curb and it's gone.
NATALIE ROY, quoted in *Washington Post*, 23 February 1991

32 Once something is mixed with trash, it becomes trash.
CHARLES F. OYLER, quoted in *New York Times*, 31 March 1991

---

125 SUBURBS
See also   13 CITIES, 129 TOWNS, 132 URBAN ENVIRONMENT

---

1 To me the country on the outskirts of the city is sweet.
MARTIAL (c. 40–c. 103), *Epigrams* 9.98.7

2 The suburbs. . . . often are leaderless. I worry more about the suburbs than about the cities. In the cities we are at least aware of and are trying to undo the errors of the past. In the suburbs these felonies are being compounded and perpetuated.
ROBERT MOSES (1888–1981), *Working for the People*, 1956

3 The whole American ethos, which once re-
volved about the dialectic of pure country
versus wicked but exciting city, seems to me
now aerated by the suburban outlook. This
produces an homogenization of both city and
country, but without full integration.
DAVID RIESMAN, *Annals of the American Academy of Political and Social Science*, November
1957

4 The ultimate effect of the suburban escape in
our time is, ironically, a low-grade uniform
environment from which escape is impossible.
LEWIS MUMFORD, *The City in History*, 1961

5 Suburban Christmas is a cheap plastic Santa
Claus in a shopping center parking lot surrounded by asphalt and a sea of cars. Suburban spring is not a walk in the awakening
woods, but mud in poorly built roads. Suburban life is no voyage of discovery or private
exploration of the world's wonders, natural
and man-made; it is cliché conformity as far
as the eye can see, with no stimulation
through quality of environment.
ADA LOUISE HUXTABLE, *New York Times Magazine*, 9 February 1964

6 Suburbs are things to come into the city from.
ART LINKLETTER, *A Child's Garden of Misinformation*, 1965

7 The disadvantages of suburban life exist
mainly in the minds of intellectual planners
and social engineers. They apply their own
criteria in judging the quality of life and conclude that, because they would not like it for
themselves, it must be bad for everyone else.
THOMAS WYNDHAM, *New Towns*, 1969

8 Let me say that I am always happy to see the
suburbs having troubles—not because I am
by nature a sadist, but simply because I think
that the suburbs have not been suffering
enough for the inner city's problems. The
suburbs, generally speaking, live off the inner city but they do not want to help out the
inner city. That is why I like to see the suburbs having the same kind of problems, such
as the problem of dumping solid waste, that
has been continuously facing the inner city.
Only when the suburbs begin to have the
same problems will they join with the inner

city to solve what are really common problems.
FRANK P. GRAD, conference, Newton, Massachusetts, 1 June 1972

9 Breaking the rigid zoning practices of most
suburbs is top priority, so that living, commerce, and work can again intermingle, leading to environments where people might
again like to walk.
RALPH KEYES, *We, the Lonely People*, 1973

10 Suburbia, the middle ground between nature's beauty and civilization's conveniences,
has been viewed as the promised land by millions of Americans over the last several generations.
PHILIP DOLCE, *Suburbia*, 1976

11 And a new set of values is now operating
among millions of young people. Their
dream isn't the half-acre lot with a picket
fence, but a townhouse in the heart of the
city. It's a Volkswagen instead of a station
wagon, a pair of skis instead of a golf course,
baking bread in an oven instead of cooking
steak on an outdoor barbecue. This is all part
of a real change in attitude among millions
and millions of young people, who find life
better lived in the heart of the city—with a
greater sense of community and relationship—than in a suburban location.
JAMES W. ROUSE, in Conservation Foundation, *Conservation and Values*, 1978

12 Suburbs . . . have become the heirs to their
cities' problems. They have pollution, high
taxes, crime. People thought they would escape all those things in the suburbs. But like
the people in Boccaccio's *Decameron*, they ran
away from the plague and took it with them.
CHARLES HAAR, *New York Times*, 16 March
1980

13 A womb with a view.
ANONYMOUS, quoted in James A. Clapp, *The
City: Dictionary of Quotable Thoughts on Cities
and Urban Life*, 1984

14 A place where the grass is greenest.
ANONYMOUS, quoted in James A. Clapp, *The
City: Dictionary of Quotable Thoughts on Cities
and Urban Life*, 1984

126 SUSTAINABLE DEVELOPMENT
See also 74 INTERNATIONAL
DEVELOPMENT

1 The principal conditions of a stable society—
one that to all intents and purposes can be
sustained indefinitely while giving optimum
satisfaction to its members—are: (1) minimum disruption of ecological processes; (2)
maximum conservation of materials and energy—or an economy of stock rather than
flow; (3) a population in which recruitment
equals loss; and (4) a social system in which
the individual can enjoy, rather than feel restricted by, the first three conditions.
> EDWARD GOLDSMITH et al., "A Blueprint for
> Survival," *The Ecologist*, January 1972

2 The principal defect of the industrial way of
life with its ethos of expansion is that it is not
sustainable.
> EDWARD GOLDSMITH et al., "A Blueprint for
> Survival," *The Ecologist*, January 1972

3 [Ecological] considerations have received inadequate attention in the strategies and plans
of development and it is imperative that all
the efforts to safeguard the environment,
whether national or regional, be fully integrated into our overall development efforts.
Such an integration is essential to assure sustained development which is dependent on
the sustained availability of natural resources.
> EMIL SALIM, Indonesian Minister for Envi-
> ronment, ASEAN Ministerial Meeting on
> Environment, Philippines, 30 April 1981

4 Any way of life we pursue must be or be able
to become ecologically sustainable. . . .
There are various options to choose from, but
there is no option that allows present trends
to continue.
> RAYMOND F. DASMANN, *Environmental Con-
> servation*, 1984

5 The World Bank has smart people. They
should devote some systematic thought to
what they mean by sustainable development. They're good at defining a lot of other
stuff. I'd like to see the Bank respond to that
challenge. We all mouth this cliché about sustainable development endlessly. I may not

fully understand it, but I don't spend $15 bil-
lion annually.
> DAVID RUNNALLS, quoted in *Conservation
> Foundation Letter*, November–December
> 1984

6 Our global future depends upon sustainable
development. It depends upon our willingness and ability to dedicate our intelligence,
ingenuity, and adaptability—and our energy—to our common future. This is a choice
we can make.
> WORLD COMMISSION ON ENVIRONMENT AND DE-
> VELOPMENT, *Our Common Future*, 1987

7 Sustainable development is . . . development that meets the needs of the present
without compromising the ability of further
generations to meet their own needs.
> WORLD COMMISSION ON ENVIRONMENT AND DE-
> VELOPMENT, *Our Common Future*, 1987

8 We have learned to our cost that development which destroys the environment eventually destroys development itself. And we
have learned to our benefit that development
that conserves the environment conserves
also the fruits of development. There is, thus,
no fundamental dichotomy between conservation and growth.
> RAJIV GANDHI, address to the UN General
> Assembly, 19 October 1987

9 Dutch environmental policy on its own can
only promote a sustainable development on a
local and regional scale. At the fluvial, continental and global levels, the international dimension becomes increasingly larger in the
policy to be pursued.
> NETHERLANDS NATIONAL INSTITUTE OF PUBLIC
> HEALTH AND ENVIRONMENTAL PROTECTION,
> "Concern for Tomorrow: A National Envi-
> ronmental Survey," 1988

10 Achieving sustainable economic growth will
require the remodeling of agriculture, energy
use, and industrial production after nature's
example.
> JESSICA TUCHMAN MATTHEWS, *Foreign Affairs*,
> Spring 1989

11 While it has been relatively easy to gather
support for the concept of sustainability at a
rhetorical level, there is the danger that the
term has become so inclusive that it runs the

risk of becoming a meaningless catch phrase, cynically regarded by development professionals as simply one more form to fill out in the project cycle.

STEVEN H. ARNOLD, testimony, U.S. Congress Joint Economic subcommittee, 13 June 1989

12 The maintenance of a livable global environment depends on the sustainable development of the entire human family. . . . [If] the poor nations attempt to improve their lot by the methods we rich have pioneered, the result will eventually be world ecological damage.

WILLIAM RUCKELSHAUS, Scientific American, September 1989

13 If this is the new environmental buzzword, it's a boring one. Sustainable—it sounds like a middle-class savings account.

ANONYMOUS, quoted in Los Angeles Times, 31 October 1989

14 Efficiency has its place, but it needs to be balanced by the competing temporal standards of sustainability if we are to properly adjust our short-term needs to the long-term needs of the planet.

JEREMY RIFKIN, The Green Lifestyle Handbook, 1990

15 When we Indians kill meat, we eat it all up. . . . When we build houses, we make little holes. When we burn grass for grasshoppers, we don't ruin things. We shake down acorns and pinenuts. We don't chop down the trees.

WINTU INDIAN, quoted in Julian Burger, The Gaia Atlas of First Peoples, 1990

16 Sustainable development, to put it simply, is a way to fulfill the requirements of the present without compromising the future. When policies of sustainable development are followed, our economic and our environmental objectives are both achieved. In fact, America's entire approach to bilateral and multilateral assistance is based on the concept of sustainable development.

JAMES BAKER, U.S. Secretary of State, speech, National Governors' Association, 26 February 1990

17 [A sustainable society] is one that shapes its economic and social systems so that natural resources and life-support systems are maintained.

LESTER BROWN, Amicus Journal, Spring 1990

18 The synthesis of environmental and economic imperatives popularly called "sustainable development" must become a reality, not just a slogan.

ROBERT REPETTO, EPA Journal, July–August 1990

19 Economic growth, which is an increase in quantity, cannot be sustainable indefinitely on a finite planet. Economic development, which is an improvement in the quality of life without necessarily causing an increase in quantity of resources consumed, may be sustainable. Sustainable growth is an impossibility. Sustainable development must become our primary long-term policy goal.

ROBERT COSTANZA and LISA WAINGER, Washington Post, 2 September 1990

20 The word development has long been used to suspend clear thinking about destructive economics and inappropriate ways of living. Trying to clean up development's larcenous image with a new adjective like sustainable is a very recent public relations job.

ANDREW NILKIFORUK, Harrowsmith, September–October 1990

21 What is and is not sustainable depends on the number of people now and in the future, the demands made on the planetary system by those people, the system's physical and biological processes, and the investment society is able and willing to make to overcome constraints in the system.

GORDON H. ORIANS, Environment, November 1990

127 TECHNOLOGY

1 The machine does not isolate man from the great problems of nature but plunges him more deeply into them.

ANTOINE DE SAINT-EXUPERY (1900–1944), Wind, Sand, and Stars, 1939

2 Technology, while adding daily to our physical ease, throws daily another loop of fine wire around our soils.

ADLAI E. STEVENSON (1900–1965), Fortune, October 1955

3 The contrast between the machine and the pastoral ideal dramatizes the great issue of our culture.
LEO MARX, *The Machine in the Garden*, 1964

4 Despite the dazzling success of modern technology and the unprecedented power of modern military systems, they suffer from a common and catastrophic fault. While providing us with a bountiful supply of food, with great industrial plants, with high-speed transportation, and with military weapons of unprecedented power, they threaten our very survival.
BARRY COMMONER, *Science and Survival*, 1966

5 The essence of technological, if not civilized, pursuits is the constant clashing with ecological principle.
ROBERT RIENOW and LEONA TRAIN RIENOW, *Moment in the Sun*, 1967

6 While we can rely on technology to compensate for depletion of certain kinds of natural resources, we cannot rely on technological progress to increase the supply of natural environments which yield utility through direct personal contact.
JOHN V. KRUTILLA, North American Wildlife and Natural Resources Conference, Houston, 1968

7 Our contemporary culture, primed by population growth and driven by technology, has created problems of environmental degradation that directly affect all of our senses: noise, odors and toxins which bring physical pain and suffering, and ugliness, barrenness, and homogeneity of experience which bring emotional and psychological suffering and emptiness. In short, we are jeopardizing our human qualities by pursuing technology as an end rather than a means. Too often we have failed to ask two necessary questions: First, what human purpose will a given technology or development serve? Second, what human and environmental effects will it have?
U.S. SENATE PUBLIC WORKS COMMITTEE, report on water pollution bill, 7 August 1969

8 America's technology has turned in upon itself; its corporate form makes it the servant of profits, not the servant of human needs.
ALICE EMBREE, quoted in Robin Morgan, *Sisterhood Is Powerful*, 1970

9 The most important and urgent problems of the technology of today are no longer the satisfactions of the primary needs or of archetypal wishes, but the reparation of the evils and damages by the technology of yesterday.
DENNIS GABOR, *Innovations: Scientific, Technological and Social*, 1970

10 Either the machine has a meaning to life that we have not yet been able to interpret in a rational manner, or it is itself a manifestation of life and therefore mysterious.
GARET GARRETT, quoted in Loren Eiseley, *The Invisible Pyramid*, 1970

11 Technology and production can be great benefactors of man, but they are mindless instruments, and if undirected they career along with a momentum of their own. In our country, they pulverize everything in their path—the landscape, the natural environment, history and tradition, the amenities and civilities, the privacy and spaciousness of life, much beauty, and the fragile, slow-growing social structures that bind us together.
CHARLES A. REICH, *The Greening of America*, 1970

12 The supersonic transport (SST) summarizes, in one project, our society's demented priorities. It is a virtual catalog of the reasons why the United States is ailing in the midst of its affluence—nationalistic vanity, pandering to corporate profit, the worship of technology, and the deteriorating human environment.
BRENN STILLEY, in Garrett De Bell, ed., *The Environmental Handbook*, 1970

13 Technology feeds on itself. Technology makes more technology possible.
ALVIN TOFFLER, *Future Shock*, 1970

14 That great, growling engine of change—technology.
ALVIN TOFFLER, *Future Shock*, 1970

15 To appeal to contemporary man to revert, in this twentieth century, to a pagan-like nature worship in order to restrain technology from further encroachment and devastation of the resources of nature, is a piece of atavistic nonsense.
NORMAN LAMM, *Faith and Doubt*, 1971

16 The sonic boom "problem," of course, cannot in principle be "solved." . . . [The] job of the ecologist is to dispel this faith in technology.
WILLIAM W. MURDOCK and JOSEPH H. CONNELL, in Clifton Fadiman and Jean White, eds., *Ecocide*, 1971

17 Technology . . . is a queer thing. It brings you great gifts with one hand, and it stabs you in the back with the other.
C. P. SNOW (1905–1980), *New York Times*, 15 March 1971

18 The predominant factor in our industrial society's increased environmental degradation is neither population nor affluence, but the increasing environmental impact per unit of production due to technological changes.
BARRY COMMONER, *Environment*, April 1971

19 It seems probable, if we are to survive economically as well as biologically, that much of the technological transformation of the United States economy since 1946 will need to be, so to speak, redone in order to bring the nation's productive technology much more closely into harmony with the inescapable demands of the ecosystem. This will require the development of massive new technologies . . . a new period of technological transformation of the economy which reverses the counter-ecological trends.
BARRY COMMONER, forum of Resources for the Future, Washington, D.C., 20 April 1971

20 There *is* a demon in technology. It was put there by man and man will have to exorcise it before technological civilization can achieve the eighteenth-century ideal of humane civilized life.
RENÉ DUBOS, *A God Within*, 1972

21 Technology can relieve the symptoms of a problem without affecting the underlying causes. Faith in technology as the ultimate solution to all problems can thus divert our attention from the most fundamental problem—the problem of growth in a finite system—and prevent us from taking effective action to solve it.
DONELLA H. MEADOWS et al., *The Limits to Growth*, 1972

22 The advance of technology, like the growth of population and industry, has also been proceeding exponentially.
CARL KAYSEN, *Foreign Affairs*, Summer 1972

23 The technology of *mass production* is inherently violent, ecologically damaging, self-defeating in terms of non-renewable resources, and stultifying for the human person. The technology of *production by the masses*, making use of the best of modern knowledge and experience, is conducive to decentralisation, compatible with the laws of ecology, gentle in its use of scarce resources, and designed to serve the human person instead of making him the servant of machines. I have named it *intermediate technology*.
E. F. SCHUMACHER (1911–1977), *Small Is Beautiful*, 1973

24 The system of nature, of which man is a part, tends to be self-balancing, self-adjusting, self-cleansing. Not so with technology.
E. F. SCHUMACHER (1911–1977), *Small Is Beautiful*, 1973

25 Even bigger machines, entailing even bigger concentrations of economic power and exerting ever greater violence against the environment, do not represent progress: they are a denial of wisdom. Wisdom demands a new orientation of science and technology towards the organic, the gentle, the nonviolent, the elegant and beautiful.
E. F. SCHUMACHER (1911–1977), *Small Is Beautiful*, 1973

26 What we are finding out now is that there are not only limits to growth but also to technology and that we cannot allow technology to go on without public consent.
DAVID R. BROWER, *Skeptic*, July–August 1976

27 People are the quintessential element in all technology. . . . Once we recognize the inescapable human nexus of all technology our attitude toward the reliability problem is fundamentally changed.
GARRETT HARDIN, *Skeptic*, July–August 1976

28 Its technical diversity, adaptability, and geographic dispersion make it resilient and offer a good prospect of stability under a wide range of conditions, foreseen or not. The hard path, however, is brittle; it must fail,

with widespread and serious disruption, if any of its exacting technical and social conditions is not satisfied continuously and indefinitely.

AMORY B. LOVINS, in support of a "soft-technology path" to obtaining energy, *Foreign Affairs*, October 1976

29 Any demanding high technology tends to develop influential and dedicated constituencies of those who link its commercial success with both the public welfare and their own. Such sincerely held beliefs, peer pressures, and the harsh demands that the work itself places on time and energy all tend to discourage such people from acquiring a similarly thorough knowledge of alternative policies and the need to discuss them.

AMORY B. LOVINS, *Foreign Affairs*, October 1976

30 The choice of technology, whether for a rich or a poor country, is probably the most important decision to be made.

GEORGE MCROBIE, quoted in *Conservation Foundation Letter*, October 1976

31 Presumably, technology has made man increasingly independent of his environment. But, in fact, technology has merely substituted nonrenewable resources for renewables, which is more an increase than a decrease in dependence.

HERMAN E. DALY, *Steady-State Economics*, 1977

32 Alaska is America's last chance to "civilize" a great region without disrupting its ecological integrity and without falling victim to the technological Leviathan in the process.

CHARLES KONIGSBERG, 1977, quoted in *Earth Ethics*, Summer 1990

33 My quarrel is with the political "environmentalism" that offers no reasonable alternatives but proposes solutions which entail delaying or abandoning present, feasible, and proven technology and "waiting for" solutions that are "soft," "attractive," and "just on the horizon."

WILLIAM TUCKER, *Harper's*, December 1977

34 We must ask whether our machine technology makes us proof against all those destruc-tive forces which plagued Roman society and ultimately wrecked Roman civilization. Our reliance—an almost religious reliance—upon the power of science and technology to forever ensure the progress of our society, might blind us to some very real problems which cannot be solved by science and technology.

ROBERT STRAUSZ-HUPE, *Philadelphia Inquirer*, 1978

35 It troubles me that we are so easily pressured by purveyors of technology into permitting so-called "progress" to alter our lives without attempting to control it—as if technology were an irrepressible force of nature to which we must meekly submit.

HYMAN G. RICKOVER (1900–1986), quoted in *The American Land*, 1979

36 How extraordinary! . . . The richest, longest-lived, best protected, most resourceful civilization, with the highest degree of insight into its own technology, is on its way to becoming the most frightened.

AARON WILDAVSKY, *New York Times*, 27 February 1979

37 It is apparent that virtually no poor society has ever been able to improve its environment. But it seems equally clear that wealth alone is not enough. . . . In addition to wealth, it is clear that *technology* is needed to reverse the trend.

JAMES R. DUNN, quoted in *Conservation Foundation Letter*, November 1979

38 The question is not whether "big is ugly," "small is beautiful," or technology is "appropriate." It is whether technologists will be ready for the demanding, often frustrating task of working with critical laypeople to develop what is needed or whether they will try to remain isolated, a luxury I doubt society will allow any longer.

ROBERT C. COWAN, *Technology Review*, February 1980

39 There is no retreat from a technological society, and the only way cities are likely to be abolished is by nuclear war. So we are saddled with a daunting problem. How can we build, into rapidly evolving technological ecosystems, components to confer stability,

fail-safe systems of the kind which preserve
natural ecosystems from extinction? It is, I believe, the top priority problem for our generation.

LORD ERIC ASHBY, *Environmental Science and
Technology*, October 1980

40 Our way of life has been influenced by the
way technology has developed. In future, it
seems to me, we ought to try to reverse this
and so develop our technology that it meets
the needs of the sort of life we wish to lead.

PRINCE PHILIP, duke of Edinburgh, *Men, Machines and Sacred Cows*, 1984

41 There are three main dangers to technocratic
solutions. First is the danger in believing
there is a complete or acceptable solution
using modern dominant ideologies and technology. The second danger is the presentation of an impression that something is being
done when in fact the real problem continues. Tinkering distracts from the "real work."
Finally, there is the danger of assuming there
will be new experts—such as professional
ecologists—who will provide the solution but
who may in fact be constrained to be public
relations spokespersons for the agenda of
profit or power of some corporation or
agency.

BILL DEVALL and GEORGE SESSIONS, *Deep Ecology*, 1985

42 We have become a people unable to comprehend the technology we invent.

ASSOCIATION OF AMERICAN COLLEGES, report,
"Integrity in the College Curriculum," February 1985

43 Technology, when misused, poisons air, soil,
water and lives. But a world without technology would be prey to something worse: the
impersonal ruthlessness of the natural order,
in which the health of a species depends on
relentless sacrifice of the weak.

NEW YORK TIMES, editorial, 29 August 1986

44 Science can amuse and fascinate us all, but it
is engineering that changes the world.

ISAAC ASIMOV, *Isaac Asimov's Book of Science
and Nature Quotations*, 1988

45 I'm not sure what solutions we'll find to deal
with all our environmental problems, but I'm

sure of this: They will be provided by industry; they will be products of technology.
Where else *can* they come from?

GEORGE M. KELLER, *Nation's Business*, 12
June 1988

46 Since we have no choice but to be swept
along by [this] vast technological surge, we
might as well learn to surf.

MICHAEL SOULE, in David Western and Mary
C. Pearl, *Conservation for the 21st Century*,
1989

47 We're finally going to get the bill for the Industrial Age. If the projections are right, it's
going to be a big one: the ecological collapse
of the planet.

JEREMY RIFKIN, *World Press Review*, 30 December 1989

48 Technology shapes society and society shapes
technology.

ROBERT W. WHITE, *Environmental Science and
Technology* 24, no. 4, April 1990

49 As powerful as modern technology makes
us, our one species (among perhaps 10 million) looks, in a Gaian perspective, like a
small cog in a very large machine.

JESSICA TUCHMAN MATTHEWS, *Washington
Post*, 22 February 1991

128 TOURISM
See also　45 ENVIRONMENTAL IMPACTS,
109 POPULATION IMPACTS

1 Do not plan long journeys because whatever
you believe in you have already seen. When
a thing is everywhere, then the way to find it
is not to travel but to love it.

AUGUSTINE OF HIPPO (354–430), *City of God*

2 Sheep are driven into Hetch Hetchy every
spring, about the same time that a nearly
equal number of tourists are driven into
Yosemite; another coincident which is remarkably suggestive.

JOHN MUIR (1838–1914), *Boston Weekly Tran-
script*, 25 March 1873

3 The sentiment for nature in the late seventeenth and eighteenth centuries is insepara-

ble from the widening knowledge of scenery that came from travel.

> CLARENCE J. GLACKEN, in Frank F. Darling and John P. Milton, eds., *Future Environments of North America*, 1966

4 [By the year 2020] very likely no inhabited, and few uninhabited, spots on earth will remain immune to what may become an infestation.

> HERMAN KAHN and ANTHONY J. WIENER, in William R. Ewald, Jr., ed., *Environment and Change*, 1968

5 The omnipresent tourist with his camera, his excessive asking of directions, his predilection for souvenir shops, gaudy restaurants, vulgar entertainment, his general addiction to tasteless, distasteful, or excessively visible activities, his foreignness, and his conspicuous idleness, can be extremely disturbing. In fact, tourism, through crowding, wear, litter, economic and psychological impacts, can cause as much contamination and degradation of the general atmosphere and environment as any physical process that is not actually physically harmful.

> HERMAN KAHN and ANTHONY J. WIENER, in William R. Ewald,Jr., ed., *Environment and Change*, 1968

6 Come and visit us again, but for heaven's sake don't come here to live.

> TOM McCALL, Governor of Oregon, on maintaining a satisfactory environment in Oregon, quoted in *Conservation Foundation Letter*, August 1971

7 Even tourism, once considered the ideal "clean" industry, has run afoul of the no-trespassing mood in places.

> *FORBES*, 15 June 1971

8 The tourist business is a trap, it is a tainted honey;
Man clearly should have stayed in bed, and not invented money.

> KENNETH E. BOULDING, "The Ballad of Ecological Awareness" in M. Taghi Farvar and John P. Milton, eds., *The Careless Technology*, 1972

9 All tourism resources are part of the heritage of mankind.

> WORLD TOURISM ORGANIZATION, declaration, Manila, 1980

10 Although no one should dispute the individual's right to leisure, it would clearly tax the world's resources if everyone had the means and the intention of travelling during his or her vacation.

> UNITED NATIONS ENVIRONMENT PROGRAM, *Industry and Environment 7*, no. 1, 1984

11 We have to define the maximum load, the point beyond which damages will become irreparable.

> GERNOT PATZELT, on the boom in Alpine tourism, quoted in *Time*, 3 September 1984

12 In seeking the unspoiled, you inevitably spoil it.

> GEORGE PACKER, *Boston Review*, August 1988

13 Tourism should be a reward for right living, not a substitute for it.

> DAVID EHRENFELD, *Conservation for the 21st Century*, 1989

14 Ecotourism means you take your ethics with you when you travel. It is environmentally and politically correct.

> *EcoSource*, January–February 1991

---

129 TOWNS

See also   13 CITIES, 120 RURAL AREAS, 125 SUBURBS, 132 URBAN ENVIRONMENT

---

1 God made the country, but man made the town.

> WILLIAM COWPER (1731–1800), *The Task*, book 1,*The Sofa*, 1782–1785

2 A town is saved, not more by the righteous men in it than by the woods and swamps that surround it. A township where one primitive forest waves above while another rots below— such a town is fitted to raise not only corn and potatoes, but poets and philosophers for the coming ages.

> HENRY DAVID THOREAU (1817–1862), *Excursions*, 1863

3 No town can fail of beauty, though its walks were gutters and its houses hovels, if venerable trees make magnificent colonnades along its streets.

> HENRY WARD BEECHER (1813–1887), *Proverbs from Plymouth Pulpit*, 1887

4 Town and Country must be married, and out of this joyous union will spring a new hope, a new life, a new civilization.
> EBENEZER HOWARD (1850–1928), *Garden Cities for Tomorrow*, 1898

5 We live in towns from choice, when we subscribe to our great civilized form. The nostalgia for the country is not *so* important. What is important is that our towns are *false* towns—every street a blow, every corner a stab.
> D. H. LAWRENCE (1885–1930), *Letters to Bertrand Russell*, 1948

6 The phrase "small town" has come itself to carry a double layer of meaning, at once sentimental and condescending. There is still a belief that democracy is more idyllic at the "grass roots," that the business spirit is purer, that the middle class is more intensely middling. . . . History, geography, and economics gave each American town some distinctive traits of style that are imbedded in the mind, and the memory of this style is all the more marked because of the nostalgia felt, in a largely urban America, for what seems the lost serenity of small-town childhoods.
> MAX LERNER, *America as a Civilization*, 1957

7 The sharply angular townscape we know so well and the plethora of sheer bad design offend the sensitive excruciatingly, but somewhere medicine and psychology could tell us that even the insensitive are being affected, made less successful human beings.
> FRANK FRASER DARLING, *Wilderness and Plenty*, 1971

8 Towns don't want to be suburbs, suburbs don't want to be cities, and cities don't want to be wastelands.
> MICHAEL DUKAKIS, Governor of Massachusetts, quoted in The Conservation Foundation, *Conservation and Values*, 1978

---

130 TREES
See also   51 FORESTRY, 52 FORESTS

---

1 Thou shalt not cut them down (for a tree of the field is man's life) to employ them in the siege.
> BIBLE, Deuteronomy, 20:19

2 Manifold origins doth nature assign them. Some spring up untended, for no man's ordering: over all the spreading landscape.
> VIRGIL (70–19 B.C.), *Georgics*, book 2

3 He that plants trees loves others beside himself.
> THOMAS FULLER, *Gnomologia*, 1732

4 Who leaves the pine-tree, leaves his friend, Unnerves his strength, invites his end.
> RALPH WALDO EMERSON (1803–1883), *The Dial*, 1841

5 A man does not plant a tree for himself; he plants it for posterity.
> ALEXANDER SMITH (1830–1867), *Dreamthorp*, 1863

6 Of all man's works of art, a cathedral is greatest. A vast and majestic tree is greater than that.
> HENRY WARD BEECHER (1813–1887), *Proverbs from Plymouth Pulpit*, 1870

7 The qualities, almost emotional, palpably artistic, heroic, of a tree; so innocent and harmless, yet so savage.
> WALT WHITMAN (1819–1892), *Specimen Days*, 1877

8 He who plants a tree
Plants a hope.
> LUCY LARCOM (1824–1893), "Plant a Tree"

9 When a man plants a tree he plants himself. Every root is an anchor, over which he rests with grateful interest, and becomes sufficiently calm to feel the joy of living.
> JOHN MUIR (1838–1914), *San Francisco Daily Evening Bulletin*, 7 September 1877

10 We all travel the milky way together, trees and men . . . trees are travellers, in the ordinary sense. They make journeys, not very extensive ones, it is true: but our own little comes and goes are only little more than tree-wavings—many of them not so much.
> JOHN MUIR (1838–1914), *Scribner's Monthly*, November 1878

11 Except during the nine months before he draws his first breath, no man manages his affairs as well as a tree does.
> GEORGE BERNARD SHAW (1856–1950), *Maxims for Revolutionists*, 1903

12 I like trees because they seem more resigned to the way they have to live than other things do.
WILLA CATHER (1873–1947), *O Pioneers!* 1913

13 I think that I shall never see
A poem lovely as a tree.
JOYCE KILMER (1886–1918), "Trees," 1914

14 A grove of giant redwoods or sequoias should be kept just as we keep a great or beautiful cathedral.
THEODORE ROOSEVELT (1858–1919), from an article in *Natural History Magazine*, 1919, quoted in Farida A. Wiley, *Theodore Roosevelt's America*, 1962

15 If a man kills a tree before its time, it is as though he had murdered a soul.
NAHMAN BRATZLAV, quoted in *Menorah Journal*, 1924

16 Trees are the earth's endless effort to speak to the listening heaven.
RABINDRANATH TAGORE (1861–1941), *Fireflies*, 1928

17 There's a tree that grows in Brooklyn. Some people call it the Tree of Heaven. No matter where its seed falls, it makes a tree which struggles to reach the sky. It grows in boarded-up plots and out of neglected rubbish heaps. It grows up out of cellar gratings. It is the only tree that grows out of cement. It grows lushly . . . survives without sun, water, and seemingly without earth. It would be considered beautiful except that there are too many of it.
BETTY SMITH, *A Tree Grows in Brooklyn*, 1943

18 Fifteen years ago the excuse of increased food production was enough to get rid of hedgerow trees in England; but at this moment the amenity value of such trees in such a populous country, needing the balm of the green leaf, far outweighs the small increase of food production which might accrue from their removal.
FRANK FRASER DARLING, speech to the British Association, Aberdeen meeting, 29 August 1963

19 A woodland in full color is awesome as a forest fire, in magnitude at least; but a single tree is like a dancing tongue of flame to warm the heart.
HAL BORLAND, *Sundial of the Seasons*, 1964

20 A tree is a tree—how many more do you need to look at?
RONALD REAGAN, speech to the Western Wood Products Association, 12 September 1965. The remark is also remembered as "If you've seen one tree you've seen them all."

21 To a Christian a tree can be no more than a physical fact. The whole concept of the sacred grove is alien to Christianity and to the ethos of the West.
LYNN I. WHITE, JR., *Science*, 10 March 1967

22 The planting of trees is the least self-centered of all that we do. It is a purer act of faith than the procreation of children.
THORNTON WILDER (1897–1975), *The Eighth Day*, 1967

23 Trees are contagious; as soon as one neighborhood or street is planted, citizen pressure builds up for action for the next street, and the next.
WILLIAM H. WHYTE, *The Last Landscape*, 1968

24 Of the 30 billion acres of land on earth, more than 9 billion are already desert. We cannot afford to lose more of this green mantle, or the water table will sink beyond recall. Trees are like the skin of the earth. If a being loses more than one-third of its skin, it dies. One third of every country should be kept in tree cover.
RICHARD ST. BARBE BAKER, *My Life, My Trees*, 1970

25 Ancient druids used to sacrifice human beings under oak trees. Modern druids worship trees and sacrifice human beings to those trees.
CHARLES E. FRASER, Hilton Head (S.C.) developer, quoted in John McPhee, *Encounters with the Archdruid*, 1971

26 A tree symbolises life which can only flourish on Earth if all the people of the world decide to defend it.
OLA'H GYORGY, World Environment Day/International Year of the Child Poster Contest, Environment Liason Centre, Nairobi, Kenya, 23 January 1979

27 They kill good trees to put out bad newspapers.
JAMES G. WATT, quoted in *Newsweek*, 8 March 1982

28 I don't think people are more important than trees or trees less important than people. We should not kill people the way we kill trees [but] we have no right to kill trees with wanton waste.

MIKE ROSELLE, quoted in *San Francisco Chronicle*, 1 November 1987

29 They absorb carbon monoxide and carbon dioxide and give out oxygen. What could be more desirable? And they look good in the bargain. Stop chopping down the rain forests and plant more saplings, and we're on our way.

ISAAC ASIMOV, quoted in *Time*, 19 December 1988

30 Tree planting teaches people that a community can make an impact. It inspires people to become more socially aware and to see that what they do really counts.

ANDY LIPKIS, *Countryside*, Winter 1990

31 The problem with city trees is that we take them for granted. We tend to notice them only when they're gone.

ROWAN ROWNTREE, *Smithsonian*, April 1990

32 President Bush knows that trees are both symbols and soldiers in our campaign to protect the environment.

MICHAEL DELAND, *Washington Post*, 18 August 1990

33 Stop beating trees to a Pulp—Recycle!
BUMPER STICKER

131 TROPICAL FORESTS
See also   22 DEFORESTATION,
51 FORESTRY, 52 FORESTS

1 [Hispaniola's] lands are high; there are in it very many sierras and very lofty mountains. . . . All are most beautiful, of a thousand shapes; all are accessible and filled with trees of a thousand kinds and tall, so that they seem to touch the sky. I am told that they never lose their foliage, and this I can believe, for I saw them as green and lovely as they are in Spain in May, and some of them were flowering, some bearing fruit, and some at another stage, according to their nature.

CHRISTOPHER COLUMBUS, (1451–1506), *Journal of Christopher Columbus*, translated by Cecil Jane, 1968

2 Amazonia is still the last unwritten page of Genesis.

EUCLIDES DA CUNHA, *Um Paraiso Perdido*, 1906

3 They had forsaken the realm of sunlight for a nether world of dark enormous greens, wild strangled greens veined by brown rivers of hot rain, the Andean rain, implacable and mighty as the rain that fell on those sunless days when the earth cooled.

PETER MATTHIESSEN, *At Play in the Fields of the Lord*, 1965

4 Between sky and forest floor is the greatest biological show on Earth—exquisite noisy birds, lithe and watchful cats, supersnakes, armies of ants and termites, more than 150 species of bats, acrobatic arboreal monkeys, "violets" as big as apple trees, myrtle with stems as thick as thighs, "roses" with 145-foot trunks, lianas and air plants, voluptuous orchids, rubber trees, multifarious hardwoods, giant domed silk-cotton, wild fig and banana trees, a lone species of willow, and even jungle cacti.

ROBERT CAMPBELL, *Smithsonian*, October 1977

5 In Brazil, there are potentially 10 cultivable acres for every family. The pressure on the Amazon forest comes not from Brazil's population growth but from a government's effort to diffuse pressures for a just redistribution of land.

FRANCES MOORE LAPPÉ and JOSEPH COLLINS, *Food First*, 1979

6 Conservation is an emotive subject likely to be expressed in dramatic language, but the current and predicted rate of depletion of tropical moist forests is so rapid that it calls for colorful comment. It represents an impact on the world's wild places unprecedented in history.

T. C. WHITMORE, in Michael E. Soule and Bruce A. Wilcox, *Conservation Biology*, 1980

7 What scientists know about tropical rainforests serves above all to convince them that they are deeply ignorant about them.

CATHERINE CAUFIELD, *In the Rainforest*, 1984

8 Those who are farthest from the jungle are most likely to idealize the impersonal workings of the rain forest, and to indict humans as mere polluters.

NEW YORK TIMES, editorial, 29 August 1986

9 Here the 'ohia trees
filled with red flowers red birds
water notes flying music
the shining of the gods.
  W. S. Merwin, *The Rain in the Trees*, 1988

10 While an ecologist may see, from a global perspective, that the Amazon is part of a world system to purify the air and conserve endangered species, the President of Brazil may regard it as part of the national patrimony, with any attempts at outside regulation regarded as a threat to the sustainability of the principle of national sovereignty. The Minister of Finance may see the rainforest as the part of the solution to financial sustainability, by promoting cash cropping or logging to earn foreign exchange to pay the foreign debt. Meanwhile, the indigenous population sees the rainforest as the home where they sustain their way of life, while the poor nearby may see it as a source of land for subsistence farming. Wealthier individuals may see it as an opportunity for investments in cattle ranching or farming to preserve their life style, while the Minister of Planning and Minister of Defense may regard it as a relatively deserted space that needs to be populated and protected to sustain their borders and provide space for a rapidly growing population.
  Steven H. Arnold, testimony, U.S. Congress Joint Economic subcommittee, 13 June 1989

11 First I thought I was fighting for the rubber tappers, then I thought I was fighting for the Amazon, then I realized I was fighting for humanity.
  Chico Mendes (d. 1988), quoted in World Rainforest Movement, *Rainforest Destruction*, 1990

12 The rain forest has plants and animals found nowhere else in the world. It has medicines found nowhere else. It also helps us breathe.
  Michael Kramer, 3d grader, *Mother Earth News*, March–April 1990

13 If the countries that contain tropical rain forests can be persuaded that there is more money to be made by extracting renewable resources from living forest than by destroying it for timber or cattle pasture, the conservation argument would be almost won.
  John Hemming, *Washington Post Book World*, 12 August 1990

14 Destroying rain forest for economic gain is like burning a Renaissance painting to cook a meal.
  Edward O. Wilson, quoted in *Time*, 3 September 1990

132 URBAN ENVIRONMENT
See also   13 CITIES, 95 OPEN SPACE

1 Our cities are a wilderness of spinning wheels instead of palaces; yet the people have not clothes. We have blackened every leaf of English greenwood with ashes, and the people die of cold; our harbors are a forest of merchant ships, and the people die of hunger.
  John Ruskin (1819–1900), *The Crown of Wild Olive*, 1866

2 The manner in which the great multitude of the poor is treated by society to-day is revolting. They are drawn into the large cities where they breathe a poorer atmosphere than in the country; they are relegated to districts which, by reason of the method of construction, are worse ventilated than any others; they are deprived of all means of cleanliness, of water itself, since pipes are laid only when paid for, and the rivers so polluted that they are useless for such purposes; they are obliged to throw all offal and garbage, all dirty water, often all disgusting drainage and excrement into the streets, being without other means of disposing of them; they are thus compelled to infect the region of their own dwellings.
  Karl Marx (1818–1883), *Das Kapital*, 1867

3 Strange to say . . . where great towns by the hundred are springing into existence, no care at all is taken to avoid bad plans. The most brutal Pagans to whom we have sent our missionaries have never shown greater indifference to the sufferings of others than is exhibited in the plans of some of our most promising cities.
  Frederick Law Olmsted (1822–1903), *Journal of Social Science*, November 1871

4 Can anything be heard in the hubbub that does not shriek, or be seen in the general glare that does not flash like an electric sign?

The life of the city dweller lacks solitude, silence, ease. The nights are noisy and ablaze. The people of a big city are assaulted by incessant sound, now violent and jagged, now falling into unfinished rhythms, but endless and remorseless.

WALTER LIPPMANN (1889–1974), *Public Opinion*, 1922

5 In the depauperate homes of the workers . . . rickety and undernourished children grew up: dirt and squalor were the constant facts of their environment. Shut off from the country by miles of paved streets, the most common sights of field and farm might be strange to them: the sight of violets, buttercups, day-lilies, the smell of mint, honeysuckle, the locust trees, the raw earth opened by the plow, the warm hay piled up in the sun, or the fishy tang of beach and salt-marsh. Overcast by the smoke-pall, the sky itself might be shut out and the sunlight diminished; even the stars at night became dim.

LEWIS MUMFORD, *Technics and Civilization*, 1934

6 How long can men thrive between walls of brick, walking on asphalt pavements, breathing the fumes of coal and of oil, growing, working, dying, with hardly a thought of wind, and sky, and fields of grain, seeing only machine-made beauty, the mineral-like quality of life?

CHARLES A. LINDBERGH, *Reader's Digest*, November 1939

7 There are no more deserts. There are no more islands. Yet there is a need for them. In order to understand the world, one has to turn away from it on occasion; in order to serve men better, one has to hold them at a distance for a time. But where can one find the solitude necessary to vigour, the deep breath in which the mind collects itself and courage gauges its strength? There remain big cities.

ALBERT CAMUS (1913–1960), *The Myth of Sisyphus*, 1942

8 We shape our buildings and afterwards our buildings shape our world.

WINSTON CHURCHILL (1874–1965), quoted in Kenneth E. Goodpaster and K. M. Sayre, *Ethics and the Problems of the Twenty-First Century*, 1979

9 The city man, in his neon-and-mazda glare knows nothing of nature's midnight. His electric lamps surround him with synthetic sunshine. They push back the dark. They defend him from the realities of the age-old night.

EDWIN WAY TEALE (1899–1980), *North with the Spring*, 1951

10 I can't even enjoy a blade of grass unless I know there's a subway handy.

FRANK O'HARA (1926–1966), *Meditations in an Emergency*, 1957

11 A neighborhood is where, when you go out of it, you get beat up.

MURRAY KEMPTON, *America Comes of Middle Age*, 1963

12 The contemporary urban region represents an ingenious device for vastly enlarging the range of human communication and widening the scope of individual choice. Urbanization thus contributes to the freedom of man.

HARVEY COX, *The Secular City*, 1966

13 Why can we not plan and build urban centers so that the first impulse of nearly everyone who has some free time on a weekend would not be to hop into a car and try to get out of them?

FRANK P. ZEIDLER, in Frank F. Darling and John P. Milton, eds., *Future Environments of North America*, 1966

14 The pathetic weekend exodus to the country or beaches, the fireplaces in overheated city apartments, the sentimental attachment to animal pets or even to plants, testify to the persistence in man of biological and emotional hungers that developed during his evolutionary past and that he cannot outgrow. . . . Historical experience, especially during the 19th century, shows that urban populations are apt to develop ugly tempers when completely deprived of such contacts [with nature]. Saving nature in both its wild and humanized aspects is thus an essential part of urban planning.

RENÉ DUBOS, speech, UNESCO Biosphere Conference, Paris, 1968

15 Since the eye does get used to almost anything, in Paris one is no longer shocked by the grievous promiscuities, the stone pimples and warts that deface our streets.

FRANÇOIS NOURISSIER, *Les Français*, 1968

16 To try to achieve a decent environment without social justice is comparable to efforts to build the city beautiful by concentrating on the boulevards and ignoring the indecencies of life that exist in the densely packed slums behind the facade.

ROBERT C. WEAVER, colloquium, U.S. Congress, 1968

17 Where and how will [the people] all live? By crowding further into our dense cities? In new layers of sprawling suburbia? In jerry-built strip cities along new highways?

LYNDON JOHNSON (1908–1973), message to Congress, 22 February 1968

18 Will urban sprawl spread so far that most people lose all touch with nature? Will the day come when the only bird a typical American child ever sees is a canary in a pet shop window? When the only wild animal he knows is a rat—glimpsed on a night drive through some city slum? When the only tree he touches is the cleverly fabricated plastic evergreen that shades his gifts on Christmas morning?

FRANK N. IKARD, North American Wildlife and Natural Resources Conference, Houston, March 1968

19 For the city is not a hostile and alien entity thrust upon the natural environment. The urban organism, like most others, depends for its well-being upon pure water, clean air, and productive soil. Problems of land use, water development, pollution, and wise use of natural resources are the concern of city and countryside alike.

ROBERT C. WEAVER, North American Wildlife and Natural Resources Conference, Houston, March 1968

20 It must be concluded that slum sanitation is a serious problem in the minds of the urban poor. . . . The point is . . . the peculiarly intense needs of ghetto areas for sanitation services. This high demand is the product of numerous factors, including: higher population density; lack of well-managed buildings and adequate garbage services provided by landlords, number of receptacles, carrying to curbside, number of electric garbage disposals; high relocation rates of tenants and businesses, producing heavy volume of bulk refuse left on streets and in buildings; different uses of the streets—as outdoor living rooms in summer, recreation areas—producing high visibility and sensitivity to garbage problems; large numbers of abandoned cars; severe rodent and pest problems; traffic congestion blocking garbage collection.

ROBERT PATRICELLI, in report of National Advisory Commission on Civil Disorders, 1 March 1968

21 The evidence of mankind's gathering environmental crisis does not have to be sought in books or in scholarly documents. City dwellers on every continent of this crowded earth see it, hear it, smell it, absorb it and suffer from it.

JAMES RUSSELL WIGGINS, speech, U.N. General Assembly, 3 December 1968

22 When the pressures of modern living become heavy, the harassed city-dweller often refers to his teeming world as a concrete jungle. This is a colorful way of describing the pattern of life in a dense urban community, but it is also grossly inaccurate, as anyone who has studied a real jungle will confirm.

Under normal conditions, in their natural habitats, wild animals do not mutilate themselves, masturbate, attack their offspring, develop stomach ulcers, become fetishists, suffer from obesity, from homosexual pairbonds, or commit murder. Among human city-dwellers, needless to say, all of these things occur. . . . Clearly, then, the city is not a concrete jungle, it is a human zoo.

DESMOND MORRIS, *The Human Zoo*, 1969

23 If American cities are to offer ample amenities for living, much stronger governmental controls of the design, quality, height, and density of buildings, and of the layout of transportation, recreation, and cultural facilities will be necessary.

NEIL H. JACOBY, *Center* magazine, November–December 1970

24 There is no single policy that deals more adequately with full resource use, an abatement of pollution, and even the search for more labor-intensive activities than a planned and purposive strategy for human settlements.

BARBARA WARD and RENÉ DUBOS, *Only One Earth*, 1972

25 We ought to learn from biology and go underground. In biology, the circulation systems are always on the inside. The idea in our cities is to take all things that have to do with machines and put them underground. This would leave the area above the ground to the walking people. Eventually, all urban transit would have to go underground, no matter what the cost.

CONSTANTINOS A. DOXIADIS, quoted in *Reader's Digest*, March 1972

26 One of the problems that has been created in inner cities has been the exodus of rural people to downtown Baltimore, Philadelphia, Detroit, St. Louis and New York, without the skills to be a productive citizen, without the cultural background to live there. They constitute a breeding ground for crime and delinquency, and cause welfare rolls to skyrocket. We should have kept them in the country. We could keep them much cheaper out there, much more productive out there than we have them in the ghettos of the inner cities.

EARL L. BUTZ, U.S. Secretary of Agriculture, *New York Times Magazine*, 16 April 1972

27 A change in the pattern of regional development is imperative. That means governmental action to inhibit free-standing shopping centers, strip-highway commerce, isolated office and educational campuses, and other such elements of spread city.

JOHN P. KEITH, *New York Times*, 9 December 1973

28 Our policies seem to be based on the assumption that poor people, especially blacks and Latins, do not even *like* greenery, except maybe watermelon rinds and plantain leaves. The logic of our policy seems to rest on this syllogism: inner cities have no greenery; poor people live in inner cities; therefore parks, open space, and wilderness are not necessary for them.

CHARLES E. LITTLE, in James N. Smith, *Environmental Quality and Social Justice in Urban America*, 1974

29 The community essential to freedom is small and palpable. It must exist within an area that can be comprehended by the senses—a place whose roads and shops, landmarks and physical hazards each inhabitant can know. It can be part of a much larger whole, as older

city neighborhoods were, but it must nevertheless be distinguishable to its inhabitants. All the immaterial benefits of a community derive from this physical base. That is why Greek philosophers were concerned with establishing the area and population of the ideal community—a concern that has now been transformed from a problem of philosophy into one of engineering.

RICHARD S. GOODWIN, *New Yorker*, 28 January 1974

30 Urban living, I think, is an anti-civilized thing. You put people in the slums of the city and lock them up in those high-rises and complexes with no outlet whatsoever for their lives. There are bound to be problems.

ERSKINE CALDWELL, *Washington Post*, 29 January 1976

31 Neighborhoods are the building blocks of cities. . . . If we want to save the cities, we must save the neighborhoods. . . . If we destroy our neighborhoods, we destroy our cities. If we destroy our cities, what is next?

PORTER BRIGGS, *American Preservation*, October–November 1977

32 The near fiscal collapse of New York and Cleveland is a sign of what lies ahead for our overgrown and outworn cities in the next two decades. The sober truth is that we can no longer afford to maintain these incredibly entropic urban environments.

JEREMY RIFKIN, *Entropy*, 1980

33 Third World cities are and they will increasingly become centres of competition for a plot to be invaded where you can build a shelter, for a room to rent, for a bed in a hospital, for a seat in a school or in a bus, essentially for the fewer stable adequately paid jobs, even for the space in a square or on a sidewalk where you can display and sell your merchandise, on which so many households depend.

JORGE HARDOY, hearing, World Commission on Environment and Development, Sao Paulo, Brazil, 28–29 October 1985

34 This is very much the age of the computer and the word processor. But why on earth do we have to be surrounded by buildings that look like such machines?

PRINCE CHARLES, PRINCE OF WALES, on much of modern architecture, speech, Royal Institute of British Architects, 1988

35 The new vision of future metropolitan growth . . . will be much more conscious of the collective impacts of individual decisions than the currently dominant perspective. Hence, it will embody individualism sensitive to collective behavior patterns, rather than unconstrained individualism.

ANTHONY DOWNS, *Synergy/Planning*, July 1990

36 Americans have an edifice complex that would make the ancient Romans blush. We have come to think that buildings and form are the solutions to our problems.

WALLY ORLINSKY, letter to the editor, *Harper's*, October 1990

133 WASTE
See also   60 HAZARDOUS WASTES,
124 SOLID WASTES

1 Though living near a river, do not waste water; though living near mountains, do not waste firewood.

CHINESE PROVERB, cited in 1875 collection

2 Only want sets a limit to waste.
LATIN PROVERB

3 Use it up, wear it out, make it do, or do without.
NEW ENGLAND PROVERB

4 Wilful waste makes woeful want.
SCOTTISH PROVERB, cited in 1721 collection

5 It is the elimination and utilization of waste, waste effort, waste time and material, the minimizing of destruction and damage, wear and tear that produce the great results in the industrial world. There is no magic in these accomplishments. The leaders in action or thought are not magicians, but steady persistent workers.

THEODORE N. VAIL, c. 1900, quoted in *Conservation Foundation Letter*, April 1973

6 The adventurer is within us, and he contests for our favour with the social man we are obliged to be. . . . We are born as wasteful and unremorseful as tigers; we are obliged to be thrifty, or starve, or freeze.

WILLIAM BOLITHO, *Twelve against the Gods*, 1929

7 Natural resources are frequently used wastefully . . . not because individual resource users do not know any better, but because they cannot help it under the influence of economic forces.

S. V. CIRIACY-WANTRUP, *Resource Conservation*, 1952

8 The predominant influence of the American socio-cultural environment upon individuals now born and brought up in it is to give them a sense of plenty, even of abundance; to encourage them to spend, to waste, even to destroy.

CHARLES E. LIVELY, "Some Reflections on the Conservation Movement," 1953

9 Our heritage of wastefulness is derived from an economy which now demands that the volume of waste be constantly increased in order that the economy itself be maintained.

PERCY H. MCGAUHEY, testimony, U.S. House Interstate and Foreign Commerce subcommittee, 29 June 1965

10 The salvation of our environment requires that we overcome our divisions and the pressure of temporary, local interests. Otherwise the Soviet Union will poison the United States with its wastes and vice versa. At present, this is a hyperbole. But with a 10 percent annual increase of wastes, the increase over 100 years will be 20,000 times.

ANDREI D. SAKHAROV, *New York Times*, 22 July 1968

11 And so when we examined the principle of efficiency as we now practice it, we see that it is not really efficient at all. As we use the word, efficiency means no such thing, or it means short-term or temporary efficiency; which is a contradiction in terms. It means hurrying to nowhere. It means the profligate waste of humanity and nature. It means the greatest profit to the greatest liar. What we have called efficiency has produced among us, and to our incalculable cost, such unprecedented monuments of destructiveness and waste as the strip-mining industry, the Pentagon, the federal bureaucracy, and the family car.

WENDELL BERRY, quoted in *Manas*, 14 March 1973

12 Despite the current ascendancy of the throw-away mentality, I feel there's a strong ethical hatred of waste among most Americans.
   THOMAS F. WILLIAMS, quoted in *Conservation Foundation Letter*, April 1973

13 Waste is not just the stuff you throw away, of course, it's the stuff you use to excess.
   JOY WILLIAMS, *Esquire*, February 1989

14 Waste isn't waste until its wasted.
   DAN KNAPP, *Sierra Club Sourcebook*, 1990

15 We have to turn the wastes of war into a war on wastes.
   GARY COHEN, *E* magazine, July–August 1990

16 "Residual" is a more neutral term than "waste."
   BLAIR T. BOWER, remarks, World Wildlife Fund, 8 May 1991

17 In the aftermath of the Persian Gulf war, Kuwait was a waste disposal company's dream come true.
   LIZ SLY, quoted in *Greenwire*, 8 May 1991

---

134 WATER

See also   21 DAMS AND WATER PROJECTS, 25 DRINKING WATER, 59 GROUNDWATER

1 The best of men is like water;
  Water benefits all things
  And does not compete with them.
  It dwells in (the lowly) places that all disdain,
  Wherein it comes near to Tao.
   LAO-TSU (6th century B.C.), *Tao-te Ching*

2 Water is the best of all things.
   PINDAR (c. 522–c. 438 B.C.), *Olympian Odes*

3 [The water commissioner in Rome] must see that no one draws water without a written authorization from Caesar. He must exercise great vigilance against manifold forms of fraud.
   FRONTINUS (about A.D. 35–about A.D. 103), *The Water Supply of Rome*, c. 100

4 Water is the principle, or the element, of things
  All things are water.
   PLUTARCH (about A.D. 46–after A.D. 119), *Placita philosophorum*

5 We made from water every living thing.
   KORAN, sura 21.30

6 And (further), thou seest
  The earth barren and lifeless,
  But when We pour down
  Rain on it, it is stirred
  (To life), it swells.
  And it puts forth every kind
  Of beautiful growth (in pairs).
   KORAN, sura 22.5

7 Praise be, my Lord, for Sister Water. Who is most useful, humble, precious and chaste.
   FRANCIS OF ASSISI (1181–1226), *The Canticle of the Sun*, translated by Matthew Arnold

8 Water is a very good servant, but it is a cruell maister.
   WILLIAM BULLEIN, *Bulwarke of Defence against All Sicknesses*, 1562

9 The green mantle of the standing pool.
   WILLIAM SHAKESPEARE (1564–1616), *King Lear*, 3.4.134 (1605–1606)

10 The thirsty earth soaks up the rain.
   And drinks, and gapes for drink again.
    ABRAHAM COWLEY (1618–1667), "Drinking," 1668

11 We'll never know the worth of water till the well go dry.
    SCOTTISH PROVERB, cited in 1721 collection

12 When the well's dry, we know the worth of water.
    BENJAMIN FRANKLIN (1706–1790), *Poor Richard's Almanac*, 1746

13 Water is insipid, inodorous, colorless, and smooth.
    EDMUND BURKE (1729–1797), *On the Sublime and Beautiful*, 1757

14 I wish to make it clear to you, there is not sufficient water to irrigate all the lands which could be irrigated, and only a small portion can be irrigated. . . . I tell you, gentlemen, you are piling up a heritage of conflict!
    JOHN WESLEY POWELL, (1834–1902), speech, Los Angeles International Irrigation Conference, 1893

15 Whiskey's for drinking, water's for fighting about.
    MARK TWAIN (Samuel Langhorne Clemens, 1835–1910), attributed, late 19th century

16 Water is the eye of a landscape.
   VINCENT LEAN, *Collectanea*, 1902

17 Water is H₂O, hydrogen two parts, oxygen one, but there is also a third thing, that makes it water and nobody knows what that is.
   D. H. LAWRENCE (1885–1930), *Pansies*, 1929

18 Water, thou hast no taste, no color, no odor; canst not be defined, art relished while ever mysterious. Not necessary to life, but rather life itself, thou fillest us with a gratification that exceeds the delight of the senses.
   ANTOINE DE SAINT-EXUPÉRY (1900–1944), *Wind, Sand, and Stars*, 1939

19 [Water is] the one substance from which the earth can conceal nothing; it sucks out its innermost secrets and brings them to our very lips.
   JEAN GIRAUDOUX (1882–1944), *The Madwoman of Chaillot*, 1946

20 This is not dead land, it is only thirsty land.
   FRANCES MARION, *Westward the Dream*, 1948

21 The earth holds a silver treasure, cupped between ocean bed and tenting sky. Forever the heavens spend it, in the showers that refresh our temperate lands, the torrents that sluice the tropics. Every suckling root absorbs it, the very soil drains it down; the rivers run unceasing to the sea, the mountains yield it endlessly. . . . Yet none is lost; in vast convection our water is returned, from soil to sky, and sky to soil, and back again, to fall as pure as blessing. There was never less; there could never be more. A mighty mercy on which life depends, for all its glittering shifts water is constant.
   DONALD CULROSS PEATTIE and NOEL PEATTIE, *A Cup of Sky*, 1950

22 If there is magic on this planet, it is contained in water.
   LOREN EISELEY, *The Immense Journey*, 1957

23 Of all tasks imposed by the natural environment, it was the task imposed by a precarious water situation that stimulated man to develop hydraulic methods of social control.
   KARL A. WITTFOGEL, *Oriental Despotism*, 1957

24 The Romans had a respect amounting almost to adoration for running water.
   MICHAEL GRANT, *The World of Rome*, 1960

25 The society which scorns excellence in plumbing because plumbing is a humble activity, and tolerates shoddiness in philosophy because philosophy is an exalted activity, will have neither good plumbing nor good philosophy. Neither its pipes nor its theories will hold water.
   JOHN W. GARDNER, *Saturday Evening Post*, 1 December 1962

26 The biggest waste of water in the country by far. You spend half a pint and flush two gallons.
   PRINCE PHILIP, duke of Edinburgh, speech, 1965

27 I earnestly believe that desalting [of water] is the greatest and is the most hopeful promise that we have for the future.
   LYNDON B. JOHNSON (1908–1973), First International Symposium on Water Desalinization, 7 October 1965

28 The crisis of our diminishing water resources is just as severe (if less obviously immediate) as any wartime crisis we have ever faced. Our survival is just as much at stake as it was at the time of Pearl Harbor, or the Argonne, or Gettysburg, or Saratoga. . . . Pure water, when and where you need it, is worth whatever it costs to get it there.
   JIM WRIGHT, U.S. Representative, *The Coming Water Famine*, 1966

29 High quality water is more than the dream of the conservationists, more than a political slogan; high quality water, in the right quantity at the right place at the right time, is essential to health, recreation, *and* economic growth.
   EDMUND S. MUSKIE, U.S. Senator, speech, 1 March 1966

30 If you gave me several million years, there would be nothing that did not grow in beauty if it were surrounded by water.
   JAN ERIK VOLD, *What All the World Knows*, 1970

31 The frog does not
   Drink up
   The pond in which
   He lives.
   AMERICAN INDIAN PROVERB, quoted in David Zwick, *Water Wasteland*, 1971

32 Human beings were invented by water as a device for transporting itself from one place to another.
Tom Robbins, *Another Roadside Attraction*, 1971

33 The bad news is that if the drought keeps up, within a few years we'll all be drinking reclaimed sewer water. The good news is that there won't be enough to go around.
Bill Miller, quoted in *Chicago Sun-Times*, 4 March 1977

34 Children of a culture born in a water-rich environment, we have never really learned how important water is to us. We understand it, but we do not respect it.
William Ashworth, *Nor Any Drop to Drink*, 1982

35 Of all our planet's activities—geological movements, the reproduction and decay of biota, and even the disruptive propensities of certain species (elephants and humans come to mind)—no force is greater than the hydrologic cycle.
Richard Bangs and Christian Kallen, *Rivergods*, 1985

36 A drought is a lack of water, but not necessarily a disaster. Whether or not a drought becomes a disaster depends on how people have been managing their land before the drought. . . . Given the overcultivation and land misuse forced on many people in the tropical Third World, one would expect drought to be a major disaster worldwide.
Lloyd Timberlake, *Africa in Crisis*, 1985

37 Water flows uphill towards money.
Anonymous, saying in the American West, quoted by Ivan Doig in Marc Reisner, *Cadillac Desert*, 1986

38 If surface water can be compared with interest income, and non-renewable groundwater with capital, then much of the West was living mainly on interest income. California was milking interest and capital in about equal proportion. The plains states, however, were devouring capital as a gang of spendthrift heirs might squander a great capitalist's fortune.
Marc Reisner, *Cadillac Desert*, 1986

39 Clean water is not an expenditure of Federal funds; clean water is an investment in the future of our country.
Bud Shuster, U.S. Representative, quoted in *Washington Post*, 9 January 1987

40 Water can stand for what is unconscious, instinctive, and sexual in us, for the creative swill in which we fish for ideas. It carries, weightlessly, the imponderable things in our lives: death and creation. We can drown in it or else stay buoyant, quench our thirst, stay alive.
Gretel Ehrlich, in Stephen Trimble, ed., *Words from the Land*, 1988

41 The next war in our region will be over the waters of the Nile, not politics.
Esmat Abdel Mequid, Egyptian Foreign Minister, quoted in *Business Week*, 18 June 1990

42 The journey of water is round, and its loss, too, moves in a circle, following us around the world as we lose something of such immense value that we do not yet even know its name.
Linda Hogan, *Northern Lights*, Autumn 1990

43 Between earth and earth's atmosphere, the amount of water remains constant; there is never a drop more, never a drop less. This is a story of circular infinity, of a planet birthing itself.
Linda Hogan, *Northern Lights*, Autumn 1990

44 Think of the tremendous amounts of water needed to keep a golf course green in a region where there is no rain during the hottest months. Isn't there something immoral about maintaining such luxuries?
Garrett Hardin, *E* magazine, November–December 1990

45 California's water system might have been invented by a Soviet bureaucrat on an LSD trip.
Peter Passell, *New York Times*, 27 February 1991

46 We should no longer think of water as a gift of nature but an industry which needs investment.
Thawat Vichaidiji, Thai water official, *Bangkok Post*, 17 March 1991

47 Water has flowed into current uses because it has been cheap relative to economic returns from using it. It has been cheap not only because it has been plentiful but because it has been allocated politically rather than economically—by legislation and litigation rather than by auction, meaning markets.
GEORGE F. WILL, *Washington Post*, 28 March 1991

48 Water will increasingly force the West to make, as no other region must, semi-socialist choices.
GEORGE F. WILL, *Washington Post*, 28 March 1991

49 You think we have bad fights over oil. Just wait until we start fighting over water. It's predicted in the Koran.
ANONYMOUS JORDANIAN, quoted in*Washington Post*, 28 April 1991

50 Our planet is shrouded in water, and yet 8 million children under the age of five will die this year from lack of safe water. The same irony will see 800 million people at risk from drought. . . . Two-thirds of the world's rural poor have no access to safe drinking water, and while millions are made homeless from floods, hundreds of millions are coping with drought.
UNITED NATIONS ENVIRONMENT PROGRAM, "What Water Shortage?" undated

135 WATER POLLUTION
See also 104 POLLUTION, 105 POLLUTION CONTROL, 106 POLLUTION PREVENTION, 134 WATER

1 Filthy water cannot be washed.
WEST AFRICAN PROVERB

2 To get clear water, one must go to the source.
FRENCH PROVERB

3 Who is there that can make muddy water clear? But if permitted to remain still, it will gradually become clear of itself.
LAO-TSU (6th century B.C.), *The Way of Virtue*, 550 B.C.

4 And let this be the law: If anyone intentionally pollutes the water of another, whether the water of a spring, or collected in reservoirs, either by poisonous substances, or by digging, or by theft, let the injured party bring the cause before the warden of the city.
PLATO (428–343 B.C.), *Laws*

5 Water that stirs not stinks.
ANCRENE WISSE, c. 1180–1200

6 Expect poison from the standing water.
WILLIAM BLAKE (1757–1827), *The Marriage of Heaven and Hell*, 1793

7 Ye nymphs that reign o'er sewers and sinks,
The river Rhine, it is well known,
Doth wash your city of Cologne;
But tell me, nymphs, what power divine
Shall henceforth wash the river Rhine?
SAMUEL TAYLOR COLERIDGE (1772–1834), "The City of Cologne," 1800

8 The sewer is the conscience of the city.
VICTOR HUGO (1802–1885), *Les Misérables*, 1862

9 Excretions of consumption are of the greatest importance for agriculture. So far as their utilisation is concerned, there is an enormous waste of them in the capitalist economy. In London, for instance, they find no better use for the excretion of four and half million human beings than to contaminate the Thames with it at heavy expense.
KARL MARX (1818–1883), *Das Kapital*, 1867

10 Don't pour out dirty water before you have clean water.
MARCUS WEISSMANN-CHAJOS, *Hokma u Musar*, 1875

11 The old swimming hole of those of us with a touch of gray in our hair is now, ten to one, polluted and the boy of today is apt to be stricken with typhoid who swims in it. Pollution is the big thing that this mighty national crusade has got to battle.
WILL H. DILIG, *Izaak Walton League Monthly*, September 1922

12 Is ditchwater dull? Naturalists with microscopes have told me that it teems with quiet fun.
G. K. CHESTERTON (1874–1936), *The Spice of Life*, 1936

13 The most ordinary sewer systems of today would have seemed like black fantastic night-

mares to the taxpayers of only one hundred years ago.

RICHARD NEUTRA (1892–1970), *Survival through Design*, 1954

14 Water has been the orphan stepchild of the entire conservation picture and our polluted streams have been a national disgrace for years.

KENNETH REID, quoted in Edgar B. Nixon, ed., *FDR and Conservation*, 1957

15 As large a body of water as Lake Erie has already been overwhelmed by pollutants and has in effect died.

BARRY COMMONER, *Science and Survival*, 1963

16 Sewage plants are built. They need steel. They need electric power. They need paperwork. They need workers. The workers get paid, and they consume.

EDWIN L. DALE, JR., *New York Times*, 19 April 1970

17 Water is the most precious, limited natural resource we have in this country. . . . But because water belongs to no one—except the people—special interests, including government polluters, use it as their private sewers.

RALPH NADER, in David Zwick and Marcy Benstock, *Water Wasteland*, 1971

18 If the clothing is not clean, if the underwear doesn't survive after it has been washed eight or ten times, the people who will suffer an adverse effect are the citizens of Indiana. . . . [If] the people of Indiana prefer to wear gray shirts and have a little hardness distilled on their glasses, so forth and so on, as a price for obtaining cleaner water, or for obtaining a chance of having lesser phosphate content which in turn may produce or may not produce, we don't know, lesser amounts of algae, that is a choice which we feel the people of Indiana should make through the Indiana Legislature.

U.S. DISTRICT COURT, SOUTHERN DIVISION, INDIANA, decision, *Soap and Detergent Association v. Offutt*, 31 August 1971

19 Let's turn the Corps [of Engineers] loose on building the regional sewage- and waste-treatment systems the nation so desperately needs.

HENRY S. REUSS, U.S. Representative, *Reader's Digest*, November 1971

20 You fellows have got to get this [phosphate-pollution problem] straightened out, because the laundry's piling up.

BETTY FURNESS, quoted in Mel Ziegler, ed., *Bella!*, 1972

21 "Sewage sludge" just doesn't sound as interesting as "night soil."

JULIE SULLIVAN, in *The Cousteau Almanac*, 1980

22 One major, overwhelming reason why we are running out of water is that we are killing the water we have.

WILLIAM ASHWORTH, *Nor Any Drop to Drink*, 1982

23 Inadequate sewer pipes and sewage treatment as well as insufficient system capacity to handle storm runoff characterize many of the nation's 15,000 wastewater treatment systems. If uncorrected, these problems could compromise federally mandated ambient water quality standards.

U.S. CONGRESSIONAL BUDGET OFFICE, *Public Works Infrastructure*, April 1983

24 If you could tomorrow morning make water clean in the world, you would have done, in one fell swoop, the best thing you could have done for improving human health by improving environmental quality.

WILLIAM C.CLARK, speech, Racine, Wisconsin, April 1988

25 What is happening underwater . . . is not for the squeamish. Scuba divers talk of swimming through clouds of toilet paper and half-dissolved feces, of bay bottoms covered by a . . . sediment . . . appropriately known as black mayonnaise.

NEWSWEEK, 1 August 1988

26 The governing classes nowadays want to talk about social justice and projects that provide jobs for lawyers. No one wants to talk about sewers.

DANIEL PATRICK MOYNIHAN, U.S. Senator, quoted in *USA Today*, 11 August 1988

27 The amount of sewage dumped into the harbor in 1986 would cover all of metropolitan Boston up to a depth of 17 feet. . . . Boston is the only major city in America to dump it right in its own harbor.

GEORGE BUSH, campaign speech, Boston, 1 September 1988

136 WEATHER

See also   15 CLIMATE

1 Praise be to Thee, my Lord, for
  Brother Wind,
  And for the air and the cloud of fair
  and all weather
  Through which Thou givest
  sustenance to Thy creatures.
    FRANCIS OF ASSISI (c. 1181–1226), *Canticle of
    the Sun*, translated by Matthew Arnold

2 For the man sound in body and serene of
  mind there is no such thing as bad weather;
  every sky has its beauty, and storms which
  whip the blood do but make it pulse more
  vigorously.
    GEORGE GISSING (1857–1903), *The Private Pa-
    pers of Henry Ryecroft*, 1903

3 We all grumble about the weather—but—
  nothing is done about it.
    MARK TWAIN (Samuel Langhorne Clemens,
    1835–1910), quoted in Robert Underwood
    Johnson, *Remembered Yesterdays*, 1923

4 [For the benefit of mankind, we need to attain the] maximum possible mastery of our
  atmospheric environment. . . . The enemy is
  hail, blizzards, floods, droughts, hurricanes.
  The enemy is the innate intransigence and in-
  scrutability of nature.
    WALTER ORR ROBERTS, speech, American
    Meteorological Society, 1965

5 How can proper account be taken of natural
  weather scenery, the stimulating, the unique
  experience of living with weather in its more
  robust forms?
    ROBERT L. HENDRICK, "Human Dimensions
    of Weather Modification," University of
    Chicago, Department of Geography re-
    search paper, 1966

6 The wilderness of weather.
    ROBERT L. HENDRICK, "Human Dimensions
    of Weather Modification," University of
    Chicago, Department of Geography re-
    search paper, 1966

7 It seems clear that the power and motion of
  severe storms provide some of the most exhilarating opportunities that the human
  mind experiences.
    ADRIAN CHAMBERLAIN, testimony, U.S. Sen-
    ate Commerce Committee, 21 February
    1966

8 Among famous traitors of history one might
  mention the weather.
    ILKA CHASE, *The Varied Airs of Spring*, 1969

9 The weather system creates a world of have
  and of have-not countries . . . similar to that
  which exists economically between the have
  and have-not countries. Some states are
  blessed with better weather than others, a situation which the less fortunate states could
  some day assert it is within their right to redress.
    E. B. WEISS, speech, American Meteorlogi-
    cal Society, Rapid City, S.D., June 1972

10 Nowadays, everybody is doing something
   about the weather but nobody is talking
   about it.
    STEPHEN H. SCHNEIDER, speech, American
    Association for the Advancement of Sci-
    ence, Washington, D.C., December 1972

11 Weather is one of the few things left in this
   world more or less completely free. It's just a
   general feeling we've fouled up everything
   else, why the weather?
    ANONYMOUS ENVIRONMENTALIST, quoted in
    Conservation Foundation Letter, January 1973

12 Nor should we let the soothing talk of spe-
   cial-interest groups or short-sighted optimists, bolstered momentarily by a good
   harvest or two, weaken our resolve. We must
   now begin urgent actions to correct the long-
   term conditions that render us vulnerable,
   sooner or later, to extended periods of unfavorable weather, which, as history has taught
   us, are inevitable.
    STEPHEN H. SCHNEIDER, on drought, testi-
    mony, U.S. Senate Public Works subcom-
    mittee, 31 March 1977

13 Innocence, I suppose, is just a response to
   landscape and weather and familiar images
   and the kiss of the wind.
    WALLACE STEGNER, in Richard W. Etulain,
    *Conversations with Wallace Stegner on West-
    ern History and Literature*, 1983

14 The weather has quite a bit to do with societal vulnerability to shortfalls in food, water, and energy supplies. These vulnerabilities, in turn, are related to complexity and maintaining a vital democracy.
> STEPHEN H. SCHNEIDER and RANDI LONDER, *The Coevolution of Climate and Life*, 1984

15 The public-domain experience—that wide openness, those lilac distances, those wild dust storms, blizzards, thunderstorms, downpours of savage hail, that sense of the largeness, wonder, mystery, danger, of the natural world.
> WALLACE STEGNER, on the West, *Sierra*, September–October 1989

16 We're having a cold spell now. That's hardly a sign of global cooling. It's just the weather changes.
> RICHARD LINDZEN, *USA Today*, 26 December 1989

17 For all its technological progress, [North] American agriculture still remains at the mercy of the weather.
> NATURAL RESOURCES DEFENSE COUNCIL, *Farming in the Greenhouse*, 1989

---

137 WETLANDS

---

1 Take a View of a Swamp in its original Estate, full of Bogs, overgrown with Flags, Brakes, poisonous Weeds and Vines, with other useful Product, the genuine Offspring of stagnant Waters. Its miry Bottom, and Harbour to Turtles, Toads, Efts, Snakes, and other creeping Verm'n. The baleful Thickets of Brambles, and the dreary Shades of larger Growth; the Dwelling-Place of the Owl and the Bittern; a Portion of Foxes, and a Cage of every unclean and hateful bird.
> JARED ELIOT (1685–1763), *Essays upon Field Husbandry in New England and Other Papers*, 1748–1762

2 The mosquitoes and other stinging insects that make the wilds of America so trying for the savages, may be so many goads to urge these primitive men to drain the marshes and bring light into the dense forests that shut out the air, and, by so doing, as well as by the tillage of the soil, to render their abodes more sanitary.
> IMMANUEL KANT (1724–1804), *The Critique of Judgment*, 1790

3 When I would recreate myself, I seek the darkest wood, the thickest and most interminable, and, to the citizen, most dismal swamp. I enter a swamp as a sacred place,—a *sanctum sanctorum*.
> HENRY DAVID THOREAU (1817–1862), *Excursions*, 1862

4 Ye marshes, how candid and simple
    and nothing-withholding and free,
Ye publish yourselves to the sky and
    offer yourselves to the sea.
> SIDNEY LANIER (1842–1881), *"The Marshes of Glynn,"* 1878

5 The marsh, to him who enters it in a receptive mood, holds, besides mosquitoes and stagnaton, melody, the mystery of unknown waters, and the sweetness of Nature undisturbed by man.
> CHARLES WILLIAM BEEBE (1877–1962), *Log of the Sun*, 1906

6 Our country includes within its boundaries 125 million acres of undeveloped wet and swamp lands which are subject to overflow. With proper drainage and protection, an estimated two-fifths of this area, or 50 million acres, would be physically suitable for crop or pasture use.
> U.S. DEPARTMENT OF AGRICULTURE, 1953, quoted in Fish and Wildlife Service circular 39, "Wetlands of the United States"

7 Only those people that have directly experienced the wetlands that line the shore . . . can appreciate their mystic qualities. The beauty of rising mists at dusk, the ebb and flow of the tides, the merging of fresh and salt waters, the turmoil of wind and weather—all unite to create an environment that man has only superficially explored.
> GOVERNOR'S TASK FORCE ON MARINE AND COASTAL AFFAIRS, "Delaware: Wetlands," 1972

8 If we fail to save the wetlands, we will be losing more than an economic and aesthetic asset that can never be recreated. The loss may

also signal an impending and crushing defeat in the larger effort to maintain an environment that civilized man can inhabit.

WILLIAM SAXBE, U.S. Attorney General, conference, Tarpon Springs, Florida, 18 July 1974

9 America's marshes and backwaters, sloughs and estuaries, provide wilderness experiences second to none, experiences that bring men as close to being at one with non-human nature as they can reasonably afford to be—awesome experiences, humbling experiences, entangling experiences, fundamentally frightening experiences.

PETER A. FRITZELL, speech, National Wetlands Symposium, November 1978

10 The interior experiences of these proto-wilderness areas also provide kinds of sublimity and picturesqueness. . . . They force you inward, both upon yourself and upon the non-human world. . . . The wetland is, then, one might argue, the kind of environment most appropriate to a people whose conventional frontiers are closed and who now must begin to look closely at what they have rather than what they might have.

PETER A. FRITZELL, speech, National Wetlands Symposium, November 1978

11 A giant sponge of biological diversity embroidering the southern coast.

CHARLES E. LITTLE, on the salt marshes behind the Carolina beaches, in *The American Land*, 1979

12 Civilization began around wetlands; today's civilization has every reason to leave them wet and wild.

EDWARD MALTBY, *Waterlogged Wealth*, 1986

13 Wetlands have a poor public image. . . . Yet they are among the earth's greatest natural assets . . . mankind's waterlogged wealth.

EDWARD MALTBY, *Waterlogged Wealth*, 1986

14 Poets who know no better rhapsodize about the peace of nature, but a well-populated marsh is a cacophony.

BERN KEATING, *Connoisseur*, April 1986

15 Edges have always produced phenomena that are among the most interesting in nature—the great migrations of fish and fowl triggered by the intersections of the seasons;

the abundance and diversity of wildlife known to any hunter who stalks the junctures of forest and field, and the fantastic habitats of the tide marshes at the merge of land and water.

TOM HORTON, *Bay Country*, 1987

16 We are cutting out our kidneys to enlarge our stomachs.

ERIC FREYFOGLE, Illinois law professor, on the destruction of wetlands, *Baltimore Evening Sun*, 12 September 1991

138 WILDERNESS

See also 68 HUMANKIND AND NATURE, 87 NATURE

1 Besides, what could they see but a hideous and desolate wilderness, full of wild beasts and wild men? And what multitudes there might be of them they knew not.

WILLIAM BRADFORD (1590–1657), *A Relation or Journal of the Beginning and Proceedings of the English Plantation Settled at Plimouth in New England*, 1622

2 A wilderness-condition is . . . a condition of straits, wants, deep distresses, and most deadly dangers.

THOMAS BROOKS, *Golden Key*, 1675

3 Away, away, from men and towns,
To the wild wood and the downs,—
To the silent wilderness,
Where the soul need not repress
Its music.

PERCY BYSSHE SHELLEY (1792–1822), "To Jane, The Invitation," c. 1820

4 In the woods a man casts off his years, as the snake his slough, and at what period soever of life, is always a child.

RALPH WALDO EMERSON (1803–1882), *Nature*, 1836

5 I long for scenes, where man hath never trod,
A place where woman never smiled or wept—
There to abide with my Creator, God,
And Sleep as I in childhood sweetly slept,
Untroubling, and untroubled where I lie,
The grass below—above the vaulted sky.

JOHN CLARE (1793–1864), "I Am," 1845

6 We need the tonic of wildness. . . . At the same time that we are earnest to explore and learn all things, we require that all things be mysterious and unexplorable, that land and sea be infinitely wild, unsurveyed and unfathomed by us because unfathomable. We can never have enough of nature.

HENRY DAVID THOREAU (1817–1862), *Walden*, 1854

7 A Book of Verses underneath the Bough,
A Jug of Wine, a Loaf of Bread—and Thou
   Beside me singing in the Wilderness—
Oh, Wilderness were Paradise enow!

EDWARD FITZGERALD (1809–1883), *The Rubáiyát of Omar Khayyám*, 1859

8 The spectacle of death, everywhere so majestic and solemn, seems to borrow from the wilderness a fresh majesty.

JULES VERNE (1828–1905), *L'étoile du sud*

9 What would the world be, once bereft
Of wet and of wildness? Let them be left,
O let thembe left, wildness and wet;
Long live the weeds and the wilderness yet.

GERARD MANLEY HOPKINS (1844–1889), "Inversnaid," 1881

10 Only by going alone in silence, without baggage, can one truly get into the heart of the wilderness. All other travel is mere dust and hotels and baggage and chatter.

JOHN MUIR (1838–1914), 1888, in William Frederick Badé, ed., *The Life and Letters of John Muir*, 1924

11 The clearest way into the Universe is through a forest wilderness.

JOHN MUIR (1838–1914), 1890, quoted in L. M. Wolfe, ed., *John Muir, John of the Mountains: The Unpublished Journals of John Muir*, 1938

12 I remember a hundred lovely lakes, and recall the fragrant breath of pine and fir and cedar and poplar trees. The trail has strung upon it, as upon a thread of silk, opalescent dawns and saffron sunsets. It has given me blessed release from care and worry and the troubled thinking of our modern day. It has been a return to the primitive and the peaceful. Whenever the pressure of our complex city life thins my blood and benumbs my brain, I seek relief in the trail; and when I hear the coyote wailing to the yellow dawn, my cares fall from me—I am happy.

HAMLIN GARLAND (1860–1940), *McClure's*, February 1899

13 The Call of the Wild.

JACK LONDON (1876–1916), title of novel, 1903

14 Leave it as it is. The ages have been at work on it and man can only mar it.

THEODORE ROOSEVELT (1858–1919), speech, Grand Canyon, 1903, quoted in William Schwarz, ed., *Voices for the Wilderness*, 1967

15 There's a land where the mountains are nameless,
and the rivers all run God knows where;
There are lives that are erring and aimless,
and deaths that just hang by a hair;
There are hardships that nobody reckons;
there are valleys unpeopled and still;
There's a land—oh, it beckons and beckons,
and I want to go back—and I will.

ROBERT W. SERVICE (1874–1958), "The Spell of the Yukon"

16 The strong life that never knows harness;
   The wilds where the caribou call;
The freshness, the freedom, the farness—
   O God! how I'm stuck on it all.

ROBERT W. SERVICE (1874–1958), "The Spell of the Yukon"

17 All the wilderness seems to be full of tricks and plans to drive and draw us up into God's light.

JOHN MUIR, (1838–1914), working as a sheepherder in 1869, *My First Summer in the Sierras*, 1911

18 Every prophet has to come from civilisation, but every prophet has to go into the wilderness. He must have a strong impression of a complex society and all that it has to give, and then he must serve periods of isolation and meditation. This is the process by which psychic dynamite is made.

WINSTON CHURCHILL (1874–1965), *Sunday Chronicle*, 8 November 1931

19 In God's wildness lies the hope of the world—the great fresh unblighted, unredeemed wilderness. The galling harness of civilization drops off, and the wounds heal ere we are aware.
JOHN MUIR (1838–1914), "Alaska Fragment," July 1890, in L. M. Wolfe, ed., *John of the Mountains: The Unpublished Journals of John Muir*, 1938

20 It is imperative to maintain portions of the wilderness untouched so that a tree will rot where it falls, a waterfall will pour its curve without generating electricity, a trumpeter swan may float on uncontaminated water—and moderns may at least see what their ancestors knew in their nerves and blood.
BERNAND DE VOTO (1897–1955), *Fortune*, June 1947

21 But all conservation of wildness is self-defeating, for to cherish we must see and fondle, and when enough have seen and fondled, there is no wilderness left to cherish.
ALDO LEOPOLD (1886–1948), *A Sand County Almanac*, 1949

22 In Europe, where wilderness has now retreated to the Carpathians and Siberia, every thinking conservationist bemoans its loss. Even in Britain, which has less room for land-luxuries than almost any other civilized country, there is a vigorous if belated movement for saving a few small spots of semi-wild land. Ability to see the cultural value of wilderness boils down, in the last analysis, to a question of intellectual humility. The shallow-minded modern who has lost his rootage in the land assumes that he has already discovered what is important.
ALDO LEOPOLD (1886–1948), *A Sand County Almanac*, 1949

23 The wilderness, the big woods, bigger and older than any recorded document:—of white man fatuous enough to believe he had bought any fragment of it, of Indian ruthless enough to pretend that any fragment of it had been his to convey. . . . that doomed wilderness whose edges were being constantly and punily gnawed at by men with plows and axes who feared it because it was wilderness.
WILLIAM FAULKNER (1897–1962), *Go Down Moses*, 1955

24 How much wilderness do the wilderness-lovers want? ask those who would mine and dig and cut and dam in such sanctuary spots as these. The answer is easy: *Enough so that there will be in the years ahead a little relief, a little quiet, a little relaxation, for any of our increasing millions who need and want it.*
WALLACE STEGNER, *This Is Dinosaur*, 1955

25 It is a commonplace of all religious thought, even the most primitive, that the man seeking visions and insight must go apart from his fellows and live for a time in the wilderness.
LOREN EISELEY, *The Immense Journey*, 1957

26 The wilderness and the idea of wilderness is one of the permanent homes of the human spirit.
JOSEPH WOOD KRUTCH (1893–1970), *Today and All Its Yesterdays*, 1958

27 The Arctic has a call that is compelling. The distant mountains [of the Brooks Range in Alaska] make one want to go on and on over the next ridge and over the one beyond. The call is that of a wilderness known only to a few. . . . This last American wilderness must remain sacrosanct.
WILLIAM O. DOUGLAS, (1898–1980), U.S. Supreme Court justice, 1960, quoted by Jimmy Carter, speech, 29 February 1980

28 The emotional aspects of a wilderness experience might be compared to a religious experience. It is particularly valuable for those people whose unconscious associations of pain and discomfort in relationships to man render a deity in human form impossible. Christianity is unacceptable to some people because of the use of the human symbol, but some who can't accept Christ can gain a tremendous sense of peace from relating to uncontaminated areas.
DONALD MCKINLEY, *Forest Industries*, February 1963

29 It may well be that . . . the Canadian north, with its vast expanses of primeval country,

can restore to modern man a semblance of balance and completeness. In the long run, these last wild regions of the continent might be worth far more to North Americans from a recreational and spiritual standpoint than through industrial exploitation. If this vision could be realized, even in part, these people might once more be proud of their heritage.

SIGURD F. OLSON, *Runes of the North*, 1963

30 Wilderness is an anchor to windward. Knowing it is there, we can also know that we are still a rich nation, tending our resources as we should—not a people in despair searching every last nook and cranny of our land for a board of lumber, a barrel of oil, a blade of grass, or a tank of water.

CLINTON P. ANDERSON, U.S. Senator, *American Forests*, July 1963

31 The "wilderness-area" mentality invariably advocates deep-freezing an ecology, whether San Gimignano or the High Sierra, as it was before the first Kleenex was dropped.

LYNN I. WHITE, JR., *Science*, 10 March 1967

32 In wilderness I sense the miracle of life, and behind it our scientific accomplishments fade to trivia.

CHARLES A. LINDBERGH (1902–1974), *Life*, 22 December 1967

33 The measure of a modern industrialized nation can be taken by observing the quality of its works in the two extremes of its environment—cities and wilderness bespeak its attitude toward the living earth. The United States is swiftly destroying its cities and its wilderness with highways.

A. Q. MOWBRAY, *Road to Ruin*, 1969

34 [Wilderness] can be a means of reassuring ourselves of our sanity as creatures, a part of the geography of hope.

WALLACE STEGNER, *The Sound of Mountain Water*, 1969

35 Something will have gone out of us as a people if we ever let the remaining wilderness be destroyed; if we permit the last virgin forests to be turned into comic books and plastic cigarette cases; if we drive the few remaining members of the wild species into zoos or to extinction; if we pollute the last clean air and

dirty the last clean streams and push our paved roads through the last of the silence, so that never again will Americans be free in their own country from the noise, the exhausts, the stinks of human and automotive waste.

STEWART L. UDALL, quoted in William Schwarz, ed., *Voices for the Wilderness*, 1969

36 Wilderness is a bench mark, a touchstone. In wilderness we can see where we have come from, where we are going, how far we've gone. In wilderness is the only unsullied earth sample of the forces generally at work in the universe.

KENNETH BROWER, in Garrett De Bell, ed., *The Environmental Handbook*, 1970

37 Canoeists and other primitive-trippers are not delighted to encounter others intent on the same private experience. How many visitors constitute the end of wilderness?

JOHN A. LIVINGSTON, in Borden Spears, ed., *Wilderness Canada*, 1970

38 We have always had reluctance to see a tract of land which is empty of men as anything but a void. The "waste howling wilderness" of Deuteronomy is typical. The Oxford Dictionary defines wilderness as wild or uncultivated land which is occupied "only" by wild animals. Places not used by us are "wastes." Areas not occupied by us are "desolate." Could the desolation be in the soul of man?

JOHN A. LIVINGSTON, in Borden Spears, ed., *Wilderness Canada*, 1970

39 Wilderness is the bank for genetic variability of the earth.

DAVID R.BROWER, quoted in John McPhee, *Encounters with the Archdruid*, 1971

40 Natural wilderness is a factor for world stability, not some remote place inimical to the human being. It is strange that it has been so long a place of fear to many men and so something to hate and destroy. Wilderness is not remote or indifferent but an active agent in maintaining a habitable world, though the co-operation is unconscious.

FRANK FRASER DARLING, *Wilderness and Plenty*, 1971

41 What a remarkably hopeless future for man when the locus of God's presence is to be found in the wilderness and not in human industry.

RICHARD NEUHAUS, *In Defense of People,* 1971

42 The wilderness holds answers to questions man has not yet learned to ask.

NANCY NEWHALL, quoted in John McPhee, *Encounters with the Archdruid,* 1971

43 The only way we can save any wilderness in this country is to make it harder to get into, and harder to stay in once you get there.

MARTIN LITTON, *The Grand Canyon,* 1972

44 So long as wilderness exists in reality . . . so long will the safeguards against an urban, industrial, mechanized ignorance of the facts of human life be effective.

HOWARD ZAHNISER, editorial, *Living Wilderness,* 1972

45 I realized that Eastern thought had somewhat more compassion for all living things. Man was a form of life that in another reincarnation might possibly be a horsefly or a bird of paradise or a deer. So a man of such a faith, looking at animals, might be looking at old friends or ancestors. In the East the wilderness has no evil connotation; it is thought of as an expression of the unity and harmony of the universe.

WILLIAM O. DOUGLAS (1898–1980), U.S. Supreme Court justice, *Go East, Young Man,* 1974

46 The exquisite sight, sound, and smell of wilderness is many times more powerful if it is earned through physical achievement, if it comes at the end of a long and fatiguing trip for which vigorous good health is a necessity. Practically speaking, this means that no one should be able to enter a wilderness by mechanical means.

GARRETT HARDIN, *The Ecologist,* February 1974

47 Throughout the history of this country, it's been possible to go to a place where no one has camped before, and now that kind of opportunity is running out. We must protect it, even if artificially. The day will come when

people will want to visit such a wilderness— saving everything they have to see it, at whatever cost.

JOHN MCPHEE, *Coming into the Country,* 1976

48 [Wilderness] is not any particular species or habitat type, but a higher class of life form with its own nobility derived from its complete independence of human beings.

DAVID EHRENFELD, *The Arrogance of Humanism,* 1978

49 I will speak for those in our nation who will not be able to journey to Alaska but who want to know that its wonders are there.

JAMES WEAVER, U.S. Representative, May 1978

50 There is no other place in the United States, and perhaps not in all of North America, where you can see vast landscapes as they come from the hand of the Creator, without any alteration by man.

JOHN F. SEIBERLING, U.S. Representative, on Alaska, quoted in *Conservation Foundation Letter,* June 1978

51 There's not one American in a thousand who has the stamina or wherewithal to use [the Arctic tundra of Alaska] as wilderness. . . . When you lock up the land, you lock up the human mind. You lock up the human spirit. And *that's* the only resource we might run short of in the future.

WALTER J. HICKEL, quoted in *The American Land,* 1979

52 They say, let's establish a wilderness, a formal, legal wilderness. But I say, why? . . . When God made this country, He zoned it Himself.

WALTER J. HICKEL, quoted in *The American Land,* 1979

53 The word "wilderness" occurs approximately three hundred times in the Bible, and all its meanings are derogatory.

RENÉ DUBOS, *The Wooing of Earth,* 1980

54 Opponents of wilderness areas often act as if these resources were being thrown away. This is simply silly. The natural resources in wilderness do not disappear. Any future generation that decides that natural resources are

more important than wilderness areas is free to change the law.

LESTER C. THUROW, *The Zero-Sum Society*, 1980

55 In my district, . . . there are some who do not like wilderness. They do not like it at all. I would try to plead with them . . . with their religious sensibilities—that we should leave some of our land the way we received it from the Creator. . . . I got a letter froma constituent right in the most conservative area in my whole district—and it is conservative. He said, "Mr. Weaver, if the Lord wanted to leave his forest lands, some of them in the way that we got them from Him, why did He send His only Son down to earth as a carpenter?" That stumped us. That stumped us until one of my aides, an absolute genius, said that the Lord Jesus before He determined His true mission spent 40 days and 40 nights in the wilderness.

JAMES WEAVER, U.S. Representative, hearing of House Interior and Insular Affairs Committee, 5 February 1981

56 The action and tone of his statement leads me to conclude that [Interior] Secretary [James G.] Watt's idea of wilderness is a parking lot without lines.

DON EDWARDS, U.S. Representative, *Progressive*, March 1981

57 We need wilderness preserved—as much of it as is still left, and as many kinds—because it was the challenge against which our character as a people was formed. The reminder and the reassurance that it is still there is good for our spiritual health even if we never once in 10 years set foot in it. It is good for us when we are young, because of the incomparable sanity it can bring briefly, as vacation and rest, into our insane lives. It is important to us when we are old simply because it is there—important, that is, simply as idea.

WALLACE STEGNER, *Las Vegas Sun*, 13 October 1981

58 Never let your love of nature overshadow your concern for human needs. I want wilderness to contribute to the American way of life.

BESTOR ROBINSON, quoted in Ron Arnold, *In the Eye of the Storm*, 1982

59 [Wilderness areas are] essentially parks for the upper-middle class. They are vacation reserves for people who want to rough it—with the assurance that few other people will have the time, energy, or means to follow them into the solitude.

WILLIAM TUCKER, *Progress and Privilege*, 1982

60 Wilderness, in the environmental pantheon, represents a particular kind of sanctuary in which all true values—that is, all nonhuman values—are reposited.

WILLIAM TUCKER, *Harper's*, March 1982

61 The wilderness concept appears valid if it is recognized for what it is—an attempt to create what are essentially "ecological museums" in scenic and biologically significant areas of these lands. But "wilderness," in the hands of environmentalists, has become an all-purpose tool for stopping economic activity as well.

WILLIAM TUCKER, *Harper's*, March 1982

62 Enjoyment of wilderness may not be spontaneous and "natural." It may be a learned process, inviting and even requiring reflection. But it is nonetheless valuable for being an aristocratic pleasure, democratically open to all.

GEORGE F. WILL, *Newsweek*, 16 August 1982

63 Pristine wilderness is an acquired taste and is incompatible with the enjoyment of some popular tastes such as dirt bikes, snowmobiles and other off-road vehicles. But surely there is no shortage of space in America for persons whose play must involve internal-combustion engines.

GEORGE F. WILL, *Newsweek*, 16 August 1982

64 Thoreau was,as far as I know, the first American who publicly concluded that wilderness as wilderness—that is, pure nature—was a good thing to have around.

NOEL PERRIN, in Daniel Halpern, ed.,*On Nature*, 1986

65 [Alaska] is a mad eugenicist's dream: take a few hundred thousand hardy, indomitable people; scatter them lightly over half a million square miles of frozen wilderness; subject them to mosquitoes the size of meadowlarks and temperatures of 50 below and 100 above; succor them with kegs of liquor; sup-

ply them ample gunpowder and guns—and see what happens. It's not particularly surprising that you end up with a citizenry—to use the term broadly—composed in large part of wild characters who have in common only their disdain for sissified city folk and pompous politicians.

MORRIS UDALL, U.S. Representative, *Too Funny to Be President*, 1988

66 In terms of wilderness preservation, Alaska is the last frontier. This time, given one great final chance, let us strive to do it right. Not in our generation, nor ever again, will we have a land and wildlife opportunity approaching the scope and importance of this one.

MORRIS UDALL, U.S. Representative, on the Alaska lands bill, *Too Funny to Be President*, 1988

67 The true wisdom is out there in the wilderness, and not in books—you need direct experience with wilderness to become enlightened.

DAVE FOREMAN, quoted in *Los Angeles Times*, 20 April 1988

68 The survival of the human race depends on the survival of Antarctica. An oil spill in Antarctic waters can damage the food chain for decades, and this affects us even in the Northern Hemisphere. It is essential that Antarctica be declared a wilderness reserve protected by all nations.

JACQUES COUSTEAU, quoted in *New York Times*, 25 September 1989

69 And I can assure you that, unlike what the Roman Catholic priest taught us, hell is not necessarily fire: For even in the cold Arctic, God's great works are destroyed, and that is also hell.

JOSIE KUSUGAK, *Mother Earth News*, March–April 1990

70 Wilderness areas in the United States can be seen as a museum of the geological and biological past, especially important to a nation that otherwise lacks a lengthy history to record.

ROBERT H. NELSON, *Policy Review*, Summer 1990

71 I wonder if all humans have a psychic layer that, given a chance, exactly corresponds to untouched wilderness. . . . The ecologists

say if wilderness goes, man goes. . . . Are they inadvertently pointing out nature's balancing power as the survival ingredient in all of us?

LYNDA W. SCHMIDT, *The Long Shore*, 1991

---

139 WILDLIFE
See also 11 BIRDS, 38 ENDANGERED SPECIES, 73 INSECTS, 102 PLANTS, 140 WILDLIFE REFUGES

---

1 No person should kill animals helpful to all. Rather, by serving them, one should attain happiness.

YAJUR-VEDA 13.47, 1000–500 B.C., quoted in *The Assisi Declarations*, World Wildlife Fund 25th Anniversary, 29 September 1986

2 But ask now the beasts, and they shall teach thee; and the fowls of the air, and they shall tell thee; or speak to the earth, and it shall teach thee; and the fishes of the sea shall declare unto thee.

BIBLE, Job 12:7–11

3 For that which befalleth the sons of men befalleth beasts; even one thing befalleth them: as the one dieth, so dieth the other; yea, they have all one breath; so that a man hath no preeminence above a beast. . . . All go unto one place; all are of the dust, and all turn to dust again. Who knoweth the spirit of man that goeth upward, and the spirit of the beast that goeth downward to the earth?

BIBLE, Ecclesiastes 3:19–21

4 The wolf shall dwell with the lamb, and the leopard shall lie down with the kid, and the calf and the young lion . . . and the lion shall eat straw like the ox. . . . They shall not hurt nor destroy in all my holy mountain: for the earth shall be full of the knowledge of the Lord.

BIBLE, Isaiah 11:6–9

5 And in that day, will I make a covenant for them with the beasts of the field, and with the fowls of heaven, and with the creeping things of the ground; and I will break the bow and the sword, and the battle out of the earth; and I will make them to lie down safely.

BIBLE, Hosea 2:18–20

6 It is not with respect to our convenience or discomfort, but with respect to their own nature, that the creatures are glorifying to their Artificer.
AUGUSTINE OF HIPPO (354–430), *City of God*

7 There is not an animal
(That lives) on the earth,
Nor a being that flies
On its wings, but (forms
Part of) communities like you.
KORAN, sura 6.38

8 It should not be believed that all beings exist for the sake of the existence of man. On the contrary, all the other beings too have been intended for their own sakes and not for the sake of something else.
MAIMONIDES (1135–1204), *The Guide for the Perplexed* 1:72, c. 1190

9 The time will come when men . . . will look on the murder of animals as they now look on the murder of men.
LEONARDO DA VINCI (1452–1519), quoted by Alice Herrington, testimony, U.S. House Merchant Marine and Fisheries Subcommittee, 9 September 1971

10 This world is like Noah's Ark
In which few men but many beasts embark.
SAMUEL BUTLER (1612–1680), "The World"

11 It is certain that God attaches more importance to a man than to a lion, but I do not know that we can be sure that he prefers one man to the entire species of lions.
GOTTFRIED WILHELM VON LEIBNIZ (1646–1716), *Théodicée*, 1710

12 Learn from the birds what food the thickets yield;
Learn from the beasts the physic of the field;
The arts of building from the bee receive;
Learn of the mole to plow, the worm to weave.
ALEXANDER POPE (1688–1744), *An Essay on Man*, 1733

13 Animals have these advantages over man: they never hear the clock strike, they die without any idea of death, they have no theologians to instruct them, their last moments are not disturbed by unwelcome and unpleasant ceremonies, their funerals cost them nothing, and no one starts lawsuits over their wills.
VOLTAIRE (1694–1778), letter to Count Schomberg, 31 August 1769

14 He prayeth well who loveth well
Both man and bird and beast.
SAMUEL TAYLOR COLERIDGE (1772–1834), "Rime of the Ancient Mariner," 1798

15 Nothing can be more obvious than that all animals were creately solely and exclusively for the use of man.
THOMAS LOVE PEACOCK (1785–1866), *Headlong Hall*, 1816

16 Happy would it be for animal creation if every human being . . . consulted the welfare of inferior creatures, and neither spoiled them by indulgences, nor injured them by tyranny!
SARAH KIRBY TRIMMER, *Fabulous Histories*, 13th ed., 1821

17 The behavior of men to the lower animals, and their behavior to each other, bear a constant relationship.
HERBERT SPENCER (1820–1903), *Social Statics*, 1851

18 The white man must treat the beasts of this land as his brothers. . . . What is man without beasts? If all the beasts were gone, men would die from great loneliness of spirit, for whatever happens to the beasts also happens to man. All things are connected. Whatever befalls the earth befalls the sons of the earth.
SEATTLE (Seathl), patriarch of the Duwamish and Squamish Indians of Puget Sound, letter to U.S. President Franklin Pierce, 1855

19 Origin of man now proved. He who understands baboon would do more towards metaphysics than Locke.
CHARLES DARWIN (1809–1882), *The M Notebook*, 1856

20 Animals are such agreeable friends—they ask no questions, they pass no criticisms.
GEORGE ELIOT (Mary Ann Evans, 1819–1880), *Scenes of Clerical Life*, 1857

21 [Animals are] nothing but the forms of our virtues and vices, wandering before our eyes, and visible phantoms of our souls
VICTOR HUGO (1802–1885), *Les misérables*, 1862

22 Bears are made of the same dust as we, and breathe the same winds and drink of the same waters. A bear's days are warmed by the same sun, his dwellings are overdomed by the same blue sky, and his life turns and ebbs with heart-pulsings like ours, and was poured from the same First Fountain. And whether he at last goes to our stingy heaven or no, he has terrestrial immortality. His life not long, not short, knows no beginning, no ending. To him life unstinted, unplanned, is above the accidents of time, and his years, markless and boundless, equal Eternity.

God bless Yosemite bears!

JOHN MUIR (1838–1914), 1871, in L. M. Wolfe, ed., *John Muir, John of the Mountains,* 1938

23 I have been studying the traits and dispositions of the "lower animals" (so called) and contrasting them with the traits and dispositions of man. I find the result humiliating to me.

MARK TWAIN, (Samuel Langhorne Clemens, 1835–1910), *Letters from the Earth,* c. 1907

24 All members of the lower classes of southern Europe are a dangerous menace to our wild life.

WILLIAM T. HORNADAY, *Our Vanishing Wildlife,* 1913

25 We have enslaved the rest of the animal creation, and have treated our distant cousins in fur and feathers so badly that beyond doubt, if they were able to formulate a religion, they would depict the Devil in human form.

WILLIAM RALPH INGE (1860–1954), *Outspoken Essays,* 1922

26 [Animals] are not brethren, they are not underlings; they are other nations, caught with ourselves in the net of life and time, fellow prisoners of the splendor and travail of the earth.

HENRY BESTON, *The Outermost House,* 1928

27 Ours is a lost cause, and there is no place for us in the natural universe, but we are not, for all that, sorry to be human. We should rather die as men than live as animals.

JOSEPH WOOD KRUTCH, *The Modern Temper,* 1929

28 In our pride we may exclude animals from our purview, but they all live a life, social and individual, like ourselves, and all life is subject to the Plan and Will of God.

ABDULLAH YUSUF ALI, interpreting the words of the Koran, *The Holy Qurān,* 1934

29 The best thing about animals is that they don't talk much.

THORNTON WILDER (1897–1975), *The Skin of Our Teeth,* 1942

30 The greatness of a nation and its moral progress can be judged by the way its animals are treated.

MOHANDAS K. GANDHI (1869–1948), *Selected Writings,* 1971

31 If animals are deprived of hope (as well as of fear), they are compensated by being given an almost endless patience for enduring, or simply for waiting.

JOSEPH WOOD KRUTCH (1893–1970), *The Twelve Seasons,* 1949

32 Those who wish to pet and baby wild animals, "love" them. But those who respect their natures and wish to let them live normal lives, love them more.

EDWIN WAY TEALE (1899–1980), *Circle of the Seasons,* 1953

33 The survival of our wildlife is a matter of grave concern to all of us in Africa. These wild creatures amid the wild places they inhabit are not only important as a source of wonder and inspiration but are an integral part of our natural resources and of our future livelihood and well-being.

JULIUS NYERERE, *Arusha Declaration, Tanganyika,* September 1961

34 You can't be suspicious of a tree, or accuse a bird or a squirrel of subversion or challenge the ideology of a violet.

HAL BORLAND, *Sundial of the Seasons,* 1964

35 Man, our most ingenious predator, sometimes seems determined to destroy the precious treasures of his own environment.

HAL BORLAND, *New York Times Book Review,* 23 February 1964

36 But if we stop loving animals, aren't we bound to stop loving humans too?

ALEXANDER SOLZHENITSYN, *The Cancer Ward,* 1968

37 We seldom see the bones of pain that hang beyond the green summer day. The woods

and fields and gardens are places of endless stabbing, impaling, squashing and mangling. We see only what floats to the surface: the colour, the song, the nesting, and the feeding. I do not think we could bear a clear vision of the animal world.

J. A. BAKER, *The Hill of Summer*, 1969

38 The tragedy of the blue whale is in the reflection of an even greater one, that of man himself. What is the nature of a species that knowingly and without good reason exterminates another?

GEORGE SMALL, *The Blue Whale*, 1971

39 Our whole moral and legal tradition is founded on the assumption that there is an unbridgeable gap between man and animals, giving us the right to own and exploit them without reference to their best interests. If our scientists now tell us that animals are different from us only in degree, then our exploitation carries far more serious implications than we have been willing to admit.

STEPHEN I. BURR, *Environmental Affairs*, Spring 1975

40 Man is modifying the world so fast and so drastically that most animals cannot adapt to the new conditions. In the Himalaya as elsewhere there is a great dying, one infinitely sadder than the Pleistocene extinctions, for man now has the knowledge and the need to save these remnants of his past.

GEORGE B. SCHALLER, *Mountain Monarchs*, 1977

41 Animals will be a liability . . . . We know that in *our* world nothing is free. In the future every animal on Earth will exist at some cost to humanity.

PAUL SHEPARD, *Thinking Animals*, 1978

42 A world where people are beginning to crowd one another intolerably is a world too small for animals. Until recent centuries, big clusters of people were widely separated. In the towns some animals, such as pets, sparrows, and cockroaches, thrived, but the realm of the wild birds and mammals was between towns. Now the planet is becoming a city. Animals that once lived on farms or simply away from civilization soon will no longer find space.

PAUL SHEPARD, *Thinking Animals*, 1978

43 There is a profound, inescapable need for animals that is in all people everywhere, an urgent requirement for which no substitute exists. It is no vague, romantic, or intangible yearning, no simple sop to our loneliness or nostalgia for Paradise. It is as hard and unavoidable as the compounds of our inner chemistry. It is universal but poorly recognized. It is the peculiar way that animals are used in the growth and development of the human person, in those most priceless qualities which we lump together as "mind." It is the role of animal images and forms in the shaping of personality, identity, and social consciousness. Animals are among the first inhabitants of the mind's eye. They are basic to the development of speech and thought. Because of their part in the growth of consciousness, they are inseparable from a series of events in each human life, indispensable to our becoming human in the fullest sense.

PAUL SHEPARD, *Thinking Animals*, 1978

44 [Wildlife cannot be saved] unless we can instill our beliefs in the people of our time and those to follow as moral and ethical issues. That they will buy. . . . [Slavery] has in less than a century become morally and ethically repugnant.

ROGER CARAS, speech, Yale School of Forestry symposium, 10 April 1978

45 The real problem is that man can get along economically without the overwhelming majority of animals and plant life, for some period of time. The economic trade-offs will not be consciously made. They are being made every day by fishermen, pastoralists, and farmers, in no orderly way.

WILLIAM T. CONWAY, quoted in *Conservation Foundation Letter*, May 1978

46 So bleak is the picture . . . that the bulldozer and not the atomic bomb may turn out to be the most destructive invention of the 20th century.

PHILIP SHABECOFF, on the destruction of wildlife habitat, *New York Times Magazine*, 4 June 1978

47 Man and beast are competing for the same living space. This in itself is a cataclysmic development equal in magnitude to those radical changes in climate, topography and vegetation that have decimated whole spe-

cies. Yet storks nest in chimneys, coyotes follow road graders to catch field mice, bears and pumas live in exurbia.
SAM WITCHEL, *New York Times*, 3 May 1979

48 When one considers that tens or even hundreds of lions, leopards, rhinos, buffalos, and so on must have died—or been killed—in transport or captivity for every one that lived to entertain the citizens, the probable scale of the Roman impact on wildlife staggers the imagination.
ANNE EHRLICH and PAUL EHRLICH, *Mother Earth News*, May–June 1980

49 Without knowing it, we utilize hundreds of products each day that owe their origin to wild animals and plants. Indeed our welfare is intimately tied up with the welfare of wildlife. Well may conservationists proclaim that by saving the lives of wild species, we may be saving our own.
NORMAN MYERS, *A Wealth of Wild Species*, 1983

50 An animal, whether real or imaginary, has a place of honor in the sphere of the imagination. As soon as it is named it takes on a dreamlike power, becoming an allegory, a symbol, an emblem.
ITALO CALVINO, *On Nature*, 1986

51 It is through the vested self-interest, tolerance, curiosity, or just plain indifference of individual land owners or users that wildlife survives alongside humanity.
DAVID WESTERN, speech, Conservation 2100 Symposium, Rockefeller University, New York City, October 1986

52 To insult someone we call him "bestial." For deliberate cruelty and malice, "human" might be the greater insult.
ISAAC ASIMOV, *Isaac Asimov's Book of Science and Nature Quotations*, 1988

53 Miners used to take a canary around the coal mines to warn them when the air was so foul that the canary died. This is the importance of wildlife to us: because if wildlife dies it is our turn next. If any part of the life of this plant is threatened, all is threatened. If you say "not interested" to wildlife conservation then you are signing your own death warrant.
PRINCE PHILIP, duke of Edinburgh, quoted in *The Times* (London), 17 May 1988

54 That promise was long since broken for passenger pigeons, and for the salmon who ran into dams on the ancestral streams, and for peregrine falcons who found their eggshells so weakened by DDT that they couldn't reproduce. But now it is broken for us, too—nature's lifetime warranty has expired.
BILL MCKIBBEN, *The End of Nature*, 1989

55 Whether we have the will or wisdom to preserve millions of hapless species is another question. To win over public sentiment, the wildlife versus people myth must be shown for what it is: a clash of human values between those who care for wildlife and those who don't, no less than rock music fans and their critics.
DAVID WESTERN, *Conservation for the Twenty-first Century*, 1989

56 The real issue is whether we can meet the universal inalienable right to a better living and save wildlife too.
DAVID WESTERN, *Conservation for the Twenty-first Century*, 1989

57 Wildlife is a personal matter, you think. The attitude is up to you. You can prefer to see it dead or not dead. You might want to let it mosey about its business or blow it away. Wild things exist only if you have the graciousness to allow them to.
JOY WILLIAMS, *Esquire*, February 1989

58 Save an alligator, kill a yuppie.
BUMPER STICKER, quoted in *Buzzworm*, September–October 1990

59 Man's predilection for the eye-catching animals of this world could leave the less charismatic creatures out in the cold.
COLIN TUDGE, *Wildlife Conservation*, September–October 1990

60 The stark truth is, if we want wild animals, we have to make sacrifices.
COLIN TUDGE, *Wildlife Conservation*, September–October 1990

61 We are the only species on Earth that can choose whether and when to be predators.
MARGARET L. KNOX, *Sierra*, November–December 1990

140 WILDLIFE REFUGES
See also   139 WILDLIFE, 143 ZOOS

1 In a very real sense, the setting aside of protected areas represents a failure in our ability
to manage land and resources so as to sustain
the rich and varied tapestry of animal and
plant life on the continent [of Africa].
    D. H. M. Cumming, speech, Conservation
    2100 Symposium, Rockefeller University,
    New York City, October 1976

2 The deliberately designated wild places, the
parks and refuges, are not sanctuaries for
wild animals in the long run because the constant presence of man slowly warps the animals, which become tamer. The wildness is
lost both by natural selection and behavioral
adjustment. As more and more pople come
to see them, their management becomes
more and more intense. Finally, they will become wild game farms. Already the refuges
are too small for wolves, grizzly bears, and
condors.
    Paul Shepard, Thinking Animals, 1978

3 [Alaska is] a pagent of life and a diversity of
fish, birds, and animal species rivaling the
marvels of Africa's Serengeti Plains.
    U.S. House Interior Committee, report, 7
    April 1978

4 In reality, the place [Arctic Natural Wildlife
Refuge] is an arctic desert covered with ice
and snow and largely uninhabitable nine
months of the year.
    Dan B. Huxley, quoted in Washington Post,
    20 June 1987

5 The oil we need to carry us into the 21st century is being held hostage.
    George N. Nelson, on the battle over the
    Arctic National Wildlife refuge, quoted in
    Washington Post, 20 June 1987

6 Even now, in the midst of an oil glut, with
gasoline cheaper in real terms than in 1950,
there is a push to explore that wildlife refuge.
This does not leave me sanguine about the
chances of protecting it in perpetuity. Is this a
bleak harbinger of what the future holds?
    Morris Udall, U.S. Representative, Too
    Funny to Be President, 1988

7 National wildlife refuges are frequently not
the pristine wildlife sanctuaries implied by

their name. While the refuges serve their primary purpose by providing habitat and safe
haven for wildlife, virtually all refuges also
host many other nonwildlife-related uses.
    U.S. General Accounting Office, "National
    Wildlife Refuges," September 1989

8 How can this generation justify tearing up
"America's Serengeti" to create a sprawling
industrial-pollution factory when a mere
two-mile-per-gallon increase in the efficiency
of new U.S. cars would save more crude than
the oil industry hopes to find in the unique
wildlife refuge?
    Gaylord Nelson, opposing opening the
    Arctic National Wildlife Refuge for oil drill-
    ing, letter, Wall Street Journal, 11 September
    1990

9 The United States invented the national park.
Have we so lost our way a century later that
we are prepared to sacrifice a one-of-a-kind
wilderness for a shot at a small and temporary supply of oil? Similarly, are we so desperate for a fast buck that other natural
treasures in Alaska are for sale to the highest
bidder?
    Jimmy Carter, Los Angeles Times, 1 Decem-
    ber 1990

10 The mission of the National Wildlife Refuge
System is to provide, preserve, restore, and
manage a national network of lands and waters sufficient in size, diversity and location
to meet society's needs for areas where the
widest possible spectrum of benefits associated with wildlife and wildlands is enhanced
and made available.
    U.S. Fish and and Wildlife Service, Refuge
    Management Issues, Issue 1, February 1991

141 WORKPLACE ENVIRONMENT

1 'Tis a sordid profit that's accompanied by the
destruction of health. . . . Many an artisan
has looked at his craft as a means to support
life and raise a family, but all he has got from
it is some deadly disease.
    Bernardino Ramazzini (1633–1714), 1705,
    quoted in Samuel S. Epstein, The Politics of
    Cancer, 1978

2 Economy of the social means of production, matured and forced as in a hothouse by the factory system, is turned, in the hands of capital, into systematic robbery of what is necessary for the life of the workman while he is at work, robbery of space, light, air, and of protection to his person against the dangerous and unwholesome accompaniments of the productive process.
KARL MARX (1818–1883), *Das Kapital*, 1867

3 Every organ of sense is injured in an equal degree by artificial elevation of the temperature, by the dust-laden atmosphere, by the deafening noise, not to mention danger to life and limb among the thickly crowded machinery, which, with the regularity of the seasons, issues its list of the killed and wounded in the industrial battle.
KARL MARX (1818–1883), *Das Kapital*, 1867

4 Yet if the beat of a metronome will depress intelligence, what do eight or 12 hours of noise, odor, and heat in a factory, or day upon day of clattering typewriters and telephone bells and slamming doors, do to the political judgments formed on the basis of newspapers read in streetcars and subways?
WALTER LIPPMANN (1899–1974), *Public Opinion*, 1922

5 Dead matter leaves the factory ennobled and transformed, whereas men are corrupted and degraded.
POPE PIUS XI (1857–1939), *Quadragesimo Anno*, 15 May 1931

6 Kant's doctrine, that every human being should be treated as an end, not as a means, was formulated precisely at the moment when mechanical industry had begun to treat the worker solely as a means—a means to cheaper mechanical production. Human beings were dealt with in the same spirit of brutality as the landscape: labor was a resource to be exploited, to be mined, to be exhausted, and finally to be discarded. Responsibility for the worker's life and health ended with the cash-payment for the day's labor.
LEWIS MUMFORD, *Technics and Civilization*, 1934

7 Workers and their families are exposed to the densest pollution zones of any population group in the country.
RALPH NADER, testimony, U.S. Senate Public Works subcommittee, 17 May 1971

8 Many of the environmental hazards begin in a far more serious concentration as occupational hazards on the job.
RALPH NADER, testimony, U.S. Senate Public Works subcommittee, 17 May 1971

9 Little testing as to the human health effects is made of chemical compounds; workers who use new chemicals are treated as human guinea pigs. Even worse than that—job-related illness or deaths go unreported, undetected, unnoticed.
FRANKLIN WALLICK, *The American Worker: An Endangered Species*, 1972

10 After three decades of unprecedented and virtually unregulated proliferation of new chemical products, American industry now confronts a frightening fact. . . . Long-term exposure to an unknown number of chemicals can produce irreparable damage to the organs of employes who work with them—and chemicals are used in every nook and cranny of U.S. industry.
BUSINESS WEEK, 11 May 1974

11 The carnage occurs in "slow motion," hidden behind the walls of the several million workplaces of this country's . . . workers.
ALAN ANDERSON, JR., on widespread illness and death from occupational diseases, *New York Times Magazine*, 27 October 1974

12 *Health, work,* and *environment* rank among the most important areas of social concern today, and the point where these concerns converge—the workplace—has become a microcosm of national conflict.
NICHOLAS A. ASHFORD, *Crisis in the Workplace*, 1975

13 The nation's largest cancer research laboratory is the American workplace.
SUSAN Q. STRANAHAN, *Philadelphia Inquirer*, 15 March 1976

14 Almost everything we know now about occupational cancer comes from counting dead bodies.
J. WILLIAM LLOYD, quoted in New York Academy of Sciences, *Cancer and the Worker*, 1977

15 Millions still work in places of duress, disease, and danger. Every year, noise, dust, dirt, fumes, gases, toxic chemicals, heat, radiation, and unsafe machinery pollute, make ill, injure, and kill more than half of the 80

million workers in our country, Here, in the bodies of workers, is where the corrupt ecology of capitalism hits home. Here is where Marx and Engels saw it at its worst. And here is where it must first be expunged, by the workers themselves.

HOWARD L. PARSONS, ed., *Marx and Engels on Ecology,* 1977

16 On-the-job hazards continue to kill, maim, and make ill our nation's workforce at an unacceptable rate . . . . Business is too willing to spend its time and resources fighting job safety and health.

EULA BINGHAM, quoted in National Wildlife Federation, *The Toxic Substances Dilemma,* 1980

17 We treat nature like we treated workers a hundred years ago. We included then no cost for the health and social security of workers in our calculations, and today we include no cost for the health and security of nature.

BJÖRN STIGSON, quoted in *The Economist,* 8 September 1990

18 The new ecological lifestyle of the future will alter our concept of work. In the modern scheme of things, work is a necessary evil, a burden that must be borne in order to earn a wage that allows us to do what we really enjoy. In a sustainable culture, work is considered to have intrinsic value. It gives us a chance to develop our creativity, to join with others in a common task.

ANDREW KIMBRELL and JEREMY RIFKIN, *Utne Reader,* November–December 1989

---

142 ZONING

See also   77 LAND USE, 95 OPEN SPACE, 101 PLANNING, LAND USE

---

1 A nuisance may be merely a right thing in the wrong place, like a pig in the parlor instead of the barnyard.

U.S. SUPREME COURT, ruling against permitting an apartment house in a single-family zone, *Village of Euclid* v. *Ambler Realty Co.,* 1926

2 Zoning law, far from accomplishing its purpose to protect the property rights of others, has become merely an instrument of special

favor, under which those with power or influence can either by special permission or by change of zoning, accomplish their own selfish purposes, regardless of the overall public good.

JOHN A. McCARTY, 48 *Massachusetts Law Quarterly* 473, 1963

3 As a purse cannot be made from a sow's ear, so also a noisy, dust-laden, restless community does not become a residential, tree-shaded quiet haven through the instrumentality of a zoning ordinance.

MICHAEL MUSSMANO, Supreme Court of Pennsylvania justice, *Board of Adjustment of the City of Harrisburg* v. *Bomgardner,* 1963

4 Zoning has provided the device for protecting the homogenous, single-family suburb from the city.

RICHARD F. BABCOCK, *The Zoning Game,* 1966

5 Zoning reached puberty in company with the Stutz Bearcat and the speakeasy.

RICHARD F. BABCOCK, *The Zoning Game,* 1966

6 If, when we speak of planning, we postulate objective standards for physical environment and let the social chips fall where they may, then zoning as an implement of planning has not merely failed but has been instrumental in the failure of planning. This failure is pernicious. Like another Noble Experiment with about the same birthdate as zoning, it erodes the civic conscience by permitting us to wrap our selfish anti-democratic aims in a garment of public interest.

RICHARD F. BABCOCK, *The Zoning Game,* 1966

7 Zoning needs no purpose of its own. . . . Zoning is a process. It is that part of the political techniques through which the use of private land is regulated.

RICHARD F. BABCOCK, *The Zoning Game,* 1966

8 There are no principles unique to zoning. . . . [The] only meaningful principles applicable to land-use planning in a democratic society are equally germane to other areas of human endeavor.

RICHARD F. BABCOCK, *The Zoning Game,* 1966

9 The basic nature and concept of zoning—restrictive and permissive rather than creative and of assistance to development—has been

responsible for much of the visual blight
around us today.

JOHN CARSON, *Urban Land*, February 1972

10 Where there is natural population growth, it
has to go somewhere, unwelcome as it may
be, and in that case we do not think it should
be channelled by the happenstance of what
town gets its veto in first. But, at this time of
uncertainty as to the right balance between
ecological and population presures, we cannot help but feel that the town's ordinance,
which severely restricts development, may
properly stand for the present as a legitimate
stop-gap measure.

FIRST U.S.CIRCUIT COURT OF APPEALS, uphold-
ing three- and six-acre zoning in parts of
Sanbornton, N.H., in the face of proposals
for denser second-home development,
*Steel Hill Development, Inc. v. Town of San-
bornton*, 24 November 1972

11 Zoning is only a negative; you can't create
something positive like a place for low-in-
come housing.

CHARLES E.LITTLE, interview, June 1973

12 Zoning is a way of keeping a lot of people occupied while somebody steals the goose.

CHARLES E. LITTLE, quoted in *Conservation
Foundation Letter*, June 1973

13 Clearly, the Virginia Supreme Court was un-
prepared to accept any land-use regulation
that on its face addressed the economic status
of housing occupants. It preferred to cling to
the naive notion that the private "market"
sorts out who will be able to afford what
housing. . . . This approach . . . denies the
reality that most private development decisions are in large measure a function of public
regulatory policy. Most zoning is, in brief,
"socioeconomic."

HERBERT M. FRANKLIN, *Zoning Digest* 25, 1974

14 A quiet place where yards are wide, people
few, and motor vehicles restricted are legitimate guidelines in a land-use project addressed to family needs. . . . The police
power [of government to limit growth
through zoning] is not confined to elimination of filth, stench, and unhealthy places. It
is ample to lay out zones where family values, youth values, and the blessings of quiet

seclusion and clean air make the area a sanctuary for people.

WILLIAM O. DOUGLAS (1898–1980), U.S. Supreme Court justice, *Village of Belle Terre
v. Boraas*, 1 April 1974

15 Zoning should be considered not as a restrictive process but as a constructive one; its goal
should be to integrate different types of land
uses that would interplay interestingly in
planned environments.

RENÉ DUBOS, *Celebrations of Life*, 1981

16 A man knocked at the heavenly gate;
His face was haggard and old.
He stood before the Man of Fate
For admission to the fold.

"What have you done," Saint Peter asked,
"To gain admission here?"
"I've been in the zoning business, Sir,
For many and many a year."

The pearly gates swung open wide;
Saint Peter touched the bell.
"Come in and choose your harp," he said,
"You've had your share of Hell."

ANONYMOUS, published in *Wisconsin* (a
county code administrators' newsletter),
June 1977

17 We thank Thee, Lord, that by Thy grace,
Thou brought us to this lovely place—
And now, dear Lord, we humbly pray
Thou wilt all others keep away.

ANONYMOUS PRAYER, quoted by Sir Desmond
Heap in Richard F. Babcock and Charles L.
Siemon, *The Zoning Game Revisited*, 1985

18 Often, zoning is put down as being political.
So, what else is new? Of course, it is highly
political; perhaps that is why it is so exciting a
game.

RICHARD F. BABCOCK and CHARLES L. SIEMON,
The Zoning Game Revisited, 1985

19 You can't zone chaos.

STEPHANIE MILLS, *What Ever Happened to Ecology?*, 1989

---

143 ZOOS
See also 140 WILDLIFE REFUGES

---

1 The sort of man who likes to spend his time
watching a cage of monkeys chase one an-

other, or a lion gnaw its tail, or a lizard catch flies, is precisely the sort of man whose mental weakness should be combatted at the public expense, and not fostered.

H. L. MENCKEN (1880–1956), quoted in New York *Evening Mail*, 2 February 1918

2 All [zoos] actually offer to the public in return for the taxes spent upon them is a form of idle and witless amusement, compared to which a visit to a penitentiary, or even to a State Legislature in session, is informing, stimulating and ennobling.

H. L. MENCKEN (1880–1956), quoted in New York *Evening Mail*, 2 February 1918

3 No HCP [habitat conservation plan] has ever led to the recovery of any endangered species in the wild. HCPs constitute little more than a developer paying for the right to turn an ecosystem into an intensively managed open zoo. We are allowing economic and political considerations to preclude the *mandated* recovery of an endangered species—and that is illegal under the Endangered Species Act.

JASPER CARLTON, *E* magazine, November–December 1990

4 Zoos are becoming facsimiles—or perhaps caricatures—of how animals once were in their natural habitat. If the right policies toward nature were pursued, we would need no zoos at all.

MICHAEL FOX, *Sierra*, November–December 1990

5 If the zoos happen to sustain [these] large vertebrates for that long, we will have done a wonderful job in giving our descendants choice as to whether they want to re-create the wild.

NATE FLESNESS, on the goal of saving 90 percent of certain species' genetic diversity, *American Way*, 1 February 1991

6 Zoos have become survival centers for endangered species.

CHARLES HOESSLE, *American Way*, 1 February 1991

7 The overall goal is to provide a hedge against extinction. You might call it a form of insurance against extinction.

MICHAEL HUTCHINS, on the species survival plans adopted in 1981 by the American Association of Zoological Parks and Aquariums, *American Way*, 1 February 1991

8 People do not go to zoos to learn about the imminent disappearance of species or to see habitats better viewed on public-television nature shows. People visit zoos, I think, to have some telling turn with the wild's otherworldliness; to look, on the most basic level, at ways we didn't end up being—at all the shapes that a nonreflective will can take. We are, by definition, such fleeting observers of evolution's slow-moving work that visiting a zoo and staring at animals can somehow stay us awhile, reinvolve us in the matter of existence.

CHARLES SIEBERT, *Harper's*, May 1991

9 According to a sign on the chain-link fence where the front gate used to be, Brooklyn's Prospect Park Zoo, first opened in 1935, is being converted into a "cageless natural habitat." This was a claim I at first thought a bit redundant and then preposterously bold, considering that most of the world's remaining natural habitats are, in fact, caged or fenced to keep us out and the animals in.

CHARLES SIEBERT, *Harper's*, May 1991

10 These are places we're designed to make *ourselves* happier about our continued keeping of them. We are, in a sense, trying to eliminate zoos even as we go on designing and maintaining them. With our new habitats, we are trying to conceal from ourselves the zoo as living evidence of our natural antagonism toward nature; the zoos as manifestation of the fact that our slow, fitful progress toward understanding the animals has always been coterminus with conquering and containing them.

CHARLES SIEBERT, *Harper's*, May 1991

INDEXES

AUTHOR INDEX

This index refers to quotations by category number and
by the number of the quotation within the category.
Thus, in "Baudelaire, Charles, 2.7," the number refers
to category 2, quotation 7.

SUBJECT INDEX

This index refers to quotations by category number and by the number of the quotation within the category. Thus, in "alligators 139.58," the number refers to category 139, quotation 58. Bold references are to entire categories.

14:23 attts/bch
3r:16. mkts
18
67:69 managent